Miss Boo Is Sixteen

BY MARGARET LEE
RUNBECK

Our Miss Boo

Time for Each Other

The Great Answer

The Secret

Hope of Earth

Pink Magic

Answer Without Ceasing

A Hungry Man Dreams

The Year of Love

Miss Boo Is Sixteen

BY MARGARET LEE RUNBECK

Miss Boo
is
Sixteen

HOUGHTON MIFFLIN COMPANY BOSTON
THE RIVERSIDE PRESS CAMBRIDGE

Second printing April 1957

𝔗𝔥𝔢 ℜ𝔦𝔟𝔢𝔯𝔰𝔦𝔡𝔢 𝔓𝔯𝔢𝔰𝔰
CAMBRIDGE • MASSACHUSETTS
Printed in the U.S.A.

For W. B.
who started stern and became heart-shaped

Contents

Contents

Miss Boo Is Sixteen

Now We Know

§❧ GETTING A LETTER from your child is often a shattering experience.

Not quite as much of a milestone as the first time you hear her voice on a telephone, for that happens, of course, when she is just recovering from babyhood. Suddenly you realize she is no longer a cunning little ventriloquist's doll for you to operate as you please. From here on she will be an unpredictable individual, running under her own power, evolving according to some mysterious hidden pattern. Every day she will become more like herself and less like what you omnisciently have decided she should be. You may have thought you had an orchid; gradually you see it is a beanstalk or a daisy. From here on, your success as a parent will depend on how willing you are to help a daisy be a daisy, and not try to make something else of it.

The letters she writes you when she is out from under your hovering influence tell you more than news. Sometimes you're unprepared for those letters, often badly spelled and curiously phrased. For instance, when Boo was not quite thirteen we let her go away to summer camp, by no means certain we had done the right thing. After all, the camp up in the High Sierras was quite primitive. We had heard of mountain lions, and even more grisly, of rattlesnakes. We were timid about asking if brushes with these were exceptions or routine. But she cleared that up for us on a postcard sent after a week of wracking silence.

"Hi folks," the postcard said giddily. "Today we found a rattlesnake under our tent. The riding master killed it. Eeek! Boo."

Ghastly as that was, a letter worried me even more. It, too, came after we had heard nothing for days and days. The letter said:

> *Today we had a talk about sex. In case you're interested, everybody has some kind. Also we found out we are all addle essence. They say that can give us a lot of trouble, and make your family mad. But you finally outgrow it. So here's hoping.*
>
> Boo

Well, she *has* outgrown quite a lot of it in the last three or four years. But we still have some distance to go. As for me, I don't want to hurry it, for I find it a delightful journey. Since I belong to Parents' Union Local 359, however, I must keep this fact to myself, and complain with the rest of them.

My experience has been that addle essence is strenuous exercise for everybody. Even when you let it get in your hair, you can't help acknowledging that its irrepressible honesty, its poetic beauty, and its radiant absurdity keep everybody in the vicinity from getting into a rut.

But it is a perishable commodity. The only thing you can be sure of, is that it doesn't last forever. For sooner or later, no matter how delightfully mad we may be in our youth, eventually we are swept off our feet by common sense.

Grownups Are Screwy

੩৯ WE WERE DRIVING up from the desert and we had been lulled by the cozy intimacy of the car into dropping down the walls of discretion that often protect children from seeing adults exactly as they are. We had forgotten Boo and were all talking unguardedly to each other as if she were not present.

Then beside me I heard a despairing sigh.

"What's the matter, darling?"

"Grownups!" she said eloquently.

"Grownups? What about them?"

She shrugged. "Grownups are so screwy," she said somewhat wearily.

"Oh? We are?" In the vacant air before me something very welcome was happening. I was seeing a magazine page with the words amusingly lettered, and under it, as by-line, our two names. As one does in the presence of material, I prodded gently.

"What are we screwy about, precious?"

"Millions of things," she said. "You're people who could

do anything you want to do, and yet you hardly ever sit all day in a bathtub full of bubbles, eating ice cream cones and reading comic books."

"No, I guess we don't," I admitted.

"And you fool around with people you just can't bear."

"What else *can* we do, if they're under foot?"

"You could do what *we* do," she said impatiently. "When we can't stand anybody, they probably feel the same way about us. So we come to an understanding."

"How do you manage that?"

"We say, 'Listen, you. Scram. You play on that side and I'll play on this, and that way we won't have any pain.'"

"Does it work?"

"Mais *natch*," she said bilingually. "There are always plenty of people we do like. But grownups . . ."

"I know what grownups do," I said. "We try to make-believe we're just crazy about everybody."

"And that makes you very cross, sometimes, with the people at home."

I thought that over and decided it was true. "How else are we screwy?"

"Oh, you buy clothes like everybody else's . . . then when *everybody* has 'em, you toss yours out. Too common. And you wash dishes. When everybody knows the best meals get eaten standing beside the refrigerator. Then all you have to do is brush the crumbs off the chest. You read books because everybody else is reading 'em, and if you missed last year's best book, you wouldn't dream of wasting your time reading it this year."

"We're too busy for that," I said defensively.

"And that business about being too busy," she said scornfully. "You have more time than we do because you don't have to do Latin and Algebra . . . and what do you do with your time? Waste it boring yourselves."

"I think you have something," I said. "Maybe you and I could do a magazine article called 'Grownups Are Screwy' . . . might even reform a few of 'em."

"I doubt it," she said, "but you always say people like to read about themselves."

"I'll tell you what. You talk to some of your friends, and see what ways they think we're crazy, and then we'll see what we can do."

"I'd be getting my money ready for college," she said with enthusiasm. "And besides, I'd sort of like to see my name in print."

But, like a lot of what seems to be good material, this was never impaled tidily on typewriter paper. About a week later she came home from school looking glum.

"I've got bad news for us," she said.

"Oh? The Latin quiz?"

"Nope. The magazine article. I asked my friends what they thought. They say grownups aren't screwy at all. *I* just spend my time with screwy grownups."

Runch Is Leddy

இ THE MORNING he came for the interview about the job, his arms were loaded with bundles. Something which looked like a brick wrapped in newspaper. Something also wrapped in newspaper which turned out to be a book. A third thing wrapped in newspaper which he didn't open throughout the encounter.

The bundles were the first thing I noticed about the small Japanese man. The second thing were his teeth. A mouthful of gleaming porcelain cubes which kept his lips from meeting, and gave him the expression of an astonished squirrel. I think he must have borrowed the teeth to make a fine first impression, for we never again saw him wearing them.

He weighed all of eighty-nine pounds, and his suit, of a mossy texture, was many sizes too big. With it, as he stood on the doorstep, he wore a Homburg hat, held up by his ears. His eel-colored eyes swam around alertly behind formidable horn-rimmed glasses which gave him a professional look.

I invited him in, not very hopefully. I had seen a great many applicants for the job during the last months. Some revealed the depths of their unsuitableness during the first interview, but some I rashly hired who stayed a few days, wreaking havoc on us. Now having exhausted the categories of couples (too expensive), widows (too morose), Scandinavians (too temperamental), attractive psychotics (too unpredictable) . . . I was venturing into the Japanese, fast vanishing from domestic employment. But this prospect didn't look very promising.

He said his name was Dr. Frank Frederick Ishinara. "Dr. only in Japan," he explained. The title supported the professional glasses, but didn't reassure about cooking and housework.

I showed him over the house, trying to make the kitchen as enticing as possible. He looked around disparagingly and made no comment, except about the eggbeater. "I buy new eggbeater," he announced. "This kind no good."

I introduced him to what might turn out to be his room and bath, and he said in his chirping voice, "Must have good light in room. Eyesight need very good light."

Then we went into the small library of our house, to discuss salary and references. He held the three newspaper-wrapped bundles on his tightly joined knees, and when I mentioned references, he unwrapped the package which was shaped like a large brick. There was his whole history, saved and yellowed. In that bundle every month of the fifty years since he had come to America was accounted for.

He handed me the references one by one, treasured, tattered, but glowing. They read like nostalgic lyrics. My first thought was that, when he left us, my reference couldn't possibly live up to the elegance to which he was accustomed. I'd have to get new engraved stationary, for one thing. . . .

Of the twenty I glanced through before I called a halt, at least seventeen said in one way or another, "We did every-thing possible to persuade him to stay on with us. But he was determined to leave."

Having just survived a shattering succession of help which lasted one week each, and most of whom had to be evicted with threats, and finally bribes, the thought of having some-one so good that we would beg him to stay simply brought tears to my eyes.

While I was reading this entrancing collection of letters, Dr. Ishinara was unwrapping the second of his bundles. This turned out to be a small yellow book, decorated with a frisky dragon eating lettuce. Across the cover, in hand-lettered script was the title, "Food for Nutritive and Pleas-ing."

He said modestly, handing me the book, "No obligation to engage author."

He tried unsuccessfully to smile around his entrenched teeth. I took the book and opened it. A recipe book. Writ-ten by Dr. Frank Frederick Ishinara.

"Avocado recipes no good," he said. "Confuse with arti-choke."

I could see why this might throw the recipes off, so I made a sympathetic noise. My heart was beating wildly, for here was offered help, like the title of his book, both nutritive and pleasing.

But I had partially promised the job to a large German

woman. She had brought me a sample of apfelkuchen . . .
I would have to dispose of her; that was all. Even if I had to
give her a week's pay. But I heard myself being businesslike,
which is always an unnatural and disastrous position for me
to try to assume.

"I'll have to let you know," I was saying. "I think we'd
like very much to hire you. But I must think it over, and
make a few arrangements. You give me your telephone
number, and I'll call you tomorrow."

"No phone number, Missus," Dr. Ishinara said. "Maybe
I telephone *you* tomorrow." His eyes twinkled mischiev-
ously through his glasses. "Maybe *I* have to think over, also."
He arose with what I think is called alacrity, the pointed
toes of his brown shoes (which must have been bought in
1913) glittering cheerfully.

"Very nice we talk," he said regretfully.

I tried to hand back the book about food for nutritive, but
he waved it off graciously. "I make you present," he said.
With every atom of my judgment screaming for me to re-
consider, I let him out the front door. I knew I was making
a mistake, but the large German woman had intimidated
me, and I *had* practically promised. Could we engage both
of them? I had a cartoonish vision of our house exploding,
blowing us all through the roof.

"I'll expect to hear from you in the morning," I said
faintly.

"House very much big," he said, saving face just in case.

I closed the door and came back to the library, trembling
with indecision. The little book lay on the desk, most
appealing in its quaintness. It was apfelkuchen against book.

Who was it that posed the choice between hyacinths and bread?

Suppose I *had* promised; it wasn't a signed contract. There must be ways of changing one's mind (as if I hadn't tried two million at least in the course of my lifetime!)

This was more than just a good houseman and cook being offered to us. This was adventure; you couldn't help knowing that. You might not guess what kind of adventure it would be, but it would surely be *some* kind. What, I wondered, had been in the third bundle? It was flat and square . . . Probably I would never know. The words in many handwritings on the sheets of embossed paper danced in my memory. "He is an original and charming cook," one had said. "He is scrupulously clean" . . . "no bad habits" . . . "faithfulness itself" . . . "cheerful and willing" . . . I must have been mad to have let him out of the house.

I tore upstairs for my car keys. The usual dragnet search through all my handbags and pockets produced nothing. I slit open the sealed envelope where I keep the extra keys (the sealing is supposed to help me treat these more respectfully as spares).

I backed the car out of the drive and roared down the street. It has always seemed a great advantage that the bus is only two blocks away . . . but now that fact was a big menace. He had probably caught a bus immediately. I could see him in my mind, sitting with his demure knees gripped together, riding farther and farther out of our life.

No eighty-nine pounds of picturesqueness, with two newspaper-wrapped parcels clutched in his arm, was waiting at the bus stop. He had caught the bus and I had lost

him. Lost him by trying to be sensible and businesslike as
people are always urging me to be. The peril of common
sense which doesn't come natural is that it waylays you
perversely at the very moments when it should be thrown
to the winds. There are persons for whom common sense is
not sensible, and I am one such.

Other people were waiting at the stop, looking impatient.
That indicated that no bus had passed recently! I jumped
out of the car and ran over to them. "How long have you
been waiting?" I gasped to nobody in particular. They
brightened up, thinking this was some quixotic way of
offering strangers a lift.

"Ten minutes at least . . . maybe fifteen . . ."

"Did you see a Japanese gentleman? Small . . . with large
teeth?"

Now they knew I wasn't kind; I was merely crazy. They
shook their heads and turned away. I hurried back to my
car and drove it aimlessly around and around the blocks
surrounding our house.

Then I saw him. Toddling along at a rapid pace. I
pulled up at the curb beside him. He looked at me, not
quite recognizing me. Also something was different about
him, so we both stared blankly. His face had a totally different expression. He looked like a very young infant. Then I
knew what the difference was. He had removed the teeth.

He beamed at me. "I take nice long walk," he said. "Ten-
cent-fare stop twelve blocks nearer town. Mariposa Road."

"Please . . . I wish you'd come back," I said. "I don't have
to think anything over."

"You like engage me?" he asked delightedly.

"I'd like it very much."

"Then we be engaged," he said. "I pleased also much." He tipped his Homburg hat courteously.

"Come, get in the car," I said.

A look of horror came over his babylike face. He stared at me a long moment, and I could see that the job was tottering in uncertainty. I had made an awkward and disgraceful mistake. If I didn't know it was improper for us to ride together, he wasn't sure by any means that he could afford to associate himself with such ignorance. Then he decided to forgive my accidental *faux pas*.

"I walk back to house, Missus," he said with dignity.

"Very good," I said, trying not to sound like a butler.

He started off at a sprightly pace, a very little and very ancient man who had obviously never considered growing old. Already I loved the spirit of him. But I knew our family would all have to prove our right to love him. For his dignity wouldn't permit any too easy familiarity of affection.

I stopped the car suddenly at the corner flowerstall. They had showery bouquets of chrysanthemums on display. I must carry home a bunch for him to arrange; chrysanthemums would be an acceptably subtle welcome for a little Japanese gentleman, wouldn't they? That transaction took me not more than five minutes, I am sure.

So I was quite unprepared for what happened when I put my key in the front door. It opened instantly. And there, beaming as if ten years of serving us lay behind the gesture of opening the door, was Dr. Ishinara. In an immaculate white coat. "I run home through alleys," he said genially. "I surprise Missus?"

"But . . . but . . .?" I couldn't frame the question so I rudely pointed at the white coat.

"I bring coat in package," he said. "I think maybe Missus like engage right away quick."

"But how did you get into the house?"

Now all the beam went out of the infant-like face. "I scold Missus. You leave back door open! Now that very bad way to be." He glared at me fiercely. *"Anybody* come in, Missus. Very bad."

I tried to apologize, meekly handed the flowers over to him, and retreated. I could see that already he had taken over the house. If we intended living in it, we were going to have to behave ourselves.

I ran upstairs and into my bedroom, breathless. Within an hour the destiny of all of us had been placed in a tiny pair of Japanese hands. I knew I had more than hired a cook. I had given us all into his keeping. We, and everything in our house, now belonged to him, for better or for worse.

A warm sunshine of well-being spread through my bones. Dr. Frank Frederick Ishinara . . . what on earth would we call him?

I must go down in a few minutes and explain the routine of the house to him. Then I must send him away to bring his bags. I would give him taxi money, of course, so there could be no slip-up . . . no changing of mind. I wished I could go down to San Pedro Street and help him pack his belongings. He must be at least seventy years old, I thought. Or maybe even older. What would the rest of the family say?

Downstairs I heard the slightest shuffle in the hall. Then a respectful, cheerful, incredible little chirp.

"Missus?" he said.

I looked over the banisters down into the foreshortened hall. An incredibly kind little face peered up at me. The formidable glasses were gone. He was not a professor now; he was our cook.

"Runch is leddy," he announced fiercely, defeated but unbowed by his *r*'s and *l*'s.

The Growing

〆➤ GROWING WAS certainly in the air! Yet it took me all day to realize exactly what it meant.

Everywhere we looked we could see that things were on the grow. That morning the gardener had had to lop off long exploring arms from the bougainvillea, because all of a sudden we couldn't see out of our bedroom windows. We had picked roses that were too tall for any of the modest vases we have in the house (our vases having been brought with us from New England, where hopes are plausible and conservative . . . and not preposterous as is the floral fact in California).

Boo got out a favorite gingham frock from the recesses of her closet, which somehow had been forgotten in her preoccupation with shorts and swim suits. She put it on exuberantly with the delight of finding something lost.

"My wonderful pink plaid!" she cried. "Imagine it spending the whole summer in the dark. Not even a moth to enjoy it."

But when she tried to button it, something was wrong.

The buttons and the buttonholes weren't within speaking distance of each other!

"What on earth can have happened to it?" she cried indignantly. "You don't suppose it could have shrunk on account of not being worn, do you?"

"I've heard of that causing shrinkage. In certain types of clothes," I said, hardly daring to tell her the sober truth.

"I know what's happened," she said elatedly, "I've grown! I've definitely grown!"

"You definitely have," I admitted, because blithesome as is that news to her, it still has a wistful meaning to me. I know she'll go on growing; I want her to, of course. And yet. . . .

By this time she was walking around, delightedly surveying the outgrownness of the frock.

"Isn't it wonderful!" she cried. "I've grown at least an octave!"

I thought she meant only that stretched distance between thumb and little finger which occurs when she sits for twenty-nine minutes a day drumming out piano scales.

"Yes," I said, sounding depressingly like a parent, "you're getting to be a big girl now."

She went out and sat in the shade of the acacia tree a long time. She came back into the house and considered whether or not she'd do some cooking; she got out her roller skates and looked at them. She finally put them on, and just sat with her elbows on her knees. Then she took them off and came inside, and said in that particular plaintive voice I haven't heard for years, "I don't know what to *do.*"

"What about?" I asked absently.

"About anything. There isn't anything to *do.*"

"Nonsense," I said, "there are hundreds of things to do."

"Not today," she said tragically. "There's nothing at all."

I looked at her, and I saw that the usual bubble and squeak had gone out of her. She looked limp and loose-endy, like a doll when nobody is home to breathe life into it.

"Well, I'll tell you what," I said. "You can come with me. I'm going into Hollywood to do some errands."

Unenthusiastically she got into the car and slumped supinely beside me, looking out from under her golden bangs indifferently. There was simply nothing on the street. But I didn't insist upon opening the subject, because I have had days myself when there was nothing on my street.

At last she said, "I'll tell you what's the matter with me. Wanta know?"

"Yes, darling."

"Well, I'm halfway between."

"Between?"

"I'm getting too big for the things I used to like to do, and I haven't found out yet how people spend their time doing that other stuff."

My heart opened to her in a flood of understanding.

"That's nothing to be alarmed about," I said. "I hope you're going to be the kind of person who never finishes growing. You're going to keep on . . . long after school is finished, and college . . . long after you're sixty and seventy. . . . There will be dozens of times like this, when you're halfway between what was big enough for you yesterday and what will be yours tomorrow."

"I s'pose so," she said listlessly, staring straight ahead of her. But it was only nominal agreement, because she couldn't see where she was going; and where she had come from was suddenly too tight for her to return to, like the pink gingham dress.

We had reached the bookstore now, and I got out. But she just shook her head when I invited her to come in with me. So then I knew how sunk she was. But I knew, too, that the remedy was at hand. I asked for my own books quickly, for now that was not the business of the day.

"But what I want mostly," I said to my friend the bookman, "is an armful of books for Boo."

"Does she ever find time to read?" he asked incredulously, remembering how only a couple of years ago she had hopscotched up and down his aisles, and worn him out with questions.

"She's about to," I said. "She just discovered time, and it's got her scared."

"We'll fix that up," he said, and the two of us hurried back to the rear of the long shop, where there are stacks and stacks of classified reading matter. He ran up his ladder and began handing me down books; I hardly had time to take them from his downstretched hand, because I was snatching up selections of my own. Then I realized that he was picking out books for himself-when-young as I was seizing books for myself. He had picked *Treasure Island* and *Ivanhoe,* and was trying to find some other title which he was muttering over and over to himself. I had found *Pride and Prejudice, The Life of the Bee, The Wind in the Willows,* and Flammarion's *Astronomy,* and was looking for *Mistress Masham's Repose,* which I couldn't find.

He came down the ladder, and I sat on the lowest step, and we talked and talked. He told me about how his father let him read anything as a boy, and about their barn with hay and a big high loading door . . . the finest reading room a boy could know, he says. And I told him about the way my father used to read aloud to us, and how many times we had read Maeterlinck's *Life of the Bee,* over and over.

"She ought to have something about the oceans," he said emphatically. "Or maybe we should save that for next year?"

After a while we both woke up suddenly and realized that we had been a long time back there in what the sign said was the Juvenile Department. We came up toward the front of the shop self-consciously, with our arms full of books.

"You don't want these wrapped do you?" he asked, and I shook my head, for we have a silent agreement that it is insulting to books to carry them out of a shop wrapped and tied with string, as if they were some kind of captive merchandise.

Then both of us happened to let our eyes fall on the adult books around us. Dyspeptic books they were, with frowning letters making up the titles; worried fat responsible-looking books, with bloated economy and disgruntled diplomacy and atomic doom in their titles. Within an arm's reach were ten of them that spoke explosively of the crowded emptiness of today and the terror of tomorrow.

He saw me realizing this, and he said, "You know sometimes I have to retreat back into that Juvenile Department, or I'd go nuts."

When she went to sleep that night, the books were on a chair beside her bed. A few beatific sentences had been read

out of each one, just to make sure each book was her own.
I knew from her politeness that some were too young. . . .

"Wanta know something?" she said. "This has been
simply a super day."

"Why do you suppose that was?"

"Well, first of all, I found out I had grown an octave."

There again was the word she had used this morning.
I had accepted it then as her way of indicating a number
of inches. But now I saw that she meant something more
than inches. I didn't try to ask her. She had given me the
word . . . she had given me the day, and I must interpret
it for myself, as she had interpreted it for herself. I turned
out her lamp and went downstairs, thinking about it.

We do seem to live through this life of ours in octaves.
There *is* a rounded octave of desires and fears and accomplishments always present at whatever stage we are. When
one scale is finished another will grow from it, recognizable
yet lifted into a higher register.

Our days are melodies made from these notes in endless
patterns. We emerge from one octave to the next so gently
that we hardly realize the transition.

Thinking about all this, I remembered that table of new
adult books with the menacing titles. In the same instant I
had a vision of that little face I love, which this morning
had looked out with listlessness and discontent at a world
outgrown. The adult books with the grim titles and the
face had something in common. Her malady had been that
she couldn't find anything to do. And this present world
whose voice speaks in the dyspeptic books, this weary, jittery, fagged-out world of the moment . . . it, too, hasn't yet

found what it wants ardently to do. They were two un-happy children together, protesting against the growing!

"I'll tell you what's the matter with me," Boo had said. " . . . I'm halfway between."

In the destiny of the race, this world we know is only a half-grown child. At this moment, it cannot find its way back to yesterday, and it is afraid to venture into tomorrow.

Perhaps they both need a kind of mothering. Perhaps this spoiled little world needs to ask its Mother what it had better do. Then she could show it what wonders lie ahead, waiting until it is ready to accept them. There are beautiful freedoms ahead, as unguessed as the armful of books that started Boo's ticking again. Surely we'll find them one by one, as we lay aside the tired inanities.

Drama

᙭᙭ USUALLY when Boo is telling us about some episode in her comic-strip existence, she unconsciously imitates all the characters. She does it so well that I think in panic, What would we do if we found we have an actress on our hands?

Boo herself has no such notion, and I doubt if she realizes that when she's telling about a squirrel she happened to meet in the park, her teeth get bigger, her cheeks bulb out, and her hands become tiny paws holding an invisible nut.

At the beginning of this school year when we were picking our electives, I suggested a course in drama.

"I thought you wanted me to be well educated," she cried in surprise. "Drama isn't education."

"Well, it might teach you to come into a room without everybody thinking the house is on fire, and sitting in a chair like a lady instead of a wad of wet noodles."

"You have to learn lines," she said distastefully.

But the more she thought about it, the more appealing the idea became. "Mostly, I think the kids just horse around with each other."

Then a sobering thought occurred to her. "Suppose they ask me if I have any talent?"

"You could always say no, then count on surprising them."

"They'd soon find out," she said. But once the idea had been mentioned, wild horses couldn't have kept her out of the drama course.

The first couple of weeks were a disappointment. The class took a quick glance at the history of the theatre since the Roman empire. It was sheer swindle; you couldn't tell it from just any ordinary history course.

Then things began looking up. They were put into little teams and given an assignment.

"Guess what? I've got a part to work out!" she said as she burst into the house. "We're supposed to present an old woman being told she can't be on relief."

"What're you . . . the relief?"

"Comedy, I suppose? Very funny," she said with dignity. "I'm the social worker who asks the questions. Quite a nice part, Miss Thugbugger says." (That isn't her name, of course, but nobody between the ages of thirteen and seventeen would pass up such an invitation to improvise.)

We didn't hear how the drama went, for hot on its heels came an assignment to be "a girl who needs glasses and won't admit it," and then "a father showing off his baby," "a woman accusing a maid of stealing," and on and on through a nerve-wracking semester until we inevitably reached *The Skin of Our Teeth,* which statistics tell us has been played by every high school in the nation except 672 backward groups, who happen not to have any stage available.

We weren't alone in the misery, for several of our friends had children also bitten by the drama. I felt especially sorry for my friend Martha Burton, whose child is what my mother used to call, "Less prit than smart."

Martha had entered her daughter in the course because she thought it would give her confidence. But, instead, it turned out that Cabby was petrified whenever she had to stand up before the class, and couldn't even get her teeth unclenched. So eventually she became the Props Committee. Martha tried to put the best possible face on that, but I knew she was humiliated.

"Cabby has so much ingenuity! It was simply inevitable that they'd make her rig up the props for their little plays," Martha said, looking very bright-eyed about it.

The appointment involved a lot of work for everybody in the family except Cabby. When they put on the sketch about Lincoln for the whole student body, Martha had a terrible time getting the items together.

"I've ridden all over town trying to borrow a paisley shawl," she said. "And would you believe it, the people who own one, won't lend it! I bought some nice copper to hang on the walls . . . *that* I didn't mind. You can always use copper for *something*. But the dough nearly threw me."

"The dough, dear?" I murmured, thinking that under the strain Martha had lapsed into slang.

"Bread dough. I couldn't seem to get a big enough batch so it would look like anything in the large yellow mixing bowl. Finally about four in the morning I threw in three more yeast cakes, and by the time we got up, dough was billowing all over the kitchen."

My heart ached for her, but I was glad she had so much manual labor that she couldn't grieve over the fact that Cabby wasn't being trusted out on the stage.

Parents were banned from attending that performance, so we never really knew how Boo came out as a shawled neighbor who dropped into the Lincoln cabin to borrow a Bible.

Her review of herself was laconic.

"I was okay," she said.

"I think on the stage they call that 'adequate,' " one of the less sympathetic members of the household said. But the point was lost on Boo, who has probably never read a drama review in her life.

Now the five-finger exercises of ad lib assignments were over, and Miss Thugbugger was bracing herself for the Spring Play.

"Have they given you your part yet?" I asked anxiously.

"We try out next week," Boo said glumly. "I don't think I'll get the female lead, so don't be disappointed."

"I won't be, dear. After all, there have to be secondary parts and good sports to play them."

"Wrong game," Boo said. "Good sportsmanship hasn't anything to do with drama. On the contrary."

She looked positively gaunt during the week of tryouts. "Don't keep asking me," she said quarrelsomely. "I'll tell you when I know for sure."

"I'm just interested," I said meekly.

"Well, don't be."

And then the suspense was over, and we knew. She came home, smugly beaming with pride and relief.

"Guess what?"

"You got the lead! How wonderful!"

"Well, no. Better than that. I'm the Chairman of the Props Committee. My name on the program, and everything."

"But . . . but I thought Cabby did the props."

"Pooh with Cabby. She's only the committee. *I'm* the chairman."

"As talented as Cabby, only more so," I said without bitterness. Then I went and phoned Cabby's mother to find out where we could borrow a paisley shawl, and how many yeast cakes to put in the bread dough.

Tumpti

క⇒ NOTHING in our house was ever quite the same after Dr. Frank Frederick Ishinara took over. He wanted to do the shopping, and at first, in an exuberance of liberation, I let him. But he was too frugal a shopper. The first week, we endured the austerity, each of us being more than delighted with what the bathroom scales had to say on the subject. But finally, because the cooking, though excellent, was so miniature, we had to speak about the size of the portions.

He looked disgusted. "Everybody too fat," he said categorically, and we couldn't very well deny it.

"Everybody eat too much."

"Yes, I suppose we do," I conceded meekly. "But we're all very active people . . . and we've fallen into the dreadful habit of enjoying food."

His little quince-like face did not change its expression in any way, but you could see by his silence that he had a volume of rebuttal he was withholding.

"I think . . . perhaps I'd better do the shopping myself,"
I said. "You see, I've always done it, and I know the situation."

"Waste money," he said laconically. "I get bargains."

"I'm sure you do," I said diplomatically. "The fact is,
you're such a *good* cook, we want to give you everything
possible to work with."

"I very bad cook," he said fiercely. So we let it go at that.

The very first day when I brought home the provisions,
I ran into trouble. I brought home lamb chops, one large
one for each of us, and one for Frank. He counted them
and then looked disgustedly at me. "Who other chop intended to be devoured by?"

"Why . . . by you, of course."

He let one of his rare expressions nearly demolish his
face. Then he said with dignity, "Dr. Ishinara would not
eat such thing."

"Oh, I'm so sorry. What would you like?"

"I provide own food," he said with dignity. "I cook nice
for me. Lice!" My horror at his diet was dispelled in a
moment, when I recalled his difficulties with *r*'s and *l*'s.

We soon took to calling him by a pet name. Frank just
didn't seem to fit, and of course that was because it wasn't
really his name. One of the Oriental's first and easiest con-
cessions when he comes to America, is to take on a good
solid American name. Frank, who never did things by half,
had taken on two.

But we called him Tumptigubben, which is what we
seemed to remember Swedish children call the good fairies
that get all the boring tasks done when nobody is around.

At first we called him Tumptigubben behind his back. But finally the name slipped out, and seemed to please him, so from then on we called him Tumpti.

In his cooking he could make absolutely anything, from ingenious canapes, which our friends called "landscapes on toast," to huge towering decorated cakes. Often he would create a birthday cake, at a time when none of us could possibly claim an anniversary. On these masterpieces he would print in Gauguin pink or neon blue frosting "Hapy Birsday, dear House." Or even "Hapy nineteen March."

Once, wanting to please him, I suggested he cook us something out of the recipe book he had sired.

"Those recipes no good," he said, grinning. "I write for show. Help get good jobs."

He couldn't bear to see any extravagance around the premises. One Friday morning, after his Thursday off, we found our table decorated with stiff paper flowers.

"I make," he said. "Real flowers waste of money."

Appalled though we were, we had them on the breakfast table for months. The eye is, alas, a great peacemaker; what can't be cured it finally renders invisible. And besides, I think all of us understood that what the paper flowers lacked in aesthetic value, they more than made up in human meaning.

Another Friday morning we found at each place when we came down to breakfast, a hard, sticky sweet roll. Made, I should think, of chipped isinglass held together by sweetened varnish.

"I bring gift," Tumpti said demurely.

We bit into the rolls with gusto, and tried not to let the

taste seep through to our expressions. Each of us cried appreciatively, and Tumpti stood there with his eyes almost lost in wrinkles of delight. We overdid our enjoyment, however, for every Friday morning after that we sat down to some indescribably horrific piece of pastry brought from First and San Pedro Streets. We became very skillful in secreting the gifts about our persons, wrapped in handkerchiefs. Once I still had mine in my sweater pocket when I took my afternoon walk. I crumbled it to offer to some sparrows who tried it and indignantly refused it, not even having the politeness to secrete the crumbs about *their* persons. I imagine these delicacies were a special breed put out by a cynical bakery especially for cooks to offer Occidentals on Friday mornings.

I'm sure Tumpti must have had acrobats in his ancestry. Of all his household tasks he most enjoyed washing windows, and our panes were scrubbed thin. It was a terrifying spectacle to watch, for he would stand on the narrow window sills with his little feet turned out in a ballet position, while he wielded the huge screens as if they were balancing parasols. The only way you could get through the nerve-wracking performance without raising your blood pressure, was to anticipate when a window washing yen was about to strike, and then arrange to be out of the house.

The larger the job, the more he seemed to enjoy it. He'd romp around the rooms with our big vacuum cleaner like a child playing hobbyhorse. We always said that if some day he turned up missing, we'd look for him first in the vacuum cleaner's dustbag.

The first time he cleaned the living room, I went down to

explain that when the time came to move the huge divan, in case he insisted upon sweeping behind it (which no one ever had attempted before), we'd borrow the neighbor's houseman to help move it.

But the huge divan, which looked like a recumbent elephant and must have weighed as much, was already standing in the middle of the floor. He, all eighty-nine pounds of him, was crouched behind it, scratching its back with a whisk broom.

"But . . . how on earth . . . ?" I gasped.

He looked at me and grinned.

"Jujitsu," he said.

If You Want To Be Boss

ᔓ CHILDREN ARE wholesomely objective about their own faults. They wear their little selves turned inside out; the patches and seams have no privacy.

Unless they've been shamed into self-consciousness about their shortcomings, they don't defend them with alibis and explanations. To begin with, they don't consider faults are permanent. After all, they live in a state of constant development from day to day. Their attitude seems to say, "I started out from scratch with nothing much to my credit, and I worked up this far. Probably keep going, making improvements along the way."

When you talk to a four-year-old, and you compare what you've accomplished by way of self-improvement in the last four years, you're apt to blush.

Since children consider their shortcomings neither permanent nor fatal, they aren't particularly embarrassed about them. If adults had the same expectation about reforming themselves, the race might really get somewhere!

A chubby child I know came home from school and said without chagrin, "No matter if I give other children my cupcake, they'd rather not eat their lunch with me."

"Why do you suppose that is?" her mother asked, trying to be as tactfully casual as possible, so her child's feelings wouldn't be bruised.

But the little girl was cheerfully impersonal about the whole situation.

"Well, I suppose they think I'm bossy," she said.

"And are you?"

"Yep," she said, taking a lollipop out of her mouth to accommodate a wide grin.

"Planning to do anything about it?" her mother asked.

She thought a minute, still grinning. "Yep," she said. "Guess I'll have to get over it. You can't boss people around if they won't play with you."

A Spy's-Eye View

ॐ **IF THERE'S** any apple polishing these days, nobody could accuse the teen-agers of doing it. Sometimes parents are guilty, however. Me, for instance. You see, I like teachers, and I can't get over a feeling of respect persisting from my own childhood. I think teachers probably know everything. When they talk to me as an equal, I feel positively giddy.

So when my friend Miss Getterson casually said I could attend the Student Government assembly meeting if I wanted to, I was pretty set up about it.

But Boo was appalled at the idea.

"I hope nobody would suspect you belonged in *my* family," she said bluntly.

"I don't expect to disgrace either you or myself," I couldn't help sounding haughty.

"Sit somewhere in the back where people won't wonder how you happened to be there."

"You needn't feel any responsibility. I'm Miss Getterson's guest."

"And if we should run into each other," she said truculently, "I hope you don't try to speak to me or anything."

"Perish the perish," I said. "If I see you, I'll duck under a seat."

"The meeting's not for outsiders, anyway," she said gruffly. "I can't imagine what you'll find interesting."

"Not the welcome, certainly," I said, cheerfully offended.

"And for pity's sake, don't try to dress up," she said, gazing into a new depth of horror. "Wear something inconspicuous."

"I was thinking of wearing a sheet, with two holes cut in it for eyes." This, naturally, she ignored.

"Thank goodness, you're an un-celebrity. We have some poor kids whose parents are celebrities," she said. "Everybody feels awfully sorry for them when their parents insist on showing up."

"How do *they* dress?"

"The really important ones try to look unimportant. Usually they wear old sports clothes. But sometimes the ones who aren't important enough to *try* to look unimportant dress the same way. That's very offensive."

I could see that no parent could possibly do the right thing at Beverly Hills High, so I just went as I was. There was one other parent present, and I guess she was pretty important, because she had on a beauty operator's white uniform. But she gave herself away completely, for she had the uniform under her nice mink coat. She and I tried not to meet each other's eye, so I knew we'd had the same briefing, and we both were trying to be invisible.

The meeting was conducted by a tall toothsome lad who was the President of the Student Council. His Board also sat on the platform, nice-looking youngsters full of confidence.

They all spoke without frills, using a kind of basic English without too much regard for the hair-splitting meanings of words. The idea was what mattered, and the words lay wherever they fell.

The President, a bland staccato youngster . . . a Rotarian in the bud, if I ever saw one, began by saying, "Once a week we more or less sit down and think things over. Good idea sometimes."

Since nobody contradicted that startling discovery, he said, "So we decided to let you all attend our regular weekly meeting. Thought we'd discuss some common problems. Any question, you can ask at the five minutes after what we have to say is finished. Anything we haven't covered, that is."

You could see he had perfect confidence that they would cover all the common problems so adequately that nothing would be left to question. Now he called on one of his colleagues, a redheaded giant who stood up and jammed his knuckles in his Levi pockets. He explained what public opinion is, and what kind of weapon it can be.

"If everybody thinks a thing is so, then you'd better get on the beam and agree," he said menacingly.

When something real difficult faced the Board, they handled it in a radical way. "When we've got something real serious to discuss, we ask the faculty to please leave the room. That way we can be democratic."

A girl, tall and smooth, was then called upon. Without preamble, she touched on what was evidently a controversial subject.

"Clothes are a private matter," she said. "But they shouldn't be inconspicuous. Real personality can rise above clothes. But the right clothes give you confidence. If people don't see your clothes, you feel insecure."

In the twenty minutes allotted to the entire discussion, these subjects were tossed into the air, to land wherever they might take root: going steady; owning a car; getting your family to let you have a telephone listed in your name; being decent to kids from other schools when their teams clashed with ours in our gymnasium; not throwing Good Humor sticks all over the parking lot; nobody booing next week when the annual Faculty Talent Show was going to be given. "Remember they're human, too," a serious-faced boy said. "Maybe that could be our motto in regard to teachers."

Nobody mentioned study in any form. They seemed to have banished that idea from the curriculum; anyway it wasn't a common problem.

During the five-minute discussion period, a bright-eyed lad stood up on the front row. "I'm innerested in getting some of you guys to volunteer as lunchroom waiters," he shouted belligerently.

"The pay depends on how big you can make it. You get your lunch . . . as much as you can eat."

A wave of nose-holding swept over the audience, but the recruiting officer went on valiantly. "Seriously now," he said quite fiercely. "About the best thing I've learned at good ole Beverly Hills High is how to carry seven bowls of soup on one tray. All a matter of confidence."

If I picked up one gem from the meeting, it was the need for confidence. I crept out as invisibly as possible, knowing my own education had been cripplingly deficient. For you never saw anybody slink out with less confidence.

The Rich People

᭏ WHEN I WAS a child there was one most conspicuous fact about our family. But I never discovered it until I was grown up and could compare our life and our house with what I saw all around me.

The fact was that we were what is commonly called "poor people." I know now that the reason this conspicuous fact was never fully grasped by us was my mother. So valiantly did she emphasize our riches that we never really found we were poor until long after the condition had passed.

And by that time I never could say to myself, "We used to be poor," because whenever I remembered our circumstances such a wealth of happiness and adventure and comfort came flooding into my heart that I could only stand silent, wishing all families were as rich as we had been.

My mother, to begin with, was born with a purseful of fun in her mind. She could make a game of anything that had to be done. She had the grace of accepting necessities so they felt like choices. Her eager little face always leaps into my mind when I read that verse in Deuteronomy which says, "I have set before you life and death, blessing and cursing; therefore choose life." She chose the "life" of enjoying what we had, instead of concentrating on the "death" of what we lacked. We never grieved over what we couldn't have; we just had something else.

We walked miles sometimes to save a five-cent carfare. But our mother taught us the joy of walking, so that economizing seemed never the reason we walked.

Drudgery didn't exist for her, yet when I remember all the "work" which flowed through her small hands, I cannot see how one woman could have accomplished it. She would tackle anything, no matter how strange a task it was, nor how large it appeared. "We'll just pitch in," she'd say. And pitch in we did.

She and my father bought a big old house when we were very small. It had to be a large house, because our only way of paying for it was to convert half of it into an apartment to be rented . . . the best half, of course. Knowing how to make the "best" of anything, we kept the darkest part, and my mother brought make-believe sunshine into it with yellow wallpaper, and white paint and ruffled organdy.

The actual paper hanging was a picnic for all of us. We hired one room done, so we could all find out how trained paper-hangers tackle their work. Then we set to. Each of us had a dinner pail we carried to our work just as the professionals had carried theirs. At noon we sat on the floor with our backs against the wall and swapped shop-talk. My mother's fables of big paper-hanging and paint jobs she had done in her time were the tallest tales of all. Her audacious imagination could scamper over any subject like a buffooning monkey.

She did everything in an original way, as if it never had been done before. I came home from school unexpectedly one morning and found her washing dishes with her best hat on.

"Just felt bored with carpet sweeping and dusting," she confessed airily. "This is to remind me that if I hurry up and get finished, I can go someplace and see sights."

Sometimes when we sat down to a meal, we found we were lunching at the Martha Washington Tea Shoppe, or the Eatum Up Lunch Counter. There would be humorous or absurdly "dainty" menu cards, listing all kinds of diverting foods. It wasn't until years later that I realized these menus appeared when our budget was particularly narrow-minded. My mother never abandoned anything to dullness and disappointment; she could dress up anything with what she had in herself.

She was a proper-looking little woman, with demure curls and a small voice. She admired propriety above all outward graces. But at home she had a mischievous talent for make-believe which never left anything as she found it. She never told a story without outrageous impersonations. Her very verbs came to life and strutted behind footlights. Yet the drama of simple neighborhood "doings" had no malice, for she could not bear to hurt anyone . . . not even with laughter. I remember once hearing her say, "It must hurt God's feelings when we laugh at each other."

Her days were filled with housework and canning and repairing and contriving, yet she always found time for countless little deeds of charity and neighborliness. "Everybody must share whatever they have. Some people can just give money, but we can give our time," she used to say proudly. There was no disparaging of either gift, for both offerings were important and valuable. Some people have money; perhaps the more fortunate have time.

Sometimes we'd come running back from school and find her not at home. There would be some kind of note pinned on our back door, suggesting we "start dinner," but suggesting it in some way that amused us. I remember one note, typewritten like a classified advertisement, which said:

Help Wanted: Two girls with exceptional ability to set table, pare potatoes, wash lettuce, slice tomatoes, open canned corn, and light oven with meatloaf inside. Lowest wages and highest praises.

The high board fence of "things we cannot possibly afford" could have hemmed us in on all sides, and made us all sorry for ourselves, and poor. But it never did, because my mother knew that what is within the heart is more real than anything which can be bought and added to the outside of living.

Yet, if there was some luxury that one of us craved unbearably, my mother usually found a way to manage it. She had a blithe way of snubbing necessities when she wanted to, in favor of luxuries. Once when I was about fourteen, there was a hat which I thought I couldn't live without. Instead of trying to persuade me that it was only a silly whim, she treated it as seriously as I did.

"You think you want it so much you'll remember it when you're a grown woman?" she asked me. I knew I never would be the same if I couldn't have that hat.

"All right, my darling. You'll have it," she said.

"But how?"

"Never mind how," she said, setting her lips firmly. "We'll give up butter and eat gravy for a few weeks. The butter would just blur into oblivion, but if you really love the hat that much, it will live with you as long as you live." It has, too.

It has been many years since I saw that merry little blue-eyed face . . . merry until the very last minute of her life. When we lost her quite suddenly, I thought the window through which I looked into heaven had been closed forever.

We were going to be apart now, and there would not even be letters. Then a curious thing happened to me. Something seemed to lay a gentle hand on my mind, and without words Something seemed to tell me that the letters would not stop at all, if I would only receive them. They would come to me somehow, but I would have to look for them and recognize them, for they would be wearing disguises. They would borrow all sorts of shapes to say themselves to me. I could not know how they would come, and my grief at first was too deep to look above itself. But they waited for me to look.

I find them now over and over in the most unexpected places. I find them in something a stranger says to me with a quick merry lift of laughter; I find them sometimes in my own thoughts. I may be cogitating on some subject and suddenly there will flash across my mind a bright parenthesis, a tucked-in comment which I recognize.

Once a year we in America celebrate Mother's Day. Those

whose mothers are still within touching distance, give flowers. The rest of us who have had to learn something of this I have tried to say, need no flowers nor any other stumbling symbols. For nothing which has helped make our heart the living thing it is, can ever be lost.

The having and then the not-having have left a knowledge that is bigger than symbols, and closer than breath.

Line Busy

క్ఠ THE PEOPLE in my house always think if you're talking on the telephone it is their chance to engage your other ear, without your being able to talk back.

Last night I was having a protracted telephone conversation, so Boo came in and sat on the floor in the direct line of my vision.

"Who're you talking to?"

I mouthed, "Relations."

She said, "We had a talk about relations in our Good Citizenship Club."

I let my eyebrows go up in an *accent circonflexe* to indicate interest.

"Premarital relations," she said. "Comes from the Latin. 'Pre' is a prefix meaning before . . . so this was about relations before marriage. Dr. Hunt is against 'em."

I became more circumflex, and let my free hand scuffle over the mouthpiece, so our kinfolks wouldn't hear anything to upset them.

"Seems funny to me," Boo said. "I assume the premarital relations are the ones you had before you acquired in-laws. Why should Dr. Hunt think in-laws are more desirable than the relations you were born with? Very puzzling."

"Don't puzzle," I said. "I'll explain it to you later."

"When?"

"Tomorrow, God willing."

The Sooplize

₨ IF HE HADN'T been undeniably the best cook on earth, we couldn't have put up with the suspense, surprise, and general emotionalism of Tumpti's cooking. Scarcely ever was a meal a routine matter, negotiated without shock of some kind. But as one of us said in defense of him, "Well, at least he shocks you *upward*."

Also he talked to himself. And not in any pleasant amiable dialogue, as one might expect between congenial comrades. He argued with himself, sometimes in crackling Japanese, and even more terrifying, in gunfire English. The part of him that did the bullying had the other meeker part completely cowed. But occasionally there was answering back.

With us he was usually pleasantness incarnate. Obviously he liked us better than he liked himself. And we intended to keep it that way, if we possibly could.

That wasn't too difficult. We had a method for getting along fine; when we inadvertently proposed something he didn't want, he tolerantly ignored the proposal.

"No good," he'd say cheerfully. "I show you how I do it." So we always came to a compromise by having it his way.

Sometimes I used to worry about his food. Every five or six days he would cook up enough for a week of his meager rations. As he had promised in the beginning, it would always be lice in some form or other. The quantity would be about enough for two normal people to eat at a sitting.

When I timidly inquired if he were getting enough to eat, he got quite mad. "You want me fat! Everybody too fat. I stay with health."

He had his own time for doing chores, and nothing could divert him from his private schedule. For instance, on Wednesday morning he put all of his Tuesday's clothes in the washing machine, and on Thursday morning Wednesday's aprons, white trousers, and shirt had to be washed, and so on through the week. Our washing machine is not one of the silent varieties you see on TV when you want to see a Spectacular. Ours rumbles and quivers and the whole house vibrates in harmony with it. Consequently when you woke up at our house, your first thought was that you were on a seagoing vessel. But it was only Tumpti taking care of his daily cleanth.

His private cooking he always did when he was in the grip of the whim. Usually it would be on the rare occasions when I had asked him to put together a tea tray, and bring it into the living room for guests. Since he usually enlivened the lice with raw fish, this wasn't the best moment for concocting his own fare.

In many ways he had a positive genius for picking an inconvenient time for doing everything. But we loved him so much, and we were so aware of his incomparable virtues, that we naturally made the quiet best of it all.

But I did think that the day he was preparing a big buffet for twenty-five people (the hungriest people imaginable, too, this being a writers' club) was hardly the time for him to cook up one of his own private recipes.

The buffet, in fact, had been his idea from the beginning.

"Not enough company," he had grumbled. "House too quiet. I go someplace else."

"Why, we've thought . . ." I said apologetically.

"You invite. I make beeg buffet supper. Turkey, ham, cleamed potatoes. Stuff for party." He danced on his little feet like a boxer, sparring in the air to indicate the size of his preparations.

He kept at me, too, until I set the date and called up the guests. Whenever I brought up the subject of the menu, he was indignant. "I fix. Nobody bother. You bring in turkey . . . twenty pounds. Also big ham. Maybe oysters, sweet potatoes. I make chelly pie. I borrow big coffeepot next door."

"I'll buy a big coffeepot," I said quickly, feeling sure that borrowing isn't done in Beverly Hills.

"Waste money. I already arrange," he said haughtily. "I rend cook next door two thlee things." His face looked greased with craftiness.

We insisted on eating our lunch out on the day of the buffet. For one look in the kitchen told us that when big events are marching, small episodes must retreat.

That's why it was such a ridiculous moment for him to decide to cook up his private "lice." Not just the little supply for a week, either, but a huge quantity, enough to see him through a month.

"What's this?" I asked innocently, as if I didn't know when I saw the kettle boiling.

"My lice," he said indignantly, just daring me to comment, for or against.

So I said in a most conciliatory voice, "Well, one thing about a buffet supper. It really doesn't matter whether or not it's served exactly on time. Don't you worry about it."

"Wully? I don't wully." He wagged his little head cheerfully, and I could see that in his mind worry is an unadmirable Occidental pursuit holding no temptations for him.

But when I told the family about his picking today to cook for himself, they weren't too indulgent.

"I think he just tries to see how annoying he can be. Why couldn't he eat a few slivers of turkey and ham? It wouldn't kill him."

"He rikes his lice," I said. "And this is a free country. That's why he's lived here for fifty years." But privately I thought there was a point in the rare criticism.

We were all prepared to have the buffet appear late, like a prima donna. But on the dot of seven, Tumpti came to the door of the living room, stiff and sparkling in fresh white.

"Buffet leddy," he said, faultlessly.

And there it was, all present and accounted for . . . the turkey, its breast rippling into snowy slices, as regular as the pages of a new-opened book . . . the ham pink-petaled and luscious with a garland of spiced crabapples ringing the platter, sweet potatoes, creamed potatoes, broccoli with flawless hollandaise, fruits in a salad which looked like a travel

folder for the Garden of Eden . . . rolls under wraps . . .
And then my eye stumbled and stopped. For in the very
center of the buffet . . . the *pièce de résistance,* supported by
the entire caste of lesser viands . . . was a mystery performer.

"What on earth is that?" I whispered in horror to Tumpti,
standing by with eager tiny hands clasped in pride under a
fatuously enthralled face.

"That *lice,*" he whispered back. "Ve'y good. I fix for
sooplize."

He had prepared an enormous flat pan of it . . . so huge
that he had had to buy it somewhere out of his own salary
(or maybe the neighbors on the *other* side were the owners?)

Everyone was dipping into it, and its hidden goodies were
being turned up to view. Tiny shrimps, almonds, mushrooms . . . heaven knows what. But principally lice.

Everybody came back and asked for more of it. And the
entrepreneur produced another immense panful, just as good
as the first. Everyone ate until the last grain and morsel was
gone, and the rest of the buffet just sat there looking morti-
fied.

Every time our paths crossed, he said, "I sooplize you!"
His face was the happiest one in the room. The writers had
been invited, but Tumpti was the honored guest.

So now day after day the family, badly outnumbered, has
been working away on an ole twenty-pound turkey, and a
ham what am, which looks as if it will continue am-ing
forever.

Apple Without Newton

తక IF YOU *must* see apples growing, you have to find a good excuse to leave California. So, when we could bear it no longer, we went back to New England. On business.

We sat on a sunny stone wall under an applesauce tree, and we ate apples, loving autumn in the heart. The perfume of apples was in the air, and occasionally we heard the solid drumbeat of one falling in the orchard, without a Newton to marvel. Naturally we talked about apples as we munched . . . that first one of Eve's, the brave one of William Tell, the ones Robert Frost picked in his poem. We recited the homely names of strains we like best . . . Russets, Grimes Golden, Baldwins, and Macintoshes. Those of us who preferred the crisp and tart lined up against the mealy and sweet.

We tossed the cores over our shoulders, then bit into another apple and opened the pearly pockets and saw the seeds. We said to ourselves, "Nobody . . . no human eye . . . has ever seen this seed before!"

We held the seed in our hand, polished as mahogany and

warm as life itself, and we thought, This is one of the wonders of the universe. I can let it become nothing, in the crack of this stone wall. Or I can plant it and someday there will be another tree for friends to sit beneath on some distant Saturday morning.

Somebody said lazily, "An apple's a wonderful thing. I was just thinking."

"So was I," the rest of us admitted.

"No matter where you happen to eat an apple, it always reminds you of home," somebody said.

Then I remembered the American apple, and the Polish schoolmaster with whom I ate it.

This was long ago when I was a young student coming back to America after a fine holiday. I boarded the ship from a tender at Southampton, just before midnight. There was that carefree excitement you always feel when you get on a ship, waiting in the ocean for you to come and possess it. I ran fore and aft, exploring; I leaned on the rail and watched the lights rocking in the water, and the luggage coming on board. It was all exciting and fun, as if we were a large family of children moving into a new house.

I kept bumping into a dark-eyed little man, more delighted even than I, and more eager to see everything at once. He kept courteously apologizing and asking me questions, and I realized he had a new vocabulary of wobbly English he wanted to try out on somebody.

So we talked. We talked as if there never would be another night for talking. And this was how he actually felt, it developed, for he belonged in Third, and this was the only time he could have the run of the ship.

He was a teacher in a boys' school in Warsaw, and he had

been saving his money for ten years to visit America. He wanted to see everything, but particularly the place where Washington crossed the Delaware, which his boys liked to hear about. He had five weeks to spend . . . and nearly $40.

"But I do not care to eat much," he said hastily. "I want only to see."

We talked and talked. Sometimes we came to the high wall of an unfamiliar word and could not climb over it to each other. He wanted to know about schools, about little boys' camps, about free concerts for children. He wanted to know how we teach reading, and what gift his wife would most enjoy from America. He wanted to have his picture taken, and he wanted to see a cafeteria.

Then he decided to share something with me. "Now you must wait here, and I shall bring up something from below. A gift given to me because I am going to America."

He disappeared, and I waited a long time, sleepy now, but not daring to be so rude as to leave when this was his only night.

He came back at last, his face pink from the long plunge down to Third. "Look . . . here it is," he said almost in awe. "An American apple." He put it gently in my hands, a very weary apple from long being more than fruit to this man and his schoolboys. I could see it was a tangible pledge, a hostage from a dream at last come true.

"We shall eat it together, and you will tell me if it tastes like all American apples," he said. Then he held it up for one last admiring look, and cut it in half.

He bit into it, and silently tested the taste. Then he nodded with satisfaction. Yes, America was going to be all that he had hoped for.

He was hilarious with enjoyment. He smacked his lips and snapped his eyes, and I, too, ate as lustily.

We tossed the halved core into the Atlantic darkness, and shared a moment's silence.

"Well," he said ceremoniously. "Now I have eaten an American apple. It is delectable. But it eats too fluently."

I had not thought of the Polish schoolmaster for years. What is he doing now, behind the iron curtain? Whatever he is doing, I know an American apple stays fresh and sweet in his memory.

Mushrooms and Metaphors

ॐ WHEN I GO BACK to New England, I tell my friends I am visiting *them*. But actually I am homesick for the woods. Not the cathedral forests of the Northwest, or the open unreticent groves of eucalyptus and palms; what I long for are the damp secretive little woods that come to your very dooryard, if you live in the suburbs, to eat out of your hand. The intimate small woods straggling thinly over the landscape . . . the shadbush and ferns, the oaks that keep their pink crackling leaves through much of the winter . . . these are what I love, and I have to find excuses for keeping assignation with them.

Like going out with neighbors to look for mushrooms, when I knew I should stay in the house and get a little work done. But there are ways of getting around getting work done and I am familiar with most of them.

For instance one says to oneself, "After all it isn't every day two officers of the New England Mycological Society invite you to gather specimen mushrooms. You would learn something new . . . that's your job, isn't it . . . learning new things, seeing new sights, turning up new figures of speech?"

As you button up the sweater, you think complacently, You wouldn't be just amusing yourself. You wouldn't even be out looking for mushrooms to *eat* . . . it's a fresh new metaphor you'd be hunting.

I've chased wild metaphors many a time; I know their trails lead into engaging bypaths, for they are untamable creatures, indigenous to no restricted climate but found in any. They cannot be caught with trap or cage; they are like leprechauns whom to look at is not to see. Metaphors, too, must be looked at out of the corner of the mind, so to speak. The art of misapplication rules them. Talking about one subject, they instruct about another. They are puns in picture form.

Metaphors are the shadow which clarifies substance. They are tiny mirrors into which imagination may look and see . . . itself. For the more you know, the more you see in a metaphor; indeed in simile it is knowing which becomes seeing.

Metaphors are as tactful as they are informative, for if you know nothing at all about the subject, you are not offended or rebuked, because they offer your eye an agreeable still life, valuable for itself. Metaphors are the diplomats of rhetoric; they lead you urbanely to the brink, but it is you who states some unique conclusion to your own discovering self. There is nothing more satisfying than finding a provocative metaphor. (Unless it be the finding of a clump of gnomish mushrooms hunched at the foot of a chestnut stump!)

Trying to explain, one often fumbles . . . then some little

picture comes nimbly to the hand and one picks it up surely like a flashlight. With its tiny, incisive ray, a good simile can illumine almost any elusive meaning. Where reason stumbles, imagination flies unfettered. One is talking about desultory reading with no program or destination . . . book after book, each all right but unassociated . . . then one has it. "Why!" you say delightedly, "it's like sewing a long seam with no knot in the end of the thread!"

Or you try to tell someone about the pleasure of keeping a journal. "But there are so many books already written," one is told. You stammer witlessly for rebuttal, then your friend the metaphor helps you.

"Of course . . . but it is the difference between planting even a windowbox of our own, and walking through the public's botanical gardens!"

Our afternoon was too full of mushrooms to think about the metaphors. There was too much beauty splashed across the sky, too many impressive Latin names bandied about . . . too many enchanted dwarfs scampering through the leaves to be transfixed into mushrooms when you pounced. . . .

We came home with baskets bulging. Then, within sight of the house I remembered on what pretext I had come out. Here we were laden with mushrooms, both edible and specimen . . . but quite quite empty of metaphor.

Well, the next best thing, then, is to learn more about mushrooms. You never know when knowledge will come in handy.

"What I don't understand," you say earnestly, "is how these little chaps grow. Are they root, branch, or flower? And where is the rest of them?"

"They're flowers," the six-foot-tall mycologist explains. "They spring from an underground plant, a white thread-like mycelium. It grows along quite unseen, under the ground, until it is ready to put out its blossoms. . . ."

"Mycelium," you repeat, and a glow of joy comes over you. "Just the way thought grows along, unsuspected and unseen until it shows itself above the surface in some sudden action. . . ."

You are delighted beyond words now. "And how in the world have historians . . . or dramatists . . . how have poets . . . or lovers . . . or even economists . . . how has *anyone* ever got along without that wonderful metaphor? Mycelium!"

This is why you went to the woods; *this* is what you were seeking under the leaves, beside the tree stumps. You have forgotten the mushrooms now. Let 'em be broiled and served on toast! What you have found was prophesied in the book of Proverbs: *A word fitly spoken is like apples of gold in pictures of silver.*

Let the mushrooms be eaten; *this* shall be framed and hung upon a page.

The Prom

இ PART OF the agony was that such an unimportant matter could loom so tragically mountainous. It rolled up and hit us without any warning; one day we were happy and carefree, and the next day our house was tense with the fact.

She herself had announced the awful absence bluntly. "Looks like I'm not going," she had blurted out suddenly.

"Going where?"

"Why to the Prom, of course."

"Why not?" I asked, not sensing the significance.

"Nobody's invited me."

I recovered instantly from the stark awfulness, and said as brightly as possible. "Oh, it's early yet. Give 'em time."

"Other people've been asked."

"Well, don't worry about it," I said.

"Who's worrying?" she growled.

"You have plenty of time for proms . . . years and years of them."

"Eeek!" she said as if I were promising years and years of toothache.

After that, she didn't mention it again. And that's what really worried me. It is painful to see anxiety treated in a mature way by your child; it means that from now on anxiety will be accepted as a normal part of existence. No longer will disappointment be met with incredulity and frankness. Grief will now be compounded with the hateful germ of shame. It will go underground, as it has long ago gone in adult make-up, and not be the wholesome lying-on-the-floor-and-screaming indignity.

I, of course, gave it my most expert worrying. For the first time, I felt completely helpless to deflect a blow which I saw whizzing like a comet toward Boo's precious peace and happiness. I kept telling myself it was trivial and unimportant but of course I couldn't deceive myself. I knew that probably nothing we'd had to face in the last fifteen years was as ghastly in importance.

I wondered how many houses in our neighborhood were quaking with this agony. Did they dare confess it? Did anybody try to handle it in an open and frank way? I saw in my mind an efficient pair of mothers making a deal. "Listen, Grace . . . your George had better ask Patricia to the prom. Then later I'll have him down to our beach house." I winnowed through my list of friends who had sons, but there were no Graces among them. And if there had been, I couldn't have baldly bargained. We just don't do things like that in my family. But even more important, Boo would never forgive me for trying.

So we all just suffered in gallant silence. I thought that Boo looked strained and pale; her voice, valiantly chirpy with pride and anxiety, seemed to be getting higher and tighter, as if it would suddenly break in a shower of sparks.

Once I dared say, "To tell you the truth" (not telling the truth at all), "I'm not sure I would allow you to go to the prom. I think you're too young."

"I've aged lately," she said, and tried to grin, but didn't manage it any better than I had managed my wobbly stand.

The days went on and other girls got bids. We knew because sometimes Boo burst into the house and said, with bright-eyed cheerfulness, "Oh, I'm so happy for Joan. And *she's* even got braces on her teeth."

We thought of making a festive family jaunt to San Francisco, on the week end of the prom.

"What would we do in ole San Francisco?" Boo asked gloomily.

"Have fun, natch."

"Doing what? Sightseeing, I suppose."

"I know people up there. My old classmate Ernestine you've heard me speak of."

"The one with the son," she said accusingly, laying bare my shameful maneuvering.

"We'd take up formals. I'd get a new one for me. And of course your *first* one. Then we'd have them, just in case."

"In case what?" she asked with dark sullenness.

"Why . . . in case anything came up."

"I don't want a formal," she said bitterly. "I doubt if I'm ever going to want one. I hate the sight of 'em. Silly sentimental net and stuff . . . practically announcing to the world you're interested in romance or something. Who's interested in romance, for golly's sake?"

So I dropped the idea of San Francisco, seeing it would be only a dismal public confession of failure on the home ground.

We knew there was no use trying to spare ourselves; we would just have to stand upon dignity and take what humiliatingly came . . . or didn't come, to be more accurate.

I considered every fantastic possibility, and rejected them all. I thought of writing a letter to our Senator, suggesting we get a bill through the legislature prohibiting proms for schoolchildren until they had reached the age of consent. This cruel situation should be stopped by law. If not by law, then by the P.T.A.

Whereas before we had had to drive her into exile for homework, now every evening Boo retired voluntarily to her room and shut the door. She didn't even care whether or not she came out to answer the telephone, and that should give you an idea how defeated and dispirited she was.

And then came a telephone call from a furry eager voice which I couldn't recognize. It said, all respectfulness, "May I please speak to Boo?"

My heart suddenly began galloping, and I said, "Why certainly. Will you wait until I go and call her?" as if I thought he might be willing to raise his voice and shout without benefit of Alexander Graham Bell.

"I'll wait," he said, sounding as if his own heart might be cantering a bit.

I ran upstairs instead of screaming, as was my impulse. "Someone on the phone," I gasped, falling through her door.

"Who?"

"I forgot to ask," I said, and kept myself from crying hysterically, *It's a boy.* But she could read it as plainly in my face as if I were passing out cigars in a comic strip.

She went down the stairs at a sedate slink, not like her

usual catapult. Obviously she was trying to tell herself, as I was, that it was *nothing*.

She said tentatively, "Hello?" and then there was a long dark silence. I thought the child had fainted. Then a dead syllable floated up to me where I was shivering over the banisters.

"Yes," she said, and her voice sounded hacked out of wood. I couldn't help making up a brilliant sentence that she could have said, but she wasn't telepathic enough to read my mind. So she said, "Yes," again, and after a wide desert of silence, she muttered, "You're welcome," and I heard her putting the phone back in its cradle.

I bounded down the stairs, trying not to look eager.

She said crossly, "What's everybody excited about?"

"Nobody's excited, dear," I lied. She stamped past me with her fists jammed into the pockets of her bathrobe. Her hair, put up in pin curls, added nothing to her winsomeness, except as touching confession that hope springs eternal.

Now the whole family had massed, waiting to be told. At the top of the stairs she didn't even turn around and look down at us, for she probably knew she would see us stripped of all decent decorum. Over her shoulder she said dully, "That was Winthrop Rawes. He's in my Probs class. He wanted to ask was the assignment what he thought it was. It was."

I gripped the banister weakly. "Maybe you hung up . . . too quick," I said in what was unintentionally a little whimper.

"Too quick for what?" she exploded. Then she began to cry. We stood congealed with agony and helplessness. "I don't see why a person can't have any privacy in her own house," she said. "You'd think my business was a public issue. I'm human, like anybody else. All I want is a little *privacy* . . ." That wasn't what she wanted by any means; it wasn't what any of us wanted. But it was as good a word as any to describe our indescribable misery.

Nail Broth

᭞ MY FATHER loves an old story from the folklore of Sweden. His mother told it to him, and he told it to me scores of times when I was a little girl. I liked it then just as a fairy tale. But since I have grown up I like it even more. When I have watched people react to each other, giving or withholding, I sometimes remember the old story and it seems to me a great parable of human relationship.

I hope you are not too far away from story days to listen to it, the way my father tells it:

"One cold twilight," he says, "a merry wayfarer came through the forest, and there on the edge of the woods he found a little cabin. A single stingy candle was squinting in the window, and a raveling of smoke blew up from the chimney. He knocked on the door, and in a few minutes it was opened a suspicious crack. A mean and meager old face peered out, and a voice, just waiting for a quarrel, said, 'What's your business, tramp?'

" 'I'm not a tramp, grandmother. I'm a human far from my home.'

" 'What's that to me?' the old woman grumbled.

" 'Well, I hoped I might sleep the night on your kitchen floor, grandmother.'

" 'I guessed as much,' she said sourly, not opening the door any farther. 'Why should I share my home with a stranger when I haven't enough for myself?'

" 'Not enough for yourself!' he cried with all sympathy. 'And you such an old woman, too!'

"Her lip trembled with self-pity, but she still didn't open the door. 'I'm about to go to bed without supper,' she said. 'So what chance have you of being fed from my cupboard?'

" 'Without supper!' he cried. 'Oh, you poor dear thing. In that case I must come in and share what I have with you.'

" 'A likely notion that *you* would have anything to share,' she said crossly. But her curiosity was sitting up and looking around greedily.

" 'All of us have more than we realize, grandmother,' he said gently. 'And we can always multiply, if we start with what we have and make something of that.'

"She found herself, in spite of herself, opening the door then. But he didn't come in until she curtly motioned with her head. Then he stepped in and glanced around the room with pleasure, admiring everything, so that the old woman herself looked around in surprise at her simple possessions.

"Then she became cautious again. 'What's all that talk about sharing, I'd like to know?' she said crossly.

" 'Oh yes. If you have nothing in the house to eat, I must have been sent especially to help you. For I have here something that is almost magic.' He took from his pocket and held lovingly in his hand a plain bent nail. She looked at it with reluctant curiosity.

" 'Give me a pot of water on the boil, and I'll make you the finest nail broth you ever ate,' he said pleasantly.

"When the pot was boiling with the nail bobbing about in the water, he stirred it carefully, and almost to himself he began remembering nourishing broths he had made that very week with this same nail. 'Of course, it may be a bit thin tonight,' he admitted, 'because only yesterday I used it in the hunting lodge of the Baron of Blekinge.'

" 'The Baron of Blekinge,' she cried incredulously. He appeared not to notice her amazement and pleasure at the aristocratic name.

" 'Wonderful broth I made for him from this nail,' he said. 'But, to be sure, he *did* have a handful of meal to add to it.'

"The old woman's eyes glinted. If only a little meal stood in the way of her having a supper as good as the Baron of Blekinge enjoyed. . . . Grudgingly, but with her pride challenged, she went to the cupboard and produced not one but two handfuls of meal.

" 'There,' she said with a chuckle, 'if the Baron has one, we'll allow ourselves two. What do you think of that?'

"The wayfarer clucked his approval, and the two of them smiled understandingly at each other over the boiling pot.

" 'The Baron said that if I had arrived but one night earlier, we should have had salt beef to add to our broth,' he mused after a few moments.

" 'Salt beef, is it?' the old woman said gruffly. Then her face flushed with excitement at the idea of excelling such aristocratic hospitality as the Baron had offered.

"While the stranger was putting in the fragments of beef, he said thoughtfully, 'I wish with all my heart I had a few grains of coffee, so I could make a cup to toast my lady's generosity. . . .'

" 'Who says we have no coffee?' she replied brusquely.

"When it was brought and the aroma admired, the way-farer said, 'Let us set out this feast on an embroidered cloth, grandmother. For such an occasion as this, we must have everything as fine as you deserve.'

"The old woman blushed at the compliment, for it had been years since anyone had said such a thing to her. In her happy confusion she went to the cupboard and brought out the best cloth, and while her guest was laying it she thought, Such a guest as this deserves a hostess in a gown, not a mean old woman in a work apron.

"She excused herself and went into the bedroom to change into her Sunday frock. On the window sill she saw the blossom of her house plant. Recklessly she broke it off and pinned it in her hair, hardly daring to look at herself in the mirror.

"Just before they sat down on either side of the table, she lighted the two candles she had been saving for her funeral bier, and stood them in the center, for she knew that she might never again be entertaining a man who had such magnificent ideas as this man had.

"He lifted his coffee cup and drank her a toast. 'Here's to a gracious and charming woman,' he said. 'People deserve the best they give to each other.'

"She beamed with pride, for here was a man at last who really appreciated her. Who understood her as she never had been understood before.

"And I shall never be poor again, she thought to herself, now that I know how to make broth out of an old nail."

Education Yet?

੨❧ MEMORY IS a slick politician who will support either side of the argument loyally. On some days when I think I probably had the best childhood ever known, my memory pops up with all kinds of corroborating evidence. Even school was a carefree paradise, as I remember it then.

At other times I recall that my school days were terribly serious business. I see myself a heroic and studious child, worrying incessantly and studying far into the night, long after everyone else was slothfully asleep. I think to myself, "Nothing I have had to face as an adult was as crucial as what I bore every day as a child. Examinations, for instance! Education is grim pain most of the way."

But it doesn't look so very grim as our children live it today. The parents' meetings I attend give the impression that it is abhorrent for anything to make our children feel concerned or responsible.

"Bringing home excellent grades is not nearly so important as students becoming well adjusted," we're frankly told.

Meanwhile the high school students I know seem dangerously well adjusted. And furthermore, let us not even mention anything so painful (though unimportant) as grades.
Let us not show our old-fashionedness, shall we? Let's take
education the way it is, concealing whatever tremors we
feel about it.

Today, for example, I heard a car pulling in with sound
effects into our drive. I was expecting someone, so I ran
out to meet what I thought would be a taxi. Instead there
was a bright scarlet car heaving with a kangaroo lurch under
our porte-cochere. It was packed with youngsters, five of
them and a beaming little man next to the driver. "Okay
. . . put on brakes, yet!" he was shouting.

I was so surprised by the banner hanging on the side of
the car that at first glance I didn't recognize the occupants.
The banner said, "Drivers Instruction. Beverly Hills High
School." There, sitting behind the wheel, was Boo, looking
pink-faced and triumphant.

"Well, I got the brakes on yet," she said explosively, and
the instructor, who turned out to be an enterprising refugee
hired by the school as part of its Social Studies program,
daubed at his forehead with a silk handkerchief.

"You expected the oleander to jump out of the way already?" he asked.

I said, "To what do we owe the honor of this unexpected
visit?" Nobody paid any attention to my nervous attempt
to be light-handed.

Boo said proudly, "We've got the champion lousy driveway. I told Mr. Manheim about how nobody hardly ever
drives in or out of it without running off onto the grass, or

mowing down the rosebushes, or nosing into the side of the wall."

Mr. Manheim said genially, "So I say if it's as bad as she says, we make it our official place for practicing getting into driveways."

"It's an honor," Boo said. "I was going to keep it as a surprise for you."

"Well, thanks very much," I beamed, trying not to anticipate what it would be like to have this onslaught every day.

"I mean the whole thing," Boo explained. "I wasn't going to tell you until I had my license, and then I was going to show you kind of casually."

A boy volunteered, "That wouldn't work, stupid. You have to have your parents' signature before you can take the driving test."

Another boy said, "It's quite a sharp idea, though. They figure now that you can't consider yourself as having a high school education unless you can drive a car."

I said humbly, "Dr. Albert Einstein never could drive a car."

Nobody heard me except Mr. Manheim, who said boastfully, "I could have taught him to drive all rightie. Dr. Einstein could have graduated from high school without any trouble already."

They backed the car down the drive, taking only a mild swoop onto the grass, and charging at one trembling rosebush.

A boy in the back seat shouted out, "Hey, there, you scared the pants off of that rosebush!"

Then there was a general reshuffling, and a new driver

slid under the wheel. I watched three out of the five wage the battle of the bushes, and then I went cravenly into the house. Everybody was having a lovely time, and I didn't want to be a wet blanket on such sport.

But that gaunt impostor my memory has invented as myself-when-young, couldn't help muttering, "This is education already?"

Prescription: Dose of Children

(shake well before using)

૨❧ I ALWAYS DID ENJOY eavesdropping. (It's legitimate if you're a writer, so no apologies.) Some of the best conversations are the ones that are none of your business.

For instance, in the beauty shop where I go to catch up on *Vogue,* I heard a little girl begging her mother, who was under the dryer, to let her have a permanent.

The mother said, "Of course not. Do you think I have a money bush somewhere?"

The child said cheerfully, in a tone too low to be heard under the dryer, "I water it every day."

Another time I overheard what was evidently a new child eagerly getting acquainted with some of the early settlers in our neighborhood.

"I'm not very well adjusted," the new little girl said. "So if I say anything you don't like, why I probably don't mean it. Okay?"

A jacaranda tree grows outside my study window, and from this I pick up some good eavesdropping. A jacaranda tree is fine for little boys to sit beneath and talk. Today they were boasting about how brave they were. Boasting, one of the most ancient masculine sports, flourishes uninhibited when males are alone. For females are all too often dismally realistic.

"Would you really sock him one?" a small chap was asking a slightly bigger boy.

"Would I?" the eight-year-old said in a fierce voice. "Just let me get the chance."

"What would you do?"

"I'd sock him one . . . then I'd run like the mischief," the boaster said.

It took them a few minutes to see the humor, then they rolled on the grass with glee.

Every adult needs a few children on his perimeter. If you've become a little top-heavy maybe you need a daily dose. The prescription says "Shake well"; it's talking about the patient, not the remedy.

Fortunately for all of us, there's no shortage of children these days. Every street, every train and plane, every supermarket teems with children ready and willing to help you with your ailment of ossified adulthood. And parents are quite willing to share their young.

A friend of mine crossed the country in a daycoach.

"However did you manage?" she was asked.

"Manage? Why, I just got on the train and forgot the kids. All kinds of people took them over."

A bachelor I know says, "Traveling is more broadening this year than ever. I had kids in my lap the whole trip."

"I thought you didn't like children," I reminded him.

He grinned sheepishly. "I used to get 'em in my hair . . . this year I've got 'em in my arms."

Sometimes people admit they're afraid of children. "I don't know how to get along with them." But all you have to do is to smile back. Nobody has ever written a juvenile book on "How to win friends and influence people." Children are born knowing.

Once you've opened this new window in your viewpoint, you've got a real hobby. Children are never too busy to have fun. You get the idea when you're with them that there's nothing more important than being happy. Just possibly they're advance pioneers with that discovery; maybe nothing *is* more important.

Children can enjoy almost anything, even mild emergency. I heard a little boy say, "We had a keen time. Had to sit for nearly two hours on a broken-down bus. More fun! I thought maybe we might have to stay there all night."

"What did you do?"

"Well, I ate a lady's lunch. Then when they got to looking at the motor, the driver let me hold the flashlight. Golly. More fun!"

A very learned man was telling me about a boy who has befriended him.

"How big is he?" I asked, trying to get a picture of this companionship.

"How big? Why, I don't know . . ." He made a vague indication of height. "Anyway he comes just about up to my funnybone."

The 200-Watt Mystery

ॐ OUR LITTLE TUMPTI was full of mysteries. When you knew him you saw why the cliché "inscrutable" sticks like a Band-Aid to the word "Oriental." Almost everything Tumpti did was a mystery, and added to that was the mystery of *how* and *why*.

But there was one abiding question furnishing speculation endlessly. How on earth did he spend his evenings in his room? The second morning he was with us, he came out to the breakfast table with indignation disfiguring his pleasant little face. Perilously he was balancing a radio on one outspread hand.

"I no rike," he said.

"Well, then don't listen to it," we suggested.

"Please take out of my loom. It get in my way."

"Sometime there might be a program you wanted to hear, and then you'd have it handy."

"Take out or I blake it," he said with a meaningful look in his eye. "I dlop it accidentally."

We took it out. Also we took out the TV set that had been the condition on which our last help had consented to give us her slipshod services.

"Perhaps you'd rather read," I suggested. "You can borrow any of the books you see around."

"I bollow no books."

"Or magazines . . . and of course we have three newspapers coming in every day."

"Newspaper I wrap up tlash in," he said with dignity.

Someone who was at that moment eating one of his excellent popovers said defensively, "So he doesn't read. What's so funny about that?"

He glared at the table in general. "I need better erectric right in my loom. No good. Luin eyesight."

"Of course," we said placatingly. "We keep the bulbs in the mop closet. Take all you need."

"I use 200 watts erectric right," he said, and we looked delighted.

When he had gone back to the kitchen, leaving the radio precariously perched on the edge of a chair, we carried on a family conversation with eyebrows.

Somebody whispered, "What on earth do you suppose he does do at night?"

"Whatever it is, he wants to see what he's doing."

Boo said, "He probably meditates. Aren't they great meditators?"

"But they do that best in the dark, don't they?"

We all shrugged our shoulders, giving up the guessing game.

But whatever it was he did, he kept at it until long after

midnight, for you could see the little magnolia tree which stands near his window, illuminated like one of Nightingale's prize-garden effects. His window blind was pulled tightly down so there was no space for even an ant to peek. But the brilliance of his two 200-watt bulbs made a Japanese lantern of the room. We just couldn't help being intrigued by the mystery.

"Probably something very simple, like playing a long game of chess with an opponent in Japan. Anyway I know we'll find out sometime. In this world stuff just doesn't stay mysterious, alas."

But we didn't find out for a very long time. And when we did the answer was so preposterous that no amount of wildest guessing would ever have uncovered it.

Carats of Kindness

ᛒᛥ WHEN WE WERE children living in a humble part of town, we soon accepted the fact that all that glitters is not gold. We had a riddle which asked: "Why is Christmas jewelry like grass?" The answer, in case you weren't a child in that naïve period, was "Because they both turn green in the spring."

This is a story, a true story, about a piece of Christmas jewelry.

We didn't have much jewelry in my family . . . my mother's wedding ring, and her engagement ring with a diamond not much bigger than a grain of rice, and my father's lodge pin.

But we *knew* people who owned jewelry. One Christmas my mother's best friend got a big round gold bracelet from her husband. We were stunned by such magnificence. But I was guilty and shamed because our mother, who was such a wonderful woman, had no bracelet . . . and little chance of ever owning one.

When she and I talked of the beauty I said passionately,

"When I grow up I'm going to buy you a gold bracelet. The most beautiful one I can find."

Then suddenly in myself I swore a reckless vow. I wouldn't wait until I grew up. I'd manage to get it for her by the very next Christmas. She would see . . . everyone would see. . . .

I was fourteen that year, the age when all one needs to ride forth on a great crusade is a deeply felt cause. I knew, of course, that I couldn't buy such a gift by any childish "saving" of my allowance, for even if I saved every penny, it would be absurdly inadequate. I would have to earn some real money. I'd have to venture out into competitive adult enterprise.

I took the newspaper into the bathroom, locked the door, and combed the column called Business Opportunities. Regular employment was not feasible for someone with school on her hands. But I could carry on a business . . . presumably from a locked bathroom. Most of the opportunities, though glowing, sought a partner with capital. Obviously I couldn't qualify. But at last I found an offer of a size I could manage.

You had to send a dollar right away. Well, I could do that, by borrowing seventeen cents. Then the Dixie Mailing Company would tell you how to multiply the investment by at least a hundred a month. My head swam.

Each day I ran home from school in a fever, hot with hope. At last my instructions arrived, a flamboyant piece of wishful rhetoric. It explained exactly what was to be done, and how to word the letters with which you started your career.

You selected small businesses, then promised the proprietors that you could increase their gross. You saved your method for the follow-up letter. At the right time you explained that you would find new customers, for which you would ask 10 per cent of the first hundred dollars each spent. As soon as you got the little businessman signed up, you went to work on the customers. You promised them a rebate of 5 per cent on the hundred dollars they spent. It sounded wonderful. I had postage enough for only eight letters, but I wrote them neatly, and the feverish waiting began again.

Of the eight, one replied . . . a postcard saying,

Dear Sir: Drop in and discuss your prop.
                                    WILHELM METZEROTH.

I walked past his store a dozen times before I got up my courage. I explained who I was, and he asked solemnly about my proposition. Then he called his *vife* from upstairs. Four round blue eyes inspected me while he told her my story in a volley of rich German. Then their roars of laughter put me out of business in nothing flat. Even now I cannot relive the moment without embarrassment.

So I knew there would be for me no easy way of wealth.

Then suddenly I remembered our pearls. We loved oysters, and whenever we bit down on a hard object, the whole family became richer by one pearl. Rather dark, of course, and sometimes lopsided. But certainly genuine, since pearls come from oysters. We kept them in a twist of tissue paper, and they belonged to us all jointly.

I counted out my one-fourth.

The next interview took even stiffer courage, for this time

it was no genial neighborhood grocer I had to deal with, but a well-dressed man in the precious-gems section of the best jewelry store in the city.

I unfolded my tissue on purple velvet; the rather grandfatherly man behind the counter looked at my pearls gravely. Then he took off his glasses and looked at me.

I said nervously, "I thought whatever the regular price of pearls is, I'd gladly sell these at a reduced rate. I know they need polishing, and of course they're not very large. . . ."

He looked at the grayish little globules again, then he asked, "May I know, Miss, why you have decided to sell these . . . gems?"

I had not expected to tell him, for it was quite a personal matter. But somehow I found the words tumbling out. He listened sympathetically and asked a few questions, and in a few minutes I was showing him the snapshot of my mother, which was the only wealth I carried in my purse.

He looked closely at her picture, and after a moment he said, "I also loved my mother very much. But I didn't have a chance to do nice things for her because she died when I was still a little shaver."

Then he became businesslike. "Look here. I've got to be honest with you because you've been honest with me. I *could* say we just don't happen to need any pearls right now. Then you'd go on hoping. But I've got to tell you . . . these aren't pearls. They're worthless. Edible oysters don't produce pearls."

The floor felt as if it were collapsing under me. Mercifully appearing not to notice, he went on talking, telling me about pearls. Then he began explaining the possibility of my earning the money I needed. He had a sister who worked in the employment office of a small department store. Did I think . . . of course I thought! I could work on Saturday afternoons. Saturday mornings we cleaned house. I could do anything. He wrote down his sister's name and gave it to me.

Then, since I was there, I thought I might just look at some gold bracelets. Together we walked to another department. Under glass was a tray on which gleaming gold bracelets nestled in velvet cradles. I stopped, breathless.

"Not these," he said hastily. "I'm afraid we'd find these rather expensive. But I have others."

He disappeared, then came back with three bracelets in his hand. They were just as beautiful as any bracelets on earth could be . . . and one especially.

"I think you might afford one of these," he said.

"But . . . how much?" I asked tremulously.

"Well, the price might possibly vary through the year . . . gold prices rise and fall, you understand. It would depend on many things." He went on with some kind of adult double-talk, the dazzle of which I couldn't quite follow. Then he said, "As a matter of fact, if you find you can earn the money, I might get a special discount for you. The wholesale price, perhaps, under the circumstances."

"But if I had some idea," I said timidly. "So I'd know how hard I would have to work."

He looked carefully at me quite a long time. Then he said something which has probably done more than any other single remark to influence me.

"To succeed in anything," he said gently, "one always **works a little harder than one feels possible.**"

Getting the job wasn't simple, even with his sister's help. A fourteen-year-old wouldn't fit everywhere. But at last I fitted. Now it was late February; much time had been wasted. Finally I had my first pay for one-half day, three precious quarters.

That winter I went in several times to look at the glorious bracelet. Each time it had become more beautiful. When I had earned five dollars, I took the fresh bill to my friend. "I'd like to have you lay the bracelet away," I said, trying to sound businesslike. "I am prepared to make a down payment. Also I don't believe you mentioned the price."

He looked at me keenly and asked how much I thought I could earn by Christmas. I computed rapidly, adding in my allowance recklessly.

"I might be able to pay twenty-five dollars," I said. "But I'd be a lot more comfortable if it cost twenty."

He said firmly, "It costs twenty-two."

"I'm sure I can make that," I said confidently.

But in October I caught diphtheria. Several nights in delirium I was tortured by gold hoops, and my mother seemed crying her eyes out about something I couldn't quite understand. The diphtheria infuriated me; it was a conspiracy against my determination. The time I had to waste just couldn't be made up before Christmas. All the work, all the Saturday afternoons when I'd given up fun with my contemporaries would just go for nothing.

The middle of December I went again to see my friend. I had decided to tell him frankly I couldn't get the twenty-two dollars by Christmas. What about the discount? Had he forgotten that?

"But the twenty-two dollars is *with* the discount," he said uneasily. "Without that, the price would be considerably higher."

I saw now he had lost faith in me. I felt utterly defeated. Maybe I should have told him about the diphtheria . . . but it sounded like an excuse, a crybaby excuse. . . .

Then I had an inspiration. "Couldn't you let me have the bracelet by Christmas, and I could go on working and paying you through January and February?" I said weakly. "You'd be perfectly safe if you trusted me."

"Unless something happened to you. Like illness, for instance."

"Nothing would happen to me," I said fiercely. "I'm healthy as a horse."

He thought quite a long time, then he said not too certainly, "Well . . . next Saturday, after you finish your work, you come in, and I think I can promise to let you have the bracelet."

Christmas came on Monday. But I couldn't endure the suspense, so my mother had her bracelet on Christmas Eve. Never on earth was a gift so adored; never was a giver so showered with love. Everyone in the neighborhood came to admire; nobody could believe such a thing belonged to my mother.

The only cloud for me was that I still owed a little more than three dollars before I could honestly consider the bracelet was hers. I think no adult could worry about an obligation as that little girl worried about hers. Suppose something *did* happen to me? Would the jewelry store send police to our house? My family would be disgraced before everyone we knew. My grades slid into ignominy that midwinter.

But in time I got the last cent paid up, without tragedy gobbling me up.

My mother wore the bracelet all her life. When she no longer was with us, my father gave the bracelet to me. I couldn't wear it at first, partly because it was too close to my grief. And also because as I grew up I had come to feel almost bitter about the salesman who had begun by being kind and had ended by exacting the last farthing from a worried half-sick child. He should have realized. . . .

Yet, often through the years I have recognized that I owed that man a great deal. For whenever I am tempted to spare myself the last cruel extra mile of effort, I have remembered him.

"Through the years . . ." One day a few months ago when I was thinking about all this, the phrase struck me. It suddenly occurred to me that this bracelet, this inexpensive piece of Christmas jewelry, had lasted an amazingly long time. I had always thought of the price in the child's terms, but suddenly I saw that something odd was here. I counted the years. . . .

Then I happened to be in a fine jewelry shop in London. On an impulse I asked the salesman to look at the bracelet. What did he think it might be worth?

"It's a very fine piece, madam," he said. "It's pure gold. Eighteen carats, actually."

I have written this now to apologize to that unknown grandfatherly man, whose 18-carat kindness I had wrongly appraised through the years.

All That's Lacking

§∽ THERE IS ALWAYS one special friend who confounds the whole family. In our case, we can see what Boo sees in Felicity; the mystery is why Felicity bothers with Boo. Felicity, contrary to her name, is a moody and devious child. Perhaps her mother had a premonition and hoped to ward off the moroseness with a name. Felicity is all agreeableness and smoothness on the outside of her behavior to adults. But already, though she is not yet sixteen, there is the fine print of shrewdness and discontent on her face.

But Boo likes her. Boo thinks she is "deep." Also cool. And in fact, crazy. (Crazy being the highest compliment of the moment.) So we do our best to make ourselves acceptable to Felicity. Which is no mean feat, and one we're never confident we've achieved.

Felicity's philosophy comes home to us, blithely borne by our own innocent-hearted child.

"Yes, but can happiness buy money?" We recognize where *that* comes from, without any quotation marks.

"Early to bed and early to rise makes a man healthy,

wealthy . . . and never around when stuff happens."

"If all history teachers were laid end to end . . . but who wants to lay history teachers?" That one we pass with no comment, afraid of cracking the cellophane and letting out the real aroma.

You know Felicity. You've probably had a few of her in your own life, along the way.

Felicity wants to be a fashion designer when she has finished what she playfully calls her education. (My private opinion is that Felicity's knowledge was present, intact, in the original chromosome.) Education, the momentarily necessary evil, is really a campus to her; classrooms are only oases where you go to replot your strategy between the delightful surging of the crowds through the corridors. By crowds, naturally, we mean crowds of boys. Felicity doesn't count girls, except possibly as inert hurdles in an obstacle race.

Felicity does enjoy working in the art studio of our big high school. This you can understand when you see the freedom and camaraderie of the place. Everyone sits in tight little skirts with neat behinds innocently outlined, before big teacher-obscuring easels, and life can be delightful. And home work can easily be construed as brooding over one's personal appearance, and planning fantastic costumes for oneself. Felicity is very good in Dress Design.

But her mother, a realistic and practical woman, is not sure. Her mother is all pulled apart and weary-looking from trying to make ends meet. You can see when you look at her that she knows how to stretch herself, but not the ends. She's determined that since Felicity will have to earn her own living at least until she can delude some man into earning it for her, she'd better be equipped to do something practical. So she says flatly, "Felicity can be a dress designer only if she shows so much talent that there's no risk about it. She can find out this year if she's good enough to go on."

So Felicity is on probation as far as dress designing is concerned.

"If she's terrific, her mother can't ignore the talent," Boo says. "And you know nobody is going to ignore anything that Felicity wants. Not permanently."

Today, as I quite often do, I found Boo waiting with Felicity deigning to be driven home in our car.

"Are you sure it's no bother?" Felicity says, pretending to wait for me to urge her. "I can easily walk home. It's only three miles, and I let all the other people drive off because I did want to help Boo with her geometry."

"We're thrilled to have you," I say. "Do get in, dear."

"Only if you're *sure.*"

"We're terribly sure," I say. And this remark at least is utterly sincere.

Once in the car, she devotes herself to talking nicely to the old folks. "Might as well cement relations, never can tell when they might come in handy," you can almost hear her little mind saying to itself.

So I try to talk nicely to her. It would be a strategic breach on my part to let Boo convict me of not being as gracious as Felicity. Boo sits demurely, her blue eyes weighing both of us, for she suspects that there is something wrong with me as far as Felicity is concerned.

"How goes the fashion designing?" I ask brightly.

"Oh wonderfully, thanks," Felicity purrs.

"How does your mother feel about it now?"

"My mother?" she asks politely, as if she'd never heard of the individual.

"You remember what she told me that day you both came to luncheon with us."

"Oh?"

"That she'd let you go on studying only if she was sure you had unmistakable talent."

Felicity is quiet a moment, then she says sweetly, "Oh, there's no doubt about my talent."

I crawl out from under the avalanche of that simple remark, and then I say, trying not to sound too acidly middle-aged about it, "Well, I'm glad to hear that. But of course talent is only part of the battle."

"Battle?" she asks gently, as if I were a savage imperfectly equipped with the language.

"Well, what I mean is, talent is important. But hard work is equally important."

"Oh, I see what you mean," she says generously. "Actually, I'm capable of almost too much hard work. I never know when to stop. That's what people tell me."

Boo rushes in here to corroborate this thumbnail sketch of her darling. "Oh you don't, Felicity! Everybody else falls by the wayside, and you go right on."

Felicity says, not really hearing Boo, "Oh, I have plenty of talent. And I certainly know how to work. But there's one thing I do lack. And that worries me."

"For heaven's sake, what is *that?*" I asked incredulously.

Felicity says with a little sigh, "I just haven't enough self-confidence."

Each to His Own Riches

ॐ PEOPLE WHO LOVE trees instantly recognize each other by an invisible family resemblance of the heart. Some of the nicest persons I know were introduced to me by my friends, the trees. Particularly the espalier trees. That word, in case you don't happen to be acquainted with that old line of aristocrats, describes the little fruit trees which have been shaped by patience, and by pruning which is art's faith in abundance. An espalier tree resembles its own shadow, having practically only two dimensions, height and width, and hardly more depth than a vine. It is as though the tree had been "pressed" like a keepsake flower, between the huge pages of the earth and the sky.

The best espalier trees . . . the ones you see in rural France and fashionable England, and on some of the most beautiful tapestries of the Gobelins . . . are geometric in design. Each little twig is planned according to pattern; they are rounded but strict right angles at the ends of perfectly horizontal limbs. When the fruits come . . . cherries, peaches, apples, or pears . . . they, too, are set in the design, like the fruit in illuminated parchments.

When you love and understand a tree, you own it, for that is the only possessorship there is. Three most publicly owned espaliers I know stand high above the Hudson, against the walls of one of the gardens of The Cloisters. The sun warms them there with a kind of double sunshine, browned on both sides. That is why spring always comes a little early to them, so that they are decked with nosegays of blossoms when blossoms are still incredible miracles in a city.

These trees introduced me to the man who cares for them, and he in turn gave me a card to his friend Nils Narvgaard, who is the head gardener on one of the big estates in Connecticut.

The day I arrived, Nils was sitting on the stone wall at the gate, waiting with a welcome. He had a deep Danish voice, a voice which no high wind could blow away, a seaman's voice. He had seaman's eyes, but a landsman's hands, strong, quick, and certain.

He knew his land . . . all the hundred acres of it . . . as intimately as you might know a beloved face, for he has lived with it for thirty-five years. They have grown up (but not old) together; they have gardened each other, you might say, for every acre which he has cultivated and cared for in the land has landscaped in him a matching acre of patience and joy, of planning and pruning and waiting-for-flower. You listen to his rich quiet words, his humor and tenderness, and the strong mastery which takes no nonsense from wanton growth, no backtalk from weeds or brambles, and you think suddenly:

Which is the garden and which the gardener?

Then you glimpse the truth about all achievement, that it is no flowing away, but a double-running current which enriches every channel through which it streams.

"The Old Man loved those," Nils said, pointing to that screen of tall espaliers standing with outstretched arms against the sky. "He used to call them our taller brothers. He used to come down here with me, and we'd work side by side all day. We knew each other, he and I." Yes, I could see that. Two of them owned this land, though only one's name was on the tax bill.

Behind the espaliers lay the garden. Walking about in it, I could see the family and the years which lay beyond all this, clear as the lines of living on Nils's weather-worn face. While the garden had been building, Nils had seen a whole generation of this family swing around the clock. He had made a riding ring for the children's ponies; he had grown white lilacs for the young mother, and purple stock for the Old Madam. He had planted holly for Christmas, and forget-me-nots for debuts; he had marked the coming of a Swede into the family with an herb garden, and the marrying of a Scottish girl with a path of heather.

But now times had changed. A new world had come thumping at the gates. A bank is paying his salary now; a board of trustees is deciding what to do with him, and what to do with his garden. When you plant trees and a man's life in a garden, you cannot uproot them quickly when their day is done.

"The gardens aren't the same now," he said after a few minutes of silence. "Since the Old Man's gone, nobody cares about it any more. Young Mr. William never even comes down to look at it. Young people aren't the same."

"Maybe he will care later," I ventured. "Maybe he's just too young now."

"Maybe," he answered sadly. "But I don't think so. He hasn't got it in him. Young people . . . they haven't got anything to see a tree with."

"How young is he, your Mr. William?"

"Well, Mr. William . . . " He thought honestly about it, trying to give Mr. William every hope of the doubt. "Well, Mr. William must be fifty or so."

I tried to picture young Mr. William, who could have known this rich old gardener, and that no-less-rich Old Man, his father, if only he had known how to be introduced by a tree. What was he like, this man who could have been rich himself, yet had chosen not to see riches?

"What kind of man is he?" I asked.

"He teaches at some university," Nils said, trying fairly to give him his due. "He writes some kind of books . . . study books, I believe. He's always shut up some place writing his books."

"Oh! What kind of books? And what does he teach?"

The honest blue eyes came back from the top branch of the espalier trees, and he looked at me a long, thoughtful moment.

"I don't know as I ever heard," he said simply, with the dignity of indifference.

An Open Letter to a Baby

(about to be born)

੨❧ MY DEAR YOUNG FRIEND (so young, in fact, you still wear a minus sign before your age!)

I've been told . . . by statistics, that is . . . that an awful lot of you little guys are making plans for arriving among us in the near future. This, in fact, is Baby Year. We've had bumper crops in cotton, wheat, and soy beans. In a massive muddled way the government deals with that. But now we're having a bumper crop of babies, and nobody knows what to do about it. Except make the best of it.

But your big business right now is to find yourself a good home. Sometimes that's not easy to do from a distance, which is supposed to lend enchantment to the view. I'm an old inhabitant around these parts, so I've lined up a few points which might help you.

It's not like hotel reservations, you know. You can't sleep a few nights and then check out if you don't like the place. Once you've unpacked your layette and signed the register, this is where you'll belong, for better or worse.

So pick your home carefully. Better still, don't bother

about the *home* at all; what you'd better do is concentrate on The Parents. They're all that's going to matter. Homes will come and homes will go, but parents go on forever. If you have the right parents, it won't make any difference to you whether you live in a trailer or a penthouse. And if you've made poor pickings in fathers and mothers, no amount of house elegance will make up for the lack.

In this world we have scientific methods for detecting all sorts of things . . . all types of Geiger counters, so to speak. Chemicals for showing up this; instruments for registering that. But nobody's ever discovered a way of detecting a Good Parent hidden behind the disguise of an Ordinary Person.

Sometimes the people who know the most about babies can't get along with them in person . . . even schoolteachers don't always make good mothers. On the other hand some of the most unlikely-looking girls . . . selfish brats, tomboys and even career girls . . . often turn out to be inspired mothers when the moment arrives. (I don't know why I say "when the moment arrives"; I mean "when YOU arrive.")

One test, however, may help you. When you're looking around for a good mother to give the job to, be sure you pick a woman who enjoys whatever she happens to be doing. They say, "If you want to get something done, ask a busy person to do it." So if you want to get a mother you'll really enjoy . . . and who'll enjoy you, pick out one that's already having fun. She doesn't necessarily have to be a baby-fancier; you can take care of that later. Babies are an acquired taste. But she should be crazy about things in general; she should throw herself into whatever she's doing. Enthusiasm; that's what she's got to have.

Don't bother about the way parents look. There never was a mother who wasn't beautiful when her child looks up into her eyes. And when you sit on your dad's knee and see him grinning down at you over the proud swell of his chest, you'll notice what a fine brave man he is. Other people may not always be able to see him clearly; but you will.

Don't bother about their age. If they're too young, you'll age 'em. If they're a bit on the oldish side, you'll soon limber them up.

Be sure they're in love with each other, if you can manage it. If they're in love with each other, they'll know how to love you. They'll love you for yourself, and in addition, each will give you a second helping of love because of the other. If they're in love with each other as they should be, they'll keep you in your own little place, not trying to make you play a part emotionally too big for you, not batting you back and forth between your own world and what should be theirs. That kind of thing confuses a child.

Look in their bureau drawers if you insist on orderly people; and into their bank accounts if you feel you're going to be an extravagance. But first of all, look into their hearts. If they are full already, there will be plenty of room there for you. A child *can* fill an empty or a shriveled heart, but it isn't nice work and it won't make you the kind of human you'll enjoy being.

Notice your dad's mouth, and his jaw and the glint in his eye. Pick him for firmness, like good fruit. Listen to the way he says "No." A man who knows how to say the right kind of "No" will also stand behind his "Yes."

You'll be terribly unsure of things for the first twenty years (and a long time afterwards, probably). There's nothing that makes a child feel as safe as good firm parents.

Pick people who play. You'll teach them new games. But you'll find your job easier if they already go picnicking, and swim, or ride bicycles, and in general *do* things. Be sure they don't mind questions. You can tell whether or not there's popcorn under a skull by the questions people ask.

Get into a big family, if possible. And be sure you have your full quota of grandparents.

I might as well admit that you're arriving among us at a very peculiar time. This is almost like another Genesis, because it seems a new world is being created. This time we'll have to take better care of it, all of us. This time we'll have to see, as God did, that it is "very good."

So, try to pick elastic people, so they can jump, and then land without breaking into pieces. Try to pick people who have their best treasures always with them, in their hearts and their minds. In the years ahead of us, the rich people will be the hard-working and the cheerful, the friendly and the ingenious . . . the ones who can make something out of whatever is at hand. Mothers who can make quick banquets, and fathers who can make "buddies" and helpers out of whatever strangers happen to be around them. People, in short, who can get along with themselves and each other, and who require little outside equipment.

Does it look like a big job you've got ahead of you, making a family out of two people who aren't even related to each other except by marriage? Well, it is a big job, but you can do it. Matter of fact, you're the only thing on earth that can accomplish it!

So come along, as many of you as dare, and get at it!

Invitation to the Waltz

ॐ WHEN ALL OF US had given up all hope about the Prom,
suddenly everything was fine.

Boo came bursting in the back door. It was Tumpti's
Thursday off and I was in the kitchen cooking dinner. I
knew when I saw her that something earth-shaking had
happened, for she had forgotten to change her gym shoes
after the sixth period, and her eyes were even wilder than
her hair.

"My goodness," I said, daring to say no more.

"Hi-ya keed," she said deliriously, evidently quoting some
contemporary. She dumped her armful of books on the
kitchen counter, and reached into the refrigerator for anything lying around loose. This insubordination could happen only on a Thursday, for Tumpti never allowed anyone
to so much as guess what was in the refrigerator. She began
chewing noisily, obviously not noticing what she was eating.
Then she turned on the spigot and gulped down a glass of
water. But still she couldn't trust herself to speak.

"What's for dinner?" she gasped at last.

"Oh, food," I said, trembling so that the lettuce leaves looked as if a high wind were whipping through them.

She now sat down with her feet far apart and her hands clutching her knees, the way the roller derby girls rest on television.

"What kind of a day did *you* have?" she exploded.

"Oh fine. Just fine," I said out of my dry mouth. "And how'd *you* get along?"

"Swell," she said. "Except in Probs. I flunked a test. First test I ever flunked in Probs. Must have had something on my mind."

She announced it so triumphantly that I murmured, "That's fine, dear."

She got up and loped around the kitchen aimlessly, bumping into things and flipping the gas burners on and off excitedly.

"Oh, by the way," she said at last, "a kid asked me to the Prom."

It was about as "by the way" as swearing before a notary public would have been. I attempted to match the casualness.

"Why, that's nice," I said. "Anybody I know?"

"Well, in a way you do know him. Sorta. You've talked to him on the telephone."

"Oh, you mean . . . ?"

"Yep," she said, and tossed a cookie into her mouth as if it were a basketball into the basket. Then around the crumbs, she grinned.

"Gosh," she said, "I was beginning to get worried."

"You were?" I cried in simulated astonishment. "I'm sure I can't imagine what about. Somebody was bound to ask you, you're so pretty and everything."

She stood absolutely still now. "Am I?" she asked at last. She opened the cupboard door where a departed house-keeper's mirror still hung, and studied her face earnestly.

"Well, it isn't much," she said honestly, "but I guess a guy could see that for himself. If he asked me he probably knows what he's getting."

I said to myself with fierce maternal prejudice, I doubt that. I doubt if any sixteen-year-old . . . even that wonder-ful life-saver whatever his name is . . . could possibly appre-ciate.

Aloud I said calmly, "We'll have to begin to think about a formal, won't we?"

"Begin," Boo cried. "Are you kidding?"

Then we encountered each other's eye, and we burst out laughing for sheer exuberance. Boo ran her fingers across her forehead and tossed off imaginary perspiration. "Eeek . . . wasn't that an experience!" she said, and fell into my arms limply, like a boxer who's just been set on his feet again after the ten-count.

A Speaking Part

శ్రి ONE OF OUR favorite people is Oliver Hinsdell, the drama coach. Outside he's a handsome and dignified-looking man. Inside . . . well, his students call him "Pop" with great affection.

It's a rare play that doesn't have at least one of his alumni appearing in it, in either a big role or a walk-on part. There are an awful lot of hopeful youngsters in our section of the world, expecting to be great actors some day. Until they really "make" it, they turn up in somewhat surprising places.

For instance, a girl student phoned Oliver to say she'd at last broken into the entertainment world.

"I suppose you couldn't really say it was *acting*," she said honestly. "But the costume is nice."

"Well, fine," Oliver said. "What's the costume?"

"I'm selling programs at the Hollywood Bowl, and they let me wear a lovely long flowing cape."

The real prize for optimistic interpretation, though,

should have been given to a pretty eighteen-year-old we met the other evening as we were coming out of the Pilgrimage Play, held in that amphitheater which is ten acres of Biblical Jerusalem miraculously created in our Hollywood Hills.

This girl, seeing her beloved teacher in the silent crowd leaving the Pilgrimage Bowl, ran over to speak to him.

"Oh, Mr. Hinsdell . . . I've got a part," she said in an ecstatic whisper.

"I'm so glad," Oliver whispered back. "What are you playing? I'm afraid I didn't recognize you."

"Well . . . you didn't really see me. I'm backstage," she said. "But it's a speaking part, all right. I'm the scream of the woman taken in adultery."

The Yellow Dog

᠃᠉ PROBABLY THE WORD I hear used more often than any other in connection with children is "security." I've come to the conclusion that security is something which, if you haven't it, you must talk about it. If you *do* have it, there's no point in mentioning it.

I don't believe we ever heard the word used about us when we were children. Yet I doubt if you could find more secure little individuals than we were. We knew it was a good world, held together by God in spirit, and by the firm hands of our mother and our father in the flesh.

Far from mentioning security, just the opposite category of words were said. But the contradictory words only made the undeniable fact more obvious to us.

One of the most lovable moments I remember went like this: Our father would be reading his newspaper after his day's work was finished, and we two children would be playing around quietly, waiting for him to notice us. Without looking at him, we could tell when he was ready for us, and we'd both hold our breath. Noisily then, he would fold up the paper.

"Ho-hum," he'd say, "I suppose there are no children in this house."

"Sure there are," we'd cry and leap at him, each of us scrambling up on a welcoming knee.

"Ugh, you kids are enough to smother a man," he'd say, making a terrible face. We'd chuckle, our noses pressed against his vest, feeling the fountain pen in his breast pocket, and hearing his heart pumping away reassuringly like the very motor that kept the universe running.

Then he'd say, "What I'd like is to find somebody who had a nice little yellow dog."

We had played this game ever since we could remember. So we would control our mirth and try to ask as seriously as possible, "What would you do if you found somebody who did have a little yellow dog, Daddy?"

"Why I'd see if he would be willing to trade it to me for two worthless, no-account youngsters."

"Us, Daddy?"

"Who else, do you suppose?"

"And then what would you do with the little yellow dog?"

"Why, I'd chase it off the premises," he'd say, and we'd snuggle deeper, and now all three of us would be heaving with merry contentment.

The Night, at Last

ॐ I DON'T KNOW how we lived through the suspense. I suppose every house that had a high schooler in it was enduring the same anguish. I had thought that if we just had an invitation to the Prom, the rest would all fall into place. But I was wrong. Every atom concerning the festive occasion was grim.

Shopping for the formal was not unalloyed joy, even though we had been told recklessly by the head of the house, "Now don't try to economize. Shoot the works."

Boo had responded to that, "Oh, we will. Put your mind to rest about that. Formals cost something fierce. Kids tell me their fathers are all furious."

Then she said, unfamiliar common sense protruding like teeth that need braces, "But I won't have to have anything else all year. Just thinking about me going to the Prom will keep me warm."

Even so, the shopping was a savage safari. After school each day we trekked relentlessly from shop to shop. Nothing would do. The formal had to be similar to everybody's, but not identical to anyone's. It had to be sophisticated, yet not *too*. Most of all, it had to be something Felicity would approve.

"What I gotta have," Boo explained tremulously, "is a dress that makes my hair look longer, and me look shorter. It's got to make my nose not so turned up, and my hands not so big. And it's got to be something real long, that will stay out of my way so I won't trip and drag us both to the floor."

As you see, it was quite an order for a mere dress. But at last we found the perfect one, pink and cloudy . . . something we could remember a lifetime, like her first hat, trimmed with a cluster of commas and long velvet streamers.

I said, "I suppose the boys' parents have to go through the same ordeal of shopping."

"Oh, no. Boys are supposed to wear rented tuxes," Boo said. "Wouldn't make any sense to buy a tux before a boy gets his growth. School fixes up the deal. Costs six dollars, without pants."

During this tense prelude Boo became a new person, difficult and moody like someone facing a great concert or a court trial. She had to be spoken to at least twice when anyone asked her a question, then she seemed to drag herself up from a well, dull-eyed and pale and dripping with worry. She couldn't eat, whereas normally she couldn't be filled up.

"All I care about eating is celery. Or maybe olives," she said languidly.

She and this mysterious Winthrop Rawes avoided each other as if they were partners in a crime about to be uncovered. Each afternoon when she came home I'd ask tactfully, "How was Winthrop today?"

"How should I know?" she said peevishly. "We don't discuss his wonderful condition in Probs. We've got better things to do."

"Did you thank him for his invitation, dear?"

"Good heavens, no," she cried in horror. "What'd you think I *am?*"

"A well-brought-up girl, I hope," I said primly.

"Perish the perish."

Then suddenly this mutual ignoring became a worry, for worries could spring up from anything like weeds on well-fertilized soil. Suppose he hadn't really asked her? Maybe she had only imagined it.

"Nonsense," I said staunchly. "Of course he asked you."

"He kind of mumbled," Boo said. "Now that I think of it, I was kind of excited. And he *didn't* ask the time he telephoned."

"He was scared," I said. "I guess boys get scared too."

She looked as if she couldn't believe such heresy.

My heart ached with pity for all of them who were suffering the terrible malady of youngness.

"Tomorrow you just say something nice to him," I suggested. But Boo paled at the thought.

"I wouldn't know what to say."

"Couldn't you just be natural?"

"Certainly not," she said. "At our age it isn't natural to be natural."

"Nonsense. You'll have a perfectly wonderful time. Do you think we should get you a nice little corsage?"

"Heavens no! A gardenia is included in the three and a half bucks the bid cost," she said. Then with a lightning quick change of mood, she went on, "I'll press it in the dictionary afterwards, and tell my children it came from my very First Prom."

"Well, all right. But tomorrow you speak to him nicely. Tell him you're looking forward."

"Oh please," she said. "I gag at the thought."

But during the night she thought of a sufficiently casual way of mentioning it. She came bounding down to breakfast. "I've got it! I'll say, 'How on earth did you find out my telephone number the time you called . . . before you asked me to the Prom?' That sound okay?"

"Perfect," I said, refraining from pointing out that anyone with the strength to open the telephone directory could have managed the feat.

At last the day was upon us. It dawned looking like just any ordinary day. "Here it is," we said to each other. "And we didn't have to bribe, kidnap, twist wrists, or skip town. Things finally straighten out, seems like."

Boo came to breakfast haggard and hysterical. "Guess what day this is?"

"Can't imagine," we said in unison.

"How'll we ever get through classes?" she asked bleakly.

"Education should be suspended, and let joy reign unconfined," I said comfortingly.

But it looked like anything but joy unconfined. Somehow the day crawled past; dinner finally was behind us, though

Boo had not been able to swallow a mouthful, and her wrist watch had been looked at every five minutes.

"He's not coming until quarter of nine," she said. "What on earth shall we do in the meantime?"

We made facetious suggestions, and she said wearily, "No humor, *please*. Just for this once."

When it was time to dress, she was so undone I thought I'd have to put her to bed. "My hair's a fright. I'd better wash it again. Maybe we could set it better."

"It looks lovely."

"I wish we hadn't got pink. Pink brings out my nose."

"Pink's lovely," I said, prepared to reinforce every collapse, one by one. At last she was dressed, with a drop of my perfume in the bend of her elbow. Everything was proper except the contents of her little evening bag, which seemed a kind of first-aid kit for any emergency that a vicious fate could think up. There were safety pins, bobby pins, two rubber bands, a needle and thread, adhesive tape, and the lucky old snail shell she used to carry in her bluejeans pocket when she played short stop on the eighth-grade baseball team. Also her lipstick, which she hoped to heaven she could remember to use once or twice.

She bore little resemblance to herself; that was what really steadied her nerves. "Why, I look positively human," she breathed in amazement.

Suddenly there was a thunderous rumbling of motor in the drive and she said, "He put it together himself from parts of one thing and another. That's what somebody told me. It's a real great car."

Actually it sounded like a space ship, but we didn't mention that. The doorbell rang, and before anyone could stir, it rang again.

Boo shrieked in a squeak, "Somebody answer it! The guy'll think he's got the wrong house. He'll leave!"

On trembling knees, I descended the staircase. When I opened the door and saw him hunched nervously in his rented coat, I wanted to take him in my arms. He was a child-type boy; he was the kind of boy that Boo is a girl. They were two of a kind.

He was huddled under the watery gleam of the porch light, a big muscular man's body with a youngster's pink face uneasily floating above it. The transparent cage for the gardenia that had "come" with the bid, twinkled in his big hand.

"Is this the residence . . . I mean does Boo live here?"

"Indeed she does," I said, trying not to sound too excessively welcoming. We shook hands tentatively.

"I hope I'm not too early . . . or late, or anything," he blurted out in that furry voice which was all I had known of him until now.

"You're just right," I said dizzily. "You couldn't be better, Winthrop."

We went into the living room and sat edgily on two chairs. We both started at once to say something, then both plunged into silence with a pardon-me, then we bumped words again. Then we laughed . . . and everything between us was fine.

"Fact is, I'm kind of nervous," he said. "You see, I've . . . well, I've never been out with a girl before. Without parents or anything."

I said, "Don't worry about it. You two'll take care of each other, and everything will be fine."

"I sure hope so," he said doubtfully.

Then without warning, Boo stood in the door, looking belligerent above her pink cloud of dress. Winthrop scrambled to his feet, fumbled with the slippery corsage box, and it bounced maliciously on the floor. He picked it up slowly and handed it, upside down, to Boo, who nearly dropped it again in the scuffle.

"Gosh," he said, "I wasn't expecting you to look so . . . well, so good." He perceived now that this was not the tactful thing to say, and he began blushing.

"Think nothing of it," Boo said. "I wasn't expecting it myself."

Somehow they managed to get out of the house without too much clumsiness, for bashfulness was a fog of silence through which they couldn't grope to reach each other. At last the door closed upon them, and in a moment the throttled thunder of Winthrop's real great motor rattled the windows of the house. I felt as if I'd like to go to bed with an ice pack.

Instead I went out to the kitchen and there everyone had gathered, even Tumpti.

"We're starved to death," they said. "Seems we haven't eaten a comfortable meal for weeks."

Tumpti was beaming. "I hungly too. I eat rittle lice, please."

The Right Man for the Job

੨ IF THERE's anywhere that the editorial "we" is precisely justified, it is in gardening in Southern California. When someone says, "We're putting in snapdragons this week," he doesn't mean that he personally will be down on his knees with a trowel in his hand. He knows you'll understand, if you too are a California gardener, that it is a corporation, and that the owner of the property is only a very small stockholder. He may make suggestions, but the Mexican or Japanese gardener has the final say, and it is practically always "no." And of course the mere owner must not tamper with the doing, in any case.

There are good reasons for this, mostly having to do with the climate. In New England a garden-loving citizen can work through a happy small segment of the year. Then there comes a nippy day when the garden has reached its zenith and all passion is spent. There comes a day, in fact, when a realistic gardener says to his creation, "What you need now is a damn good frost."

Then he can go in and curl up comfortably by the fire, and forget the whole strenuous subject for at least eight months.

But in California it's different. You can't forget it for a minute. There is desert drought to be kept at bay; there are hordes of garden pests which are never decently thinned out by the law of survival of the fittest because nothing . . . *but nothing* . . . ever wipes out any of their eggs or young; and there is also the adobe soil, always eager for a chance to become heavy clay again unless you keep leavening it expensively with commercial nourishment which the gardener adds to his towering bill every single month. So gardening is a twelve-month-a-year pursuit, and you've no choice about it.

The gardener himself is imperatively necessary. I've longed to hear of a house owner who revolted, and said, "Just let nature fight it out on my land. Let the bushes become Frankensteins and strangle the windows. Let the soil either go mad with galloping growth or sulk back to destitution, whichever it pleases. As for me, I've finished bowing down and serving the situation."

I expect if such a rebel did arise, the neighbors would get up a petition and have him evicted. At any rate, all houses are surrounded by neatly barbered lawns and embellished by shrubs, flowers, succulents, and trees (which have to be pruned once a year at a cost of a hundred and seventy-five dollars, at least). So the gardener is the least of your worries. You just add his salary and expenses to the other costs of blessedness, and try not to be harassed by the whole subject.

You soon learn it wouldn't do you any good to want to be

creative and participating. Gardeners have their own inflexible ideas, and if you do propose something, they have two ways of rejecting it. They either argue the idea to death, or if you persist in your folly, they expensively plant and then sit on their heels watching the stuff die. *That* will show you.

Our first gardener was a Japanese we inherited when we bought the house. He was a neat, tightly built little chap of no discernible age. His name was Yosh, he said, turning on the brightness of his teeth. When Tumpti took over the inside of the house we expected that he and the gardener would be friends. But Tumpti had other ideas. Tumpti would have liked taking charge of the gardening himself, if there had only been more hours in the day. As it was, he gave infuriating orders and even planted sprouts and cuttings which he gleaned from the alley. But Yosh would have none of him.

We just kept the windows closed while the war went on, for wild Japanese flew back and forth between them and any innocent bystander was liable to be felled.

"They'll eventually come to peace," we assured each other. "Dogs, roosters, and Japanese have to fight it out until they find out who's the boss."

"I bet on Tumpti."

"But Yosh is a third of his age."

"You wait and see."

So the battle went on. To supplement the treasures he picked up in our alley, Tumpti would bring home on Friday mornings after his Thursday off little flats of Japanese herbs. These he planted in the choicest part of the garden and outlined with whitewashed stones. But the next Tuesday when Yosh appeared, they would disappear, and the battle would wage hotter.

Tumpti said, "I leave. That gardener clazy."

"Sure he is," we said placatingly. "Just ignore him."

"I do gardening in spare time," he proposed, his ancient hands quivering with eagerness to take on more work.

With rank cajolery we persuaded him that such work was unworthy of his talents. But peace didn't reign.

Then suddenly, to everyone's surprise, harmony stretched over the domain. The tall skinny Japanese in the big straw hat would pass the tiny dimunitive one in the starched white clothes, and not a word would be exchanged.

"You see!" we said knowingly to each other. "They're just like dogs and roosters."

Then one day I went out to speak to Yosh about maybe if he didn't mind, he wouldn't sprinkle the terrace today because we were having people for tea out there.

He stood up respectfully and took off his big straw hat. Something was slightly different in his appearance, but I couldn't put my finger on the change.

Was it his teeth? Good heavens, had Tumpti . . . ? We talked for quite a long time while I cogitated on his slightly changed appearance, calling him Yosh with all politeness.

At last he said, "I'm not Yosh. I'm Tosh. Yosh's brother."

"Oh? What happened?"

"I work for you now."

"You do? What became of Yosh?"

He avoided looking up at the house. "He got another job," he said courteously.

"Well . . . I hope you enjoy working for us," I said timidly.

"I wait and see. I only work one month, then I see."

I worried through that month, confiding in nobody. Any kind of upheaval in the help is a bother, to coin a classic understatement. I felt relieved every time I saw the tall figure in the big straw hat appear draped in his serpents of garden hose, with his power lawn mower and the truck load of implements he carries to impress any neighbors who might be thinking of changing gardeners. Occasionally, of course, there would be noisy flare-ups between Tumpti and Tosh. But at least we still had them both.

Two months went by, and I forgot we had had trouble. In fact it seemed that Tosh now had a foolproof technique. If Tumpti went out and screamed at the squatting gardener, he paid not the slightest attention, never even looking up.

Eventually, once again, I had to go out and speak to Tosh, and once again as I tentatively stated my errand, I became conscious that there was a slight difference in appearance. After I finished what I had to say, there was a long silence. Then the tall figure smiled, and in a high, rocking voice said, "Please, I not Tosh. I'm Tosh's brother. My name Kosh."

"Why . . . when did this happen?" I cried in surprise.

He looked at me blankly. I could see he wanted to answer me, but for some reason wasn't sure of what to say. Then he smiled a pleased confidential smile.

"I deaf man," he said. "Tosh hear too good. So he give up job. I leave hearing aid in truck when I come work for you, please."

The Money on the Mantel

໐ WE HAD a gift given to us when we were children that was a rather strange thing. We had many things given to us and we loved them all. But this was something we still use years later. It happened like this.

One wintry afternoon our mother was baking fruitcake, and she found she was all out of citron. The "tea store" was the best place to buy citron, and that was quite a long way from our house, so both of us children went after it, to keep each other company.

"I'm going to have to give you a five-dollar bill," our mother said, while we were pulling on our overshoes, "and please be careful of the change. Five dollars is a lot of money. So listen to me, please, and stop monkeying-and-fooling." (That was a wonderful verb of hers . . . monkey-and-fool! Do mothers use it still?)

There were more instructions, and we half listened to them. I put the leather change purse in my pocket because I was the bigger, and we started off, monkeying-

and-fooling along the snowy streets, and thoroughly enjoying ourselves.

The tea store was a wonderful place, smelling of travel. On the walls were painted scenes from Ceylon and China and Siam. Tall burlap bags of coffee and peanuts, and beans, kidney and lima and navy, stood around invitingly open, and as you waited, you dribbled the beans through your fingers and nobody told you not to. The spices and the big, cloudy amber globes of citron lived in little glass-fronted bins, lined with lace-paper doilies.

There were always grownups in the store, for it was a place where people enjoyed shopping. We waited and waited our turn, and at last it came. The clerk got out the big citron, carved off a delicious sugar-coated crescent, and weighed it. We gave him the bill, and he gave us the change.

We scampered along toward home, and suddenly I remembered that he had given me only a handful of coins. No bills. We ran back; we told him timidly.

"Oh no, little girl. You only gave me a dollar bill," he said cheerfully, but firmly. And he went on weighing peanuts and tea and spice.

We went out of the store utterly crushed. We stumbled along, holding tight to each other's hands and trying not to cry. Then we gave up and did cry, huddled together on the curbstone. People stopped and spoke to us, then went on about their business. But one big man with a white mustache kept at us until he understood what the grief was about.

"You wait here," he said. "I'll go back and tell that clerk." He took the hot handful of change and strode down the street. We waited. We waited quite a long time; but finally he came back, and sure enough he had four one-dollar bills.

"There," he said, "and next time you girls pay attention."

He scowled at us and walked away. We held the money, stunned with relief. Then suddenly our manners prodded us, and we ran after him.

"Please, sir, we ought to thank you."

He glared down at us. "All right. And so now you've thanked me."

"But our mother would want to thank you, too," we said. "She'd probably like to write a little note and thank you." Our mother was a great note writer.

"Not necessary at all."

"But she wouldn't like it," we said. "She'd be pretty cross if we didn't have your name, so she could."

We insisted; he resisted. But finally, and very gruffly, he took out a crumpled paper and scribbled a name and address on it.

When we got home, we gave our mother the paper bag, and she looked in approvingly. Then she opened the big purse to count the change.

"Why, for pity's sake," she said, "this isn't right!"

"Oh, yes," we said, "it's. . . ."

"Why there's too much here! I gave you children only a one-dollar bill. This is change from a five."

"But you said . . ."

"Yes, and then I said I'd better not trust you with it."

So we explained, and we got out the slip with the address, and she said when supper was over we'd take the money back to the man with the white mustache. Our father himself would thank him.

"Such kind people there are in the world," our mother said, after she had scolded us properly.

After supper we all put on our overshoes. Our father thought the paper said "Felix Zurich"; our mother said his name was "Felix Sunage." But the address at least was plain — 439 Fourth Street. We hurried along. At Fourth Street we found no 439; the numbers ended at 325. We rang doorbells; we asked and asked. But there was no such address, and nobody ever heard of such a man.

We were all quiet, going home. Before he took off his overcoat, our father put the money on the mantel.

"It doesn't belong to us," he said. "We'll leave it there awhile."

It stayed there for days. We looked at it and thought of things we could buy with it for ourselves. After all, the man had given it to us. Timidly we mentioned it several times to our father.

"It doesn't belong to us," he said. "We'll have to do something special with it."

It stayed there for weeks.

"We'll have to do something kind with it," our mother said.

We all thought of things we could do with it. We proposed some of them.

"Yes, that's a good idea," our father said. "But as long as you thought of it, maybe you'd like to have it for your own kind deed."

So we did our own kind deeds, and the stranger's deed lay on the mantel.

It stayed there year after year. We did many things with

it. But always when the moment came for us to reimburse ourselves, we somehow didn't, and it stayed on, spent over and over.

When our mother dusted the mantel she often said, "There are such kind people in this world." When visitors mentioned it and we told them about it, they, too, added it to themselves.

And it went on and on, and still goes on and on, I hope.

We Buy a Car — Almost

ᔥ You CAN easily tell which house is ours when you look down our street; we're the people who usually have a beat-up jalopy standing in our drive.

Not that we own one . . . yet. But we're working at it. It's a long story, finance-wise (that know-how sounding term I'm always hearing in the conversation of people entirely at home in significant subjects! I'm trying to learn to use it myself, population-wise . . . procrastination-wise . . . calorie-wise . . . but on me the terms never look real).

Well, as I was saying . . . we've come to the car-buying business down a devious route, finance-wise. It got its start because Miss Boo suddenly decided to take a course in summer school instead of going to camp as usual. So commendable did this intention seem to me, I felt that in all fairness, she should be rewarded.

"As long as education has won out over recreation," I said, "I think you're entitled to the money that a month at camp would have cost."

"How much would that be?" she asked, evidently adjusting the gauge on her pleasure.

"A hundred and eighty dollars, dear. It'll be yours."

"To do what I *want* with?" she cried incredulously.

"Within reason," I said cautiously.

"Whose reason, for instance?"

"Well, I wouldn't want you to buy something fancy from the Thousand Oaks Circus Animal Farm."

"Natch not. I'm entirely reliable now," she agreed. Evidently she too was remembering the time she confidently expected to be given what she most wanted for Christmas . . . a lovely baby monkey.

"We'd open a savings account in your name," I said brightly.

"Oh, that!" she said morosely, "that wouldn't be like having it be my own."

"Of course it would. It would give you a feeling of independence and security."

"I have that already," she said gloomily, "and what good does it do me? What can you do with ole independence and security?"

I chose not to venture out into that quagmire of a theme.

"Of course if I could draw out the money now and then."

"That's what having an account in your name implies," I said with dignity. "You can either draw it out and fritter it away, or you can let it sit there quietly getting fatter by the minute as the interest piles up."

"Sounds fine," she said, and I could see her doing mathematical gymnastics.

So the money was deposited and it sat and got fatter and

fatter for about nineteen days.

Then she had an idea. You could see it fermenting in her the minute she appeared for breakfast.

"How'd you like to go into a partnership with me?" she suggested.

"What kind?"

"Well, how'd you like the two of us to buy a car together?"

"Do I need a car? I use the family car."

"Yes, of course. But this would be your own. Half of it anyway."

"That's a thought. What'd each of us have to contribute?"

"Well, I've got a hundred and eighty dollars, and a driver's license," she said. "You've probably got the rest of the money we'd have to have. Then besides, the nicest thing about you is that you never want to tell people how to drive, or how to get someplace."

"Oh, is that so?" I said, pleased that such a nice thing was nice about me.

"That's quite a consideration," she said. "Most grown-ups, especially women, always want to give directions. Especially if they don't know for sure."

"So we'd own the car together," I said, not giving any directions, but guiding us back on the route.

"That's the idea."

"I'll think it over."

"Of course, it would have to be a suitable car," she said.

"Such as what?" I asked, thinking of the Jaguars that zoom up and down our street with an aura of arrogant extravagance around them.

"Well, we wouldn't want a fancy show-off car. I'd be embarrassed if we got something snobbish and new-looking."

"That's embarrassing?" I asked, willing to learn.

"That's what *we* consider it," she explained, invoking her contemporaries to support her opinion. *"We* like a nice casual car. Of course, *boys* our age think it's sharp to have something comical, maybe a T-model painted pink, with some gag printed on the door. 'This way out' or 'Walk, don't run to the nearest exit.' But that's *boys*. They'll get over it."

So we discussed the subject a bit farther, decided not to say anything to the rest of the family, smuggled the morning paper upstairs and read six or seven columns of advertisements, put through a few telephone calls, and eventually forgot all other normal activities while we searched for the one perfect vehicle.

Within a matter of hours, word got around among the used-car dealers, it seemed, and we were in business. Frenziedly in business. The house was convulsed with it; our telephone line was tied up, you couldn't get in or out of our driveway, and a strange assortment of car owners who wanted to dispose of their particular headache sat waiting in various rooms of our house to tell us their stories. Some were pretty ingenious; their wives were now pregnant, so they needed a more sedate car; their children had just married, and the only thing the new in-law brought into the family was another car just like this one; they were leaving our part of the country to take up work in the East; no place to park on their street, so they were buying a motorcycle. The prize reason for wanting to sell, I thought, should have gone to a man who said he now had a hernia, so he needed less frisky transportation.

In between interviews we dashed around to the car lots.

All in all, we must have tried out and rejected three score and ten cars; anyway it *felt* like a lifetime to me.

And then the perfect one was brought to our door. It was painted robin's-egg blue, and had nice butter-colored seat covers. It was a convertible, but the owner frankly said that the buttons which were supposed to raise the top no longer worked. But that was all right; we don't have much rain in California.

We wanted to put a down-payment on it immediately, even though we had promised Jonesy, our trusted mechanic, that we wouldn't buy *anything* until he'd looked it over. But for some reason, the owner wouldn't take the money.

"You kids better think it over a little bit," he said, hoping to dazzle me, I suppose, by his bald-faced flattery.

"We have thought it over," Boo said. "We'll take it."

"It's against my principles to sell something without the buyer having plenty of time to think."

"We don't need time," she said. "We're trained to think fast."

But still he wouldn't get down to business, finance-wise.

"You'd better look around a little more," he said. "How do you know the price is right? Anyway, you phone me this afternoon. Or better still, I'll phone you."

In spite of us, he drove away, and we could barely keep from running down the street after the beautiful pale blue thing, disappearing.

"I don't understand the man," Boo said. "He acted like he didn't want to sell it after all."

I didn't understand him either. He acted as if he couldn't get away from us fast enough. Needless to say, we didn't wait until he telephoned us. We called him. His wife answered, a disgruntled-sounding woman. She didn't beat around the bush. She came right out and dispelled the mystery.

"My husband doesn't want to sell," she said flatly.

"But why not?" Boo cried in indignation. "He took up our time."

"I can't help that," she said. "But Bill says the car's cuter than he thought it was. He says that as soon as he saw that little blonde in the driver's seat. . . ."

"That's silly," Boo said.

"Sure it's silly. But wait'll you hear the rest. *Now* he's trying to get me to go over to a beauty shop and have myself made into a blonde!"

The Escalator

᪗ Now THAT she was a woman who had *lived* (that is, who had had a genuine date which had kept her out until twelve-thirty) Boo took a much wider view of the world. A view, to be specific, which now included another sex.

A day or so earlier she used to say, "Oh, boys!" as one would throw a rock. Now she gave the same words a different reading. "Oh, boys?" she said and the word had two syllables, and was played on melodious little flute notes conveying all kinds of rich, wistful meaning.

To begin with, she told me confidentially that she had decided to "go steady."

"With whom?" I asked apprehensively.

"Oh, I suppose I'll have to begin with Winthrop Rawes," she said resignedly. "I don't know anybody else. Yet, that is."

"But didn't you meet other boys at the Prom?"

"Heavens no," she said. "You're not supposed to notice anybody else is there except the boy you're dancing with."

"You mean you had to dance all the dances with Winthrop?"

"Of course. He brought me, didn't he?"

"I see," I said dimly. "And now is he persuading you to go steady?"

"Oh no," she said, all feminine. "He hasn't thought of it yet. But he'll think of it. Just give him time. A boy has more prestige if he's going steady. And Winthrop just loves prestige. He uses the word."

"Well, just to brief me on the customs of the day . . . what does going steady involve?"

"Oh, movies once in a while, and cokes after school. And sitting together at games. And if people happen to have classes near each other, they walk along the corridors together. They don't have to talk. They just have to walk together."

"Sounds like Siamese twins."

"It is, in a way. But it gives you prestige."

"So you said."

"To tell you the truth, I wouldn't *pick* Winthrop. But he'll do."

"Not a nice attitude."

"Realistic. Also honest. Can't you say out loud what you think inside?"

"Well, maybe you could think about some more favorable aspects of the situation."

"For instance, that I owe him something?" she said trying to be fair. "He did get me started." This attitude didn't seem much of an improvement over the original standpoint, so I made no comment.

But she didn't need any comment, being quite able to make her own. "You see, it's like an escalator. When you're just a girl you have to stand there doing nothing but *frustrating,* watching everybody else going up and up. But once a boy asks you to something, you're on the escalator. Then it's up to you to stay on."

I tried to digest this graphic description, then I went back to the original announcement.

"So you've decided to go steady with Winthrop?"

"Until something better turns up," she said. "Fact is, I saw something better at the Prom. Whatta guy! He's a senior. I couldn't expect him to look at me. But anyway. . . . It's wonderful to know there *are* such people." She drifted off in an age-old sigh. Then she got back to her realistic program.

"So . . . I'll just go steady *temporarily.*"

Aunt Fay

and the Men in My Life

ᕽᕽ WHEN I WAS just past thirteen, Aunt Fay came to visit us. She was exactly what I was looking for, a porthole from our safe life which would give a terrifying view of what surrounded us. For I was a drama-starved child, ripe and honing for picturesque tragedy. I was almost overwhelmed in it that autumn, for through my Aunt Fay I nearly lost my father.

He was the sun of our private firmament; all our orbits circled around him willingly. He had an opinion on every subject; as far as we were concerned, they were absolutely correct. In his presence everything became fun. Everything except work, of course. For at thirteen I had heavy sluggish syrup in my bones so that even lying still was an effort. I had strength enough for everything except work. At the very thought of work I buckled at the knees. But laziness had to be a fugitive in my father's house; to say you were tired was worse than confessing theft.

From the time we were toddlers, his family had competed

for his displays of affection. I was the healthy one who never "caught" anything, so I never saw his dear face bent anxiously above my bed. I used to pray to have a long illness, so my father would worry about me and bring home a half-pint of vanilla ice cream when he came from work. It sometimes happened to my little sister, but not to me. Anything that ever ailed *me* could be cured by a dose of hard work.

When my father opened the front door and gave his special little whistle, the very air sprang to life, and we all came running, throwing ourselves on him and demanding kisses.

We did exactly what he told us to do, about everything. Our only chance of exercising our own perilous judgment was not to be exposed to him at all. For if we came within sight of him, we were putty in his hands. And we loved being putty! My mother lived solely for him. His joy was hers, his slightest wish her own. And he would have said the same thing in reverse. "I want whatever Jet wants," he would say. "She's my boss."

This unanimity gave a wonderful feeling to us children, as if the universe were in perfect agreement with itself.

Into this Eden came my Aunt Fay. Armed to the teeth from birth. Hating men and envying them, she was nettled to a frenzy by the sight of man-and-woman happiness. She was so allergic to it that she broke out in splotches of torment and wit.

My Aunt Fay was married to my father's brother Andrew. He had the size in the family; he was big and also handsome, with a golden wishbone-shaped mustache, a double chin and a militant pompadour. But behind that façade of ornate flesh, cowered a docile spirit.

He and Aunt Fay were destined for each other, as mur-
derer and victim. Or, to be less grim about it, as ventriloquist and dummy. Aunt Fay demanded a handsome man to
operate and humiliate, and Uncle Andrew was looking for a
buxom knee on which to live a safe and supine life.

Although Aunt Fay quite frankly said she "had no use
for men," there was still plenty of primitive female in her,
so that she yearned to be throttled by some male. She lived
on the edge of constant danger of such throttling; the fact
that she could come so close without ever being touched is
a tribute to the self-control of the sex she despised.

She often let it be known that she had brought to her
marriage an inheritance. She had been quoted as saying,
"Poor Andrew . . . he'd have had quite a different career if
he hadn't married an heiress."

From the first hour of their visit in our house, our happiness was an outrage and a challenge to Aunt Fay. We were
all pitifully vulnerable and she mowed us down right and
left. We had been used to believing that relatives were
people who liked you. This left us wide open to attack. At
first we just couldn't believe our own wounds.

Just to get squared off during our first meal, she lashed
out at each of us. "Good heavens, Jessie, why are you dressing that puny child in blue? Makes all the veins stand out
in that pale, miserable face of hers," she said about my
precious little sister. Before we could attempt a defense,
she started on me.

"Sit up straight, child. Don't get round in the back
before you get round in the front." I, who was beginning
to be pretty conscious of my timidly rounding front, wilted
with embarrassment.

My father said, "Fay, if you were one of my own children you'd have to leave the table for that kind of talk."

This was the matador's red cape to Aunt Fay. She whirled upon him and beamed delightedly. "Well, Willie!" she said with a horn thrust of laughter goring his tenderest spot. "You're quite a little man, aren't you?"

My father's face flamed with anger, for she had selected the one word which had a sharp point for him. But our faces flamed even brighter, and my mother looked as if she would burst into tears. Nobody ever before had dared to call my father by the patronizing diminutive. My mother called him Will, and it had almost deific implications in the name. He was her Will . . . will incarnate.

Aunt Fay went on. "Let's get this straight at the start, shall we? I'm *not* one of your obedient little women, Willie. You've made quite a little kingdom here, but I'm afraid you'll never find *me* curtsying to you."

Uncle Andrew, glad of a diversionary attack, cackled encouragingly. Anticipation like cream spread over the oatmeal of his expression. He was going to enjoy his visit to the hilt.

"You tell him off, Fay," he cried, shivering with the excitement of danger. "W.B.'s never had any woman tell him off before."

Neither of the adversaries so much as glanced at him. My father was cutting his meat fiercely. His strategy was badly hamstrung because he was the host at this table, but at last he did permit himself to say, "Well, Fay, it might give you a real experience to find yourself curtsying to *something* for once."

"Not me," Aunt Fay said. "I've been independent since the day I was born."

"Independent?" My father tested the fabric of the word, and in his face you could see him saying to himself, "Hmmn . . . the stuff's heavy tweed, and a woman should wear silk." Then aloud he said, "I never thought independence was very becoming on a woman. Besides, it's lonely."

"Nonsense," she said, and now it was her face which flamed. You could see her fumbling frantically for something to turn back the thrust. "You've got away with murder, Willie. But these females of yours will get on to you one of these days. The girls will, anyway. Jessie's always been too much in love with you to have an ounce of sense."

"Now Fay," my mother protested feebly, trying to draw the fire away from my father. "I guess I just can't help it."

That meal marked the first bout, and it ended in a draw. Neither my Aunt Fay nor my father had shown the full fierceness of the fight that was waiting between them.

Throughout the next days the battle went on. My father was always at a disadvantage because he had a basic instinct that it is unthinkable to strike back at a woman even when she is trying to push in a man's teeth. He couldn't help pulling his punches, which were usually in defense of someone other than himself. For instance, when Aunt Fay was belittling Uncle Andrew by lavish intimation about her inheritance, my father said, "Fay, since you mention the inheritance so often, I assume you'd like to talk frankly about it."

"Why what do you mean!"

"Well, I mean maybe you'd like to be definite about the

situation. I've heard about your inheritance ever since Andrew married you. Seems he's never been able to do anything without being bolstered up by that money of yours."

Uncle Andrew looked ready to faint. "Well, W.B., it did help me at first. The time I bought that laundry. Fay gave me a few hundred dollars. . . ."

"*Which* you promptly lost," Aunt Fay said witheringly.

"Which I lost," Uncle Andrew amended meekly.

"Then how about the money I lent you to buy into that sugar beet business? What became of that, I'd like to know?"

My father, enjoying his brief inning, said, "Never mind what became of the money, Fay. I'd like to hear just how much of a fortune it was." It was a remark so far from my father's customary courtesy that it showed his utter desperation.

In the silence that blotted out everything else, you could have heard a handkerchief fall. And indeed you did hear it, for my mother frantically tried to furnish a saving diversion.

"Will dear, I've dropped my handkerchief," she said faintly. But for once my father was deaf to her.

For Uncle Andrew, probably for the first time in his life, was daring to talk back about Aunt Fay's money.

"I'll tell you how big it was, W.B.," he cried, looking white around the mouth. "It was just big enough to ruin my life."

Aunt Fay's face was seething with anger, and her eyes were whittled down to sharp points of hatred. "What a fine spectacle of gratitude *that* is!" she cried.

Now that Uncle Andrew had opened an inch of reckless-
ness, the dam within him broke with a roar. He said with
terrible deliberateness, "Fay's Ma left her just under five
thousand dollars, a diamond ring, and a piano. She lost the
diamond ring in the washroom of a theater. The piano
made the neighbors so mad that somebody set fire to our
house. And the money . . . well, she's still got a few hundred
which she holds over my head all the time."

Aunt Fay said with deadly quietness, "So *you've* fallen
under the spell of that domineering little tyrant . . . that . . .
that. . . ."

Her fury ricocheted off her husband insultingly. He
wasn't worth getting into a first-class rage over. My father
was the real adversary, the triumphant embodiment of all
the maleness which she detested.

So Aunt Fay said explosively to him, "I'll thank you to
leave Andrew out of this. *You're* the one! You're so spoiled
by these simpering little ninnies of yours that you're unbear-
able!"

My father bowed his head in mock meekness. "Thank
you, Fay, I call it a real compliment when you say my
girls love me enough to spoil me."

"Love you!" Aunt Fay sniffed. "The children are scared
to death of you, and Jessie's been in a trance since the first
time you looked at her."

Then into her eyes came a new gleam, for in that moment she saw her most effective strategy. She could never
get the best of my father by scoffing at him. There was
a better way of getting even with him for being a man.
So in that moment, the battle went underground. Far

underground, where it struck its blows through a child's defenseless heart. Mine.

The next morning Aunt Fay got up for breakfast, and there couldn't have been a more charming companion. She asked my father about his work in a flattering way; she complimented my mother on her morning prettiness.

"We relatives ought to stick together," she said. "You know I've nobody of my own except you dear people."

My father was quite undone by this change in her. When he got up to leave the table he touched her shoulder timidly. Aunt Fay quivered under his affectionate touch, then said, "Bye-bye, Willie. Have a fine day."

My father left his hand on her shoulder a moment. "I think I ought to apologize to you, Fay. I got off on the wrong foot with you. Fact is, I guess I kind of forget you're a woman, because you play rougher than any woman I've ever known."

For a moment she wavered, unable to decide whether this was a declaration of peace, or a further attack. Then she put up her hand and gave my father's arm a shy pat.

My mother's eyes were misty with relief. Plainly she knew the lovableness of her Will had finally won over this peculiar sister-in-law. She knew no woman in her right mind could resist him for long. . . .

The day continued as it had started. Aunt Fay announced she was going to kidnap me and take me to luncheon and a matinee. I had never been to a matinee in my life, and I'd been "downtown to lunch" only twice. My mother was as pleased as I was.

It was a baffling day. My Aunt Fay was witty and disarming. She made me feel this was not woman and child on naïve holiday, but experienced contemporaries passing the time pleasantly. She let it be understood that from the first she had recognized me as the only worldly-wise member of my family. The moment she said it, I realized with dazzling joy that it was true.

She intimated that only shocking blindness kept my parents from appreciating me. Now that I thought of it, I quite agreed with her. My father especially, she said. How could I stand it, the way he made fun of all my best attempts to improve conditions around me?

Well, it did grieve me, I admitted. And that insulting nickname he called me. *Mugsie!* Didn't my friends tease me about it? Or perhaps I never brought them home so they could *see?*

The way he ordered me about as if I were a child . . . the menial chores, like lugging the wood upstairs for the fireplace in the sitting room. Aunt Fay really admired the way I didn't throw the wood in his face. A big strong man like my father asking a frail young woman like me. . . .

She didn't make a frontal attack on my father; that would have brought out defense. Instead she flattered and sympathized with me, weaving bonds which lashed me to her. I was enraptured. She bought me a green velveteen suit, very grown-up in cut. Just the thing to get me started right in high school in a few weeks.

"That is, if you don't blow up and run away or something before school opens!" she said laughingly.

I saw for the first time that my father was a strong-willed villain who had ruined my mother's life. I saw my father for what he was, a strutting little male, getting his way in everything. It was as much of a shock to me as it must have been to Adam and Eve to discover they were naked. I had thought we were living in a happy home, and all the time we were miserable, without ever suspecting it!

The climax of all this disillusionment came the next night at dinner. My father, telling an anecdote said, "It was him all right."

I said icily, "Father, please!"

"What's the matter, Mugsie? Bad grammar?"

"My name's Margaret, if you don't mind," I said bitterly.

After dinner he said, "Princess Margaret, how about some wood upstairs? It's chilly tonight." He rubbed his hands together with crude good humor, and I gritted my teeth and stamped down the basement stairs.

"So help me, this is the last time," I said to myself. "I'm only giving in because we have company."

I dragged the wood in its canvas carrier noisily up the basement stairs. My father and Aunt Fay were talking in the hall, in loud jolly tones.

"Pardon me, please," I said with ironic politeness, shoving between them with my degrading load.

"Certainly, Mugsie!" my father said, bending low. Just as our eyes passed each other, he winked. That infuriated me, for his eyes were full of laughter.

I could feel the adult gazes following me upstairs; I knew they were watching my bulging calves, which were not my best point. I felt my father laughing at my rebellion, but I also felt Aunt Fay encouraging me.

At the landing I turned and looked down, and my father said, "Did I call you Mugsie? Forgive that. I should have said 'Your Highness.'"

Something in me broke then, a combination of shame and whipped-up bewilderment, and loyalties attempting violent suicide.

"I don't care what you call me," I said angrily. "I don't care what you do to me. I'm going to run away from here just as soon as I can. Then you can carry your own heavy old wood upstairs." Before I quite realized what I was doing, I had let loose of one strap of the carrier, and the whole load went rolling down the steps, bouncing thunderously and gouging the wallpaper.

Somehow then I was crying, and the three of us were gazing at the havoc. I expected my father would come bounding up the stairs and give me a good sound spanking.

But he did nothing of the kind. He looked from me to Aunt Fay. Then with deliberation he put one foot on the lowest step, and over his raised knee he managed somehow to bend the formidable torso of Aunt Fay. Then, not too gently, he gave *her* the spanking. At first she tried to believe it was one of his crude jokes.

But he said, "You've had this coming for years, woman. If nobody else will do it, I guess I'll have to."

She let out strange cries and yelps, half horror and half delight. There was nobody to save the situation, for my mother had stepped over to a neighbor's. Uncle Andrew, who was having his usual nap after dinner, came running to the parlor door. When he saw what was happening he said, "Now W.B. . . . you can't do a thing like that. . . ." Then he began to laugh, with a bellow that must have echoed throughout the whole street.

I myself was crying hysterically. Everyone had forgotten

I was the cause of the trouble. I ran from the scene of devastation to my room, and shut the door. Now Aunt Fay would surely leave us. I would lose my only friend, the only person on earth who appreciated me. I fell into bed sobbing. Nobody came near my room, and after a long while I fell asleep.

From a dream I roused up because my mother was taking off my clothes. "Don't wake up, darling," she said. "You've had a hard day, haven't you?"

Nobody called me in the morning, and when I woke up I was miraculously ill. Nothing serious, only a bad sore throat which gave me a pathetic little voice and made me interestingly flushed. Aunt Fay and Uncle Andrew had taken an early train, my mother said, her eye so innocent I felt sure she hadn't heard about the spanking. . . .

I had my luncheon in bed, and all afternoon I lay under the blanket, trying not to think. Everything in my world had collapsed, and it would be years before I would be a real woman able to cope with my own destiny.

In the late afternoon, with the house deliciously fragrant from a cake and a meatloaf in the oven, my mother came and sat beside my bed, sewing. We didn't talk about anything much. I just let the comfort of her serenity soak into my bruises. When she got up to set the table, she leaned over my bed and looked into my eyes. She put both her warm hands around my cheeks.

"It's not hard to be a woman, darling," she said. "It feels strange at first. But there's nothing better you ever could be."

I couldn't think of anything to say, so I closed my eyes

and let two tears leak out from under my eyelids. Thoughtfully my mother bent down and kissed me. Then in her light and gentle way she said something which I never would forget.

"There's only one kind of woman who has a bad time of it," she said. "That's a woman who wants to belittle men. A woman who is against men has the loneliest time on earth."

With that one light finger touch she put a mark on my life which set the design of it as long as it will last.

She closed my door, and I lay there and let her words explain themselves in my mind. I saw my Aunt Fay's face, tight and alert with hostility. And I saw my mother's face, soft and pleased with life, gentleness written in every line, love that would not knowingly hurt any creature, large or small. One face was angry and starved, and the other filled with the rich delights of being a woman who knew her estate. One was convulsed with trying to prove some point; the other never needed to prove anything, for it was all self-evident.

I must have fallen asleep, for when I heard a noise and opened my eyes the windows were violet and the room was nearly dark. The door was pushing open and my father's face was peering around the edge almost timidly. I said nothing to welcome him, but my heart was unclenched like a hand opening to take a treasure.

He came over to the bed and looked down at me. "Who's that hiding under the covers?" he said, as he used to say when I was four, and seven, and sometimes even when I was ten.

"It's me," I said. "It's Mugsie."

He didn't say anything for a moment, then he whispered, "I could call you Margaret, if you wanted me to."

My opened heart spilled light throughout my body, for there was more than a heart could hold.

"Not yet," I said. "You better wait until I'm grown up. I'm still just your little girl."

"Just my little girl," he said thoughtfully. "That's okay for a long time yet."

I reached for his hand and held it tight against my cheek, and it didn't matter at all if tears splashed on it, for this was my father's safe and wonderful hand. There was a cold square of a box in his hand, and it smelled deliciously of vanilla.

"I thought I'd lost you, Mugsie," he said.

"I thought I'd lost you, too."

But I had not lost him. My mother had helped me safely over a dark abyss so that I never could lose my father. And because of that, I did not lose the other men who came through the years and made my life beloved and merry and rich.

Off-Color

꒳ IT IS a sobering catastrophe when you detect a flaw in a friend you believed was perfect. Years finally make you a bit resilient in this crisis, but Boo hasn't been worked on by too many years as yet.

I suspected something was wrong the moment she came in the house before dinner. It had been a day much anticipated. She was on a specially chosen committee of four public-spirited members of the Good Citizenship Club. Their assignment was to go to our airport to welcome a high school student arriving from Australia to be a delegate at a Youth Congress in New York.

Felicity was the other girl on the committee and there were two boys. This neat balancing in itself was enough to make the occasion delightful. Felicity naturally had selected what she and Boo would wear. This was no simple decision; it required long daily telephone conferences for a week before the day arrived. First, Felicity thought they should look very sophisticated. "After all, we'll be the first actual American girls he'll see. First impressions, you know."

Boo wasn't very sure she could look sophisticated, but she was willing to try. "I could wear my heels," she said doubtfully. "But they don't seem quite right for an airport."

"I'll let you know about that," Felicity said.

One day they were to be pony-tailed; the next day Felicity wanted new haircuts, very short and Continental looking. One day they were to wear gloves, and the next Felicity thought they'd better embody California informality. Only more so.

"I think we've got to be either stinking with style, or else real casual," Felicity decreed.

"You don't mean boys' shirts with the tails out?" Boo asked in horror.

"Possibly," Felicity said, and you could almost hear her considering how piquant are the twin melons of her neat little derrière, unexpectedly apparent in the boys' shirt motif.

The Good Citizenship Club had appropriated funds so that they could take the Australian delegate for a snack in the coffee shop. That would give them a chance to get acquainted before the adult hostess, who was to provide an overnight view of an American family, would arrive and spoil everything.

It should have been a lot of fun. But somehow it wasn't. Boo came into the house on dragging feet. I heard the feet but I called out cheerily, "How'd it go?"

"How'd what go?" she asked with that perverse obtuseness that a teen-ager uses so maddeningly to ward off intrusion into privacy.

"Why, meeting the delegate, of course," I said.

"Oh, that! All right, I suppose."

"Why, darling . . . I thought. . . ."

"Oh, *please,*" she said impatiently. "Everything that happens has to be beat to death in this house. Talk, talk, talk . . . that's all we have around here!"

So I knew it had been literally unspeakable. I warned the rest of the family, and we ate dinner discussing national politics. The silence around Boo was thunderous.

Usually she breaks down after a half-hour or so, when anything is troubling her, for she is a serene child who doesn't cherish her troubles as some of us do. But tonight she dried the dishes in silence, and if she spoke at all it was only a weary, "Oh, I suppose so," or a noncommittal "Okay."

She went upstairs to study, and I knew homework would have a bad time of it. At nine o'clock, as is our custom, I brought up what we call the "midnight snack," usually milk and graham crackers, or the last piece of the pie.

"Just put it somewhere," she said without looking at me. "I'm not very hungry."

"Is something worrying you?" I asked, as if I had just noticed it.

"Not particularly," she said.

"Don't you feel well, dear?"

"I feel okay."

"Did Felicity enjoy herself?"

She considered snubbing me for the question, and then she burst out angrily, "Felicity! *She* was practically hysterical."

Then it came tumbling out. "The boy from Australia wasn't much of a mixer. I guess they must have picked him because he was a brain. Anyway he couldn't think of anything to say. And when one person can't, then nobody can. So we all just kind of congealed. We goggled at each other, and couldn't think of a *thing*."

"Not even Felicity?"

"Oh sure, Felicity finally thought of something all right." Her voice was razor-edged with sarcasm now, made sharper by her adoration of Felicity. *"She* finally thought of an off-color story."

"I see," I said, trying not to let my horror show. The fact was, I didn't suspect that Boo even knew the term.

"Very far off?" I asked stupidly.

She nodded in misery. "What will he *think?* Felicity herself said that his first impression of American kids was pretty important."

I tried to think of some comfort to offer. "Well, maybe he didn't know it was off-color," I suggested. "Maybe he didn't get the point."

Boo shook her head. "He guffawed," she said. "In case you're not familiar with the verb, it means he laughed so loud everybody looked at us. It was the only time he opened his mouth, except to eat." She threw back her head and gave a gloomy imitation of the Aussie guffawing. "Everybody was embarrassed. Except Felicity."

Then my curiosity got the best of me. "What *was* the story," I asked unguardedly. "Could you tell it to me? Maybe it's not as bad as you think it is."

"Oh, it's off-color, all right," she said. So then she told it. "Seems it was Christmas Eve, and three little lady cats were sitting before a fireplace talking about what they wanted for Christmas. The first one said, 'Know what I'd like? A nice little blue-eyed kitten with pretty little white paws.'

"The second one said, 'Well, what I want is *two* sweet little baby kittens, with pointed ears.'

"So the third one said, 'As long as you're dreaming, why not dream big? I'd like to have *three* little kittens, with curly tails and nice whiskers.'

"Just then an old tomcat was walking along the roof. So he leaned over the chimney and called down, 'Watch out, girls! Here comes Santa Claus.'"

To her surprise, the telling of the story cheered her considerably. When she finished it, her eyes were sparkling and her mouth, so lately sad, gave up trying not to smile. She put her head on her desk and shook with laughter.

I said, "Well, it could have been worse."

"But don't you realize," she said sternly, "we're too young to know what it meant. In *mixed company* anyway."

Feesh

෫ WE'RE NOT by nature fishermen. But because we now live in California, we *are* by nature hosts. For very soon after you acquire a permanent California address you realize that Horace Greeley's advice, "Go west, young man," is still ringing down the centuries, heeded by all and sundry. Sooner or later everyone (including our New York dentist) checks in, hoping transparently to be invited at least to luncheon, and at best to occupy the guest room. California architects have become wary now, and recommend that in the new, ideal, functional houses no guest room should be provided.

Eventually a couple we just loved in the East arrived. In New York City we had no way of finding out that they adored fishing. But our first hour together here, revealed the fact.

"Dave's just mad to go deep-sea fishing," Elaine said.

"Albacore," Dave explained in rapture.

So we could do no less than get up a party. And when

I say "get up" that's precisely what I mean, for we had to rise at 3 A.M., drive chilled through the night to Malibu, meet ghostily with characters we scarcely recognized in their fishing clothes, and be out where the Albacore gather, before the sun was up. Dave had gear in abundance to lend our family, and nothing I could say kept him from rigging up one of his best pieces of equipment for me. I knew gloomily that somehow I'd either break it or lose it, or both, and I had a feeling that no matter what I would do to try to make up for the mishap, our beautiful friendship would be damaged.

The large commercial fishing boat would have been fun except for the fishing. Besides our party there were about twelve experienced fishermen, each with a lump in his hip pocket which was lunch, and liquid refreshment. The skipper was a wordless expert, and the crew was a copper-blond giant, who plays in Westerns between fishing trips. The crew took one look at me, and said, "Don't worry about anything. I'll do the baiting for *you*."

As soon as the engines started, the crew collected a dollar from everyone who wanted to go in on the jackpot. I knew I was throwing my dollar down the drain, but there wasn't much choice. So I took off my borrowed leather gloves, snatched the opportunity to dab the sniffles from my nose, and got a dollar bill out of the all-too-snug hip pockets of my Levis.

We chugged out into the darkness, and just as pearly streaks were beginning to crack the surface of the sky, we came up alongside another boat.

"What's this?" I asked.

"We get the chums here . . . fish, you know." For a happy moment I thought we were going to buy our catch, and then just enjoy a sea trip. But of course it was the bait boat.

Several bushels of chums were ladled into our bait tank, a few sportsmanly remarks were shouted back and forth between us and the bait boat, then we were off again.

This is not an account of a fishing trip, so I'll skip past the next four hours (as I was not able to do in fact), merely listing the items . . . the gutteral mutterings of the absorbed fishermen, the choreography of snarl between me and my line, constantly shaping and reshaping in large and more intricate patterns, the cumulus clouds of nausea floating up from my stomach, my dread of what would happen when one of our companions got out his lunch and unwrapped it before my eyes, the slapping of the caught fish six inches past my horrified face . . . and finally my own delirium when *I* began to catch. The frenzy of greed that possessed me . . . my reckless bout with the chum as I forgot all squeamishness and tried to bait my own hook . . . and suddenly the noonday sun beating down on salt-sprayed skin. It was an unforgettable morning made up of revulsion and delight, of physical unwillingness and atavistic lust.

Albacore weren't biting . . . but sea bass were; also a few plebeian mackerel and groupers. Biting and gamy. Which was the reason I broke Dave's expensive reel . . . the first one, that is. The second accident, when I dropped the whole thing into the sea was really the fault of a gull who looked as if he were going to attack me over possession of my chum.

When the boat turned around and began wallowing toward home, I was the one who got sulky because we had to take the sissy landlubbers back to shore, as per agreement.

The skipper and the crew weighed in the individual catches, and the jackpot went to a small Mexican chiropractor, who probably was the master of special grips denied to us laymen. Some of the fishermen had their catches expertly cleaned and filleted. But we carried ours home with heads and tails on, because that way they looked more like genuinely caught fish.

We had twenty-two pounds of them going to our house, and when someone suggested we'd better call up friends and offer them fish, I was shocked. Give away our own privately caught fish? If anybody insisted on making fish gifts to friends and neighbors, the Farmers' Market would oblige.

"They'll be utterly delicious for tonight's dinner," I said. "Wonderful brain food. We ought to get on some quiz program tomorrow. . . ."

But we reckoned without Tumpti. He took one look at the catch, and appropriated it.

"I fix," he said.

"Naturally. Cook up *plenty,*" I said.

He looked at me in disgust. "Ham tonight," he said firmly. "I make salt feesh for later. Ver' good."

The guests expected me to take command of the situation. But the rest of us knew that if Tumpti said salt fish for later, that's what it would be.

He sent Dave out to buy a special stone crock . . . T"lee gallons. Also salt. Not civilized salt packaged in neat cylinders, but big white bags of biting salt which could be found only on the wharf at Santa Monica.

Meantime he cleaned fish. After dinner, he turned on the garden lights, and set himself up tidily in business, working in sharp illumination far into the night, while a ring of us and neighbor cats were held at bay by his expression and the gleam of his knife.

The next day I dared to ask, "Tumpti, when can we eat the salt fish?"

"Plitty soon. You be ve'y glad. Salt feesh ve'y good."

So we waited. Dave and Elaine extended their visit a few days hopefully. But they finally had to give up. "Maybe we can send you a few by air mail," we promised doubtfully, knowing that Tumpti would be in charge of the supply and would dole it out as he saw fit.

He kept the big crock down in our dungeon-like basement, safe from cats, us and other unspecified marauders. He did let us go down with him and look at it once.

"Two, thlee weeks now," he said happily. So we waited, our salivary glands going mad every time we thought of the fish.

Now plenty of time had passed, and we told each other we just ought to be firm. Nothing had been said about the fish for nearly a week. Maybe he had forgotten them entirely. After all, he was a pretty old man.

As usual, the being firm fell to me.

"Think no more of it," I promised. "Tomorrow I'll just *tell* him we expect the fish for dinner."

Early in the morning I went out boldly to his domain.

"Now . . . about dinner," I said. "We'll have the fish tonight, Tumpti."

"Today not Fliday," he said sullenly. "No good feesh in market."

"We don't need the market," I said faintly. "I'm talking about our *own* fish . . . in the basement."

He looked at me with steel mildness in his eyes. He set his little toothless jaw.

"Feesh?" he asked in a rasping voice. "What feesh?"

So then I knew the worst.

Salt had come to grips with the forces of nature. But nature had carried out her irresistible cycles of deterioration, unheeding all human efforts to interfere.

One Search Ends, Another Begins

ᘰ THE SEARCH kept up.

Boo's friends now knew that she was in the market for a car, and that widened the horizon of possibility by cousins, neighbors, and occasionally (if the girl felt well enough entrenched) by a boy friend. Seemed as if everybody knew somebody who wanted to sell a car.

In between looking at the cars, Boo looked at her bank book. Occasionally she dallied with the delicious possibilities of other things besides cars which a hundred and eighty dollars would buy. A piece of make-believe, almost-not-quite mink, for instance.

"You're too young for fur," I said sternly. "Besides, this is California."

She looked at jewelry. She even went into the hushed sanctuary of our most expensive shop and asked to see some nice modest lady-like pearls. Or even diamonds. . . .

There was a girl from Denmark in her high school class who was said to have had an operation which improved the shape of her nose. Boo went over all her own features to see where transformations might be worth a hundred and eighty dollars.

It was a nerve-wracking period for all of us. For a little money, like a little learning, is a dangerous thing.

I even presented the stock market to her. I was careful to do my explaining in private, because my knowledge is more inspirational than factual, and this was no moment for ridicule from eavesdroppers. She listened to my come-on quite soberly, and I thought perhaps I had succeeded in getting the money out of harm's way.

"You could buy some lovely stock," I said. "While a car bought with the same money would just be depreciating before your very eyes, the stock would be getting better and better."

"I'm not interested," she said. "Money is for old folks. Young people like the stuff money will buy."

So we went on dizzily exploring the stuff money will buy. Especially on four wheels.

Then suddenly the search was over. I could scarcely believe what I was hearing when she answered the telephone and said wearily, "I'm sorry, sir. I'm not buying a car just now."

As soon as she put up the phone, I cried breathlessly, "You're *not?*"

"Not what?"

"Not buying a car!"

"Nope."

"How'd you reach that conclusion?"

"I made a big discovery."

"That's fine," I said, not caring what the discovery was, just so it was doing what it seemed to be doing.

"It's about sex," she said.

"Oh?"

"Yep. I found out something."

"What on earth?" I said, trying not to sound too apprehensive.

"Which would you rather do . . . own a car, or have a boy drive you around in *his?*"

As simple as that. But it's pretty profound, after all. And if she can just remember the discovery and let it take over, I think she's going to have a pretty good time out of life, woman-wise.

"Okay?" she asked.

"Entirely okay," I agreed.

So now we still have jalopies cluttering up the driveway, making the whole street look rakish. But there's variety in the clutter, here today and gone tomorrow, each replaced by another just as dilapidated. But that's the way we like it.

Take Time by the Tail

ટ્ય I WENT TO SEE some early American clothes in a museum. A sobering experience, for somebody who fastens loose buttons with a safety pin on the wrong side of the material, and who lives in nylon. In the exhibit were miles of ruffles on petticoats, each edged with handmade tatting. Some woman sewed on every inch by hand, and she also made soap and candles, and bread, then spent the afternoons driving behind a team of horses, on long leisurely calls from house to house.

They were just better women than we are.

We are knee-deep in labor-saving devices and ready-mixed food, and we haven't a minute to spare. With all the complex abundance we endure, we have one crying shortage . . . *time*. The most common plaint you hear nowadays is, "I just haven't time . . . I'd love to do it, if I had the time. . . ."

So I began to study time a little, to find out what kind of commodity it actually is. Gradually a rebellion rose up

within me, for I realized that most of us have time for
necessity but not for delight.

Time, it seemed to me, is a tyrant who admits duties,
obligations, and bores into its presence, but banishes as many
of the frisky pleasures as possible. Time usually strains out
the camels and swallows the gnats. For most of us duti-
fully waste the best parts of our time on things we wish
we didn't have to do.

I announced my discovery to the family with the smug-
ness that usually accompanies such declarations.

"Don't anybody count on me on any Tuesday evenings
from now on," I said. "I'm taking one evening a week to
do nothing except what I enjoy."

They said with sarcastic sympathy, "What a dismal life
you lead, you poor dear."

"Okay. But on Tuesday night I'm nobody's business. I'm
going to paint, or read some old books I never have time
for, or do up some preserves, or maybe just sit and stare
into space."

"That's what I like to do," Boo said. "I love to just sit
and frustrate."

And when Tuesday came, that's about what I did. The
evening was all worn out from the day just spent. My attention was a ragbag, a bowl of mincemeat, a shattering
yarn.

Boo said with masterly simplicity, "The trouble with your
free evening is that it comes at the wrong end of the day.
Why not have your evening in the morning?"

So that's what I did. And that's how I discovered on the
clock a big jackpot of time . . . three extra hours a day. In

eight days it adds up to an extra twenty-four-hour day. In a year it amounts to much more than a month . . . nice fresh hours that nobody has yet fingermarked . . . rich hours dehydrated of all perverse interruptions and distractions . . . private hours mailed special delivery from eternity itself.

Naturally, you couldn't waste such untarnished time on anything but work. So inadvertently I found that my rebellion had rebelled against me. Time had got the best of me again.

So, filled with self-righteousness, I now got up at five o'clock and plunged into work in a whisper so the rest of the house wouldn't be disturbed. I had to huddle in a warm robe because heat hadn't got up yet. Seems as if nobody else in the world is awake except some birds with insomnia. There is a lovely novelty about the familiar houses across the street, for at this hour the light is a splash of level sunshine and the shadows all point west instead of east.

After I got accustomed to the new light-angle outside, I discovered new light-angles in me. I found curiosity is livelier in the early morning; appreciation keener, and the windowpane that seems to divide one's own small thinking from the lucid effortless light of Mind is more transparent. There's elated voluntariness and a rush of thinking outward to meet what's new. The mind . . . even a lazybone's mind like the one I know best . . . is an athlete in the morning, performing out of sheer joy in strength. It's hardly recognizable as the heavily fed sulky servant who does only what it must.

I wanted to tell everybody what I'd discovered. And for

a few days I did just that, making a bore of myself. Then, for the thousandth time I conceded again that the best things in life are secret. And must stay that way, until we find them for ourselves. But we never give up trying to put up our fine discoveries in patent medicine bottles and passing them out for free.

I wanted to say, "Listen, honey . . . you're wasting your early morning thinking on routine stuff! You're throwing away your best on matters that concern the 'creature' and his tiresome maintenance . . . his bath, his clothes, his trek through town. Your keenest blade of the mind is hacking through dull tedium."

Nobody can measure an early morning hour. It's not just the length of four fifteen-minute radio programs. One reason it's so big is that you apply yourself immediately, knowing nothing is going to save you, no phone, no doorbell, no pleasant aimless conversation. You rose up to work and you plunge right in. Nobody, it goes without saying, would dawdle or doodle at five o'clock in the morning.

People said to me, grumblingly, "What's the matter with you anyway? What makes *you* so doggoned cheerful?"

That was the problem, all right. You have to dim your exuberance because the sight of anybody with work done and self-respect under the belt is infuriating to people just out of bed. You must speak gently so you won't rile the invalids suffering from the malady of being-too-busy-to-be-human.

You refrain from making the speech that wants to be said. "Listen, sleep is often a symptom of boredom. Don't you remember? People in love . . . with each other or with life . . . don't require much sleep. . . ."

You dare not say any of it. And if you yawn . . . as you do about eleven o'clock . . . you do it with a polite pardon-me.

And that, matter of fact, is one of the many advantages of the system. You have a perfectly legitimate right to an afternoon nap. If anybody questions, you can mention Thomas Edison, and give the impression you're inventing a new kind of light bulb. And perhaps, you really are!

Real Live Money

ᕤ Now THAT Boo had made her big discovery about money, I thought we'd better go on with the education.

We would now venture into the chapter called "Money and Clothes."

We have passed through that period when the question of clothes was "*Must* I put on something else? Comp'ny won't care. Nobody looks at a child . . . except to make improvements, of course."

"*I* look at you. And I think you're perfect . . . practically," I used to say gently. "But today let's have a kind of dress rehearsal for when you become . . . well, civilized."

"Okay," she used to say dolefully, "but can I wear blue-jeans?"

We *have* now become civilized as far as clothes are concerned. It is a fearsome state. The clothes question which used to be an unwelcome foundling on our doorstep has become the honored guest in our house. It has first place. Boo comes down late to breakfast looking pale from trying to decide which pearls, the large or the small, should go with the sweater . . . or do I like the silver chain with the elephant?

"Give me your undivided attention," she pleads.

"I have only one kind," I say. "One-piece."

"No comedy, please. Now look . . . *this* . . . or *this?*" She holds up each ornament in breathless suspense. If I can't make up my mind instantly, with good substantiating reasons, we have to go through it several times. The same mountainous importance, naturally, is given to shoes, to scarf, to handkerchief-in-pocket-or-out. Life is a complex business.

And shopping, up to the time of my *invention,* was delicious agony. Every item in her size was tried on thoughtfully and courteously. She could have closed her eyes and picked at random. After all, how can anything be unbecoming when one has blue eyes and golden hair, and every ounce is accounted for (and if an alien ounce sneaks in on the morning scales, it is routed by night like a pickpocket in Utopia).

But to her, and to all her friends, there are hundreds of shades of difference between the one perfect swim suit or sweater, and all the others on earth.

Sometimes if *two* utterly perfects appear we strike a crisis. "It would save you a shopping trip later," she says, always considerate, "and if you say so, I'll just hang the extra one in the closet and not wear it until you say I definitely need a new one. Okay?"

We have been known to be guilty of three when we went to buy one. These were the Saturdays when she said,

"Wasn't our luck absolutely *fab* today! I just love to shop with you, darling."

If we took a kibitzer on the trip, we naturally had to buy a little souvenir for her. Not a major item, of course. But a blouse she adored, or a handbag like Boo's, only in green. "It seems so selfish not to think of someone else," Boo always says afterwards. "You wouldn't want me to be selfish, I'm sure."

In spite of all this she never had a thing to wear. None of them have. When an occasion arises everyone phones everyone else and discusses the problem at length. I hear her saying, "But I haven't a thing, Felicity . . . absolutely nothing. My closet looks like Old Mother Hubbard. Speaking of O.M.H., I suppose Connie will wear that *bag* her mother brought her from Paris." Poor Connie, her mother selects her clothes.

But a while ago, everything changed in our house. Because I had an inspiration, so stunning and so wonder-working that I felt as if it should be marked "Pat. pending."

Next time the despotic subject of clothes came up, which it did within the hour, I was ready with my invention.

"Speaking of clothes . . . we're going to work on a new system."

"Oh? Something loathsome and sound, I expect."

"No. I think you're going to like it."

"So? Tell."

"I've figured out how much we spend for your clothes in a year. Hereafter we're going to give it to you in monthly installments."

"You mean real live *money?*" she uttered the electric word in a whisper.

"I don't mean hay," I said, aiming at her language and missing it by a year or two.

"Gosh," she looked starry-eyed with awe, and found nothing to say for quite a while. "You mean I'll handle actual money! In amounts you can see with the naked eye."

"The thing is, you've got to plan your spending," I said. "If you know you're going to need a large item . . . say a winter coat, you'll have to go lightly on buying, to be ready for it. If I were you I should draw up a yearly budget."

"Now, please," she said politely, "if I'm going to manage it, I'd better do it."

"It will give you fine experience, so when you have your own family." Right there was where I made my big mistake. For when we talk about her family of the future this present always fades into dwarfed insignificance. "My husband will be proud of the way I handle his money," she said with that lovely guilelessness which her "husband" always brings out in her.

"Exactly. Anybody can spend money. But the really smart women . . ."

"Say no more," she said, for she was already making a list and crossing things off and scribbling in improvements. Before she went to bed, she had drawn up an elaborate spending plan, and set up books to handle the checks coming and going each month. There was nothing simple about this; it was double-entry bookkeeping . . . triple-entry, in fact, for there was a column frankly marked "borrowed."

The first month's check sent her whole gang out shopping. I shuddered to think. She was quite capable of shooting the works on a new sweater for everybody . . . "just to get things started right."

But I completely misjudged her. She would have been capable of generosity on my money. But this was of a different breed. This was hers. This was money which screamed with pain if you touched it carelessly. This was money which bruised easily if you came too near it.

They all came home looking grim.

"Your child is a monster," Felicity said. "Presents for nobody. Not even light refreshments."

"Naturally not," Miss Boo said. "Refreshments are not wearing apparel."

Sally said sheepishly, "On me they are. A heavy layer between my bones and my underwear."

"What did you buy?" I asked, realizing that from now on things would be different in this house.

"One very sensible slip. Tailored. No silly lace to wear out and fall to pieces," Boo said defensively.

"The way it does on the slips I always buy you."

"Exactly," she said. "I don't think lace is appropriate for a schoolgirl. I expect to have a few lace-trimmed slips in my trousseau, which naturally I assume you'll provide when the time comes. . . . Or do I have to start saving for that?"

The tailored slip covered the first month's buying. "I don't seem to need very much," she said innocently. "I seem pretty well outfitted at the moment."

The next month she looked at swimming suits, and they were a terrible temptation. But the old white one was still pretty good, and the best one could be passed down to everyday wear, and replaced when the markdowns came. The month passed without a purchase. Not without shopping. But without buying.

I took the matter in hand now. I went with her on the next shopping trip. She tried on lovely things as always, and made the most of her brief reflection in the mirror. But nothing was completely irresistible. The sales person, I thought, looked a bit fed up. I stole out of the dressing room where this intoxicating nonsense was going on, and apologized to her.

"Think nothing of it. They all try on *everything!*" she said over an armful of new candidates. "But at least you're in there pitching for a sale. When they come alone, they usually haven't the slightest intention."

Pitching or no pitching, we left without a purchase.

"I'm frightfully sorry," Boo said pleasantly to the limp saleswoman, "they're all charming. But nothing seems to look just right on *me.*"

When we were outside, before I had a chance to scold her, she said meekly, "But you wouldn't want me to buy something that wasn't completely perfect, would you?"

"The red one was."

"Not quite," she said, trying to keep the honest regret out of her voice. "Besides it makes such a difference when what you're spending is *money.*"

"I can't seem to remember what it was we *used* to spend," I said mildly.

"That was just that green stuff grownups sling around for people they love," she said with a twinkle. "But kids' money is practically sacred."

The next month I mentioned pj's. "Who'd waste money on clothes nobody sees?" she said with finality. "Anyway, I've matched up the green tops with the yellow-striped bottoms. They're not legally married, but they're very happy together."

Ignoring this, I said, "And of course you'll need something rather special for the Faculty Tea. You know last year I got you the taffeta skirt with the gold nylon blouse."

"Ideal for this year," she said. "No *people* would see it. Only teachers. Besides, teachers think it's refined to look shabby."

"You mean you're not buying anything this month?" I thought we might as well get the cards on the table.

"My husband wouldn't approve," she said. "Not while I have all that silly stuff you bought me."

Her money began piling up. "I get dizzy when I think of it," she said. "I expect I'll be able to help start my husband in business, or something."

Each month she enters the sum in her book, and there it stays intact. "My frozen assets," she calls them. "And *do* they keep me *warm?*"

Every Saturday she goes shopping, and when she comes home, she has a list of things she could have bought.

After five or six months I began getting positively ashamed of her.

"What do people think? Probably that we're just too mean to dress you decently."

"Oh no. I tell 'em. The ones that matter," she said. "Anybody can *spend* money. It takes strong character to resist it. That's what you always told me."

Things didn't get better. Saving can become as pernicious a habit as spending.

" I belong to Spendthrifts Anonymous," she said. "The way to stay sober is not to spend the first dollar."

"You'll have to spend some next month," I said sternly. "You need a new raincoat, a dress for Sunday School, new shoes, and a skirt."

"Who looks at anybody in the rain?" she asked feebly, skipping the rest.

"Never mind that. I'm warning you."

"Okay," she said agreeably. "I'll shop next Saturday."

"I'll come with you."

Her face congealed in horror. "You wouldn't like the places I patronize," she said. "Very low altitude. Basement, in fact."

She came home from the trip, beaming. As she burst through the door, she cried, "I bought something."

"I should hope so. Raincoat? Shoes and skirt?"

"Well, not exactly," she hedged. "I got something for you. A lovely scarf. Marked down."

"And for you?"

"Well, I'll tell you." She always begins this way when she wishes to evade the issue. "I looked and looked. But to tell you the truth, nothing looks so good on me as . . . *money.*"

I could see by the convulsed merriment in her face that she was thinking about her "husband" and hoping that when he arrives, he will know how to read between the lines of her hard-earned shabbiness.

The Best Intentions

৪৯ SOMETIMES WHEN I find myself trying too hard, I remember the Perry family and Martha Brown, who had been the maid, comforter, friend, and unacknowledged mainstay of that house for nearly thirty years. Martha asked and expected nothing but her small weekly wage, and the right to go on serving as long as she had breath in her body. (You can see this is a story that didn't happen very recently.)

The Perry family, however, had shrunk in size and finances until all that was left was one daughter, Miss Charlotte Perry, and a big gloomy mansion on a street from which fashionableness had long ago packed up and moved away.

A large mortgage had been put on the old house, and meeting the monthly payments was a major crisis. Miss Charlotte knew the sensible adjustment was to dismiss Martha, sell the house for whatever it would bring, and settle herself in some modest apartment. But this Miss

Charlotte could not bear to do because she knew Martha was too old to find a new job, and the family had considered it a moral responsibility to see that she always had a home in the big old house, and a place in the bosom of the Perry family.

Naturally Miss Charlotte, who was far from young herself, told the loyal old servant nothing of this daily financial struggle. Night after sleepless night she was haunted by the forlorn vision of poor Martha without home or job, too old and friendless to find another life. She worried along month after month, always for Martha's sake, and always with the bleak hope that something would pop up to solve things.

What did pop up, finally, was severe illness for herself. She had no choice then, for the matter was out of her hands. The bank sent Miss Charlotte to a resthome in the country, then put the house and the furniture up for sale. Martha effaced herself as quietly as possible from the scene.

In a couple of months Miss Charlotte was well enough to resume worrying, beginning just where she had left off. She telephoned the bank to see if they could get in touch with old Martha Brown, who she knew must be desperate.

Within a few hours Martha herself arrived at the resthome. The same old Martha, soft-spoken and drab and cheerful.

"Oh, Martha, how did you get here so quickly?" Miss Charlotte asked, her eyes filling with weak tears at the sight of her old friend.

"Well . . . my husband took the day off from his work and drove me down," Martha said with an economical blush.

"Your husband! What on earth do you mean?"

"Well, you see, Miss Charlotte . . . I just thought I'd take a little rest before I looked for another job. So I got myself a light-housekeeping flat in a roominghouse. I thought it would be nice to sit and listen to the radio, and cook myself whatever food I liked." Her eyes pecked timidly at her late employer's face, to make sure she was giving no offense.

"After about a week, I noticed a nice-looking, white-haired man living in the front room of the second floor . . . we got to saying good morning when we met on the stairs . . . and one day he asked me was I cooking lamb stew up in my little flat . . . so I invited him to come up and have dinner with me . . . and well, he came, and we got acquainted." She was galloping shyly now through her story to the end, and Miss Charlotte was sitting there with her ears unbelieving.

"He said he just loves hearing a woman running about her housework humming, and I guess I do hum when I cook . . . and anyway. . . ."

"You married him!" Miss Charlotte concluded in amazement.

"Yes. But what I wanted to tell you, dear . . . we've got a lovely big room waiting for you in our house. We've just bought a real nice house." She gulped a minute. "Henry's never had a real home before." Then she brought out the truth. "You see . . . it's our *old* house, where we all lived for such a long time."

Miss Charlotte could say nothing, for the miraculous, droll wonder spreading through her mind.

Martha was saying gently, "So now we have our own home again, you and I."

"And we wouldn't have had it, if we hadn't lost it," Miss Charlotte said.

They sat there quietly, not knowing how to explain what had happened. A miracle had been forced upon them by what they thought was disaster.

When Miss Charlotte told me about this she said timidly, "People like me can only go so far with our good intentions. When things become unmanageable, Something else has to take over. Good as human intentions are, they sometimes stand in the way of a better working out. Maybe we have to learn we can trust life even more than we trust ourselves.

"After all, we inherit our own good intentions from Something which has even better intentions than our own."

The Public Spirit

હ્ર THE BEST THING about the Good Citizenship Club was
that you mingled. You mingled with some very odd subjects, but you also mingled with all sorts of people. Even
with seniors, who normally wouldn't have been caught
dead looking at you.

"It gives you experience," Boo said. "Makes you feel
terrible. But Felicity says that's fine experience."

Besides the personal element, it also exposed you to aspirations and desires bigger than you could handle. It
stretched you till you ached. Boo came home from the
meetings starry-eyed and moody, sometimes expecting us
to drop everything and enlist in some world-wide humanitarian work they had discussed, sometimes finding us
loathsomely complacent and selfish because we were just
idly sitting on Uncle Sam's lap, like over-fed, spoiled
babies.

"This house simply disgusts me," she said. "Everything in it is smug. Don't you realize that three out of
every five people in the world are barefooted? And you've

got a whole closet full of shoes! Why don't you *do* something?"

I tried to defend myself. "I'd give 'em away, darling, if that would help. But it's not as simple as all that. It's a very complex problem."

"Oh certainly. The well-fed man can always think of good reasons for going on being well fed. Why, Dr. Hunt says. . . ." Sociology strained through Dr. Hunt was quite a thing; but when you got *that* further strained through Boo, it became sheer fantasy. But I always listened respectfully, remembering how repulsive my own safe family had seemed to me when *I* was sixteen and had discovered there are baffling inequalities on this planet.

Usually after a meeting of the G.C.C. she was in despair because no big heroic act could be attempted that very day.

"Education! That's much too slow," she said. "We ought to *do* something. And all anybody offers us is words. . . . 'Let's have a debate' . . . 'Let's get up a round table discussion.' . . . I'm sick of talk."

"What would you like to do?"

"Something drastic. Maybe send my allowance to some little village in Africa every month. Maybe stop wearing silly clothes and just go into Levis and saddle shoes. Maybe if people saw us all wearing some kind of uniform, they'd get to *thinking!*"

I knew exactly how she felt. I knew well the humiliating absurdity of the deed compared to the need. For a few weeks it looked as if we were going to have a permanently disgruntled, out-of-joint humanitarian on our hands.

Then good old Dr. Hunt came to our rescue. He gave

the club something to do. He got everybody working on a committee, and the next thing we knew there was going to be an Event. Committees met after school every day, and the atmosphere seethed with civic industry.

"We're inviting the public," Boo said. "We're arousing."

There would be a giant mass meeting on a Friday night when normally people just waste their time having fun. . . .

She got home late for dinner, and her eyes were glowing with public-spirited zeal.

"Guess what? Dr. Hunt picked me and the President of the club — he's a senior! — to go around town today putting up posters. Everywhere they'd let us — beauty shops, delicatessens . . . specialty shops, bus stops . . . anywhere the public will notice them. We want everybody to know about the wonderful speaker we're going to have."

"That's fine," I said. "Who *is* the speaker?"

She looked completely deflated for a long moment. Then she had the grace to blush. "Well, I haven't the faintest idea," she admitted, "but Joe, the President of the club — he's certainly a doll!"

The Having and the Doing

ভ🦢 WISDOM COMES in through small doors sometimes. . . .

Two of our favorite friends are the small sons of one of *your* favorite motion picture actors. The other day these youngsters went to visit a couple of contemporaries who live like little princes, in the midst of every conceivable weary luxury that wealth and lack of imagination can provide.

The governess, who had taken Bill and Mike from their own ranch to visit, brought back amazed accounts of the wonderful mechanical toys, the swimming pool, the gymnasium and the riding horses with which the hosts were encumbered. But what Bill and Mike brought home was the wanting of a two-wheeled cart.

"If we had one, I could pull Mike around in it," Bill told his father excitely. "And maybe we could haul wood up to the house for the fireplaces."

"Sure you could," their father said. "How did you think you could get one?"

"Well, we could call up and ask 'em where they bought

theirs," Mike said casually, measuring his father out of the corner of his eye.

"You fellows happen to have any money?" the father asked.

They admitted they had a little. . . . But it was pledged to pay Cub Scout dues, and their mother's birthday was coming. . . .

"Tell you what we *could* do," their father said thoughtfully. But before he had finished the sentence, both boys were ahead of him.

"Sure we could, Pop," they said. "We could make it easy as anything." When you are nine and seven, and used to hammer and nails, there's nothing you couldn't make!

"That's right," Pop said. "I know where there are a couple of wheels down in the barn."

Plans for the Saturday carpentry filled the whole week. Never was a cart so dreamed about and planned for. They drew the pattern on smoothed-out wrapping paper; they measured, and sawed and perspired. Pop helped with suggestions, but they did the work.

They built it all themselves. And they built much more than a slightly wobbly cart out there on the sunny barn floor with the doors flung open and the sky smiling down on the hotly clutched nails and the sandpapered boards.

You'd hardly expect that two small boys would understand that they were building more than just a toy cart. But they did. For at the end of the afternoon, when the cart was almost ready for a triumphant trip around to the front of the house to be shown to the rest of the family, Mike said, "Which do you think will be more fun? Makin' or havin'?"

Bill sat back among the sawdust, and thought about it. Then he grinned through his big new far-apart teeth.

"Makin'," he said.

People go to lectures and read books heavy in the hand and heavier in the mind. They discuss and argue, and move big cumbersome pieces of mental furniture about from side to side. And then, unannounced and unheralded, wisdom blows in through some small opened window in the mind, casual as a petal from the tree.

We live whole lifetimes groping among wise syllables. Then one day a child says the sum quite simply.

"Which will be better? Havin' or makin'?"

"Why, makin'."

They don't need to explain it. They've found it out by doing. The thing proves itself.

Making must come from within, while having is an external circumstance which may or may not be worth its weight in satisfaction. The happiest people of the earth are those who learn that difference early. There's nobody so right, so safe from the whims of discontent as a man mated to his work. A man and his work are like a lock and a key. Useless without each other.

The "born" mechanic, the natural housewife, the "green-thumbed" gardener . . . these are the real kings of the earth, the people who love what they are doing. So are doing it well.

If work is not its own reward, there comes no other pay worth having. Thousands of years ago the Preacher said it like this:

There is nothing better for a man than that he should eat and drink, and that he should make his soul enjoy good in his labour. This also I saw, that it was from the hand of God.

Ecclesiastes 2:24

The Gift

꒰꒱ TUMPTI HAD BEEN with us about a year, when we found that up to now we had been on probation, and hadn't realized it.

"I tly you out. Now I stay," he announced one morning at breakfast.

We responded to that surprising news according to our varying natures. Most of us said, "Well!" and let it go at that. Boo said, "So we didn't flunk out!"

Tumpti, all his features coagulating in merriment, said, "Now I send for my tlunk. Fit very nice in loom."

That very afternoon the trunk arrived from a storage warehouse. It was so heavy two burly giants could barely wrestle it into the room, much to Tumpti's disgust; he plainly felt that if they'd just step aside he could heave it to his shoulder and run in with it.

Now that we had him anchored in our life by a trunk, we felt he really belonged to us.

"It's something like when you get the last installment

paid, and the mink's all yours," we said, honoring one of our family jokes.

Whatever else was in the trunk, there was one article which he brought out at dinner and showed with pride. At first glance it appeared to be a large gilt-framed picture; but when you looked more carefully, you saw it was like no picture you'd ever seen before. It was made up entirely of semiprecious stones, some cut and polished, others in their primitive state. The stones had been carefully mounted, and the whole effect was like an exquisite sampler made in a language you couldn't quite read.

"Why, Tumpti, that's a beautiful thing! Where on earth . . . ?"

"I make," he said humbly.

"But where did you get such wonderful stones?" We could identify amethysts, carnelians, different kinds of quartz, and a few choice pieces of turquoise.

"I find," he said. "U.S.A. Government send all Japanese people to Arkansas while war bangs." He clutched the big sampler to him to free his hands in order to act out the last verb, "Bang bang." Obviously there was no malice in the memory.

We tried to make sympathetic sounds, not taking our eyes off the collection of stones.

"I have fine time at U.S.A. Government vacation. Nothing to do."

"So you collected these beautiful stones. Did everybody make a collection?"

He looked haughty. "Ten sousand people in camp. I only one corrects locks. People too razy!"

The conversation came to a stop now, but he still stood there looking down at his treasures.

"So now I give you pleasant," he said gruffly. "You take locks. I find prenty, some other day maybe." He thrust the frame at me, and with it came a stream of his muttering, half Japanese, half English, for his own generosity was embarrassing to him.

"Why, we can't accept such a beautiful thing, Tumpti. It must have taken you a long long time to find such extraordinary stones."

"You take," he said belligerently. "Stone no good. Maybe you punch holes and make string of beads."

"I wouldn't let anyone *touch* it," I cried. "It's a work of art exactly as it is."

I added lamely, "But of course we can't accept it."

"Then I dlop on froor," he threatened, looking as if he intended to do exactly that. I seized the frame just in time, and he beamed with joy. Then his little face flushed pink.

"I got nobody else I rike to give pleasant to," he said. "I got nobody else anyplace."

"We'll put it on the mantel in the living room," said Boo, who also cannot bear emotion. "And when people admire it, we'll tell them it was given to us by one of our best friends."

He bowed then, all dignity. "Sank you ve'y much," he said, as if it was *we* who had given *him* the gift.

Love

ह&~ LOVE CAME AT US without warning. At any age, love is
a shock when it attacks you. But when you're just past sixteen, it almost unhinges the universe.

To begin with, anyone on the outside is entitled to stare
at it . . . and not see it as it is. In the prose of ordinary living,
it is a typographical error, yet it makes so much sense that
for the first time one understands why the world was
created. The most profound of all events, from the outside it
appears to be just nonsense.

In amazement you perceive that you are suddenly wearing
the classical robes of poetry and drama and music; but if you
are a sixteen-year-old, on you love is a most comical costume.
It hasn't even the wistful pathos of a Pagliacci's domino; it
is grotesquely too big, laughably too beautiful. You know
you look absurd in it. You know that every gesture you
make is full-fledgedly ridiculous. But you cannot help it.
If you could help it, it would not be love. You just have to
be recklessly ridiculous, moaning helplessly inside where no
one can hear.

When love strikes a sixteen-year-old, it hits the whole family. Nothing is the same for a few days. And what can the others in the family do about it? Nothing. If you are blind to what damage you do to everything precious you and your child have felt about each other, you can resort to the vandalism of humor. You can try to laugh it off. But love doesn't laugh off. All that happens is that you become forevermore someone in your child's eyes who must not be allowed to come close to what is important.

Actually, there is no right way for a family to behave when love knocks at the front door, and bursts in without waiting to be invited. You may try your best to strike a balance between your child's illumined viewpoint and ordinary common sense . . . but you'll say the inspiredly wrong thing every time you open your mouth. I can't even picture what right conduct *could* be. Perhaps the ideal behavior would be to put yourself in the deep freeze and just wait until a day when she is hungry again for the plain bread of normal living and loving and being.

There *is* no right behavior. So if you're sensible, you just try to be as inconspicuous as possible. She'll not be noticing you much anyway. She'll not be noticing anything, for suddenly she has stepped across an imaginary line into a world that has never before existed. A world beyond dimension, beyond geography . . . long dreamed toward but never before touched.

The funny-paper symptoms of love are all present, the not-eating, the not-hearing, the bemused enchantment. But it would be crass and gauche and fatal for them to be diagnosed as if they ever before had been experienced. They are new; no one since the world began has felt *this* way. If you catalogue them blithely and say, "Oh . . . so you're in love! Now don't be silly, darling," you only show how insensitive and ignorant you are. So you try to say nothing at all. The hardest job an adult is ever asked to do about a child. An almost impossible assignment at any time, and *now. . . .*

But if you are wise you'll try. You'll listen mutely if you're offered any confidence. You'll wear dark glasses, but you mustn't look like a panhandler standing with a beggar's cup. You'll take what you're offered, and make no comment, either in word or look.

It happened in our house with practically no warning. One day she was our irrepressible roller skater, with a flying pony tail and a farmhand's unfillable appetite. The next day she was a sleepwalker, listening to music that nobody else could hear. One day she was full of jokes and pranks and happy earthiness; the next she was a poet whose stanzas were silence. And we, sad battered humans that we were, could only stand aside and wait, remembering how we had felt once . . . or even twice.

There comes a time, of course, when love *has* to be talked about. When nothing else is worth doing. That's when the door of danger swings wide open and you're liable to throw yourself into the pit of destruction. For then it's almost impossible not to say the wrong thing.

I had been waiting for that moment; I had been practicing my reticence so I'd have it perfect when the moment came. Because I knew that sooner or later, it would come, and I'd be offered a view of this wonderful thing. I could look — but I mustn't touch. I would be offered it, and then

be denied it because I would not understand. No matter
how I behaved, it would be evident that I didn't understand.
Or else that I understood intrusively well.

The moment came just after dinnertime on a long twilight.

"I wish we could go out walking someplace," she said.
"Just the two of us. You and me, I mean." I knew what
"just the two of us" really meant, but I didn't let that show
in my face.

"We could," I said.

"I wish we could walk someplace in the country. I hate
all these nice proper houses. They disgust me."

"I know, dear."

"They don't disgust you," she said almost angrily, to
warn herself she was going to walk with an alien spirit.
"You like 'em!"

"I like woods better," I said contritely.

We walked, and neither of us talked, and I could see tall
woods growing up invisibly on either side of us in the places
where houses were imagining *they* were.

At last she said, "Do you think a person who is a senior
could really notice a junior? I mean *really?*"

"He might."

"I mean not just to think she was a doll, or something
silly like that? I mean really *recognize.*"

"He might," I ventured again. "After all, *you* recognize."

She thought that over for a block, her face pink with
feeling.

"Yes, perhaps," she said at last, like someone in a very
slow-paced play, where the audience has all evening to

spend and there isn't much plot to get in the way of the lines.

I was cold, because in my eagerness to get out into that imaginary forest for our walk, I had shrugged into my too thin jacket. But when I shivered, I saw that she read it as my unexpected awareness of Life all around us. So I shivered again.

"He spoke to me this morning," she said.

"What about?" I asked, by mistake.

"What about? Why, nothing, of course. He just spoke to me. He said 'Hi.' That's exactly what he said. He came up behind me. I could feel him from the minute he sort of zoomed into the corridor from the Chem Lab. He kind of slowed up and walked along behind me, and then he sort of leaned down . . . he's awfully tall . . . even for a senior . . . and he said 'Hi.' " She was quiet, then she asked ardently, "Do you suppose he . . . meant anything?"

"Of course he did," I said, hoping I'd not be asked to translate.

"Oh gosh," she breathed. "I hope so. He said 'Hi' . . . Just like that."

I shivered again. Life was pretty wonderful.

The Diploma

ҍ҉ WHEN YOU'RE PRAYING to be wise yourself, it sometimes helps to think of the wise people you've known. So I remembered an old-fashioned woman I know. Nothing about her is modern; even her virtues are rather out of style. But her children think the world of her, for she has always been the kind of mother they could depend on. No matter how boyish and complicated were her son's emotions, somehow Toots could always be relied upon to understand.

But one day there came to her the greatest test she had ever faced in all her years of being a mother.

Steve's letter, pages and pages scrawled over with feverish handwriting, arrived special delivery. Trustingly he poured out all his innermost reasons for a dramatic action he wanted to take. He was certain what her answer would be.

But she was not so certain.

He began by telling her about a girl. Joan's name had popped up frequently in Steve's letters all through the winter. But not until now did Toots have the secret of the mysterious sudden failure of Steve in this, his last year at the university. Now it all came out; he was enthusiastically in love, and he wanted to be married next week.

It could have gone along in the ordinary way, he said, except that Joan's family was moving to another city. Too, her father had offered him the big chance of going into the new business. He knew his mother would agree that the last five months of college were utterly unimportant compared to this wonderful opportunity.

Besides, Joan's father said a college education was all bunk. He had made his pile, and he hadn't got past the first few months of high school. So that showed you. What Steve wanted was to stop being a student, and be a man with a fine new job and a wonderful family of in-laws. He knew his mother would see it as he did. The letter went on, page after rhapsodic page.

More than anything else Toots wanted her son to continue thinking of her as he always had, somebody to be depended upon to see his point of view, and to support it against the world if need be. She walked the floor, trying to look into the future and realize what might grow out of this moment which lay in her hand like an unplanted seed.

Then she sat down and wrote what she probably would not have had the strength of character to say if Steve had been standing there before her, his eyes ardent and reproachful. She wrote it like a business letter.

Dear Steve:
You and I entered into a gentlemen's agreement when you started your college education. We did not draw

up any contract, but we both understood that I was investing the money which I had saved all my life to put into something in which I had faith. You, for your part, were guaranteeing that you would invest four years of your time. I have spent all my money, and you have spent part of your time.

What you have got out of your share of this investment has been as large or as small as your own effort. I am unable to alter or change your dividend. Nobody but you can say whether or not it has been worthwhile. But I am entitled to my return from our business partnership.

If these new friends of yours are worth going into business with, they will recognize that you have a prior commitment, which will not be terminated until the day after your commencement. If this is an honest opportunity, it will wait for its proper time.

But whether it waits or not, I insist upon my legitimate dividend from my investment. All I can get for my money is your diploma. I want that.

Very truly yours,
MARCELLA BOWMAN

She sent the letter and spent a sleepless night, remembering all the little-boy Steves who were gone now . . . the lad with the run-over puppy, the nine-year-old who had made her a rickety footstool for Christmas. . . . She nearly sent a wire telling him not to read the letter. But she didn't send the wire, and a week went by somehow, uncomforted by the conviction that she had done the right thing. Two weeks passed without any word from Steve.

When his letter came, it was scrupulously courteous; it said he would live up to his side of the "business bargain." It made no mention of Joan, or the renounced opportunity.

It was a miserable four months for both of them. When June came and Toots went down for commencement, Steve was formal and tragic as only a very young person can be. When she asked about Joan he evaded the question elaborately to show her how much he had been hurt.

Never once did he call her by her old pet name; she was Mother, and the word held her at arms' length.

Commencement Day was probably the most forlorn day of her life. At the end of it, she had the diploma, which she had said was all she would get from their partnership. It was indeed all she had.

They drove five hundred miles home together. Steve was faultless in his courtesy toward her, but all the old camaraderie and confidence had gone. All the fun and quickness had gone.

She told herself: "when we're home . . . when he finds his work . . . we'll slip back into our old life, and all this will be forgotten."

All summer the dead body of the diploma lay between them.

No really good job seemed available in their town. So he finally went to work in a gas station. He came home at night, dirty-faced and tired. He would look in the mirror and say, "Well, college man, you're a distinguished-looking individual."

That job blew up and there were others, equally routine. The winter dragged along and Steve was getting nowhere.

Listlessly he tried this and that, and finally became an insurance salesman. But his heart wasn't in it.

The breach between them had started by being only as wide as a sheepskin; now they were separated by unplowable acres of despair.

Then a new girl came to town. This romance didn't happen quickly. This friendship was a slow-growing, patient plant, not an exotic cut flower. Toots and Elizabeth understood each other long before Steve saw what was happening to him.

In his happiness he went out and sold insurance harder than ever. For now he had stopped trying to prove how wrong his mother had been.

He got an appointment to tell the principal of a school about insurance.

The principal said, "Say, boy, you explain this stuff like a teacher. I happen to be an authority on recognizing good teacher material when I see it."

Steve said earnestly, "I'd like to be a teacher, matter of fact."

"Fine. Have you a college diploma?"

"Well, no," Steve said slowly. "But my mother has one. With my name on it."

The Big Walk

$\Bbbk$ People are always reminding me that I live a very sedentary life. It's an insulting phrase, especially when one's picture of oneself is an animated cartoon of frenzied activity.

"What you ought to do is take a nice long walk every day," various well-meaning advisers said. I ignored the good advice cheerfully for years, because walking seems a ludicrous waste of time to me, unless there is no other form of transportation available except dogsled. But came a day when I couldn't help admitting that my taking-a-long-walk apparatus needed using, or it might become obsolete.

"But I do walk," I said. "I walk all over the house."

"That doesn't count. The walking that's good for you has to be done out in the open, with chin up, stomach in, and legs swinging in long strides."

"You can't live in a house and dash back and forth between housekeeping and a desk without doing some walking," I said sulkily. Mentally I traced my steps through an

ordinary average morning . . . shower, run downstairs, out
to get newspaper usually tossed on the neighbor's lawn, back
to breakfast room, rush to the front door to tell the little
boy from next door that we can't buy any more Boy Scout
peanuts, back to breakfast room, up to workroom in rear of
house, perching on typewriter chair, running length of
house to see if the noise at the patio gate is the postman, out
on balcony to view mailbox, back to desk, up the hall to find
the dictionary borrowed for a Scrabble game, back to desk,
out on balcony to see if mail carrier has arrived, back to
desk, across room to pencil sharpener, run through length
of house to balcony to see, etc., back to desk, and on and on,
through the whole day of chores and errands. Carried on
at a dog-trot because there is too much of it to be accomplished at a mere walk. And yet they said that what I
needed. . . .

"The way to do it," I was told, "is to make a lively game
of it. Try to walk a little farther each day. Get a pedometer,
and keep a chart. You can enjoy anything if you'll put some
thought into it."

So I got the pedometer. That in itself took quite a lot of
walking around the shopping district, because Beverly Hills
is a place where walking has become practically an extinct
folk custom. But at last in a golf equipment shop I found a
pedometer, not to measure walking, the salesman said, but
to check on the distances between tee and green.

He showed me how to adjust it, and how to measure my
own step. My idea of the interesting way to measure was
to step in a puddle of muddy water, then walk nonchalantly
across a white rug. But he said there were easier ways, and

laid down a yardstick on the floor, then crouched beside it while I strolled past. Turned out that 24 inches was about right for me, a sedate-walking woman past her first youth.

Then, diffidently, he suggested that the pedometer would work best if I could attach it to my leg. On my garter, say, with the little instrument slipped in the top of my hose, perhaps. I tried it, and I must say it gave off a most business-like click. Anyone passing me would think I had a defectively jointed artificial limb which creaked with every bend of the knee.

I promised myself that I'd take a long walk the next afternoon. Maybe two miles, to start with. But in the morning, just for fun I would wear the pedometer around the house. Down to breakfast, up to my bedroom, back to my workroom, through the house to look out my balcony door for the mail carrier . . . just the customary routine hither-and-yoning.

At three I put on my jacket for the Big Walk. Before I started I had better check on the pedometer's reading.

And guess what? Just living my ordinary sedentary life, I had chalked up more than four miles!

So now I don't have to listen to anybody's good advice. So now I just sit and sit, enjoying my sedentary life and clicking off mileage on my pedometer.

Poor Winthrop

ҍ✒ LOVE IS NOT BLIND. Love is a super way of seeing. It makes everything dear and unique, which is hidden to other eyes, stand out in billboards visible only to the one who loves. Joe may have looked like a pretty average senior to anyone else, but to Boo he was a masterpiece up to which the race had been working for long centuries. He was smarter than anybody else, more relaxed, more witty, more everything. He was, to borrow a teen-ager's own cliché, The Most.

But that left everyone else suddenly deficient. Poor Winthrop especially.

"How could that silly *child* expect me to go to the movies with him?" Boo asked in honest astonishment. "Can't he *see?*"

"He probably thinks you're still going steady with him, dear."

"Eeek," she said. "How could I have given such an impression?"

I dared not mention the escalator which had seemed such a sound idea a few weeks ago.

"He's a child," she said again, obviously having found the perfect word to describe his total ineptitude.

I refrained from reminding her that he is eight months older than she. But she read my mind. "Even so," she said bitterly. "Some boys stay immature all their lives. Immaturer than girls anyway."

I tried to be practical. "Why couldn't you just go to the movies with him? After all, you're not dated up to go with anyone else, are you?"

"Suppose I went to the movies with this child . . . and I met someone? What would anybody think, seeing me? They'd think I was satisfied. They'd probably see me laughing at his corny jokes and stuff . . . the way you just naturally do to be polite . . . and they'd think I was just like him."

"Quite a predicament," I said, indulging in the relief of sarcasm since for one moment we were not standing on holy ground.

"He bores me," she said, becoming more irately specific. "He talks about stuff just the way a girl does. His voice has changed all right, but his mind hasn't. What he says is just like what a girl would say."

"Such as?"

"Oh, I don't know. He talks about food. He loves macaroni and cheese, and some kind of eggplant his pore ole mother cooks. Imagine talking about *food*."

"Felicity talks about food."

"See! That's just what I'm saying. He talks like a girl.

He just loves green. 'Whyn't you get a nice green sweater, Boo. I bet you'd look like a doll.' Eeek."

"That's his way of paying you a compliment about your hair."

She held her nose expressively. "If I want to talk with a girl, I'd go to the movies with a girl. Girl-talk!"

"George Bernard Shaw once said that was a good test. If you want to know whether or not attraction will survive the years, just ask yourself, 'Would I find this person uniquely interesting if we were of the same sex?' "

She looked utterly disgusted. "George Who-who What? I never heard of him," she said conclusively. "He probably said it when he was good and old, too."

"Maybe," I conceded, remembering that practically everything GBS had to say he said when he was good and old. But I had done my best for Winthrop. I had even called in George Bernard Shaw to help his cause. But I could see it was lost beyond recall.

We Flunk Out

ঔ➤ SHE GAVE US our chance, and we muffed it. I don't know by what stages the lovely affair became mundane enough for Joe to be invited to our house. But there came a day when Boo said, with giant economy-sized casualness, "Oh by the way, a boy's going to drop around tonight."

No need to ask *what* boy. From her face you could see there was only one.

"Happens he's a senior. He knows I'm having some trouble in Math, so he's going to help me."

"Naturally," I said with panting heart. "I suppose that's just part of being fellow members of the Good Citizenship Club."

"That's it," she cried, grateful for the device.

I said, going all out, "Why not ask him for dinner?"

She brooded cautiously. "What're we having? He doesn't just eat anything."

I wanted to say, "Neither do we," but I knew that could be an estranging remark, so instead I asked intelligently about his preferences.

We discussed that rich subject and then she said cannily, "I wouldn't want him to think we were *anxious* to have him."

"How could he ever get such an impression?" I inquired blandly.

"Well, you never can tell. Some boys think friendliness is pursuit. That's what Felicity says."

"I can hear her saying it."

"But Felicity doesn't know Joe," Boo said in experimental triumph. "None of 'em know him. Because he doesn't have any time for girls. That's what everybody says."

"Except maybe a member of the Good Citizenship Club who is weak in Math."

"Something like that," she said, and met my eye with bold innocence.

Everybody in the house was excited about his coming, and we all confessed it by not mentioning him, nor appearing to realize. We were in fact, just normally hysterical with tenseness.

Boo had a few last-minute instructions, and she gave them like a coach getting his team ready for an ordeal. "Most families keep out of sight when a boy's in the house," she said.

"That seems rude."

"I don't say you have to. I'm just telling you what's customary."

"We'd like to do the right thing," we assured her. "But on the other hand, we're naturally friendly people. We'd speak pleasantly to *anybody* in the house and pass the time of day a little."

"Well . . . let him indicate," she said. "If he acts like he'd like to talk to you, you can listen real politely." I saw that her grammar had been murdered by anxiety. I recalled what had happened to mine in the few really pivotal moments in my life.

"You can count on us, darling," I ventured reassuringly.

"Oh for heaven's sakes . . . don't act like it's important!" she cried in dire distaste.

"Of course not," I promised. "It is, but we won't."

She herself answered the doorbell when it rang, and for a long time they stood in the hall, with a tent of muttered undertones protecting them from the family climate. Then they came nonchalantly into the living room, and we felt ourselves being expertly inspected. Boo, gulping rather badly, introduced us, and Joe made good-citizenly acknowledgments. We mumbled shyly but robustly, trying to weigh out just the proper grams of unconcern and hospitality.

Apparently our blend was exactly the right mixture to intrigue him for, to everyone's amazement, he motioned Boo to a chair and then sat down himself.

He tossed his glance around at the reading matter behind which we had all been cowering. He had a few intelligent remarks to make on each subject. You could sense he was doing everything possible to put us at our ease.

Though I was positively shy about looking at him, I could see he was a nice boy, not too sure of himself. Wordlessly I warned myself that his not-too-sureness would probably take the form of brash blustering.

He had blond hair, almost whitened by the sun, and his thin face was tanned to the color of cork. With this he wore honest blue eyes, and a smile that blew briefly across his mouth, like the wind where it listeth. With great relief, I liked him. But no doubt some of that liking was just the fall-out from Boo, whose liking was sending out radar waves in every direction.

At precisely the right moment, he and his pupil adjourned to the library, after he had courteously corrected a few opinions we had been cherishing:

(a) that our farmers need government help;

(b) that, compared to the Old Masters' work, modern paintings are members of the Jukes family;

(c) that Airacobras will resist obsolescence longer than some other planes;

(d) that riboflavin builds mental health.

After they left, we sat stunned, trying to picture what would now happen to Math. If it was mentioned, of course.

At nine o'clock I thought of taking in the usual midnight snack served to a homework-doer at this hour. Then I rejected the notion in horror. Joe probably wouldn't approve of cookies and milk. And if he didn't, I certainly should be perpetrating a political or a cultural boner.

They thought of food themselves, however, and on Joe's way out of the house at nine-thirty, they passed the refrigerator and in passing ate practically all the remains of the roast chicken Tumpti was planning to serve the next day. So . . . we would have a tantrum from him in the morning. . . . Well, better to suffer that than to mar our child's entire life.

We thought resignedly, "This is the beginning of the new order. We'll have Joe on our hands . . . or somebody like him . . . every night from now on."

But we were wrong.

We didn't even find out the facts for nearly a week. During that week homework was done in the afternoon. The two of them sat in Joe's mongrel car, parked at our curb or on some street nearby, Boo on the back seat, Joe on the front, studying earnestly.

"But why?" I asked helplessly. "It doesn't sound comfortable."

"It's very comfortable," Boo said. "And besides our minds are at rest."

"Your minds?" I cried incredulously. "What on earth have your minds got to do with it?"

"Why, we both know where each other *is*," she said. "This way we don't have to wonder. It puts your mind to rest."

I tried to accept that without writhing. "But . . . but wouldn't your minds be just as much at rest if you studied on each side of our library table?"

She shook her head earnestly.

"The space in the car belongs to us," she said. "At least it belongs to Joe. It's the only place that is really ours. It's kind of our own home . . . temporarily."

"I see," I said dismally.

"And besides . . . Joe knows perfectly well that you people don't like him. Don't even understand him."

"Why . . . wherever did he get such an idea? We're . . . we're just crazy about him."

"Don't be insincere, please," she said patiently. "He knows all right."

"But we do like him. We think he's simply wonderful. We never saw anybody like him."

"I know all that," she said confidently. "That's hardly what we're discussing. I just happened to remark that he knows you don't like him."

"What gave him such an idea?"

"You'll find as you know him better that Joe's hardly ever wrong about things."

"This may be the only thing he's wrong about . . . us not liking him," I protested.

"He can tell. Joe says there's a kind of atmosphere when people don't like you. For one thing, the night he was here, you never offered us a midnight snack. Joe says that was your subconscious mind wanting not to feed our friendship."

"My subconscious mind wasn't in it at all," I said helplessly. Then I admitted the truth, almost in tears. "You see, darling, I had forgotten to ask you and I couldn't bear to do the wrong thing."

As I heard myself making this shameful confession I saw in a blaze of clarity what is basically wrong with most of us parents these days. *We're scared to death of displeasing our children.*

She saw nothing demoralized or abnormal in my attitude. She was used to seeing all kinds of adults backed into a corner by the young. No wonder they feel insecure, these addle essence. The very persons who should be towers of certainty for them are crumbling down before them. Adults are bowing down to consult the vacillating judgment of the very young. And the youngsters, knowing what shifting quicksand their own judgment is, naturally feel unsure and alarmed within themselves.

Corroborating my own quick analysis, she tried to reassure me. "Well, don't worry about it," she said. "If Joe ever changes his mind, he'll come into the house."

"Try to persuade him, dear," I said. I couldn't bear to think of them living their whole lives through in a beat-up tin carcass born a Chevvy and now a confused monstrosity of Ford-Oldsmobile-Chrysler. It seemed like a drafty, claustrophobic life. And sedentary as the mischief.

Long Live Joe

ভ I DON'T KNOW when love came down from Olympus
and began walking with the mere mortals in our house.
But at any rate, it made the descent safely. For suddenly
Joe was reconciled to us. Now the whole house was filled
with his tall rangy presence, his winsome grin askew on his
lovable face. And also the house was filled with his absence
when he just couldn't avoid being somewhere else. Occasionally he simply had to run home . . . to change his clothes,
for instance. When he wasn't with us, the air was as filled
with talk about him as a blizzard is filled with snowflakes.

Joe knew everything; final authority on all subjects.

"Joe says. . . ."

"Joe doesn't believe. . . ."

"Joe foresees a time. . . ."

This stage was our crucial test. One utterance of doubt or
disagreement and we would have banished ourselves as hope-
less half-wits. Our eyebrows got weary with the acrobatics of
credulity; our smiles ached with admiring astonishment;

our voices constantly climbed ladders of "Is that so?" and "Well, well!"

"What difference does it make?" we reminded each other indulgently. "All knowledge is relative."

"*And* they laughed at Fulton when he sat down to play."

"So we won't laugh," we agreed. "We may burst, but we won't laugh."

I think Joe was a little in love with all of us. For after all, such total approval is heady intoxication, and pathetically rare in the experience of most of us. Anyway he obviously enjoyed sitting in our living room or our kitchen and holding forth on any and all subjects. He probably felt he had never before been in the presence of such delightfully uninformed yet receptive people. In knowledge we were all virgin forests.

Everybody but Tumpti, of course. When Joe expounded in the kitchen he had to make sure what day it was. Only on Thursday could he speak freely there. Otherwise, Tumpti would flip his all-encompassing white apron as if shooing off a flock of jabbering hens.

"Sklam," Tumpti would say. "Young boy know nothing. Better keep hole in head shut. Few blains reak out."

Joe magnanimously forgave him (forgiving as he ate, naturally). "Quite a character," Joe said. "I might write a play about him sometime."

Boo cried, "*Oh Joe* . . . are you going to write a play?"

"Sometime," he said. "When I get around to it."

"You didn't tell me!" she cried with accusing rapture.

"Lots of things I haven't told you, Woman," Joe said. That didn't seem possible to us.

"I knew he was going to write music," Boo confided happily. "But he hadn't mentioned any plays. Gosh."

"It's nothing," Joe said modestly. "Besides, let's wait until I've done 'em."

"But if you say you will, why you will!" Boo breathed. "Remember how you told me yesterday you were going to eat six ham sandwiches for lunch — and you did!"

"That's right," he conceded. "Well, we'll see."

Whenever we opened the front door, or answered the telephone, or went into the garage, there was Joe, arriving or leaving.

Felicity, slightly bitter on the subject, expressed it in her own way. "It's like a whodunnit. Every time you people open a closet, Joe falls out."

Even so, the day . . . and the night . . . just wasn't long enough to see all we wanted of Joe.

One of us recklessly asked, "When does Joe study, Boo?"

And was answered by the others, "Is there a comma in that sentence?"

Boo, naturally, ignored that heavy-footed adult wit. Boo said, raising her golden eyebrow, "Study? Why should Joe study? He gets A. In the subject he likes, anyway."

Undaunted, adult humor persisted. "What subject is that? Boology?"

Even more undaunted teen-age tolerance persisted. She tried courteously to smile, but the smile was slightly rancid.

I thought to myself, Oh, the poor gallant young. What they endure from us. We're two races utterly alien. No wonder there's the taint of race prejudice between us.

Writers

ဦ ONE THING about writers: they like to be invited to meals with other writers. (Or probably with anybody!)

Anyway, I was invited to lunch to meet an eight-year-old prodigy, equipped with a lot of natural talent and a somewhat breathless mother. I anticipated a rather confounding time, although my hostess assured me we'd have fun. So much in common, she said, not specifying just *what*.

The guest of honor wore a ruffled pinafore, and she had yellow curls and eyes the color a paper doll would have if you drew them in with a nice blue pencil.

"I've decided to be a writer," she said confidently.

"Have you begun working at it?" I asked, trying not to sound patronizing.

"Of course. I've written about two hundred poems."

"Good ones?"

"Well, they're not spelled right, and the punctuation is terrible. But some of them are quite good. Not all of them, of course."

Whenever writers have a chance at would-be writers, they break out a certain monologue; all about how important it is to have discipline, to write something every day whether you feel like doing it or not . . . the business about keeping the pen limber and obedient . . . the paragraph comparing writing to other work in which one wouldn't expect to succeed by only working when you feel like working.

Paula listened to this with great courtesy. But with equal courtesy, she disagreed.

"Yes, but I'm not going to be that kind of writer," she said.

"You're not? What kind are you going to be?"

"I'm going to be a good writer," she said simply.

We were all staggered by that. It whirled us back to the wistful beginning when we were all going to be good writers.

"You see," she said earnestly, "you can't write well unless you wait for inspiration."

Her blue eyes are honest and unafraid; she doesn't suspect she has said something profound. But a montage thunders across my vision . . . huge oppressive volumes and masses of writing cascading across the weary world day after day . . . then like a blessed lilt of calmness and joy, the few winged words of grace written in a lifetime. Never any words written but those few. . . .

What a wealth of silence . . . what a waiting and a treasuring there would have been if only all of us had kept that standard we started with. Never a word written except the inspired words!

Someone dared ask, "But what is inspiration, Paula?"

She thinks awhile. "Well . . . inspiration is where . . ."

she speaks slowly because she is thinking deeply. I like the beginning of the definition. "Inspiration is where . . ." a locality in the geography of the mind. . . .

"I guess . . ." she has it now; it goes more quickly. "Inspiration is where you look at something, and you see it more beautiful than it usually is."

Her eyes consult my face to see if I agree. I doubt if she would amend her definition if I didn't. But she is glad that I do.

"And why do you suppose it's more beautiful than it usually is?" I'm half afraid of asking.

But I need have no fear, for she says, "Because . . . well, because you're there to see it. Wanting to tell about it makes you see it better."

It was a good definition before, but now it has wings of wisdom. Now it has in it the very essence of beauty, which has trinity of being . . . the object, the eye, and finally the word brought back from that journey into a mental place so that others may see it . . . more beautiful than it usually is.

I say to her, "Paula, you *be* that kind of writer."

Then Boo brings us back, "Let's us all eat our ice cream shall we?" she says. "I have to meet Joe in twenty minutes."

So we eat.

Crisis

౿ LOVE WENT ON, gathering momentum every day. There was time now for nothing but Joe. Math may have brought them together, but *they* kept everything else apart. Boo's grades went into a nosedive. She couldn't even seem to concentrate on that fact.

"So I'm not a brain," she said contentedly.

"But at least you don't have to be a moron."

"Maybe morons are happier. Joe says . . ."

"Don't tell me what Joe says, please. Your *report card* says!"

But she told me anyway. "Joe says the happiest race on earth are the Polynesians. And he doubts if any of them could pass an aptitude test. And as for IQ's . . . they never heard of them."

"So you want to be a Polynesian? You're starting about sixteen years . . . and nine months . . . too late."

"Don't be anatomical, please," she said wearily. "Joe says the scourge of present-day humor is that it's anatomical."

"We're not discussing humor," I reminded her grumpily. "We're discussing your slump in intelligence."

We knew something had to be done. But what, was the question. We wished frantically for an expert to help us. But we knew only one expert, and he was already on the case. We alternated between thinking that this very day we must act decisively, then weakly deciding that we'd just better let Nature take her course. But we trusted Nature even less than we trusted ourselves.

"This won't go on at such a pace," we said to each other with spurious consoling. "When a trend hits its peak, where can it go but down?"

"That's the stock market you're thinking of," we said gloomily. *"This* can go plenty of places. All of 'em in the direction of disaster."

I worried in the night; I made drastic decisions. "What do mothers in fiction do?" I asked myself desperately. But no inspired precedent seemed to occur to me. Knowing how it looks in the making, I just don't take fiction as gospel truth.

Days passed; everything passed, except this infatuation.

"Well, there are only a few more weeks of school," we reminded each other.

"How will that help? Then they'll have all day to put their minds at rest about each other. We've got to *do* something."

"What did the Capulets and the Montagues do?"

"And look what happened there!"

"We just ought to put our foot down. They're children."

"So was the Capulet's little girl a child."

"All right. This afternoon I'll go over and have a frank

talk with Mrs. Montague . . . I mean, with Joe's mother."

"What'll you say to her?"

"I don't know yet. But I'll issue some kind of ultimatum. I'll tell her to keep her crazy little boy at home."

"That'll be just fine."

But while I was making up my mind what I *could* tell her, she came to see me. The visit was a shock. For all of us had overlooked the most obvious fact . . . that Joe's family was probably just as worried as we were. And even more so, because Joe was two years older. And as independent as a drunk sprinkling banana peels under his own feet.

Amazingly enough, she thought it was all our fault. A girl's parents should keep a tight hand on things. Boys' parents were different. They didn't dare.

"One word from us, and Joe does as he pleases," his mother said frankly. "He's always been like that. But now, with Boo in there encouraging him, he's worse than ever. I know what they're thinking of," she went on, her voice balancing on a ladder to keep from toppling into tears. "They're thinking of eloping."

"They can't be," I cried in revulsion.

"Why can't they?" she asked realistically. "*We* eloped when Joe's father was nineteen. And we made the mistake of telling Joe about it. Laughing about it, and making quite a story."

"They couldn't," I said dully. "Not Boo."

"You don't know her," she said ominously. "You just don't see her the way I do."

But it was that which gave the whole conversation its exhilarating unreality.

It all sounded so fantastic that I kept thinking we were

talking about two other guys. Why, the girl Joe's mother was so bitter about was obviously not our dear reasonable child! So naturally, what were *we* worrying about?

She may have been a small and birdlike woman with a tired little ineffectual face, but at least she had a positive idea.

"So we have decided," she said firmly.

"Oh, I'm glad to hear that." I rallied up at the words. "What have you decided?"

"That the minute school is out, you had better just send Boo away for a vacation."

I improvised nimbly then, seeing the solution in a blast of clarity. "Why . . . that's exactly what we think you should do about Joe."

"Joe?" she cried indignantly. "That's out of the question."

"And why, may I ask?" I did ask, sounding like one of those fictional mothers I had already rejected as impractical.

"Joe has to go to work this summer. He's got to earn part of his tuition for his first year at college. If they'll let him in, with the grades he's got since Boo took hold of him."

I wanted to scream my protest at these ill-chosen, libelous words, but I restrained myself.

"Besides, there's no place we could send him, even if we had the money," she said, dabbing at her pinched little nose. "We're not people like *you*. We can't gratify every whim. Joe's father works hard for his money. He doesn't just pull it out of the air the way some people seem to."

I swallowed that, trying to keep the real issue and nothing else on the agenda. Always a difficult feat between women. Especially women worried mutually about the bad effect each other's children are having on their own.

"You've probably got dozens of places you could send her. Relatives . . . or to some lovely camp . . . or off to Europe. Anywhere . . . just so it's away!" she said in a crescendo.

"Of course we could send her," I said soothingly. "But how much would that help? Don't you realize what happens when people who're infatuated with each other are forced to be apart?"

"They get over it," she said firmly, obviously not having read much fiction.

"On the contrary. Imagination just takes over. Fancy and fantasy paint up dreams that are unlimited when there are no realistic facts to be faced every day."

She looked at me with the pity in her face which most sensible people reserve for writers. I could see her forcing herself not to say what was in her mind. Obviously she wished *both* of us would go somewhere . . . anywhere, just so it was away.

We went on battling the mist for another hour, each of us delicately stabbing the other through the heart. Then it was dangerously near the time high school lets out. She didn't want Boo to find her here, because of course Boo would then tell Joe and Joe would be furious. So she left.

"Please think about what I've said. And you'll see I'm right," was her parting remark. She was positive she had the one perfect solution. She left me to see how valid it was. But all I saw was where Joe got his congenital authoritativeness.

I got through the rest of the day, shaken and uncertain. I wanted my own mother more than I've needed her for years.

Unexpectedly, when I went up to say goodnight to Boo,

I found myself telling her. She looked so solid and sensible lying in her little bed in the moonlit room. We had faced so many minor crises, she and I. Surely this one could be dispelled by the two of us together. . . .

I blurted it out.

"Joe's mother came to see me today."

Boo sat up in bed, and the moonlight fell across her face, making it ageless and beautiful in wisdom.

"Poor darling. That must have been trying for you."

"She's worried about Joe," I said.

"What kind of worried?"

"She's afraid you two youngsters are planning to elope."

Boo shook her head sadly. "That just shows how little she knows about him," she said.

My heart leaped up like a Roman candle, and drops of relief, green and golden began running down my private sky.

"She doesn't understand the boy," Boo said gently.

I wanted to hug her in my too quickly thawed worry. I wanted to laugh and sing with joy.

"Do *you* understand him?"

"Of course I do," she said. "Joe would never elope."

"He wouldn't?" I said, stretching out the balm to cover all my old aching worry.

"Of course he wouldn't elope," she said, sipping her own words as if they were delicious honey. "Joe says that when people really are proud of loving each other, they want everybody in the world to know it."

"Is that what he says?"

She nodded, and impulsively I kissed the top of her head,

which smells as it did when she was a baby, like sweet summer clover in sunshine.

"Joe says that when we get married we're going to have the biggest wedding money can buy," she said happily.

So then I knew that Joe's mother had been right. Sooner or later, however we chose to manage it, Boo would have to go off somewhere. Anywhere, just so it was away.

The Suitcase and the Key

ঽ৶ WHILE I WAS LYING AWAKE nights trying to think out the best way for me to behave toward Boo during these dangerous days, I remembered something that happened when *I* was sixteen.

You would never guess to look at me now that I had ever tottered precariously on the edge of being a problem juvenile. I look horribly wholesome now, as if I had been *born* in my right mind. But once I walked blindly along a precipice in blank darkness, never realizing.

There was an alien life which I came within an inch of living, and all that saved me was a wise whisper in a little hallway.

I was having fun; tomorrow's world felt uncertain to me as it always feels to a sixteen-year-old. And besides I was terribly in love.

On Tuesday I had been a chubby-cheeked youngster with no secrets from anybody; by Thursday I was a mysterious woman and a strange man (not quite twenty whom I'd never seen until three weeks before) was in love with me.

Naturally my family couldn't understand it; they were middle-aged people almost forty. What did they know about life?

My father's way of dealing with the sudden thing was to dismiss it indignantly. But when he found it wouldn't be dismissed, he got angry. I got tragic. He forbad; I defied, and suddenly in our peaceful little house we had star-crossed lovers. I knew the thrilling beautiful pattern, for I had read some Shakespeare the semester before.

By Friday we wanted to be engaged; my father said if that slippery so-and-so with the Southern accent came around to our front door once more, he'd put the dog on him. My mother tried tactfully to talk to me. But I was enjoying tragedy. Besides, for the first time in my young life, I felt really important, with a stranger and all the grownups in my world upset about me.

It went on for another week, fast and furious. Harvey met me outside the high school gymnasium and we planned everything. I shut myself in my bedroom and packed a little bag . . . Harvey would wait in the drugstore three blocks away, and we would go over to the Union Station in Washington and get a daycoach for Alabama. We'd have a week with Harvey's kinfolks, and when we came back, I'd be the only married woman in the whole high school!

We all went to bed early that night, and when the house was finally quiet, and all the lights were out, I got up and dressed in the dark. I was doing it, but, being sixteen and romantic, I was also *watching* myself do it. I was so excited I could hardly breathe.

I took the little bag out of the closet and opened my bedroom door noiselessly. I could hear my father's healthy breathing down the hall. There was not another sound in the sleeping house. My Sunday shoes in one hand, my bag in the other, I crept along beside the wall. Then I stopped dead. For there, leaning silently against her door, with her long curly braids over her shoulders, my mother was waiting.

She looked like either a ghost or a girl, certainly no middle-aged mother. She was smiling, and her hands were warm, and she put her finger against her lips and tiptoed along to the head of the hall.

"Ssh," she said as if we were two conspirators. "Don't wake anybody."

"No. I won't," I whispered back, embarrassed because she had caught me. She didn't appear to be alarmed at what I was doing, and she didn't ignore the suitcase.

"I thought you'd need my key," she said. She reached down and took my suitcase, so I could have a free hand to take the key. She laid the key in my hand and it was warm from hers. I think it was the first time I had ever held the key to our family's house.

"Put it in your pocket," she said. "I thought you'd want to go out and think it over, darling. You'll need the key to get in with when you come back, so you won't have to wake up anybody."

I stood there, ready to weep, looking into her kind dear eyes and then down at the key, which somehow seemed to stand for our whole shabby precious house, and our whole family, and all its goings and comings.

"You go out and talk to Harvey," she said, "and then you come in quietly and go to bed."

"All right, Mama," I said, and I took the suitcase which she offered me.

But it was more than a suitcase she gave into my hand; it was her trust in me. She had given me the suitcase and the key, the way out of my own life and the way back into it. She gave them both to me because she trusted me.

I don't know how long I was out of the house; I don't remember what I said to Harvey, drinking cokes in the drugstore. Maybe he was relieved; maybe the whole thing had got a little out of hand for him, too. I don't remember much about Harvey, to tell you the truth, for I didn't know him very well.

But I do remember that I came tiptoeing up the stairs in our house after a while, and down the hall was my father's good innocent breathing. And my mother's blessed little whisper in the darkness.

"That you?"

"Yes, Mama."

"That's my good girl."

She and I never mentioned it as long as she lived. And my father, of course, sublime in his understanding of how to handle women, had never known that it happened.

I have wavered on the brink of lots of temptations since then. Every once in a while I try impetuously to take steps in the wrong direction, hoping I can fool myself. But sooner or later there comes the moment when I remember the suitcase and the key. Then, not wanting to at all . . . being often annoyed with myself because of my inconvenient memory, I hear that little whisper in the darkness.

"That's my good girl."

Hands

ह‰ WHENEVER I'M too worried to think intelligently, I work with my hands. It is one of the oldest and best remedies mankind has discovered.

So I ironed today. Usually I have to forego this simple pleasure. I am "spared" this kind of work, alas, so that I can do other things. I am spared it but oftentimes I am homesick for the woman-comfort of it.

Lilliam would never allow me to iron when she was around.

"Jes' you leave that arnin' be," she would say sternly. "You kine of browse when you arn. We ain't got time for you to arn today."

"Nonsense," I used to say defensively. "I can iron either fast or slow. Today I'll do my fast ironing."

"Nome, honey. You better jes' let me arn. I kin arn better than smart people."

I know why I can't iron fast, all right. Lilliam knew also, and sometimes when she was in a frank mood she would tell me plainly. "The whole trouble with you doin' work," she would say, "is you enjoy yo'self too good."

I suppose I am guilty of that. Except when I am worried as I am now, I do enjoy myself pretty good. And enjoyment certainly does use up time.

The stage must be properly set to get the most out of ironing. I know the unleashed architects are building home laundries which look like laboratories or studios, or even like clinics, where ironing may be done scientifically. But for my taste, ironing belongs in a big old-fashioned kitchen, with something good for lunch on the back of the stove. Bean soup, maybe, chuckling in a black iron kettle. Under clean red-checked tea towels, loaves of bread should be "setting," rising and rounding for an hour before they go into the oven.

Outside the kitchen windows there should be a bright dazzle of snow coming down. If there can be a hill in the distance, put children there (children who will never grow up and fall in love). Have them in red mittens, shouting and running with their sleds. While you're imagining, it's no more trouble to include a dog hysterical with joy, capering at their heels.

The kitchen should be warm and smelling of the clean fragrance of starch on a little girl's ruffles. There should be a canary singing somewhere in another part of the house, and if you are blessed by having an old-fashioned grandmother in the family, it is lovely to think of her rocking in a sunny window, with the darning trudging steadily through her fingers. On one side of her is the tangle of unmatched stockings, each condemned by a hole. She picks them out and scrutinizes them serenely, clucking affectionately at the way people do wear things out; then through one after another she weaves her flash of needle, and mates them into tidy pairs, restoring order to her share of the universe.

If she is a humming grandmother, as my mother would have been, so much the better. It is a comfort to feel that someone who has lived a long time in this turbulent world has a contented heart, singing like a teakettle. Indeed, there is no sight on earth more reassuring than a happy grandmother . . . an old-fashioned one.

I am not an ironer who likes conversation with my work. Talk spoils the whole thing for me, much as I love it at other times. And I certainly do not want any radio turned on, to make me forget what I am doing. No, I want to remember what I am doing, for that is part of the charm of it.

"But the radio is so wonderful."

"Yes, but not so wonderful as thinking."

So there is no daytime serial in my kitchen while I iron. I live my own daytime serial, musing along from subject to subject as my iron travels over the clothes which are dear to me because of the people who wear them. They are dear, yet comical as cartoons, on my ironing board, crippled with wrinkles when I unroll them from the laundry basket, and then plumped into their right shape by my iron. My thoughts are built along with this parade that passes under my hands; the precious present and the lovely past meet here, and I think with a rush of gratitude that I would not trade my living, troublesome and crowded as it sometimes feels, for any better way on earth.

I see with a pang how far along the ironing board Boo's skirts extend now, and I remember the time, so lately past, when a skirt was only a little more than a foot long.

Just a little while ago, clothes were made to play in. Now they are chosen to be the lyrics set to the music of living. They are romantic as valentines, because the girl who wears them has discovered that life is to be lived by the heart.

I remember those little clothes with wistfulness. An absurd little woolen frock she once adored, with a fluff of angora around the neck. "Fliff," she used to call it. "I simply love the fliff! It's *practically* fur, isn't it? Well, baby fur, anyway."

And the ridiculous little pink things.

"You know Mary-Jane Francy?"

"Yes."

"Well, do you know her mother?"

"Um-hum."

"Well ... do you know *what?*"

"No. What?"

"Well. Her mother lets her wear silk wonderwhere ... with lace on the panties!"

Why should those memories make my eyes prickle? I have her still, and this agony of mine will pass, as the measles came and went ... and the little girl who maliciously forgot to invite her to the birthday party ...

My mother before me liked to iron. I probably inherit the joy, as I inherit much else from her overspilling heart. I remember how happily I used to see her at this work, her face flushed, her hair curly with warmth.

My mother used to say, "I hope we never get to be so prosperous that I can't do my own ironing."

We girls would look at her in amazement. "Why, Mrs,

Davidson says she simply loathes ironing," we would tell her. "I don't believe I ever heard of anyone really liking ironing."

"Well, *I* like it," my mother would say. "It gives you such a good chance to just stand quietly thinking about the people you love best in the whole world. What could be better than that?"

"But, of course, you *could* think about us without the bother of ironing," we reminded her.

"No. It's not the same," she'd say wisely. "Ironing gives you a chance to think your love, and then a chance to do something about it."

My mother reveled in the way she loved her home and us. She never made any secret of it. She never said anything about giving us the best years of her life. On the contrary. She often told us that *we* were giving *her* the best years of her life.

"I love every day that passes," she used to say. "I wouldn't want to skip one day of having you children small and then getting bigger. This is the very best time of my life, and I know it."

And this, I know, is the best time of *my* life. Despite the comical-tragic nonsense that is so serious to us all at this minute . . . I know it is the best, for our hearts are being exercised, whether we want them to be or not.

I have gone a long way from the ironing. And suddenly I know I feel better. I cannot say just why I do, for nothing is really changed. The big worry waits patiently to be looked at and honored. But somehow I feel the deep abiding happiness of being alive.

The Bible explains it very simply; it says, "Lift up your heart with your hands."

Maybe that's what hands are for, when minds admit defeat.

The Bookkeeping

❧ Now I COULD THINK more calmly. Which is another way of saying, Now I could pray, and not just run in circles.

Should we all just go to Europe? Even if we had the money, would that be the cure? Could I find some counter-revolution at home . . . some boy who would out-joe Joe? Winthrop? Obviously that was wistful wishing.

Summer camp at this stage of the conflagration would be much too juvenile and tame; sending her to visit practically any of our friends would be unjust and unfair . . . to them. Like the feeble-minded boy in the story who found the lost cow by imagining where he himself would go if he were a cow, I tried to picture what would have diverted me when I was sixteen . . . in such a situation. I got out a pencil and wrote down the emotions involved, balancing them on each side the page, the way people balance debits and credits. (I discovered then that one reason I've never been able to fathom mathematics in any form except intuition is that I've always done bookkeeping with emotions instead of figures.)

But somehow that seemed to clarify the problem. Not the
solution, but the problem. What we needed here was an
emotion stronger than love. What emotion would that be,
for pity's sake? Well, how about the Joan of Arc urge? The
clarion call of doing-something-heroic-to-help. . . . But what
could Boo help? And what had she to help *with*? I
thought over her assets, my pencil poised to write them
down in my crazy mathematics. Then across my mind
floated a wisp of dialogue she and I had had a while ago
when she wanted us to buy a car in partnership.

" 'What've you got to contribute?' " I had asked.

" 'Why . . . I've got a hundred and eighty dollars . . . and
a driver's license.' "

There it was, all her assets. Now I was feverish with a
plan. I would have to begin with a telephone call across the
country to my father.

I could barely wait for Boo to come home from school.

By miracle she came in alone. Joe was having to take a
special examination to see if he could possibly get through
Chemistry and graduate.

"Maybe I should have sat on the steps and waited for
him," she said. "But I thought that might just worry him
more."

"Is he worried?"

"Of course. Who isn't?" she said, and my heart twisted
painfully at the touching terribleness of being young, with
all the cards stacked against you. But I had to keep my end
of them more firmly stacked.

"I'm worried here, also," I said.

"About us?"

"What would I be worried about you for?"

"Well, I just thought."

"No. I'm worried about Granddaddy."

"What's the matter?" All her sympathies sprang to attention, for she loves that gallant little man, as do we all.

"He needs some help right now. I talked to him on the phone this morning."

"What kind of help? Just tell me. I'm old enough. I've got a right to worry about other people, you know. I'm not a child."

"W.B. can't drive his car for a few weeks. He's having some treatments for his eyes. And meantime he can't drive at all."

"Oh the poor darling," she said. "And he's somebody that likes to get around. You know he's always got a lot of projects and stuff. And there he'd be stuck out in the country!"

I said, not being quite enough of a culprit to meet her dear eyes, "You know what? If I had the money . . . and didn't have so much work to do here . . . I'd just. . . ."

"What would you do?"

"I'd just go out there and drive for him myself this summer."

"What would we do here without you?"

"You'd just have to manage."

"Yes, I suppose we would," she said, her face brooding over the problem. It looked then that we had come to a dead-end street. Ineptly I had put out a suggestion and had included an alternative that canceled out the whole thing. For the twentieth time in my life, I realized that for me not only is honesty the best policy, but the only one. If shenanigans are required, I can be counted on to muff the whole thing.

She went into her own room, and I heard her puttering around aimlessly. I yearned for an X-ray that would show me what was going on inside her mysterious little head.

I sat on at my desk, more discouraged than ever. Then she came to my door and looked in apologetically.

"I've been thinking," she said. "What's the matter with *me?*"

"What'd you mean?"

"What's the matter with me going out to drive Granddaddy?"

"Why . . . what an idea!"

"I've got a driver's license . . . and I've got a hundred and eighty dollars for my fare across the country."

"Oh, but darling . . ." I protested, for sheer luck-stretching. "I think maybe I'd better just forget the work, and go myself."

"May I speak frankly?" she asked, and I said, "Of course."

"I wouldn't have a comfortable moment, for worrying about you. You're a nice woman, but you're beyond the pale as a driver."

"Am I?" I said, making a mental note that when I next counted up my own personal credits and debits, I'd put my driving stupidity at the top of my list of assets.

"I'm the logical one to go," she said firmly. "And besides. . . ."

"Besides?"

"Joe would want me to do it. Joe always wants me to do the right thing."

I almost put down my head on my desk and wept at the goodness of the two of them.

But she didn't notice. For already her mind had begun making pictures about the whole thing.

"We could write to each other," she said.

My honesty, almost extinct in this scene, aroused itself.

"You know you're not at your best in writing," I said.

"I know that," she admitted. "I'm practically illiterate."

"Would Joe find it repulsive that you can't spell?"

She thought morosely about that horrible danger. Then she said bravely, "Well, he would have to know it someday."

"You'd be taking a terrible chance with Joe," I warned, trying in spite of caution to lay the situation bare.

Then she said something that almost undid me.

"If this thing is as good as we hope it is, neither distance nor spelling can chop it down."

So then I knew we were facing eternity itself. But for now, we had to deal with time expediently.

Too Much Particular

ৡ◈ WE HAD our ups and downs with Tumpti; that was just normal. Indeed, if someone had been keeping a graph of our life together, it would have resembled a precipitous mountain range. But Everest occurred when we didn't expect it. Our big worry was Boo, and we gullibly assumed that every other trouble would momentarily retreat. But that was reckoning without Tumpti.

Trouble with him usually followed a reliable pattern. If it was suggested that Tumpti do something that he didn't choose to do, our seventy-year-old houseman placidly said, "I leave. You get nother boy." Then, naturally, we let him do exactly as he pleased. We usually felt frustrated, but we were always well cared for and well nourished. And our household, always tottering on the threat of explosion, didn't have a moment of boredom.

This trouble struck just after we passed through one of our regular crises, brought about because we had invited friends for a barbecue. Tumpti had appeared to be cooperating. But at the last moment he unaccountably decided to serve a black-tie dinner in the dining room, setting the table with our only imported linen and our precious Irish Belleek china, which we usually keep behind glass.

The effect was ludicrous, for we had urged our guests to come wearing Levis and plaid shirts, either in or hanging out. So, dead-pan, we sat down to the restrained occasion looking as if Amy Vanderbilt had meticulously composed her most formal table and dinner, absent-mindedly forgetting that she had invited as guests a gang of sharecroppers on relief.

The only correct person in the room was Tumpti, and he rebukingly looked down his nose at us all (or as down as a little man not quite five feet tall *can* look).

But he had had his way, and he was happy. And the meal he served was so excellent that you couldn't possibly mention any discrepancies to him. Especially since the discrepancies were *ours,* and in no way his. Furthermore, you couldn't mention them on a full stomach, purring with pleasure.

I was working at my desk the next day, thinking this was a perfect example of the right strategy in dealing with our help. You see, I had picked up some of his necessity for saving face, and I called our method "strategy." But suddenly my harmless, time-wasting musing was shattered.

Boo came to the door of my workroom.

"Sorry to trample over your working hours," she said. "But you'd better come downstairs. Tumpti is leaving."

"What about?"

"He says you're much too particular. In some ways I agree with him."

Apprehensively I got up from the desk, knowing I wouldn't get back before tomorrow.

"He's real mad," she warned me. "Profanity . . . both Japanese and American."

"It's called English," I said automatically.

"This is American."

I started militantly downstairs, my steps becoming more tentative and timid as I approached the kitchen. I mapped out my battle plan. Would I need bribery . . . flattery . . . or *more* flattery? Tumpti was standing beside the kitchen counter muttering to himself in a whisper that could be heard next door.

"What's all this?" I asked in a craven voice.

"Too much particular," he said, his eyes gray as eels and angry as serpents. "Embroidered table linen too hard to iron. Straw mats better. Just wipe straw mats." He pantomimed the carefree wiping.

A drench of relief poured over me. "Oh . . . table linen!" I said, trying to sound as indignant as he did. "Who cares about table linen?" Naturally I wouldn't remind him that he was the one who had injected the big linen tablecloth into the scene. "We send tablecloths out to the laundry."

"Can't go to raundry," he said bitterly. "Raundry tear 'em up. Raundry Chinese."

Now I perceived this was an international incident. "Oh, I know a very good French laundry. I'll take everything down there this afternoon."

He shook his head furiously. "I trust nobody with best linen. I have to wash it myself. You too much particular."

In this dilemma I thought that looking meek was indi-

cated. So I looked loathsomely meek. But that only reminded him of other indignities he was suffering.

"China too thin," he said. "Break like eggshells. Man
busts out in perspiration when china in dishpan." With
sinking heart, I had a clue to what all this meant. We were
going to be punished because some of the precious Belleek
china had been broken! I could have wept about that. But
I didn't. I went on looking craftily meek.

"We won't use that china again," I said as if I were making a great concession. "Old china anyway. Hundred years
old. Too thin besides. Makes everybody uncomfortable.
Everybody burst out in perspiration."

He let his eely eye swim around and look at my face, and
almost he relented. But then he shook his head and whipped
up his anger. His whole face seemed to explode in rage.

"No!" he shouted. "I stay here too long anyway. I rike
new job. New people. I tiled of you."

At that moment I thought recklessly that I'd like to tell
him I was pretty tiled of him. But I didn't. Instead, I surprised myself by saying, "Well, Tumpti, you're a free man.
You'll have to work wherever you please. If you're tired of
us, I guess you'd better just leave. . . ." Then my firmness
came unstarched, and I heard myself muttering in a quick
gulp, ". . . and after you've tried some other family for a
while, maybe you'll want to come back to us."

He was shaking his head vigorously, and to my amazement I saw tears were also in *his* eyes.

"I work too long here," he said stubbornly. "I need new
place. Place where I just pay 'tention to the cooking and
the looms and the raundry. No bother about the people."

Incredulously I heard what he was not saying; he was admitting that he loved us all too much for his own Oriental comfort. I felt like putting my arms around him as I would have around any other lonely little waif and saying, "Don't be afraid of loving people too much. It won't hurt you. And even if it does. . . ." But of course I couldn't do any of that; I couldn't trespass upon his dignity by letting him see that I understood him.

We stood there helplessly, two human beings tragically separated by the incongruity of age and sex and nationality. So we just stood there, both trying our best to look angry and indignant.

"So I reave. You get nother boy," he said, taking out a handkerchief and blowing his tiny nose.

"All right, if that's the way you want it," I muttered fiercely.

Then we both rallied up to make the moment less tense and difficult for each other. We both spoke at once.

I said, "Perhaps you have a point, Tumpti. And you could come and see us whenever you wanted to."

He was saying, "Anyway, I go back to Japan plitty soon. State Department of U.S.A. say maybe I can go. Maybe not. But can't come back again."

"Oh, you wouldn't want to leave the United States for good!" I cried. "You told me you've been away fifty years."

"Since 1903 . . . I rike to see if anything happen while I gone away."

We talked about that obliquely for a few minutes, and then suddenly he wanted to tell me something very important.

"Now I leave your house, I tell you my big pran. You keep secret?"

"Of course," I said, having no idea what was coming.

"You wait here. I show you something." He went into his room, and I heard him unlocking his trunk. In a few moments he came back, holding in his arms a huge paper-wrapped parcel. His face was utterly beaming; all the anger of a moment ago had ebbed away and now he was beatific as a man is in the presence of his greatest treasure, whether it be a faded photograph or a bank book with the newest ink still damp.

"I show you," he said, and laid the huge parcel on a chair while he got out a clean cloth and wiped the already spotless counter energetically. He was murmuring in a counterpoint of Japanese and English, not to me, but to his valuable bundle.

He laid the big package, which looked like some kind of a rug or counterpane on the counter and untied the string around it. Eagerly then he opened the wrappings and took out what now appeared to be a huge flag.

But it was like no flag I've ever seen before. It was made of heavy rich silk, and it was embroidered all over in tiniest petit point. The flag itself had stars, and a rising sun and a rainbow, also a moon and cloud-tipped mountains. A flattened-out globe which included all the continents occupied the center space. It was quite well drawn, and fastidiously embroidered. A garland of flowers framed a kind of banner across the top, and on this was a motto which said "New World of Brotherly Peace." At the bottom of this remarkable creation was a modest inscription, embroidered in sky blue, which said, "Dr. Frank Frederick Ishinara, First President of New World."

One last corner of the flag was still unfinished, like the cloudy portion at the bottom of the Stuart portrait of George Washington.

Tumpti gazed at it lovingly, and in his thin little neck I could see a pulse wildly beating. This was one of the great moments of his life.

"I never show frag before," he said reverently. "Some day I show Plesident of U.S.A. Then I give him my pran for New World of Brotherly Peace. Then he make me First Plesident."

I gazed at it in silence, unable to speak.

"You made it?" I gasped.

"I make," he beamed, and with one finger he delicately touched a spray of minute lilies-of-the-valley which he had embroidered on the garland. "I begin ten years ago when U.S.A. Government send all Japanese people to stay in Arkansas. I have big dleam then. I make pran."

Now the mystery of his long evenings in his room without newspaper, radio, or book was explained. Now was explained his eccentricity about insisting upon big 200-watt bulbs in his lamp.

But over all that . . . a horrifying thought was spreading across my mind. Why, the dear little man into whose hands we had literally given our lives, was obviously quite insane. For months at the helm of our house had been a madman!

A frightening montage swept over me . . . his rages, his eccentricities which had seemed mere conversation pieces with which we amused our friends . . . his determination to

have his way. . . . All of it, I saw in the light of this monu-
mental madness to which he had devoted his last ten years,
fitted together now, the parts of a picture of mental derange-
ment.

He was looking at me expectantly. I was supposed to say
something worthy of what he had just shown me.

"I . . . I just haven't any words," I said in all sincerity.

That seemed to satisfy him, and he chuckled, and once
again his fingers moved lovingly over the infinitesimal
stitches.

"Sometime I tell you all about my pran," he said ex-
pansively. "Now you know. So now I cannot work in
your house. Not be light. You feel bad because First
Plesident of New World of Brotherly Peace do raundry in
your house."

"No, I don't believe it would be right," I said in some
relief. Then he had a big thought and he said to me, bowing ceremoniously, "Maybe when I be First Plesident, I
make you Secletally of Rabor."

I went back upstairs to my desk, shaking all over. Boo
was sitting on the floor trying to read one of the French
books people deludedly give me for Christmas.

She said, not looking up, "Expect you fixed everything.
Hmn?"

"You mean about Tumpti?"

"I don't mean Rock Hudson," she said absently, this being
the correct answer these days to a stupid question.

"He's leaving," I said, trying not to sound too stunned.
"We're driving him over to a storage warehouse to arrange
something about some trunks he has there. He's leaving

this very afternoon. You're driving me to the hairdresser's at three, and we'll drop him off at the warehouse first."

"Whee . . . when that little guy makes up his mind, he doesn't loiter, does he?"

"We both made up our minds," I said.

"Yeah? I can imagine," she said cheerfully. "When Tumpti's around, there's only one mind to make up."

It wasn't a comfortable, relaxing permanent I had that day. All the time my favorite operator was telling me about her social life I was worrying about our home situation. Here for months we had been exposed to a completely mad person, and we had never suspected. Anything could have happened. Horror headlines danced before my imagination. Something had spared us all, including poor little Tumpti.

Well, tonight he would be sleeping in the stark Japanese roominghouse where once a week he paid for a modest pocket of a room. His mysterious trunk and the framed sampler of stones he had collected while he was the government's guest in Arkansas would be safely out of our house. Should I warn anyone, and if so, whom?

When my permanent was finished (looking too pristine), I telephoned home for someone to come and get me in the car. Boo, always expecting (and usually getting some momentous private call), answered the phone.

"Oh . . . it's you," she said in disappointment.

"Sorry," I said glumly.

"Well, I've got a lovely surprise for you," she cried brightly. "Guess what?"

"You know I never can guess anything."

"Tumpti's not leaving."

"He's not?"

"Nope. He came from the warehouse about half an hour ago. I persuaded him to stay."

"You did? What did you say to him?"

"I just persuaded him," she said happily. "I said, 'Tumpti, please don't go.' So he said, 'Ar-light. I stay.' "

Nother Boy

᠍᠍᠍ OUR VERY HOUSE seemed to be crumbling to pieces between the two problems, Boo and now Tumpti. I couldn't decide what was the best thing to do about Tumpti. Suppose I fired him, and that made him really angry enough to do something desperate? I could not face such a vision.

On the other hand, suppose I didn't fire him. And *then* something violent happened?

In the dilemma, I told nobody about the flag and the world plan. In some moments I called myself criminally irresponsible; at other times I assured myself that we had been at his mercy a couple of years with nothing serious happening. Just because I now understood the situation, the danger had not heightened. But of course I wasn't comfortable about it all.

As days went past and he seemed gentler and more mild, I decided that the world plan was probably not much worse than the private madness which most of us cherish in one form or another. Certainly it was no worse than a few of the schemes that the press expose as motivating some of our senators and congressmen. Arousing no suspicion, some of the hermetically sealed skulls around us every day may actually be time bombs ticking silently toward catastrophe. The dream of Utopia has plagued the race for centuries, and it usually seems a ludicrous dementia when it seeps out of a fermenting brain into speech or deed.

The light shining through the tightly drawn blinds in Tumpti's room continued to illumine the magnolia tree until midnight. So I knew the empty space at the bottom of the flag was being meticulously filled in, stitch by almost invisible stitch.

And then the United States Government stepped into the situation. In the years that he had been with us, no mail ever had come for him. But on this morning there was a legal-sized envelope, with the insignia of our State Department engraved in the corner. It was addressed to Dr. Frank Frederick Ishinara. He received it with silent dignity, as if he were quite accustomed to such missives. I could barely control my curiosity, but I knew I must not ask until information was volunteered.

I could not read in the ancient puzzle of his face whether my government was saying, "Now, my children, you will be safe from having a dear madman in your house. We are letting him go to Japan," or whether it was decreeing, "He cannot leave the country. Keep him until something ghastly happens, and then blame yourself the rest of your life."

I had to wait nearly a week, full of suspense and anxiety. Then one afternoon a huge truck drove up to our house,

and men began carrying in three heavy trunks from the
storage warehouse. Still we said nothing, as if this were
ordinary daily procedure. But the next day I heard strange
noises in the patio, and there was Tumpti, dressed in his
best suit with his big scholarly glasses on his little nose, and
he was working at an amazing business. He had tape measure and saw, and standing around waiting were enormous
garden tools, almost as tall as he was. An opened empty
trunk was ready to be packed. Methodically he was taking
measurements, and in a few minutes he was sawing the
handles off the big forks and hoes and rakes, and fitting
them into the trunk. How he had managed to bring all this
garden equipment into the house without anyone seeing
him, I couldn't imagine.

He had sacks of seeds, and boxes of bulbs waiting to be
packed, and even some bare-root shrubs and fruit trees.
With incredible efficiency he got the whole trunk put together, and one knew that somewhere across the world
there would soon be a garden planted from America in
Japanese soil.

But mostly what I knew was that the answer to our
dangerous question had been decided by the omnipotent
government. He had been given permission to go back to
Japan, and he was taking as much of America with him as
possible.

Within a half-hour, as I peeped through the venetian
blinds at him, I saw the trunk securely locked. Then he
brushed up the sawdust with a whisk broom, and carried it
tidily away. He and I never mentioned the trunkful of
garden which would link his America with his Japan, but

I couldn't help knowing it was more than mere garden to him.

What went into the other trunks I never happened to discover, but I am sure it was equally symbolic merchandise. When all his preparations for departure were finished, he got around to telling us about it, as casually as if he was saying he was going to a motion picture on his day off.

"Nex Monday I reave for Japan," he said. "You want I help you find nother boy?"

"No. I'll look," I said. "It won't be easy to find someone like you, Tumpti. You've been so good to us."

"I no good," he said fiercely. "I ve'y bad cook. Mebbe I too old to crean looms good." It was the first time he had ever suggested he had any age at all. And of course we all denied it from our hearts.

I spent the week talking to impossible applicants. We half expected that Tumpti would change his mind at the last moment, even though we knew his going was officially stamped and sealed by the Japanese Consulate and our own State Department. We just couldn't believe it would really happen. For he was part of us, and we couldn't imagine it any other way. Even I, knowing what I did about him, couldn't want him banished beyond our care.

He was supposed to leave at eleven o'clock Monday morning. Nobody in our house made any pretense of going down to the office, or off to school, or upstairs to work at a desk. There wasn't anything we could do to help him, for he wouldn't even let us drive him down to Terminal Island, where he was embarking on a Japanese freighter.

"I take taxi," he said. "Dr. Ishinara got plitty much

money saved up. Work fifty-four years and don't spend much money."

To our knowledge he had spent practically no money, except for the varnished little pastries and such gifts which he brought to us on Friday mornings after his days off.

At last he was ready and standing in the hall with one very small satchel beside his highly polished brown shoes. He was wearing the too big Homburg, which we hadn't seen since the day he came applying for the job. And he had ensconced the huge teeth in his old babyish mouth.

Somehow he looked like a beloved child disguised as an old man for a make-believe journey. At the last moment he seemed much too small and much too old for us to let him venture out alone into a world he expected to find unchanged while his back had been turned upon it. I held my hands gripped before me, so they wouldn't stray out and touch him with helpless affection, for I knew that would disgrace us all beyond remedying. I would lose face forever, and he would lose face with himself because he had spent time working for such people . . . and even forgetting his principles so far as to love them.

"Well, goodbye," we all said, much too loudly. "Now you take care of yourself, Tumpti."

Boo said desperately, still with a remnant of faith in her power to persuade, "Don't go, Tumpti . . . dear."

His way of dealing with that was to pretend not to hear it.

"Everybody has to go someplace. But please don't you go. We need you here, Tumpti dear," she said, and *she* didn't care if she did lose face, for she frankly scuffed tears across her nose.

"You get along fine after I reave," he said. "I no good for anybody." He grinned with desperation matching Boo's. And as if he were on a tightrope he balanced his enormous teeth astride the grin.

"Now I go Japan," he said explosively. "U.S.A. Government tell me go, but don't come back ever. U.S.A. Government say they get nother boy."

The End

ﾞ THE LAST NINE DAYS of school were a merry-go-round
gone crazy. Nobody was sure Joe was going to graduate.
His father wouldn't let him buy the required blue coat and
gray trousers until it was definite.

"If I didn't have to use my money for the railway fare,
I'd buy 'em for him," Boo said. "What's convention anyway? We're here to help each other, aren't we?"

Meantime her cheerless, brave preparation for her trip
went on. She was to leave the day after school closed. With
Joe's troubles hanging over her, she couldn't seem to care
about buying new clothes, or thinking about the ones she
had. For all of us, it was the end of the world.

But we got through it somehow. At least we got through
seven days of it. But we hadn't reckoned on Joe. For suddenly when we thought everything was going to work out
safely, Joe smashed it all to smithereens.

I don't know what he actually said to her. I only know
that she came home from school looking utterly tragic.

And this time it wasn't play-tragic. This was real.

"Joe's finished with me," she said.

"What on earth do you mean?"

"Just that. He's through. He doesn't want anybody in his life who's such a . . . a pushover."

My hands went suddenly cold. "You'd better explain it, dear."

"You know, all right," she said bitterly. "Joe's mother told him all about it. She said that you and she agreed that I had better be sent away someplace this summer. Out of Joe's way."

"We didn't agree," I said lamely.

"Whatever you want to call it. Anyway, you fixed up a little trap and let me walk into it. You fixed it so I would think I was getting a big ole inspiration about helping Granddaddy this summer. And all the time. . . ."

She angrily snatched the tears off her eyelashes, and turned her face from me. It was the first time in our sixteen years together that I had deceived her. It made not the slightest difference to me that I had done it for what I thought was her sake. I had deceived her, and that was the truth. I had committed that most heinous of all affronts . . . I had meddled and managed in such a way that it looked like her free choice, when it was not.

I have no idea what I said about it. But she wouldn't accept it at all. She just stood there with her face turned away, and she kept shaking her head in rejection. Rejecting what I said, and me along with the words.

"Don't talk about it," she kept saying. "There's nothing anybody can say. So just don't let's talk."

I never felt worse in my life. I just sat helplessly convicted with no defense to offer. She went out of the room, and walked around the house a few minutes, and then she came back.

"But I'm going on the trip anyway," she said. "The only honest thing in the situation is that Granddaddy really needs me. Or is that just part of your trap?"

"No. That's the truth," I said shakily.

"So I'm going. And I'm glad to be out of this house. As a matter of fact, I'll need a few weeks to feel better about what you did to me."

"Please, darling. . . ."

"Besides . . . with Joe through with me, what would I do in this place? What could I possibly do?"

Bon Voyage

ЗӘ SCHOOL CLOSED. Joe got his job in the supermarket. At the last minute, it was decided he was going to graduate after all. But none of that changed his mind about Boo.

"I don't blame him," was her only comment.

I couldn't get near to her. We talked pleasantly; we did everything we had to do; the surface looked normal and fine. But underneath there was nothing but chasm, she on one side, a tiny lonely figure, and I on the other side, guilty and sick at heart.

Everything I had learned from my own life had seemed to fail me. The very rocks of my conviction had become shimmering mists. I had failed; with all the wisdom I thought I had . . . inherited, borrowed, and sculptured from my own experience . . . I had failed when the real test came. Unlike the victorious British, I had won all the battles, but I had lost the war.

My optimistic common sense tried to tell me that someday we should both remember this spring and be able to laugh together. A whole childhood of understanding had bound us together; surely nothing this size could separate us forever.

But for this moment, nothing helped. There were times when she threw herself totally into the idea of being important to her grandfather. When she talked on the telephone to her friends, she sounded like her real self. She even mentioned Joe once or twice on the phone.

"Oh, Joe? Why, he'll get along okay," she said to Felicity. "I'm not the only girl in the world."

"I'll say you're not," Felicity said, practically licking her chops.

But Joe didn't telephone once. A few days ago he had been expecting to take her to the Union Station to make sure everything was in order and her roomette was going to be comfortable. Joe had planned to check on the Southern Pacific and hold 'em up to their contract . . . Every time the phone or the doorbell rang, my treacherous hopes sprang up. But it was never his lazy casual voice that said, "Hi there, folkses." When Joe was through, he was finished.

During her last afternoon, she suddenly decided that she didn't want anybody but our own family to see her off at the station. I know that was because she was too proud to let her contemporaries see how things were. She called up all the youngsters she had invited and asked them not to come.

"Okay," they said obligingly, not caring too much one way or the other.

To me, she said brutally, "Let's don't make any more of this than we have to. I'm going away and that's all there is to it."

"You're going to have a fine summer, darling. And after

you finish helping W.B. you'll have that lovely visit in New York."

"Yep."

The station with everyone hurrying and laden with luggage, was exciting. Every once in a while she looked behind us through the crowd, as if she were expecting someone . . . as if she hoped, by some miracle, someone tall and tan would be coming through the crowd . . . maybe just *happening* to be there. But there was no Joe.

The roomette was a diversion. The whole train was a novelty, for she had never actually been on a train before. There was all the etiquette of tipping and ordering meals, and having a ginger ale in the club car, to be considered. And in spite of our crushing trouble, it was quite thrilling. We admired everything, and said what we needed to say in an aside to the big fatherly porter, and then we got off the train. And still she had not looked into my face with recognition.

We huddled drearily on the dark platform. Each lighted window along the car had a happy-looking traveler mouthing messages to a group like ourselves on the platform. I looked up at the row of small lighted stages, and I saw a number of youngsters like our own. There were both boys and girls, and the sight cheered me. She would have fun; in a few hours she would have forgotten us all. Even Joe. She'd feel the welling up of that lively curiosity of hers about everything new. She would soon be humming along the back of her mind, the way she always does. This nightmare would fade in a day or so, and both of us would know that it wasn't as ghastly as it seemed now. When we met again in a couple of months one of us could say to the other, "What was that all about?"

I tried to believe all this, but somehow I couldn't manage it. Suppose she never forgave me, as I never should forgive myself? I wanted to beg her . . . I wanted to explain . . . but I knew that words are sometimes the most expensive and dangerous luxuries between the generations. She herself would have to make the journey between hurt and understanding, and I would have to stand by and wait humbly.

She stood up and pulled down the little folding hook provided on the wall for her coat. But really she was trying to look along the platform, hoping that Someone would happen to be arriving at the last minute. But Nobody was.

I yearned to give her something right now which she could accept. So I decided to tell her about all the other youngsters on the train. Then she would put on her new lipstick and go out to dinner expecting adventure. Then she could shake off the memory of all of us who had hurt her.

I spoke the good news with elaborate pantomime. "The train is jumping with kids," I said. She couldn't understand. For one thing her roomette was brightly lighted, and we were standing in the twilight of the dusky platform. I repeated it several times, and still she wrinkled her eyebrows and shook her head uncomprehendingly.

Then I opened a book I was carrying and wrote the message in big letters along the flyleaf.

"Kids! Millions of 'em on the train." I held it up over my head for her to read. She tried her best to make out the words. She tried and tried, and finally shrugged her failure. I know despair was shameless on my face. Then a look of understanding spread over her face. She got out a piece of note paper from her handbag, and I watched her golden hair sift across her cheek as she bent her face to answer what she believed I had written.

She wrote and wrote, with her tongue clamped between her teeth the way she wrote when she was seven. At last she held up the big-lettered words for me to read.

"I love you, too," she had written.

Everything was going to be all right. It didn't matter now whether or not she saw that I was crying. She had correctly read the words I had not dared to write, so I could trust her also to read the tears. . . .

The conductors bawled their last "All aboard," the train gave a shudder, and suddenly began to move, groaning heavily like a fat rheumatic. Her little window became foreshortened; she pressed her forehead against the glass, we waved in a frenzy and then we couldn't see her at all. We turned away and started up the long platform, looking, I am sure, weary and middle-aged and already lonely. But I was not feeling weary nor middle-aged. I wanted to run and do nip-ups, for now at last I felt happy and forgiven.

Then someone crashed into us, someone tall and tan, carrying a gardenia in a transparent box.

"Gosh, I'm a little late," Joe said.

"You're awful late, honey," I cried deliriously.

"I've . . . I've got a corsage for her," he stammered. "I think they're awful silly. But I knew she wanted one."

Joe, the super-authority, was gulping and looking as if he were going to cry.

"I wanted to say goodbye to her," he muttered lugubriously. "I thought maybe I'd kiss her goodbye. That's silly, too, but girls like it."

"Well, kiss me goodbye," I said. For his worried young face shook my heart. After all, you cannot love one youngster without loving them all.

That's the life sentence given you when you take one of them into your life forever.

LEA'S COMMUNICATION SERIES
Jennings Bryant/Dolf Zillmann, General Editors

For a complete list of other titles in LEA's Communication Series, please contact Lawrence Erlbaum Associates, Publishers

Research in Media Promotion

Edited by

Susan Tyler Eastman
Indiana University

 LAWRENCE ERLBAUM ASSOCIATES, PUBLISHERS
2000   Mahwah, New Jersey   London

Lawrence Erlbaum Associates, Inc., Publishers
10 Industrial Avenue
Mahwah, New Jersey 07430

Library of Congress Cataloging-in-Publication Data

Research in media promotion / edited by Susan Tyler Eastman.
   p. cm. — (LEA's communication series)
   A collection of 11 original studies.
   Includes bibliographical references and indexes.
   ISBN 0-8058-3382-X (cloth : alk. paper)
   1. Advertising — Television programs — United States.
   I. Eastman, Susan Tyler. II. Series.
PN1992.8.A32 R47 2000
659.1'930223 — dc21   99-087341
                                      CIP

Printed in the United States of America
10 9 8 7 6 5 4 3 2 1

Contents

PART II   Applications of Research in Promotion

Preface

This book is the first in a series that will focus on research about program promotion. Once disdained in news and television programming, but long of prime concern in the radio business, effective promotion had become strategically important for the television industry by the mid-1990s as a result of intensified competition on the domestic and international fronts. The next frontier, without question, will be the online medium, and promotion will be particularly crucial to success on the Internet and its offshoots and successors. It is now a truism that the greater the number of competitors, the more critical effective promotion becomes.

This book brings together a decade of scholarly studies and trade articles published in a wide range of journals and magazines with the goals of providing a forum for discussion and fostering more research that utilizes promotional materials. In both theory and application, a great quantity of additional research is needed to understand promotion's range of effects in the three media—on-air, print, and online. Moreover, the short length and special characteristics of on-air promotion makes it ideal for many studies of cognitive processes. Most of the original studies reported in this book are exploratory rather than theory testing only because so little has been accomplished in this area so far, but it is expected that these studies will provoke follow-up studies and new investigations that will be contributed by the book's readers to subsequent volumes. The impact of program promotion on ratings has surfaced as a new variable in the arena of programming research, supplementing—but not supplanting—such traditional concerns as inheritance and audience-flow strategies. Promotion research is likely to receive even more industry attention in the coming decade and become the direction of much fundable scholarly research.

The first people to thank for their enormous contributions to this book are the authors who reviewed a wide range of literatures and conducted original studies for their chapters: William J. Adams, Robert V. Bellamy, Jr., Andrew C. Billings, Paul D. Bolls, Joseph G. Buchman, Douglas A. Ferguson, Walter Gantz, Charles A. Lubbers, Gregory D. Newton, Elizabeth M. Perse, Robert F. Potter, Nancy C. Schwartz, Paul J. Traudt, and James R. Walker. Then I also want to thank Glenda C. Williams for her enthusiasm about the proposal and finished product and for her useful suggestions for polishing the text. Lastly, I want to thank Lawrence Erlbaum Associates' Acquisition Editor, Linda Bathgate, the production editor, Mary F. Martis, and the copyeditor, Kevin Gilligan, for their commitment to this new series and their attention to the details that make the book a polished and reliable source for researchers.

— Susan Tyler Eastman

Author Biographies

William J. Adams is an Associate Professor in the School of Journalism & Mass Communication at Kansas State University. His BA is from Brigham Young University, his MA from Ball State University, and his PhD from Indiana University. He has published extensively as a journalist and scholar, especially focusing on network television programming for prime time. His work includes chapters in the area of television and movie programming in four editions of *Broadcast/Cable Programming: Strategies and Practices* (Wadsworth, most recently, 1997) and on promotion in *Promotion & Marketing for Broadcasting & Cable* (Focal Press, 1999). He has also published articles in the *Journal of Broadcasting & Electronic Media*, the *Journal of Communication*, and the *Journal of Media Economics*. Professor Adams brings considerable expertise with television programming and marketing to his analysis of the means and methods of promoting movies and syndicated series on television.

Robert V. Bellamy, Jr., is an Associate Professor of Media Studies in the Department of Communication at Duquesne University in Pittsburgh. His BA is from Morehead State University, his MA from the University of Kentucky, and his PhD from the University of Iowa. His current research interests include television programming and promotion, media globalization, media and sports, and the impact of technological change on media industries. He has published several articles about network branding, U.S. media economics and institutions, and international media communication. His work has appeared as chapters in several books, most recently in *Promotion & Marketing for Broadcasting & Cable* (Focal Press, 1999) and *MediaSport* (Routledge, 1998) and such publications as the *Journal of Broadcasting & Electronic Media*, the *Journal of Communication*, the *Journal of Sports & Social Issues*, and *Journalism Quarterly*. Professor Bellamy is coauthor of *Television and the Remote Control: Grazing on a Vast Wasteland* (Guilford, 1996) and coeditor of *The Remote Control in the New Age of Television* (Praeger, 1993).

Andrew C. Billings is an Assistant Professor in the Department of Speech and Communication Studies at Clemson University. His BA was in Education and his MA and PhD in Speech Communication at Indiana University. He served as director of Indiana's award-winning forensics team for many years and coached the 1998–1999 team to third place in the National Forensics Association tournament. His research focuses on issues of gender and identity in sports announcing and promotion and in public speaking. Professor Billings has published in the *Journal of Sports & Social Issues, Ecquid Novi, The Forensic*, and *National Forensics Journal*.

Paul D. Bolls is an Assistant Professor in the Department of Mass Communication at Southern Illinois University at Edwardsville. His BA is from Montana State University, his MA from Washington State University, and his PhD from Indiana University. His research analyzes cognitive processing of media, including applications to television programming and promotion, especially utilizing laboratory experiments with physiological measures. Professor Bolls has published in the *Journal of Broadcasting & Electronic Media, Communication Education, Communication Research, Media Psychology*, and the *Journal of Marketing Communication*.

Joseph G. Buchman is an Associate Professor in the Department of Business Management at Utah Valley State College, and he also teaches in the Multimedia Communications Technology program there. His BS is from Indiana University, his MS from Purdue University, and his PhD from Indiana University. His research and teaching focus on communication technologies, especially radio news, talk, and promotion. Professor Buchman authored the chapters on commercial radio promotion in two editions of *Promotion & Marketing for Broadcasting & Cable* (most recently, Focal Press, 1999), and he coauthored two editions of *Broadcast & Cable Selling* (Wadsworth, most recently, 1993). He has published primarily in the trade press, including articles on radio, the Internet, and legal issues in *Next* and *Virtually Alternative*.

Susan Tyler Eastman is Professor of Telecommunications at Indiana University in Bloomington. Her BA is from the University of California at Berkeley, her MA from San Francisco State University, and her PhD from Bowling Green State University. She is senior author/editor of six editions of *Broadcast/Cable Programming: Strategies and Practices* (Wadsworth, most recently, in press for 2001) and three editions of *Promotion & Marketing for*

Broadcasting & Cable (most recently, Focal Press, 1999). Professor Eastman has published over a hundred book chapters and articles, many of which focus on the structural, content, and industry factors affecting promotion of programs in television, radio or cable. Her articles have appeared in such journals as the *Journal of Broadcasting & Electronic Media*, *Critical Studies in Mass Communication*, the *Journal of Communication*, the *Journal of Applied Communication Research*, *Sociology of Sport Journal*, the *Journal of Sport & Social Issues*, the *Journal of Educational Technology Systems*, and the *Journal of Research and Development in Education*.

Douglas A. Ferguson is Professor and Chair of the Department of Communication at the College of Charleston. Formerly, he was Chair of the Department of Telecommunications and Assistant Dean for Resources and Planning in the College of Arts & Sciences at Bowling Green State University. His BA and MA are from Ohio State University and his PhD from Bowling Green State University. Early in his career, he was program director of NBC-affiliated WLIO (TV) and a station manager. He co-authored *The Broadcast Television Industry* (Allyn & Bacon, 1998) and was coeditor/author of *Promotion & Marketing for Broadcasting & Cable* (Focal Press, 1999) and *Broadcast/Cable Programming: Strategies and Practices* (Wadsworth, 1997, in press for 2001). Professor Ferguson's scholarly work has been published in the *Journal of Broadcasting & Electronic Media*, *Communication Research*, *Journalism Quarterly*, the *Dowden Center Journal*, and *Communication Research Reports*. He has authored several chapters on aspects of information technology and currently teaches, researches, and writes about the Internet and other new media technologies.

Walter Gantz is Professor and Chair of the Department of Telecommunications at Indiana University in Bloomington. His BA is from Brooklyn College, his MA from the University of Michigan, and his PhD from Michigan State University. His research has focused on the media's impact on families, including children, on the diffusion of information, on audiences for sports, and on television advertising and the family as the audience for public service messages. He has also published a study about television promotion. He is coauthor of *Desert Storm and the Mass Media* (Hampton, 1993). Professor Gantz's articles have appeared in such journals as the *Journal of Behavioral and Social Sciences*, the *Journal of Broadcasting & Electronic Media*, *Sociology of Sport Journal*, the *Journal of Sport & Social Issues*, *Journalism Quarterly*, the *Journal of Communication*, and *Health Communication*.

Charles A. Lubbers is an Associate Professor of Journalism & Mass Communication at Kansas State University. His BA and MA are from South Dakota State University, and his PhD is from the University of Nebraska–Lincoln. His research and teaching specialty is public relations, especially the marketing of television and other media to the industry and to audiences, but he also teaches about the movie industry. Professor Lubbers has published in *Public Relations Review*, the *Journal of Corporate Public Relations*, and the *Journal of Social Behavior and Personality*.

Gregory D. Newton is an Assistant Professor in the H. H. Herbert School of Journalism and Mass Communication at the University of Oklahoma. His BA is from Northern Illinois University, his MA from Northwestern University, and his PhD from Indiana University. His specialty is radio, including programming, promotion, and law. In addition to industry experience at several radio stations, he has been Associate Editor of the *Federal Communications Law Journal* and has published in the *Journal of Broadcasting & Electronic Media*, the *Journal of Communication*, the *Journal of Radio Studies*, and the *Journal of Applied Communication Research*. Many of Professor Newton's studies have explored the structural factors affecting the promotion of television programs.

Elizabeth M. Perse is an Associate Professor of Communication at the University of Delaware, Newark. Her BA is from Northwestern University and her MA and PhD from Kent State University. Her current research and teaching focus on the uses of newer communication technologies and on investigating cognitive and emotional dimensions and aspects of activity and involvement. In addition to more than 35 book chapters and journal articles, she has coauthored 2 textbooks — *Communicating Online* (Mayfield, 1998) and *The Mayfield Quick Guide to the Internet for Communication Students* (Mayfield, 1998) — and is completing a book on media effects for Lawrence Erlbaum Associates. Professor Perse's articles have appeared in such journals as the *Journal of Communication, Communication Research*, the *Journal of Broadcasting & Electronic Media*, and *Human Communication Research*, and for 3 years she was the Review and Criticism Editor for the *Journal of Broadcasting & Electronic Media*.

Robert F. Potter is an Assistant Professor of Telecommunication and Film at the University of Alabama. His BA and MS are from Eastern Washington University and his PhD from Indiana University. Prior to his academic career, he served as promotion director for radio stations in the Pacific Northwest. His research and teaching have focused on the cognitive processing of media, particularly experimental studies of imagery and processing of radio commercials and radio messages. Professor Potter has published in the *Journal of Broadcasting & Electronic Media, Media Psychology, Psychophysiology*, and the *Proceedings of the American Academy of Advertising*.

Nancy C. Schwartz is an Instructor in the Department of Telecommunications and a doctoral candidate in Instructional Systems Technology at Indiana University, Bloomington. Her BS is from Ball State University and her MEd from Arizona State University. She has 18 years of teaching experience accumulated in the American public schools, the Department of

Defense Dependents School overseas, and with the Broadway touring company of *Annie*. Her current research interests center on media processing and effects and the impact of technology on teaching and learning. She has published in *Teaching and Change* and the *Journal of the American Society of Information Science*.

Paul J. Traudt is an Associate Professor of Mass Communication in the Hank Greenspun School of Communication at the University of Nevada at Las Vegas. He has a BA from the University of Colorado, an MA from the University of Utah, and a PhD from the University of Texas at Austin. He teaches, writes, and consults in the area of the processes and effects of mass media and evolving communications technologies. He has published and conducted research across the spectrum of programming and audience concerns, including the use of remote control devices on the part of cable televiewers, qualitative ethnographies of family decision-making processes and television program viewership, and survey-based analyses of the audiences for public and government access television. Professor Traudt's recent publications include a study in the *Journal of Media Economics* on programming and audience factors related to donors to public radio and a chapter on interactive television in *Communication Technology Update* (Focal Press, 1998).

James R. Walker is Professor and Chair of the Department of Communication at Saint Xavier University in Chicago. His research has focused on the impact of remote control devices on television viewing behaviors and the television industry, on television programming practices, and on the effectiveness of television program promotions. He has published over 20 articles in national and regional journals, including the *Journal of Broadcasting & Electronic Media*, *Journalism Quarterly*, *Communications Law Review*, and the *Journal of Popular Culture*. Professor Walker coauthored *The Broadcast Television Industry* (Allyn & Bacon, 1998) and *Television and the Remote Control: Grazing on a Vast Wasteland* (Guilford, 1996) and coedited *The Remote Control in the New Age of Television* (Praeger, 1993).

INTRODUCTION TO RESEARCH ABOUT PROMOTION

This half of the book provides a framework for scholars and practitioners seeking to understand research to date about program promotion on television, radio, and online. The first chapter consists of practical background on industry programming and the conventions of promotion, and it introduces the terminology of the field. The second chapter supplies a theoretical background by detailing the passive and active conceptual approaches. The third chapter reviews what has been researched so far about structural aspects of on-air promos, summarizing what has been learned about the variables contributing to the salience model. The fourth chapter turns to the topics of sex and violence in the content of on-air promotion. And the fifth and last chapter examines the topic of media branding. Taken together, these five chapters will help readers new to the field to understand published articles about promotion, as well as the chapters in the second half of the book. In addition, three of the chapters in Part I contain original studies to be added to the literature they review.

1

Orientation to Promotion and Research

Susan Tyler Eastman
Indiana University

Fred Silverman, the legendary programmer for CBS, ABC, and NBC in the 1970s, has been quoted as saying, "Fifty percent of success is the program and fifty percent is how the program is promoted" (Bedell, 1981, p. 141). He meant that capturing high ratings is not just a function of program scheduling and appeal, but is also a function of how the audience is told about the programs. On-air promotion has become a big-budget item for the U.S. television industry, occupying airtime that could otherwise be sold for commercials, and print and online promotion incur costs with no direct return. Moreover, the marketing of images has become one of the central concerns of program suppliers. NBC has spent billions of dollars linking itself to the Olympics, for example. Such leading broadcast and cable networks as Disney (owner of ABC and ESPN), Time Warner (owner of CNN), General Electric (owner of NBC), and Westinghouse (owner of CBS), as well as Japan's AsiaNet and Murdoch's Star Network, among others, are devoting enormous financial resources to developing the value of their brand names around the world. The industry's professional association for those in the business of media marketing, Promax, now holds annual conventions in South America, Europe (England), and Asia, as well as in the United States — conventions that swell annually in the number and prominence of their participants. More savage competition, rising program costs, and the rapid growth of the Internet have been spurs to increased concern about media marketing around the world.

Industry analyses show that the proportion of time devoted to promotion has been growing in the last decade. An hour on ABC or NBC carried 5 more minutes of promotion in 1999 than it did in 1989 (Associated Press, 1999). On average for the six broadcast networks, the amount of promotion now exceeds 4½ minutes an hour in prime time and many more minutes in some other dayparts (Fleming, 1997).

CHANGES AND EXPECTATIONS

It is an industry truism that the best program without promotion has no audience. At heart, promotion on-the-air, online, and in print is the way that stations and networks announce the availability of their programs, but promotion does much more. It creates a mood, identifies a provider, and generates attitudes that reach far beyond a single program. Although promotion can be seen as a mere adjunct to television and radio programming, conceptually, it is a subset of the larger arena of marketing of products and images via advertising and is related to, but not identical with, publicity and public relations. But in the media business, promotion refers particularly to the on-air, online, and print activity of media outlets, and it has a particular characteristic not commonly associated with other products: Not only can programs be promoted externally in television and radio guides and on billboards and other signs, programs can be also promoted within and adjacent to other programs on the air.[1] On-air spots (*promos*) are widely thought to be the most valuable kind of self-advertising possible and are unique to the broadcast and cable industries. It has been estimated that the U.S. broadcast networks were collectively airing more than 30,000 promos a year by the late 1990s (see Eastman & Newton, 1998a). To carry those promos, the Big Four were collectively foregoing as much as $4 *billion* in annual advertising revenue they might have earned—unequivocal evidence of the importance they assign to on-air promotion.

The study of promotion is not merely about how the industry reaches viewers and listeners, however. Promotional messages are short bursts of communication that can be examined for their implications about basic processes of communication. They can be studied for what they reveal about how human cognition works, how social persuasion works, and how cross-national images are created and embedded in world culture. Nonetheless, a knowledge of contemporary strategy and practice in tele-

---

[1]The term "promotions" with an "s" is used more widely in the advertising business to refer to store displays, consumer contests, and related point-of-sale activities to spur sales of products.

vision, radio, and Internet programming is essential to understanding most of the studies of promotion that have been published so far. Recognizing how the industry works, how it measures its successes, and how it has changed in recent years explains why increasing industry and scholarly attention has been directed toward promotion.

Five Recent Changes

Just as movie producers spend tens of millions of dollars marketing their big-budget films, the broadcast television and cable industries, and to a lesser extent radio, devote a large percentage of their revenues to promoting their images, their programs, and their services. Five key industry changes have contributed to the increasing significance of broadcast and cable promotion:

1. the rising costs of program production and licensing;
2. the expanded number of program channels;
3. the rapid rise of the online media;
4. federal and state deregulation of the media;
5. the impact of adoption of new user technologies.

First, the cost of original production continues to escalate. Rising prices for content mean that attracting the maximum number of viewers becomes more and more crucial in order to charge the highest possible rates for advertising, since it is that advertising that, in the usual way of things, pays the cost of licensing programs.[2] Although the broadcast networks have begun producing more of their own programs or requiring equity positions in licensed programs in order to improve their control of costs and expand revenues, promotion becomes even more important as a tool for gaining all possible viewers for every program as the cost of those programs rises.

Second, the increase in broadcast networks from four to seven, counting UPN, the WB, and the fledgling Pax, make competitive positioning at the broadcast level essential. At the same time, PBS appears to be maintaining its ability to attract viewers, and the flood of cable networks, with dozens more on the threshold, makes the rivalry for viewers even more dependent on effective program promotion. These changes in the industry have both reduced the dominance of the established services and simultaneously made promotion of programs and images of greater importance.

---

[2]Cable has the advantage of a second revenue stream from subscriptions, a pattern that broadcasters are trying to emulate by expanding beyond spot advertising to marketing other services.

Third, the rapid expansion of the Internet has introduced a wholly new set of online competitors. Indeed, cable and broadcasters even compete with themselves by having online promotion because the total amount of time television viewers have available for entertainment and information (from whatever source) remains relatively stable. Although the shape of promotional practices within the online industry has yet to be fully realized, if the past is a guide, the online media will borrow promotional tactics heavily from the broadcast media, just as cable has done, and promotion will become only more important as a way of distinguishing one service from another and attracting audiences—whether they are called viewers or online users.

Fourth is the impact of government deregulation of on-air media and ownership limits. Relaxation or removal of impediments to active self-marketing has had the effect of increasing the importance of that self-promotion. Radio stations can now change their call letters relatively easily to meet marketing objectives, and limits on patterns of scheduling of nonprogram material (including promotional spots, jingles, and teasers) have been removed, allowing stations to exercise creative control of their airtime and to utilize it to promote themselves as much as they wish. At the same time, the concentration of station ownership into larger and larger groups places even more focus on marketing. Most managers of electronic media services are well indoctrinated with the importance of effective promotion and marketing, and the fostering of innovative promotional practices as well as increased salaries for top promotion executives and bigger departmental budgets are evidence of their acceptance of promotion as the third leg of the media business, along with programming and advertising sales.

Finally, the fifth big change has been in the audience's rapid incorporation of the new media into their daily lives. For a decade or more, television viewers have been able to tape programs for later viewing and change channels at whim, disrupting the impact of program lineup strategies and reducing audience manipulability. The widespread use of videotape recorders and remote controls has ratcheted up the importance of promotion as a tool for distinguishing among competing services and for making multiple uses of the media possible. The likelihood of technological media convergence creates still another capacity in which promotion will be important—the educational function of teaching users how the newest electronic world operates.

Promotion Sets Expectations

Promotion is important because it is part of the *frame* that governs how programs are perceived and understood by any group or individual (see Scheufele, 1999). As extended to promotion, framing refers to the idea that on-air, online, and print communications exist within a large framework of audience and industry expectations about programs, commercials, and other messages, and cannot be fully understood out of context (see Goffman, 1974, 1979). Programs and commercial messages provide a frame for promotional messages. At the same time, aspects of language, visuals, sounds, and narrative structures themselves provide frames that affect the interpretation of the messages conveyed in promotion. These are often called the executional features, or presentational aspects of promotion, and they act on reception of the message. Moreover, a broad conception of framing encompasses the notion that promotion itself may provide a crucial part of the larger frame for programs and advertising messages. How audience members feel about promotional spots can affect how they feel about the promoted program. Cues within all kinds of messages imply levels of power to be ascribed to individuals and social groups and affect how audiences see both characters in programs and programs themselves (see Entman, 1993). From a programming scholar's or practitioner's perspective, understanding audience viewing (and listening), and thus how to decode industry programming, necessitates weighing the impact of promotion. Promotion profoundly affects what audiences, advertisers, and affiliates expect from media producers and services and, simultaneously, what those producers see themselves as providing. Producers of messages can be victims of the images they create. In the media business, promotion has become part of a two-way street at several levels.

Audience activity models presume that promotion partakes of both advertising and programming in structure and content, and that measuring the effectiveness of promotion must encompass variables from both advertising and programming research. Most research about promotion to date has presumed that audiences are relatively minimal in the amount of their self-driven activity, and thus able to be impacted to a limited extent by external motivators such as on-air promos. Essays by Kubey and Csikszentmihalyi (1990) refer to "the intense competition for the attention of prospective consumers" that "also leads producers to try to outdo the competition with each new commercial or promotional ad lest their ad . . . be lost in what they themselves call the 'clutter' of everything else appearing on the screen" (pp. 198–199). But as this book shows, only a few social scientists so far have taken the next step of investigating the phenomena of program and image promotion.

Congruent with decades of practice by the major networks and stations, a small body of scholarly studies have demonstrated the undeniable contribution of on-air promos and print advertising to program viewership, as measured by fluctuations in Nielsen ratings. The amount of that contribution has been shown to vary by type of program and network and depending on whether a program is new or established and how popular the program is (see Eastman & Newton, 1998a, 1998b, 1999; Walker, 1993). Moreover, while promotion's impact on ratings appears modest, it is clearly significant, given that differences of 1 to 2 rating points shift the comparative rankings of national networks or broadcast stations in a market and materially affect broadcast and cable revenues.

BASIC TYPES AND FUNCTIONS

For those new to the field of promotion, some basics about hows and whys of promotion might be useful (see the textbook by Eastman, Ferguson, & Klein, 1999, for an amplified treatment of fundamentals of scope, design, and application). Promotion divides into two main types: There is *image* promotion intended to enhance the brand name of the parent service and create a positive attitude among viewers, advertisers, and other groups. It is typified by slogans and themes that may position the station as integral to the community ("Your Good Neighbor") or characterize the entire lineup (for example, "Must See TV"). The second type is *program* promotion, which may involve supporting newspaper and magazine ads, billboards, radio or television spots, online materials, and so on, but which is primarily comprised of on-air promos (spots for one or more programs to induce viewing or listening or foster retention). The promotion of specialized services by cable operators or online companies could become a third type, but it has yet to materialize in any widely recognized way. In the movie business, some outside forces such as critics are part of the promotion process, but for the most part, promotion is an activity of program distributors — whether they be stations, networks, or syndicators.

Most broadcast, cable, and movie promotion focuses either on brand images or on specific programs (or films). On television and radio, individual promos (on-air spots) range in length from a few seconds (as in a logo or other identifier) to as long as 15 or 30 seconds, but all take up time that could otherwise be sold to advertisers (on commercial stations, or be occupied by programs on noncommercial stations). Indeed, some station managers insist on annual calculations of the total value of promotional time, using their advertising rate cards to impress staff with the value of that commodity.

Audience Acquisition and Retention

Although image building through network branding is central to long-term network strategy, programs are the focus of everyday promotional strategy by networks, stations, cable systems, and movie distributors. Program promotion's main goals are to achieve sampling (to get viewers to try an unfamiliar program), to activate interest in upcoming episodes of ongoing programs, to announce changes in the program schedule, and to build viewer satisfaction with the programming. Whereas established television programs carry some audience from week to week if there is no change in their time slots, all newly acquired or produced programs, any shows that have been moved in day or time in the schedule, and those that change content (movies, magazine news) or guests (talk, games, variety entertainment) necessitate on-air and supplementary external promotion. For television, program promotion functions to increase the amounts of both new and inherited viewing, but movies are like a group of television specials airing one time only. Because its effectiveness is directly related to audience size as well as audience viewing patterns, promotion thus has considerable monetary as well as conceptual significance.

Still another body of research has as its primary purpose the retention of viewers or listeners. Radio stations host near-daily giveways to keep their audiences satisfied and coming back, a practice being copied by some cable networks and television stations. The distribution of program guides by cable systems and public broadcasters is another retentive device intended to make the use of media more convenient and thus more fulfilling. There is little more than anecdotal evidence of the success of various retentive strategies, making this a likely subject for future research.

Promotion to Affiliates and Advertisers

Not all promotion is to audiences, however—or one must redefine the term to include more groups than just listeners, viewers, and users. A great deal of promotion is directed toward the industry itself.

The goal of some promotion is to get stations and cable networks to buy program series and specials. Slick ads in trade magazines, glossy print brochures, and video press kits are among the primary means of reaching those who license syndicated programs, both domestically and internationally. The large distributors (syndicators) of programs have full-time staff whose job is to market their programs to American and other television or radio outlets using elaborate promotional materials. The content of such promotional materials discusses aspects of programs of interest to potential purchasers of the programs but not viewers (such as which demographic group a show appeals to, which other stations have already purchased the show, and so on). In consequence, the materials are distributed via trade-only publications, convention presentations, and mail, fax, and online—reaching the targeted group but not the general audience. Similarly, the newer broadcast and cable networks also promote their value to potential affiliates to increase their coverage and maintain existing affiliations.

The goal of still other promotion is to convince advertisers to buy commercial time or underwriters to fund programs. The promotional materials that sales executives take or mail to existing and potential advertisers display such things as the audience demographics of the best rated programs or a cable interconnect's coverage area in hopes of persuading time buyers to purchase commercial time. Much of trade magazine advertising is directed primarily to advertisers, and booths and displays at industry conventions are among the common tools for reaching advertisers and underwriters. On the noncommercial side, promotional materials attempt to lure potential underwriters into financing new program series and specials. These kinds of promotion are also not normally seen by the general public.

As mentioned earlier, still another body of promotion has the goal of building a brand name around the globe by associating it with desirable events, people, and programs. For example, Disney has long fostered use of its classic cartoon figures (especially the Mickey Mouse ears) to signal its appeal to children and to identify its English-language name to citizens of non-English-speaking countries. NBC has branded itself by associating its name with the Olympics. Such promotion generally reaches all three groups — potential audiences, affiliates, and advertisers.

SCHOLARLY PERSPECTIVES

Promotion, in particular on-air promos, can be analyzed from several theoretical perspectives. Television and radio promos and movie trailers can be explored for their contribution to academic understanding of human perceptual, aesthetic, and cognitive processes, for their impact on industry programming strategies, and for their impact on vulnerable social groups such as children, the elderly, and the disadvantaged. But most studies to date have assessed promotional activities for their value and function within a media industry.

Promotion as Programs, Commercials, or Motivators

Although promotion can be in magazines and newspapers or online or in movie houses, the brief on-air promos that take up a significant portion of television airtime have attracted the most scholarly interest. There are three reasons for this interest.

First, television *program promos are miniprograms*. Most are preproduced units possessing beginnings and endings, characters, sets, and a bit of plot—typically suspenseful to foster viewing. They may incorporate clips from a series episode or clips from news segments or may involve direct address to viewers or listeners by an actor, player, or station talent (nearly all promos also incorporate a "voice-over" produced by the station to identify time and station and often to tease or lure by drawing out the suspenseful element). Because the preponderance of promos are a type of miniprogram, under traditional royalty concepts, their creators/producers (the networks or stations) can be said to have inherent rights as creators/producers, and such rights can be expected to have monetary value under copyright law. Legal scholars concerned with copyright may find the topic of on-air promos of particular interest, and critical scholars focusing on media narratives and aesthetics should find promos a fruitful area for analysis.

Second, contrarily, *promos can be seen as commercials for programs.* Clearly, product sales demonstrate that advertising influences buyer behavior. Promos' purposes are to attract new viewers to programs, to maintain viewing of an entire schedule, and to create an image either for a program or a set of programs (or for the network/station as a whole), and as commercial messages, they clearly have monetary value because they occupy time (or space) that could otherwise be sold. As objects of scholarly research, promos possess characteristics paralleling and differing from other product advertising and have significance for scholarly study of business practices and behavior responses.

Third, *promos are clearly related to viewing.* They have been demonstrated to influence viewing in empirical studies, and they have the weight of decades of industry tradition behind them. Entire departments at networks and stations are devoted to the production (and scheduling) of promotion, and their use in the industry has matured to the stage that some companies specialize in the production of promotional spots (and associated print and online promotion). When the television researchers evaluate their impact on viewing, promos are said to possess the rating of the program containing them. (Promos have largely moved out of the transitions between programs to be located within the breaks inside programs, but when occurring between programs, the usual method of calculating a spot's viewership—whether a commercial or a promo—is to average the ratings for programs on either side of the break.) Empirical scholars interested in factors affecting programming and audience behavior can explore the structure, content, and impact of promos, and they need to incorporate the functions and practices of promotion within their theories and models.

Although Nielsen ratings have been the most common dependent measure utilized in research about promotion to date, such research has commonly been limited to content analysis or survey methods. Other measures, such as recall tests and physiological assessments of attention and involvement, are more suited to experiments testing fundamental aspects of the communication and thinking processes. As the rest of this book shows, the study of promotion bears on many aspects of cognition, behavior, and attitudes.

Factors Affecting Ratings

Because the most common dependent measure used to evaluate the success (or lack thereof) of on-air television promotion has been ratings, it is necessary to understand where ratings come from and what limitations they have. As the reader probably knows, ratings are a measure of the size of an audience, and many factors affect the size of media audiences. How to increase size is a central concern of the industry, and how to understand the conditions and characteristics that affect size is a central concern of media scholars.

First, unquestionably, the appeal of a program (often called its "quality") dominates all other factors. How programs have been scheduled on television, however, has also been shown to profoundly affect audience size (see Webster, Lichty, & Phalen, 1999; Webster & Phalen, 1997). For example, the size of the audience of a preceding program affects the next program's viewership; placement of a new show between two hit programs almost invariably raises the number of viewers of the intervening program. Two related factors are the compatibility of adjacent programs and the challenge posed by competing programs on other channels. In addition, the character of widely available technology and the nature of the market probably affect audience size. For example, Cooper (1997) demonstrated the impact of network affiliation (possibly a surrogate for program appeal) and the impact of whether a channel is UHF or VHF or cable-only on audience size. The degree of market concentration and cable/satellite penetration also affect audience size.

The new thing that this book adds to this list of impact is the effect of promotion. Early research has reinforced the industry convention that on-air is the most important means of communication to audiences about programs and thus directly encourages or discourages viewing in ways that research now needs to measure for each of the media.

In addition to a complexity of factors affecting audience size, the measurement tool of ratings themselves is problematic (see Ferguson, Meyer, & Eastman, 1997; Webster et al., 1999). Most ratings still come from diaries for local markets and for all radio. For network and large-market television, broadcast and cable ratings come from meters, but many of those continue to be traditional meters, not the most elaborate peoplemeters that were recently developed. All ratings share problems in response rate, cooperation rates, and response bias. Diaries tend to be good measures of promotional impact but not accurate gauges of listening or viewing. Traditional meters tell whether the television set was on and what channel was tuned in, but not who was watching. Peoplemeters attempt to record who was watching, but button-pushing fatigue soon sets in, and peoplemeters cannot reveal how distracted the potential viewers were. Realities such as these explain why quantitative calculations of promotion's impact will continue to be imperfect, and will lead to calls for better measures of viewing and influence.

OUTLINE OF THIS BOOK

The remaining chapters in this book make a start at collecting, organizing, and interpreting the available scholarly and applied research about media promotion. Each chapter reviews and analyzes published research in a broadly defined area, suggesting what can be predicted or hypothesized about promotion from wider but related literatures and analyzing whatever studies specifically about promotion are available. Then, in all chapters save the first two, the authors report original studies conducted for this book on some aspect of promotion. These studies go a long way toward supplementing the slender framework of research that now exists. Each chapter concludes with an extended outline of the theoretical and methodological issues in that area and poses specific questions, topics, and concerns for future research. These concluding sections include recommendations about the means and methods for conducting specific studies as a way of triggering interest in further research. For the convenience of readers, works cited appear in a list of references at each chapter's end.

Framework and Concepts

The chapters in Part I are intended to supply a grounding in theories, models, and findings to orient the reader to the field of promotion studies. In the chapter following this one, Elizabeth M. Perse uses the audience activity paradigm to frame a discussion of theories that account for promotion's impact. Her analysis incorporates a very large body of media and psychology literature, and through examinations of conceptions of cognition and persuasion, she spells out the implications regarding media promotion. She looks first at orienting and salience assumptions, as well as processing and attitudes toward messages. Then, these passive research approaches are contrasted with a second group of approaches related to selective attention and intentionality, bringing in channel loyalty and program satisfaction. Of particular research value are the outlines she provides of the benefits and limitations of each of the two main perspectives. This chapter provides a crucial theoretical background for most subsequent chapters, and the authors in later chapters refer back to this material rather than repeating it at length.

In the third chapter, this author in conjunction with Paul D. Bolls shows how the findings in the advertising and programming literatures provided a solid basis for assumptions about how to measure the effectiveness of on-air promotion using ratings. The authors focus on theories of expectation and excitation transfer as the foundation for structural studies of promotion's effects, but they acknowledge that the line between structure and content blurs. After analyzing most of the existing structural studies about on-air promotion, the authors take a first step in investigating the content of on-air promotion. Using open-ended interviews with viewers while screening promos, they assess the appeals within promos for situation comedies for various adult demographic groups. This original study explores the factors that attract viewers to television programs or repel them, including the roles of story line and actor visibility, as well as familiarity with program content. Lastly, the authors outline options for future research into the structure and content of on-air promotion, specifying particular theoretical approaches and practical methods that test in the laboratory and the field what has already been shown in the research. This chapter serves as a backdrop for many of the remaining chapters because it shows the origins of the salience model of structural promotional effectiveness on which some other authors draw.

Moving to other aspects of content in the fourth chapter, James R. Walker evaluates the roles of violence and sexual content in on-air and print promotion and compares the amount of those characteristics in studies of prime-time promotion from the early to late 1990s. Adding a new study to the scant literature, the author tracks the quantities of aggressive actions, sexual behavior, and sexually related language in televised promotional materials. Walker makes the case that promos have particular potency because they utilize the most extreme portions of programs (as do movie teasers). The author summarizes scholarly conclusions about the likely impacts of portrayals of excessive violence and sexual content on society and explains why the television industry continues to use such potentially harmful content in promos. The chapter concludes with useful suggestions for future studies of the content of promos on cable television and other media.

In the fifth chapter, Robert V. Bellamy, Jr., and Paul J. Traudt tackle the crucial topic of media brand equity and provide one of the first quantitative studies of television branding in the literature. The authors provide a thorough review of complex conceptions of branding and brand equity in the marketing literature and then measure the relative equity of the major broadcast and cable television networks in the United States. The study they report in this chapter is an initial attempt at measuring aspects of recall, recognition, share of mind, and extension of brand for television networks. At the chapter's end, they delineate specific aspects of media brand equity amenable to research, as well as other approaches to conceiving and measuring media branding with implications beyond the United States.

Applications by Genre and Medium

The six chapters in Part II consider narrower applications of promotion, focusing either on a single type of television programming or on another medium than television. In the sixth chapter, Walter Gantz and Nancy C. Schwartz explore promotion within and about children's programs, detailing the unique aspects of children as a television audience. After a comprehensive review of the existing literatures on cognitive processing and advertising as they relate to promotional message reception and processing, they detail an exhaustive descriptive study of promotion to children prepared for this book. Their study provides an exceptionally valuable baseline for future extensions of research in this area, and their suggestions for future studies outline as yet unexplored questions in cognitive processing, children's special susceptibility to media messages, and the particular effectiveness of the Internet as a tool both for captivating children and for investigating their motivations and behaviors.

In the seventh chapter, Andrew C. Billings and this author examine sports promotion. They review the existing studies in three areas: sports marketing and the media, the impact of promotion of sports within sports programs, and the impact of promotion for prime-time shows carried within sports. They supplement the previous studies with an analysis of the effectiveness of prime-time promotion within the 1998 Nagano Olympics, looking at the percentage of promos for prime-time shows that improved or maintained their ratings and testing the individual and collective impact of salience variables. Like the preceding and following chapters, they lay out an extended agenda for additional research related to sports and promotion, covering the areas of gender and racial bias in structural and content effects and in international sports marketing.

William J. Adams and Charles A. Lubbers look at industry practices in promoting theatrical movies in the eighth chapter. Because this topic will be unfamiliar to most readers, they provide a useful primer on movie promotion, analyzing the roles of premieres, awards, previews, merchandising, and product placement as types of promotion especially critical to the movie business. Then they illuminate the interesting influences of movie critics on ticket sales and on the Academy Awards in the dual study they conducted for this book. Concluding with detailed suggestions for additional studies in the areas of critics' influences and audience, they illustrate the complex relationship between critics and movie attendance. Their chapter will be especially helpful to readers for its detailed analysis of the kinds of archival and trade information that are readily available and can aid in scholarly investigations of movie promotion.

In the ninth chapter, Joseph G. Buchman analyzes news promotion, focusing particularly on the promotion of local newscasts because local news is key to most stations' ratings, revenues, and expenses. Drawing on literature about motivations research and the social impact of media, the author shows how local news promotion can exemplify the targeting of instrumental and ritualized news viewers as well as depict utilitarian and diversionary news consumption. From a practitioner's perspective, the short quotes of news themes used to illustrate various promotional approaches are especially useful. After reviewing the few studies about news promos, teases, and bumpers, he describes the promotion of newscasts in depth and then recommends future studies that assess promotion from the perspective of different types of viewers and in varied contexts.

Stepping away from television, Gregory D. Newton and Robert F. Potter analyze studies of factors affecting the promotion of radio in the 10th chapter. After an exceptionally clear exposition of related cognitive processing theory, they explore aspects of short- and long-term memory for sound in the context of radio promotion via stations' own airwaves. Utilizing a strong theoretical foundation, their study focuses on the effect of auditory complexity on listeners' memories and adds another layer to scholars' understanding of how cognitive processes function. Their chapter has particular value because it provides readers with a model for reporting experimental research while also spelling out the meaning of their research in ways that have practical applications for radio producers. Their chapter concludes with recommendations for the next steps in the same line of research, as well as other directions for needed radio research.

In the 11th and final chapter, Douglas A. Ferguson explores promotion of programs and station images on television stations' web sites. He focuses on current efforts by stations to use online to supplement their traditional on-air and print media, but shows how many stations lack a clear focus to their promotional use of the online medium. His study adds to the small body of scholarly research about features of the Internet and shows how particular attributes relate to the promotion of programs. Program promotion surfaces as a wholly unexplored topic to date, much in need of examination because of its unrecognized importance to station audience growth and retention as well as its value to research about the impact of new media technologies. The author's extended comparison of on-air and online promotion will be particularly useful to readers as well as producers of program promotion. In addition, the chapter alludes to the unique kinds of online-only programs to be promoted in the future and the ways in which their marketing might differ. The chapter concludes by outlining directions for future research about program promotion in the online medium.

Looking Ahead

Each of these chapters brings original thinking and fresh scholarship to a swelling area of industry and academic interest. Scholars will find fruitful ideas for their own research studies and suggestions for theoretical approaches and appropriate methods in the chapters in this book. This literature has been collected and supplemented in the hopes that it may aid other researchers in building on the work that has already been accomplished. But interpreting many of the studies necessitates a firm grasp of current industry practice as well as research methodology. Much work still lies ahead to understand the processes and effects of promotion, and the coming together of several media technologies in the near future means that there will be altered processes and perhaps drastically new effects to investigate in the decades to come. New studies should be significant for what they reveal about the industry as well as for what they reveal about human thinking and behavior.

REFERENCES

Associated Press. (1999, April 12). Clutter of commercials growing in prime time. *Herald Times*, p. A10.

Bedell, S. (1981). *Up the tube: Prime-time TV and the Silverman years*. New York: Viking.

Cooper, R. (1997). The structural determinants of television ratings share: Network affiliation, broadcast band, cable penetration, and market concentration. In C. Warner (Ed.), *Media management review* (pp. 29–38). Mahwah, NJ: Lawrence Erlbaum Associates.

Eastman, S. T., Ferguson, D. A., & Klein, R. A. (Eds.). (1999). *Promotion and marketing for broadcasting and cable* (3rd ed.). Boston: Focal Press.

Eastman, S. T., & Newton, G. D. (1998a). The impact of structural salience within on-air promotion. *Journal of Broadcasting & Electronic Media, 42*, 50–79.

Eastman, S. T., & Newton, G. D. (1998b). Estimating the contributions of inheritance and promotion. In S. T. Eastman (Ed.), *Report on compilation valuation for distant television signals* (pp. 3.15–3.27). Copyright Board of Canada, re Retransmission 1998–2000.

Eastman, S. T., & Newton, G. D. (1999). Hitting promotion hard: A network response to channel surfing and new competition. *Journal of Applied Communication Research, 27*, 73–85.

Entman, R. (1993). Framing: Toward clarification of a fractured paradigm. *Journal of Communication, 43*(4), 51–58.

Ferguson, D. A., Meyer, T. P., & Eastman, S. T. (1997). Program and audience research. In S. T. Eastman & D. A. Ferguson (Eds.), *Broadcast/cable programming: Strategies and practices* (5th ed., pp. 32–65). Belmont, CA: Wadsworth.

Fleming, H. (1997, March 31). PSA slice shrinks as commercial pie grows. *Broadcasting & Cable, 19*, 22.

Goffman, E. (1974). *Frame analysis: An essay on the organization of experience.* New York: Harper & Row.

Goffman, E. (1979). *Gender advertisements.* New York: Harper Colophon Books.

Kubey, R., & Csikszentmihalyi, M. (1990). *Television and the quality of life: How viewing shapes everyday experiences.* Hillsdale, NJ: Lawrence Erlbaum Associates.

Scheufele, D. A. (1999). Framing as a theory of media effects. *Journal of Communication, 49*(1), 103–122.

Walker, J. R. (1993). Catchy, yes, but does it work? The impact of broadcast network promotion frequency and type on program success. *Journal of Broadcasting & Electronic Media, 37*, 197–207.

Webster, J. G., Lichty, L. W., & Phalen, P. F. (1999). *Ratings analysis: Theory and practice* (2nd ed.). Mahwah, NJ: Lawrence Erlbaum Associates.

Webster, J. G., & Phalen, P. F. (1997). *The mass audience: Rediscovering the dominant model.* Mahwah, NJ: Lawrence Erlbaum Associates.

2

Applying Theory to the Practice of Promotion

Elizabeth M. Perse
University of Delaware

Most of the work on television programming and promotion has been drawn from a "loose body of beliefs—supported by some tested propositions—that the practitioners of programming use to make predictions" (Eastman, 1998, p. 324). Although this area of industry practice has been driven mainly by practical consideration and guided by rules of thumb, there are several communication theories that offer guidance to scholars and professionals alike.

This chapter takes a conceptual orientation to the promotion process, with an emphasis on on-air television promotion. Central to this discussion is the concept of *audience activity*. Audience activity describes how intentionally and purposely people select and attend to different media and different programs. Guided by the uses and gratifications perspective (e.g., Blumler, 1979; Levy & Windahl, 1985; Perse, 1990a; Rubin, 1984; Rubin & Perse, 1987b) as well as evidence drawn from almost 50 years of research (see Eastman, 1998, and Webster & Phalen, 1997, for summaries), it is clear that audience activity is an important concept in understanding promotion effects because activity varies—across media, across people, across time, and even within individuals. Different theoretical models of promotion grow out of different assumptions about audience activity.

CLASSIC AUDIENCE PROMOTION

Audience promotion is the set of messages directed toward the audience that is initiated by a station or a network. Promotional messages are a type of commercial—short, persuasive messages designed to influence the audience to sample specific programs. The goal of audience promotion is ratings, or increases in audience size. Promotion works to increase ratings in several ways: (a) by creating awareness of unfamiliar programs, (b) by creating awareness of the schedule for both familiar and unfamiliar programs, (c) by activating interest in a program, (d) by encouraging sampling of programs, and (e) by building satisfaction with programs, leading to loyalty and repeat viewing (Ferguson, Eastman, & Klein, 1999, and Eastman, chap. 1, this volume). Audience promotion, then, is intended to have cognitive (awareness), affective (positive attitudes), and behavioral (sampling) aims.

Beyond the limited research on the effects of news teasers (Cameron, Schleuder, & Thorson, 1991; Schleuder, White, & Cameron, 1993), virtually all the research on the effectiveness of promotional messages has focused only on behavioral effects: ratings of promoted programs (e.g., Billings, Eastman, & Newton, 1998; Eastman & Newton, 1998, 1999; Eastman, Newton, & Pack, 1996; Eastman & Otteson, 1994; Walker, 1993; Williams, 1989). A focus on ratings is certainly an important one, especially in this era of channel competition and extraordinary costs for special media events (e.g., Eastman et al., 1996). This focus, however, neglects other, longer term goals of promotion: to create a positive image and loyalty for a channel or network.

In the current demassified, multichannel media environment, audiences are more selective in their media use; technology allows easy selection of preferred channels and avoidance of others (e.g., the "favorites" button on the remote control device). Audience polarization, or specialization that leads to consumption of one type of content to the exclusion of other types, is already common in music, film, radio, and books (Webster & Phalen, 1997). This selectivity may emerge in the television audience. In the long run, another goal of promotion is channel loyalty—to lead audiences to place the channel or network in their channel repertoire, or the set of channels that they regularly view. This is no small feat; no matter how many channels are available, channel repertoires are relatively limited, typically to fewer than a dozen (Ferguson & Perse, 1993).

The dual aims of audience promotion, sampling specific programs and building channel loyalty, are certainly interrelated, but the routes to each are somewhat different. Marketing communication has recognized that consumers follow different processes to make purchasing and consumption decisions. Two of the dominant models in marketing communication highlight the importance of audience involvement in the process (Ray, 1973). Depending on the audience's interest in the topic and the personal relevance of the message, audience behavior results from two different processes. The *low-involvement process* works by creating awareness of an alternative (in the case of promotion, a program), leading to some low-level familiarity with that program. That familiarity leads to selection, if and when the program is encountered, for two reasons. First, audiences can only select from among the program alternatives of which they are aware. Second, audiences are likely to select familiar programs over unfamiliar ones (Krugman, 1965). The low-involvement process, then, moves from cognitive to behavioral effects. Attitudes, if they are formed, grow out of behavior, or experience with the program.

The *learning process*, on the other hand, is based on an interested and involved audience. This model explains program selection as growing out of a process marked by progressive cognitive and affective effects (McGuire, 1985). The audience first learns about program alternatives, forms attitudes about the program, then decides to watch that program. If expectations are met by the program, attitudes are strengthened and loyalty (or repeat viewing) should result.

Both the low-involvement and the learning processes have ratings as their ultimate goal. They differ, however, in at least two important ways. First, the low-involvement process characterizes program selection as a passive act. Television viewing is more a function of audience availability than of specific programs (Webster & Lichty, 1991). That is, people watch television when they have time to watch. Availability is linked to time of day, where people are, their access to television, and the other constraints on their time. People do not decide to watch programs. First, they decide if they will watch television. Once they decide to watch television, viewers engage in an orienting search, or set of channel-changing patterns to check out which programs are available (Heeter, 1985). They select programs that are either the "least objectionable program" or a familiar alternative.

The learning process characterizes program selection as a mindful act that occurs before television viewing begins. People watch programs, and decide to watch television, if there is a program that they want to watch. People become aware of program offerings, either through guide use or promotional messages (Gantz & Eastman, 1983; Heeter, 1985), they decide which programs they are interested in watching, and then form intentions to watch. Watching a specific program is a function of awareness, attitude, and intention.

The low-involvement and learning processes also differ in relevant outcome variables. Table 2.1 summarizes the two processes and the variables relevant to each. The different assumptions about the audience, coupled with concerns about different outcomes, point out that the concept of audience activity is central in understanding the different communication theories guiding the practice of audience promotion.

TABLE 2.1
Outcome Variables of the Promotion Processes

	Outcome Variables	
	Passive Low-Involvement Model	*Active Learning Model*
Cognitive	Awareness of program/schedule	Attention to the promo
	Familiarity with program	Memory for the promo
Affective	Attitude toward the promo	Attitude toward the program/ network
		Satisfaction with the program/ network
Behavioral	Selection while watching	Intention to watch
		Channel/program loyalty

AUDIENCE ACTIVITY

One enduring concern of media scholars has focused on the nature of the audience. Over the past half-century, there have been two competing views of the audience. One, growing out of sociology's concept of the mass society and psychology's notion of classical conditioning (e.g., De-Fleur & Ball-Rokeach, 1989), considers the audience as exploited by mass communication producers. This passive audience is relatively unselective in their use of mass media and reacts to powerful media messages in predictable ways. The other, growing out of the idealism of libertarianism, considers the audience rational, selective, and self-determining. The active audience selects and uses media content in accordance with their own goals and interests and, generally, is able to resist its influence.

Most programming and promotion research has grounded its research in an assumption of a more passive audience. Effective programming and promotional strategies were seen as able to funnel passive viewers into certain programs and through an evening's programming. A good deal of research supported various approaches to audience flow, such as inheritance effects, channel loyalty, repeat viewing, and double jeopardy (see Webster & Lichty, 1991, and Webster & Phalen, 1997, for summaries). Increases in the number of broadcast and cable television channels, increases in in-home sources for video (VCR and now online delivery), and increased ease in program and channel selection due to the remote control device have all begun to decrease the power of the traditional audience-flow approaches to predict program ratings (see Walker, 1988). Eastman (1998) characterizes the current shifts in the relative activity of the audience as a tension between an active audience and an active media industry. Duality of audience activity is a concept that has been embraced across a range of disciplines. Several theoretical approaches have found value in recognizing that audiences can be more or less active and that different types of activity lead to different communication effects.

Media-Directed Mental Processing.   Perhaps the earliest recognition of variations in audience activity emerged from the study of the effectiveness of television advertising. Krugman (1965, 1966), the originator of the low-involvement model of marketing communication effects, noticed that, unlike advertising in print media, television advertising needed to be reinforced regularly, because it was quickly forgotten. Krugman proposed that mental reactions to media content (specifically advertising) depended, to a large extent, on the medium of advertising. Certain attributes of different media enable or reduce cognitive activity. Print, according to Krugman, is an "inanimate" medium, with consumption controlled by the "animate" audience. The print audience uses its left brain, analytical mental processing, and learns the material and makes personal connections to it. Television, on the other hand, is "animate" while the audience is "inanimate." The television audience uses its right brain, keeping focused on the changing images. The pacing of television engages the audience perceptually, but does not allow them to learn the content or make very many personal connections to it. Audience activity, then, is a function of the audience control over consumption of the medium's delivery of content.

Uses and Gratifications.   Uses and gratifications research recognizes that audiences vary in their willingness and ability to plan, select, attend to, become involved with, and use media content (e.g., Blumler, 1979; Levy & Windahl, 1984; Rubin & Perse, 1987b). Scholars have identified two types of television use, based primarily on audience activity (Rubin, 1984; Rubin & Perse, 1987b). *Ritualistic television use* is a more passive use of television, marked by lower levels of audience activity (Perse, 1990a, 1998; Rubin, 1984; Rubin & Perse, 1987b). Ritualistic television use grows out of desires to fill time by watching television or to use television as background to accompany other tasks. There is little planning of what to watch before viewing and little evidence of polarization of content; a wide variety of different types of programs are viewed—excluding news. While viewing levels are high, attention levels are low and channel changing is common.

Instrumental television use, on the other hand, is a more active use of television (Perse, 1990a, 1998; Rubin, 1984; Rubin & Perse, 1987b). It grows out of desires for information and entertainment. It is a selective approach to watching television, marked by watching specific programs, especially favorite programs and news-oriented programs. Television viewing is planned and attentive. Viewing levels are lower than with ritualistic viewing, but instrumental viewers think about the programs they are watching and do not change channels as much.

Ritualistic and instrumental television uses also differ in the responses they evoke. In general, instrumental use is linked to higher levels of satisfaction with certain television programs and a heightened sense of parasocial interaction (pseudofriendship) with television personalities (Kim & Rubin, 1997; Perse, 1990c; Perse & Ferguson, 1993; Perse & Rubin, 1988).

Elaboration Likelihood Model of Persuasion.   The Elaboration Likelihood Model (ELM) is a general model of persuasion that attempts to explain the contradictory findings of decades of persuasion research. Prior research had found that different types of variables had different effects across different studies. Petty and Cacioppo (1986) proposed that there is no single route to persuasion and that different variables do not have single, predictable impacts on attitudes. According to Petty and Cacioppo, attitude change results from two different routes or processes: central and peripheral routes.[1] The route followed depends on the likelihood that people are going to elaborate, or devote mental energy to considering the message. Petty and Cacioppo recognized that people are rational; they want to feel that their attitudes have some nonrandom basis. But, people are not always motivated or able to devote a good deal of mental energy to forming attitudes. So, elaborating on messages, and the route to attitude change, depends on personal and situational factors.

The *central route* to attitude change is the more cognitively active route. When people are motivated and interested in a topic, they are likely to devote mental energy to paying attention to messages about that topic, considering carefully the information in the message, and forming attitudes based on their mental evaluations of the message. The central route leads to fairly long-term attitude change with resulting actions that conform to attitudes. In the case of television promotion, centrally motivated people would pay attention to promotional messages about programs or topics that are personally important. They would think about the information in the promotion (e.g., topic of the show, stars, plots, time and date), remember the information in the promotional message, form an attitude about the promoted program, and plan to watch or not, based on their own evaluations of the promotional message. If positive attitudes are formed, the central viewer is likely to plan to watch the program. And, because attitudes formed via the central route are fairly predictive of behavior (Petty & Cacioppo, 1986), these viewers are likely to watch.

In this information-saturated world, it is impossible for people to devote a good deal of mental energy to every message that they encounter.

---

[1]Central and peripheral routes of the ELM are conceptually similar to systematic and heuristic processing proposed by Chaiken (1980).

People are not always motivated to follow the central route, especially about topics that lack personal relevance. Moreover, people are not always able to devote the mental energy needed to follow the central route. Sometimes there is no time; decisions have to be made quickly. Or, people may be pressed by other demands on their attention — the distractions of everyday life. But, people still want to feel that their attitudes have some rational basis. When people are not motivated or able to follow the central route, they follow the *peripheral route*. The peripheral route is a less careful consideration of messages. People do not pay attention to the information inherent in the message. Instead their attention is caught by peripheral cues. Peripheral cues are salient production elements of the message. They typically involve the source or spokesperson of the message; source credibility and attraction are peripheral cues. Another peripheral cue can be based on bandwagon effects, or representations of the number of people endorsing an idea (e.g., "the most watched channel in the Delaware Valley"). Based on the positive or negative impressions formed by the peripheral cues, people form attitudes. But, attitudes formed via the peripheral route are relatively short-term. And, they are not necessarily predictive of behavior.

In the case of television promotion, relaxed television viewers might not be motivated to expend a good deal of mental energy considering promotional messages. But, certain salient peripheral cues might capture their attention. The presence of a favorite personality, the hint of sexual innuendo, or the promise of action might lead viewers to feel positively about an upcoming show. Because this attitude was formed without a good deal of mental activity, though, specific intentions to watch the promoted program are not formed. But, the positive feelings about the program could be brought to mind again, especially if those attitudes are cued while viewers are searching for something to watch the evening the program airs.

Automatic and Controlled Mental Activity. Cognitive psychologists recognize that people are neither always highly aware nor always totally mindless. At times we are attentive to the world, consciously alert to our environment and our own responses to it. At other times, we are on "automatic pilot," operating almost unconsciously. This is the distinction between controlled and automatic mental processing (Anderson, 1995; Bargh, 1988; Fiske & Taylor, 1991). *Controlled mental processes* are those that are intentional, deliberate, and require conscious attention. *Automatic mental processes* are relatively effortless, involuntary, and outside our conscious control. The concept of schematic processing helps explain the distinction between controlled and automatic thought.

Cognitive psychologists envision memory as "a large and permanent collection of nodes that become complexly and increasingly interassociated and interrelated through learning" (Schneider & Schiffrin, 1977, p. 2). These associations of nodes of information are termed schemas. A schema is a mental network of concepts that relate to a particular domain (e.g., object, person, or event) developed as a result of prior experience. Schemas are important to cognitive activity because they guide how new information is perceived, interpreted, and learned. Schemas direct how people encode new experiences, how and what they remember and learn from those experiences, and the inferences they draw. Common schemas relate to gender (expectations about males and females), social roles (e.g., politicians, police officers), and specific settings (e.g., restaurant or theme park). People respond to their environment based on the schema, or mental frame, that is top-of-mind.

There are two ways that schemas are brought to mind: through controlled or automatic processes. When people are highly mindful, deliberate, and goal-oriented, their goals direct the selection of the schema, or mental frame, that they will use to evaluate and deal with a situation. For example, a job candidate carefully plans strategies to get information and to make favorable impressions. Or, a politically involved viewer looks for candidate statements about specific issues while watching a televised presidential debate. When people's goals direct the schema that they use, controlled processing results. Controlled processing is similar to the central route of the ELM; it is careful consideration of information that may have longer term effects. Within the context of audience activity, controlled processing is the mark of the active audience.

When people are not so mindful or goal-oriented, schemas are activated or primed by salient cues in the environment. Priming is automatic processing. When a schema is primed and brought to top-of-mind, it is, in a sense, energized. As long as it is top-of-mind, that schema will be used to interpret the environment. Priming is unconscious and relatively short-term; a schema rarely is top-of-mind for more than a few hours. But, once a schema has been primed, it retains some of its energy, and is more easily brought to top-of-mind again. Media content can serve as a potent prime. Much media use serves entertainment and relaxation purposes (Kubey & Csikszentmihalyi, 1990; Rubin, 1984), when people are not necessarily particularly mindful. The less active audience may be more likely to engage in automatic processing.

Implications

Audience activity should be treated as a variable. Audiences can be more or less active depending on the medium that they are using. Television, by the nature of its continuous presentation controlled by the cable or broadcast signal, may not facilitate activity. Greater control, though, offered by technological developments, such as videotape and remote control devices, may have altered Krugman's (1965) propositions. Audience activity may also vary based on the reasons that people have for using media and its content. Programming for which audiences have little affinity may be used ritualistically and passively. Programming that is more important, however, because audiences anticipate learning something, being entertained, or seeing a favorite performer (e.g., Rubin, Perse, & Powell, 1985), is more likely to be instrumental and watched actively. Similarly, active viewers may process television content centrally and in a controlled manner, and form more longer-term attitudes, based on their pre-existing schemas. On the other hand, ritualistic viewers may pay attention to and be affected by more peripheral cues in programs and promotional messages that prime schemas with salient content cues. Because audience activity varies, and different types of activity are associated with different outcomes (see Table 2.1), it is important to consider how to promote to both active and passive audiences.

PROMOTING TO THE PASSIVE AUDIENCE

Most programming research is based on the assumption that television is minimally active. That is, most people watch television for relaxation and watch television relatively passively; while watching, they change channels infrequently. So, the ratings of any program are mainly explained by the ratings of its lead-in program. There are three theoretical approaches that explain how program promotional messages have additional impact on ratings beyond the impact of lead-in program ratings: salience theory, excitation-transfer theory, and the ELM. Table 2.2 lists key research from this perspective.

Salience Theory and Orienting Response

If program promotion is to have any impact on program ratings, it must capture the attention of this passive audience. Salience theory (e.g., Eastman & Newton, 1998, 1999) notes that the location and placement of promotion (among other variables such as genre, station, clutter, and frequency) can increase the ratings of a program significantly. Salience theory is based on the assumption that certain structural and content features of promotional messages attract the attention of the audience. Although attention itself does not ensure the promotion will be effective, it is clear that a promotional message cannot have an effect unless it is noticed. So, salience theory builds on cognitive and perceptual psychology to ex-

TABLE 2.2

Theory and Research Assuming a Passive Audience

Author(s)	Year	Theory/Approach/Findings
Anderson, Alwitt, Lorch, and Levin	1979	Children's visual attention to television is influenced by aspects of program content.
Anderson and Levin	1976	Children's visual attention to television is influenced by aspects of program content.
Brown and Stayman	1992	Attitude toward the ad: A_{ad} affects product purchase intentions.
Bryant and Comisky	1978	Limited capacity: Exciting story content limits recall of subsequent commercials.
Cantor, Bryant, and Zillmann	1974	Excitation transfer: Arousal associated with sexual content increases enjoyment of humor.
Eastman and Newton	1998	Salience theory: Content, structure, and placement of promos influences audience awareness.
Eastman and Newton	1999	Salience theory: Content, structure, and placement of promos influences audience awareness.
Finn and Hickson	1986	Excitation transfer: Interesting commercials have some limited impact on television program appeal.
Goldberg and Gorn	1987	Mood carry-over: Viewers of happy programs rated embedded commercials more effective.
Huston and Wright	1983	Children's visual attention to television is influenced by aspects of program content.
Lang	1990	Orienting response: Structure and content of television commercials affects OR and arousal.
Lang	1991	Limited capacity: Memory for political ads affected by structural features that influence OR.
Lang, Dhillon, and Dong	1995	Orienting response: Positive messages have only limited impact on OR.
Lang, Geiger, Strickwerda, and Sumner	1993	Orienting response: OR affected by video techniques, such as cuts and edits. Limited capacity: OR limits reaction time after orienting content.
Lang, Newhagen, and Reeves	1996	Limited capacity: Negative news stories are associated with greater attention and reduce attention to subsequent stories.
Lang, Sias, Chantrill, and Burek	1995	Limited capacity: Simple narrative structures are more easily remembered.

Levin and Anderson	1976	Children's visual attention to television is influenced by aspects of program content.
Lorch, Anderson, and Levin	1979	Children's visual attention to television is influenced by aspects of program content.
MacKenzie and Spreng	1992	Attitude toward the ad: A_{ad} affects product purchase intentions.
Mathur and Chattopadhyay	1991	Mood carry-over: Congruency between program- and commercial-induced moods.
Mattes and Cantor	1982	Excitation transfer: Commercials after arousing program segments rated more enjoyable.
Muehling and Laczniak	1988	Attitude toward the ad: A_{ad} affects product purchase intentions.
Mundorf, Drew, Zillmann, and Weaver	1990	Limited capacity: Negative news stories are associated with greater attention and reduce attention to subsequent stories.
Newhagen and Reeves	1992	Limited capacity: Negative news stories are associated with greater attention and reduce attention to subsequent stories.
Norris and Colman	1993	Mood carry-over: Congruency between program- and commercial-induced moods.
Pavelchak, Antil, and Munch	1988	Limited capacity: Involvement in viewing football game limits recall of commercials.
Perry, Jenzowsky, Hester, King, and Yi	1997	Excitation transfer: Interesting commercials have some limited impact on television program appeal.
Reeves, Newhagen, Maibach, Basil, and Kurz	1991	Emotional tone of message affects attention and recall.
Reeves, Thorson, and Schleuder	1986	Reaction time to secondary tasks affected by audio and visual complexity of television commercials.
Thorson and Lang	1992	Orienting response: Videographics affected OR and thus led to better recall for familiar material.
Thorson, Reeves, and Schleuder	1987	Limited capacity: More complex audio tracks in television commercials associated with slower reaction times to secondary tasks.
Williams	1989	Sex and violence in TV Guide ads have mixed effects on promoted program ratings.
Zillmann	1980	Excitation transfer: Arousal increases enjoyment for suspense.
Zillmann and Mundorf	1987	Excitation transfer: Arousal associated with sexual content increases enjoyment of music.

Note. OR = orienting response.

plain that certain features of promotional messages will increase the likelihood that they will be noticed and attended to.

Salience theory builds on the concept of *phasic attention* (Lang, 1990). Phasic attention to television involves short-term increases and decreases in the level of attention paid to television during exposure. Phasic attention to television is primarily involuntary and is stimulated by the structural and content features of television.

There are two dominant lines of mass communication research that focus on phasic attention. The first has concentrated on the child audience. This body of research was designed to identify the kinds of content and formal (noncontent) features of television that are associated with children's visual attention to the screen. Based on direct observations of children watching television, researchers found that children's visual attention to television is usually stimulated by the presence of females, other children, puppets, familiar animals, animation, "peculiar" voices, dancing, singing, rhyming, repetition, alliteration, sound effects, and the "fade-to-black" (e.g., Anderson, Alwitt, Lorch, & Levin, 1979; Anderson & Levin, 1976; Huston & Wright, 1983; Levin & Anderson, 1976; Lorch, Anderson, & Levin, 1979).

Although this research has been limited to the child audience, the explanations for the salience of these program features offers insights into the effectiveness of salient program elements for all audiences. Certain aspects of program promotional messages might be more salient, that is, associated with heightened visual attention, for two reasons. First, certain content is associated with stimuli that are rewarding. Women on television attract children's attention, and men depress children's attention, because women are typically children's caretakers, and so are associated with pleasant feelings (Levin & Anderson, 1976). Sexual content is a common aspect of program promotion that has been linked modestly with increased ratings that might be associated with rewards and pleasure (Williams, 1989; see also Walker, chap. 4, this volume). Second, certain content and formal features signal the intended audience for the material (Condry, 1989).

The second line of research on phasic attention to television holds that attention varies mainly because of the *orienting response* (e.g., Lang, 1990; Thorson & Lang, 1992). The orienting response was first described by Pavlov (1927) as an "orientation" to a stimulus that is a "what is this!" reaction. It is viewed as a kind of adaptation to the environment that increases survival because it alerts one to changes that may call for some kind of response. The orienting response is a reflexive and automatic reaction to a stimuli that leads to attentional engagement, or a focus on the stimulus. When an orienting response to television content occurs, viewers focus visual and auditory attention on the television screen, they stop paying as much attention to other distractions in the area, and if the messages are not too complex (taxing the limited capacity of the human brain to process quickly), the message that stimulated the orienting response will be remembered.

Memory and the orienting response are related because certain physiological changes signal that cognitive resources are being devoted to perceiving and processing the stimulus evoking the OR. In television viewing, the orienting response is associated with physical orienting toward the screen. Breathing pauses for a moment, then resumes with shorter, faster breaths. There is increased blood flow to the head and brain, and reduced blood flow to the limbs. Brain activity changes; although there is increased electroencephalogram (EEG) activity, there are lower alpha wave amplitudes (for alpha blocking, see Reeves, Thorson, & Schleuder, 1986; Thorson & Lang, 1992).

Certain aspects of television content can stimulate the orienting response. Novel, surprising, puzzling sights and sounds attract the orienting response as viewers try to figure out what they are and what they mean (Reeves et al., 1986). Even cuts, edits, and other video techniques capture attention because they are unusual in the real world (see Lang, Geiger, Strickwerda, & Sumner, 1993).[2] Movement toward the screen is also associated with the orienting response, perhaps because the moving elements appear, even briefly, to mimic real-world threats (see Lang, 1990). Dramatic content changes, such as commercial onsets, result in orienting responses (Lang, 1990). Emotional content is also associated with heightened arousal, which also increases attention (Lang, 1990).

People become habituated quite readily to certain stimuli, so that they no longer elicit the OR.[3] But, the orienting response is also linked to interesting and meaningful stimuli. For example, when television viewers first encounter the harsh, intrusive, and annoying tones used by many local television stations to signal weather alerts, the orienting response directs attention to the screen. After time, viewers can be habituated to the tones, but they still orient to the screen because they have learned that there is informational value associated with them. So the tones continue to evoke the OR. Similarly, the squeal of tires during a car chase attract the orienting response, because we have learned that those sounds signal danger while driving and action while viewing.

---

[2]The 1999 Gap clothing ad for khaki pants was certainly attention-getting because it was the first to use the multiple-camera technique that appeared to freeze the dancers while the camera moved around them.

[3]As Reeves and his colleagues (1986) pointed out, habituation is adaptive. It would be difficult to manage in everyday life if we were constantly oriented to various stimuli. Humans become familiar with aspects of their environment and learn which ones are deserving of attention.

Although emotion has been associated with the orienting response, there have been questions as to whether the valence (positive or negative) of the emotion matters. Reeves, Newhagen, Maibach, Basil, and Kurz (1991) proposed that positive emotional messages would be remembered better than negative ones for two reasons. First, negative messages, because they have survival value, are processed more automatically. In other words, people can automatically avert themselves from negative stimuli. Moreover, people have a preference for approaching positive stimuli and avoiding negative stimuli, so positive emotion-evoking stimuli should elicit stronger orienting responses. There is only limited support for the superior OR potential of positive messages (Lang, Dhillon, & Dong, 1995). More research finds heightened orienting to and greater memory for negative messages (e.g., Lang, Newhagen, & Reeves, 1996; Newhagen & Reeves, 1992). Some explanations for the impact of negative emotion-invoking stimuli may be the novelty and surprise inherent in negative events. And, perhaps the survival value in paying attention to negative images does override the desire to avoid unpleasant stimuli.

Caution: Limited-Capacity Theory. People have a limited ability to pay attention to and cognitively process information (Broadbent, 1982). Short-term memory, for example, can handle typically no more than seven (plus or minus two) bits of information (Simon, 1974). If viewers are oriented toward something, they cannot be paying full attention to anything else.[4] Television content that elicits the OR, then, has the potential to distract attention from other content. That is, context makes a difference in what will be attended to and remembered.

In studying the effect of video "cuts" on viewers' memory, Lang and her colleagues (1993) found that cuts did attract the orienting response. But, when related material followed a cut, it was associated with slower reaction times to a secondary task, indicating that viewers were devoting more cognitive resources to the material surrounding the unrelated cut. Consistent with limited-capacity theory, material following a related cut was remembered better than material following an unrelated cut. In another study, Lang (1991) found that memory for aspects of political ads was related to position in the ad. Because scene changes lead to orienting responses, ad information distanced from a scene change was remembered better. So, memory for items improves if they are separated a bit from another structural feature that elicits the OR. Similarly, because neg-

---

[4]One research technique used to assess attention to television is reaction time. Viewers engage in a secondary task while watching television. When their performance on the secondary task decreases, it is assumed that they are devoting more time to what they are watching on television (e.g., Reeves et al., 1986).

ative video requires more attention and increases arousal, the orienting response that it evokes can distract viewers from other material in the newscasts. Several studies have found decreased memory for news stories presented before (Newhagen & Reeves, 1992; Lang et al., 1996) and after negative stories (Mundorf, Drew, Zillmann, & Weaver, 1990).

Limited-capacity theory points out that sensory input can tax the cognitive abilities of television viewers and reduce memory for material too close to an OR-eliciting program feature. But, television content can overtax the passive television viewers in other ways. Complex messages can tax not only sensory inputs, but also the ability to derive meaning from the message. Complexity includes "more words and/or pictures per unit time, less familiarity with those words and pictures, [and] the number of sensory channels activated" (Thorson, Reeves, & Schleuder, 1987, p. 368). So, messages that are so complex that they elicit repeated orienting responses will be associated with cognitive overload and confusion. Complex messages will not be consistently attended to or remembered. In fact, attention can also be affected by the complexity of the narrative structure of the material. Simple story lines are more easily remembered (Lang, Sias, Chantrill, & Burek, 1995).

Limited-capacity theory also offers a paradox to professionals who decide where to place advertisements and promotional messages. Although the most popular television programs offer the largest audience and greatest reach, the most popular programs may often be among the most mentally engaging. Involving television programs, however, may require cognitive energy and interest. Viewers who are "caught up" in the action of the program lack the cognitive resources to devote to commercial messages. Bryant and Comisky (1978) found an inverse relationship between how involving program content was and memory for commercials in the programs. Commercials placed at the most suspenseful part of an action-adventure program (after the climax, but before the resolution) were remembered far less than commercials placed after the climax and resolution. Commercials in a control condition of minimally involving video were remembered the best. These findings were supported by research on memory for ads in Super Bowl XX (Pavelchak, Antil, & Munch, 1988). Viewers who were less involved in the action of the game were more likely to remember the ads. People clearly have limited capacity for attention and also for more complex mental engagement.

Implications for Promotion. Salience theory has received some support in studies of promotional message effectiveness. In general, promotional messages are more effective at raising (or maintaining) ratings for familiar, or continuing, rather than new programs (Billings et al., 1998; Eastman & Newton, 1999). Familiarity may signal attention to promotion for programs that viewers have found interesting or rewarding (e.g., Levin & Anderson, 1976). Promotional messages that have salient positions and constructions (first or last in a pod or those that stand alone) are also more effective (Eastman & Newton, 1998, 1999). The effects of limited capacity have been less directly explored with program promotion. The findings that promotional messages are more effective when they stand alone, instead of being combined with other promos (Eastman & Newton, 1998, 1999), offer indications that clutter may tax cognitive resources. The effects of pod position and clutter may be difficult to isolate, however. As Eastman and Newton (1998) pointed out, in this era of remote control devices, the first or last element of the pod may not be the first or last item seen by channel surfers. When taped programs are viewed, zipping may reduce even more exposure to promotional messages with desirable first and last positions (e.g., Cronin & Menelly, 1992). Future research should consider limits on salience theory.

Clearly, though, salience theory offers important advice for program effectiveness. But, research has also found that, in general, salience effects are rather fleeting. That is, when promoting to the passive audience, effects are typically short-term. Promotional messages tend to be more effective when there is a shorter time between promotion and program airing (Billings et al., 1998; Eastman & Newton, 1998; Eastman et al., 1996).

Excitation Transfer

Excitation transfer is a theoretical approach based on physiological response, specifically *arousal*, as a result of mass communication. Arousal is an affective, nonspecific physiological response that is marked by alertness, faster breathing, and increased heart rate (Lang, 1994). Scholars hold that arousal becomes emotion when it is labeled (Schachter, 1964). People label arousal based on context. For example, an exciting sporting match is associated with a good deal of arousal. A viewer will label that arousal as either positive (happiness or joy) or negative (sadness, disappointment, or anger) based on the outcome of the game. Arousal is a relatively short-term state, but it does take some time for it to dissipate. One important implication of excitation transfer is that residual arousal can increase affective reactions to subsequent events. Arousal can be relabeled based on a changing context. So, arousal produced by an exciting sports contest can first be labeled as disappointment, but then be relabeled as anger, if one is cut off by another car when leaving the stadium parking lot.

Excitation-transfer theory recognizes that mass communication has the ability to arouse and that the arousal produced by one message can transfer to another and increase the emotional response to the later message (Zillmann, 1991). One example is the positive emotional responses to suspenseful movies and television (Zillmann, 1980). In real life, suspense is not a pleasant experience. In entertainment, though, it can be satisfying and appealing to audiences. Zillmann (1980) used excitation transfer to explain the appeal of suspense. A well-done drama can heighten arousal, which, in the face of uncertainty, viewers label as suspense. When the suspense is resolved satisfactorily, the residual arousal is labeled as enjoyment. The more arousal, the greater the enjoyment.

There is a good deal of evidence that arousal produced by one aspect of a message can transfer to another. Excitation-transfer effects have been identified with several different kinds of media content: Arousal associated with sexual images leads to greater enjoyment of music (Zillmann & Mundorf, 1987) and humor (Cantor, Bryant, & Zillmann, 1974). Researchers have even found that interesting commercials can increase the appeal of television programs somewhat (e.g., Finn & Hickson, 1986; Perry, Jenzowsky, Hester, King, & Yi, 1997).

Most relevant to program promotion, evaluations of commercials are affected by the programs in which they are embedded. Norris and Colman (1993) found positive evaluations between programs and commercials on such dimensions as boredom and stimulation. Program-produced feelings appear to carry over to commercials. Mathur and Chattopadhyay (1991) noted a congruency between program-induced and commercial-induced moods. Similarly, Goldberg and Gorn (1987) noted that viewers of a happy program, compared to viewers of a sad program, rated embedded commercials more effective and were somewhat more likely to remember the ads. Mattes and Cantor (1982) observed that, compared to nonarousing film segments, 45-second commercials viewed after arousing segments were rated as more enjoyable and more effective. Interestingly, the effect was observed only for the third and fourth commercials out of the five-commercial pod. The researchers explained these effects according to excitation transfer. For the first two commercials (the first 90 seconds of the pod), viewers were aware that their arousal was due to the exciting film. But, for the next two 45-second commercials, they had forgotten and attributed the arousal to the commercials. By the end of the pod, however, the arousal produced by the film had dissipated.

Implications for Promotion.   Excitation transfer offers an interesting counter to limited-capacity theory. From a cognitive, limited-capacity viewpoint, arousing material should inhibit memory for material that follows it. From a more physiological, excitation-transfer viewpoint, when promotional messages follow arousing content, viewers should be more aroused by those promos. Cognitive psychology points out that arousing messages are more memorable (e.g., Lang et al., 1996). Coupled with carry-over effects of program-produced mood, excitation-transfer theory suggests that promotional messages might be more effective in happy, exciting, emotionally-arousing programs. The arousal and mood produced by those programs can transfer to the promotional messages, and may lead those promos to be more effective. Although excitation transfer has not been directly applied to the study of promotional messages until now (see Eastman & Bolls, chap. 3, this volume), there is some modest evidence that program-produced arousal might enhance promotional message effectiveness. Promotional messages airing in a program's end-credits have been found to be more effective (compared to promotional messages in program segments) in programs of midrange ratings (not the highest or lowest rated quartiles; Eastman & Newton, 1998). Perhaps the arousal of the program climax and resolution transfers to the promo. And, the genre compatibility between program and embedded promos modestly linked promotion effectiveness (Eastman et al., 1996) may signal some mood carry over effects. But, once again, it is clear that excitation-transfer effects are fleeting. Arousal does not transfer or mood carry over to promotional messages more than 3 or 4 minutes or so from an arousing program.

Peripheral Route Processing and Attitude Toward the Ad

The learning model of communication effects (McGuire, 1985; Ray, 1973) holds that advertising effects can be explained by a cognitive, deliberate, and involved response to advertising. But, much advertising is for products that are not particularly involving or important. Moreover, consumers encounter most advertising in media exposure situations accompanied by various distractions and at times when they are not particularly willing to invest a good deal of cognitive effort and activity to thinking about commercials. Research that has applied the Elaboration Likelihood Model to advertising effects has led scholars to recognize that central processing of commercials is not the only route to commercial effectiveness. Commercial messages can have effects via the peripheral route. A primary peripheral route to advertising effectiveness is through attitude toward the ad (A_{ad}). Attitude toward the ad is an affective response to a particular commercial generated at the time of exposure (Lutz, 1985). Attitudes toward ads affect consumer behavior indirectly. Liking an ad (A_{ad}) is related to forming more positive impressions about the product that it promotes (attitudes toward the brand) and has also been found to be associated with intentions to purchase products (Brown & Stayman, 1992). Scholars have found that as involvement with products and messages decreases, the impact of A_{ad} on attitudes about brands becomes more important than the thoughts about the brands generated during the commercial (MacKenzie & Spreng, 1992; Muehling & Laczniak, 1988). Quite simply, under conditions of low involvement, liking an ad can lead to favorable impressions of brands.

Research has made it clear that A_{ad} has some antecedents in central processing (e.g., Lord, Lee, & Sauer, 1995); the learning model reinforces the idea that thoughts about products result in attitudes. But, Lutz (1985) pointed out that, during peripheral route processing, A_{ad} is affected by several other responses to the advertisement: impressions of the credibility of the advertisement (e.g., source credibility, a peripheral cue; Petty & Cacioppo, 1986); prior attitudes about advertising, in general, and about the advertiser, in specific; impressions about the execution of the ad (how the ad was created); and moods produced by the ad.

Affective responses appear to be particularly predictive of A_{ad}. Chattopadhyay and Nedungadi (1992) pointed out that, at times, the content of ads is often more complex and not very effective when attention levels are low or distracted (under conditions of low involvement). On the other hand, emotional responses require little effort. Because emotional responses to ads require less attention, affect-laden cues are likely to be more salient. So, affect is the most common peripheral effect. Lutz (1985) summarized some of the affective reactions that grow from exposure to commercials: entertainment, irritation, familiarity, empathy, confusion, dislike, and warmth. According to Lutz, these affective reactions can transfer to attitudes toward the ad through a contextual evaluation transfer: Under conditions of low involvement, some salient aspect of an ad attracts viewers' attention. As a result, viewers have an emotional reaction to the ad (A_{ad}). Attitudes toward the ad transfer to the brand through a priming process (Yi, 1990) in which affective schemas are primed and affect responses to the ad, or through a kind of conditioning, where the positive feelings toward the ad are associated with the product.

Implications of Peripheral A_{ad} Effects. The sheer number of promotional messages as well as the clutter that surrounds advertising (e.g., Eastman & Newton, 1998) suggest that peripheral processing is an important response to watching promotional messages. It would be difficult, if not impossible, for viewers to centrally process all the promotional messages that they encounter. Peripheral processing of salient promos, however, can have some effects on viewers. Viewers can form attitudes toward promotion based on their affective reactions to emotional cues in the promotional messages. Under these conditions, these attitudes toward the promotional messages themselves can be linked to impressions about, attitudes toward, and intentions to watch the program being promoted (e.g., Brown & Stayman, 1992).

A consideration of the peripheral effects of A_{ad} offers additional theoretical information about the effectiveness of promotional messages.

Whereas salience theory focuses, in part, on the attention-attracting features, attitudes toward promotional messages may also be affected by emotional content features (e.g., humor, poignancy, danger) that capture the attention of the more passive viewer. The positive feelings associated with these emotional content features transfer, directly, to positive feelings about the promotion and, indirectly, to positive feelings about the promoted program. But, peripheral effects are generally short-term (Petty & Cacioppo, 1986). In fact, studies have found that A_{ad} is not very enduring (Chattopadhyay & Nedungadi, 1992).

Assumption, Benefits, and Limitations of Promoting to a Passive Audience

These three theoretical approaches to explaining promotional effectiveness are built on the assumption of a passive audience that is responsive to cues inherent in media content. Together, these three approaches focus on cognitive and affective outcomes considered important by the low-involvement model of communication effects (Ray, 1973). Salience theory focuses on the effects of promotional message elements on memory for the messages. If viewers remember the promotional message, then it has made some sort of impression and, perhaps, viewers have become more familiar with the promoted program. Excitation transfer and peripheral attitudes toward the promotional message (A_{ad}) focus on the affective responses by the passive audience to promotional messages. Excitation transfer suggests that arousing programs may lead to enhanced emotional responses to subsequent promotional messages and that positive responses to programs may carry over to subsequent promotional messages. The Elaboration Likelihood Model explains that emotional cues in promos may lead viewers to form positive attitudes toward those messages, which can then carry over to the program. Awareness of programs, familiarity with programs, and positive attitudes about the programs may have their largest impact during orienting searches, when viewers are trying to find something to watch (Heeter, 1985). A program's memorable cues, associated with positive feelings, may be noticed while viewers are searching among different channels in their repertoires, and viewers may decide to stop searching and sample the promoted program.

There are several benefits to using theories that aid promoting to a passive audience. Certainly, there is a good deal of evidence that television viewing is a rather passive activity. Much television viewing fills time or is used for relaxation. Because passive approaches focus on effective message creation, many of the effects of promotional messages are under the control of media producers. That is, they can control the program clips and emotional tone of the promotion, thus affecting the salience of different cues. The kinds of things that attract people's attention, for the most part, are, in theory, if not in practice, rather predictable, as are the affective responses to those cues. So, there is less likelihood of widespread boomerang effects; knowledgeable producers should not encounter unexpected effects from their promotion. Most important, there is evidence that these theories explain audience effects. Salience and affective responses lead to awareness, familiarity, and program sampling.

There are some limitations to relying on passive approaches to program promotion. First, different theories offer contradictory guidelines. Salience theory suggests that if on-air promos are placed first or last in a pod, they are more likely to be noticed. But, limited-capacity theory points out that last memory of the last items in a pod might be limited because of salience of earlier items "clogging" short-term memory and rehearsal. And, excitation transfer holds that affective reactions to first and final items might be lost. Even the salience of stand-alone promos during the end-credits of programs might be negatively affected by the distraction of mental activity devoted to plot resolution.

Another limitation of promoting to a passive audience is the impact of surrounding media content on promotional effectiveness. If audiences are responsive to the salience of content elements, executional cues, and emotional aspects of promotional messages, then they are equally responsive to those aspects of programs and other commercials. In other words, context has an important impact on the effectiveness of promotional messages. Although producers have a good deal of control over creation of the promotional messages, they may have less control over the other content surrounding them. Salience theory and excitation transfer both caution producers to be aware of interactive effects of surrounding material. The interaction of context and promotion may lead to unanticipated impacts on the attitudes toward the promotional messages.

The major limitation of promoting to a passive audience is the short-term nature of the effects of promotion. It is clear that the effects of salience, excitation transfer, and A_{ad} are all relatively brief. Although there are conflicting findings about the effects of frequency on promotion effectiveness (see Eastman & Newton, 1998; Walker, 1993), reinforcement may be an important component of promotion. Repetition reinforces salience and emotional cues and keeps familiarity at top-of-mind. At any rate, there is one clear way to benefit from promotion's short-term effects — the most effective promotional messages are those fairly close to the program airing.

A final limitation of passive approaches is that they focus only on a single goal: encouraging sampling of programs. In order to satisfy a second goal of promotion — to build program and channel loyalty — we need to consider theoretical approaches that build on notions of an active audience.

PROMOTING TO THE ACTIVE AUDIENCE

Audience activity has several dimensions: (a) selectivity, especially selective exposure and attention to media content; (b) utilitarianism, or selecting media content to satisfy personal goals; (c) intentionality, planned and goal-directed media use; and (d) involvement, cognitive effort and affective responses (Blumler, 1979; Levy & Windahl, 1985; Rubin & Perse, 1987b). When audiences are active, they are more attentive to media content that helps them achieve their goals, select media content based on expectations and attitudes that they have, and respond cognitively and affectively (e.g., Perse, 1990b, 1998). The concept of the active audience implies "a vigilant, self-directed, rationalistic consciousness aware of its needs and motivations, bending media materials in pursuit of these motivations and in the maintenance of cognitive independence" (Biocca, 1988, p. 63).

Audience activity is a core concept of the uses and gratifications perspective. As an audience-centered approach to the study of mass communication, it focuses on what people do with mass media, rather than what media do to people. Uses and gratifications research focuses on many of the same questions as other media perspectives (e.g., program selection and media effects), but focuses on the deliberate action of the audience. Audience activity can offer insights into how to promote to the active viewer: (a) to attract the attention of the selective viewer; (b) to encourage intentionality, or planning to watch programs that have been promoted; and (c) to develop program and/or channel loyalty through satisfaction. Table 2.3 lists key research utilizing this research perspective.

Selective Attention to Promotional Messages

Most of the research that considers the active audience has focused on selective exposure, or selection of specific programs or genres. Research on *selective attention* to television content has been, for the most part, limited to research that focuses on automatic, or involuntary attention (Lang, 1990). Cognitive psychology, though, has emphasized a distinction between automatic and controlled processing (e.g., Anderson, 1995; Wyer & Srull, 1986). Whereas automatic processing builds on involuntary attention to salient program cues, controlled processing is directed by the goals of the individual viewer (Wyer & Srull, 1986). Cues in the environment are noticed and attended to because they have relevance.

Research in marketing has shown that the goals that people have when they watch advertisements affect their attention to certain aspects of the ads. Park and Young (1986), for example, found that, compared to participants who were focused on their own affective responses to commercials, participants who were focused toward trying to learn about product at-

TABLE 2.3

Theory and Research Assuming an Active Audience

Author(s)	Year	Theory/Approach/Findings
Blumler	1979	Audience activity: Dimensions.
Galloway and Meek	1981	Expectancy value: People watch programs that have valued attributes.
Garramone	1983	Selectivity: Motives for watching political ads affects selective attention to aspects of the ads.
Levy and Windahl	1985	Audience activity: Dimensions.
Palmgreen and Rayburn	1982	Expectancy value: People watch programs that have valued attributes.
Palmgreen and Rayburn	1985a,b	Satisfaction: Based on programs meeting expectations.
Park and Young	1986	Selectivity: Motives for watching commercials affects selective attention to aspects of commercials.
Perse	1990a	Selectivity: Instrumental viewing motives associated with greater selectivity. Intentionality: Instrumental viewing motives and affinity associated with greater intentionality.
Perse	1990b	Selectivity: Motives for watching local news affects selective attention to different news reports.
Perse	1992	Selectivity: Motives for watching local news affects selective attention to different news reports.
Perse	1998	Selectivity: Favorite programs associated with greater attention and less channel changing.
Perse and Ferguson	1993	Satisfaction: Satisfaction related to instrumental viewing motives.
Perse and Rubin	1988	Satisfaction: Satisfaction related to affinity and attentions.
Rubin and Perse	1987b	Audience activity: Dimensions. Selectivity: Instrumental viewing motives associated with greater selectivity. Intentionality: Instrumental viewing motives and affinity associated with greater intentionality. Parasocial interaction: Associated with greater intentionality.
Rubin, Perse, and Powell	1985	Parasocial interaction: Associated with greater exposure to programs and instrumental viewing motives.

41

tributes remembered more of the attributes. Similarly, Garramone (1983) noted that, compared to "issue-oriented" viewers of political ads, "image-oriented" viewers of the same ads paid more attention to the video (rather than the audio), had more confidence in their abilities to recall the video, and formed impressions of the candidate based more on the video information.

Uses and gratifications explains that the goals, or *motives*, that people have for using media affect their attention to certain program aspects. Perse (1990b, 1992) noted that local news viewers who were motivated to seek useful information while watching local news were more likely to pay attention to the government reports in the news than those viewers watching for entertainment or to pass time. Instrumental viewing motives, or those that focus directly on the benefits of watching specific program content, are associated with higher levels of selective attention (Perse, 1990a, 1998; Rubin & Perse, 1987b). Instrumental motives typically include information, or seeking program content for learning or social utility, entertainment, and excitement and arousal. In the case of promotion, then, the active audience may be more likely to pay selective attention to promos for programs that focus on the useful information in and the excitement of the promoted program and subsequently remember details about the promoted programs (e.g., schedule).

Another aspect of instrumental viewing motives is relevant to program promotion. When people watch favorite programs, they are more likely to watch for instrumental reasons, pay greater attention to the program, think more about the program content, and change channels less (Perse, 1998). As the television programming becomes more diverse and specialized, the audience will most likely become more polarized and instrumental, that is, seek specific content and avoid others (Webster & Phalen, 1997). Program promotion can take advantage of the specialized audience to promote specific programs to those viewers who already prefer certain content. Or, targeted promotional messages can be created for different outlets to promote the same program using different strategies to attract specialized audiences.

Intention to Watch a Promoted Program

One of the major differences in promoting to an active rather than a passive audience is that the active audience is selective and *intentional*. That is, the active audience plans to watch programs and "makes appointments" for certain programs (e.g., Levy & Windahl, 1985; Perse, 1990a). Promotional messages may be most effective when they increase intentionality, that is, lead audience members to become more active — to plan to watch specific programs. There are several guidelines from uses and gratifications to enhance intentionality. First, intentionality is linked to instrumental viewing motives (Perse, 1990a; Rubin & Perse, 1987b). Promotional messages that emphasize instrumental benefits to viewers may increase intention and planning to watch programs. Second, affinity for a specific program, or feelings that the program is important, is a potent correlate of intentionality (Perse, 1990a; Rubin & Perse, 1987b). Promotional messages directed toward the active audience should aim to increase program affinity and attempt to convince viewers that the program content is important and meaningful because it will help satisfy instrumental goals (e.g., information, social utility, excitement, and entertainment).

A third strategy drawn from uses and gratifications is the concept of *parasocial interaction*. Parasocial interaction refers to a sense of pseudo-friendship with a specific television personality. Although some of the initial writings on parasocial interaction assumed that only certain television viewers formed parasocial relationships — viewers with a lack of social connections to others (e.g., Horton & Wohl, 1956; Rosengren & Windahl, 1972; Rubin et al., 1985) — it is clear that parasocial interaction is a normal and typical response to television viewing (Perse & Rubin, 1989). People naturally form "relationships" with others who are appealing and enjoyable. Parasocial interaction is a response to selective and instrumental use of specific television programs (e.g., Rubin & Perse, 1987b; Rubin et al., 1985). It is a particularly valuable concept for researching and producing promotion because it is also related to higher levels of viewing programs that feature the favorite character as well as higher levels of intentionality (Rubin & Perse, 1987a). So, people are likely to plan to watch programs that include their favorite personalities. To build on these preferences of the active audience, promotional messages might sacrifice salient cues associated with the orienting response to focus on the appearance and likability of performers with audience appeal — those with whom targeted viewers are likely to have developed parasocial relationships.

Expectancy-Value Theory. Expectancy-value theory is a cognitive approach to understanding why people act. The theory views behavior as a function of (a) *expectancy*, or the perceptions that a certain object or action has certain attributes or consequences, and (b) *evaluation*, or the positive or negative value placed on the attribute or consequence (Fishbein & Ajzen, 1975; Palmgreen & Rayburn, 1985a). Uses and gratifications researchers have noted the similarities between expectancy-value theory and uses and gratifications (e.g., Galloway & Meek, 1981; Palmgreen & Rayburn, 1982). Uses and gratifications holds that people select media content based on expectations that it will help them achieve their goals (e.g., Katz, Blumler, & Gurevitch, 1974). Research has demonstrated that the beliefs that people have about the attributes of specific television programs, coupled with their evaluations about the value of those attributes, is linked to watching those programs (Galloway & Meek, 1981). The more strongly valued attributes are believed to be present in certain programs, the more likely people are to watch those programs.

Fishbein and Ajzen (1975) argued that expectancy-value theory should not necessarily consider behavior as its only dependent variable. Instead, intention to act is the single best predictor of whether someone will act. People, however, may not necessarily act in accordance with their intentions. But, certain conditions may enhance the connection between intention and behavior. First, the shorter the time period between the time that the intention is formed and the behavior, the more likely intention will translate into action. So, the time between promotional messages and the program they promote should be relatively short. Second, intentions are stronger when they are at the same level of abstraction as the behavior. That is, an intention to watch a specific episode of a dramatic episode of a program on a specific night is more likely to be linked to viewing than an intention to watch the program sometime. Thus, promotional messages should be more likely to be linked to episode ratings if they promote specific episodes. Third, attitudes formed via a more central route with more cognitive energy and effort are more likely to be long lasting and are more predictive of behavior (Petty & Cacioppo, 1986). Programmers can be somewhat more secure that the active audience is more likely to watch programs that they intend to watch.

Channel/Program Loyalty and Satisfaction

Promoting to an active audience allows for different types of outcome variables than promoting to a more passive audience (see Table 2.1). With an active audience, it is possible to consider such long-term effects of promotion as channel/program loyalty. *Channel loyalty* is one kind of audience duplication that marks the nonrandom tendency of viewers to watch different programs on the same channel/network. Channel loyalty is a reality; Webster and Lichty (1991) report that "the audience for one network show is 50% to 60% more likely than the population in general to watch that network on another day" (p. 172). Program loyalty is repeat viewing, the nonrandom tendency for audiences of one episode of a program to watch another episode. On daily programs, repeat viewing is typically around 50% (60% for soap operas). For weekly programs, repeat viewing is lower, about 25% to 30% (Webster & Lichty, 1991). Structural aspects of television, such as audience availability (represented by the time of day the program airs), program rating, and story line (continuing or not) account for a majority of the variance in repeat viewing (e.g., Webster & Lichty, 1991; Webster & Wang, 1992), but some individual factors, such as satisfaction with a program, could contribute to channel/program loyalty.

Satisfaction is an "affective emotional reaction that grows out of confirmation or disconfirmation of product expectations" (Perse & Rubin, 1988,

p. 368). Satisfaction is important because it affects purchase and consumption. With mass communication "products," more satisfied newspaper subscribers spend more time reading the papers (Burgoon & Burgoon, 1980), more satisfied cable subscribers are less likely to discontinue service (LaRose & Atkin, 1988), and more satisfied soap opera viewers spend more time watching their favorite serial (Perse & Rubin, 1988). Promotion may contribute to channel/program satisfaction because it is one of the "loyalty-producing factors" that can increase viewership (Cooper, 1993).

Promotion may contribute to satisfaction by enhancing the gratifications, or benefits, the viewers obtain from watching a program. Promotion, by its nature, is made up of snippets of programs that emphasize certain themes, personalities, plots, or action. According to expectancy-value theory, promotional messages may lead to program selection, as viewers believe that the program has certain valued attributes (those highlighted in the promotion). If those expectations are met, satisfaction with the program follows (Palmgreen & Rayburn, 1985b; see also Eastman & Bolls' explanation of expectancy theory in chap. 3, this volume).

Interestingly, program satisfaction seems to grow out of a transactional process (Wenner, 1985). That is, the gratifications obtained from watching a television program are not the sole predictors of program satisfaction. Satisfaction is also linked to affinity, or perceived importance of the program (Perse & Rubin, 1988); program affinity and satisfaction go hand in hand. Satisfaction is linked to higher levels of voluntary attention while watching the program (Perse & Rubin, 1988). And, satisfaction is also a consequence of the gratifications sought from the program, or the reasons for watching (Palmgreen & Rayburn, 1985b; Perse & Ferguson, 1993; Perse & Rubin, 1988). More instrumental reasons for watching a program are associated with greater satisfaction. There are two explanations for motives' impact on satisfaction. First, more instrumental viewing motives signal a more active viewer who anticipates watching the program and is more attentive while watching. Intentionality and attention are both linked to satisfaction. Second, the motives, or expectations, that people have color their experience (Eastman & Bolls, chap. 3, this volume). That is, anticipation can shape experience. Cognitive psychology would explain that processing goals guide controlled information processing (Wyer & Srull, 1986). If a viewer watches a program expecting to learn something, that goal activates schemas and attentional effort appropriate to satisfying that goal. In other words, viewers contribute to their own satisfaction, perhaps as much as the program content.[5] Promotion can work to increase satisfac-

---

[5]Certainly content is not irrelevant to program satisfaction. If a viewer plans to learn or be excited by a program, and he or she is not, disconfirmation of expectations will lead to dissatisfaction with the program that may transfer to other content from the same source.

tion, then, by increasing viewers' realistic expectations about the program, so that viewers will watch for instrumental, more active reasons.[6]

Benefits and Limitations of Promoting to an Active Audience

The clear benefit of promoting to an active audience lies in the nature of the effects. Effects are likely to be long-term. Memory for upcoming programs and their schedules may be more enduring, leading to intention to watch. Because active audiences are more selective and intentional, programmers will not have to rely as much on salience to result in program sampling during orienting searches for something to watch. Instead, the active viewer knows ahead which programs he or she is planning to watch. Another benefit is that promotion can aim for different, longer term goals — especially satisfaction leading to channel/program loyalty and repeat viewing.

The major limitation to directing promotional messages at an active audience is that, for now, structural features of television still account for most of the variance in ratings. Much program selection is still passive and ritualistic (Bellamy & Walker, 1996; Ferguson & Perse, 1993). Individual factors account for only small amounts (Webster & Lichty, 1991; Webster & Wang, 1992). But, as the audience becomes more fragmented and polarized according to taste and interest, the enhanced potential for activity may increase promotion's impact on ratings. The online audience of web-based content appears to be a very active audience, sampling quickly and moving rapidly through web pages (Huberman, Pirolli, Pitkow, & Lukose, 1998). The wealth of content options and ease of access encourage sampling, but also polarization (i.e., bookmarks and favorites). Promotion may alert interested viewers to sample offerings on new outlets, remind them of interesting material on familiar outlets, and lead them to place certain channels in their channel repertoires. Because the changing media environment enhances audience activity, active strategies may become more valuable.

DIRECTIONS FOR FUTURE RESEARCH

Marketing communication scholars have long recognized that the concept of audience activity is central to understanding not only the effects of

---

[6]Similarly, promotion designed to appeal to certain demographic groups that repeatedly features sexual innuendo or extremely aggressive behavior from program episodes, even though those elements do not reflect the overall program, sets up unrealistic expectations that might generate dissatisfaction with the source in the long-term. NBC learned this lesson in the early 1980s.

communication, but the processes through which audiences are affected. The tension between the active audience and the active media industry (Eastman, 1998) is becoming more relevant, as the newer media environment offers more choices and ease of accessing those choices. Theories that assume promotion toward a passive audience have been and will continue to be useful. Their focus on salient content features that attract involuntary attention and produce arousal and moods still leads to awareness, familiarity, and sampling. But, as the audience becomes more fragmented and selective, creating low-level, short-term awareness and familiarity may not be sufficient to result in sampling. Promotional messages directed toward a more active audience may lead to more long-term effects, especially intention to watch a program and satisfaction leading to channel and/or program loyalty.

Research into the effects of promotion offer a fruitful area for testing theories based on both passive and active audiences. Although most research on program promotion is based on effectiveness, or how promotion increases audience size, future research should be undertaken to resolve inconsistencies among theories and to identify the processes involved in effects.

Promoting to the Passive Audience

For future research adopting the passive perspective, questions such as the following stand out: Does the genre of the promoted program affect the effects of promotion? Are there differences between the processes and effects of promotion for news and entertainment? On a broader front, researchers should ask what the nature of the cognitive effect is according to salience theory. Is it memory, recall, impression, or familiarity? Or should some of these concepts be reconceptualized? Can research resolve the contradictory hypotheses proposed by salience, limited-capacity, and excitation-transfer theories? How do the processes of effects proposed by these three approaches differ?

The industry will be interested in how attitudes toward promotion, in general, and to specific promotional messages, in particular, affect program sampling. Practitioners want to know what kinds of affects produced by promotion are most likely to lead to program sampling. More theoretically, scholars need to ask when program contexts increase cognitive and affective effects of promotion and when they decrease those effects.

Promoting to the Active Audience

From the active audience perspective, the questions are quite different. Researchers need to investigate how cognitive (recall) and affective (attitude) effects of promotions differ for instrumental and ritualistic television viewers. Here the key question is whether different types of promos are more effective for instrumental and ritualistic television viewers. Further in this vein, researchers should identify the predictors of intentionality and the ways that promotion increases intentionality.

A related question is whether parasocial interaction increases the effectiveness of promotion that highlights program personalities. For example, does parasocial interaction increase program sampling and loyalty? And in relation to viewer expectations, studies need to investigate the ways in which confirmation and/or violation of program expectancies created by promotion affect channel/program loyalty.

Newer Media Technologies

The newest media technologies raise further questions and reassessments of the answers to old ones. For example, how effective are promotional messages that are viewed at fast speed (while being zipped on videotape)? Can channel switchers be affected by brief glimpses of promotional messages? In sum, researchers need to explore the factors that can increase effects of brief exposure to promotion.

Much of the research on the effectiveness of promotion has been based on content analysis of promotional messages. Future research should use other research methods, such as cross-sectional and panel surveys and laboratory and field experiments, to uncover how the active and passive audience responds to promotion. Understanding the context and process of effects will not only increase theoretical understanding of message effects in general, but also offer practical information to industry practitioners.

REFERENCES

Anderson, D. R., Alwitt, L. F., Lorch, E. P., & Levin, S. R. (1979). Watching children watch television. In G. Hale & M. Lewis (Eds.), *Attention and cognitive development* (pp. 331–361). New York: Plenum.

Anderson, D. R., & Levin, S. R. (1976). Young children's attention to Sesame Street. *Child Development, 47,* 806–811.

Anderson, J. R. (1995). *Cognitive psychology and its implications* (4th ed.). New York: Freeman.

Bargh, J. A. (1988). Automatic information processing: Implications for communication and affect. In L. Donohew, H. H. E. Sypher, & E. T. Higgins (Eds.), *Communication, social cognition, and affect* (pp. 9–32). Hillsdale, NJ: Lawrence Erlbaum Associates.

Bellamy, R. V., Jr., & Walker, J. R. (1996). *Television and the remote control: Grazing on a vast wasteland.* New York: Guilford.

Billings, A. C., Eastman, S. T., & Newton, G. D. (1998). Atlanta revisited: Prime-time promotion in the 1996 Summer Olympics. *Journal of Sport & Social Issues, 22,* 65–78.

Biocca, F. A. (1988). Opposing conceptions of the audience: The active and passive hemispheres of mass communication theory. In J. A. Anderson (Ed.), *Communication yearbook* (Vol. 11, pp. 51–80). Newbury Park, CA: Sage.

Blumler, J. G. (1979). The role of theory in uses and gratifications studies. *Communication Research, 11,* 51–80.

Broadbent, D. E. (1982). Task combination and selective intake of information. *Acta Psychologica, 50,* 253–290.

Brown, S. P., & Stayman, D. M. (1992). Antecedents and consequences of attitude toward the ad: A meta-analysis. *Journal of Consumer Research, 19,* 34–51.

Bryant, J., & Comisky, P. W. (1978). The effect of positioning a message within differentially cognitively involving portions of a television segment on recall of the message. *Human Communication Research, 5,* 63–75.

Burgoon, J. K., & Burgoon, M. (1980). Predictors of newspaper readership. *Journalism Quarterly, 57,* 589–596.

Cameron, G. T., Schleuder, J., & Thorson, E. (1991). The role of news teasers in processing TV news and commercials. *Communication Research, 18,* 667–684.

Cantor, J., Bryant, J., & Zillmann, D. (1974). Enhancement of humor appreciation by transferred excitation. *Journal of Personality and Social Psychology, 30,* 812–821.

Chaiken, S. (1980). Heuristic versus systematic information processing and the use of source versus message cues in persuasion. *Journal of Personality and Social Psychology, 39,* 752–766.

Chattopadhyay, A., & Nedungadi, P. (1992). Does attitude toward the ad endure? The moderating effects of attention and delay. *Journal of Consumer Research, 19,* 26–33.

Condry, J. (1989). *The psychology of television.* Hillsdale, NJ: Lawrence Erlbaum Associates.

Cooper, R. (1993). An expanded, integrated model for determining audience exposure to television. *Journal of Broadcasting & Electronic Media, 37,* 401–418.

Cronin, J. J., & Menelly, N. E. (1992). Discrimination vs. avoidance: "Zipping" of television commercial. *Journal of Advertising, 21*(2), 1–7.

DeFleur, M. L., & Ball-Rokeach, S. (1989). *Theories of mass communication* (5th ed.). New York: Longman.

Eastman, S. T. (1998). Programming theory under stress: The active industry and the active audience. In M. E. Roloff (Ed.), *Communication yearbook* (Vol. 21, pp. 323–377). Thousand Oaks, CA: Sage.

Eastman, S. T., & Newton, G. D. (1998). The impact of structural salience within on-air promotion. *Journal of Broadcasting & Electronic Media, 42,* 50–79.

Eastman, S. T., & Newton, G. D. (1999). Hitting promotion hard: A network response to channel surfing and new competition. *Journal of Applied Communication Research, 27,* 73–85.

Eastman, S. T., Newton, G. D., & Pack, L. (1996). Promoting prime-time programs in megasporting events. *Journal of Broadcasting & Electronic Media, 40,* 366–388.

Eastman, S. T., & Otteson, J. L. (1994). Promotion increases ratings, doesn't it? The impact of program promotion on the 1992 Olympics. *Journal of Broadcasting & Electronic Media, 38,* 307–322.

Ferguson, D. A., Eastman, S. T., & Klein, R. A. (1999). Marketing the media: Scope and goals. In S. T. Eastman, D. A. Ferguson, & R. A. Klein (Eds.), *Promotion and marketing for broadcasting and cable* (3rd ed., pp. 1–28). Boston: Focal Press.

Ferguson, D. A., & Perse, E. M. (1993). Media and audience influences on channel repertoire. *Journal of Broadcasting & Electronic Media, 37,* 31–47.

Finn, S., & Hickson, T. M. (1986). Impact of arousing commercials on perceptions of TV news. *Journalism Quarterly, 63,* 369–371.

Fishbein, M., & Ajzen, I. (1975). *Belief, attitude, intention and behavior: An introduction to theory and research.* Reading, MA: Addison-Wesley.

Fiske, S. T., & Taylor, S. E. (1991). *Social cognition* (2nd ed.). New York: McGraw-Hill.

Galloway, J. J., & Meek, F. L. (1981). Audience uses and gratifications: An expectancy model. *Communication Research, 8,* 435–449.

Gantz, W., & Eastman, S. T. (1983). Viewer uses of promotional media to find out about television programs. *Journal of Broadcasting, 27,* 269–277.

Garramone, G. A. (1983). Issue versus image orientation and effects of political advertising. *Communication Research, 10,* 59–76.

Goldberg, M. E., & Gorn, G. J. (1987). Happy and sad TV programs: How they affect reactions to commercials. *Journal of Consumer Research, 14,* 387–403.

Heeter, C. (1985). Program selection with abundance of choice: A process model. *Human Communication Research, 12,* 126–152.

Horton, D., & Wohl, R. R. (1956). Mass communication and para-social interaction: Observations on intimacy at a distance. *Psychiatry, 19,* 215–229.

Huberman, B. A., Pirolli, P. L. T., Pitkow, J. E., & Lukose, R. M. (1998). Strong regularities in World Wide Web surfing. *Science, 280,* 95–97.

Huston, A. C., & Wright, J. C. (1983). Children's processing of television: The informative functions of formal features. In J. Bryant & D. R. Anderson (Eds.), *Children's understanding of television: Research on attention and comprehension* (pp. 35–68). New York: Academic Press.

Katz, E., Blumler, J. G., & Gurevitch, M. (1974). Utilization of mass communication by the individual. In J. G. Blumler & E. Katz (Eds.), *The uses of mass communications: Current perspectives on gratifications research* (pp. 19–32). Beverly Hills, CA: Sage.

Kim, J., & Rubin, A. M. (1997). The variable influence of audience activity on media effects. *Communication Research, 24,* 107–135.

Krugman, H. E. (1965). The impact of television advertising: Learning without involvement. *Public Opinion Quarterly, 29,* 349–356.

Krugman, H. E. (1966). The measurement of audience involvement. *Public Opinion Quarterly, 30,* 583–596.

Kubey, R., & Csikszentmihalyi, M. (1990). *Television and the quality of life: How viewing shapes everyday experiences.* Hillsdale, NJ: Lawrence Erlbaum Associates.

Lang, A. (1990). Involuntary attention and physiological arousal evoked by structural features and emotional content in TV commercials. *Communication Research, 17,* 275–299.

Lang, A. (1991). Emotion, formal features, and memory for televised political advertisements. In F. Biocca (Ed.), *Television and political advertising: Vol. 1. Psychological processes* (pp. 221–243). Hillsdale, NJ: Lawrence Erlbaum Associates.

Lang, A. (1994). What can the heart tell us about thinking? In A. Lang (Ed.), *Measuring psychological responses to media* (pp. 99–111). Hillsdale, NJ: Lawrence Erlbaum Associates.

Lang, A., Dhillon, K., & Dong, Q. (1995). The effects of emotional arousal and valence on television viewers' cognitive capacity and memory. *Journal of Broadcasting & Electronic Media, 39,* 313–327.

Lang, A., Geiger, S., Strickwerda, M., & Sumner, J. (1993). The effects of related and unrelated cuts on television viewers' attention, processing capacity, and memory. *Communication Research, 20,* 4–29.

Lang, A., Newhagen, J., & Reeves, B. (1996). Negative video as structure: Emotion, attention, capacity, and memory. *Journal of Broadcasting & Electronic Media, 40,* 460–477.

Lang, A., Sias, P. M., Chantrill, P., & Burek, J. A. (1995). Tell me a story: Narrative elaboration and memory for television. *Communication Reports, 8,* 102–110.

LaRose, R., & Atkin, D. (1988). Satisfaction, demographic, and media environment predictors of cable subscription. *Journal of Broadcasting & Electronic Media, 32,* 403–413.

Levin, S. R., & Anderson, D. R. (1976). The development of attention. *Journal of Communication, 26*(2), 126–135.

Levy, M. R., & Windahl, S. (1984). Audience activity and gratifications: A conceptual clarification and exploration. *Communication Research, 11,* 51–78.

Levy, M. R., & Windahl, S. (1985). The concept of audience activity. In K. E. Rosengren, L. A. Wenner, & P. Palmgreen (Eds.), *Media gratifications research: Current perspectives* (pp. 109–122). Beverly Hills, CA: Sage.

Lorch, E. P., Anderson, D. R., & Levin, S. R. (1979). The relationship of visual attention to children's comprehension of television. *Child Development, 50,* 722–727.

Lord, K. R., Lee, M., & Sauer, P. L. (1995). The combined influence hypothesis: Central and peripheral antecedents of attitude toward the ad. *Journal of Advertising, 24*(1), 73–85.

Lutz, R. J. (1985). Affective and cognitive antecedents of attitude toward the ad: A conceptual framework. In L. F. Alwitt & A. A. Mitchell (Eds.), *Psychological processes and advertising effects: Theory, research, and application* (pp. 45–63). Hillsdale, NJ: Lawrence Erlbaum Associates.

MacKenzie, S. B., & Spreng, R. A. (1992). How does motivation moderate the impact of central and peripheral processing on brand attitudes and intentions? *Journal of Consumer Research, 18,* 519–529.

Mathur, M., & Chattopadhyay, A. (1991). The impact of moods generated by television programs on responses to advertising. *Psychology and Marketing, 8,* 59–77.

Mattes, J., & Cantor, J. (1982). Enhancing responses to television advertisements via the transfer of residual arousal from prior programming. *Journal of Broadcasting, 26,* 553–566.

McGuire, A. J. (1985). Attitudes and attitude change. In G. Lindzey & E. Aronson (Eds.), *The handbook of social psychology: Vol 2. Special fields and applications* (3rd ed., pp. 233–346). New York: Random House.

Muehling, D. D., & Laczniak, R. N. (1988). Advertising's immediate and delayed influence on brand attitudes: Considerations across message-involvement levels. *Journal of Advertising, 17*(4), 23–34.

Mundorf, N., Drew, D., Zillmann, D., & Weaver, J. (1990). Effects of disturbing news on recall of subsequently presented news. *Communication Research, 17,* 601–615.

Newhagen, J. E., & Reeves, B. (1992). The evening's bad news: Effects of compelling negative television news images on memory. *Journal of Communication, 42*(2), 25–41.

Norris, C. E., & Colman, A. M. (1993). Context effects on memory for television advertisements. *Social Behavior and Personality, 21,* 279–296.

Palmgreen, P., & Rayburn, J. D., II. (1982). Gratifications sought and media exposure: An expectancy value model. *Communication Research, 9,* 561–580.

Palmgreen, P., & Rayburn, J. D., II. (1985a). An expectancy-value approach to media gratifications. In K. E. Rosengren, L. A. Wenner, & P. Palmgreen (Eds.), *Media gratifications research: Current perspectives* (pp. 61–72). Beverly Hills, CA: Sage.

Palmgreen, P., & Rayburn, J. D., II. (1985b). A comparison of gratification models of media satisfaction. *Communication Monographs, 52,* 334–346.

Park, C. W., & Young, S. M. (1986). Consumer response to television commercials: The impact of involvement and background music on brand attitude formation. *Journal of Marketing Research, 23*(1), 11–24.

Pavelchak, M. A., Antil, A. H., & Munch, J. M. (1988). The Super Bowl: An investigation into the relationship among program context, emotional experiences, and ad recall. *Journal of Consumer Research, 15,* 360–367.

Pavlov, I. P. (1927). *Conditional reflexes: An investigation of the physiological activity of the cerebral cortex.* London: Wexford University Press.

Perry, S. D., Jenzowsky, S. A., Hester, J. B., King, C. M., & Yi, H. (1997). The influence of commercial humor on program enjoyment and evaluation. *Journalism Quarterly, 74,* 388–399.

Perse, E. M. (1990a). Audience selectivity and involvement in the newer media environment. *Communication Research, 17,* 675–697.

Perse, E. M. (1990b). Involvement with local television news: Cognitive and emotional dimensions. *Human Communication Research, 16,* 556–581.

Perse, E. M. (1990c). Media involvement and local news effects. *Journal of Broadcasting & Electronic Media, 34,* 17–36.

Perse, E. M. (1992). Predicting attention to local television news: Need for cognition and motives for viewing. *Communication Reports, 5,* 40–49.

Perse, E. M. (1998). Implications of cognitive and affective involvement for channel changing. *Journal of Communication, 48*(3), 49–68.

Perse, E. M., & Ferguson, D. A. (1993). The impact of newer television technologies on television satisfaction. *Journalism Quarterly, 70,* 843–853.

Perse, E. M., & Rubin, A. M. (1988). Audience activity and satisfaction with favorite soap opera. *Journalism Quarterly, 65,* 368–375.

Perse, E. M., & Rubin, R. B. (1989). Attribution in social and parasocial relationships. *Communication Research, 16,* 59–77.

Petty, R. E., & Cacioppo, J. T. (1986). *Communication and persuasion: Central and peripheral routes to attitude change.* New York: Springer-Verlag.

Ray, M. L. (1973). Marketing communication and the hierarchy-of-effects. In P. Clarke (Ed.), *New models for mass communication research* (pp. 147–176). Beverly Hills, CA: Sage.

Reeves, B., Newhagen, E., Maibach, E., Basil, M., & Kurz, K. (1991). Negative and positive television messages: Effects of message type and message context on attention and memory. *American Behavioral Scientist, 34,* 679–694.

Reeves, B., Thorson, E., & Schleuder, J. (1986). Attention to television: Psychological theories and chronometric measures. In J. Bryant & D. Zillmann (Eds.), *Perspectives on media effects* (pp. 251–279). Hillsdale, NJ: Lawrence Erlbaum Associates.

Rosengren, K. E., & Windahl, S. (1972). Mass media consumption as a functional alternative. In D. McQuail (Ed.), *Sociology of mass communications* (pp. 166–194). Middlesex, England: Penguin.

Rubin, A. M. (1984). Ritualized and instrumental television viewing. *Journal of Communication, 34*(3), 67–77.

Rubin, A. M., & Perse, E. M. (1987a). Audience activity and soap opera involvement: A uses and effects investigation. *Human Communication Research, 14,* 246–268.

Rubin, A. M., & Perse, E. M. (1987b). Audience activity and televison news gratifications. *Communication Research, 14,* 58–84.

Rubin, A. M., Perse, E. M., & Powell, R. A. (1985). Loneliness, parasocial interaction, and local television news viewing. *Human Communication Research, 12,* 155–180.

Schachter, S. (1964). The interaction of cognitive and physiological determinants of emotional state. In L. Berkowitz (Ed.), *Advances in experimental social psychology* (Vol. 1, pp. 49–80). New York: Academic Press.

Schleuder, J. D., White, A. V., & Cameron, G. T. (1993). Priming effects of television news bumpers and teasers on attention and memory. *Journal of Broadcasting & Electronic Media, 37,* 437–452.

Schneider, W., & Shiffrin, R. M. (1977). Controlled and automatic human information processing: I. Detection, search and attention. *Psychological Review, 84,* 1–66.

Simon, H. A. (1974). How big is a "chunk." *Science, 183,* 482–488.

Thorson, E., & Lang, A. (1992). The effects of television videographs and lecture familiarity on adult cardiac orienting responses and memory. *Communication Research, 19,* 346–369.

Thorson, E., Reeves, B., & Schleuder, J. (1987). Attention to local and global complexity in television messages. In M. L. McLaughlin (Ed.), *Communication yearbook* (Vol. 10, pp. 366–383). Newbury Park, CA: Sage.

Walker, J. R. (1988). Inheritance effects in the new media environment. *Journal of Broadcasting & Electronic Media, 32,* 391–401.

Walker, J. R. (1993). Catchy, yes, but does it work? The impact of broadcast network promotion frequency and type on program success. *Journal of Broadcasting & Electronic Media, 37,* 197–207.

Webster, J. G., & Lichty, L. W. (1991). *Ratings analysis: Theory and practice.* Hillsdale, NJ: Lawrence Erlbaum Associates.

Webster, J. G., & Phalen, P. F. (1997). *The mass audience: Rediscovering the dominant model.* Mahwah, NJ: Lawrence Erlbaum Associates.

Webster, J. G., & Wang, T. Y. (1992). Structural determinants of exposure to television: The case of repeat viewing. *Journal of Broadcasting & Electronic Media, 36,* 125–136.

Wenner, L. A. (1985). Transaction and media gratifications research. In K. E. Rosengren, L. A. Wenner, & P. Palmgreen (Eds.), *Media gratifications research: Current perspectives* (pp. 73–94). Beverly Hills, CA: Sage.

Williams, G. A. (1989). Enticing viewers: Sex and violence in TV Guide program advertisements. *Journalism Quarterly, 66,* 970–973.

Wyer, R. S., Jr., & Srull, T. K. (1986). Human cognition in its social context. *Psychological Review, 93,* 322–359.

Yi, Y. (1990). Cognitive and affective priming effects of the context for print advertisements. *Journal of Advertising, 19*(2), 40–48.

Zillmann, D. (1980). Anatomy of suspense. In P. H. Tannenbaum (Ed.), *The entertainment functions of television* (pp. 133–163). Hillsdale, NJ: Lawrence Erlbaum Associates.

Zillmann, D. (1991). Television arousal and physiological arousal. In J. Bryant & D. Zillmann (Eds.), *Responding to the screen: Reception and reaction processes* (pp. 103–133). Hillsdale, NJ: Lawrence Erlbaum Associates.

Zillmann, D., & Mundorf, N. (1987). Image effects in the appreciation of video rock. *Communication Research, 14,* 316–334.

3

Structure and Content in Promotion Research

Susan Tyler Eastman
Indiana University

Paul D. Bolls
Southern Illinois University at Edwardsville

On-air promotion's relevance to prime-time television ratings has been beyond question for the last 3 decades. To date, most scholarly research about promotion has focused on the structural characteristics of on-air promotion. Studies have attempted to describe and measure such attributes as style and frequency (Owens & Bryant, 1998), frequency and ratings (Walker, 1993), and design and placement (Eastman & Newton, 1998a). The studies have generally looked at the impact of on-air promotion on the subsequent ratings for a program, looking either for up/down movement of ratings or the variance accounted for as in regression analyses, and one line of studies culminated in the testing of the salience model (also described in Perse, chap. 2, this volume). Much of this research presumes that self-driven channel-changing activity by television audiences is relatively minimal and thus viewers are able to be impacted to a modest extent by such external motivators as on-air promos that subtly influence viewers' enjoyment of programs.

To provide a context for additional research, this chapter begins by reviewing the two literatures that led to the development of the variables that comprise the salience model. First, the advertising, marketing, and information-processing literature is surveyed for studies about structural and content factors affecting advertising spots that might apply to on-air promotional messages. Then, the chapter explores the programming literature for clues to attributes that might impact promotional effectiveness. It goes on to summarize the findings in previous studies about structural factors affecting the impact of on-air promos.

Turning in a new direction, the chapter then approaches promotion from a content perspective through the available literature and reports an original study of on-air promo content. Other than sports promotion and violence and sex, the topics of subsequent chapters, the content of promos has merely been described, and no previous studies have attempted to measure the contribution of content features to ratings. This relatively unexplored area supplements structural studies of salience because content and structure are divisions of convenience, not rigorous conceptual distinctions. In general, *structural* is the term used when variables seem exogenous or external to the promotional spot or ad, and *content related* is applied when the variables appear to be endogenous or internal. For example, external factors — such as location and frequency — are determined by network and station executives, whereas internal factors — such as pacing and camera angle — are normally in the hands of those who actually create and produce the promos. However, many variables used in the studies described later can readily be considered as features of both structure and content. This section closes with a proposed model for assessing some content features of on-air promos. Finally, in the third section — as is the pattern for the book — the chapter concludes with an agenda for studies assessing promotional effectiveness for future research.

To provide a convenient overview of the relevant research, Table 3.1 summarizes the main analyses and studies that are discussed in the chapter. Listed from oldest to most recent, the studies relevant to this chapter subdivide into (a) key studies about features of advertising, programming, and cognition relevant to promotion, and (b) key studies about the features and impact of on-air promos for prime-time programs — limited to studies of promos carried within prime-time television; additional studies of promotion appear in other chapters.

CLUES IN THE ADVERTISING LITERATURE

Consumer response to television advertisements is the subject of a large body of research. Those working in this area have sought to reveal the impact of different structural and content characteristics in advertisements that impacted message effectiveness. This line of research can be extended to television program promotion because both advertising and promotional messages are intended to influence decisions made by a target audience. Admittedly, there are differences between the decision to buy a product and the decision to view a program that place limits on generalizing conclusions about effective television advertisements to the problem of designing and producing effective television program promotions. However, at a basic level, both effective advertising and promotional mes-

TABLE 3.1

Summary of Studies Relevant to Promotion Research

Author(s)	Year	Subject, DM, and Sample	Relevant Findings
Colley	1961	Discussion of advertising goals.	Proposed Hierarchy of Effects model for advertising messages.
Love	1981	Experimental comparison of on-air promos by light and heavy TV viewers.	Concluded that heavy viewers made more use of on-air promos than light viewers.
Gantz and Eastman	1983	Telephone survey of 521 adult TV viewers about their use of promotional media.	Found that most viewers valued and actively used on-air media, that women used printed guides more than men, that older viewers used guides, whereas younger viewers focused on on-air program selection.
Stewart and Furse	1986	Examined the relationship between 155 executional features of over 1,000 TV commercials on message effectiveness.	Concluded that individual executional features have differential effects on different measures of message effectiveness.
Bellamy	1992	Analysis of changes in three networks' TV promotion resulting from economic pressures and success of Fox.	Identified promotion as the "third leg" of network strategy; outlined rising industry questions about traditional emphasis on promotional push for new fall season and sweeps, use of generic network image campaigns, role of promotional giveaways tied to retailers.
Walker	1993	Impact of frequency and program type for 386 prime-time promos on ratings for 62 network series.	Found that frequency of promotion per episode overall was negatively correlated with ratings, but was positively correlated for returning programs; showed the importance of viewers' familiarity with programs.
Kent and Allen	1994	Experimental examination of the differential effects of clutter on television ads for similar and different products.	Showed that clutter in advertising has differing effects when for competitive rather than noncompetitive products.
Laskey, Fox, and Crask	1994	Comparison of executional style of 1,178 TV advertisements on message effectiveness.	Found individual-oriented executional style to have positive effects on memory for the advertisement but no strong effects across all product categories.
Laskey, Fox, and Crask	1995	Comparison of message strategy of 1,178 TV advertisements on message effectiveness.	Found limited positive effects for an informational strategy compared to transformational strategy, but showed that neither strategy was effective across all product categories.

(Continued)

TABLE 3.1
(*Continued*)

Author(s)	Year	Subject, DM, and Sample	Relevant Findings
Taylor, Miracle, and Wilson	1997	Experimental comparison of the information level of TV advertisements on an American student sample and Korean student sample.	Concluded that Americans prefer advertisements with a high level of information, but that Koreans do not exhibit strong preferences for advertisements with very high or very low levels of information.
Zhao	1997	Experimental examination of Super Bowl TV ads for the effects of clutter and serial position.	Showed that both clutter and late pod positions lead to lower brand memory in advertising.
Eastman and Newton	1998a	Regression analysis of 5,365 promos for 966 episodes of prime-time programs on ratings.	Established major variables affecting prime-time program promotion and demonstrated a significant impact on network ratings for Salience model and variables of position, distance, location, carriage program rating, frequency, clutter, and construction, especially for midrated programs; demonstrated significant changes in network promotional practices over time and difference by network, genre, and familiarity of the program.
Eastman and Newton	1998b	Regression analysis of 4,860 promos for 825 high-, mid-, and low-rated network prime-time programs.	Revealed that most impact on ratings occurs over two midquartiles of prime-time programs; established overall impact of promotion at about 11%, varying from 0% to 22% with time of year and ratings rank of programs.
Yoon, Bolls, and Lang	1998	Experimental investigation of the effects of production pacing and content arousal on attitude toward the advertisement.	Found that fast and arousing TV advertisements resulted in more favorable attitudes than slow and calm advertisements.
Eastman and Newton	1999	Regression analysis of 223 promos for network prime-time sitcoms.	Demonstrated significant impact of method of construction, familiarity, amount of clutter, position of promo, rating of program carrying the promo on the promoted sitcom's ratings; proposed a six-part Salience model.
Eastman, Newton, and Bolls	2000	Regression analysis of 1,297 promos for prime-time sitcom promos looking at impact of presentation, appeals, and type of humor on sitcom ratings.	Revealed the selective impact of network popularity, familiarity, suspense, reality of characters, and novelty on ratings; showed strong differences between networks in type of humor used in comedy promos.

sages must persuade people to make a decision that requires an investment of resources in the form of time and money. An obvious difference between the decisions product advertisements try to influence and the decisions program promotions try to influence concerns the level of involvement the decisions require. Product advertisements attempt to influence both very high-involvement purchase decisions requiring the investment of thousands of dollars, such as which car to buy, and very low-involvement decisions, such as which candy bar to buy. Program promotions only attempt to influence a relatively low-involvement decision — which program to view.

These types of involvement are known to influence the processing of persuasive messages (see Petty, Cacioppo, & Schumann, 1983). Further, different advertising strategies are believed to be more or less effective under different levels of involvement (Gill, Grossbart, & Laczniak, 1988). Despite this difference, much advertising and all promotion messages are designed to influence relatively low-involvement decisions and, therefore, share at least some degree of similarity. Based on the assumption of a logical connection between television advertising and television program promotion, this section attempts to extend the conclusions of research on television advertising effectiveness to television program promotion and suggest ways that advertising research might influence future research on program promotion.

The Hierarchy of Effects Model

Television advertisements and television program promotion probably influence consumer decisions through a similar pathway. The Hierarchy of Effects model (Colley, 1961), shown at the top of Fig. 3.1, is the most commonly accepted model of how television advertisements are believed to work. Colley proposed that features of a persuasive message evoke *attitudes toward the message* (Aad) which impact *attitudes toward the advertised brand* (Ab) and then lead to *purchase intentions* (PI). This basic model has been used to explain how television advertisements eventually impact consumer behavior and can logically be extended to television program promotion. In a similar vein, the structural and content features of a promotional message probably evoke a variety of attitudes toward the message that get incorporated into attitudes toward the show being promoted and then influence intentions to view the program. The bottom of Fig. 3.1 shows the Hierarchy of Effects model extended to the context of program promotion.

It is important to understand how advertising researchers define message effectiveness in contrast to how effectiveness has been defined in promotion research. An effective message, whether it is an advertisement

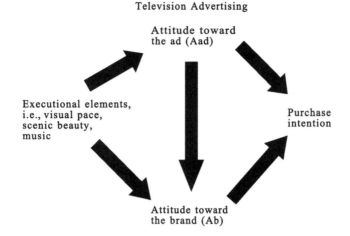

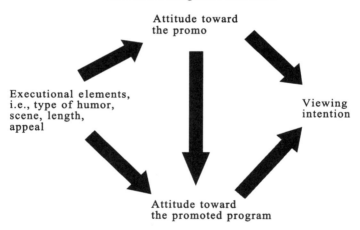

FIG. 3.1.   The Hierarchy of Effects model adapted for promotion. Originally developed by R. H. Colley (1961).

or program promotion, obviously is one that achieves the goal of either increasing product sales or program viewership. For the most part, advertising researchers have not studied message effectiveness by directly measuring product sales. Researchers have instead measured variables like attitudes, intentions, and memory as indicators of message effectiveness. On the other hand, researchers studying television program promotion have usually used program ratings as an indicator of effectiveness, which could be likened to directly measuring product sales. The methodological implication of this difference to researchers who study program promotion is that it may be important to include other measures besides ratings in order to more accurately assess overall message impact.

Television Advertising Content

Advertising researchers have examined message content at two different levels. One level focuses on the examination of specific types of content like humor, sex, and fear, whereas the other level examines content at a more general level, focusing on what researchers have termed *message strategy* (Bolls & Potter, 1998; Laskey, Fox, & Crask, 1995). Research on the impact of specific content types on message effectiveness is inconclusive. Research on the effects of humor on advertisement effectiveness serves as a prime example. Some studies on humor report positive effects on attention and attitudes toward the ad (Madden & Weinberger, 1982). However, for every study reporting positive effects of humor, there is a study reporting nonsignificant or negative effects of humor, usually attributed to humorous appeals distracting attention away from key information in the message (Duncan & Nelson, 1985; Gelb & Zinkhan, 1986). The inconsistency of research findings related to the effects of humor has led some researchers to call for a reconceptualization of humor in more general terms by looking at general humor mechanisms and variables such as product category (Spotts, Weinberger, & Parsons, 1997).

Information level as a specific feature of message content has also been examined. Taylor, Miracle, and Wilson (1997) compared the effects of advertisements with high and low levels of product information on attitude toward the ad, attitude toward the brand, and purchase intentions. They concluded that advertisements with high levels of information are more effective for Americans, whereas advertisements with low levels of information are more effective for Koreans. This should remind researchers that the decision to view a program is influenced by both message features and individual viewer characteristics. Certain types of program promotion may only be effective with specific target audiences that, at a minimum, might be defined by their cultural background or general demographic descriptors.

A second group of researchers who also examined the effects of content on message effectiveness conceptualized content at a more general level so that it reflected message strategy. This line of research divides content according to either an informational or transformational strategy (Puto & Wells, 1984). Informational content focuses on presenting specific, tangible product strengths, whereas transformational content focuses on building a link between a brand image and consumer personality. Johar and

Sirgy (1991) examined the impact of these two kinds of content on message effectiveness and concluded that it depends on certain product and consumer characteristics. Specifically, they claimed that informational content is most effective for products that are highly differentiated from competing products and/or when consumers are highly involved in the purchase decision. The latter rarely applies to television viewers, but the condition of high differentiation may apply to some shows and channels but not others. This suggests that measures of program and channel competition may be essential in promotion research.

More recently, Laskey et al. (1995), using a pool of 1,178 television advertisements, examined the impact of informational and transformational content on memory for the advertisement. They found some limited positive effects for informational content on memory, but concluded that neither type of content is highly effective across all product categories. This leads to the inescapable conclusion that, at a minimum, different television genres should be studied separately.

Research on Message Execution

A second area of research that examines factors affecting message effectiveness looks at message execution, or "how" a message is communicated. Stewart and Furse (1986) have done one of the most extensive studies in this area. Using a pool of over 1,000 advertisements, they analyzed the effects of 155 individual executional elements on message intrusiveness, comprehension, and persuasiveness. They found that different executional elements, such as visual pace, the number of words, scenic beauty, and the use of music to create a mood, affect different aspects of advertising message effectiveness. In a less extensive study of executional elements, Laskey, Fox, and Crask (1994) examined the effects on memory of four specific executional styles for a pool of 1,100 television advertisements. The four styles were individual oriented, story oriented, product oriented, and technique oriented. In the individual style, a spokesperson talks about the product; in the story style, the product is featured in a short drama. The product style relies on a demonstration of the product, and the technique style presents the product in a fantasy manner or through the use of an analogy. As in Stewart and Furse (1986), Laskey et al. (1994) did not find strong positive effects for any executional style across product categories. However, the individual-oriented style appeared to have relatively greater impact on memory compared to the other executional styles. The implications for promotion research are twofold: First, using spokespeople in promotional spots for special event programming (where remembering when the show airs may be crucial to building an audience) may be an effective strategy. Second, findings of strong effects for any promotional message feature on message effectiveness are unlikely, but as Eastman and Newton (1998a, 1998b) have pointed out, even small effects carry practical significance in the form of economic impact on the broadcast industry.

Another executional feature that has been examined is message pacing. Yoon, Bolls, and Lang (1998) examined the effects of the number of cuts (defined as a change in visual scene) in television advertisements on attitude toward the ad, attitude toward the brand, and purchase intentions. Yoon et al. found that fast-paced messages resulted in significantly more positive attitudes toward the ad as well as the brand and higher purchase intentions compared to slow-paced advertisements. As applied to program promotion, this suggests that MTV-style spots are more likely to result in more favorable attitudes toward the message, which may carry over to attitudes toward the program being promoted.

CLUES IN THE PROGRAMMING LITERATURE

The principal conclusion of virtually all programming research is that inherited viewing matters more than any other factor. In other words, the lead-in program's ratings have a powerful impact on the next program's ratings, and inherited viewing strongly influences general patterns of television behavior (see Eastman, 1998; Webster & Phalen, 1997). The relevance of these consistent findings to promotion is that efforts to counter inherited viewing by attracting viewers to competing channels are fighting an uphill battle.

Countering Inheritance

Nonetheless, broadcasters have developed strategies to negate inheritance. In particular, the tactic of scheduling specials, miniseries, and other stunt programming usually has two goals: first, to draw in *new* viewers, generally those who watch little television or use a lot of other media (thus raising the total number of homes using television), and second, to attract viewers not committed to viewing programs on other channels (see Eastman & Ferguson, 1997). That means that only part of the population of potential viewers can be reached by promotion, and much of that promotion has to forego on-air spots (at least on the home channel) in favor of external media and other channels. The conclusion for promotion is that only modest effects should be expected, even for the most spectacular and most promoted programs. Moreover, the strong patterns characterizing viewing behavior suggest that promotion may have different results for different kinds of programs. Eastman and Newton (1998b) found that promotion had little impact on very high-rated or very low-rated programs and most affected those in the lower-middle quarter of programs.

Along the same lines, Ferguson (1992a) and Ferguson and Perse (1993) explored the problem of channel repertoires (the number of channels regularly viewed) in a series of studies and found that repertoires continued to be quite small, as in earlier research, and ranged from 8 to 10 or so channels. This finding, corroborated by informal proprietary reports in the trade press, confirms that the power of promos to draw viewers to channels outside their regularly viewed ones is inherently limited. It also implies that promotion has marginal power to attract viewers to programs of types different from those regularly watched. Another study by Ferguson (1992b) on selective exposure showed that the new media environment (largely cable television at the time) had a negative impact on inherited viewing, meaning that people chose their programs and channels more purposefully than in the past, an effect likely to be exacerbated by the recent proliferation of Internet use. On another front, Webster and Wang (1992) examined repeat viewing of television programs, and the high correlation they found between scheduling and repeat viewing also suggests that the size of any effects of promotion will necessarily be small. Such viewing practices and context-related characteristics suggest that each promo has only a limited opportunity to reach people. Nonetheless, the high cost of licensing prime-time programs and the escalating clash among new and old media competitors for the viewing audience makes even the tiniest effect from on-air promotion significant to the networks. This is evident from the fact that the six broadcast networks forego about $4 billion a year in commercial revenues to air promotion for their programs. Moreover, the cumulative impact of promotion on viewing behavior merits scholarly interest in and of itself.

Preference or Structure

Two opposing views underlie much of the programming research that raises questions about how promotion operates. As articulated by Adams (1993), audience preference and habit are the keys to audience choice of programs and thus account for ratings variance. In contrast, Cooper (1993) argued that structural characteristics of program scheduling—such as lead-in, network affiliation, cable penetration, and market concentration—are the keys to audience viewing patterns. If Adams is right, then constant monitoring of viewers is needed to determine the trajectory of their program preferences, and on-air promos should concentrate on encouraging habitual viewing. If Cooper is right, then strategies for the arrangement of programs are crucial, and on-air promos should focus on relating programs to one another, as with vertically or horizontally scheduled shows. The practice of blocking similar programs within adjacent hours (all sitcoms, all sports) is thus an attribute of industry practice that magnifies the impact of promotion. Indeed, promos both encourage habits and encourage inherited viewing at present, though promotion by the national networks tends to embody Cooper's structural view, whereas local station promotion tends to reflect more of Adams' view of preference and habit. The primary implications are that if Adams is right, then the content of the promos matters most; if Cooper is right, then the environment of the promos matters most.

User Technology

The other branch of programming studies that has relevance for promotion is that concerned with how viewers use remote control devices. Walker and Bellamy (1993) and Bellamy and Walker (1996) showed that the remote control both facilitates the evasion of promotional messages (as well as commercials—a distinction not always significant to viewers) and simultaneously heightens the value to industry programmers of whatever promotion does reach audiences. As Bellamy and Walker pointed out, increased selectivity on the part of viewers will demand increased impact from advertising—and consequently promotion—to command attention, raising but not answering the question of what features might generate increased impact.

An observational study of 159 adults by Eastman and Newton (1995) showed that most channel changing took place between programs, not within them, a finding with direct import for on-air promotion. It implies that promos should be scheduled within commercial pods, rather than in the breaks between programs, to achieve maximum reach. Although some viewers do use remote controls to zap commercials or watch multiple programs, some types of programs are more vulnerable to this manipulation, and others—probably more involving programs such as dramas and sports—are less vulnerable because viewers stay with the channel to avoid missing any content. It follows that promos in breaks within highly involving programs have a better chance of being seen by more viewers. Another inference is that first and last position will matter less in breaks within highly involving programs; middle positions might be perfectly satisfactory for on-air promos.

COGNITIVE THEORIES

At the deeper level of theory, research in cognition can provide explanation for structural phenomena. The relatively new field in cognitive neuropsychology called expectancy theory provides a broad theoretical framework for content-related studies of promotion. Expectancy theory deals with what the brain believes about the future. As in classical conditioning theory, people develop expectations by association with previous experiences (called associative learning). Studies of conditioning show how expectations are acquired; they come by association and extension from previous experiences. For example, in medical science, the medical treatments people get during their lifetimes set up expectations about how medicines will behave and set up expectations of relief, and this has led to some astonishing results in studies of placebo effects. People's internal states (health) have considerable ambiguity, as does the outside world. Neuroscientist Marcel Kinsbourne explained that "expectancies are embedded in the brain's neurochemistry" (Blakeslee, 1998, p. D1) and said that anticipation is derived from both information from the external world and internal memories and feelings (p. D4).

Applying Expectancy and Excitation-Transfer Theories

When applied to television programs, in essence, expectancy theory explains *why* what people expect influences their behavior and thus that viewing choices are, in large part, the result of conditioning or learning. There are a myriad of sources for acquiring expectations about television programs, including a lifetime of previous experience watching television shows, beliefs about the various networks and program genres, word of mouth from other viewers, and (of course) on-air and print promotion about programs provided by their suppliers. Because most individual television programs do not cause much critical comment or generate conversations among friends (though the exceptional programs certainly do both), on-air promos have become powerful conditioning tools that set up expectations within the framework of previous viewing and beliefs.

As mentioned by Perse (chap. 2, this volume), Palmgreen and Rayburn (1982) identified a variant on the general expectancy-theory to explain television viewing called expectancy-value theory. It accounts for viewing by assessing the relative positive and negative value that viewers place on having their expectations met. For example, watching an R-rated movie would have very negative valence if one happened to be watching with an 8-year-old child, but positive valence, perhaps, in other circumstances. Expectancy-value theory is very general, like broad "motivations" for television viewing (see Rubin, 1994); such perspectives explain but do not predict much about actual viewing. Examining the impact of promotion permits analysis of more specific spurs to viewing in a way that allows them to be tied to changes in program ratings. Because it is normally necessary to measure effects, not processes, accounting for the impact of promos on viewing behavior becomes a practical and logical method of understanding expectancy theory at the level of individual and mass audience viewing.

A related theory comes from the study of arousal and involvement (Mattes & Cantor, 1982; Mundorf, Zillmann, & Drew, 1991). Excitation-transfer theory implies that messages able to evoke emotions may lend those emotions to the programs by affecting viewers' attention, processing, and storage of information. Mattes and Cantor found that viewers who watched highly arousing programs rated subsequent commercials significantly more enjoyable and effective than those who watched less arousing programs. By inference, a promo might benefit from placement within highly arousing programs or after exciting commercials. Mathur and Chattopadhyay (1991) demonstrated such transference of emotion between programs and commercials, and, going in the other direction, Eastman, Newton, and Bolls (2000) found it to a limited degree between promos and situation comedies. Such a theory helps explain what may be happening at a cognitive level when promotion has an impact on program ratings.

Salience Theory and Model

Exploring the impact of structural features of promotion on viewing choices led Eastman and Newton (1998a, 1999) to develop salience theory. In outline, salience theory claims that certain characteristics contribute to prominence (i.e., salience) in promotion and that promotion with these characteristics has more impact on viewing choices—as measured by higher ratings—than promotion with none or lesser amounts of the same characteristics. To date, the studies have focused on the impact of on-air promos, setting aside the role of the print media. Nonetheless, the model developed from on-air studies shows that midrated programs, rather than the hits or bottom-rated programs, tend to be significantly affected by promotion. Hence, maximal salience in certain structural and content variables can create an advantage that positively affects a promoted program's ability to attract an audience—compared to a less advantaged program—usually measured as increases or decreases in ratings and shares for the promoted programs.

More specifically, the set of characteristics (or attributes or features) affecting salience can range from especially high levels to very low levels in on-air promos, and at higher levels the promo is more likely to affect the decision to view—if it is possible to affect that decision at all. No promos, no matter how effective, are likely to convince a 10-year-old to watch *60 Minutes*, for example. However, if someone often watches sitcoms, has made the decision to watch television tonight, and is faced with choosing among several sitcoms at 8:00, some of which have been previously viewed and others of which have not, on-air promos become a key source of reminders about how the viewer felt about the previously watched shows—how much pleasure they got, how funny they were, and so on—and promos set up expectations about new episodes and totally unfamiliar programs. Print and online media promoting program viewing can, presumably, do the same thing. Promotion can, accordingly, influence, to some small or not-so-small degree, what viewers watch.

Salience Variables

The first study to examine some features of on-air promotion was Walker (1993), and building on his work, Eastman and Newton and other colleagues tested the effectiveness of various features of on-air promotion in a series of studies conducted in the 1990s. In these studies (Eastman, 1994; Eastman & Newton, 1995, 1998a, 1998b, 1999; Eastman, Newton, & Pack, 1996; Eastman, Newton, Riggs, & Neal-Lunsford, 1997), they identified a series of nine characteristics of on-air promotion that appear to be related to higher ratings.

Clutter. Eastman and Newton (1998a, 1998b) calculated the amounts of clutter within pods and breaks by enumerating the commercials, promos, and public service announcements. One problematic area is whether to count separately all the programs mentioned in a multiple spot (as do Eastman & Newton) or assign them a fractional value (as does Walker, 1993). Using the former method generates averages of about 8.3 elements per break.[1] One study (Eastman & Newton, 1998a) showed that the amount of clutter significantly affects the impact of promos on the ratings of *new* programs, but another study (Eastman & Newton, 1998b) found no impact for clutter when programs were separated by high, mid, or low ratings.

Construction. This variable refers to the number of different programs that are touted in one spot. It is becoming common today to find 30-second prime-time promos pushing several programs. Many promos pair hits and new shows—in the hope that association will result in greater sampling of the new show—or combine an evening's lineup—in the expectation that a carry-over effect will occur among blocked programs (those who want to watch one show will tune in early and stay longer for shows that appear to be similar). Eastman and Newton (1998a)

---

[1]Trade reports note that the networks' commercial programs occupied nearly 5 more minutes per hour in 1999 than a decade earlier, bringing the total commercial and promotional time per prime-time hour to 15 minutes 44 seconds (Associated Press, 1999).

conceived of promo construction as the distinction between spots promoting one program (a *single*) or more than one program (a *multiple*). The variable can be operationalized dichotomously or ordinally, or, as in Walker (1993), programs promoted in multiple spots can be assigned fractional weight. Eastman and Newton found that typically about 40% to 50% of prime-time promos were multiple spots, a proportion slightly lower than the 55% found by Walker. However, the former found a notable increase in the use of singles in May when many movies are promoted, and a marked decrease in singles in December holiday promotion. But analyses to date have not clearly demonstrated a statistically significant impact from construction on program ratings. It seems that a comparison of ways of operationalizing promo construction is needed.

Design. Studies by Eastman, Neal-Lunsford, and Riggs (1995) and Eastman, Newton, Riggs, and Neal-Lunsford (1997) tracked the changing patterns of network program scheduling in the transitions between programs. They analyzed the shift of network spots out of the transition and into the closing credits of the preceding program and into longer breaks within programs, and noted a greater focus on specific rather than generic promotion. Although the industry has long avowed its belief in the efficacy of specific (also called topical or episodic) promotion, the industry-wide focus on branding the network's image might have resulted in the persistence of generic spots. What Eastman et al. (1997) noted, however, was a diminution of differences in practice among the networks, which was confirmed by Eastman and Newton (1998a). Despite varied proportions of specific spots in earlier analyses, uniformity appeared in the practices of all six networks by the mid-1990s: Five separate analyses of databases from 1994 to 1997 showed that between 95% and 99% of promos aired within prime time consistently were specific and only 1% to 5% were generic. Such standardization eliminates the possibility of locating statistical variance in prime-time ratings, whatever the theoretical merits of the variable. No examinations of spot design in other dayparts have yet been undertaken.

Distance. Several studies have taken note of the importance of the length of time between the promotion and the airdate of the program (see Eastman & Otteson, 1994; Billings, Eastman, & Newton, 1998). This distance (in time) variable has usually been operationalized as same night, same week, next week, or further away. Whereas Eastman and Otteson found no impact for promotion carried within an Olympics, Billings et al. found a modest impact for promotion of prime-time shows close in time to the promotion's airdate. The studies concluded that promos have virtually no impact on programs distant in airdate, although the networks continue to subscribe to the theory that advance promotion of new fall shows and special programs serves to increase the audience's excitement about them and encourage tune-in.

Familiarity. Testing the assumption that more frequent promotion should have a positive impact on program ratings, Walker (1993) found that the attributes of program type (genre) and success (the status of the program as measured by ratings) interacted when measuring the impact of the frequency of promotion. He concluded that frequency of promotion had more impact for *established* than *new* programs, probably because the networks promote weaker shows more than stronger ones. This finding was corroborated by Eastman and Newton (1998a, 1998b), and the variable has subsequently been called *familiarity* or *status* in subsequent research, and analyses generally separate continuing from new programs. It appears clear that top-rated programs and bottom-rated programs are treated far differently by network promoters than midrated programs in several ways, probably because the latter are more susceptible to positive impact from promotion. It makes sense to distinguish the groups because hit programs have little ability to grow in ratings since they are already at the top, whereas bottom-rated programs can show little benefit from promotion exactly because they are not popular. It is the midrated shows that have been shown to benefit measurably from promotion.

Frequency. This variable can either reflect the raw number of promos aired for each program or can be subdivided dichotomously into high and low frequency or into multiple levels, as in high, mid, and low frequency, by applying some criterion for division. Tertiary and quartile splits are common devices useful for reflecting the real range of a variable in particular circumstances. For example, the likely range of frequency of promotion of any given show will probably be shorter for WB than for, say, CBS, merely because of the fewer hours programmed by WB. It is possible to classify all of WB's efforts as low in frequency or to compare within the internal range of WB's own efforts. Although it seems obvious that increased frequency of promotion ought to raise ratings, the findings to date have been ambiguous. Walker (1993) found that the impact of more frequent promotion was greater during the first few weeks of the fall season and that it was strongest for moderately successful returning series, and concomitantly weakest for low-rated new series. Similarly, Eastman and Newton (1998a) concluded that frequency had only a negative impact on new programs, but they found a very modest positive impact on audience size for one-time-only programs (specials, miniseries, and sports). In contrast to Walker, they found no impact for frequency on the ratings of continuing programs.

Genre. Virtually all studies have suggested, at a minimum, that promotion operates somewhat differently for different types of programs. The variables affecting the promotion of sports programs, for example, are likely to differ substantially from those affecting prime-time series. Indeed, Eastman and Newton (1998a) found that such one-time-only programs as movies, games, and specials were little impacted by promotion, although it may serve the traditional informational function of telling when and where to viewers who have already decided to watch the programs. In contrast, prime-time series that air regularly have been shown to be most affected by promotional tactics. The impact of promotion—and the features that most affect it—has not yet been explored for genres that predominate outside of prime time.

Location. One of these features is the exact location of a promo within a program—whether it appears in a commercial pod in a program break, in the end-credits (often sharing a split screen), or in the transition between programs. Conceptually, the idea is that pod positions get more viewing and thus lend more prominence to promos, and it appears that about three fourths of promos are located in pods, whereas only about 10% to 15% are in end-credits and about 10% in transitions between shows. The amount in the transitions may be falling as the use of seamless flow from show to show increases (see Eastman et al., 1995, and Eastman et al., 1997). Location appeared as one of the most significant variables in Eastman and Newton (1998a) for midrated shows. They reported that the mean rating or share of a program promoted primarily in midprogram pods ran as much as 5 percentage points higher than the mean audience for programs promoted largely in end-credits or transitional locations. They also noted the much smaller percentage of shows with end-credit or transitional promotion, suggesting that this finding may have appeared in proprietary research and be leading toward a standardization of industry practice.

Position. Eastman and Newton (1998a) also examined the role of position of a promo within pods, distinguishing between placement as in first, middle, or last. The theory is that first and last take advantage of primacy or recency, attributes conferring more prominence than midpositions. Although position proved a significant variable in contributing to ratings, results showed that midposition was equally good for promos. This unexpected finding may have been exacerbated by the method of operationalization of position as merely first, mid, or last, which fails to take account of network contracts giving affiliates last position in some time periods, thus making "second to last" the latest position possible for some network spots. Future studies should attack this variable more aggressively.

Although the so-called salience variables need more study, their collective significance in affecting ratings has been shown in sufficient numbers of analyses using different databases that the value of this line of research is established. This leaves, chiefly, the need for clarification in how to operationalize certain variables in certain circumstances — such as for different networks and dayparts.

Measuring Effect Size

In a set of analyses with a different thrust, Eastman and Newton (1998b) compared the impact of promotion on programs with different ratings in order to determine the actual size of the promotional effect. Comparing four different databases, they concluded that promotion explained about 5% of the overall variance in ratings. A number like 5% may seem small, but a difference of that much in ratings represents millions of dollars in revenue for a major broadcast network.

They found, not unexpectedly, that promotion's impact varied by season of the year and by the ratings of the program being promoted (in other words, by whether the show was a hit or a loser). Whereas they found promotion had no impact on May ratings, perhaps because of the large number of specials and movies aired in May sweeps, they found an impact as high as 8% in February — one of the key months for stations and networks in determining the next year's schedule. But overall, their most reliable and conservative estimate of impact was 5%.

When Eastman and Newton (1998b) tested for the impact of promotion on programs in the middle of the ratings spectrum, they found that shows ranked high on the salience variables tended to be more affected by promotion than programs at either extreme. They found division by quartiles — into high-rated, upper-mid-rated, lower-mid-rated, and low-rated programs — most useful in locating the exact programs most impacted by promotion. They found a high of 20% impact for programs in the lower-mid quartile — the shows on the bubble, the ones with hopes of rising in ratings or in danger of cancellation. The researchers found an impact of 7% in the upper-mid quartile; these may be established second-tier shows or those with rising expectations that may swing over into hits. They found impacts of 7% for both the upper quartile (the hits) and the lower quartile (the bottom-ranked shows). Because of cancellation effects (a variable that impacts one quartile positively may impact another quartile negatively), the overall impact for promotion stayed at 5%.

In addition to showing up in statistical analyses, Eastman and Newton's (1998a, 1998b) findings follow logically from two facts about network promotional practices: First, most new programs fail — for a variety of reasons — and are canceled in a few weeks or not renewed for a second season. Clearly, analysis of the impact of promotion on the ratings of these programs is not going to locate positive results. Second, the top-rated programs are at the peak of popularity and need audience maintenance but probably cannot grow in ratings. Commonly, such shows appear in on-air promos merely to boost other lower rated programs (or provide information about changes in day or time). In addition, not surprisingly, the Eastman and Newton (1998a, 1998b) studies revealed substantial differences by network and by program genre — the latter is another area where more study should be fruitful.

In a different approach to the impact of ratings, several studies compare the percentages of ratings that rose, stayed flat, or fell after promotion. These studies are discussed in detail in the chapter on sports promotion (Eastman & Billings, chap. 7, this volume), but they also show that the impact of promotion is measurable and that it varies by network and program genre. These studies fit neither under the rubric of structural nor content-related examinations of promotion, but may encompass the features of both.

A STUDY OF THE CONTENT APPEALS IN ON-AIR PROMOS

Although other studies (see Walker, chap. 4, this volume) have looked at the amounts of sex and violence in promos or the effectiveness of teasers (see Buchman, chap. 9, this volume), no other studies have assessed the ways in which on-air promos appeal to people. The classic mass-media appeals utilized in analysis of advertising and programming consist of such broad concepts as conflict, comedy, information, sex, and human interest.[2] Preliminary testing showed that these classic concepts were too sweeping to reveal much about effectiveness in promos for humorous programs. Moreover, pilot analyses also showed that promos for various genres of programs would have very different appeals, and nonvideo media might stress certain aspects of programs as part of reaching a narrower target audience than that of prime-time television. These factors necessitated focusing on a single genre and medium to limit the range of possibilities to a practical total, a decision supported by previous advertising and promotion research (Laskey et al., 1995; Walker, 1993). It was also expected that particular age and gender groups would tend to react differently than other demographic groups to elements within promos. Consequently, to establish a baseline in this little-explored area, this study

---

[2]See S. T. Eastman, S. W. Head, and L. Klein (1989, pp. 17–21) for a review of the classic primary and secondary audience appeals in mass media.

looked only at the appeals within network on-air promos for the genre of situation comedies (sitcoms) but explored the reactions of a wide range of adults. The goal of the study was to locate the range of appeals in the content of on-air promos for televised comedies and to compare the appeals across demographic groups.

As discussed above, although not previously applied to promotion, excitation-transfer theory implies that when viewers' reactions to promos are strong, enhanced feelings should affect the desire to watch a program — and thus raise audience size (as measured by ratings), an outcome devoutly desired by industry programmers and of scholarly interest for what it reveals about the uses and gratifications of programming. Because promos are both commercials for programs and miniprograms in themselves, and because they affect viewing decisions, they are appropriate for serious investigation. At the same time, a countervailing force is that involvement with television programs is likely to be low rather than high.

Research Questions

The study's purpose was to reveal some of the aspects of on-air promos that encourage people to watch new (unfamiliar) programs or put them off, thus fostering viewing of other programming options. Because this study was exploratory, hypotheses were inappropriate, but several research questions were suggested by previous advertising and programming studies (see Bellamy, 1992; Bolls & Potter, 1998; Johar & Sirgy, 1991; Taylor, Miracle, & Wilson, 1997; Zhao, 1997). Four questions in particular guided the method and analysis:

R1: What aspects of on-air promos for unfamiliar network programs (situation comedies only) do potential viewers identify as positive and negative influences on their likelihood of viewing?

R2: In what ways do women and men and adults of different ages differ in their responses to on-air promos?

R3: What role do such features as humor, identification, and information play in making promotion more likely to be effective?

R4: What role does the provider of the program (the network or producer) play in influencing the likelihood that promotion will be effective?

Although this approach can reveal only what people *say* about their reactions and likely future behaviors, at a minimum, their comments should provide some clues to the triggers contained in the content of program promotion. Given that they are intended for a mass audience, the appeals in on-air promos for situation comedies would probably not provoke much by way of a social-acceptability bias in responses. Ultimately, it was hoped that these clues would suggest a multifaceted model to guide practitioners and provide a starting place for subsequent research studies.

Method

Each of approximately 300 students in two sections of an undergraduate class showed six adults a prerecorded promo and then asked the adults to write out their reactions in their own handwriting. Each of the six people approached had to fit into one of six prespecified age and sex categories. The respondents could be acquaintances, family, neighbors, or university students, faculty, or staff, creating a large convenience sample. After data collection and transcription was completed, each student wrote a paper on the experience for a grade.

Stimulus and Protocols

The stimulus videotapes were network promos for new situation comedies, taped off-air, and the study was conducted in September before the programs premiered. It was presumed that lack of familiarity with a program would make the promo the biggest single influence on the person's reaction, after such factors as habits and personal preferences. It was expected that the impact of such external factors as the presence of friends and family and other available activities would not markedly influence the respondent's reactions.

The research protocol was detailed in writing and multiple oral presentations to the student researchers to establish the importance of rigorous consistency, and it was presumed that the very large sample would allow for some inconsistencies without serious contamination of the results. According to the protocol, a respondent who agreed to participate was given an *Information Sheet* explaining the study's general purpose, the respondent's right to refuse to continue, and the names and contact information for the responsible university officials. Next, the research protocol called for the respondent to be handed a *Response Form* headed (in large type) "Interview with Adult WOMAN 45–64 years old" (or another of the six groupings) that directed the respondent to refuse to participate if she or he had already been surveyed. Then the respondent was asked to watch the *videotaped promo* and answer (in his or her *own* handwriting) the question, "*Based on this promo, why might you watch or not watch this show?*" This question appeared in large bold type at the top of every response page. The remainder of the page was blank to allow for extended responses and variations in handwriting, except for a brief line of thanks at the bottom and a

request for a telephone number to be used to (randomly) confirm participation.

Responses were obtained from people fitting into the following six
demographic groups: a man and a woman in the 18 to 24 age group, a man
and a woman 25 to 44 years old, and a man and a woman 45 to 65 years
old, providing a convenience sample of nearly 2,000 adults. Randomly
assigned copies of network promos for the following six programs were
utilized:

Encore! Encore!	30 sec	NBC
The Hughleys	20 sec	ABC
The Secret Lives of Men	10 sec	ABC
Sports Night	10 sec	ABC
Maggie Winters	20 sec	CBS
Will & Grace	30 sec	NBC

Follow-Up Interviews

As a second step, after about 2 hours of in-class training, 32 different
students in an advanced course interviewed three more adults in the same
set of six age groups to further explore the meaning of additional respondents' comments. Conducted interview style and audiotaped (rather than
written out by the respondent), and utilizing screening of one of the same
videotaped promos and the same protocols, these one-on-one question-
and-answer sessions were intended to elicit longer (and perhaps more
thoughtful or more complete) responses for analysis by demographic
group. After transcription, printing, coding, and analysis, these responses
were compared across the six age and sex groups to see what distinctions
and similarities appeared in relation to the first sample and among subgroups.

Means of Analysis

Handwritten and audiotaped responses were transcribed and printed
by the students and analyzed by the researchers, who employed a modified form of grounded inductive content analysis (see Glaser & Strauss,
1967). A random set of 200 typed printouts were scanned for the reasons
or explanations alleged for the respondent's response to the promo. A single respondent might provide one or many explanations, in simplistic or
detailed form, with or without additional examples from his or her television viewing. A preliminary set of 66 global and specific adjectives and
phrases with both positive and negative connotations was developed and
later reduced to 30 groupings (with examples) as related explanations
were clustered or removed to "other" because their appearance was so in-

frequent. The goal was to obtain a set of appeals (or uses and gratifications) that applied specifically to the televised promotion of situation comedies.

Analysis of the 1,847 first-stage interviews was conducted by means of the extended category schema developed in several iterations from preliminary analysis of the first 200 interview sheets. Using the final set of 30 categories (with exemplars), the researchers tallied from one to many appeals from every response interview, depending on the length and variety of the respondents' comments. Although additional terms/adjectives could be added to the category schema at any time, that proved unnecessary. Although some variation in how to tally the responses could occur, the initial coding was conducted jointly by the researchers until a 97% level of agreement was reached. Then one researcher tallied the remaining 85% of the sheets, providing a high level of consistency of analysis. For the additional 92 second-stage interviews, analysis was conducted using the same category schema by the same researcher, but each age and sex group was analyzed separately from the others. The purpose was to locate responses that characterized particular age and gender groups. In addition, special emphasis was placed on locating additional explanations of appeals.

This process follows the general method used by Greenberg (1974) with British children when he first obtained the set of gratification items still generally used in research of this kind, but this study refines the method to apply to a single program genre—as many researchers (see Walker, 1993) have insisted is needed. The process lends itself to the development of sets of uses/motives/gratifications (usually called *appeals* in promos) that should then be suitable for use by scholars in subsequent research about promoting television comedies and useful for comparing the appeals in promos for other program genres.

Validation

To verify that the research protocols had been followed and to eliminate falsified transcripts, two procedures were employed. First, all handwritten original responses were examined by a researcher for completeness and variety in handwriting styles and telephone numbers to assess the likelihood that they were written by the purported writer. Second, a total of 100 randomly selected respondents were called back to confirm their participation in the study. In three cases, the interview could not be confirmed or the administrator had not followed directions. In addition, unlikely information on the original response sheets (such as the identical handwriting on more than one response sheet, unlikely telephone numbers, mentions of telephone rather than in-person interviewing) triggered

11 additional callbacks to verify the interviews. Altogether, one or more interviews conducted by five students were found to have been falsified (or conducted contrary to directions), and these interviews were dropped from the study. Generalizing from 9 out of 111 to the full database means that 92% of the data appeared to have been obtained according to the research protocol.

Results

A total of 351 students completed all or part of the assignment (99% of 356 enrolled). Interviews were successfully conducted with 1,939 adults. In the first stage, the 1,847 interviews were distributed as in Fig. 3.2.[3] Although more than half the respondents (61%) were located in Bloomington, especially those in the youngest groupings (men and women ages 18–24), more than one third of the sample (37%) resided outside Bloomington, according to the home or office telephone number they provided. (A further 2% of interview sheets lacked a phone number.)

Responses

Respondents in the initial wave made 3,679 codable (interpretable and recordable) responses, with from 1 to as many as 6 per interview. Of those, half (1,815, or 49%) were generally positive, whereas the other half (1,864, or 51%) were generally negative. The researchers used the typed transcript in analysis, so the exact context of comments was always available to aid in determining the thrust of a particular comment. At the conclusion of analysis, it became obvious that the responses readily fit into three broad categories of positives and negatives, as shown in Fig. 3.3, with no unattributed explanations.

As Fig. 3.3 shows, most comments (46%) were about the appeal of the plot or program (as implied by the promo). But a substantial proportion were about the actors or the source of the program (network or producer) (17%), and still more were about the promo itself (37%), as hoped. In the tables that follow, imagine negative versions of each idea (omitted for lack of space) to correspond with the positive versions included in the table. For example, the negative side of "identifies with or relates to story line or characters" was "does not relate to actions or plot or characters," whereas the negative side of "unexpected/original/fresh" was "formulaic/too common/trite."

The category of *story lines/programs*, as shown in Table 3.2, is a composite of many kinds of comments (*N* = 1,696), and whether some comments

---

[3]A total of 12 interview sheets had too little response information to be usable ("I don't watch TV," etc.) and were excluded from the analysis.

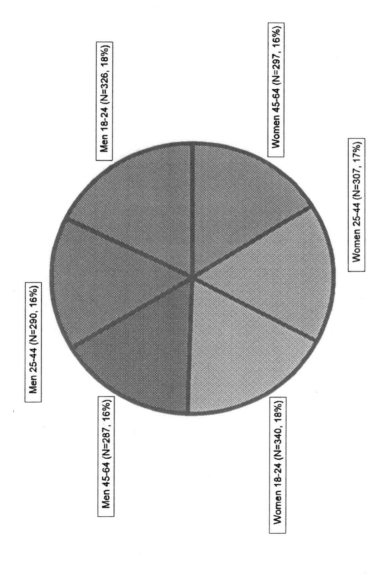

Men 18-24 (N=326, 18%)

Women 45-64 (N=297, 16%)

Women 25-44 (N=307, 17%)

Men 25-44 (N=290, 16%)

Men 45-64 (N=287, 16%)

Women 18-24 (N=340, 18%)

FIG. 3.2. Distribution of responses by gender and age. $N = 1{,}847$.

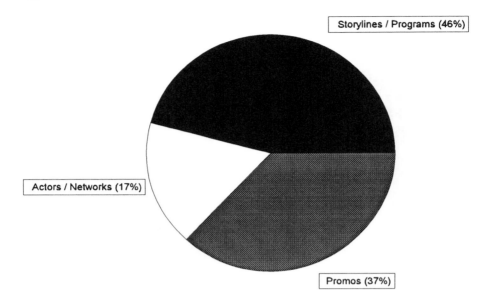

Comments

Topic	Slant	
	Positive 49%	**Negative 51%**
Storylines/Programs	1,166	1,088
Actors/Networks	366	251
Promotion	283	525

FIG. 3.3.   The distribution of responses in interviews. N = 3,679 comments.

might better have been placed with the *promos* group is an open question. Clearly, genre and title are characteristics of the program, and in context, "family orientation or cuteness," "idea seems somewhat interesting," and "unexpected/fresh" seemed to be more about the program than about how it was promoted, and consequently, they were grouped under *story lines/programs*. Similarly, "identifies with" seemed to be more about the characters in the program than about the actors or outside associations and not directly a function of their portrayal in promos.

As Table 3.2 shows, more than a third of respondents mentioned (without prompting) that they identified positively with the characters or action (39% of positives), whereas 47% (of negatives) used not-identifying as

TABLE 3.2
Explanations Relating to the Story Line or Program

| | Story Lines/Programs | | | | | |
| | Positive | | Negative | | Total | |
	n	%[a]	n	%[a]	N	% of All
Identifies with/relates to	297	39%	443	47%	740	44%
Lighthearted/cute/human weaknesses/ family oriented	167	22%	104	11%	271	16%
Somewhat interesting	105	14%	87	9%	192	11%
Witty/frank/adult/ironic/suggestive	52	7%	101	11%	153	9%
Unexpected/original/fresh	51	7%	100	11%	151	9%
Genre						
sports	67	9%	74	8%	141	8%
religion	6	1%	15	2%	21	1%
Title appealing	14	1%	13	1%	27	2%
	759	100%	937	100%	1,696	100%

[a]Percentages based on the number of positives or negatives in this category, not on the overall quantity of responses.

an explanation for not wanting to watch the show. Interestingly, twice as big a proportion of people found lightheartedness/family orientation a positive (22%) as found it a negative (11%). But somewhat more people mentioned adult content (of the very mild sort revealed in sitcom promos) as a put-off (11%) than as a positive appeal (7%). One promo was for a new sports-oriented sitcom, and about equal percentages of respondents found the subject matter appealing as found it unappealing. It was somewhat surprising how relatively few people mentioned originality or its lack as an appeal for a new program (accounting for just 9% of all *story lines/programs* responses), but perhaps sitcom viewers as a whole do not expect much originality.

In contrast, the category of *actors/networks* shown in Table 3.3 is a composite of direct and associative comments ($N = 617$), including mentions of specific programs under the rubric of "show/hit" and names of frequently mentioned networks. As in Table 3.2, the categories had negative sides. The negative side of "attractive/vivacious actors" was "unattractive/stupid character"; the other side of "associated with liked actor/show/hit" was "disliked or not-watched show or actor." The occasional associations with specific networks could be either positive or negative. However, it is clear that respondents took note of (positive or negative) associations with known and liked actors and programs more than of any other aspect of the new programs, although finding unknown actors "attractive or vivacious" was a relatively strong positive appeal and thus also a trigger for potential viewing.

TABLE 3.3
Explanations for Relating to the Actors
or a Specific Network (or Producer)

	Actors/Networks					
	Positive		Negative		Total	
	n	%[a]	n	%[a]	N	% of All
Associated with liked actor/show/hit	159	43%	153	61%	312	51%
Attractive/vivacious actors	75	20%	33	13%	108	18%
Good lead actor	44	12%	29	12%	73	12%
Good chemistry/comradery	46	13%	4	2%	50	8%
Associated with producers of Frasier	31	9%	13	5%	44	7%
Associated with "good" comedies on						
ABC	4	1%	15	6%	19	3%
NBC	7	2%	1	0	8	1%
CBS			3	1%	3	0
	366	100%	251	100%	617	100%

[a]Percentages based on the number of positives or negatives in this category, not on the overall quantity of responses.

Finally, the category called *promos* was the one of greatest interest to this study (*N* = 1,366). Summarized in Table 3.4, the results show, not surprisingly, that the biggest categories of *positive* responses revolved around finding a particular story line "funny/amusing/humorous" (41% of all promo-related comments, but predominantly commented on in a positive way — 59% to 22%). The opposites of the categories are generally predict-

TABLE 3.4
Explanations Relating to the Promo Watched

	Promotion					
	Positive		Negative		Total	
	n	%[a]	n	%[a]	N	% of All
Funny/amusing/humorous	407	59%	151	22%	558	41%
Attention-getting/intriguing	133	19%	257	38%	390	29%
Generates anticipation/						
exciting/memorable	71	10%	140	21%	211	15%
Has catchy music/effects	66	23%	37	6%	103	7%
Informative	3	1%	77	11%	80	6%
Original	10	4%	14	2%	24	2%
	690	100%	676	100%	1,366	100%

[a]Percentages based on the number of positives or negatives in this category, not on the overall quantity of responses.

able—the other side of "attention getting" was "unappealing/uninterest-ing" (often captured as "I have better things to do"). The other side of "generates anticipation, exciting, memorable" was "boring, dreary, for-gettable," a calumny that was twice as important as the positive side. Some respondents mentioned that the music was especially "catchy" or especially "irritating." Promos were appealing when "original" but unap-pealing when "too similar to other promos," but as with programs, origi-nality didn't really seem to be expected. Finally, some respondents men-tioned that the promos they saw were unexpectedly "uninformative/confusing/ambiguous," though very few brought up such characteristics as clarity or informativeness on the positive side.

Table 3.4 shows that being successfully humorous (59%) and not being boring (38%) were the strongest determinants of promo effectiveness, ac-cording to the respondents. Similarly, being exciting or memorable and thus generating anticipation (10%) was less important than being dull or forgettable (21%). However, catchy music was primarily a positive influ-ence (23%), whereas being uninformative was primarily a negative influ-ence (11%), according to the explanations the respondents gave.

Discussion

Clearly, the results of this portion of the exploratory study have shown, first, that viewers have to be able to identify with characters and situations in order to be willing to watch a situation comedy. Moreover, the humor in a promo is terrifically important because it seemed to be taken as a reli-able key to the program's humor. But a promo has to attract attention and intrigue viewers in its own right; it has to make viewers curious. As the analysis shows, a promo created a particularly negative reaction when it was perceived as uninteresting or lacking in excitement or confusing. It appears that some viewers were put off by the very short promos (10–15 sec) used for some shows. The plot and script, as implied by the promo, were important because they created expectations about the promoted program. In addition, because viewers tended to identify with some char-acters and plots more than others, promos showed whether those ele-ments were to be expected in the program.

In addition, how the promo attracted attention and conveyed informa-tion were important because they led viewers to identify the target audi-ence of the program. The perceived target audience of the program, based on the promo, was important because viewers quickly determined whether the program was "for them" or "not for them." Lightheartedness, cuteness, and playing on human weaknesses were perceived as appropri-ate for promos for situation comedies by more people than those who saw those attributes as weaknesses. However, twice as many people found

suggestive, witty, adult themes a put-off in sitcom promos as were attracted by them.

Analysis by Demographic Groups

In the second wave of open-ended interviews, more details appeared in
the 345 transcribed reasons given for why the subjects reacted as they did.
Table 3.5 shows the distribution of the 92 second-stage interviewees in
each age and gender grouping. Although the sample was strongly skewed
by gender, with three fourths women (76%) and one fourth men (24%), it
was neatly divided into thirds by age (34%, 32%, 35%).

Results of separate analyses of comments by each of the six gender and
age groups (not included for reasons of excessive length) reveal some interesting differences by subgroups but, as a whole, very closely parallel
the much larger sample of 1,847 respondents in the distribution of comments. As in the large set of first-stage handwritten explanations, most
taped second-stage respondents also focused on identification with characters or situations, with the actors' chemistry or particular liking for an
actor, and with humor, excitement, and information in promos.

Gender. The first point is that women and men both gave nearly proportional numbers of explanations for their likely viewing decisions based
on the promos they saw (70% of comments were by women, 30% were by
men). Some clear differences in explanations by gender did appear, but it
is important to note that the women tended to make twice as many positive comments as they did negative ones, whereas men were very evenhanded. For example, funniness was about equally important to women
and to men, though women more often found promos funny and men
were more nearly evenhanded.

Identification, interestingly, was more important to men, somewhat
more on the negative side, because it constituted 20% of men's mentions
and only 12% of women's mentions — though women, predictably, placed
it twice as often on the positive side. Women also reported that chemistry

TABLE 3.5
Age and Gender Distribution of Subset of Interviewees

Age Groups	Gender Groups		Total	
	Women	Men	N	%
18–24	22	9	31	34%
25–44	23	6	29	32%
45–64	25	7	32	35%
	70 (76%)	22 (24%)	92	(100%)

between the actors was an important positive characteristic of promo appeal (10% of women's mentions), but men ignored the subject (there were no mentions of chemistry, comradery, or similar comments at all by the 22 men interviewed). Similarly, women cited the liking of a particular actor as a key characteristic of appeal (11%), but few men mentioned it.

Finally, how informative a promo was mattered to men (it constituted 10% of men's mentions), mostly on the negative side. The remaining responses were scattered among the many categories or were distributed in the same proportions and directions as the respondents.

More qualitatively, women particularly commented on characters that seemed to them to have energy or dynamism, about spin-off charactors they already liked, about the parallel between a current show and a much older show such as *I Love Lucy* or *The Odd Couple*, and about the fun of having TV characters do something they would never have the nerve to do in real life.

Age.   On the age side, responses also differed by group, though generally in ways that might be predicted. For example, funniness in promos mattered most to the youngest and midaged groups, especially on the positive side, whereas humorousness was less important to the oldest of the three age groups. Being able to identify or relate to the characters or situation was almost equally distributed across the three groups as both a positive and negative appeal—except for the midaged group, who reported it less frequently as a negative appeal. Perhaps the midaged group is somewhat more tolerant than the youngest and oldest, and thus more willing to consider exposing itself to programs about "other" people.

Informativeness mattered exactly equally across all three age groups, but particularly as a negative matter. Being uninformative or confusing was a significant negative attribute of some promos, and was applied particularly to those that were too short or too fast.

Chemistry showed up in the comments of all three age groups, but only in the explanations by women. Having appealing and/or exciting promos mattered most to the youngest group, but having promos be unmemorable mattered most to the oldest group. Recognizing a liked actor mattered most to the midaged group, largely as a positive appeal.

Qualitative Analysis.   In sum, the results show that the younger respondents focused particularly on the degree to which the show appealed to their sense of humor and the extent to which the promo itself intrigued them. Older respondents pointed out notably that some promos made them feel cheerful.

On the negative side, most respondents insisted that promos need sufficient length to explain a story line, that short teaser promos for unknown programs were unsuccessful in reaching them because they were too quick to get the viewer involved or too quick to get the show's concept across. Those respondents who did not find a promo appealing frequently commented on two features: the promo's formulaic nature—on the absence of an original story line—and on the absence of excitement in the promo itself. Sarcasm as a form of humor put off some respondents, though others (mostly young men) liked it. With regard to one promo, several respondents said they were annoyed by a character's apparent arrogance and willingness to make fun of others. In a similar vein, other respondents spoke of friendliness or its absence as the key to their potential identification and the program's appeal. Other negative comments had to do with the credibility of the script and acting. When respondents perceived that the jargon of the streets or some other aspect of speech or acting was not accurate or not up-to-date, they were put off by the promo.

Despite wanting television comedies (and thus the promos for them) to mirror their lives in some respects—especially in friendships, work situations, and home lives—respondents noted that television shows should not be *too* real. They serve a function as escape from daily life, and those who like sitcoms apparently value the convention of magically solving all the problems satisfactorily in 30 minutes. (Fans of dramas such as *ER* and *Homicide* may feel differently and thus choose other genres to watch.)

Overall, these respondents commented more often than expected about the importance of the music and of the need to identify with the characters in order to want to watch a new program. In particular, some older respondents felt free to comment on the race of characters when it did not match their own. However, identification—as a positive attribute—occurred across wide age groupings: The characters could be much younger than the respondents, yet the latter might feel able to identify with their personalities, actions, or situations. Similarity to megahit shows was considered a positive, but similarity to lesser shows (midrated or lower) was considered a negative. Revealing strong chemistry between actors seemed to be crucial to a successful promo for an unknown program.

Proposed Model for Comedy Promos

The study shows that several general conclusions apply to promotion as well as to advertising. Creating messages with characters or situations that viewers can identify with is crucial to effectiveness, as is grabbing the viewers' attention at the start of on-air spots. Associations with known celebrities or megaevents (or actors and hit shows in the case of promotion) and with popular brand names have long been recognized as keys to successful appeal. In addition, production features (executional elements in the Hierarchy of Effects model as adapted for promotion in Fig. 3.1) are

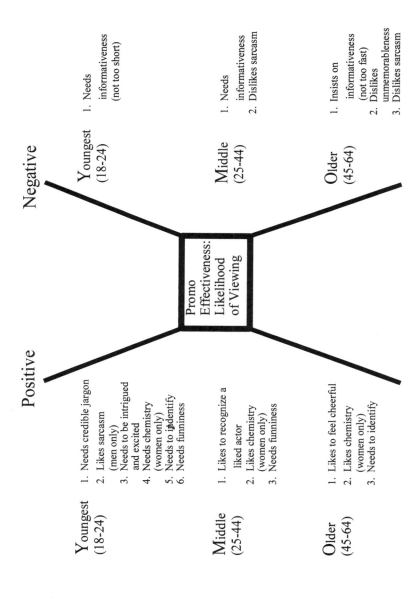

FIG. 3.4. Proposed content model for on-air comedy promotion.

Positive

Negative

Youngest (18-24)
1. Needs credible jargon
2. Likes sarcasm (men only)
3. Needs to be intrigued and excited
4. Needs chemistry (women only)
5. Needs to identify
6. Needs funniness

Middle (25-44)
1. Likes to recognize a liked actor
2. Likes chemistry (women only)
3. Needs funniness

Older (45-64)
1. Likes to feel cheerful
2. Likes chemistry (women only)
3. Needs to identify

Youngest (18-24)
1. Needs informativeness (not too short)

Middle (25-44)
1. Needs informativeness
2. Dislikes sarcasm

Older (45-64)
1. Insists on informativeness (not too fast)
2. Dislikes unmemorableness
3. Dislikes sarcasm

Promo Effectiveness: Likelihood of Viewing

central to the effectiveness of promotional messages, though which specific features are most crucial may differ from those important to advertising messages.

Clearly, promotion for television programs brings out special characteristics related to the intention to view that are not necessarily part of successful advertisements. Having humor that the target viewers find funny is necessary to foster a viewing intention for promos for comedies, though naturally not for dramatic series. Generating excitement and anticipation is necessary to develop a positive attitude toward the promo and the program but not necessary for commercial advertisements. Among production features, music was particularly important as an accompaniment to on-air program promotion, as was adequate length in time for spots introducing new programs.

Moreover, the specific findings about production features differed for particular different demographic groups, as the study showed, and the findings are reflected in the proposed content model for comedy promotion shown in Fig. 3.4. The model indicates that the impact of executional features on likelihood of viewing varies considerably for the youngest age group compared to the middle and older age groups, and that specific features differ by gender.

The positive and negative elements listed in the model suggest attributes that can guide practitioners of promotion. They also suggest characteristics that should be kept in mind by researchers when assessing attitude toward promotion, attitude toward the program, and viewing intentions.

Significance of the Study

For the television industry, these findings reveal the wide variety of attitudes people have toward the genre of situation comedies and the kinds of content in on-air promos that capture their attention. In promoting a new situation comedy, a key ingredient appeared to be an association with something familiar and already well liked—such as a known actor, a hit show, or a watched show. It can safely be assumed that viewers expected familiar actors to continue to be stars in new programs. Even the bare fact of being produced by the same people who had created another favorite was noticed by a few people. However, association with a particular network did not seem a very strong indicator except in a minor negative sense for ABC. It was largely younger people who perceived some networks as having programs they might want to watch and others as not having such programs. However, older viewers took little note of sources, implying that older viewers might be more flexible than younger ones, although ratings show that younger viewers try more channels. A paradox!

The findings reinforce the view that promos directly influence viewing decisions. Specifically, they demonstrate the importance of having a high-quality show, with a good story line and appealing characters. And given that, in promos producers need to make effective use of production elements like music and sound effects, to include basic information about a show as well as a good joke, and to associate the show with known and liked actors or other hit shows. Several *unexpected* aspects to the responses appeared. First, it was expected that sexual innuendo might play a stronger positive role than it appeared to. Second, it was expected that the particular network would play a stronger role than it seemed to, although no promos from Fox or UPN were included, so that subject remains to be explored. Third, it was expected that the subject matter of a particular episode or a series might be more frequently identified as either an attraction or a repellent, but relatively few people mentioned it, even when a promo was about a very specific subtopic such as sports. Fourth, it was a surprise that a relatively large proportion of people noticed and commented on the music or special effects in promos. And fifth, it was an eye-opener that the most interesting and relevant responses were the *minor* ones (not the common ones of "because the promo is funny" or "I can identify with a character"), which leads to the next research step.

AN AGENDA FOR FUTURE RESEARCH

The topics of the size of promotion's impact and the range of factors impacting ratings are of great interest to the creators and schedulers of programs and promotion. Writers and producers are understandably interested in what content and arrangements of the parts of a promotional spot contribute to its effectiveness. Executives of the broadcast and cable television industries not only set the guidelines for the scheduling of on-air promotion and the purchase of print promotion, but are more generally concerned because of promos' impact on ratings. Increased competition across the board — from new networks and new media and increasing use of the new media — is driving the traditional services toward more rigorous examination of every aspect of their businesses. Conventional practices deriving from the way practitioners *think* audiences behave and the way networks *ought to* behave are no longer sufficient justification. The arena of promotion stands to become a highly fruitful area for research that has theoretical implications and industry application.

Genre, Time, and Daypart Effects

Although many studies have implications about promotion's varying impact according to the genre of the programs, very few studies have directly approached promotion from a genre perspective. Eastman et al. (2000) explored promotion of situation comedies; Billings et al. (1998) and Billings and Eastman (1998) tackled the impact of promotion within sports programs, as discussed by Eastman and Billings (chap. 7, this volume). But dramas and movies may have special characteristics that affect the impact of promotion. Reality shows and news magazines may be other special kinds of programs. Gantz and Schwartz (chap. 6, this volume) explore the promotion of children's programs and reveal how little that phenomenon has been studied. Adams and Lubber (chap. 8, this volume) suggest some implications for promotion of television movies, and Buchman (chap. 9, this volume) suggests implications for promotion of local newscasts. But promotion's impact and effectiveness in most local programming and non-prime-time network programming remains to be investigated.

Drawing on excitation-transfer theory, Mundorf et al. (1991) concluded that the standard industry practice of interrupting exciting programming with commercials (and promos) might have a negative impact on reactions to those messages, leaving many questions for subsequent studies. A study by Kaid, Chanslor, and Hovind (1992) of political advertising found an interaction between the program carrying the political message and the genre of the program, a finding that raises many questions for research into program/message compatibility, with implications beyond program promotion for entertainment and information.

Longitudinal studies, content studies, and structural studies by daypart are particularly needed. Bellamy (1992) called for time-line studies of promotion in order to track changes as a reflection of changes in television economics. He also called for daypart studies for the purpose of tracking operational changes in network television. Walker (1993) pointed out the need to analyze the impact of promotion on ratings for rerun programs separately from first-run series and to distinguish new from continuing programs, because in both cases — reruns and new programs — the ratings are substantially lower.

Eastman and Newton (1998a, 1999) called for analyses by program daypart, taking into account program ratings and network. The discussion earlier in this chapter took note of the difficulties in determining how to operationalize several variables. For example, promotional spots promoting several programs have been treated in different ways by different researchers. Design and pacing are also susceptible to multiple interpretations. Moreover, analyses of local dayparts might suggest very different strategies from those the networks follow.

Clutter and Position Effects

Even though studying clutter and position effects is already part of the agenda for research on promotion, one area that has not been considered is the impact of clutter and promo position on other important variables.

Zhao (1997) concluded that clutter and position have the following effects on television advertising effectiveness:

1. Placing an advertisement in more crowded pods (clutter) leads to lower brand memory.
2. Placing an advertisement in a later position in a pod leads to lower brand memory.
3. Audiences like an advertisement less when they have more advertisements placed before them.

An examination of clutter and serial position effects for promos on memory and liking for the promo should be part of future research on promo effectiveness. One way to go about it would be through direct replication of advertising experiments on clutter and serial position effects. Researchers could conduct experiments where the number of other messages in a break and the position of the promo in the break would be manipulated and then measure attitudes toward the promo and memory.

This form of replication would be worthwhile because previous research has shown that clutter and position effects are not always the same across product types (Zhao, 1997). Television promos are different enough from product advertisements that the clutter and position effects found for promos could be slightly different than the clutter and position effects found for product advertisements. Television program promos are likely to stand out in a commercial break because they are so different from product advertisements. For example, promos are more likely to be shorter than many product advertisements, more likely to incorporate a short narrative scene, and more likely to have subjects that are more familiar than the subjects of many commercials. In other words, more people have had the direct experience of watching the show *Home Improvement* than have had the direct experience of driving a Mercury automobile. These differences — message length, narrative style, and familiarity with the subject of the message — could lead audiences to view promos differently than product advertisements, which in turn could lead to differing serial and position effects.

Future research on clutter and position effects for promotions should also develop more specific conceptualizations of clutter and position. Previous research on television program promotion has counted the total number of spots (advertisements and promos) in a break and coded serial position of promos, whereas advertising researchers have moved to more specific conceptualizations of clutter and position effects. Zhao (1997) proposed that clutter effects are really the result of two different processes — a proactive effect, caused by a change in the number of preceding spots, and a retroactive effect, caused by a change in the number of succeeding spots.

If these two different processes have differing effects on message impact for television advertisements, researchers investigating promotion's impact should also consider them. Future content analysis should specifically code the number of spots before a promotion and the number of spots after a promotion in addition to coding the overall number of spots. This would enable researchers to more precisely examine clutter and position effects in promotion by searching for proactive and retroactive effects and seeing how measures of promotional effectiveness differ.

A second way that future research on television program promotion should move toward more specific conceptualizations of clutter and position effects is by looking more closely at the nature of the spots within a break. Advertising researchers have proposed examining competitive clutter (messages for a similar product) and noncompetitive clutter (messages for different products) because competitive clutter tends to have stronger effects (Kent & Allen, 1994). This distinction in type of clutter is relevant to television program promotion because of the industry practice of promoting several shows within the same spot and even within the same break. Future research should continue to examine the effects of what Eastman and Newton (1998a) termed *multiple spots* (promoting several shows in the same promo) on promotion's impact but should consider the effects in light of competitive clutter rather than general clutter. It could be that competitive clutter for television program promotion has particularly strong effects on some of the new dependent measures of promotion impact that will be discussed in a following section.

Testing the Hierarchy of Effects Model

No research has been done yet that applies Colley's (1961) Hierarchy of Effects model to the specific context of television program promotion. There are several reasons why testing the Hierarchy of Effects model should be part of the agenda for future research in promotion. One reason is that the model offers an alternative and possibly complementary framework to the salience model. Whereas the salience model proposes in general terms that some features of promos are more salient than others, the Hierarchy of Effects model proposes specific relationships that could be used to define what it means to be a "salient" feature of a promo. In other words, the salient features of promos could be conceptualized as features that have strong relationships with attitudes toward the promo, attitudes toward the promoted program, and viewing intentions. A second reason is that the model has untapped heuristic value for organizing a research agenda. The Hierarchy of Effects model provides a framework for conceptualizing structural variables (i.e., executional features) separately from message impact variables and provides three clear areas of research — research that identifies structural features of promos, research that investigates the relationship between structural features and message impact, and research that investigates interrelationships between message impact variables. A third reason for including the Hierarchy of Effects model in the agenda for future research is that testing the model directly addresses the question of the extent to which conclusions from advertising research can be generalized to promotion. Earlier in this chapter, it was proposed that television program promotion influences decision making and behavior through the pathways proposed by the Hierarchy of Effects model. If this is true, future research that validates the Hierarchy of Effects model in the context of promotion also validates generalizing conclusions from advertising research to the area of promotion. A final reason for testing the Hierarchy of Effects model on promotional messages is that the model examines a broader context of message impact than has previously been considered in research on promos. Whereas most previous research on television program promotion has only measured ratings and shares as indicators of message impact, the Hierarchy of Effects model involves other variables such as attitudes that are also important indicators of overall message impact.

If the Hierarchy of Effects model is to be incorporated into the agenda for future research on promotion, how might testing the model proceed? Testing this model on television program promos would most logically proceed in two steps. The first step would involve some reconceptualizing and formulating of proper operational definitions of elements in the model as applied to television program promos. The second step would consist of conducting experiments to test the relationships in the model using television program promos.

Three primary areas in the traditional Hierarchy of Effects model will probably require some reconceptualization by researchers wishing to extend the model to television program promos. The first problematic part of the model lies in the definition of executional elements. The opportunity exists for researchers to conduct massive content analyses of television program promos in order to discover what executional elements promo producers are using and how to best conceptualize them. Researchers cannot take all of the executional elements that have been identified in television advertisements and apply them to promos. Television program promos have at least some unique executional elements related to message length and the practice of promoting several shows in a singly produced message. Content analysis needs to be done to identify these unique executional elements that can then be used in studies of message impact.

A second area of the Hierarchy of Effects model that may need to be rethought is attitude toward the message—traditionally conceptualized in terms of attitude toward the advertisement. Attitude toward the adver-

tisement is often further broken down into attitude toward claim components and attitude toward nonclaim components of the advertisement.
Researchers in the area of promotion need to develop their own conceptualization of attitude toward the message. As the study conducted for this
chapter shows, two possibly distinct dimensions of attitude toward the
promo are attitude toward stars/characters in the promo and attitude toward the plot or plot segment (if present) portrayed in the promo. As was
done in early work on advertising, researchers need to investigate
whether attitude toward the promo is a uni- or multidimensional construct. If it is a multidimensional construct, the specific dimensions will
need to be named and validated.

The third problematic area for researchers lies in developing a useful
measure of viewing intentions. Advertising researchers, rather than directly measuring purchases, generally measure purchase intention; in the
development process, they explore the correlation between purchase intention and actual purchases. Researchers in promotion should do the
same thing. That is, they should explore the correlation between measures
of viewing intention and ratings. The correlation between a measure of
viewing intention and ratings would be an indication of the measure's validity.

Studies that assess the correlation between viewing intentions and ratings would be relatively easy to conduct. One such study could be done
by obtaining a sample of broadcast promos and, before the episodes being
promoted are aired, showing them to a large sample of potential viewers,
perhaps in a manner similar to that used in the study reported in this
chapter. After viewing each promo, the potential viewers would complete
a measure of viewing intention. After the promoted episodes are aired,
the researcher could do one or both of two things: Ask each viewer
whether he or she actually watched the promoted program, and obtain
the ratings for each episode in order to calculate the correlation coefficient
between viewing intention and ratings.

Once researchers are comfortable with their conceptualization of the
Hierarchy of Effects model as it applies to television program promotion,
the second step of conducting direct tests of the relationships described in
the model can proceed. Once content analyses have identified executional
features of television program promos, for example, experiments can be
conducted that test the effects of different executional features on attitude
toward the promo and attitude toward the promoted program. For example, researchers could examine the impact of different lengths of scenes on
attitudes by obtaining a sample of broadcast promos with three different
lengths of scenes from the promoted program. Ideally, the researcher
should obtain several promos containing each length of scene in order to
gain the validity associated with a repeated measures experimental de-

sign. The researcher would then expose a group of participants to the promos and analyze the impact of scene length on attitude toward the promo and attitude toward the promoted program. Other experiments should also be conducted that assess the rest of the relationships described in the Hierarchy of Effects model, such as the relationship between attitude toward the promo and attitude toward the promoted program, as well as the relationship between both types of attitudes and viewing intentions.

New Dependent Measures

As stated earlier, ratings are the primary dependent measure that researchers studying television program promotion have used, and they have served as a useful indicator of promotion's impact, but they cannot provide precise insight into the complex relationship between executional features of promos and message impact. Future research on television program promotion must incorporate new dependent measures in addition to assessing program ratings.

One obvious reason for obtaining new dependent measures is to provide a more thorough assessment of promotion's impact. Viewing behavior as measured by program ratings is likely not the only important variable affected by promos. The primary goal of program promotion is to impact viewing behavior, but focusing research exclusively on examining viewing behavior is shortsighted because it is necessarily limited to short-term effects. New dependent measures that assess longer term promotional impact might include character identification and parasocial interaction. These measures could be considered for program genres and specific shows. For example, it might be interesting to investigate the effects of narrative style in promos on identification with characters in the promoted programs. It could be that direct announcements to the audience by one or more of a show's characters in a promo positively affects viewers' identification with characters in the show, but researchers have not yet investigated such a possibility.

An additional reason researchers need to look for other dependent variables in addition to ratings is to be able to argue in favor of a causal relationship between structural features of promos and promotional effectiveness. Research on promotion that only measures ratings as an assessment of promotional impact establishes correlational relationships between executional features and promo impact rather than causal relationships. The most valid way to establish a causal relationship is through experimental research. Program ratings are not variables that it is practical to assess in an experiment. The establishment of causal relationships between executional features of promos and promo impact will require developing measures of emotional response, attention, memory, and other variables that are practical to obtain during experiments. The inclusion of such variables expands the field of promotion research by allowing researchers to use promos to study how the human cognitive system works and how people cognitively process persuasive messages in general. The practical value of promotion research in providing valuable information to promo producers will persist as long as the new dependent measures are significantly correlated to direct measures of viewing behavior like ratings.

If developing new dependent measures is so important for future research on television program promotion, what are examples of possible new dependent measures? Attitudes are a new dependent measure that has already been suggested. In the previous section, it was proposed that both attitude toward the promotion and attitude toward the program be measured in future studies. It would also be interesting and valuable to measure other potential dimensions of attitude, such as intrusiveness and wear-out, as indicators of attitude toward television program promotion at large rather than attitude toward specific promotions. One such study might obtain a random sample of heavy, medium, and light television viewers and survey the sample's attitudes toward television program promotion at large. Advertising researchers have done similar studies to assess public attitude toward television advertising at large and used the information as an indicator of the difficulty advertisers face in reaching the television audience. The field of television program promotion could likely benefit from similar information regarding public attitude toward program promotion.

It would be interesting to see if attitudes toward promos are more or less positive than attitudes toward advertisements. Gantz and Eastman (1983) conducted a survey of people's use of promotional media to find out about television programs that is now nearly 2 decades old, but unreplicated. They found that most people considered on-air promos somewhat useful in making viewing decisions. Because the number of available channels and amount of promotion that viewers are exposed to has substantially increased since 1983, this study needs to be updated. Future research needs to get a handle on how useful the viewing public presently perceives on-air and print promotion to be in making viewing decisions. Researchers could then also examine the effects of different structural features of promos on perceived usefulness of the on-air spots and print ads for programs.

A second new dependent measure that could be assessed is attention. Knowledge regarding which executional features of promos are effective at grabbing and holding attention is vital to designing effective promotions because attention is a necessary but not exclusive prerequisite for promo impact. In studying attention, researchers could use such physiological measures as heart rate as indicators of attention allocated during online cognitive processing of a promotion, along with self-report measures of attention to and involvement with a promotion. One interesting study would be to examine how different executional features of television program promos affect perceived relevance, an important dimension of attention and involvement.

A third new dependent measure future research on promotion should assess is memory. A key research question asks which executional features of on-air television program promotion influence top-of-mind awareness for television programs? For program producers, this question has practical relevance at the start of each new season of television programs. A study could be conducted that combines a content analysis of promos for new programs with a telephone survey that measures recall of the new season's television programs. Analyzing the executional features of promos for new programs that have a high rate of recall in the telephone survey could suggest the features that effectively influence top-of-mind awareness for specific types of television programs. Another question future research on promotion should address that involves the assessment of memory is which executional features of promos foster or interfere with recall of such specific information as day and time of the program. This question would be especially relevant to the study of promotion for television specials and new or moved prime-time programs.

New dependent measures such as the ones just discussed not only spark interesting research questions but play significant roles in the persuasion process — which is a primary goal of television program promotion. Attitudes, attention, and memory are not the only potentially important new dependent measures, but it is hoped that discussing them will provoke additional ideas and encourage researchers to vigorously pursue other measures that will lead to a more thorough investigation of promotion's impact.

REFERENCES

Adams, W. J. (1993). TV program scheduling strategies and their relationship to new program renewal rates and rating changes. *Journal of Broadcasting & Electronic Media, 37,* 465–474.

Associated Press. (1999, April 12). Clutter of commercials growing in prime time. *Herald Times,* p. A-10.

Bellamy, R. (1992). Emerging images of product differentiation: Network television promotion in a time of industry change. *Feedback, 33*(3), 22–26.

Bellamy, R. V., Jr., & Walker, J. R. (1996). *Television and the remote control: Grazing on a vast wasteland.* New York: Guilford.

Billings, A. C., & Eastman, S. T. (1998). Marketing the Olympics within the Olympics. *Ecquid Novi* (University of South Africa), *19*(2), 74–87.

Billings, A. C., Eastman, S. T., & Newton, G. D. (1998) Atlanta revisited: Prime-time promotion in the 1996 Summer Olympics. *Journal of Broadcasting & Electronic Media, 42*, 50–78.

Blakeslee, S. (1998, October 13). Placebos prove so powerful even experts are surprised: New studies explore the brain's triumph over reality. *New York Times*, pp. D1, D4.

Bolls, P. D., & Potter, R. F. (1998). I saw it on the radio: The effects of imagery-evoking radio commercials on listeners' allocation of attention and attitude toward the ad. In D. D. Muehling (Ed.), *Proceedings of the 1998 Conference of the American Academy of Advertising*.

Colley, R. H. (1961). *Defining advertising goals for measured advertising results*. New York: Association of National Advertisers.

Cooper, R. (1993). An expanded, integrated model for determining audience exposure to television. *Journal of Broadcasting & Electronic Media, 37*, 401–418.

Duncan, C. P., & Nelson, J. E. (1985). Effects of humor in a radio advertising experiment. *Journal of Advertising, 14*(2), 33–40.

Eastman, S. T. (1994). Evaluating premium performance. *Journal of Broadcasting & Electronic Media, 28*, 201–213.

Eastman, S. T. (1998). Programming theory under stress: The active industry and the active audience. In M. E. Roloff (Ed.), *Communication yearbook* (Vol. 21, pp. 323–377). Thousand Oaks, CA: Sage.

Eastman, S. T., & Ferguson, D. A. (1997). *Broadcast/cable programming: Strategies and practices* (5th ed.). Belmont, CA: Wadsworth.

Eastman, S. T., Head, S. W., & Klein, L. (1989). *Broadcast/cable programming: Strategies and practices* (3rd ed.). Belmont, CA: Wadsworth.

Eastman, S. T., Neal-Lunsford, J., & Riggs, K. E. (1995). Coping with grazing: Prime-time strategies for accelerated program transitions. *Journal of Broadcasting & Electronic Media, 39*, 92–108.

Eastman, S. T., & Newton, G. D. (1995). Delineating grazing: Observations of remote control use. *Journal of Communication, 45*(1), 77–95.

Eastman, S. T., & Newton, G. D. (1998a). The impact of structural salience within on-air promotion. *Journal of Broadcasting & Electronic Media, 42*, 50–79.

Eastman, S. T., & Newton, G. D. (1998b). Estimating the contributions of inheritance and promotion. In S. T. Eastman (Ed.), *Report on compilation valuation for distant television signals* (pp. 15–31), filed as part of the Statement of Case and Exhibits regarding retransmission 1998–2000, on behalf of BBC, CBRA, and CRRA, with the Copyright Board of Canada.

Eastman, S. T., & Newton, G. D. (1999). Hitting promotion hard: A network response to channel surfing and new competition. *Journal of Applied Communication Research, 27*, 73–85.

Eastman, S. T., Newton, G. D., & Bolls, P. D. (2000, June). *Assessing transference from promos to ratings: The impact of humor, appeals, and presentation*. Paper presented to the International Communication Association, Acapulco, Mexico.

Eastman, S. T., Newton, G. D., & Pack, L. (1996). Promoting prime-time programs in megasporting events. *Journal of Broadcasting & Electronic Media, 40*, 366–388.

Eastman, S. T., Newton, G. D., Riggs, K. E., & Neal-Lunsford, J. (1997). Accelerating the flow: A transition effect in programming? *Journal of Broadcasting & Electronic Media, 41*, 305–323.

Eastman, S. T., & Otteson, J. L. (1994). Promotion increases ratings, doesn't it? The impact of program promotion in the 1992 Olympics. *Journal of Broadcasting & Electronic Media, 38*, 307–322.

Ferguson, D. A. (1992a). Channel repertoire in the presence of remote control devices, VCRs, and cable television. *Journal of Broadcasting & Electronic Media, 36*, 83–91.

Ferguson, D. A. (1992b). Predicting inheritance effects from VCR and cable penetration. *Dowden Center Journal, 1*, 28–40.

Ferguson, D. A., & Perse, E. M. (1993). Media and audience influences on channel repertoire. *Journal of Broadcasting & Electronic Media, 37*, 31–47.

Gantz, W., & Eastman, S. T. (1983). Viewer uses of promotional media to find out about television programs. *Journal of Broadcasting, 27*, 269–277.

Gelb, B. D., & Zinkhan, G. M. (1986). Humor and advertising effectiveness after repeated exposures to a radio commercial. *Journal of Advertising, 15*(2), 15–20.

Gill, J. D., Grossbart, S., & Laczniak, R. N. (1988). Influence of involvement, commitment and familiarity on brand beliefs and attitudes of viewers exposed to alternative ad claim strategies. *Journal of Advertising, 17*(2), 33–43.

Glaser, B. G., & Strauss, A. L. (1967). *The discovery of grounded theory: Strategies for qualitative research*. Chicago: Aldine.

Greenberg, B. S. (1974). Gratifications of television viewing and their correlates for British children. In J. G. Blumler & E. Katz (Eds.), *The uses of mass communications* (pp. 71–92). Beverly Hills, CA: Sage.

Johar, J. S., & Sirgy, J. M. (1991). Value expressive versus utilitarian advertising appeals: When and why to use which appeal. *Journal of Advertising, 20*(3), 23–34.

Kaid, L. L., Chanslor, M., & Hovind, M. (1992). The influence of program and commercial type on political advertising effectiveness. *Journal of Broadcasting & Electronic Media, 36*, 303–320.

Kent, R. J., & Allen, C. T. (1994). Competitive interference in consumer memory for advertising: The role of brand familiarity. *Journal of Marketing, 58*(3), 97–105.

Laskey, H. A., Fox, R. J., & Crask, M. R. (1994). Investigating the impact of executional style on television commercial effectiveness. *Journal of Advertising Research, 34*(6), 9–16.

Laskey, H. A., Fox, R. J., & Crask, M. R. (1995). The relationship between advertising message strategy and television commercial effectiveness. *Journal of Advertising Research, 35*(2), 31–39.

Love, G. D. (1981). *A comparison of the responses of selected heavy and light viewers to on-air television promotional materials*. Unpublished master's thesis, Temple University.

Madden, T., & Weinberger, M. G. (1982). The effects of humor on attention in magazine advertising. *Journal of Advertising, 11*(3), 8–14.

Mathur, M., & Chattopadhyay, A. (1991). The impact of moods generated by television programs on responses to advertising. *Psychology and Marketing, 8*(1), 59–68.

Mattes, J., & Cantor, J. (1982). Enhancing responses to television advertisements via the transfer of residual arousal for prior programming. *Journal of Broadcasting, 26*, 553–566.

Mundorf, N., Zillmann, D., & Drew, D. (1991). Effects of disturbing televised events on the acquisition of information from subsequently presented commercials. *Journal of Advertising, 20*(1), 46–53.

Owens, J. W., & Bryant, J. (1998, April). *The on-air promotion of college and professional football: A content analysis*. Paper presented to the Broadcast Education Association, Las Vegas, NV.

Palmgreen, P., & Rayburn, J. D., II. (1982). Gratifications sought and media exposure: An expectancy value model. *Communication Research, 9*, 561–580.

Petty, R. E., Cacioppo, J. T., & Schumann, D. (1983). Central and peripheral routes to advertising effectiveness: The moderating role of involvement. *Journal of Consumer Research, 10*, 135–146.

Puto, C. P., & Wells, W. D. (1984). Informational and transformational advertising: The differential effects of time. In T. C. Kinnear (Ed.), *Advances in consumer research* (Vol. 9, pp. 638–643). Provo, UT: Association for Consumer Research.

Rubin, A. M. (1994). Media uses and effects: A uses-and-gratifications perspective. In J. Bryant & D. Zillmann (Eds.), *Media effects: Advances in theory and research* (pp. 417–436). Hillsdale, NJ: Lawrence Erlbaum Associates.

Spotts, H. E., Weinberger, M. G., & Parsons, A. L. (1997). Assessing the use and impact of humor on advertising effectiveness: A contingency approach. *Journal of Advertising, 26*(3), 17–32.

Stewart, D. W., & Furse, D. H. (1986). *Effective television advertising: A study of 1000 commercials.* Lexington, MA: Heath.

Taylor, C. R., Miracle, G. E., & Wilson, D. R. (1997). The impact of information level on the effectiveness of U.S. and Korean television commercials. *Journal of Advertising, 26*(1), 1–18.

Walker, J. R. (1993). Catchy, yes, but does it work? The impact of broadcast network promotion frequency and type on program success. *Journal of Broadcasting & Electronic Media, 37,* 197–207.

Walker, J. R., & Bellamy, R. V., Jr. (Eds.). (1993). *The remote control in the new age of television.* Westport, CT: Praeger.

Webster, J. G., & Phalen, P. F. (1997). *The mass audience: Rediscovering the dominant model.* Mahwah, NJ: Lawrence Erlbaum Associates.

Webster, J. G., & Wang, T. (1992). Structural determinants of exposure to television: The case of repeat viewing. *Journal of Broadcasting & Electronic Media, 36,* 125–136.

Yoon, K., Bolls, P., & Lang, A. (1998). The effects of arousal on liking and believability of commercials. *Journal of Marketing Communications, 4,* 101–114.

Zhao, X. (1997). Clutter and serial order redefined and retested. *Journal of Advertising Research, 37*(5), 57–73.

Sex and Violence in Program Promotion

James R. Walker
Saint Xavier University

The high school shootings in Littleton, Colorado, stimulated a new round of governmental and media scrutiny of the entertainment media's role in the creation of violence in the United States (Oldenburg & Snider, 1999). The effects of mediated violence have been studied extensively since the rise of television in the early 1950s and continue to be the subject of much interest (Gunter, 1994; Rowland, 1983; Walker & Ferguson, 1998).

The Issues for Society

As early as 1972, the surgeon general of the United States proclaimed a causal linkage between violence on television and aggressive behavior in children (Lowery & DeFleur, 1988). But just as the cigarette industry denied the role of the cumulative effects of its frequently lethal product, the television industry has always shifted the blame to other sources, often parents, and away from their own profit-driven creations. Despite its use of a public resource (the electromagnetic spectrum), the television industry advises parents to "just say no" to their children by turning off the set if they are anxious about the negative impacts of the entertainment media (Oldenburg & Snider, 1999).

Concerns about the sexual content of television have existed since the birth of the medium. Often, this criticism has been raised by conservative religious groups. Since the rise of AIDS as a major health risk in the 1980s, however, the irresponsible nature of much of the sexual activity presented on television also has been seen as a health issue. Since television frequently presents sexual passion, but rarely deals with its consequences, the sexual content of the medium has been seen as a causal agent in the rise of sexually transmitted diseases and high levels of teen pregnancies.

For decades, media scholars have studied the levels of sexual and/or violent content in television. By 1980, this concern had produced numerous studies of the antisocial impact of media violence (Comstock, Chaffee, Katzman, McCombs, & Roberts, 1978; Rowland, 1983) as well as of the sexual (Fernandez-Collado, Greenberg, Korzenny, & Atkin, 1978; Franzblau, Sprafkin, & Rubinstein, 1977; Sapolsky, 1982; Silverman, Sprafkin, & Rubinstein, 1979) and violent (Gerbner & Gross, 1976; Greenberg, Edison, Korzenny, Fernandez-Collado, & Atkin, 1980) content of network television programs.

As the development of cable television in the 1980s produced such new television forms such as music videos, interest in sex and violence on television intensified (Baxter, DeRiemer, Landini, Leslie, & Singletary, 1985; Brown & Campbell, 1986; Caplan, 1985; Gunter, 1994; Sapolsky & Tabarlet, 1991; Sherman & Dominick, 1986; Walker, 1987; Walker & Ferguson, 1998; Wartella, 1996). More recent public discussions have reflected expanded concerns about violent video games (Provenzo, 1991) and proliferation of sexual content on the Internet (Oldenburg & Snider, 1999).

The Issues for the Industry

The response of the television industry to research documenting the medium's negative effects typically has been to ignore the findings of researchers (Cantor, 1971) or to question their validity (Milavsky, Kessler, Stipp, & Rubens, 1982) and to characterize the issue as a matter of freedom of expression. At several congressional inquiries, the industry couched its vigorous defense as a protection of First Amendment rights (Rowland, 1983). However, some efforts at self-regulation, such as the now defunct National Association of Broadcasters Code and network self-censorship, have been utilized in the past. More recently, the television industry has adopted a voluntary content-labeling system similar to the one long used by the Motion Picture Association of America ("Few Are Tuned," 1999; see the detailed discussion of content labeling by Gantz & Schwartz, chap. 6, this volume).

The industry's vigorous defense of its right to use questionable content may be the result of economic necessity. For commercial television, the use of violent and sexual content is simply one of the surest ways to attract and maintain an audience for its programming. Because the industry's revenues are determined primarily by the size and demographic composition of the audience it sells to advertisers, sex and violence are seen as necessary components of at least some of its programming. In addition, cable and home video introduced a level of explicitness in content that was previously prohibited on broadcast television. As competition for viewers among cable, broadcasters, and home video rose, any content that could attract any audience became more essential. Thus, broadcasters presume they must "push the envelope" of sexual and violent content to keep up with new competitors. Although social concerns about the negative effects of violent and sexual content may be increasing, the perceived need for such content from a programmer's perspective has become greater than ever.

The Significance of Promotional Content

Missing from all but a few of scholarly and industry discussions of sex and violence on television are analyses of the content of the on-air promos used to attract viewers to television programs. As competition for an increasingly fragmented television audience intensified in the last 2 decades, the number of on-air promos soared. By the end of the 1990s, Ferguson (1999) estimated that each broadcast network produced over 7,000 on-air promos per year. The rapid proliferation of remote controls since the early 1980s has made promos even more important for programmers attempting to arrest the attention of the increasingly restless viewer (Bellamy & Walker, 1996).

The content of promotional spots and its potential impact are of special significance for three reasons. First, since promos are aired repeatedly, a promotion containing sexual or aggressive clips from program content is seen by a far larger and more diverse audience than the actual program. For example, viewers who watch a situation comedy at 8:30 may see several promos for the medical drama that follows at 9:00. Although the on-air promo may fail in its manifest purpose — to convince them to stay tuned and "flow through" to the next hour — there may be negative effects from viewing the sexual and violent content in the promo. Thus, the industry advice to parents to just turn off the set to avoid exposure to harmful content is not effective for on-air promos because parents have no advance warning of when the offending promotional spots will air. Thus, if violent television messages cultivate the perception of a "mean and scary world" (Gerbner & Gross, 1976) or encourage children to play more aggressively (Bandura, 1994; Gunter, 1994), then researchers should scrutinize television promos as closely as actual programming, which heretofore has been the sole target of most television effects studies.

Second, the frequent repetition of promotional messages also increases the potential impact of the message. Earlier research has shown that more frequent repetition of promos is related to the manifest intent of the message, higher program ratings. This is especially true for established, and thus widely viewed, programs (Walker, 1993). Thus, if repetition increases the intended effects of the promo, it is reasonable to assume that any unintended effects of sexual or aggressive content may increase as well.

Finally, the short length and disjointed nature of most on-air promos means that much of their sexual and/or aggressive content is not viewed in the context of the larger story and/or character development (Davis & Walker, 1991). Sexual behavior and violent outbursts often appear gratuitous, as on-air promos rarely give the reasons for or consequences of these dramatic actions. Viewers may be tantalized by a passionate encounter without realizing the nature of the relationship previously established between the lovers. As discussed by Gantz and Schwartz (chap. 6, this volume), some researchers have seen such separation of effects from causes as a major reason why violence in television programs has stronger effects on younger children, who do not understand the motivations for the violence, than on adults, who comprehend the larger context (Lowery & DeFleur, 1988). Thus, the potential negative impact of sexual and aggressive content in program promos may be greater than for similar content in programs.

PREVIOUS RESEARCH ON SEX AND VIOLENCE IN PROMOTION

Although sexual and violent content in television programs has been the subject of a vast body of research, the quantity of sexual and violent content in program promotional announcements or print advertisements for network or other programs has been analyzed in only a few studies. Table 4.1 summarizes the results of these studies.

The Content of On-Air Promos

In a general descriptive analysis of a wide variety of content in on-air promos, Brown (1989) examined 605 promotional announcements aired in prime time by ABC, CBS, and NBC during one week of the 1984 television season. He found slightly more than a quarter of all promotional announcements contained sensuality expressed in either actions or words. Aggression occurred in about one third of the promotions. For both sexuality and aggression, ABC had the incidents with the longest average duration in seconds.

In a more detailed analysis of aggressive and sexual content, Davis and Walker (1991) looked at both physical aggression and sexual behaviors in

TABLE 4.1
Studies of Sexual and Aggressive Content

Author(s)	Year	Samples	Relevant Findings
Tabarlet and Gottshall	1996	1,705 prime-time promos in 171 hours on ABC, CBS, NBC, and Fox.	Demonstrated that sexual content was more common in nonsweeps than in sweeps programming, and results significant.
Sapolsky et al.	1994	1,705 prime-time promos in 171 hours on ABC, CBS, NBC, and Fox.	Found slightly more than three incidents of sexual content per hour; NBC had the most sexual content, and 22% of nonsweeps and 16% of sweeps promos contained sexual content.
Davis and Walker	1991	1,204 promos for prime-time and non-prime-time shows in 320 hours of prime-time and non-prime-time shows on ABC, CBS, NBC, Fox, and cable networks.	Found physical aggression in 30% of promos, with sexual behavior (not including language) in 12% of spots; NBC had the most promos with sexual behavior, CBS the most with physical aggression.
Brown	1989	605 prime-time promos in 1 week of programs on ABC, CBS, and NBC.	Reported sensuality in slightly more than 25% of promos.
Williams	1989	625 TV Guide ads for network prime-time programs.	Found sexual content in 21% of ads, violent content in 22% of ads.
Soley and Reid	1985	806 TV Guide ads for prime-time and non-prime-time network and local programs.	Reported sexual content in 20.8% of ads, violent content in 19.9% of ads; concluded that network programs had 50% higher levels of both sex and violence.

1,204 promotional announcements recorded from August to October of 1990. Their sample was drawn from both broadcast and cable network programming, including prime time, network news, late fringe, and weekend sports programming on four broadcast networks (ABC, CBS, NBC, and Fox), and prime-time programming on four cable networks (ESPN, TBS, TNT, and USA). The promos included spots for broadcast and cable network programs aired in both prime-time and non-prime-time periods. Physical aggression was found in 30% of the announcements, with the Fox network using aggression in nearly half of its promos. The other broadcast and cable networks used physical aggression in approximately 3 of every 10 announcements. The most common form of physical aggression was physical threat (such as pointing a gun), followed by assault with an object (not including shooting), shooting, and assault without an object (hitting, scratching, pushing, etc.). Sexual behaviors were less common. Some type of sexual behavior was featured in 12% of the promos. NBC had the highest percent of promos with sexual behavior (17.8%), whereas the Fox network featured the fewest (9.6%). Not surprisingly, the most common type of sexual behavior was kissing.

Sapolsky, Tabarlet, and Kaye (1994) studied the sexual content in 1,705 promotional spots in 171 hours of network (ABC, NBC, CBS, Fox) prime-time programming aired between September and December of 1990. The promos included spots for both network and syndicated programs aired in both prime-time and non-prime-time slots. For each promotional spot, the researchers recorded the number of incidents of six sex acts (touching, kissing, implied intercourse, explicit intercourse, prostitution, rape) similar to those categories used by Davis and Walker (1991). Arguing that sexual content is often composed of verbal references and displays of the body, the researchers also added four types of sexual language (verbal references to sexual anatomy, touching/kissing/hugging, intercourse, prostitution/rape) and two types of sexual innuendo (verbal innuendo and suggestive displays) to their content analysis. In addition, they recorded references to three types of sexually responsible practices: safe sex/sexually transmitted diseases, contraception/pregnancy, and sex education.

The results of Sapolsky et al.'s (1994) study showed slightly over three incidents of sexual acts or language in the promos embedded in every hour of network programming. A sex act occurred 1.7 times per hour, some type of sexual language was used 0.47 times per hour, some type of sexual innuendo was presented 0.67 times per hour, and sexually responsible references were made only 0.16 times per hour. Of the specific types of sexual content, the most common was kissing (1.12 incidents per hour), followed by suggestive displays (0.46 per hour) and verbal innuendo (0.21 per hour). NBC had the most sexual content in its promos (4.56 per hour), followed by ABC (2.86 per hour), Fox (2.05 per hour), and then CBS (2.00 per hour). Despite frequent claims that sex is used to bait viewers during highly competitive ratings sweeps, sexual content was actually less common in promos aired during sweeps months (16% of promos contained sexual content) than in nonsweeps months (22%). Using the same data set, Tabarlet and Gottshall (1996) reported that these sweeps/nonsweeps differences in sexual content were statistically significant.

The Content of Print Promotion

In addition to studies of sex and violence in on-air promos, two earlier studies analyzed the content of program advertisements published in *TV Guide*. Soley and Reid (1985) examined 806 *TV Guide* advertisements published during the 1982 and 1983 fall promotional seasons. They found sex in 20.8% and violence in 19.9% of all program ads, with a higher percentage of network program ads (excluding local and syndicated programs) containing both sex (35.5%) and violence (34.9%). At that time, NBC had the highest percentage of ads with sexual content, whereas CBS had the highest percentage of ads with violent content. In addition, advertisements containing sex and violence had larger sizes than advertisements without these enticers.

Williams (1989) analyzed 625 *TV Guide* advertisements for network prime-time shows published during the 1980 to 1985 November and February sweeps. Twenty-one percent of the advertisements included sexual material, whereas 22% had some violent content. Williams also concluded "that the sex and violent ads do have a positive impact on ratings" (p. 973). However, the evidence of this impact was weak. Only 22.7% of the programs using sex and/or violence in their ads produced higher ratings after these advertisements were published, whereas 36.4% of the programs using other appeals showed ratings improvement.

A COMPARATIVE STUDY OF SEX AND VIOLENCE IN NETWORK ON-AIR PROMOS

Although the studies reported earlier examined the sexual and aggressive content of network program promos and print advertising, they have become dated and the competive situation has intensified. In order to update and extend this body of research, three new content analyses of program promos were undertaken.

Theoretical Approach

The theoretical approach used here involves the application of Becker's Mosaic Model of Communication (Becker, 1978) to the impact of a variety of media messages (see also Walker, 1987; Walker, 1989; Walker, 1990; Walker 1993). As many scholars have noted (Walker & Ferguson, 1998), television and the other mass media have a significant role as sources of information and socialization in modern societies. Becker argued that communication can be conceptualized as information bits that are disseminated by mediated (television, newspapers, radio) and nonmediated (family, schools, churches, and other) sources. The information bits about any particular topic interact with information in memory on that topic and related topics to help form "pictures in our heads" (Lippmann, 1922) that become people's reality for that topic.

Central to Becker's Mosaic Model is the role of the repetition of those information bits. Some information bits are repeated frequently in many different sources (mediated and nonmediated), whereas others receive limited circulation and repetition. Information bits that are frequently repeated, such as program promos, and that are received by more people, are more likely to be remembered and more likely to produce some cognitive, attitudinal, or behavioral effects. The repetitive nature of program promos and any violent or sexual content in them makes them of special interest to those studying television effects.

Their repetitive nature means that program promos are likely to have gradual, less apparent effects over time. Schramm (1954) argued that many of the effects of the mass media are gradual, comparing them to the water dripping from a cave that builds a stalagmite:

> The stalagmite builds up from the calcareous residue of the water dripping on it from the cave roof. Each drop leaves only a tiny residue, and it is very seldom that we can detect the residue of any single drop, or that any single drop will make a fundamental change in the shape or appearance of the stalagmite. Yet, together, all these drops do build the stalagmite, and over the years it changes considerably in size and somewhat in shape. (p. 28)

Whereas one exposure to a message (such as a program promo) may have limited influence on deeply held beliefs and values, frequent repetition may produce significant cognitive and behavioral change. Thus, the impact of aggressive and sexual content in program promos may be negligible from one exposure, but of consequence after several viewings.

Research Questions

Despite the potential impact of promotional announcements predicted by this theoretical approach, the aggressive and sexual content of on-air promos has received little attention from scholars. Previous content analyses of this aspect of on-air promos are nearly a decade old. The 1990s have been a period of rapid change for broadcast television networks, with the introduction of two new broadcast competitors, the WB and UPN, and increasing competition from cable and direct broadcast satellite systems. Networks have responded with more promotional announcements, and it is likely that levels of sexual and violent content have changed. Prior studies of sexual and violent content in television program promotion and in print advertising for these programs led to four questions concerning the content of network promotional announcements:

R1: What percent of on-air promos contain sexual and physically aggressive content?

R2: How do these levels compare with the levels in previous studies of network promos?

R3: How do these levels compare with the levels in previous studies of *TV Guide* advertisements for television programs?

R4: How do promos on the four broadcast networks compare in sexual and physically aggressive content?

Method

Because the most recent data on the aggressive and sexual content of program promos was collected in 1990, more recent promos embedded in prime-time programs from the 1994 and 1998 network television seasons were analyzed for this study. Using the results of earlier studies and these new data, comparisons of aggressive and sexual content could be made using the 4-year intervals of 1990, 1994, and 1998. Analyses over time should establish whether aggressive and sexual content has been consistent over the years or varied from season to season. Given the variation in levels of violent content documented in previous studies of network programs — often dropping after congressional investigations of televised violence (Rowland, 1983) — it would not be surprising to see similar ups and downs in the aggressive content of program promos.

In addition to the 1994 and 1998 prime-time samples, promotions embedded in National Football League (NFL) games aired in 1998–1999 were examined in this study. Televised sports is often seen as a valuable means for programmers to reach predominately male viewers. Indeed, networks have accepted the NFL games as a "loss leader" (in which broadcast rights and production costs exceed advertising revenue) because of their extraordinary value for promoting new and returning prime-time programming (Carter, 1998). The inclusion of promos from a sample of NFL games allowed for comparison of promos aimed at the predominately male audience watching the NFL with promos aimed at the more heterogeneous audience of prime-time programming.

Three Samples and Comparative Database

Promotional announcements from two sets of prime-time programs (1994, 1998) from the four largest broadcast networks (ABC, CBS, NBC, Fox) and one set (1998–1999) of weekend sports programming (NFL games, predominately on CBS) were examined in this study. The 1998 prime-time (Monday–Saturday, 7:00–10:00 p.m. CST) sample included promos embedded in two weeks of nightly programming (September 20–October 3, 1998) on ABC, CBS, NBC, and Fox for a total of 137 hours.[1] The 1994 prime-time (Monday–Saturday, 7:00–10:00 p.m. CST) sample included 1 week of nightly programming (October 17–23, 1994) on ABC, CBS, and NBC, and 6 nights of programming on the Fox network (October 17–22, 1994), for a total of 75 hours.[2] The weekend sports programming included 27 NFL regular season and play-off games (2 on ABC, 20 on CBS, and 5 on Fox) recorded between September 27, 1998, and January 31, 1999, for a total of approximately 88 hours.

Coding Procedures

The unit of analysis was the individual promotional announcement, which usually lasted 10 to 30 seconds. Only announcements separated from program content were examined. Generic network promos that did not promote any specific programs were not included in the study. A promotional announcement was counted only once regardless of how many different programs were promoted in the announcement. Although several studies of promotional effectiveness have used each program promoted in the promo as the unit of analysis (see Eastman & Newton, 1998), the entire promo was used here to facilitate comparison of the findings in this study to prior studies of sexual and aggressive content in program promotions (Davis & Walker, 1991; Sapolsky, 1982).

For each of the three samples, one coder viewed each evening of prime-time television programming or NFL game, identified the promotional announcements, and then coded them for either sexual content or physical aggression. For the 1998 prime-time and 1998–1999 NFL samples, trained undergraduate students, as part of a graded project, coded one evening of prime-time television or one football game for either sexual or aggressive content. For the 1994 program sample, a trained undergraduate student was paid to code the entire sample first for sexual and then again for aggressive content.

Most promos were aired several times, and each airing was included in the sample. After a particular promotion's initial coding, coders were instructed to record the same information each time that promotion was viewed.

---

[1]No promos were coded for sexual content for ABC on 9/20/98, CBS on 9/27/98, for NBC on 9/28/98, and for Fox on 9/26/98, 9/29/98, 10/02/98, and 10/03/98. No promos were coded for physical aggression for CBS on 9/25/98, for NBC on 9/28/98, and for Fox on 9/26/98, 9/29/98, 10/02/98, and 10/03/98.

[2]There was no Fox network programming aired on 10/23/94.

Content Categories

Using detailed descriptions of each category of physical aggression, sexual behavior, and sexual language, coders recorded the presence or absence of each kind of category of content in each promotional announcement. Within the three major categories, a total of 14 subdivisions were utilized.

Physical Aggression.   Following the guidelines of Greenberg, Edison, et al. (1980), physical aggression included "any overt behavior intended to frighten, injure, or damage oneself, another individual, an animal, or property" (p. 107). Socially tolerated forms of physical aggression (contact sports, hunting and fishing for game animals, butchering of domestic animals, legal demolition of property) were not included. Four specific subcategories of physical aggression were coded: (a) assault without an object (e.g., hitting, kicking, shoving, strangling, biting, pinching, scratching, jerking, grabbing), (b) assault with an object other than a firearm (e.g., stabbing, use of machinery to inflict pain or injuries), (c) shooting (i.e., use of any kind of firearm), and (d) physical threat (e.g., pointing a gun, physically menacing someone, holding a knife against a person).

Sexual Behaviors.   Categories and descriptions of the sexual behaviors coded were derived from prior research (Davis & Walker, 1991; Fernandez-Collado et al., 1978; Franzblau et al., 1977; Greenberg, Graef, Fernandez-Collado, Korzenny, & Atkin, 1980; Sapolsky et al., 1994; Silverman et al., 1979). Following Sapolsky (1982), sexual content included all incidents that "contained a depiction of sexual behavior, seductive display of the body, or an explicit or implied reference to intimate sexual behavior, sexual organs, or sex-related activities" (p. 216). Specific sexual behaviors included (a) sexual contact, including any of the following: kissing (the kissing of any part of the body as part of any sexual behavior), hugging/embracing as part of sexual behavior, and other sexual touching (any sexual touching, other than kissing and hugging); (b) sexual intercourse, either implied in the scene or explicitly presented; (c) rape (a forced act of intercourse, usually accompanied by assault or threat);[3] and (d) prostitution, including the portrayal of pimps and prostitutes.

Sexual Language.   Sexual language included verbal references to (a) sexual organs (including any sexual part of the body), (b) sexual contact (kissing, hugging, other touching), (c) sexual intercourse, (d) rape or pros-

---

[3]To be consistent with prior research, rape was coded as sexual behavior here. However, the author subscribes to the more prevalent contemporary interpretation of rape as an act of physical violence rather than a sexual behavior; thus, it clearly could be considered physical aggression.

titution, (e) sexual innuendo, and (f) sexual display (revealing displays of the body and situations that had sexual suggestion as their implicit intent).

Intercoder Agreement Levels

To assess intercoder reliability, approximately 20% of each of the program samples were coded by a second coder. Intercoder reliability was assessed by recording the percent of agreement between the coders for the various sexual and aggressive content categories (see Holsti, 1969). The percents of agreement ranged from 79.4 to 100 across the specific content categories, and are presented in Table 4.2.

Results

Altogether, a total of 1,445 promos were coded for sexual content and 2,158 for violent content. Specifically, from the 1998 2-week program sample, 985 promotional announcements were coded for sexual content and 1,076 promotional announcements were coded for aggressive content. For the 1994 1-week program sample, 460 promotional announcements were coded for both sexual and aggressive content. For the 1998–1999 NFL sample, 622 promotional announcements were coded for aggressive con-

TABLE 4.2
Percent of Intercoder Agreement

	1994 Sample	1998 Sample	NFL Sample
Physical aggression	79.4	90.5	88.6
Aggression without object	80.9	90.8	90.0
Aggression with object	92.6	97.6	92.9
Shooting	89.7	97.0	94.3
Physical threat	94.1	92.3	90.7
Sexual behaviors	92.8	89.1	
Sexual contact	94.2	87.6	
Intercourse	97.8	95.6	
Prostitution	100.0	100.0	
Rape	100.0	100.0	
Sexual language	95.7	81.8	
Sex organs	98.6	98.5	
Sexual contact	100.0	100.0	
Intercourse	98.6	94.2	
Rape/prostitution	99.3	97.8	
Innuendo	98.6	82.5	
Display	99.3	87.6	

tent. For each type of content, the percents of promos containing at least one instance of a particular content are presented in Tables 4.3 to 4.5.

Physical Aggression Findings

Table 4.3 shows the percent of network promos that contained some physical aggression (in any of the four specific categories), aggression without an object, aggression with an object, shooting, and physical threat. Data from Davis and Walker's (1991) diverse sample (144 prime-time broadcast network programming, 140 hours of non-prime-time broadcast network programming, and 36 hours of cable programming) were included in the table for comparison.

As the table reveals, overall, the percent of promos that contained any kind of physical aggression declined from 1990 (30.0%) to 1994 (17.8%) and then increased slightly between 1994 and 1998 (20.0%). In NFL games, the percent of promos with physically aggressive content (23.2%) was slightly higher than in the 1998 prime-time sample. Some types of aggression increased, whereas others decreased. For example, aggression without an object (hitting, kicking, pushing, etc.) increased between 1990 and 1994, with similar levels reported in the two most recent samples (1998 prime time and 1998–1999 NFL). Shooting shows a steady decline between 1990 (9.3%) and 1998 (5.4%), with the exception of promos in the 1998–1999 NFL broadcasts (8.0%). Aggression with an object (other than shooting) also declined from 11.0% in 1990 to 7.2% for the 1998 prime-time sample and 5.9% for the 1998–1999 NFL sample. Physical threat showed a sharp decrease between 1990 and 1994 but went back up to three fourths of the 1990 levels in the most recent samples to over 9%.

Sexual Content Findings

Table 4.4 presents the percent of network promos with various kinds of sexual content. Promos with any kind of sexual behavior were virtually the same in 1990 (12.0%) and 1994 (13.3%) but rose sharply to 21.5% in 1998. The dramatically increasing pattern held for sexual language of any kind. In 1994, 11.3% and in 1998 23.4% of the 1998 promos featured such content. Between 1994 and 1998, there were particularly sharp increases in sexual contact (touching, hugging, or kissing) and sexual intercourse among the sexual behaviors.

For sexual language categories, sexual innuendo and sexual display (presentation of the body for sexual stimulation) showed the sharpest increases between 1994 and 1998, whereas talking about sexual intercourse showed the sharpest decrease. Presentation of prostitution and/or rape,

TABLE 4.3
Number and Percent of Network Promos With Physical Aggression

	1990[a] Prime-Time, Non-Prime-Time, and Cable (N = 1,204)		1994 Prime-Time (N = 460)		1998 Prime-Time (N = 1,076)		1998–1999 NFL (N = 622)	
	n	%	n	%	n	%	n	%
Aggression without object	94	7.8	57	12.4[b]	119	11.1	87	14.0
Aggression with object	132	11.0	10	2.2[c]	77	7.2	37	5.9
Shooting	112	9.3	36	7.8[d]	58	5.4	50	8.0
Physical threat	164	13.6	4	0.9[e]	99	9.2	58	9.3
Any physical aggression	361	30.0	82	17.8[f]	215	20.0	144	23.2

[a]From Davis and Walker, 1991. [b]For aggression without an object, the chi-square for the 1994 and 1998 prime-time and 1998–1999 NFL samples was χ^2 = 3.2, df = 2, p = .204. [c]For aggression with an object, the chi-square for the 1994 and 1998 prime-time and 1998–1999 NFL samples was χ^2 = 14.8, df = 2, p = .001. [d]For shooting, the chi-square for the 1994 and 1998 prime-time and 1998–1999 NFL samples was χ^2 = 5.7, df = 2, p = .058. [e]For physical threat, the chi-square for the 1994 and 1998 prime-time and 1998–1999 NFL samples was χ^2 = 36.8, df = 2, p = .000. [f]For any physical aggression, the chi-square for the 1994 and 1998 prime-time and 1998–1999 NFL samples was χ^2 = 4.9, df = 2, p = .087.

TABLE 4.4
Percent of Network Promos With Sexual Content

	1990[a] Prime-Time, Non-Prime-Time, and Cable (N = 1,204)		1994 Prime-Time (N = 460)		1998 Prime-Time (N = 985)	
	n	%	n	%	n	%
Behaviors						
Sexual contact	NA	NA	55	12.0	193	19.6
Intercourse	12	1.0	7	1.5	60	6.1
Prostitution	2	0.2	0	0.0	4	0.4
Rape	7	0.6	0	0.0	1	0.1
Any sexual behavior	144	12.0	61	13.3[b]	212	21.5
Language						
Sex organs	NA	NA	6	1.3	15	1.5
Sexual contact	NA	NA	2	0.4	22	2.2
Intercourse	NA	NA	36	7.8	24	2.4
Rape/prostitution	NA	NA	10	2.2	12	1.2
Innuendo	NA	NA	6	1.3	68	6.9
Display	NA	NA	5	1.1	138	14.0
Any sexual language	NA	NA	52	11.3[c]	230	23.4

[a]From Davis and Walker, 1991. [b]For sexual behavior, the chi-square for the 1994 and 1998 prime-time samples was $\chi^2 = 14.0$, $df = 1$, $p = .000$. [c]For sexual language, the chi-square for the 1994 and 1998 prime-time samples was $\chi^2 = 29.0$, $df = 1$, $p = .000$.

as behaviors or subjects of talk, and verbal references to sex organs were very low in all years.

Cross-Network Findings

Table 4.5 compares on-air promos on the four largest broadcast networks over the three time periods to show differences and similarities by network. For both the 1994 and 1998 samples, the findings reveal statistically significant differences ($p < .01$) in physical aggression and sexual behavior among the four networks. For the 1998 sample, significant differences also were found in the use of sexual language. In 1994, Fox had the greatest percent of promos with physically aggressive content (27.5%), and NBC had, by a substantial amount, the fewest (4.8%). However, the percent of Fox promos with aggressive content dropped sharply by 1998 to 10.6%, whereas CBS jumped to 26.6%. A substantial percent of NBC's promos (22.5%) also included physical aggression by 1998. However, all four networks show decreases in the percent of promos with physical aggression between 1990 and the later samples (1994, 1998), with NBC and Fox showing especially sharp declines.

TABLE 4.5
Percent of Promos With Physical Aggression
and Sexual Content by Network

	Physical Agression	Sexual Behavior	Sexual Language
1990 Sample[a]			
ABC	27.1	8.9	NA
CBS	30.0	12.1	NA
NBC	28.2	17.8	NA
Fox	47.4	7.2	NA
1994 Prime-Time Sample			
ABC	22.8[b]	7.1[c]	15.7[d]
CBS	20.0	10.7	10.0
NBC	4.8	21.8	8.9
Fox	27.5	14.5	10.1
1998 Prime-Time Sample			
ABC	16.5[e]	16.1[f]	18.2[g]
CBS	26.6	15.2	20.5
NBC	22.5	33.5	27.3
Fox	10.6	25.7	33.1

[a]From Davis and Walker, 1991. No χ^2 were reported. [b]The chi-square for physical aggression for the 1994 sample was $\chi^2 = 21.3$, $df = 3$, $p = .000$. [c]The chi-square for sexual behavior for the 1994 sample was $\chi^2 = 12.9$, $df = 3$, $p = .005$. [d]The chi-square for sexual language for the 1994 sample was $\chi^2 = 3.6$, $df = 3$, $p = .313$. [e]The chi-square for physical aggression for the 1998 sample was $\chi^2 = 22.5$, $df = 3$, $p = .000$. [f]The chi-square for sexual behavior for the 1998 sample was $\chi^2 = 34.3$, $df = 3$, $p = .000$. [g]The chi-square for sexual language for the 1998 sample was $\chi^2 = 15.8$, $df = 3$, $p = .001$.

As Table 4.5 shows, among the results for sexual behaviors in promos, NBC had the highest percent in both 1994 and 1998 (twice as much as ABC or CBS), but all four networks showed substantial increases over time. In 1998, Fox had the highest percent of promos (33.1%) that included sexual language, but 27.3% of NBC's promos also used sexual language. For the 1994 sample, there were no significant differences among the networks in sexual language.

Discussion of This Study

This study showed that aggressive and sexual content is common in broadcast network television promos but far from universal. Although most of prime-time promos contained neither aggression nor sexual content, a fourth of all promos in the most recent prime-time sample contained some type of aggressive content, and about a fifth of the sample contained some type of sexual behavior or language. Not surprisingly given the predominately male audience, physical aggression was even more common in the sample of promos aired during NFL games.

Graphs are heuristic for illustrating comparative trends over time (recasting the data from Tables 4.3 to 4.5). Figure 4.1 shows that acts of physical aggression in promos dropped sharply between 1990 and 1994, though they had climbed back up somewhat by 1998. As the results showed, among categories of physical aggression, aggression without an object (hitting, pushing, kicking, etc.) was the most common in the 1998 prime-time and 1998–1999 NFL samples, followed by physical threat.

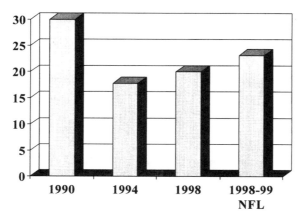

Percent of On-Air Promos with Physical Aggression

FIG. 4.1. Physical aggression in network television promos, 1990 to 1998.

However, both shooting and aggression with an object had a substantial presence. Compared to the 1990 sample, aggression without an object increased, whereas all other categories of physical aggression decreased. Thus, over time the trend has been for more fighting, but slightly less shooting, stabbing, and threatening.

And as social critics might predict, Fig. 4.2 shows that depictions of sexual behaviors in on-air promotion nearly doubled between 1990 and 1998. Moreover, the use of sexual language in promos also has shot up since 1994, a pattern probably characteristic of the programs being promoted. As the previous reports of results demonstrated, among specific sexual behaviors, sexual contact (kissing, hugging, touching) remained the most common kind of sexual behavior, but intercourse (implied or explicit) showed a surprising fourfold increase between the 1994 and 1998 prime-time samples. The most common kind of sexual language was sexual display, which appeared in a seventh of on-air promos, whereas sexual innuendo, the next highest category, appeared in about half as many promos.

When the oldest network sample (1990) is compared to the most recent (1998), it appears that the major networks have substituted sexual content for physical aggression. This is evident in the one-third decline in promos with physical aggression, and the near doubling of the percent of promos with sexual behavior. However, it should be noted that the 1990 sample contains promos from some non-prime-time and cable programming, and this difference may account for the divergent findings. Given the more specialized audiences of cable and non-prime-time programming, aggres-

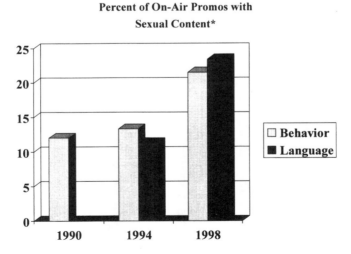

Percent of On-Air Promos with Sexual Content*

* No 1990 data available for sexual language.

FIG. 4.2.   Sexual content in network television promos, 1990 to 1998.

sive and sexual depictions may be used differently in promotion aired outside of network prime time.

Comparison to Previous Studies

Interestingly, the proportion of 1998 promos with sexual and aggressive content is very similar to those found in prior studies of print advertisements and on-air promos. Studies by Soley and Reid (1985) and Williams (1989) found sexual elements in approximately one fifth of the *TV Guide* advertisements for television programs. The percent of advertisements with violent elements was 19.9% in Soley and Reid's study and 22% in Williams' study. These figures are similar to the 20% to 23% range for sexual and aggressive content found in the most recent samples reported here. However, Soley and Reid examined promotion of all types of programs advertised in *TV Guide*. When they examined only advertisements for network programs, the percent of advertisements with sexual and/or violent content increased to approximately 50%. In addition, both *TV Guide* studies used samples of print advertisements from the 1980s and different operationalizations of physical aggression than those used in the studies of on-air promos.[4]

In addition to the 1990 data (Davis & Walker, 1991) reported here, two other studies have examined levels of sexual content in prime-time promos. Although they reported most of their findings in frequencies per hour rather than in the percent of promos reported here, Sapolsky et al. (1994) found that 16% of promos during ratings sweeps and 22% of promos during nonsweeps periods contain some kind of sexual content (sexual behaviors and/or language). The average of those two figures (19%) is very close to the percent of sexual behavior and language found in the 1998 prime-time sample. In an earlier study, Brown (1989) reported that about a fourth of his sample of network prime-time promos contained some form of sensuality. Again, although sexual content was operationalized differently, the proportion of on-air promos with some sexual content is similar to the 1998 season findings reported here. In sum, then, the proportion of promos with sexual content appears to have stayed relatively consistent for more than a decade.

Network Differences

Clear differences emerged among the networks, but these differences were not always consistent over time. As the network-by-network bar graphs in Fig. 4.3 illustrate, for the years studied here, CBS replaced Fox as

---

[4]Soley and Reid (1985) and Williams (1989) coded only violent behavior, using Gerbner and Gross' (1976) definition and not the wider range of physical aggressions coded here.

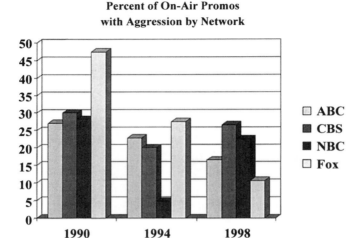

FIG. 4.3. Comparative proportions of aggressive content in promos on ABC, CBS, NBC, and Fox.

the network with the greatest percentage of promos with physical aggression. But Fox slashed violent content in its prime-time promos by about three fourths between 1990 and 1998, a dramatic fall from over 47% to just over 10%. It is clear that all the networks carried lower levels of violent content in their 1998 promos than in their 1990 promos. NBC, however, quadrupled its violent content between 1994 and 1998, and the amount on CBS grew somewhat. These changes may reflect Fox's attempt to age and expand its audience base in the 1990s, NBC's efforts to retain its top-rated position, and CBS's well-documented (and ultimately successful) attempt to lure younger males into its predominately older audience with NFL football and action programs (e.g., *Martial Law, Buddy Faro, Nash Bridges*), as well as aggressive content.

As Figs. 4.4 and 4.5 show, in the 1998 prime-time sample, NBC and Fox continued a pattern set in the 1994 sample by having the highest and next highest percent of promos with sexual behavior, and they also had the greatest percent of promos using sexual language, by far, in the 1998 prime-time sample. NBC also had the greatest amount of sexual behavior (Davis & Walker, 1991) and sexual content (Sapolsky et al., 1994) in the 1990 season. The "sexiness" of their promos reflects the network's programming, which abounds in urban professional situation comedies with strong sexual themes, and which generally gets high Nielsen ratings. But by 1998, it had been outdone by Fox in the matter of sexual language in promos. Whether the other networks will soon emulate Fox and NBC cannot be deduced from these data, but the trend toward substituting sexual

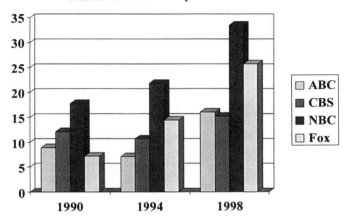

FIG. 4.4. Comparative proportions of sexual behavior in promos on ABC, CBS, NBC, and Fox.

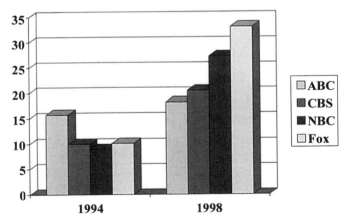

FIG. 4.5. Comparative proportions of sexual language in promos on ABC, CBS, NBC, and Fox.

content for violent content seems clear in ABC's promotion as well as in NBC's and Fox's.

Importance and Limits of the Findings

The purpose of this study was to update older research on the sexual and aggressive content in broadcast network promos and examine changes in content over time. However, several limitations should be noted. The prime-time samples used in this study were limited to relatively brief periods of 1 or 2 weeks, whereas the weekend sports programming was limited to NFL games. In addition, only the four most-established broadcast networks were examined. Although usually over 90%, agreement between the coders concerning the presence or absence of particular kinds of content was not perfect. In addition, the use of more detailed, but differing, definitions of physical aggression/violence somewhat limits the validity of comparisons to previous studies of print advertising.

Even with these limitations, this study of promos embedded in network prime-time and weekend sports programming shows that physical aggression, sexual behaviors, and sexual language are fairly common in on-air promos, appearing in at least 20% to 23% of all announcements. Parents concerned about such content should take note that NBC is the network that uses sexual content most frequently, whereas CBS has replaced Fox as the network using physical aggression most often. Also, when compared to earlier studies of both physical aggression and sexual behavior, the networks appear to be using more sex and less aggression in their promos. In U.S. television, both sex and violence are used to "sell" programs, but the four major broadcast networks increasingly prefer to market with sex.

SUGGESTIONS FOR FUTURE RESEARCH ON SEX AND VIOLENCE IN PROMOTION

The systematic examination of the content of on-air promos is in its infancy. Prior research has focused almost exclusively on promotions for network prime-time programs on the four largest networks. Newer broadcast networks (the WB, UPN, Pax) have been ignored, and only one study (Davis & Walker, 1991) has given any attention to promos embedded in non-prime-time broadcast network or cable network programs. The dearth of non-network, non-prime-time studies is a likely result of the considerable resources necessary to cover this broad viewing vista. However, given the increasing proportion of the viewing audience drawn to cable channels and newer broadcasters, as well as the declining audience shares for traditional broadcast networks (Walker & Ferguson, 1998), future research must expand the sample of programs used in studies of promo content.

Cable Network Promotion

Future studies of on-air promo content should certainly include a sample of cable networks that reflects their popularity among viewers. Because previous studies have documented the levels of sexual and violent content in network prime-time promos, researchers might want to use their limited resources to study cable network promos exclusively, examining promotions in the 10 most highly rated cable networks. Although 10 networks hardly covers the expanding cable network universe, the top-10 cable networks would encompass a solid variety of networks, including the major general interest networks (TNT, TBS, USA Network), sources of specialized content (ESPN, A&E, Discovery, the Cartoon Network), and those aimed at particular demographic groups (Lifetime, MTV, Nickelodeon; "Top 10 Basic Cable Network Rankings," 1999). Because cable network ratings are not necessarily highest in prime time, the promo sample should be drawn from both prime-time and non-prime-time dayparts.

In addition, the cable promotion sample should include the most popular pay-cable networks (HBO, Showtime). These services air unedited motion pictures with higher levels of sexual and aggressive content than is typical for advertiser-supported services. It is important to determine if this more explicit content is reflected in the promotional spots on premium channels.

Other Dayparts

As with cable networks, the content of promos in non-prime-time network programming remains an underexplored area. Davis and Walker (1991) included some promos from non-prime-time programming in their sample but did not separate them from prime-time promos in their analyses. In the study reported here, slightly higher levels of aggressive content were reported in promos aired during NFL games. With the exception of this data, nothing about the differences among network promos aired in different dayparts is known. Given the more homogeneous audiences (women and teens in daytime, adults in late night, men on weekend afternoons) and program genres (e.g., daytime soap operas and talk shows, late-night talk/variety shows, weekend sports) in non-prime-time dayparts, differences in sexual/violent content of the promos used can be expected. Thus, the evaluation of the aggressive and sexual content in non-prime-time dayparts is another rich area for new research.

In addition to non-prime-time network programs, promos embedded in programs originating from local stations (primarily local news) and syndicated programs have also been ignored in previous research. Future studies might well fill this vacuum.

Other Media

On-air promotion is only one of the techniques used in the television industry to promote programs. Substantial resources are allocated to radio, billboard, and print advertising. Currently, only two studies have examined any of this material, and both of these now-dated studies focused on *TV Guide* advertisements. Although other print outlets, radio spots, and billboard advertising have been increasingly used by the television industry to attract viewers to its programming, they have been ignored in previous promo research. Whereas the absence of studies of radio or billboard advertising is not surprising, given the limited attention these media have received in media studies to date, the area of paid advertising for both television and radio programs is ripe for further study.

In conclusion, studies of the aggressive and sexual content of program promos and advertising need to shift from their current myopic focus on the Big Four networks. The landscape of television changed dramatically between its network-dominated, broadcast-only first generation and its fragmented, cable-ready third generation (Walker & Ferguson, 1998). Future research needs to reflect that change.

REFERENCES

Bandura, A. (1994). Social cognitive theory of mass communication. In J. Bryant & D. Zillmann (Eds.), *Media effects: Advances in theory and research* (pp. 61–89). Hillsdale, NJ: Lawrence Erlbaum Associates.

Baxter, R. L., DeRiemer, C., Landini, A., Leslie, L., & Singletary, M. W. (1985). A content analysis of music videos. *Journal of Broadcasting, 29,* 333–340.

Becker, S. L. (1978). Visual stimuli and the construction of meaning. In B. S. Randhawa & W. E. Coffman (Eds.), *Visual learning, thinking, and communication* (pp. 39–60). New York: Academic Press.

Bellamy, R. V., Jr., & Walker, J. R. (1996). *Television and the remote control: Grazing on a vast wasteland.* New York: Guilford.

Brown, D. (1989). *Broadcast network television promotion during prime time of prime-time network programs.* Paper presented at the convention of the Speech Communication Association, San Francisco, CA.

Brown, J. D., & Campbell, K. (1986). Race and gender in music videos: The same beat but a different drummer. *Journal of Communication, 36*(1), 94–106.

Cantor, M. (1971). The role of the producer in choosing children's television content. In G. A. Comstock & E. A. Rubinstein (Eds.), *Television and social behavior: Vol. 1. Media content and control.* Washington, DC: U.S. Government Printing Office.

Caplan, R. E. (1985). Violent program content in music videos. *Journalism Quarterly, 62,* 144–147.

Carter, B. (1998, August 31). Can football revive CBS? *New York Times,* pp. C-1, C-6.

Comstock, G., Chaffee, S., Katzman, N., McCombs, M., & Roberts, D. (1978). *Television and human behavior.* New York: Columbia University Press.

Davis, D. M., & Walker, J. R. (1991, November). *Sex, violence, and network program promotion: A content analysis.* Paper presented at the annual meeting of the Speech Communication Association, Atlanta, GA.

Eastman, S. T., & Newton, G. D. (1998). The impact of structural salience within on-air promotion. *Journal of Broadcasting & Electronic Media, 42,* 50–79.

Ferguson, D. A. (1999). Network television promotion. In S. T. Eastman, D. A. Ferguson, & R. A. Klein (Eds.), *Promotion and marketing for broadcasting and cable* (3rd ed., pp. 79–95). Boston: Focal Press.

Fernandez-Collado, C. F., Greenberg, B. S., Korzenny, F., & Atkin, C. K. (1978). Sexual intimacy and drug use in TV series. *Journal of Communication, 28*(3), 30–37.

Few are tuned into TV's ratings. (1999, May 4). *USA Today,* p. 6D.

Franzblau, S., Sprafkin, J. N., & Rubinstein, E. A. (1977). Sex on TV: A content analysis. *Journal of Communication, 27*(2), 164–170.

Gerbner, G., & Gross, L. (1976). Living with television: The violence profile. *Journal of Communication, 26*(2), 173–199.

Greenberg, B. S., Edison, N., Korzenny, F., Fernandez-Collado, C., & Atkin, C. K. (1980). Antisocial and prosocial behaviors on television. In B. S. Greenberg (Ed.), *Life on television: Content analyses of U.S. TV drama* (pp. 99–128). Norwood, NJ: Ablex.

Greenberg, B. S., Graef, D., Fernandez-Collado, C., Korzenny, F., & Atkin, C. K. (1980). Sexual intimacy on commercial TV during prime time. *Journalism Quarterly, 57,* 211–215.

Gunter, B. (1994). The question of media violence. In J. Bryant & D. Zillmann (Eds.), *Media effects: Advances in theory and research* (pp. 163–211). Hillsdale, NJ: Lawrence Erlbaum Associates.

Holsti, O. (1969). *Content analysis for the social sciences and humanities.* Reading, MA: Addison-Wesley.

Lippmann, W. (1922). *Public opinion.* New York: Macmillan.

Lowery, S. A., & DeFleur, M. L. (1988). *Milestones in mass communication research* (2nd ed.). New York: Longman.

Milavsky, J. R., Kessler, R., Stipp, H., & Rubens, W. S. (1982). Television and aggression: Results of a panel study. In D. Pearl, L. Bouthilet, & J. Lazar (Eds.), *Television and behavior: Ten years of scientific progress and implications for the eighties* (Vol. 2). Washington, DC: U.S. Government Printing Office.

Oldenburg, A., & Snider, M. (1999, May 4). Entertainment in the cross hairs. *USA Today,* pp. 1D, 6D.

Provenzo, E. F., Jr. (1991). *Video kids: Making sense of Nintendo.* Cambridge, MA: Harvard University Press.

Rowland, W. D., Jr. (1983). *The politics of TV violence.* Beverly Hills, CA: Sage.

Sapolsky, B. S. (1982). Sexual acts and references on prime-time TV: A two-year look. *The Southern Speech Communication Journal, 47,* 212–226.

Sapolsky, B. S., & Tabarlet, J. (1991). Sex in primetime television: 1979 versus 1989. *Journal of Broadcasting & Electronic Media, 35,* 505–516.

Sapolsky, B. S., Tabarlet, J., & Kaye, B. K. (1994). *Sexual behavior and references in program promotions aired during sweeps and nonsweeps periods.* Paper presented at the annual convention of the Broadcast Education Association, Las Vegas, NV.

Schramm, W. (1954). Procedures and effects of mass communication. In N. B. Henry (Ed.), *Mass media and education: II. 53rd yearbook of the national society for the study of education* (pp. 113–138). Chicago: University of Chicago Press.

Sherman, B. L., & Dominick, J. R. (1986). Violence and sex in music videos: TV and rock 'n' roll. *Journal of Communication, 36*(1), 79–93.

Silverman, L. T., Sprafkin, J. N., & Rubinstein, E. A. (1979). Physical contact and sexual behavior on prime-time TV. *Journal of Communication, 29*(1), 33–43.

Soley, L. C., & Reid, L. N. (1985). Baiting viewers: Violence and sex in television program advertisements. *Journalism Quarterly, 62,* 105–110, 131.

Tabarlet, J. O., & Gottshall, C. (1996). *The effects of ratings sweeps periods on the number and type of sexual incidents in television programs and program promotions.* Paper presented at the Southern States Communication Association convention.

Top 10 basic cable network rankings. (1999, July 19). *Electronic Media, 29.*

Walker, J. R. (1987). How viewing of MTV relates to exposure to other media violence. *Journalism Quarterly, 64,* 756–762.

Walker, J. R. (1989). The impact of a mini-series: A quasi-experimental study of "Amerika." *Journalism Quarterly, 66,* 897–901.

Walker, J. R. (1990). Developing a new political reality: Political information and the 1988 southern regional primary. *Southern Communication Journal, 55,* 421–435.

Walker, J. R. (1993). Catchy, yes, but does it work? The impact of broadcast network program promotion frequency and type on program success. *Journal of Broadcasting & Electronic Media, 37,* 197–207.

Walker, J., & Ferguson, D. (1998). *The broadcast television industry.* Boston: Allyn & Bacon.

Wartella, E. A. (1996). *The context of television violence.* Needham Heights, MA: Allyn & Bacon.

Williams, G. A. (1989). Enticing viewers: Sex and violence in *TV Guide* program advertisements. *Journalism Quarterly, 66,* 970–973.

5

Television Branding as Promotion

Robert V. Bellamy, Jr.
Duquesne University

Paul J. Traudt
University of Nevada at Las Vegas

The concept of branding is hundreds of years old, and can be traced to a time when labels or brands were used to exert property rights on such things as land and livestock (Keller, 1998). Brands also were used to identify the crafter of a product in the early mercantile system. In time, the brand name became a form of shorthand signifier in commercial enterprises and an important element in business expansion supported by nationwide transportation systems and mass advertising.

IMPORTANCE OF BRANDING

Branding is perhaps the "hottest" of contemporary marketing strategies. Branding involves the building, maintenance, enhancement, and exploitation of brand equity, which has been defined as the "value a brand name adds to a product" (Broniarczyk & Alba, 1994, p. 214). The fundamental concept is that a recognizable brand will more easily attract and retain customers than an unrecognizable one. A strong brand is said to enhance "the value of a product beyond its functional value" (Cobb-Walgren, Ruble, & Donthu, 1995, p. 25), and serve "as a powerful heuristic cue for evaluation and choice decisions" (Park, Jun, & Shocker, 1996, p. 453). That value accrues both to existing products or services and to *brand extensions*, whereby a strong brand is leveraged to introduce new products.

127

According to Kapferer (1992), the value of brands is "something invisible, intangible and unwritten" (p. 1) and, yet, brands are the "real capital of business" (p. 3). Aaker (1991) elaborated on the corporate value of brands by arguing that "for many businesses the brand name and what it represents are its most important asset — the basis of competitive advantage and of future earnings streams" (p. 14). He justifies this by discussing how the selling price of many firms is much more than earnings would justify because of the value of the brand assets. The "incredible . . . remarkable" staying power of old, mature brands is also an indicator of the value of a brand to a company (Aaker, 1991, pp. 69–71). One only need look around the home for evidence of the staying power of such corporate or product brands as Kraft, Crest, Sears, RCA, Tylenol, and so on. Or one can turn on the television to sample NBC, CBS, ABC, Fox, HBO, MTV, and an increasing number of television brands.

The importance of the brand name has increased exponentially in the last 20 or so years due to the clutter of products in the marketplace, the ever-rising cost of new product introductions, and the method of corporate valuation that gives weight to nontangible assets (Aaker, 1991, 1996; Kapferer, 1992; Keller, 1998). Branding is particularly relevant for television because this industry, more than most others, has experienced an enormous amount of marketplace clutter in the last 10 to 20 years due to technological diffusion, deregulation, and globalization.

Branding and Television Promotion

In television, *brand identification* (i.e., branding) has been called "the key strategic thread" in promotion (Ridgway, 1998, p. 16), and has been a theme at several recent industry conferences (Ducey, 1997; Schneider, 1998). In television, the brand can be represented by call letters or an acronym, logo, company wordmark (name), theme, jingle, sound, or some mixture of these, often in combination with individual program promotion, designed to differentiate one station/channel/program from another. As explained by television promotion executive John Ridgway (1998), brands are "sign posts" for the viewer and a successful brand "incorporates comfort, originality and awareness of how one fits into the overall media environment" (p. 16). Frank (1999) said that brands "are special things to Americans, interactive myths that earn our loyalty through endless repetition and constant adjustment" (p. 74).

Although individual programs are sometimes referred to as brands or, more commonly, franchises (Spring, 1998), the television brand most often is considered to be an individual channel or network. For example, NBC executive Garth Ancier defines the NBC brand as the program source for "adults 18 to 49 [who are] 'a little more upscale' and 'a little smarter' than the [viewers of] other networks" (Schneider, 1999, p. 3). In contrast, Fox's brand has been described by one of its top executives as "a cutting-edge, irreverent broadcast network that gave teens and young adults a rebellious voice they'd never had before" (Chernin, 1998, p. 9). Despite such supposed differences, broadcast television networks remain relatively homogeneous as brands because of the need to attract large audiences. Clearly, the more specialized cable/satellite-delivered services have an advantage over traditional broadcast networks in branding. Brand awareness and image can be regarded as closely linked in services with such highly focused editorial content as CNN, MTV, the Food Network, the Golf Channel, and so on. Cable can exist and often prosper with highly specialized programming because of its dual-revenue stream of advertising and subscriptions. By comparison, brand knowledge of any of the traditional Big Three networks (NBC, CBS, ABC) or even the somewhat more specialized Little Three (Fox, the WB, UPN) is more difficult to define. Networks must walk a fine line between (a) the need for differentiation in the multichannel era, and (b) the need to maximize audiences in most time periods in order to attract advertisers to pay the total bill. Overspecialization or extreme brand differentiation would be the "kiss of death" to a broadcast network under the industry's present economic model.

The major networks provide an interesting landscape of different forms of television branding. In one vein, they promote overall network themes, such as NBC's "Must See TV" or ABC's "Television Is Good" campaigns. Of perhaps more interest are the brand or network-group extensions such as the Fox Family Channel and CNBC. Here the networks can use their "goodwill" to extend core brand equity to specialized cable content (Loken & John, 1993). An interesting form of brand extension is the *composite brand extension* (CBE), the "combining of two existing brand names to create a composite brand name" (Park et al., 1996, p. 453). Such brand alliances have recently occurred in television with the creation of MSNBC between Microsoft and NBC and CNNSI between CNN and *Sports Illustrated*. Despite the lack of strong product differentiation, the Big Three networks can be expected to have a large store of brand equity due to their long history as the only national networks. How that equity is both a help and a hindrance to the Big Three is a subject of considerable interest at a time when many see the reconfiguration or even end of the old network structure as inevitable (Roberts, 1999).

In the last 20 years, the television industry has been transformed into an entirely new form by technological convergence and economic consolidation, both of which are the result in part of technological diffusion and changes in government regulatory policy. Without a doubt, the major entities in the television industry are well aware of these problems caused by the increased number of outlets and the active use of VCRs and RCDs. They are aggressively taking measures to minimize the perceived negative impact of competitive pressures and to target the active viewer/user. On the macrolevel, the continuing consolidation of media companies both domestically and internationally is a reaction to audience choice, with the rationale being that if the viewer is going to graze, let her/him graze to other channels or, at least, programming controlled by the same company. In addition, the search for new revenue streams and niche marketing opportunities in a time of declining viewing levels for individual channels is a growing strategy (Owers, Carveth, & Alexander, 1993). The continuing leverage of brands into new channels and other businesses both domestically and internationally is a very important strategic element in industry expansion. For example, AT&T's acquisition and conversion of TCI into AT&T Broadband and Internet Services exemplifies ongoing attempts to "marry" television to electronic and Internet commerce (Mermigas, 1999). Another example can be seen in Big Three investment in Internet portals or content providers (ESPN SportsZone, CBS Sportsline, NBC's SNAP, Disney's GO).

Of critical importance in the cluttered television environment is getting television users *to sample* programs and channels — the traditional function of promotion. Long recognized as one of the most important components of television, promotion's value has increased exponentially in the multichannel age. This is particularly true with brand promotion, as it lends itself to all types of both on-air and off-air efforts. Network brand logos in the form of ubiquitous on-air "bugs" allow for promotion within programs. Likewise, the network brand name can be easily applied to new channels, outdoor advertising, cooperative promotion/advertising, and spin-off products and services (such as ESPN Zone sports bars and Disney Stores). These strategies provide constant brand exposure in a time of an RCD-wielding audience ready and often willing to change the channel. For example, the well-known NBC brand does not need much time to make an impression on a viewer. The viewer has already internalized the value of the brand and, in the best-case scenario, it is a positive association that need only be prompted through the appearance or sound of the name. The value of this level of audience association becomes obvious at a time when contemporary promotion practice supports the "Big Bang" theory — which holds that a promotional spot has only 3 seconds to gain the attention of the viewer before she or he changes the channel (Bellamy & Chabin, 1999; J. B. Chabin, personal communication, February 17, 1998).

More specific and quantifiable *consumer targeting* is one of the present marketing imperatives in a cluttered environment for nearly every product or service. The problem of reaching consumers is further compounded in television by the increasing amount of on-air clutter (i.e., nonprogram material) that provides the major on-air outlet for promotion while simultaneously encouraging viewer avoidance (Bellamy & Walker, 1996; "Prime Time," 1999; see also Eastman & Bolls, chap. 3, this volume). In addition, successful targeting is essential to television, and particularly broadcast television, because creation/generation of audiences for resale to advertisers is the medium's primary (or only) commodity. If unable to maintain or increase the sheer quantity of product (audience) in an era of much greater competition for the attention of viewers, the television network must try to improve the "quality" of the audience through much more specific demographic and psychographic targeting and the extension of the brand to new channels and other products and services. In fact, a singular focus on grabbing the attention of the audience is said to be shifting "to incorporating technological change by creating content for enhanced TV, cross-promoting on new media platforms or launching new digital and high-definition program services" (Spring, 1999, p. 14). A strong brand obviously is a very important entry point to these new services.

Despite the increasing emphasis on branding in television and in marketing in general, academic studies of television branding are scarce in both media and marketing literatures. Among the few television branding studies are those conducted or published by the National Association of Broadcasters (Ducey, 1997; McDowell & Batten, 1999) that focus on explaining the importance of branding to NAB members, along with advice on how to conduct brand studies. Notwithstanding the value that branding is said to give corporations, it has also been essentially ignored in media economics literature on corporate valuation or channel or program selection criteria (see, for example, Bates, 1993; Owen & Wildman, 1992; Picard, 1989). This can be partially explained as a reflection of a rapidly changing industry that only recently has begun to recognize the necessity of brand identity and equity in the crowded television marketplace. In addition, research on television promotion, the strategic practice that includes branding, is also in its infancy due to the long-held belief that promotion meant relatively little in an oligopolistic industry structure that is tightly controlled. Only in the last 10 years or so have studies of television promotion moved from the descriptive to quantitative measurements of effectiveness and analysis of individual promotional types (Eastman, Ferguson, & Klein, 1999).

Clearly, the social, political, and economic importance of the television industry would itself be justification for brand studies. Added to this, the contrast between a television brand (with both its ubiquity and intangibility) and other consumer brands, which generally are more tangible and less ubiquitous, is worthy of investigation to fill in some of the gaps on general brand research. The intent of this chapter is to (a) offer an analysis and explanation of the importance of branding in the television industry,

(b) present the results of a preliminary study of television network brand awareness, and (c) suggest specific areas for future research.

Market Structure and Branding

Branding is a form of *product differentiation*, whereby firms attempt to make their product "stand out" from competitors by such means as pricing, packaging, and brand image. As Freeman (1999) explained, in discussing television "you need to differentiate yourself from the other 200 channels of programming by creating a distinct personality" (p. 18).

Channel branding is vital in a crowded television environment because research indicates that most people, even those who graze a lot, only pay attention to a limited number of channels that become part of the individual or family *channel repertoire* (Ferguson, 1992). A highly differentiated service with a strongly recognizable brand image has a much better chance of becoming part of the channel repertoire of the intended viewer. Obviously programs and accompanying advertising on a repertoire channel have a much greater chance of being consumed by the viewer.

Product differentiation is typically emphasized in industries whose structure is relatively competitive (Gomery, 1989). Generally, the more entrants in a market, the greater the amount of product differentiation. In the "glory days" of the Big Three, the U.S. television industry was an oligopoly with three dominant "sellers" in an enormous market. NBC, CBS, and, to a somewhat lesser degree, ABC programmed for a mass undifferentiated audience, providing "something for everyone." Until the diffusion of satellites and cable, barriers to entry were so high that there was little chance of substantial competition for the viewer's attention. Because of this, strong product differentiation was not needed or, to be more exact, was counterproductive to network goals. Although the concept of *positioning*—of finding a conceptual location in the public's mind that separates one program service from another—is an old idea that was central to advertising and promotion in the Big Three era, there was no recognition of brand image promotion as a key element in the long-term viability of a network.

Although varying due to market conditions, a highly differentiated product can be a significant barrier to entry by *owning* a market position. For example, MTV (and its co-owned VH1, M2, and international services) *owns* the music video/lifestyle niche. Although the ongoing proliferation of digital channels might encourage a competitor, a successful challenger to MTV's position at this stage is difficult to imagine. Interestingly, a strong brand also can be a means of reducing entry barriers (Aaker, 1991). Disney's entry into the sports publishing and restaurant/bar businesses by leveraging the strong brand identity of ESPN is a powerful example. There is little likelihood that Disney would have been willing to take the risk of competing in these difficult business segments without the ESPN connection.

The ongoing consolidation of the media industries is suggestive of the emergence of a new oligopoly operating globally across media (Bellamy, 1998). Although product differentiation traditionally has been less important in oligopolies, there is little likelihood that there will be any decrease in the emphasis on branding because of the deterrent and entry reduction effects of differentiation. In addition, and arguably most important, is the nature of the emerging media oligopoly. It seems likely to be one of few owners and many channels. This means that branding will be essential to differentiating the "sibling" services of one corporation, a function that may be more important than differentiating the offerings of competing corporations.

Defining Brand Equity

The added value that a brand gives to a product or service is called *brand equity* (Cobb-Walgren et al., 1995). More specifically, brand equity "is a set of brand assets and liabilities linked to a brand, its name and symbol, that add to or subtract from the value provided by a product or service to a firm and/or to that firm's customers" (Aaker, 1991, p. 15). The measurement of brand equity is one of the major concerns of corporations and marketing scholars in the last decade (Aaker & Biel, 1993; Aaker & Keller, 1990; Broniarczyk & Alba, 1994; Brown & Dacin, 1997; Carpenter, Glazer, & Nakamoto, 1994; Derbaix, 1995; Keller, 1993; LeClerc, Schmitt, & Dube, 1994; Loken & John, 1993; Machleit, Allen, & Madden, 1993; Mela, Gupta, & Lehmann, 1997; Papatla & Krishnamurthi, 1996; Park et al., 1996), a reflection of the perceived increase in competitive pressures amid which most businesses operate. However, the development of a comprehensive brand measurement methodology has so far been an elusive goal. This is largely because of the nature of brands and brand equity. Measurement of the price premium (i.e., how much extra a consumer would pay for an established branded product or service vs. one that is not established) is considered by some to be perhaps the best measure of brand equity (Aaker, 1991). But there is general agreement that brand equity is too complicated a concept to be subject to the measurement of one variable. For example, equity has been recognized as being based on both "hard" (i.e., tangible/functional) attributes such as speed, premium prices, and user function, and "soft" or emotional attributes such as excitement and trustworthiness (Biel, 1993). Obviously, the hard attributes are much more subject to measurement than the soft ones. Broniarczyk and Alba (1994) have argued that brand equity is based on both present and potential value, further complicating measurement.

There is general consensus in the marketing literature that brand equity derives in large part from brand knowledge, which consists of both brand awareness and brand image (Keller, 1993). *Awareness* is made up of the amount and type of recall and recognition a brand has among consumers. *Image*, a more difficult concept to measure, consists of subjective conceptions of the quality of the brand and its role in the lifestyle of the consumer. High levels of awareness coupled with positive image associations equal substantial *brand equity*.

TELEVISION BRANDS

No published studies have examined media branding in television, and few are even closely related. Table 5.1 lists some of the major general studies of branding that relate in some way to the branding of television networks. As the comments below and in the table show, however, the authors generally are speaking of broader principles without direct ties to the special case of television.

There are both inherent and historical variables that make the conceptualization and definition of television brands special and different from brands in other industries. First, if we define the brand in television as a network, the continuous, never-ending nature of television allows for near constant brand promotion through in-program "bugs," and, more generally, the fact that brand and "purchase/choice" location is the same. The source of the brand is itself the brand. Although factory outlet and theme stores (the Disney Store, Niketown) are retail equivalents, most re-

TABLE 5.1
Studies of Media Brands

Author	Year	Database/Method	Relevant Findings
Owen	1993	Survey of top 25 brands.	NBC averages seventh across all adult age groups.
Aaker	1996	Discussion of Young & Rubicon's brand equity study, examining each brand using 32-item questionnaire.	CNN ranked second and PBS ranked eighth in brand strength compared to all measured brands.
Keller	1998	Brand personality survey assessing 114 traits for 37 brands.	MTV and CNN are among the brands scoring highest on one factor (MTV on excitement, CNN on competence).
Ryan	1999	Trade press account of Equitrend brand equity survey.	Big Three highest in familiarity; Discovery highest in perceived quality.

tail brands have to compete within a location with other brands and for shelf space from the storeowner.

Second, price is rarely a consideration in television with the exception of pay services such as HBO and Showtime. This may change as networks are provided on a more à la carte basis via cable, satellite, or Internet distributors, and broadcast networks develop new revenue streams. The general lack of the price issue probably is the most distinguishing characteristic of the television brand, because price, rather than brand, is often seen as the most important variable in consumer choice behavior.

Third is the degree of loyalty a consumer has for a brand. One of the key benefits of branding is the building of consumer loyalty. This loyalty for most products or services is characterized by the consumer's exclusive preference for one brand. Procter & Gamble (P&G), for example, generally expects that if it can get someone to sample Crest toothpaste, she or he might be satisfied with the qualities and image of the product, which have been reinforced through promotion and advertising, and only buy Crest in the future. Part of the reinforcement is in the brand extensions (Crest for Kids, Crest Gel, Crest Mint, etc.) that were developed in large part to keep loyal customers from sampling other brands. Obviously, this type of loyalty is nonexistent in television. Television has always operated with the assumption that viewers will sample other channels/networks—an assumption even more relevant with the rise of multiple channels and more user-friendly RCDs and other navigation devices. Market share in television is not based on exclusive customers, but rather on the number and type of grazers a network can convince to sample its wares—at least for long enough to be measured by Nielsen ratings.

Finally, television is more ephemeral and nontangible than most other products and services. Branding arguably is more important in television than in many other businesses, as awareness and image essentially are all television has to "sell" to the viewing audience that it must create. As explained by Keller (1998), "branding plays an especially valuable function in the arts and entertainment industry. These offerings are good examples of experience goods—prospective buyers cannot judge quality by inspection and must use cues such as the particular people involved, the concept or rationale behind the project, word-of-mouth, and critical reviews" (pp. 18–19). These factors also contribute greatly to the problems of definition that exist in television branding.

The Problem of the Television Brand

Clearly, most anything can be a brand. A corporate name can be a brand, such as in the case of General Electric and GE lightbulbs. An alternative is for a division or segment of a larger corporation to be emphasized as a brand. What is emphasized as a brand for any product or service is part of each brand's unique history and the influence of the exigencies of leadership, product category, and market factors. For example, General Motors Corporation (GM) differentiates such brands as Chevrolet, Buick, Cadillac, and Saturn. Chevrolet then differentiates various automobiles (e.g., Cavalier, Lumina, and Malibu). In this model, it is the Chevrolet (or Chevy) brand that is emphasized over larger umbrella-like corporate names or individual automobile brand names (i.e., advertising and promotion is always for the Chevy Lumina, never just the Lumina). A television equivalent would be the linking of network (corporate) name to specific programs (*Dateline NBC, CBS Sunday Movies*) or program genres (Fox Sports, ABC News). In both cases, the corporate owner (e.g., GM, GE) is obscured by a segment or divisional brand name (Chevrolet, NBC) linked explicitly to a specific product or program (Aaker, 1991; Kapferer, 1992). Of course, in television the linkage does not have to be program specific, as all promotions of network programs contain network identification and specifics regarding program airdates.

The increased integration of broadcast networks and their affiliate stations (both through ownership and more explicit contractual arrangement) also demonstrates a form of branding. NBC5 Chicago (rather than WMAQ-TV) and Fox53 in Pittsburgh (rather than WPGH-TV) are the equivalent of Chevrolet dealers. The importance of the network as brand can also be seen in brand and line extensions such as CBS Sportsline, CNBC, and Fox Sports Net, as well as in the formation of composite brands such as MSNBC and CNNSI.

Conventional wisdom in the television industry and in much research is that "people watch programs not networks." Although refuted in part by the study and practice of scheduling strategy (see Eastman & Bolls, chap. 3, this volume), the emphasis on the program is ingrained within the industry and supported in part by the ability of hit programs such as *Seinfeld* and *Home Improvement* to carry and increase audiences in different time spots and support entire nights of programming. The logic is simple. People tune in to watch *Home Improvement*, not ABC. By extension, *Home Improvement* is the brand of interest and contributes significantly to the network's overall brand equity, leading viewers to sample the programs following it. Popular programs can also be used as a form of brand extension through such means as spin-off programs and off-air merchandising.

Emphasizing programs over networks is parallel to how P&G brands its products. In contrast to GM/Chevrolet, P&G emphasizes neither a corporate or divisional/segment brand identity for its many products. What is emphasized is the specific name of individual products (e.g., Tide, Crest, Pampers). The success of P&G's "precision positioning" (Kapferer, 1992, pp. 149–150) in contributing to brand equity was discussed by Aaker

(1991), who asked the reader to consider "how much more value is represented by the P&G brands than a set of brands such as P&G bar soap, P&G laundry detergent . . ." (pp. 226–227).

Although specific program promotion is the main form of television promotion, a P&G strategy is highly problematic for the industry. Tide can exist as a brand indefinitely, at least in terms of most product life cycles. In contrast, television network programs (with the exception of some daytime soaps and more generic news and sports programming) have a comparatively short life span, in part because there are so many of them. Although programs do "live forever" in reruns, this is a benefit to the program owner, which is not necessarily the network. This divorce between provider (manufacturer) and product is another decided difference in the application of the P&G model to television. Of course, the recent elimination of the network financial interest and syndication rules has given networks the ability to control and own programming, which might make the emphasis on individual program promotion more prominent in the future.

The bottom line is that the brand of interest is "something that resides in the minds of the consumers" (Keller, 1998, p. 10) and is essentially whatever the corporation wishes it to be and whatever the researcher wishes to study as long as it meets the definition of brand. In television, both networks and programs can be brands. However, at this time, the logical emphasis seems to be on network as brand because of the enormous equity built over generations (whereas *Frasier* may be a long-lived program at 6 years, NBC is over 70 years old). The secondary emphasis is to make use of that equity to expand both domestically and internationally.

Broadcast and Cable Differences

The proliferation of new channels delivered to homes via satellites and cable is the proximate cause of the marketplace clutter that has made branding such an important part of the television industry. Because non-broadcast television providers receive a direct monetary subsidy from viewers in addition to advertising revenues (i.e., a dual-revenue stream), cable networks have been able to become financially successful with very small audience levels, as compared to broadcast media, and with highly specialized content. The high level of product differentiation that is the bread and butter of many cable channels allows branding to serve as a powerful barrier to entry. Although digital transmission and an even greater amount of channel capacity make it economically feasible for existing television providers to recycle existing content through new channels (e.g., the old NBC News footage that makes up a large part of the MSNBC schedule), certain brand names in cable are now so well established that we can assume that: (a) they have a high level of specific image recognition and perception and (b) it is very difficult to compete against them. Included here are such cable stalwarts as CNN, ESPN, and MTV. This makes brand leveraging very attractive for these channels both on- and off-air, as most everyone knows that CNN is 24-hour news, ESPN is about sports, and MTV is about contemporary rock/pop music.

A specific image/persona is, of course, highly desired as a brand concept and something that traditional broadcast networks lack. However, the vagueness of broadcast network images may allow their brand identities to be extended in new and lucrative directions that the more specific niche networks cannot follow. For example, NBC may be a more credible Internet service provider (ISP) or content provider than MTV because of its age (resulting in a kind of marketplace veneration) and, conceivably, exactly because of its lack of clear and established identity. This is not to imply that a clear and specific brand identity is a negative, as there is far too much evidence to the contrary. ESPN, for example, has instant credibility as a sports magazine publisher, purely from its reputation as an authoritative expert in sports coverage. However, analyses of the differences between broadcast and nonbroadcast networks should attempt to take into consideration all of the potential benefits and drawbacks of consumer brand knowledge and market equity, and not simply assume that the niche/narrowest brand is always superior.

AN EXPLORATORY STUDY OF THE TELEVISION NETWORK BRAND

Exploratory studies serve to empirically test concepts, terms, and variables as well as reveal more sophisticated questions and hypotheses. Keller (1998) defined the brand exploratory study as "research activity directed to understand what consumers think and feel about the brand and its corresponding product category to identify sources of brand equity" (p. 376). The research reported here concerns methods most appropriate for the study of *network brand awareness,* a component part of brand equity, along with loyalty, quality, and brand associations (Aaker, 1996). *Brand awareness* is the "strength of a brand's presence in the consumer's mind" (Aaker, 1996, p. 10). A brand's strength in the marketplace is directly related to the consumer's ability to identify component parts of the brand, including brand name (Keller, 1998).

The Graveyard Model

Brand awareness can be assessed in a number of ways. One of the simplest methods is to have a respondent list, via unaided recall, all the brands they can remember for a particular product or service category. The results provide a top-of-mind rank ordering of brands suitable for further analysis. Another method for measuring brand awareness is with the use of aided-recognition measures where respondents indicate their recognition of brand names from a list provided to them. The combination of these two measures, brand recall and recognition, can be used as coordinates on an x- and y-axis to plot brand awareness. This technique has been used in proprietary studies of dozens of product categories by advertising agencies (Aaker, 1996). Results typically show a positive and curvilinear slope typical of the model found in Fig. 5.1 (Aaker, 1996).

Suppose Fig. 5.1 represented recall and recognition measures for the so-called "near-luxury" automotive class ($25,001–$40,000 range). Those brands and corresponding models with highest recall and recognition would be found in the upper middle and upper right-hand portion of the slope and would include brands (and corresponding models) such as the BMW 3-Series, Buick LeSabre, Chrysler 300M, Lexus ES 300, and Mercedes C-Class. These brands currently dominate consumer share of mind compared to most competitors and have high consumer awareness, one of the characteristics of strong brand equity. Brands located in the lower left-hand portion of the slope demonstrate lower brand recall and recognition when compared to most competitors, brands such as Acura 3.2 TL, Infinity I30, and Mitsubishi Diamante. These are generally new or tired brands that may be susceptible to increased brand awareness via increased promotion and advertising, repositioning, or product redesign. More problematic is the brand located in the upper left-hand portion of the slope. Here reside brands with high recognition but very low recall. Although recognized by potential consumers, these brands fail to register in tests of recall. Brands falling into this area have established images, but these images contribute little if anything to brand awareness and may even have a negative effect on brand equity. Current efforts on the part of such automotive products as the Mazda Millenia and Oldsmobile LSS come to mind. Every effort to reposition the brand through promotion may fail. This is the so-called *Brand Graveyard*. As the model visibly demonstrates, high recognition with corresponding low recall can spell the demise of an established brand.

Aaker (1996) argued for an exception to this general rule, the case of a "healthy niche brand" (p. 12) where a brand demonstrates high recall and recognition for only a portion of the larger consumer group. Returning to our automotive example, such a case might be predicted in the near-luxury class for aficionados of such brands as Audi, Saab, or Volvo.

Research Questions

Are television network brands amenable to measurement via recall and recognition tests typical of other goods and services? Does the Graveyard

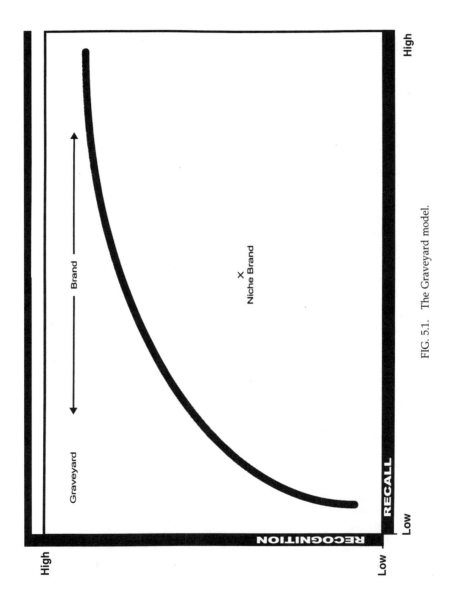

FIG. 5.1. The Graveyard model.

model shed light on respondent awareness of television network brands? The importance of awareness in the television industry is such that a Nickelodeon executive recently argued that "the battleground for tomorrow is not for share of TV audience, but for share of mind" (McConville, 1999, p. 33). The following research questions were posed in order to address these concerns:

R1: How useful is unaided recall in measuring network brand awareness?

R2: How useful are unaided-recall and aided-recognition measures in assessing network brand awareness?

R3: How useful are recognition and weighted recall measures in assessing network brand awareness?

Method

Participants for the current study were two groups of students in communication and mass communication courses. One group was enrolled in undergraduate courses in communication at a midsize private university serving a large urban and suburban population in the Middle Atlantic United States. The other group included undergraduate and graduate students in communication and mass communication at a major state university serving a largely suburban population in the western United States. The well-recognized limitations inherent in overuse of college-aged populations for survey research were offset partially in this study by the fact that adults 18 to 34 are one of the primary and most important targets of television promotion.

Survey Instrument

A two-part survey instrument was used. The first part was designed to measure network recall and to collect basic demographic and television viewing data. This portion of the survey included a page with three columns of numbered blank spaces. The instructions directed each respondent to write down the names "of all television networks you can recall. This includes broadcast networks, cable networks, and satellite networks." Each group of respondents was specifically reminded that a television network could be delivered via broadcast, cable, or satellite to avoid any possible confusion as to the definition of network. Pretests with instrument drafts indicated that most individuals were capable of generating no more than 25 network names. Consequently, space was provided for nearly double this number (48) in the actual survey instrument in a clean and uncluttered layout. Data for standard media age categories

(18–24, 25–34, 35–49, 49–54, and 55+) and gender were collected during this part of the survey. Respondents were also asked to indicate whether they watched television and their sources for television programming, including over-the-air, basic cable, premium channels, or satellite television. Each copy of the recall portion of the survey included an assigned survey number. Respondents were asked to remember this number prior to exchanging the recall portion for the recognition portion of the survey.

The recognition portion of the survey contained five pages. The first page provided instructions and asked each respondent to enter the assigned survey number from the first part of the survey into a space provided. Respondents were then informed that this portion of the survey was designed to measure their recognition of a television network. They were reminded that recognition did not necessarily mean that they watched a particular television network, only that they remembered hearing or seeing something about a particular network. They were also reminded that many networks look and sound familiar and to be certain that they actually recognized the specific network before placing a large "X" over the name and logo. The remaining four pages of the recognition portion of the survey instrument contained 91 network brands. Each brand was represented by the network's logo and name, surrounded by a box to distinguish it from neighboring brands. Brands were arranged randomly, with an average of 26 brands on the majority of pages. A total of 410 surveys were completed.

Data Coding

Each respondent's network recall responses were entered into a spreadsheet format as string data. Up to eight alphanumeric names were entered as string variable data to represent each television network (e.g., ABC, ESPN2, FOODNET, SCI-FICH). Some items listed by respondents were eliminated during data entry because they did not qualify as television networks (i.e., TCI, Primestar, and Superstation). In other cases, the respondent had provided a partial name for a network and a scheme was developed to determine whether or not to include the item. For example, some respondents would list Comedy Network instead of Comedy Central or Food Channel instead of Food Network. These items were considered recalled networks because the respondent had provided a key network identifier. In other cases where, for example, the respondent would list Cooking Channel instead of Food Network, the item was not included for analysis.

Results

The demographics of the respondents were as expected. More than four out of five respondents (84.6%) were between 18 and 24 years of age. The remaining respondents were between the ages of 25 and 34 (12.2%), with less than 4% aged 35 or older. More females (59.6%) responded to the survey than males (40.4%). Almost all respondents (96.7%) indicated that they watched television, including over-the-air broadcast channels (79.9%), basic cable offerings (91.1%), premium cable channels (62.2%), and direct broadcast satellite services (17.6%).

Unaided Recall–Top-of-Mind

The first research question concerned the utility of unaided techniques in measuring network brand recall. One method of measuring network share of mind is to identify the first network recalled by respondents, the so-called top-of-mind brand. Table 5.2 shows the results of the network first mentioned by respondents.

This table shows what might have been anticipated. The Big Three networks dominated almost 70% share of mind, and ABC and NBC combined for over 55% top-of-mind for all respondents. Fox, HBO, CNN, ESPN, and MTV combined for another 20% share, with WB, PBS, and TNN each registering slightly more than 1% share of mind. The remaining

TABLE 5.2
Network Brand Awareness: Top-of-Mind

Network	%	Cumulative %
ABC	31.1	31.1
NBC	24.7	55.8
CBS	13.6	69.4
Fox	6.2	75.6
HBO	5.4	81.0
CNN	4.1	85.1
ESPN	3.1	88.2
MTV	2.3	90.5
WB	1.5	92.0
PBS	1.3	93.3
TNN	1.0	94.1
Spice	0.8	95.1
MSNBC	0.5	95.6
Nickelodeon	0.5	96.1
TBS	0.5	96.7
TNT	0.5	97.2
UPN	0.5	97.7
USA	0.5	98.2
WGN	0.5	98.7
A&E	0.3	99.0
BET	0.3	99.2
CNBC	0.3	99.5
Fox Family	0.3	99.8
Lifetime	0.2	100.0

13 networks combined for less than 6% share of mind for all respondents. These results suggest that unaided recall as a stand-alone measure of network brand awareness is insufficient.

The results are similar on the high end of the scale to Equitrend's proprietary study of television brands, which measures "brand familiarity" by the percentage of people who are familiar enough with a brand to also rate it for quality (Ryan, 1999). For example, among a broadly representative group of people, each of the Big Three networks had a 95% familiarity rating in the Equitrend study, followed by NBC News (a category we did not use because a network news division is not a network), Fox, ABC News, CBS News, PBS, Discovery Channel, and CNN. For further comparison, ESPN ranked 15th (at a 74% familiarity score), TNN 19th (71%), and MTV 24th (69%). Neither HBO nor the WB were listed in the top 25 in Equitrend's familiarity rankings (Ryan, 1999).

Unaided Recall and Aided Recognition

The second research question concerned the most rudimentary of recall and recognition measures as surrogates for awareness, which led to a graveyard plot of network television brands. The 24 network brands generated in the top-of-mind analysis were used as the recall measure and plotted on the x-axis. Recognition was operationalized as the frequency with which respondents chose a network logo/name in the second phase of survey administration. This frequency was plotted on the y-axis. Figure 5.2 depicts the respondents' awareness of television networks.

The results from this scattergram plot also reflect the dominance of the traditional Big Three in terms of respondent awareness. A number of factors may be contributing to these results. First, and most obvious, there is little doubt that the traditional Big Three still dominate the brand landscape when it comes to television networks. Years of repetition have led the Big Three to be ingrained in the historical memory of the respondents. Further, respondents may be employing one or more metacognitive tools to recall television network brands, including the use of mnemonic devices based on *initial* alphabetical sequencing of network acronyms (i.e., A before B before C, as in ABC before CBS or NBC). Cable or direct broadcast satellite penetration in different markets as well as cable system channel capacity and channel position may also influence the recall. Top-of-mind as a recall measure places too much emphasis on the respondent's first response, particularly in a televiewer's world of multichannel clutter. Accordingly, network brand recall measures must go beyond first-glimpse strategies and take into account the host of channels respondents provide in recall tests, while remaining sensitive to the *order* in which network brands are recalled. Simple top-of-mind measures may work in the study of toothpastes, shoes, or even near-luxury class automobiles, when

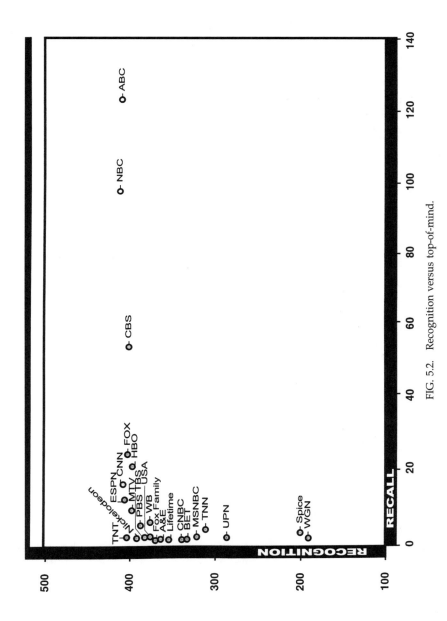

FIG. 5.2. Recognition versus top-of-mind.

the range of choices is relatively few. The dozens of television brands available to the majority of respondents force the development of a more complex measure of network brand recall.

Recognition and Weighted Recall

Previous research suggests televiewers incorporate a repertoire of up to about a dozen channels (Ferguson, 1992; Heeter, 1988; Lochte & Warren, 1989). Not surprisingly, the average respondent recalls more channels than she or he probably watches. Analyses of the current sample indicated that the average number of networks recalled by all 410 respondents was 21 ($M = 21.08$, $SD = 9.21$). This value was used in a weighting process to develop a more sensitive recall measure. Twenty-one frequency tables of recalled networks were generated. The first list represented the first network recalled by respondents, the second list the second network recalled, and so on. Each list consisted of a list of recall networks and the corresponding frequency for each network. The frequency value for each network appearing in list one was multiplied by a factor of 21. The frequency value for each network appearing in list two was multiplied by a factor of 20. This procedure was completed for each of the 21 lists (with list 21 frequency values multiplied by a factor of 1). The product within each frequency list for a particular network was then summed across all lists where the network appeared. This weighted value was used as the recall measure for each network. Some networks were dropped from consequent analysis because not one respondent listed the network in the unaided-recall portion of the survey.[1] The weighted recall measure was used in the plotting of coordinates for the x-axis value and the summed recognition measure was once again used for the y-axis value.

The third research question concerned the utility of using a weighted value for network brand recall. Recall and recognition of television networks for all respondents are illustrated in the Fig. 5.3 graveyard plot. Seventy-one networks were included in the analysis. Although not amenable to more advanced statistical tests, the graveyard plot provides a visual representation of the relative position of network brands in a crowded product/service category.

In theory, the Graveyard model is a curvilinear slope approaching that of a diagonal bisecting a rectangle. Figure 5.3 shows a curvilinear shape more akin to a hard right angle, with very few brands showing both high

---

[1]The following networks were dropped from consequent analysis for all respondents: America's Health Network, BET Jazz, the Box, CBS Eye on People, CBS Telenoticias, Flix, Galavision, Goodlife Network, INSP, International Channel, Much Music, Nick at Nite, Nostalgia, Outdoor Life Network, Product Information Network, Satellite Sports Net, Westerns, WPIX New York, and WSBK Boston.

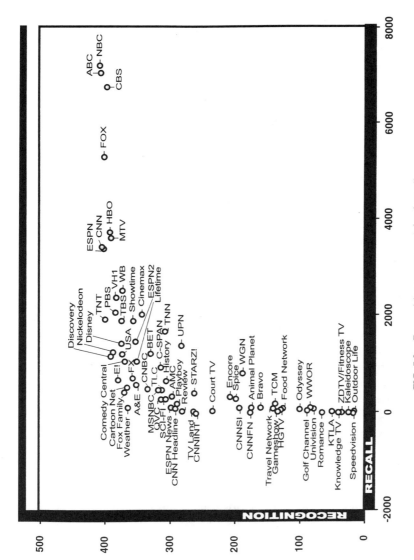

FIG. 5.3. Recognition versus weighted recall.

147

recall and recognition. Once again, the Big Three dominate all other networks in terms of brand awareness, adding validity to the results. The Fox brand appears in an island position midway between the Big Three and the next cluster of networks, suggesting that it shares many of the characteristics of brand awareness enjoyed by the Big Three but also showing that it is a newcomer among the major broadcast networks. Next, these four networks were removed in order to generate yet one more graveyard plot in an attempt to further discern television network awareness for the majority of cable and fledgling broadcast networks.

Recognition and Weighted Recall— Omitting Big Three and Fox

Figure 5.4 depicts the graveyard plot for network brand analysis after the Big Three and Fox were excluded from the analysis. It shows that the relationship between network history and brand awareness is strongly reflected in the cluster of cable networks comprised of ESPN, MTV, CNN, and HBO. Ranging widely in editorial content, nonetheless, these networks have in common their relatively long existence compared to most other cable networks as well as their wide-audience appeal, including appeal to the young adults sampled in this study.

Two other network clusters also emerge from the analysis. One is comprised of the WB, VH1, TNT, PBS, TBS, Showtime, and Cinemax. Movies, music, and young adult comedies and dramas are the dominant types of programming in this cluster, genres that are popular with the respondents of this study. Many of these networks also support the argument that a network's longevity is positively related to awareness. This can be seen in the inclusion of the more diverse PBS and TBS networks, as well as the appearance of long-lived pay channels in the cluster. The other more eclectic cluster is made up of ESPN2, the Disney Channel, Nickelodeon, the Discovery Channel, USA Network, Comedy Central, Lifetime, and BET. With the exception of USA and, to a lesser degree, Discovery, these networks may have a lower awareness level because of their specialized programming or relatively short life spans. Alternately, ESPN2 might have a higher awareness level than its longevity would suggest because of its direct name sharing with its well-established "parent."

The 24 brands in the lower half of the plot have low recall, but show a pattern of incremental recognition. This is the case whether or not the Big Three and Fox are included in the analysis, indicating that their low recall and recognition are a reliable and stable finding. Most of these networks provide single-genre editorial content to niche or microniche target audiences. Many are new or relatively new networks and have yet to reach the carriage threshold of 20 million households. Another factor in their low re-

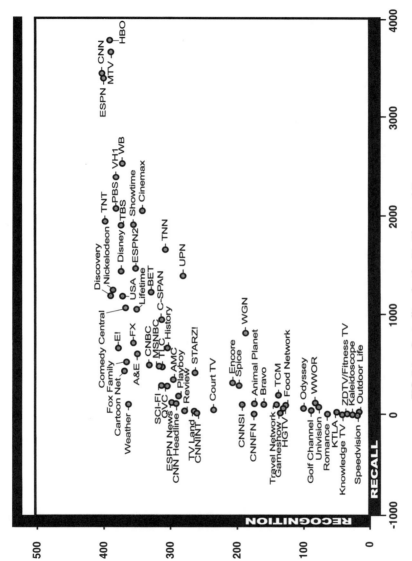

FIG. 5.4. Controlling for the Big Three and Fox.

149

call and recognition is that many of these networks are not available on the cable systems serving one or both of the geographic areas sampled.

More unclear is the pattern exhibited in the group of networks found in the traditional graveyard portion of the scattergram plot (upper left). The Weather Channel shares this position with the Cartoon Network, Fox Family Channel, E! Entertainment Television, A&E, and FX, with Discovery, Nickelodeon, and Disney close by. These networks exhibit high recognition but low recall. One possible interpretation of this cluster is that most of these channels use names that clearly identify the content, thus enhancing recognition. Another factor may be that at least some of these channels lend themselves to short bits of viewing. Viewership of the Weather Channel, for example, is predictably high in overall audience reach, but low in terms of time spent viewing, helping to explain its position in the graveyard. It does not share top-of-mind recall compared to most other networks, but ranks among the highest in brand recognition. Other networks in the graveyard, indeed networks extending slightly above and below this section in terms of awareness, might suffer from rookie status, undistinguished or unfocused editorial content, or poor promotion.

The Graveyard model reported here revealed no definitive healthy niche brands — networks exhibiting moderate to high recall with moderate recognition. Figure 5.4 indicates that TNN, UPN, and WGN are close to the niche brand position. At first glance, this is somewhat surprising in that each of these networks lacks a clearly distinctive programming focus. However, the result for UPN may be based on the young, urban, primarily African American identity the network abandoned in the 1998–1999 season in order to expand its base, although the strategy failed. UPN's modest level of recognition demonstrates the perils of changing brand identity. WGN may be in this group because of its status as the flagship for the WB network, a network that specifically targets a viewing niche of teens and young adults. The results for TNN and WGN might also be based on their large amounts of sports coverage (basketball and professional wrestling on TNN, major league baseball on WGN). Basketball and professional wrestling, in particular, are popular among younger viewers. In each case, it appears that a niche can be developed *within* a more diverse channel.

The performance of composite brands can also be examined in Figs. 5.3 and 5.4. CNBC and MSNBC rated higher, with CNNSI much lower on recall and recognition, a reflection of its low level of clearance in the tested markets. The three composite brands generated low recall, but average to above average recognition compared to all other brands. This suggests some support for the effectiveness of composite branding strategies. Extension brands also varied in terms of brand awareness. Not surprisingly, ESPN2 led all other extension brands in terms of recognition and recall, placing among the top 20 networks. Fox Family showed low recall but high recognition, making it a potential candidate for the awareness graveyard. ESPNEWS, CNN Headline News, and CNN International were part of a mixed-venue cluster exhibiting midrange recognition but very low recall. CNNFN was part of the lower third of all networks in terms of awareness. Again, the use of a college population no doubt contributed to these results.

Performance Assessment of This Study

A primary goal of the current study was to test the efficacy of simple recall and recognition measures as techniques for determining television network brand awareness. To that end, the study was both successful and limited. Results from the current study reveal high awareness for a limited set of brand choices in the television landscape. Much of this was to be expected, given the wide range of television choices available today compared to other product or service categories. Indeed, at this time, ratings data might provide the functional equivalent for most of the brands. The current results provide little if any surprises in terms of which brands demonstrate strong brand equity (and, therefore, generate strong recall) on the part of potential viewers.

Why the Graveyard model for television-network brand awareness deviates from the ideal model depicted in marketing literature can be explained. First, most product and service categories consist of merely a half dozen or so major brands. Such is the case for tennis shoes, jeans, toothpaste, and even competing classes of automobile brands. As explored in previous sections, the television network "product or service" category can include many dozens of brands for consideration. Low recall for a considerable number of brands for a particular portion of the television audience might be predicted. Second, many network brands are new and have yet to build and may never achieve brand equity levels comparable to the Big Three. Third, the youthful subjects of this study are unlikely to be as brand conscious as older viewers because they have grown up in a time of many channels competing for their attention rather than that of a stable network oligopoly. Television network brand equity takes years to accumulate. Fourth, awareness of specific programs may be more relevant than network or channel awareness. This is the conventional wisdom in programming, which may be increasingly valid as the number of programming conduits increases.

Finally, another explanation for the current shape of the network-brand awareness plot is that the data weighting procedure used in the generation of recall data may have been inadequate to assess network brand recall. However, other techniques were explored to visually "unpack" the dense clustering of most other networks with little success. For example, the same 21 frequency tables were generated with the frequency value for each network squared. This procedure was completed for networks appearing in each of the 21 lists. The resulting products for each network were summed across all lists. The weighted values of the same 71 networks were used in a plot with the existing recognition measure. The results compounded the spatial distance between the Big Three and the other networks and created tighter clusters of the remaining networks, particularly along the y recognition axis.

Most studies conclude with a call for far larger samples. The call is merited here as well, but with certain qualifications. Results from the current study document strong network brand awareness for a handful of old and new broadcast networks and the most venerable of the basic-cable networks, penetrating most, if not all, cable systems in the United States. It makes sense that these were the most dominant networks to surface across the two sampled markets in the current study. One would predict similar results in data generated in other markets. To that end, the current sample was adequate to confirm certain predictions about the brand dominance of a select handful of television networks, even if those networks were not part of the local cable array in the two markets studied. What the current study does not accomplish is an unraveling of the dense pack of second-wave cable networks geared to niche audiences/markets. The current study also deleted from the analysis specially promoted niche-programming blocks that make up a portion of a larger network's overall programming (e.g., the brands-within-the-channel of Fox Kids, Nick at Nite, etc.) and that might have triggered higher recognition. Finally, this study makes clear the need to study diverse audience groups in the media brand research. One could easily predict that the scattergram plot results would be much different given a sample of business people, children, or senior citizens.

AN AGENDA FOR FUTURE RESEARCH

This exploratory study confirms some basic branding assumptions, provides a baseline, and points dramatically to the need for more in-depth research into media branding. Recall and recognition measures isolate brand awareness, but they do not shed light on *why* some network brands dominate share of mind. What are the component parts of brand image that work with awareness to constitute brand equity?

Measuring Brand Equity

The definitive measurement of brand equity value is an elusive goal because it is often based on nontangible, qualitative variables. The quantification of brand equity is even more problematic than measuring advertising effectiveness, as network brands exist outside of specific campaigns to increase programming viewership.

Despite these difficulties, most every recent study of brand equity has identified the categories of brand awareness and brand image as being fundamental to any form of measurement. As such, the current effort has isolated a handful of dominant network brands amenable to more advanced brand-image analysis. The next step in research is to measure brand equity for television's most dominant network brands, including ABC, CBS, NBC, Fox, HBO, MTV, CNN, and ESPN. Another promising approach is to concentrate on the clusters of niche brands competing for the same audience subgroups (e.g., sports fans, investors, seniors).

Brand Equity Research and Television Networks

Aaker (1996) provided a conceptually sound technique for measuring brand equity in manufactured goods and marketplace services. However, these techniques have yet to be applied to the study of television networks. Aaker's "Brand Equity 10" is comprised of price, satisfaction, loyalty, perceived quality, leadership, value, personality, organizational association, awareness, and market share (Aaker, 1996, pp. 318–319). Data collected for these constituent parts of brand equity might be useful to specific efforts to position or reposition networks relative to the competition.

Pricing. Pricing as a measure confronts an obvious dilemma when comparing television networks and programs to other consumer and industry goods and services. Most marketing measures of pricing pose relational dilemmas for respondents, asking them to place a dollar valuation on one brand in a product or service category compared to one other brand. The technique is highly problematic when comparing television networks. How much is Fox worth compared to Comedy Central? Who is the primary competitor for ABC? Is it another member of the Big Three? How is the answer for any respondent influenced by the roles played by affiliate stations in individual markets? Are the competitors all cable networks or a select few? In addition, broadcast television is still "free" in the minds of many viewers, probably making pricing measures too abstract to generate much usable data. However, televiewers are ever more familiar with entertainment pricing in the form of premium channels, pay-per-view, videocassette rentals, and so on. A compromise can be achieved by designing measures intended to determine relative network value. Network valuation is more fully explored in a following section.

Viewer Satisfaction and Loyalty. Select satisfaction and loyalty measures hold great promise in the evaluation of network brand equity — and seem particularly suitable for measuring brands showing high awareness for groups of television viewers. Satisfaction can be measured in a number of simple ways. Viewers can be asked to rate their satisfaction with a particular brand, how well a brand meets their expectations, and how likely they would be to recommend the brand to other viewers. Network loyalty can be measured in a similar fashion. Brand viewers can be asked if they consider themselves loyal to a network, if they mostly view the target network compared to other networks, or if the target network shares a mental space among a select few others viewed by the respondent. Also of interest would be a comparison of relative network loyalty when measured by current brand measurement techniques as opposed to channel loyalty studies previously conducted in an era of many fewer channel choices, which at the time found a limited degree of channel loyalty (Barwise & Ehrenberg, 1989). How much do network loyalties change over time or with changes in lifestyle? What is the effect of local-market-station affiliation changes on network loyalty?

Network Quality and Leadership. Considered a central component of brand equity, attempts should be made to measure the dimensions of network quality and leadership. The quality dimension is amenable to the use of scales (high/low quality, best/worst, consistent/inconsistent, finest/inferior, etc.) and can be combined to create a quality index for television networks. An example from proprietary research is Equitrend's television brand research where respondents rate channel quality on an 11-point scale. The Discovery Channel (8.11 average vs. base channel average of 6.9), Learning Channel, and History Channel are at the top of the quality ratings, demonstrating the differences in awareness and image measures. Leadership is seen as comprised of two potentially related dimensions. First, leadership is a measure of dominant ranking in the product or service category. Second, brand innovation is also a quality of leadership. A network's leadership in its program category or genre can be measured, as can its growth or decline in prominence relative to the competition. Network brand innovation can be measured similarly, along programming, format, and technical dimensions. Studies of such attributes might shed light on the importance of quality and leadership dimensions as used by televiewers in assigning network brand equity value.

Value, Personality, and Organizational Association. Brand associations include value, personality, and organization. Brand value is related to brand pricing and can be modified to measure "value in my life" as compared to "dollar value." Brand personality appears to be one of the most important areas for assessing network brand equity. Respondents might be asked to rate a particular network brand in terms of whether or not it has a personality, whether they find the brand interesting, reliable, informative, entertaining, and so on. Brand personality has been central to persuasive campaigns for such consumer products as DeBeers, Saturn, and Godiva. Respondents might be asked to rate a particular network in terms of how they perceive the company behind the network. Do they consider the company trustworthy, admirable, secure, concerned about viewers, and so on. Complementary to the concept of brand personality is brand differentiation. Do viewers distinguish one network from another? Is a particular network seen as the same as other networks? Results from such analysis may shed light on the importance of network organizational personality on network brands — particularly if future study includes the examination of composite brands such as CNBC, CNNSI, and MSNBC and extension brands such as Fox Family, CNNFN, and ESPN2.

Network Brand Awareness. The results of the present study point to the need to further examine a handful of dominant network brands. However, additional venues of inquiry should be initiated to study brand equity for nondominant networks. Recall measures such as those employed in the current study could be combined with and compared to ratings data.

Market Share. Pricing policies and market share data, as mentioned, need to be incorporated in a complete brand equity measurement method. In addition, distribution is worthy of study, but complicated by the differences between broadcasting, nationwide cable penetration, and variances in cable network carriage across cable systems. Although the proliferation of digital transmission should serve to equalize distribution over time, brand equity would obviously be affected by a brand's availability to its intended audience.

Conclusions and Recommendations

This chapter provided a starting point for defining branding for national television services and measuring television brand equity. The not surprising finding of Big Three dominance indicates the staying power of well-established brands. Clearly ABC, CBS, and NBC are in an advantageous position compared to their cable brethren in terms of brand equity. Although specific measures of image are needed, this is perhaps a hidden strength of the networks at a time when their share of the television audience is in serious decline. Also in the Big Three's favor are recent Nielsen Media Research data suggesting that viewers engage broadcast networks differently than cable networks. Broadcast network televiewing seems to be "appointment TV," characterized by weekly and program-length scheduling behaviors (Schneider & McConville, 1999, p. 3). The continuing strength of the Big Three network brands leads to the preliminary conclusion that ABC and CBS should follow NBC's lead in leveraging their brand by developing other television channels and that all three should continue to use their valuable names to brand other products and services.

Although a few of the cable brands are close to the niche category of the Graveyard model, the awareness level of some other well-established brands has to be considered surprisingly low. This is a clear indication of how difficult it is to establish a new brand in a crowded market. Although HBO, ESPN, CNN, and several other of the major cable brands are economically successful and able to leverage their brand identity/equity, it seems likely that the industry is near the saturation point for the introduction of "original" brand names. Brand extensions and composite branding, both of which make great use of existing brand equity, are likely to be the main method of channel expansion. If this analysis is correct, the obvious result is a powerful barrier to entry for new television competitors that do not already have a well-established brand name.

This study was limited to national U.S. television network brands, although branding is a key element of marketing for all media and most other businesses both domestically and internationally. Brand studies of other electronic media raise interesting questions not asked in this study. For example, studies of local television stations could tell us much about how local news and other local programming, the network affiliation, and off-air promotion/community involvement contribute to brand equity. Off-air promotion would also be an important element in brand equity studies of the consolidating radio industry. With more and more television and radio channels (stations) making use of the World Wide Web as a promotional platform, the web's contribution to equity, if any, also needs to be explored.

As the once disparate media industry segments continue to merge into what appears to be an emerging global media oligopoly, studies of international branding will be needed to explore possible variations in the interpretation of the meaning of brands. An important element of this will be the evaluation of corporate efforts to leverage brands across cultures.

This chapter focused on consumer evaluation of television brands. There are other important issues of brand equity that do not directly relate to the viewer/user. For example, the effect of brand equity on business-to-business and industry-governmental relations needs to be examined. What effect might brand equity have on advertising rates (controlling of course for ratings variations)? How is brand equity expended to obtain desired results from regulators? More generally, how does and how much does brand equity contribute to the political economic power of television distribution entities?

The importance of branding is difficult to overestimate in the present cluttered media industry and consumer markets. Television and other electronic media branding, with all its idiosyncrasies in consumer payment and brand definition, will be of continuing interest and importance for three main reasons. First, a strong brand identity is critical to producing audiences in a multichannel environment, an environment that is becoming more and more crowded as television converts to digital delivery. It is perhaps the only means of gaining a place in a television viewer's/user's channel repertoire.

Second, brands are vital in expanding markets. Brand extensions marry an established brand to a new service as a means of establishing instant market credibility. In addition to the many domestic examples (Fox Family Channel, CNN International, MSNBC), brand extensions are commonly used by major U.S. and multinational television providers to extend their influence around the globe. Examples here include MTV Germany, Nickelodeon Latin America, and NBC Europe. The failure of the latter could be interpreted as an indicator that brands as amorphous as NBC do not translate well to other nations.

Finally, branding is necessary in the leveraging of corporate assets to open new markets. These markets may be related to the present business of a branded entity (e.g., *ESPN Magazine*, CBS Sportsline web site), or may be nonrelated, if not totally separate (e.g., logo apparel and other merchandise, Fox Sports restaurant/bars). With the traditional advertiser-supported model of television under increasing pressure, television providers, and especially broadcasters, are constantly looking for new revenue streams.

Ultimately the study of branding, brand equity, and promotion is a way of tracking the effects of the recent structural changes in the media industry. Studies of industry structure and consequent conduct and behavior are of use both to the industry and to anyone who wants to understand the dynamics of an ever more powerful global industry.

REFERENCES

Aaker, D. A. (1991). *Managing brand equity*. New York: Free Press.

Aaker, D. A. (1996). *Building strong brands*. New York: Free Press.

Aaker, D. A., & Biel, A. L. (Eds.). (1993). *Brand equity and advertising: Advertising's role in building strong brands*. Hillsdale, NJ: Lawrence Erlbaum Associates.

Aaker, D. A., & Keller, K. L. (1990, January). Consumer evaluations of brand extensions. *Journal of Marketing, 54*, 27–41.

Barwise, P., & Ehrenberg, A. (1989). *Television and its audience*. London: Sage.

Bates, B. (1993). Valuation of media properties. In A. Alexander, J. Owers, & R. Carveth (Eds.), *Media economics: Theory and practice* (pp. 91–113). Hillsdale, NJ: Lawrence Erlbaum Associates.

Bellamy, R. V., Jr. (1998). The evolving television sports marketplace. In L. E. Wenner (Ed.), *MediaSport* (pp. 73–87). London: Routledge.

Bellamy, R. V., Jr., & Chabin, J. B. (1999). Global television promotion and marketing. In S. T. Eastman, D. A. Ferguson, & R. A. Klein (Eds.), *Promotion and marketing for broadcasting and cable* (3rd ed., pp. 211–232). Boston: Focal Press.

Bellamy, R. V., Jr., & Walker, J. R. (1996). *Television and the remote control.* New York: Guilford.

Biel, A. L. (1993). Converting image into equity. In D. A. Aaker & A. L. Biel (Eds.), *Brand equity and advertising: Advertising's role in building strong brands* (pp. 67–82). Hillsdale, NJ: Lawrence Erlbaum Associates.

Broniarczyk, S. M., & Alba, J. W. (1994, May). The importance of the brand in brand extension. *Journal of Marketing Research, 31,* 214–228.

Brown, T. J., & Dacin, P. A. (1997, January). The company and the product: Corporate associations and consumer product responses. *Journal of Marketing, 61,* 68–84.

Carpenter, G. S., Glazer, R., & Nakamoto, K. (1994, August). Meaningful brands from meaningless differentiation: The dependence on irrelevant attributes. *Journal of Marketing Research, 31,* 339–350.

Chernin, P. (1998, July 6). How Fox built its brand. *Electronic Media, 9,* 26.

Cobb-Walgren, C. J., Ruble, C. A., & Donthu, N. (1995). Brand equity, brand preference, and purchase intent. *Journal of Advertising, 24*(3), 25–39.

Derbaix, C. M. (1995, November). The impact of affective reactions on attitudes toward the advertisement and the brand: A step toward ecological validity. *Journal of Marketing Research, 32,* 470–479.

Ducey, R. (1997, April 8). Co-branded joint ventures: Internet age business strategies. Presentation slides from Eizo Shuimbun Seminar, Las Vegas [Online]. Available at the National Association of Broadcasters' web site: http://www.nab.org/research/Research/Reports/InternetBusinessStrategy/index.htm

Eastman, S. T., Ferguson, D. A., & Klein, R. A. (Eds.). (1999). *Promotion and marketing for broadcasting and cable* (3rd ed.). Boston: Focal Press.

Ferguson, D. A. (1992). Channel repertoire in the presence of remote control devices, VCRs, and cable television. *Journal of Broadcasting & Electronic Media, 38,* 83–91.

Frank, T. (1999, July). Brand you. *Harper's,* 74–79.

Freeman, L. (1999, June 7). On TV, image is everything. *Electronic Media,* 18.

Gomery, D. (1989). Media economics: Terms of analysis. *Critical Studies in Mass Communication, 6,* 43–60.

Heeter, C. (1988). The choice process model. In C. Heeter & B. S. Greenberg (Eds.), *Cableviewing* (pp. 11–32). Norwood, NJ: Ablex.

Kapferer, J. (1992). *Strategic brand management and new approaches to creating and evaluating brand equity.* New York: Free Press.

Keller, K. L. (1993, January). Conceptualizing, measuring, and managing customer-based brand equity. *Journal of Marketing, 57,* 1–22.

Keller, K. L. (1998). *Strategic brand management: Building, measuring, and managing brand equity.* Upper Saddle River, NJ: Prentice Hall.

LeClerc, F., Schmitt, B. H., & Dube, L. (1994, May). Foreign branding and its effects on product perceptions and attitudes. *Journal of Marketing Research, 31,* 263–270.

Lochte, R. H., & Warren, J. (1989). A channel repertoire for TVRO satellite viewers. *Journal of Broadcasting & Electronic Media, 33,* 91–95.

Loken, B., & John, D. R. (1993, July). Diluting brand beliefs: When do brand extensions have a negative impact? *Journal of Marketing, 57,* 71–84.

Machleit, K. A., Allen, C. T., & Madden, T. J. (1993, October). The mature brand and brand interest: An alternative consequence of ad-evoked effect. *Journal of Marketing, 57,* 72–82.

McConville, J. (1999, June 14). Networks play in a brand new game. *Electronic Media,* 33.

McDowell, W., & Batten, A. (1999). *Branding TV: Principles and practices.* Washington, DC: National Association of Broadcasters.

Mela, C. F., Gupta, S., & Lehmann, D. R. (1997, May). The long-term impact of promotion and advertising on consumer brand choice. *Journal of Marketing Research, 34,* 248–261.

Mermigas, D. (1999, June 14). Cable honchos bet on "big pipe." *Electronic Media,* 1, 42.

Owen, B. M., & Wildman, S. S. (1992). *Video economics.* Cambridge, MA: Harvard University Press.

Owen, S. (1993). The Landor imagepower survey: A global assessment of brand strength. In D. A. Aaker & A. L. Biel (Eds.), *Brand equity and advertising: Advertising's role in building strong brands* (pp. 11–32). Hillsdale, NJ: Lawrence Erlbaum Associates.

Owers, J., Carveth, R., & Alexander, A. (1992). An introduction to media economic theory and practice. In A. Alexander, J. Owers, & R. Carveth (Eds.), *Media economics: Theory and practice* (pp. 3–46). Hillsdale, NJ: Lawrence Erlbaum Associates.

Papatla, P., & Krishnamurthi, L. (1996, February). Measuring the dynamic effects of promotions on brand choice. *Journal of Marketing Research, 33,* 20–35.

Park, C. W., Jun, S. Y., & Shocker, A. D. (1996, November). Composite branding alliances: An investigation of extension and feedback effects. *Journal of Marketing Research, 32,* 453–466.

Picard, R. G. (1989). *Media economics: Concepts and issues.* Newbury Park, CA: Sage.

Prime time clutter up. (1999, April 12). *Electronic Media,* 59.

Ridgway, J. (1998, April 20). Name of the game is branding. *Electronic Media,* 16, 37.

Roberts, J. L. (1999, April 26). Out of the box. *Newsweek,* 42–45.

Ryan, L. (1999, June 14). Experts say be bold, but be careful. *Electronic Media,* 36, 38.

Schneider, M. (1998, March 23). Digital success means brands. *Electronic Media,* 38, 39.

Schneider, M. (1999, March 22). Ancier's agenda: Wooing top talent. *Electronic Media,* 3, 45.

Schneider, M., & McConville, J. (1999, April 12). Nielsen study probes loyalty. *Electronic Media,* 3.

Spring, G. (1998, June 15). "*Friends*" for sale. *Electronic Media,* 1A, 49.

Spring, G. (1999, June 7). Promax, industry facing changes. *Electronic Media,* 14, 23.

II

APPLICATIONS OF RESEARCH IN PROMOTION

The second part of this book contains six chapters that focus on promotion within a particular genre, such as news or sports or movies, on a particular audience, such as children, or on a particular medium, such as radio or online. These chapters apply many of the theoretical concepts introduced in Part I to a particular situation, and several draw on the activity theories and salience models previously described. Chapter 6 begins by looking at promotion within children's programming; chapter 7 continues with promotion in and about sports programming; chapter 8 surveys promotion of movies; chapter 9 examines promotion of local news; chapter 10 concerns promotion of radio programming; and lastly, chapter 11 scrutinizes promotion on the Internet. Each of these chapters contains an original study prepared especially for this book to enrich the cumulative database. Each chapter also concludes with specific ideas for further studies that might be conducted by readers.

6

Promotion in Children's Programming

Walter Gantz
Nancy C. Schwartz
Indiana University

Children watch television. In a *Time* review, Richard Corliss described television as "the baby-sitter of a spoiled kid's dreams: it promises everything, never says no and lets you change the channel if you don't get what you want . . ." (Rushkoff, 1994). Although not everyone feels as strongly as Corliss, few people would disagree with the statement that children watch television—and lots of it. According to Nielsen reports, children watch 22 hours 11 minutes of television per week (Nielsen, 1998). It is widely recognized that by the time they graduate from high school, American children will have spent more time in front of a television than in a classroom.

Children also are major consumers. Children under 12 years of age now spend $24.4 billion of their own money and influence the spending of another $300 billion annually (McNeal, 1997). Television courts the buying power of children. The average American child watches over 5 hours of advertising each week and sees over 30,000 commercials each year (Robinson & Bianchi, 1997). A portion of those messages are promotional spots intended to encourage children to watch even more television programming.

Together, the viewership and purchasing power of children is big business. As competition within the medium increases, young viewers are less loyal to individual programs and certain channels (Abelman, 1995). With hundreds of millions of advertising dollars at stake annually, broadcast and cable networks and stations engage in a variety of strategies to obtain, maintain, and expand their young audiences. Tactics include aggressive scheduling (Adams, 1993), counterprogramming (Littleton, 1996), product-based programming (Greenfield et al., 1993), branding (Abelman & Atkin, 1998), and program promotion (Eastman & Newton, 1999; Katz, 1997). Program promotion provides a means for networks and stations to speak to their viewing audience and to deliver messages they hope will entice future viewership.

Very little has been written about program promotion aimed at children. Because of their varying ability to understand messages and their susceptibility to influence, children constitute a special audience. As discussed by Eastman and Bolls (chap. 3, this volume), to gain the attention and buying power of this audience, television programmers and advertisers make use of what is known about children's viewing patterns. Program promotion is a hybrid of programming and advertising. As a snapshot of the program it is publicizing, the promo is likely to utilize the characters and media elements prevalent in the show. Analogous to a commercial, a promo must deliver a sales message in a short amount of time. Thus, the same demands and opportunities that a young audience presents to programmers and advertisers are inherent in program promotion.

The combination of increased competition among networks and stations and an audience of young viewers who are simultaneously, and perhaps contrarily, both powerful and susceptible deserves closer examination. This chapter examines the nature of children as an audience by exploring the characteristics that make children a unique audience for promotional messages. It then reports an original analysis of on-air program promotion directed toward children, and it concludes with ideas for subsequent research.

CHILDREN AS A UNIQUE AUDIENCE

Children are a special audience in two ways. The first has to do with how they process information. Table 6.1 summarizes the implications of significant studies in programming and advertising for understanding how children take in promotional messages.

Cognitive Processing

Although early media scholars suggested that television viewing was an effortless, passive activity, more recent research has tended to support the premise that television viewing is a complex information-processing task (see discussion by Perse, chap. 2, this volume). To understand a television

TABLE 6.1
Studies of Children as Audiences

Author(s)	Year	Topic	Collective Implications for Promotion
Lang	2000	Information processing	When processing tasks exceed the viewer's capacity, messages will not be completely processed.
Alwitt, Anderson, Lorch, and Levin	1980	Production features	Television forms influence children's attention and comprehension. Audio attributes such as peculiar voices, laughter, and sound effects elicit attention to television. Visual attributes such as rapid action, the presence of women and/or children, and special effects promote and maintain attention. Appropriate use of salient features in production will assist children in processing.
Bryant, Zillmann, and Brown	1983		
Huston and Wright	1983		
Lang	1990		
Wartella and Ettema	1974		
Anderson, Lorch, Field, and Sanders	1981	Content	Comprehensibility of program content is a driving force in determining viewing behavior. Children's ability to understand relationships, make inferences, and construct meaning for television content increases with age and cognitive ability.
Collins	1983		
Dorr	1986		
Rolandelli	1989		
Anderson, Choi, and Lorch	1987	Attentional inertia	If one part of a program is interesting and holds a child's attention, the child is likely to continue watching after a change in content or presentation.
Anderson and Lorch	1983		
Buckingham	1996	Emotion	Emotional content in television messages intensifies viewer response.
Lang, Dhillon, and Dong	1995		

message, the viewer must encode auditory and/or visual signals and transfer them into short-term memory. Then, in order to make sense of this incoming information, previously stored information must be retrieved and integrated with the new information. The combination of new and old information is then concurrently stored in long-term memory for future use. These acts of encoding, retrieving, and storing require the allocation of processing resources. As discussed by Perse (chap. 2, this volume) and Newton and Potter (chap. 10, this volume), the limited-capacity theory of television (Lang, 2000) contends that these processing resources are limited, and that when the tasks of encoding, retrieving, and storing exceed the viewer's capacity, messages are not completely processed. With fewer experiences than adults and less stored knowledge to draw on, a child's ability to understand television messages is inherently limited.

Because children bring limited prior knowledge and varying levels of cognitive abilities to the television viewing experience, television programmers and advertisers use the medium itself to attract attention and attain processing resources through the elicitation of orienting responses. An orienting response is a reflexive response to a change in environment or to a stimulus that signals important information (Lang, 1990, 1991). As discussed by Eastman and Bolls (chap. 3, this volume), orienting responses are elicited via such structural features of television as cuts, edits, sound, and movement (Geiger & Reeves, 1993; Lang, 1990; Thorson & Lang, 1992).

Production Features.   Several studies have been conducted to identify the production features that attract children's attention (Alwitt, Anderson, Lorch, & Levin, 1980; Anderson & Levin, 1976; Barcus, 1980; Bryant, Zillmann, & Brown, 1983; Levin & Anderson, 1976). Elements found to promote attention in young children include rapid action, special effects, the presence of women and/or children, the use of magic or fantasy, the incorporation of humor, the portrayal of "fun," peculiar voices, laughter, music, singing, sound effects, and changes in audio level. Studies also have examined the effects of audio and visual features in programs and commercial messages (Calvert, Huston, Watkins, & Wright, 1982; Calvert & Scott, 1989; Huston & Wright, 1983, 1994; Rolandelli, Wright, Huston, & Eakins, 1991; Smith, Anderson, & Fischer, 1985; Wartella & Ettema, 1974). These studies reveal that audio changes or sound effects are the best means for gaining a child's attention, whereas visual attributes are best at maintaining it. In other words, some kind of change in the sound may cause a child to look at the screen, but the child will continue to look only if what happens visually is interesting (Gunter & McAleer, 1997).

Singer (1980) argued that the attention-getting production features used for sensory stimulation limit television as an information medium, and the fast pace at which material typically is presented does not leave sufficient time for cognitive processing. According to Singer, the concurrent presentation of information through action, dialogue, voice-overs, and/or captions is often too much to process, thus keeping the viewer from making efficient use of what is seen and heard. This point of view is commensurate with Lang's limited-capacity theory. Lang and Basil (1998) suggest that structural features associated with television increase the allocation of resources to the process of encoding the message, whereas content variables may increase the allocation of resources to storage.

Content.   Message content also affects the allocation of processing resources. Reeves and Thorson (1986) suggested that the distinction between structure (sensory) processing and content processing is useful;

structural change increases the need for immediate processing resources, whereas content has little effect on immediate processing, but rather increases processing costs over the entire message. Rolandelli (1989) argued that comprehensibility of content is more important than form in determining children's viewing behavior, and Anderson and his colleagues (1979, 1981, 1983) argued that children make active choices about what to watch based on their understanding of the content. Thus, content, as well as structural features, determines what children attend to.

As discussed by Collins (1983; Collins, Wellman, Keniston, & Westby, 1978) and Dorr (1986), preschoolers remember isolated events rather than complete stories, are unable to focus on important or useful information and ignore incidental information, and have difficulty with time order. For these reasons, preschoolers prefer segmented, magazine-style shows to plotted programs. Throughout childhood, steady improvement occurs in attending to content that is central to the plot, with concurrent gains in ignoring nonessential information and sequencing the events of a program correctly. As comprehension increases, children begin to prefer "stories" to segmented magazine shows. Inferences about events that are implied but not depicted require not only more complex processing, but also knowledge about relevant real-world activities. Children younger than 8 or 9 rarely infer missing content, and when they do their inferences are often incorrect (Dorr, 1986).

These findings associated with children's responses to television can be examined from the perspective of a child's stages of cognitive development. Up to the age of 5, children tend to operate from a perceptual basis. Their attention is invoked by visual and sound effects, suggesting that short scenes and frequent changes are the best way to gain and hold their attention. As children grow older, these features become only part of television's attraction. With increased cognitive development, children become more aware of relationships between characters and events and are more able to understand and follow story lines; thus, content becomes increasingly important.

Program Preference. Children's program preferences change over time. In his review of the literature, Comstock (1991) elaborated on the three-stage model of "fuzzy animal," "superhero," and "realistic content" from Wolfe and Fiske's 1954 study of comic book reading to show how children's preferences shift as they grow older. The programming of *Sesame Street* and animal cartoons for young children is representative of the "fuzzy animal" stage. The preference for cartoons declines with age and is replaced with adventure programs, commensurate with the "superhero" stage. Both groups also name family-formatted situation comedies as a favorite program genre — a format missing from the comic book study. The appeal of sitcoms is not surprising, as children are attracted to programs with characters their own age with whom they are able to identify (Dorr, 1986). Sitcoms often cater to children by featuring child actors of various ages. Furthermore, the story lines in sitcoms tend to be about events that children may well experience in their own lives (Weiss & Wilson, 1996). As children enter their teen years they prefer the "realistic content" of general audience programming, continuing to enjoy sitcoms and adventure programs, but also naming variety shows and music videos as favorite programs.

Capitalizing on what is known from research on television programs and commercials about children's attention, understanding, and preferences to maximize their impact, promos need to explicitly depict major messages, presenting little to no incidental information. Promos targeting young children are likely to be for cartoons and sitcoms and will be most effective if they employ women and/or children, rapid action, special effects, unusual sounds, laughter, music, and changes in audio level. Promos for shows aimed at older children will feature adventure and more realistic characters. These promos can require children to make inferences and draw on prior knowledge; however, given the limited time frame in which a promo is presented, the fewer resources required for retrieval of prior knowledge, the more resources that will be available to store the message, making the promo's message available for future recall—and possibly prompting viewership.

Attentional Inertia.   The longer a viewer continuously looks at television, the more likely it is that he or she will continue to do so. Conversely, the longer a viewer does not look at the screen, the less likely it is that he or she will look back. Researchers (Anderson, Choi, & Lorch, 1987; Anderson & Lorch, 1983) believe that attentional inertia is an important aspect of the way children watch television. If one part of a program is interesting and holds a child's attention, the child is likely to continue watching after a change in content or presentation, even if the new material is less interesting or more difficult to understand. Thus, attentional inertia sustains attention longer than it might otherwise be engaged, and in so doing may introduce the child to material or concepts he or she would not otherwise encounter. Programmers can take advantage of this phenomenon by placing promos in the first position of the nonprogramming pod, when children's attention is likely to carry over from the preceding program.

Emotion.   On a macrolevel, children's emotional responses to television are tied to their understanding of television as a medium (Buckingham, 1996). The ways children make sense of events they see dramatized on television and learn to cope with them are products of both their cognitive and social development. At a microlevel, emotional responses to television content can occur with little to no thought by the viewer and can elicit automatic allocation of processing resources (Lang, Dhillon, & Dong, 1995; Lang, Newhagen, & Reeves, 1996). When a moderate level of arousal occurs, children pay more attention to content, process it better, and remember it better. When arousal is low, information processing is less efficient because children fail to invest enough energy to make sense of the content. On the other hand, when arousal is very high, information processing is less efficient because children are distracted by whatever aroused them (Dorr, 1986; Lang et al., 1995). These findings suggest that promos eliciting a moderate level of arousal will be most effective with children.

Vulnerability

The second way in which children comprise a unique audience for television messages lies in their vulnerability. As children learn about the world around them, television is a potential source of information. What children see on television may influence their knowledge, beliefs, values, attitudes, and behavior. The depiction of violence, the stereotyped presentations of characters, and the nature of advertising are prominent topics in the debate about the impact and regulation of television. This debate is amplified by the fact that children regularly view programs targeted toward general or adult audiences. Promotion of programs that contain violence or other questionable content, the use of stereotypes, or the glib appeals of advertising are of concern to parents, educators, policymakers, and child advocates. Table 6.2 summarizes significant studies in this area that have implications for on-air promotion.

Violence. Research shows that children regularly watch television programs that feature violence (Cantor, 1998b). Research also shows that children are given ample opportunity to view programming containing violence. According to Woodard (1999), 28% of children's shows contain four or more instances of violence. The viewing of violent content has been at the forefront of advocacy activity and research agendas.

Viewers of different ages respond in different ways to television portrayals of violence. Children between the ages of 2 and 7 do not readily distinguish between fantasy and reality and are therefore often frightened by images of monsters, transforming characters, or animals that might attack them (Cantor, 1994, 1998a). Yet, both are standard content in promos for cartoons and programs such as *Animal World*. Older children, who are able to distinguish between fantasy and reality, are frightened by portrayals of realistic threats, such as kidnapping, assault, and natural disasters, the fare of some news promos and of so-called reality-based police shows.

TABLE 6.2
Studies of Influences on Children as Audiences

Author(s)	Year	Topic	Collective Implications for Promotion
Cantor	1998a,b	Violence	Numerous researchers working in diverse settings have found *some* relationship between violence and the media. Portrayals of violence can incite feelings of insecurity and anxiety or of domination and power. Such responses indicate a need for programmers and advertisers to responsibly police their materials for violent content.
Gerbner and Gross	1976, 1980		
Paik and Comstock	1994		
van der Voort	1986		
Barcus	1983	Roles/ stereotypes	Television is a powerful influence on children's beliefs about gender roles and ethnic groups. The ways in which women and minorities are portrayed in television programs and commercials has changed somewhat but does not come near to reflecting current demographics or social roles.
Ferrante, Haynes, and Kingsley	1988		
Greenberg and Brand	1993		
Riffe, Goldson, Saxton, and Yu	1989		
Atkin	1980	Advertising	There is ample evidence that advertising stimulates requests for food and toy products. The way children process and respond to advertising information is of increasing interest as their role as consumers in a market-driven society grows.
Seiter	1995		
Ward, Wackman, and Wartella	1977		
Young	1990		

Though many studies and analyses (Cantor & Nathanson, 1997; Dorr & Kovaric, 1980; Geen, 1994; Gerbner & Gross, 1976, 1980; Gunter, 1994; Paik & Comstock, 1994; van der Voort, 1986; Wilson et al., 1998) indicate that television violence and children's reaction to it is far from unidimensional, the need for programmers and advertisers to responsibly police their material for violent content is not negated, and it could be argued that this responsibility ought to extend particularly to program promos. Although parents may exercise some control over the programs their children watch, it is more difficult for them to censor the promotions for other programs, which are delivered during program breaks. Promos for programs geared toward general or adult audiences, which are aired during children's programs, may expose children to violent content that many are ill prepared to handle. To further complicate matters, as noted by Geoffrey Cowan, dean of the Annenberg School for Communication, in a *TV Guide* roundtable discussion ("Hollywood Under Fire," 1999), promos often take violence out of context as a way of promoting the program. Cantor

(1998a) related an account by one subject that illustrates that even a movie promo can incite fear:

> When I was about eleven years old there was a movie on TV called The Burning Bed. It was, I believe, the story of an abused wife who gets fed up and douses her husband with gasoline while he's sleeping. She starts the bed on fire and he burns to death (I assume). I never watched the movie but I saw the ad for it on TV and it scared me to death. . . . I never really worried that someone would start my bed on fire, but I was suddenly certain that we were going to have a house fire which would eventually reach my bedroom and my bed. I would lie awake as long as I could, trying to stay alert, trying to smell the smoke that I knew was going to come creeping under my door. (p. 35)

In response to concerns about violence in children's television, the Telecommunications Act of 1996 included a section for the creation and adoption of a television programming ratings system. In January 1997, the networks began voluntarily labeling their shows with age-based ratings similar to the rating system used by the Motion Picture Association of America (e.g., TV-Y7, TV-PG). Parents and advocacy groups wanted more information about the content of programs and criticized this system for its merely age-based designations. As a result, a revised rating system was instituted in October 1997 that added program-specific content indicators to the original age-based structure, resulting in the following guidelines:

Children's Programming
    TV-Y: All Children
    TV-Y7: Directed to Older Children
       FV: Fantasy Violence

General Programming
    TV-G: General Audience
    TV-PG: Parental Guidance Suggested
       V: Moderate Violence
       S: Some Sexual Situations
       L: Infrequent Coarse Language
       D: Some Suggestive Dialogue
    TV-14: Parents Strongly Cautioned
       V: Intense Violence
       S: Intense Sexual Situations
       L: Strong Coarse Language
       D: Intensely Suggestive Dialogue
    TV-MA: Mature Audience Only
       V: Graphic Violence
       S: Explicit Sexual Situations
       L: Crude Indecent Language

The Telecommunications Act also mandated that within 2 years each new television set sold in the United States contain a V-chip (a programmable chip that allows consumers to block shows on the basis of prior encoded ratings).

Although this system does provide information about the content in a program, the lack of specific criteria for rating programs remains a concern. The differences between "moderate violence" and "intense violence" or "some sexual situations" and "intense sexual situations" are arbitrary. Without more specific criteria, the ratings are not helpful in guiding parents to make viewing decisions for children. In the same way, they are not effective in determining what programs are blocked. Furthermore, because the system is voluntary, there is the issue of those programs that are not rated. This issue extends to commercials and program promos—components of television that are not addressed by the Telecommunications Act.

Though the content of program promotions are not restricted by law, programmers could better serve their young audiences and concerned parents by agreeing not to air promos for shows with more intense levels of content than the content in the existing show (Cantor, 1998a). At the least, the display of program ratings on promotional spots would give children and parents a "heads up" about the nature of the upcoming program.

Roles and Stereotypes.   Because television characters may influence children's beliefs and attitudes toward social roles and conventions, parents, educators, and politicians have also expressed reservations about the stereotyped presentations of characters in television programming and advertising. Many studies have concluded that television is a powerful influence on children's beliefs about gender roles (Signorielli, 1993) and ethnic groups (Graves, 1993). Harris (1999) noted that there is a "basic gender asymmetry," with men presented approximately twice as often as women in prime time, and three times as often in Saturday-morning children's shows. Greenberg and Collette (1997) investigated the major characters added to broadcast lineups throughout 27 seasons and found that although equity was nearly achieved in 1980 (52% male; 48% female) and 1984 (51% male; 49% female), the overall population of television programs over 3 decades was 65% male and 35% female. This disproportion extends to educational/informational (E/I) programming for children. Barner (1998) found males outnumbered females by 59.3% to 40.7% in E/I programs. More notably, he found males appeared in significantly more scenes than females and that although 6 of the 11 programs sampled featured a male as the central character, there were no E/I programs that featured a female as the central character. Gender asymmetry extends to commercials. Riffe, Goldson, Saxton, and Yu (1989) found, excluding animated characters, 61% of the characters in Saturday-morning commercials were male and 39% were female. In their study of nonprogram content during children's television, Kunkel and Gantz (1992) found males outnumbered females by almost three to one.

In 1972, Dominick and Rauch found the voice-over announcer in nonprogramming content was male 87% of the time. Replicating their work in 1988, Ferrante, Haynes, and Kingsley found a slight drop in this percentage to 83.1%. This inequality is possibly explained by the belief held by many programming executives that the male voice is considered more authoritative than the female voice, and thus is better at selling. However, this reasoning is counter to evidence that young children prefer the voices of women and children.

In addition to being underrepresented, women are often portrayed in stereotypical ways (Davis, 1990; Greenberg, 1980; Vande Berg & Streckfuss, 1992). Although there now are more positive role models for girls in such programs as *The Secret World of Alex Mack* and *The Mystery Files of Shelby Woo*, many children's shows continue to portray females as the lesser characters supporting their male counterparts. Consider, for example, Baby Bop of *Barney and Friends* and Smurfette of *The Smurfs* (Douglas, 1994). Barner (1998) found male characters more often exhibited aggression, autonomy, and attention-seeking behaviors, whereas female characters more often exhibited deference, dependence, or nurturing behaviors. Ferrante et al. (1988) found that while advertisers were beginning to acknowledge the changing roles of women in society, commercials predominantly portrayed women in the home, whereas men were more frequently shown in the business world. Concerned parents, educators, and activists believe such portrayals can limit the career aspirations and attitudes of children.

In comparison to census data, minorities are also underrepresented (Greenberg & Brand, 1994). From the mid- to late-1970s, Barcus (1983) found 3% of the characters in weekday programming for children were African American and 1% to 4% of the characters represented other minorities. In weekend programming, 7% were African American and 4% to 8% represented other minorities. Greenberg and Brand (1993) found that of the 20 children's Saturday-morning programs on the three commercial broadcast networks, three programs featured African American males and one program featured a Hispanic American male. No Asian Americans and no Native Americans appeared. Representation of minorities in commercials has been somewhat better. Riffe et al. (1989) found 86.5% of the real (nonanimated) characters in Saturday-morning TV advertisements were White and 13.5% were other minorities. Greenberg and Brand (1993) found at least one advertisement in nearly every commercial break included a minority character.

In addition to underrepresentation, minorities are often segregated from White characters. Barcus (1983) found minority characters interacted with European characters in only 18% of children's programs. Greenberg and Brand (1993) found African American girls and White girls did not play together in commercials. Segregation of African American characters also prevails in all-minority situation comedies. Such portrayals provide limited opportunities for children to observe interracial interactions (Graves, 1993).

If program promotion reflects current programming, it seems reasonable to expect that the promos will feature far more males than females and that minorities will be underrepresented. Given that promos emulate the programs that they advertise, it is unreasonable to expect a more equitable portrayal unless there is a change in the representation of females and minorities in programming. Although this issue may not be grounded in promotion, it nonetheless remains a concern.

Advertising.   Unlike most television programming, advertising messages are deliberately persuasive. Numerous analyses have documented the persuasive power of commercials, showing that children request products that they see advertised on television (Atkin, 1980; Comstock, 1991; Guber & Berry, 1993; Gunter & McAleer, 1997; Seiter, 1995; Wartella, 1980; Young, 1990). Because the ability of children to comprehend a message and critically evaluate content depends on how well they understand the characteristics of the message, young children in particular are vulnerable to selling messages. Although they are able to identify commercials at a very early age, children under the age of 8 years are seldom able to describe the difference between programs and advertisements, and they believe that ads show what products are really like (Dorr, 1986; Robertson & Rossiter, 1974; Stephens & Stutts, 1982; Ward, Wackman, & Wartella, 1977).

In response to the concerns of parents and child advocates about young children's inability to differentiate between programs and commercials, program "separators" — material inserted between the program and commercial break — were designed to inform children that the program was stopping and would "be right back after these messages." However, studies indicate that the insertion of separators has not increased young children's ability to recognize commercial segments (Palmer & McDowell, 1979; Stutts, Vance, & Hudelson, 1981). Such findings are more evidence that children are not likely to recognize promos as selling messages.

Whether or not children recognize the difference between programs and commercials, they do desire products and are persuaded by ads to ask their parents for them. In a manner similar to commercials, program promos are designed to persuade viewers to watch the promoted programs. This makes promotion an important first link in the business of television. Promos lure viewers to programs; by watching programs, viewers are likely to see commercials, and by doing this, commercial television accomplishes its mission of delivering audiences to advertisers. Thus, the content of both the promos and the advertising is worthy of careful investigation.

APPLICABLE PROMOTION RESEARCH

A number of academic and marketing researchers have examined program promotion aimed at general audiences. Katz (1997) found that the six commercial broadcast networks (ABC, CBS, Fox, NBC, UPN, and WB) aired approximately 4 minutes per hour of on-air promotion during prime time. Eastman and Newton (1998) reported that those same networks aired between 6 and 10 program promos per hour, collectively offering more than 30,000 on-air promos a year. Perhaps because research on promotion has focused on prime-time programming directed to general audiences, the work in this area has centered on the salience variable (the structural features of the promos) and the impact of promos on ratings (Eastman & Newton, 1998, 1999), rather than on their particular content or the content-based ratings of the shows being promoted. Table 6.3 summarizes studies of program promotion to children.

Relatively little is known about program promotion aimed at children. Throughout the 1970s, F. Earle Barcus conducted several studies for Action for Children's Television (ACT) to describe the nature of commercials on television directed to children (see Table 6.3). In 1978, he reported the average American child is exposed to an average of 15 commercial messages, 5 program promos, and 2 public service announcements per hour. He found the most frequent type of promo (60%) was an excerpt from the program being promoted. The remaining promos were nearly equally distributed as voice-overs over closing credits and voice-overs over station IDs. Most of the promos were for other programs on the same station (69%), with 17% for the upcoming show. Promos emphasized action-adventure dramas on the weekend and comedy programs on weekdays. Nearly half of the weekend promos and more than three fourths of the weekday promos were for programs commensurate with the time period they were broadcast. Almost no promos were for programs which aired after 9:00 p.m.

In analyses of nonprogram content of children's television on the three major commercial broadcast stations from 1983 to 1987, Condry, Bence, and Scheibe (1988) found the distribution of nonprogram content remained relatively stable until 1987 when commercial time increased and promotional time decreased. They reported that the average hour of chil-

TABLE 6.3
Studies of Program Promotion to Children

Author(s)	Year	Sample and Method	Findings About Promotion
Barcus	1978	61.5 hours of children's television programming were videotaped in October 1997. Three network-affiliated and 3 independent stations in Boston, MA, were recorded on a Saturday and a Sunday morning, and 10 independent stations across the country were recorded on weekday afternoons. All program and nonprogram content was logged and coded.	Children were exposed to an average of five promos per hour. Promos emphasized comedy programs on weekdays and action-adventure on the weekend.
Condry, Bence, and Scheibe	1988	86.5 representative hours of children's television broadcast on Saturday mornings and weekday afternoons in 1983, 1985, and 1987 were drawn from the Human Development and Television Archive at Cornell University. Content was divided into categories and coded.	Children were exposed to an average of 4.1 promos per hour. The percentage of nonprogram time devoted to promos stayed relatively constant until 1987 when commercial time increased and promotional time decreased.
Kunkel and Gantz	1992	604 hours of programming from February and March 1990 were examined. Programming from three network affiliates, two independent broadcasters, and two cable channels was videotaped at each of seven sites throughout the country. Each nonprogram segment was coded on a number of dimensions.	Children were exposed to 1 to 3 min of promotional messages per hour. Independent and cable channels averaged nearly 3 min per hour and the networks averaged just under 1. The amount of nonprogramming time devoted to promos increased nearly 10%.

dren's programing in 1987 contained 20.03 commercial messages, 4.10 program promos, and 2.10 public service announcements.

In a study of nonprogramming content located in 604 hours of children's programming aired in the early 1990s, Kunkel and Gantz (1992) found broadcast and cable channels devoted between 1 and 3 minutes per hour to program promotion, with significant differences between the broadcast networks on the one hand and independent stations and cable on the other. Whereas the broadcast networks featured just under a minute of promotional messages (0:58), independents and cable channels offered nearly three times as much, 2:52 and 2:53 minutes per hour, respectively. In a follow-up study conducted during the pre-Christmas season, Kunkel and Gantz (1994) found the broadcast networks offered slightly more than a minute of promotion (1:10), with independents and cable channels again offering more (1:59 and 3:03 min per hour, respectively). Unfortunately for the purposes of this study, in both their studies, Kunkel and Gantz (1992, 1994) focused on the content of the advertisements and did not analyze the content of the program promos.

A STUDY OF PROMOTION IN CHILDREN'S PROGRAMMING

Kunkel and Gantz's (1994) data suggest that an increasing amount of television time is being devoted to program promotion. This is consistent with Eastman and Neal-Lunsford (1993), who, after interviewing 96 industry practitioners, concluded that as a result of remote control devices, program promotion would become shorter and more frequent. With the broadcast network share of the television audience eroding rapidly, it also seems reasonable to expect fewer differences between the broadcast networks and their cable counterparts than in the past.

Given the increasingly competitive marketplace of viewing options (with more TV channels, computers, video games, and Internet access), it behooves programmers to consider what is known about the abilities and interests of children in their efforts to win the viewership of this young audience. It also seems prudent to cater to the concerns of parents by minimizing the amount of violence depicted, being sensitive to gender and minority portrayals, and using program ratings in promos. These are issues of both program and promo content.

Research Questions

To further explore these issues and to investigate the nature of program promotion directed toward and accessible to children, this study was conducted in the spring of 1998 to examine on-air program promotion aimed at children. As the first of its kind, there was reason to anticipate certain outcomes, but it seemed more prudent to be guided by research questions rather than by theoretically or empirically derived hypotheses. Five groups of research questions concerning the quantity of promos, the kinds of shows promoted, the attributes of the characters, the placement of promos, and the amount of cross-promotion guided the study.

R1: How heavily do broadcast and cable networks and stations promote their programming to children? What differences exist across channels in terms of the amount of airtime each devotes to program promotion?

R2: What types of shows are promoted during children's programming? Are program promos within children's programming primarily for other children's programs or are children frequently encouraged during these shows to view programs suited for general and/or adult audiences?

R3: What are the characteristics (animated or real, age, gender, race) of the major characters in these program promos? And, what is the gender of the voice-over used in the promos?

R4: Where are promos placed within children's shows? Are there placement differences between promos for the station/network's own programming and promos for programs airing on competing stations/networks?

R5: To what extent do broadcast and cable networks and stations promote programs airing on competing networks and stations?

Method

All children's programming on a 38-channel midwestern cable system was identified and videotaped for analysis. The sampled programming consisted of 186.5 hours of children's programming offered on the 16 channels that carried children's programs (see Table 6.4). These included affiliates for seven major networks (ABC, CBS, NBC, Fox, UPN, WB, and PBS), two independent stations, and seven cable networks (A&E, the Discovery Channel, the Family Channel, Nickelodeon, TBS, TNT, and USA). Children's programs airing from 6:00 to 10:00 a.m. and 2:00 to 5:00 p.m. Monday through Friday, and 6:00 a.m. to 12:00 p.m. on Saturday and Sunday were taped. These times were selected because they represented the periods during which programming aimed at children (2–11 years old) typically falls. Decisions to tape or to exclude programming during these blocks of time were made on the basis of information from two sources: the Internet's *Excite* TV listings, which indicates programs for children by color coding the program listings, and *TV Guide*, which provides descriptions about program series and specials. One week of programming between April 19, 1998, and May 8, 1998, was taped on each channel.

Two graduate students viewed the programs, identified the promos, and coded the data. A trial coding session that involved 616 decision points revealed seven discrepancies (99% intercoder agreement): four were on promo length, two on the type of show promoted, and one on the

TABLE 6.4
Description of the Sample

Station	Affiliation	Hours of Programming Coded
WTIU	PBS	28.5
WXIN	Fox	26.5
WGN	WB	22.5
WNDY	UPN	16.5
WRTV	ABC	3.0
WISH	CBS	2.0
WTHR	NBC	1.5
WHMB	IND	2.5
WIIB	IND	2.0
Nickelodeon	Cable	47.0
TBS	Cable	14.5
USA	Cable	8.0
TNT	Cable	6.0
Discovery	Cable	4.0
Family	Cable	1.0
A&E	Cable	1.0
		186.5

age of a character. After the trial session, coders began working independently. Intercoder reliability checks were conducted periodically, and agreement levels were maintained at the 99% level during coding.

Variables. Drawing on previous research into children's programming and structural studies of promotion to adults, 16 variables were coded for each promotion:

1. Channel
2. Airtime of program being watched (day of the week and time of day)
3. Program type (cartoon, variety, game, sports, news, nature, education, drama/action, other)
4. Program target audience (preschool or elementary)
5. Rating of the program being watched (using the Federal Communication Commission's content system, e.g., TV-Y, TV-Y7, TV-Y7/V)
6. Airtime for the program being promoted (day of the week and time of day)
7. Feature being promoted (same show, different show same network, different show different network, same show on-line, different show on-line, no specific show same network, no specific show different network, no specific show on-line)

8. Type of show being promoted (new show or series, continuing show or series, one time special, special series)

9. Target audience for the show being promoted (preschool, elementary, adult, general)

10. Rating of the show being promoted

11. Length of the promotion in seconds

12. Format of promo (animated, nonanimated, mixed)

13. Location of the nonprogram pod within the program (before program begins, within the program, end-credits)

14. Position of the promotion within the nonprogram pod (first, middle, last)

15. Age and gender of the voice-over (adult male, adult female, child male, child female, mixed adult, mixed child, none)

16. Format (animated, nonanimated, both), Age (child, teenager, adult, cannot tell), Gender (male, female, cannot tell), and Race (White, Black, Hispanic, Asian, other minority, cannot tell), of up to three primary characters in the promo

Results

Almost all of the programs recorded (94%) were aimed at elementary-school-aged children. The remaining 6% were geared to preschoolers. As shown in Fig. 6.1, nearly 3 in 4 (73%) of the programs taped were cartoons. One in 8 (12%) was action or drama (for example, *Power Rangers*, *Are You Afraid of the Dark?*, *Real Kids, Real Adventures*); 1 in 10 (10%) was educa-

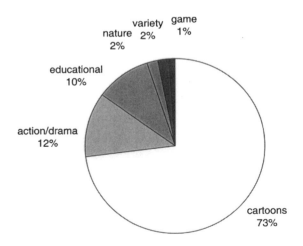

FIG. 6.1. Program types.

tional (such as *Sesame Street*). There were few nature (2%), variety (2%), or game shows (1%). Almost all (98%) of the shows recorded featured a program rating. As Fig. 6.2 shows, a majority of 60% of the programs had a TV-Y rating. One in 7 shows (14%) received a TV-Y7 rating; the same proportion earned a TV-Y7/FV rating. Nine percent of the programs were rated TV-G, and 1% were rated TV-PG.

Quantity. A total of 1,387 program promos were coded, an average of 7.4 promos per hour. As Table 6.5 shows, a slight majority (54%) of the promos were aired on the commercial broadcast networks (ABC, CBS, NBS, Fox, UPN, and WB). Promos on the cable channels (A&E, Discovery, Family, Nickelodeon, TBS, TNT, and USA) accounted for an additional 37% of the spots, and promos on the PBS affiliate accounted for 8% of the total. There were almost no promos (*n* = 14) on the two independent stations coded, in part a function of the small number of hours of children's programming recorded on these stations. Because there were so few promos on these stations, they were excluded from discussions in the text of subsample differences based on channel type.

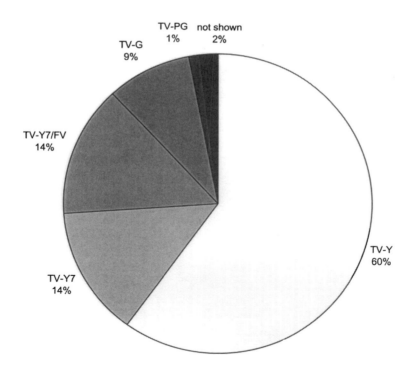

FIG. 6.2. Program ratings.

TABLE 6.5
Distribution of Promos

Channel	Number of Promos	Percent of Promos
Commercial networks	748	54
ABC affiliate	25	2
CBS affiliate	23	2
Fox affiliate	300	22
NBC affiliate	3	0
UPN affiliate	91	14
WB affiliate	206	15
Cable channels	514	37
A&E	6	0
Discovery	18	1
Family	10	1
Nickelodeon	276	20
TBS	81	6
TNT	49	4
USA	74	5
PBS affiliate	111	8
Independents	14	1
WHMB	10	1
WIIB	4	0

The promotions ranged in length from 5-sec. to 60-sec. spots. As Table 6.6 shows, half (51%) were 30 sec. long, and nearly 4 in 10 (38%) were 10 to 20 sec. in length. Few promos were longer than 30 sec. (5%) or as short as 5 sec. (3%). There was some variation across channels. Just over half (53%) of the promos aired on the six commercial networks (ABC, CBS, Fox, NBC, UPN, and WB) were 30 sec.; an additional 44% were no more than 25 sec. in length. The corresponding figures for the cable networks (A&E,

TABLE 6.6
Length of Promos

	Percentage of Promos				
	Commercial Networks	Cable Channels	PBS Affiliate	Independents	Average
5 sec.	6	1	0	0	3
10 sec.	15	20	1	0	16
15 sec.	7	24	9	0	14
20 sec.	11	6	6	0	8
25 sec.	5	2	0	0	4
30 sec.	53	44	66	100	51
45 sec.	3	4	17	0	5
60 sec.	0	0	1	0	0

Discovery, Family, Nickelodeon, TBS, TNT, and USA) were nearly reversed: 44% were 30 sec. and 52% were no more than 25 sec. In contrast, only 16% of the promos on the PBS affiliate were less than 30 sec. Instead, 66% of the promos on PBS were 30 sec. and 17% were 45 sec. All eight of the promos found on the independent stations were 30 sec. long.

Source Comparisons. On average, stations aired 3.0 min. of promos per hour during children's programming; this represents 5% of the airtime during their shows. Figure 6.3 shows marked differences across stations, with station averages ranging from zero to nearly 5 min. per hour. The Fox affiliate led the way with 4:51 min. per hour, or 8% of its airtime devoted to program promos. It was followed closely by the UPN affiliate with 4:49 min. of promos per hour. In sum, three channels featured at least 4 min. of promos per hour, two had between 3 and 4 min. of promos per hour, five offered between 2 and 3 min., four aired between 1 and 2 min., and two broadcast less than a minute per hour of such content.

Collectively, the six commercial networks aired slightly over 4 min. per hour (4:05) of promos (see Fig. 6.4). However, this number masks differences between the traditional three commercial networks (ABC, CBS, and NBC) and their younger counterparts (Fox, UPN, and WB). Whereas the traditional commercial networks featured 1 min. 45 sec. of program promos per hour, the newer networks more than doubled that, offering 4 min. 23 sec. of program promos per hour. The cable networks and the PBS affiliate featured over 2 min. per hour (2:25 and 2:07, respectively). Independents spent the least amount of time on promos, offering 53 sec. per hour.

Types of Programs. Many of the promos aired during children's programs featured programs geared to a wider audience. Whereas 60% of the promos featured shows targeting children (54% for elementary-school-aged children, 6% for preschoolers), 40% presented programs with considerably less restrictive target audiences. As Fig. 6.5 shows, one in three (34%) of the programs promoted were targeted at a general audience. Six percent, the same proportion geared to preschool children, were aimed at adults (such as *Pacific Blue*). Moreover, few (7%) of the promos displayed a rating for the show being promoted. On the commercial networks, 5% of the promos featured a program rating; typically that rating was TV-Y7. In contrast, 10% of the promos on the cable channels offered program ratings. In addition to TV-Y7 ratings, these included TV-G, TV-PG, and TV-14 rated programs. It was interesting that none of the promos on the PBS affiliate mentioned the rating for the program being promoted.

Consistent with the data about target audiences for promoted programs, a number of the shows being promoted were to air outside the hours traditionally used for children's programming. As Fig. 6.6 shows,

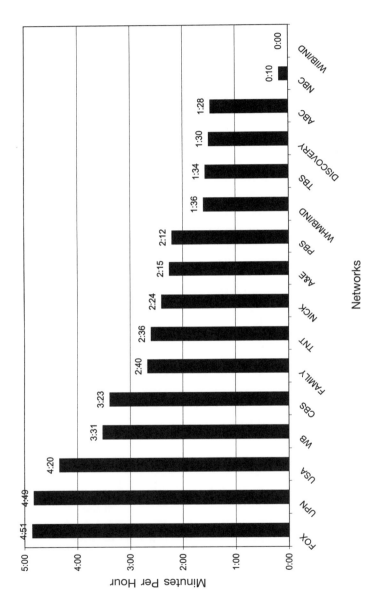

FIG. 6.3. Time devoted to promos.

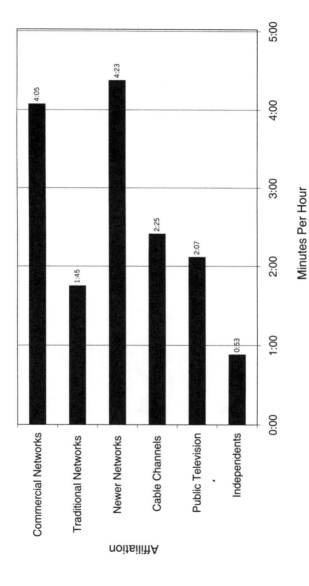

FIG. 6.4. Time devoted to promos based on station affiliation.

185

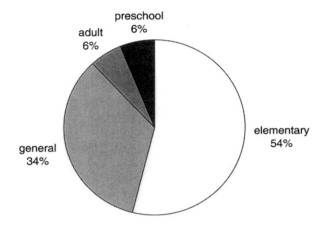

FIG. 6.5.   Audience targeted by promos.

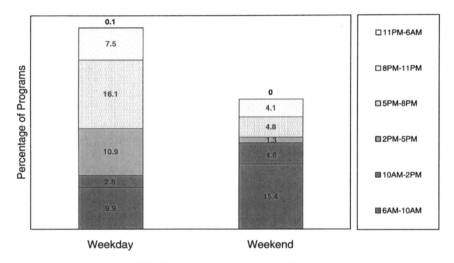

FIG. 6.6.   Promoted program airtimes.

almost one in four (23%) of the promoted shows aired on weekdays between 5:00 p.m. and 11:00 p.m., with 7.5% airing during or after prime
time (8:00–11:00 p.m.). An additional 10% of the promoted programs were
to air on weekends between 2:00 p.m. and 11:00 p.m., with 4% airing during prime time. Surprisingly, 17% of the promos coded did not indicate
the time the program being promoted was to be broadcast. Eight percent
did not even provide information about the day or days the program was
to air.

Almost all (89%) of the promos publicized an ongoing series. Few promoted new series (3%), one-time specials (4%), or special series (4%). Results here are likely to be related to the time frame in which data were collected. In April and May, with the television season winding down, there were few new series to promote. Conversely, with the pro-basketball playoffs heating up (coded as a special series), channels broadcasting the games had reason to promote the upcoming action even within children's programs. This appeared to be the case, with cable channels most likely to promote special series (10% of their promos).

Characters and Narrators. At least one major character (human or animal, real or animated) was found in 64% of the promos. Half (49%) of the promos featured at least two major characters; 31% offered at least three major characters. All told, coders assessed the demographic attributes of 2,006 characters.

Table 6.7 shows that more than half (56%) of the characters were nonanimated. PBS featured the largest proportion of nonanimated characters (85%), with the commercial networks and cable channels much closer to a 50:50 mix of animated and nonanimated characters. Children were

TABLE 6.7
Description of the Characters

	Percentage of Characters				
	Commercial Networks	Cable Channels	PBS Affiliate	Independents	Average
Format					
Animated	41	54	15	0	44
Nonanimated	59	46	85	100	56
Age					
Child	21	26	15	0	22
Teenager	27	21	0	0	24
Adult	38	32	70	100	37
Can't tell	16	22	15	0	18
Gender					
Male	67	72	78	75	70
Female	29	26	22	25	28
Can't tell	3	2	0	0	3
Race					
White	48	63	59	100	54
Black	21	12	9	0	17
Hispanic	4	1	0	0	3
Asian	2	1	2	0	2
Other minority	0	0	0	0	0
Can't tell	26	23	31	0	25

TABLE 6.8
Gender and Age of the Voice-Over Narrators

	Percentage of Promos				
	Commercial Networks	Cable Channels	PBS Affiliate	Independents	Average
Adult male	90	77	64	88	83
Adult female	1	9	20	0	6
Child male	4	3	3	0	3
Child female	0	0	3	0	0
Adult male and female	0	0	1	13	0
Child male and female	0	0	4	0	0
No voice-over	5	11	6	0	7

featured in 22% of the promos. Interestingly, adults were featured more often than children, appearing in 37% of the promos. Perhaps of even greater interest is that the PBS affiliate featured the greatest proportion of adults (70%), about twice as many as the commercial networks and cable channels. Most (70%) of the characters were male, and this proportion was relatively consistent across stations. A majority (54%) of the characters were White—again, a proportion that was relatively consistent across stations. Minorities appeared on the commercial networks more often (27%) than on the cable channels (14%) or the PBS affiliate (11%).

Voice-over narrators were used in almost all (93%) of the promos. Table 6.8 shows that the voice was overwhelmingly (83%) an adult male. Adult female voices were used in just 6% of the promos. The voice of a boy was featured in 44 promos (3%), and a girl's voice was used in only 4 promos (less than 1%). There were several differences across channels. The commercial networks featured the greatest proportion of adult male voices, using them in a prodigious 90% of the promos. PBS employed the largest proportion of adult female voices (20%) and was the only channel to use adult female voices more than 10% of the time. In contrast, the commercial networks used female voice-overs in a mere 1% of the promos.

Promotion Locations and Positions. Most promos (71%) were located in a pod in the middle of the program. As Fig. 6.7 shows, nearly one in three promos (28%) was located within a pod at the beginning of a program (prior to the program itself), while almost no promos (1%) were in a pod at the end of a show (during the end-credits, on split screen). PBS, having no breaks within regularly scheduled shows, aired all of its promos at the beginning of programs (after the credits of the preceding program, before the start of the next program). In contrast, over 8 in 10 (84%) of the promos aired on the commercial networks were featured in the middle, with only 14% aired at the beginning. The cable channels fell

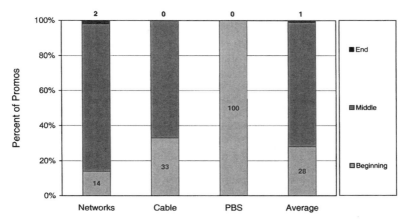

FIG. 6.7.   Promotion location in program.

in-between the commercial networks and PBS; 67% of the promos were aired in the middle of programs and 33% aired at the beginning.

Within pods, slightly more than half (51%) of the promos held a middle position. Approximately one in four promos (27%) was first in the pod, and just over one in five promos (22%) was last. Promos on the PBS affiliate were most likely to be found in the middle of a pod (93%). For the commercial networks and cable channels, the corresponding figures dropped to 66% and 29%, respectively. The location of the remaining promos was split almost evenly. For the networks, 18% started a pod and 16% completed one; for cable channels, 40% started a pod and 31% came at the end (Fig. 6.8).

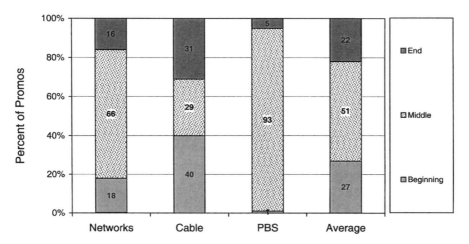

FIG. 6.8.   Promotion position in pod.

Promos for Competing Programs.   A large majority (86%) of promos were for different shows on the same network. One in 10 (10%) was for the same show, either airing later in the day, later in the week, or the next week. The commercial networks almost always (97%) promoted other programs on their schedule, rarely promoting (2%) the same show. In contrast, PBS and the cable networks more frequently promoted the show being telecast (18% and 19%, respectively). However, like the commercial networks, both most often promoted their other programs (72% and 74%, respectively). Two percent of the spots promoted the network generically without promoting a specific show; nearly all of these were on the PBS affiliate. Only 1% promoted a show on another network, and all of these were on cable networks. Fewer than a handful of spots promoted an on-line site, and again, all of these were on cable networks.

Discussion of Findings

These data clearly point to an upsurge in program promotion targeted to children. The 3 min. per hour devoted to program promos is greater than the number reported earlier in the decade by Kunkel and Gantz (1992, 1994) and nearly on par with the figure reported by Katz (1997) for prime-time programs. Such a change is not surprising. Given today's increasingly competitive television and media environments, with more channels and media competing for the same audiences, it is altogether reasonable for programmers to offer a multitude of short messages in hopes that they will lure the television audience into future viewing. Perhaps surprising to some is the extent to which the PBS affiliate promoted its lineup of shows. Although PBS bills itself as a noncommercial network and rarely interrupts its programs in midstream, it regularly promoted its product, devoting more airtime to program promos than six other channels in the study.

The length of the promos coded was commensurate with the typical television ad; almost all were 30 sec. or less. Strategists may be following the approach employed by many national advertisers: 30-sec. ads to establish a campaign, followed by short spots used as ongoing reminders. If this comparison holds, longer promos would be expected to air in the late summer and early fall as channels push their new series. To do so though, programmers would have to contend with corporate bottom-line pressures, as time devoted to program promos cuts into time for advertising.

As Fig. 6.4 showed, the newer commercial networks (Fox, UPN, and WB) clearly outdistanced both cable channels and the traditional commercial networks in terms of the amount of time each devoted to on-air program promos, and cable channels devoted more time to program promos than did the traditional commercial networks. Given these differences, it seems reasonable to infer that the newer broadcast networks and, to a lesser extent, the cable channels are making a more concerted effort to get young viewers to sample additional fare. To the extent that program promos are relatively short, with nearly half under 30 sec., more on-air promotion time suggests a more cluttered nonprogramming environment on these channels. However, it cannot be concluded that the total nonprogramming environment on the channels devoting more on-air time to program promos is more cluttered than on other channels. As documented elsewhere (Kunkel & Gantz, 1992), time allocated to program promotion may reflect deliberate programming decisions or may be the result of shortfalls in the amount of advertising time sold.

The fact that only 1% of the promos were for programs which aired on other channels suggests that programming executives zealously guard against promoting viewing options that would take viewers away from their channels. This figure may be lower than for general audience promotion because, as discussed by Bellamy and Traudt (chap. 5, this volume), with frequent cross-ownership of channels, cross-channel promos still keep viewers within the same corporate coffers. Should the trend toward consolidation continue, cross-channel promos among children's programs are likely to increase.

Promos were fairly well distributed in the first, middle, and last positions within pods of nonprogramming content. Nonetheless, if pod position matters as some suggest (Eastman & Newton, 1999; Singh & Cole, 1993), then the cable channels are likely to reap greater benefits from their on-air promos than the broadcast networks. Compared to their counterparts, cable channels were more likely to air promos at the beginning of nonprogramming pods, a time when viewership and attention is likely to be carried over from the program. Cable channels also aired more promos in the last position in the pod, a desirable spot because it is the last thing the viewer sees before returning to the program.

A sizable proportion of the programs promoted during children's shows (40%) are for programs that target general or adult audiences and air during prime time. This is perhaps to be expected, as children's viewing is not limited to the Saturday-morning "children's block" of programming. Indeed, although the Saturday-morning time period still yields the greatest concentration of children, only about 5% of children's total viewing takes place on Saturday morning. Fifteen percent of viewing is devoted to weekday afternoons, and close to 25% occurs during prime time (Nielsen, 1998). Because the total number of afternoon and prime-time hours is significantly greater than the number of Saturday-morning hours, children are exposed to a substantial amount of programming created for general or adult audiences.

Only 9% of the promotional messages identified in this study included rating labels. Stations are well within their rights to promote their entire lineups and are under no mandate to stick rating labels on their promos. However, even when the prime-time program promoted is not offensive and does not arouse the ire of parents, by not offering the rating for the promoted fare, these promos may alienate parents who do not want their young children even being tempted to watch prime-time programming. Moreover, a few stations are likely to stretch the boundaries of suitable fare without parents having any signals about the content of the promoted programs.

The preponderance of adult male characters is likely to be a reflection of the demographic makeup of the characters in current programming. Nonetheless, this is likely to be disturbing to those who are concerned about the basic gender asymmetry on television. The overwhelming dominance of the adult male voice-over suggests that little has changed in the strategies that programming executives employ to connect with potential audiences. At least with young children, this strategy flies in the face of evidence that suggests children are more likely to turn away from adult male voices than they are from female voices or from children's voices. The same critique can be leveled against the age composition of the characters featured in the promos. Because children are attracted to programs that feature characters their own age and events likely to transpire in their own lives, present-day TV promos may not be particularly compelling.

All told, this study provides a baseline for assessing program promos aimed at children. The data suggest that programming executives treat young audiences in much the same way they do adults, anticipating that the frequent use of short promos will persuade viewers to watch other content aired throughout the day on their channels. Given the differences in the way children and adults attend to and respond to mediated stimuli, such an approach may not maximize the return on each station's investment in promotions.

IDEAS FOR FUTURE RESEARCH ABOUT PROMOTION TO CHILDREN

Program promotion is a combination of programming and advertising. As such, the challenges faced by program promoters may be greater than those faced by their peers in the programming and advertising arenas. These challenges are further compounded by the unique characteristics of a young audience. Further research is needed to help scholars understand promotional impact and to aid program promoters in maximizing the effectiveness of on-air promotion to children.

Unexplored Questions in Cognitive Processing

Advertisers need to convey the names of their products and reasons for consumers to buy them. Names and reasons constitute two pieces of information that viewers must remember. Program promoters, on the other hand, must convey the name of the show, the day and time it airs, the channel or station it airs on, and a compelling reason for the viewer to tune in—five pieces of information. Given the short time frame in which to present all of this information and the limited processing abilities of children, this is likely too much information to be successfully processed and recalled. To minimize the processing load, research needs to determine which of these components is key to future viewership.

With surveys and in-depth interviews, researchers can determine just what each of these five components means to children of various ages. For example, do 5-year-olds know what "Thursday" or "5:00 p.m." means? Although they might be able to explain that Thursday is a day of the week, young children may not comprehend its relationship to a program that they have just seen promoted (e.g., how many days from now the program will be on). Likewise, it is important to study children's notions of channels and stations. How do they identify particular channels—by an icon or logo, call letters, a slogan, or a channel number? If young children are unable to comprehend day, time, and channel information, it may behoove program promoters to stick with promoting shows that are "next" on the same channel. Knowledge about children's ability to comprehend these components of scheduling information at various developmental stages will allow promoters to focus on the elements most likely to deliver viewers.

Once the key elements are identified, experiments are needed to determine the amount of exposure necessary for children to retain the program information. Almost all of the promos in this study were 30 sec. or less. Is this enough time for children to process the essential information? Once a program is established are shorter promotional spots sufficient? Manipulations on frequency and duration of children's exposure to programming information and measures of their subsequent ability to understand, recall, and act on this information will further inform programmers about the most appropriate methods for promoting programs to younger audiences. More important, such information may also provide new clues to the effective use of television for teaching young people in the home and in the classroom.

Current promotional practices aimed at children minimize the program's broadcast date, time, and station information and emphasize characters or action. Though the relative importance of the components of promotional messages is yet to be determined, it is possible that this practice interferes with processing in two ways. Not only is exposure to date, time, and channel information limited, but also the presentation of content (especially fast-paced or arousing content) may actively interfere with children's ability to attend to and remember when and where to view the show they have just been attracted to. Studies that manipulate the pacing and arousal level of content with varying presentations of broadcast date, time, and channel are needed to examine the effects of these variables on recall.

Unexplored Questions Relating to Vulnerability

Research examining the way age-based (TV-Y, TV-Y7, TV-PG, TV-14, TV-MA) movie and television ratings affect children's viewing decisions has found that cautionary labels tend to attract children — the forbidden-fruit effect. Research to determine how the new rating system influences children's choices is in its infancy. Though few promotional messages currently display ratings, this line of research needs to extend to the use of rating labels on promos.

Given the amount of information presented in a program promo in a brief amount of time, researchers must first determine whether children even notice the rating information. Because this information is often located in a corner of the screen, it may fail to capture attention — especially if the child is intent on viewing the more appealing action occurring elsewhere on the screen. As with the promotional message components discussed in the previous section, experiments are needed to determine how much time is necessary for rating information to be identified and processed. Experiments could also determine the optimal screen placement for rating information, and whether or not it is advantageous to present the rating information orally.

Surveys and interviews can help programmers (and parents, advocates, and legislators) understand the influence of rating information at various ages. Is a 6-year-old child more or less aware of rating information on a promotional message than a 10-year-old child? Are 6-year-old children more likely to be encouraged or discouraged to view programs based on promo rating labels than 10-year-old children are? At what age do children begin to have a sense of what programs are appropriate for children and what programs are appropriate only for adults, and what role does rating information play in helping them make that determination? If ratings help children identify which programs they can view, it will be important for program promoters to work this information more prominently into their promotions.

Commensurate with past research on advertising, studies need to be conducted to determine whether children recognize program promos as "selling" messages, the effect of the messages on children's choices, and the effect of these choices on other people. Interviews with children about their attitudes toward and understanding of promotional messages, and surveys of both children and their parents concerning responses to promos, will prove helpful to both programmers and policymakers.

The New Playing Field of the Internet

Although the arrival of the Internet has increased competition among media, many television programmers have found ways to work cooperatively with Internet programmers and to leverage the power of this dynamic medium. As discussed by Ferguson (chap. 11, this volume), television spots announce the presence of web sites for their programs, and web sites provide supplemental information for television programs. In many respects, the Internet may be the greatest promotional tool of the decade. Unlike television, where program promos are forced to be brief, the Internet provides a virtually unlimited opportunity to "sell" programming to an audience. Chapter 11 describes the elaborate promotion for broadcast and cable programs on web sites. For example, in addition to program "teasers," broadcast times, and local channels, Internet program promotion provides cast information, plot summaries, and previews of upcoming events. Some sites even provide an opportunity to post messages or chat with other viewers.

This trend is certainly present, perhaps even more prominent, for children's programs and web sites. Children are generally less intimidated by technology and have the curiosity to explore the expanding Internet universe. Five of the seven major networks and three of the seven cable stations in this study have sections of their web sites devoted to children's programming. In fact, children's programming is producing some of the most innovative collaborations between television and the Internet. For example, Disney has introduced a block of television programming called Zoog Disney that has an accompanying Zoog Disney web site. At the Zoog Disney web site, users have the opportunity to learn more about Zoog Disney television programs, as well as to become part of the program. Each week, messages, chat excerpts, and game scores collected on the Zoog Disney web site are inserted into the television program.

Statistics of "visitor hits" on web sites for children's television programs are an indication of the number of viewers making the jump from television to a promotional web site. Online surveys for site visitors can be used to obtain information about motivations for accessing the site, reactions to site content, and the site's level of impact in influencing children to view the related program(s). Are web sites less, equally, or more effective at enticing viewers than on-air promotion? Do children remember promotional material presented online better than they remember on-air television promos? Phone surveys or interviews could be used as an alternative to collecting data online. As Internet programmers become more skilled at capturing and maintaining audiences and as the web moves to the living-room screen, television programmers are likely to rely on the Internet more as a source of program promotion.

The Significance of the Issues

With the ongoing proliferation of large capacity cable and satellite systems and the growing access to computer games and online media, television viewers will become increasingly elusive for broadcast and cable programmers, and winning an audience will become increasingly competitive. To successfully endure the competition, program promoters must better understand how audience members make viewing decisions and intensify their efforts to reach potential viewers. Scholars can play a crucial role in furthering knowledge about children's decision making by bringing together information from the spheres of education, cognitive science, advertising, and programming. More important than helping producers promote effectively, such knowledge is necessary to teach children to be wise consumers.

This chapter has explored the unique challenges faced by program promoters targeting children and by scholars researching promotion to this young audience. Today's children have grown up in a media-rich environment and are sophisticated media connoisseurs by the time they reach adolescence. Yet, despite their media sophistication, children's ability to process messages and understand content is linked to their cognitive development. Although they may be able to discern between media messages that do or do not appeal to them, children are less able than adults to identify and understand all of the information presented to encourage future viewership.

The groundwork for future research on program promotion for children has been laid. Media scholars and industry practitioners must take the next steps in order to more fully understand the nature of program promotion directed to children. Greater understanding will help programmers figure out the optimal strategies for reaching children and convincing them to watch. Greater understanding will enable television executives to market programs successfully, and safely, to children. Greater understanding will aid parents and teachers in guiding children's television viewing.

REFERENCES

Abelman, R. (1995). *Reclaiming the wasteland: TV and gifted children*. Cresskill, NJ: Hampton Press.

Abelman, R., & Atkin, D. (1998, April). *Evaluating the impact of affiliation change on children's viewership and perceptions of network branding.* Paper presented at the annual meeting of the Broadcast Education Association, Las Vegas, NV.

Adams, W. (1993). Television program scheduling strategies and their relationship to new program renewal rates and rating changes. *Journal of Broadcasting & Electronic Media, 37,* 465–474.

Alwitt, L. F., Anderson, D. R., Lorch, E. P., & Levin, S. R. (1980). Preschool children's visual attention to attributes of television. *Human Communication Research, 7,* 52–66.

Anderson, D. R., Choi, H. P., & Lorch, E. P. (1987). Attentional inertia reduces distractibility during young children's TV viewing. *Child Development, 58,* 798–806.

Anderson, D. R., & Levin, S. R. (1976). Young children's attention to "Sesame Street." *Child Development, 47,* 806–811.

Anderson, D. R., & Lorch, E. P. (1983). Looking at television: Action or reaction? In J. Bryant & D. R. Anderson (Eds.), *Children's understanding of television: Research on attention and comprehension* (pp. 1–33). New York: Academic Press.

Anderson, D. R., Lorch, E. P., Field, D. E., & Sanders, J. (1981). The effect of TV program comprehensibility on preschool children's visual attention to television. *Child Development, 52,* 151–157.

Atkin, C. K. (1980). Effects of television advertising on children. In E. L. Palmer & A. Dorr (Eds.), *Children and the faces of television: Teaching, violence, selling* (pp. 287–305). New York: Academic Press.

Barcus, F. E. (1978). *Commercial children's television on weekends and weekday afternoons.* Newtonville, MA: Action for Children's Television.

Barcus, F. E. (1980). The nature of television advertising to children. In E. L. Palmer & A. Dorr (Eds.), *Children and the faces of television: Teaching, violence, selling* (pp. 273–286). New York: Academic Press.

Barcus, F. E. (1983). *Images of life on children's television: Sex roles, minorities, and families.* New York: Praeger.

Barner, M. R. (1998, April). *Sex-role stereotyping in FCC-approved children's educational programming.* Paper presented at the annual meeting of the Broadcast Education Association, Las Vegas, NV.

Bryant, J., Zillmann, D., & Brown, D. (1983). In J. Bryant & D. R. Anderson (Eds.), *Entertainment features in children's educational television: Effects on attention and information acquisition* (pp. 221–240). New York: Academic Press.

Buckingham, D. (1996). *Moving images: Understanding children's emotional responses to television.* Manchester, England: Manchester University Press.

Calvert, S. L., Huston, A. C., Watkins, B. A., & Wright, J. C. (1982). The relationship between selective attention to television forms and children's comprehension of content. *Child Development, 53,* 601–610.

Calvert, S. L., & Scott, M. C. (1989). Sound effects for children's temporal integration of fast-paced television content. *Journal of Broadcasting & Electronic Media, 33,* 233–246.

Cantor, J. (1994). Fright reactions to mass media. In J. Bryant & D. Zillmann (Eds.), *Media effects: Advances in theory and research* (pp. 213–245). Hillsdale, NJ: Lawrence Erlbaum Associates.

Cantor, J. (1998a). *Mommy I'm scared: How TV and movies frighten children and what we can do to protect them.* San Diego, CA: Harcourt Brace.

Cantor, J. (1998b). Children's attraction to violent television programming. In J. H. Goldstein (Ed.), *Why we watch: The attractions of violent entertainment* (pp. 88–115). New York: Oxford University Press.

Cantor, J., & Nathanson, A. I. (1997). Predictors of children's interest in violent television programs. *Journal of Broadcasting & Electronic Media, 41,* 115–167.

Collins, W. A. (1983). Interpretation and inference in children's television viewing. In J. Bryant & D. R. Anderson (Eds.), *Children's understanding of television* (pp. 125–150). New York: Academic Press.

Collins, W. A., Wellman, H., Keniston, A. H., & Westby, S. D. (1978). Age-related aspects of comprehension and inference from a televised dramatic narrative. *Child Development, 49,* 389–399.

Comstock, G. (with Paik, H.) (1991). *Television and the American child.* San Diego, CA: Academic Press.

Condry, J., Bence, P., & Scheibe, C. (1988). Nonprogram content in children's television. *Journal of Broadcasting & Electronic Media, 32,* 255–270.

Davis, D. M. (1990). Portrayals of women in primetime network television: Some demographic characteristics. *Sex Roles, 23*(5/6), 325–332.

Dominick, J. R., & Rauch, G. E. (1972). The image of women in network TV commercials. *Journal of Broadcasting, 16,* 259–265.

Dorr, A. (1986). *Television and children: A special medium for a special audience.* Beverly Hills, CA: Sage.

Dorr, A., & Kovaric, P. (1980). Some of the people some of the time — But which people? Televised violence and its effects. In E. L. Palmer & A. Dorr (Eds.), *Children and the faces of television: Teaching, violence, selling* (pp. 183–199). New York: Academic Press.

Douglas, S. J. (1994). *Where the girls are: Growing up female with the mass media.* New York: Times Books.

Eastman, S. T., & Neal-Lunsford, J. (1993). The RCD's impact on television programming and promotion. In J. R. Walker & R. V. Bellamy (Eds.), *The remote control in the new age of television* (pp. 189–209). Westport, CT: Praeger.

Eastman, S. T., & Newton, G. D. (1998). The impact of structural salience within on-air promotion. *Journal of Broadcasting & Electronic Media, 42,* 50–79.

Eastman, S. T., & Newton, G. D. (1999). Hitting promotion hard: A network response to channel surfing and new competition. *Journal of Applied Communication Research, 27,* 73–85.

Ferrante, C. L., Haynes, A. M., & Kingsley, S. M. (1988). Image of women in television advertising. *Journal of Broadcasting & Electronic Media, 32,* 231–237.

Geen, R. G. (1994). Television and aggression: Recent developments in research and theory. In D. Zillmann, J. Bryant, & A. C. Huston (Eds.), *Media, children, and the family: Social scientific, psychodynamic, and clinical perspectives* (pp. 151–162). Hillsdale, NJ: Lawrence Erlbaum Associates.

Geiger, S., & Reeves, B. (1993). The effects of scene changes and semantic relatedness on attention to television. *Communication Research, 20,* 155–175.

Gerbner, G., & Gross, L. (1976). Living with television: The violence profile. *Journal of Communication, 26*(2), 173–199.

Gerbner, G., & Gross, L. (1980). The violent face of television and its lessons. In E. L. Palmer & A. Dorr (Eds.), *Children and the faces of television: Teaching, violence, selling* (pp. 149–162). New York: Academic Press.

Graves, S. B. (1993). Television, the portayal of African Americans, and the development of children's attitudes. In G. L. Berry & J. K. Asamen (Eds.), *Children and television: Images in a changing sociocultural world* (pp. 179–190). Newbury Park, CA: Sage.

Greenberg, B. S. (1980). *Life on television: Content analysis of U.S. TV drama.* Norwood, NJ: Ablex.

Greenberg, B. S., & Brand, J. E. (1993). Cultural diversity on Saturday morning television. In G. L. Berry & J. K. Asamen (Eds.), *Children and television: Images in a changing sociocultural world* (pp. 132–142). Newbury Park, CA: Sage.

Greenberg, B. S., & Brand, J. E. (1994). Minorities and the mass media: 1970s to 1990s. In J. Bryant & D. Zillmann (Eds.), *Media effects: Advances in theory and research* (pp. 273–314). Hillsdale, NJ: Lawrence Erlbaum Associates.

Greenberg, B. S., & Collette, L. (1997). The changing faces on TV: A demographic analysis of network television's new seasons, 1966–1992. *Journal of Broadcasting & Electronic Media, 41*, 1–13.

Greenfield, P. M., Yut, E., Chung, M., Land, D., Kreider, H., Pantoja, M., & Horsley, K. (1993). The program-length commercial: A study of the effects of television/toy tie-ins on imaginative play. In G. L. Berry & J. K. Asamen (Eds.), *Children and television: Images in a changing sociocultural world* (pp. 53–72). Newbury Park, CA: Sage.

Guber, S., & Berry, J. (1993). *Marketing to and through kids.* New York: McGraw-Hill.

Gunter, B. (1994). The question of media violence. In J. Bryant & D. Zillman (Eds.), *Media effects: Advances in theory and research* (pp. 163–211). Hillsdale, NJ: Lawrence Erlbaum Associates.

Gunter, B., & McAleer, J. (1997). *Children and television.* London: Routledge.

Harris, R. J. (1999). *A cognitive psychology of mass communication.* Mahwah, NJ: Lawrence Erlbaum Associates.

Hollywood under fire. (1999, July 10). *TV Guide,* 35–42.

Huston, A. C., & Wright, J. C. (1983). Children's processing of television: The informative functions of formal features. In J. Bryant & D. R. Anderson (Eds.), *Children's understanding of television* (pp. 35–68). New York: Academic Press.

Huston, A. C., & Wright, J. C. (1994). Educating children with television: The forms of the medium. In D. Zillmann, J. Bryant, & A. C. Huston (Eds.), *Media, children, and the family: Social scientific, psychodynamic, and clinical perspectives* (pp. 73–84). Hillsdale, NJ: Lawrence Erlbaum Associates.

Katz, M. (1997, February 24). Networks prefer promos to PSAs. *Broadcasting and Cable,* 20–21.

Kunkel, D., & Gantz, W. (1992). Children's television advertising in the multichannel environment. *Journal of Communication, 42*(3), 134–152.

Kunkel, D., & Gantz, W. (1994, July). *Children's television advertising at Christmas time.* Paper presented at the annual meeting of the International Communication Association, Sydney, Australia.

Lang, A. (1990). Involuntary attention and physiological arousal evoked by structural features and mild emotion in TV commercials. *Communication Research, 17*, 275–299.

Lang, A. (1991). Emotion, formal features, and memory for televised political advertisements. In F. Biocca (Ed.), *Television and political advertising: Vol. 1. Psychological processes* (pp. 221–244). Hillsdale, NJ: Lawrence Erlbaum Associates.

Lang, A. (2000). The information processing of mediated messages: A framework for communication research. *Journal of Communication, 50*(1), 46–70.

Lang, A., & Basil, M. D. (1998). Attention, resources allocation, and communication research: What do secondary task reaction times measure anyway? In M. Roloff (Ed.), *Communication yearbook* (Vol. 21, pp. 443–474). Beverly Hills, CA: Sage.

Lang, A., Dhillon, P., & Dong, Q. (1995). Arousal, emotion, and memory for television messages. *Journal of Broadcasting & Electronic Media, 38*, 1–15.

Lang, A., Newhagen, J., & Reeves, B. (1996). Negative video as structure: Emotion, attention, capacity, and memory. *Journal of Broadcasting & Electronic Media, 40*, 460–477.

Levin, S. R., & Anderson, D. R. (1976). The development of attention. *Journal of Communication, 26*(2), 126–135.

Littleton, C. (1996, February 6). Stations will play games in daytime. *Broadcasting & Cable,* 34–36.

Lorch, E. P., Anderson, D. R., & Levin, S. R. (1979). The relationship of visual attention to children's comprehension of television. *Child Development, 50,* 722–727.

McNeal, J. U. (1997, December). Kids' market. *American Demographics, 20,* 36–42.

National Science Foundation. (1997). *Research on the effects of television advertising on children.* Washington, DC: U.S. Government Printing Office.

Nielsen, A. C. (1998). *1998 report on television.* New York: Nielsen Media Research.

Paik, H., & Comstock, G. (1994). The effects of television violence on antisocial behavior: A meta-analysis. *Communication Research, 21,* 516–546.

Palmer, E. L., & McDowell, C. N. (1979). Program/commercial separators in children's television programming. *Journal of Communication, 29*(3), 197–201.

Reeves, B., & Thorson, E. (1986). Watching television: Experiences on the viewing process. *Communication Research, 13,* 343–361.

Riffe, D., Goldson, H., Saxton, K., & Yu, Y. (1989). Females and minorities in TV ads in 1987 Saturday children's programs. *Journalism Quarterly, 66,* 129–136.

Robertson, T. S., & Rossiter, J. R. (1974). Children and commercial persuasion: An attribution theory analysis. *Journal of Consumer Research, 1*(1), 13–20.

Robinson, J., & Bianchi, S. (1997, December). The children's hour. *American Demographics, 20,* 22–24.

Rolandelli, D. R. (1989). Children and television: The visual superiority effect reconsidered. *Journal of Broadcasting & Electronic Media, 33,* 64–81.

Rolandelli, D. R., Wright, J. C., Huston, A. C., & Eakins, D. (1991). Children's auditory and visual processing of narrated and nonnarrated television programing. *Journal of Experimental Child Psychology, 51*(1), 90–122.

Rushkoff, D. (1994). *Media virus.* New York: Ballantine.

Seiter, E. (1995). *Sold separately: Parents and children in consumer culture.* New Brunswick, NJ: Rutgers University Press.

Signorielli, N. (1993). Television, the portrayal of women, and children's attitudes. In G. L. Berry & J. K. Asamen (Eds.), *Children and television: Images in a changing sociocultural world* (pp. 229–242) Newbury Park, CA: Sage.

Singer, J. L. (1980). The power and limitations of television: A cognitive-affective analysis. In P. H. Tannenbaum & R. Abeles (Eds.), *The entertainment functions of television.* Hillsdale, NJ: Lawrence Erlbaum Associates.

Singh, S. N., & Cole, C. A. (1993). The effects of length, content, and repetition on television commercial effectiveness. *Journal of Marketing Research, 30*(1), 91–104.

Smith, R., Anderson, D. R., & Fischer, C. (1985). Young children's comprehension of montage. *Child Development, 56,* 962–971.

Stephens, N., & Stutts, M. A. (1982). Preschoolers' ability to distinguish between television programming and commercials. *Journal of Advertising, 11*(2), 16–26.

Stutts, M. A., Vance, D., & Hudelson, S. (1981). Program-commercial separators in children's television: Do they help a child tell the difference between Bugs Bunny and the Quik Rabbit? *Journal of Advertising, 10*(2), 16–48.

Thorson, E., & Lang, A. (1992). The effects of television videographics and lecture familiarity on adult cardiac orienting responses and memory. *Communication Research, 19,* 346–369.

Vande Berg, L. R., & Streckfuss, D. (1992). Prime-time television's portrayal of women and the world of work: A demographic profile. *Journal of Broadcasting & Electronic Media, 36,* 195–208.

van der Voort, T. H. A. (1986). *Television violence: A child's-eye view.* Amsterdam: Elsevier.

Ward, S., Wackman, D., & Wartella, E. (1977). *How children learn to buy: The development of consumer information-processing skills.* Beverly Hills, CA: Sage.

Wartella, E. (1980). Individual differences in children's responses to television advertising. In E. L. Palmer & A. Dorr (Eds.), *Children and the faces of television: Teaching, violence, selling* (pp. 307–322). New York: Academic Press.

Wartella, E., & Ettema, J. (1974). A cognitive developmental study of children's attention to television commercials. *Communication Research, 1,* 69–88.

Weiss, A. J., & Wilson, B. J. (1996). Emotional portrayals in family television series that are popular among children. *Journal of Broadcasting & Electronic Media, 40,* 1–29.

Wilson, B., Kunkle, D., Linz, D., Potter, W., Donnerstein, E., Smith, S., Blumenthal, E., Berry, M., & Federman, J. (1998). The nature and context of violence on American television. In

U. Carlsson & C. von Feilitzen (Eds.), *Children and media violence* (pp. 63–79). Kungälv, Sweden: UNESCO International Clearinghouse on Children and Violence on the Screen.

Woodard, E. H. (1999). *The 1999 state of children's television report* [Online]. Available: http://www.appcpenn.org/kidstv99/rep28.htm

Young, B. (1990). *Television advertising and children*. Oxford, England: Clarendon.

Promotion In and About Sports Programming

Susan Tyler Eastman
Indiana University

Andrew C. Billings
Clemson University

Most of the audience experiences sporting events via television. It is the mediated event that attracts tens of thousands, even millions of people, far more than could ever attend events in person. But for decades, only a relatively few sports events were available on television. Eastman and Meyer (1989) argued a decade ago that cable sports programming would drastically change both the amount of interest in sports and the ways in which audiences view sports, and, needless to say, their predictions came true. Although some scholars have explored the impact of sports as television programming (see Rader, 1990; Real, 1989; Wenner, 1989, 1998), few studies have examined the on-air and print promotion that attracts viewers to televised sports events. Yet, on-air and print promotion are broadcasters' and cablecasters' essential tools for drawing attention to upcoming programming. They use promotion to try to convince viewers of the value *to them* of watching, and they use promotion more directly to remind viewers of the day and time of a televised event.

Eastman and Meyer (1989) also pointed out that promotion had become one of the key factors affecting the size of audiences for televised sports events. Historically, the factors associated with Nielsen ratings were presumed to be (a) inherited viewing from the preceding program, (b) close compatibility between programs, and (c) the attractiveness of competing network programs. But by the late 1980s, the impact of on-air and print promotion had joined this basic group. In mid-decade, Webster (1985) first estimated the size of *inheritance* within U.S. prime-time television (measured as the impact of lead-in ratings) as about 50%. In other words, about half the viewers of one program watched the next program, although falloff occurred as the hour got later. *Compatibility* between adjacent programs was found to significantly affect the amount of inheritance. Later on, compatibility between the program carrying the promotion and the program being promoted became an issue in research related to sports. Most sports-promotion studies to date have looked at prime-time entertainment programs promoted within sporting events, which can be presumed to have minimal compatibility (except in such cases as *Monday Night Football* promoted within other sporting events).

Once cable television became widespread, moreover, the factor of *competition* was largely put aside in analyses because of the difficulty of specifying it (there being wide variations across markets and households). In a three-network race, it made sense to attempt to account for competing programs; in a 60+ channel universe, the variety of competing programs usually becomes too great to measure in satisfactory ways. Promotion was then seen as a way to attract viewers despite schedule clutter, and that promotion might have a direct impact on ratings.

Looking at the on-air promotion of prime-time programs in the only available analysis of its kind, Eastman and Newton (1998b) calculated that promotional spots contributed, on average, at least 5% to network ratings (see Eastman & Bolls, chap. 3, this volume). As Eastman and Newton (1998b) noted, 5% may sound small, but it is more than enough to alter the rankings among the major broadcast networks and thus be worth millions of dollars in advertising revenue and have value in changing network image and prestige. No scholars have calculated any impacts specifically for promotion carried within sports, but lacking data to the contrary, similar-sized contributions for inheritance and promotion might be expected from promotion carried in sporting events.

This chapter examines the studies with findings about the structural features that affect the relative success of on-air promotion in sporting events (going beyond the studies covered in chap. 3, this volume). Some studies are about sports marketing, some about promotion for other televised sporting events, and some about promotion for prime-time entertainment shows that were publicized within sporting events. Then the chapter reports a new study analyzing the impact of on-air promotion carried in the 1998 Nagano Olympics and concludes with suggestions for future research.

RESEARCH ABOUT MEDIATED SPORTS MARKETING

Because so few studies have focused on the particular topic of promotion, looking at a broader array of mediated sports research is useful in the search for implications for studies of promotion. Moreover, the subject of promotion is generally considered to be a subset of the larger arena of marketing, which stretches beyond program audiences into social and economic issues of sponsorship, political manipulation, globalization, and commercialization. Thus, sports marketing encompasses the selling of sporting events to advertisers and to television distributors, and several studies have focused on the increasing commercialization of sporting events (see Wenner, 1998).

Although widespread implementation of televised marketing of professional and college sports had saturated the networks and local media by the early 1990s, oddly, little research has been conducted about the effects of televised sports marketing. Farrell (1989) characterized the marketing of televised sports as the creation of modern-day spectacles; McAllister (1997, 1998a,b) looked at televised sports as a vehicle for product sponsorship; yet no studies have addressed the link between sports marketing and on-air program promotion. Because the prices for television rights to megasporting events continue to skyrocket (Goldstein, 1996), much of sports marketing research has logically focused on how the networks pay for these exorbitant telecasts.

NBC, for instance, paid over $3.5 billion for the right to broadcast the Olympics from 2000 to 2008 (Nelson, 1995). In addition, Olympic host cities have paid well over a billion dollars to attract the games (*Fortune*, 1996).[1] The ways in which NBC and Olympic host cities plan to turn enormous losses into profits necessitate marketing the games on a worldwide scale. In 1976, for example, sponsorship revenue made the difference between a billion dollar loss and a $215 million profit for the city of Montreal (Gelman, 1984). *Fortune* magazine (1996) estimated that the city of Atlanta spent close to $2 billion to host the 1996 games but turned a profit through sponsorship. Although the television networks have other sources of income, none is larger than sponsorship. Contrasting it with spot advertising, McAllister (1998a) defines sponsorship as "the funding of an entire event, group, broadcast, or place by one commercial interest in exchange for large amounts and special types of promotion connected with the sponsored activity" (p. 357). The result in sports has been such aberrations as the Winston Cup racing series, the Sunkist Orange Bowl, the Virginia Slims tennis tournaments, and the positioning of Visa as the official credit card of the 1998 Winter Olympics. Clearly, sports marketing is big business, and deserving of increased attention from researchers.

Research by O'Neal, Finch, Hamilton, and Hammonds (1987), on the topic of the attributes of sports that make them attractive to corporate

---

[1]In addition, untold millions have been paid "under the table," as government investigations of the awarding of the 2002 games to Salt Lake City and the 2000 games to Sydney have shown.

sponsors, drew particular attention to the notion that sports heighten excitement, which concomitantly lowers the guard of many viewers, thus making them more susceptible to the effects of advertising. If this process operates between program content and commercials, it should also operate between sports content and promos for other programs (see studies cited by Eastman & Bolls, chap. 3, this volume). But the transference of excitement may operate in two directions: The environment of sports may make program promos more effective, and conversely, promos that build excitement may make televised sporting events even more exciting. On the one hand, expectancy theory (discussed by Perse, chap. 2, this volume) suggests that expectations about programs — perhaps particularly sports programs — might enhance (or diminish) the impact of program promos. On the other hand, excitation-transfer theory (detailed in chap. 3, this volume) implies that promos that are able to stir viewers' emotions may transfer those emotions to the programs themselves. Thus, promos for televised sporting events help generate excitement about upcoming sporting events and, therefore, potentially increase sports ratings, while at the same time, promos for other programs — such as prime-time series and movies — should gain enhanced effectiveness just by being within the environment of a sporting event. These aspects of promotion deserve more direct testing in laboratory and field settings, but expectancy and transfer theories provide a framework for understanding the importance of research about promotion to scholars and to the industry.

The significance of the topic of marketing-mediated sports itself lies in scholars' concern with questions of cultural dominance, mythology, and commercialism. Wenner (1989) wrote that televised sports easily relates to "issues of socialization, interpersonal communication, value formation, racial and gender assessments, and the balance of political and economic power" (p. 16). Gruneau (1989) delineated the ways in which television generates sports spectacles; Riggs, Eastman, and Golobic (1993) showed how an Olympics both creates and reflects political attitudes; and as Real and Mechikoff (1992) explained, "the relationship between the media sports fan and the sporting event closely parallels the position of the ritual participant acting out a mythic celebration" (p. 323). In writing of the Barcelona Games, Moragas Spa, Rivenburgh, and Larson (1995) pointed out that "the event has gravity, and each ritual holds great symbolic import . . . [in which] sport is a symbol for transcendent, universal values" (p. 105). Addressing the differences among national telecasts, Larson and Rivenburgh (1991) showed how views of internationalization are shaped by television, and Izod (1996) revealed how broadcasters were able to present myth as fact and shape the audience's view of the Olympic Games. Expanding the focus, Puijk (1997) showed how the 1992 Lillehammer Olympics shaped the image of the host country, and similarly, after analyzing the staging of the 2000 Olympics, Stevenson (1997) predicted that the mythology of the Olympics would have a dramatic impact on worldviews of Sydney as a city and a culture. Clearly, megasporting events have the power to shape cultures, identities, and attitudes, giving research into the marketing of mediated sports particular social as well as economic significance.

PROMOTING SPORTS WITHIN SPORTS TELEVISION

The criteria for effective on-air promotion have long included the need to match the target audience for the program carrying the promotion with the audience for the program being promoted, often called the *compatibility* factor (Klein, 1991; Webster & Phalen, 1997). It seems self-evident that promos in programs watched mostly by men are hardly the right place to promote shows watched mostly by women. Going beyond gender, such factors as age and other lifestyle characteristics also differentiate the audiences targeted by the major networks. However, sports programming raises some interesting questions in regard to on-air promotion.

Whereas most researchers looked at the effects of promotion carried *within* sports programming, Owens and Bryant (1998) studied the promotion *of* sports programming, specifically college and professional football. They analyzed over 400 promos for upcoming football games and found that networks relegated these promos to spots within other games of the same type and in other sports programming on weekends (see Table 7.1). Owens and Bryant concluded that the times in which the promos aired suggested that the networks were focused on maintaining their steady fan bases of men, ages 18 to 49, and did not attempt to attract new viewers to football. Thus, audience retention was viewed as promotional success in this venue.

One further study explored a different aspect of sports promotion: Billings and Eastman (1998) analyzed NBC's on-air promos for upcoming Olympic events carried *inside* the 1996 Olympics. Looking for an explanation of the highest rated nights of the Olympics, they found that the traditional characteristics of superstars, superevents, controversy, and high Sunday-night viewing accounted for only five of the nine highest rated nights and demonstrated that promotional content favoring women athletes and women's events, as well as the structural characteristics of more specific (as opposed to generic) promotion, accounted for the remaining four high-rated nights. The authors concluded that targeting women audiences had the largest impact on ratings. The presumption seemed to be that men would generally watch the Olympics regardless of telecast con-

TABLE 7.1

Summary of Studies About Promotion Within Sporting Events

Authors	Year	Programs and Promotion	Primary Findings
Wise	1999	124 promos for upcoming sports events carried on ESPN, TNT, USA, and TBS.	Broadcast salience model applies to cable; high compatibility of carriage and promoted event (wrestling in wrestling, tennis in tennis); more specific than generic promos.
Billings and Eastman	1999	303 promos for future Olympics events carried within the 1996 Atlanta Olympics (17 days, 55 hours).	Top women's events accounted for increased ratings; specific promos accounted for higher ratings; women athletes were promoted 7% more than men athletes; promos were more likely to emphasize women's sports than host or reporter narratives.
Owens and Bryant	1998	400 promos for upcoming college and pro football games.	High compatibility of carriage and promoted event (football in football only); networks did not attempt to attract new viewers, but stuck with 18 to 49 men football fans.
Billings, Eastman, and Newton	1998	183 promos for NBC's prime-time programs carried within the 1996 Atlanta Olympics (17 days, 55 hours).	Promotion in the Olympics was successful for continuing but not new programs because of the great distance in time to the new shows' airdates; higher ratings (bigger audiences) for the Olympics resulted in greater effectiveness for promotion.
Eastman, Newton, and Pack	1996	677 promos for broadcast network prime-time programs carried within megasporting events.	Promos had a modest impact on program shares/ratings: one third of shares went up, half stayed flat, less than 10 prime-time programs' percentages went down; a six-part model accounted for one third of the ratings variance; lead-in was a less important factor in share variance for new series than for continuing series.
Eastman and Otteson	1994	277 promos for broadcast network prime-time programs carried in the 1992 Winter and Summer Olympics on CBS, TNT, and NBC (103 hours).	Promotion was not successful over the long term for either new or continuing series, but had positive impact on the short-term ratings of one continuing show; promos in the Olympics greatly favored singles over multiple, generic over specific spots, and acquisitive over retentive spots, but was closely balanced between promos for new and continuing series.
McCollum and McCollum	1980	59 min of network promos for new and continuing ABC prime-time programs carried during the 1976 Montreal Summer Olympics (64 hours).	Points to the large percentage of time (15%) devoted to commercials, promos, and PSAs (nonsports content) during an Olympics; during late-night Olympic wrap-up shows, over one fifth of time was devoted to a combination of commercials and promos; noted commercials directed solely at women as early as 1976.

tent, whereas women were more likely to watch when women athletes were given increasing salience by network executives.

Insofar as these studies can be compared with regard to promotion, they are listed in Table 7.1, along with other studies of promotion within or about sports programs discussed in the next section. The table shows a growing body of work with contradictory results about promotional effectiveness, ranging from highly ineffective (Eastman & Otteson, 1994) to highly effective (Eastman, Newton, & Pack, 1996). Whether these conflicts reflect differences in the historical times, and thus network practices, or differences in the sports studied is not yet clear. As a result, there is a continuing need to analyze sports promotion in order to determine which variables most closely affect ratings.

PROMOTING PRIME TIME IN SPORTS

One oft-used justification by the broadcast networks for paying billions of dollars for sports rights fees is that sporting events are invaluable vehicles for promoting prime-time programs (Carter, 1996; Eastman & Meyer, 1989; Sandomir, 1992). This rationale makes immediate sense for promoting other *sports* programs, such as the next occurrence of the same event (an upcoming game of the same type) or for promoting such events as *Monday Night Football* and championship games of all kinds (NBA, NCAA, World Series, and other sports) that are scheduled in prime time. It also makes sense to promote sports scheduled outside of prime time, such as weekend events. In addition, the annual Super Bowls have regularly been shown to generate enormous ratings for whatever entertainment shows immediately follow them (Carter, 1996). The rationale has less face validity, however, when referring to promotion of traditional situation comedies, dramas, and other prime-time fare within sports because prime-time audiences tend to skew heavily toward women (Adams & Eastman, 1997).

As Table 7.1 shows, several scholars have investigated these issues. Eastman and Otteson (1994) analyzed the before-and-after ratings for prime-time series promoted in the 1992 Winter and Summer Olympics and found significant losses in ratings, especially for programs promoted during the Summer Games. They concluded that the extended distance in time between the promos (July) and the airdates of the new programs (fall) probably contributed greatly to the lack of positive impact for these promos. *Distance* (or elapsed time) has since been utilized as a critical variable in structural studies of promotional impact (see Eastman & Newton, 1998a). Eastman and Otteson also found that lead-in ratings had virtually no impact on the promoted programs' ratings, despite a long history of both academic and industry studies confirming the importance of the inherited audience (see Eastman, 1998; Webster & Phalen, 1997).

Looking beyond the Olympics to a broad range of sporting events, Eastman, Newton, and Pack (1996) tested the impact of 677 on-air promos for prime-time shows carried within 51 megasporting events on the broadcast networks. Eastman et al. analyzed the impacts of program promotion carried in college and pro football games, major auto racing events, World Cup Soccer, and major golf and tennis tournaments, finding modest yet significant gains in ratings and shares of promoted programs. They found that about one third of ratings for promoted prime-time programs went up, over one half stayed flat, and less than 10% went down. They concluded that staying flat was a positive achievement when a program was off-the-air for more than a few days—such as during a 16- or 17-day Olympics, a World Series, or the many nights of playoffs of various kinds. Indeed, retaining viewers becomes especially crucial to broadcast networks when cable is increasingly attracting larger shares of prime-time viewership.[2]

In an attempt to resolve the conflicts between these earlier studies, Billings, Eastman, and Newton (1998) analyzed 183 on-air promos for prime-time shows carried within the 1996 Summer Olympics in Atlanta. They found the expected impact for lead-in ratings and demonstrated that promos for continuing series had a surprisingly large effect on NBC's prime-time ratings. Promotion had no identifiable impact, however, on the ratings for NBC's new fall lineup, supporting Eastman and Otteson's (1994) finding regarding the negative effect of the distance between promos and program airdates. Several other factors noted by Billings et al. contributed to the partly positive effect in 1996, in particular, NBC's exceptionally high ratings for the Olympics itself and its top-rated prime-time program schedule. Having hit programs to promote is always an advantage.

Approaching the problem of identifying promotion's impact on ratings from another direction, Eastman and Newton (1998a, 1998b, 1999) examined structural features contributing to promotion's effectiveness (see Eastman & Bolls, chap. 3, this volume). Utilizing a series of nine attributes (clutter, construction, design, distance, familiarity, frequency, genre, location, and position) in addition to the widely recognized phenomenon of inherited viewing, they posited that more desirable levels of these attributes contributed significantly to prominence (or salience) for promotion and that increased salience would lead to increased impact on promoted program ratings. Indeed, based on analysis of a very large database, they

---

[2]In July 1998, for the first time, the collective rating of the cable networks was larger than that of the four major broadcast television networks (Petrozzello, 1998).

concluded that on-air promos contribute at least 5% to ratings, and much higher percentages for subsets of programs. Although their salience theory has been demonstrated for promotion carried within prime time, it has not been tested for promotion carried within sporting events.

A STUDY OF PROMOTION IN THE 1998 NAGANO OLYMPICS

As a follow-up to previous studies, these researchers wanted to clarify the role of the on-air promotion within the CBS prime-time broadcasts over the 16 days of the Nagano Olympics to see whether the promos functioned much as they had in the 1996 games in Atlanta or as they had in the 1992 games in Albertville and Barcelona.[3] They also wanted to test the collective impact of the so-called salience variables. The theoretical model for this study drew on the ideas of excitation transfer and expectation (see chaps. 2 and 3, this volume), and the methodology closely matched that of Billings et al. (1998) and Eastman and Otteson (1994) in order to provide results that could be compared to those from the previous Olympics. In a secondary analysis looking at separate variables, Eastman and Newton's (1998b) method was adopted to permit comparison of promotion's contribution. It was expected that examining yet another Olympics would help distinguish the influence of promotion from other circumstances affecting prime-time program ratings and test the relevance of key salience variables.

Special Characteristics

However, the 1998 Winter Olympics had some special characteristics. The Nagano Games did not achieve outstanding television ratings in the United States (Barnhart, 1998), in part because winter sports have not traditionally appealed as greatly as summer events to American television viewers, and in part because the time difference between Japan and the United States created delayed broadcasts of key events. On the positive side, these Olympics aired in February, in the midst of a national sweeps ratings period when the networks and stations air their strongest programs, and thus promotion carried within these games might be expected to have considerable impact on subsequent viewing. On the negative side, top-ranked NBC carried the Atlanta Games and was promoting the most popular programming on television at the time (Huff, 1996), whereas the

---

[3]1992 was the last year in which both the Winter and Summer Olympics occurred. Beginning in 1994, Winter and Summer Games were scheduled alternately every 2 years (1994 in Lillehammer, 1996 in Atlanta, 1998 in Nagano, 2000 in Sydney, 2002 in Salt Lake City, and so on).

Nagano Games were aired by CBS, a network with considerably lower ratings and a far less popular prime-time schedule in the 1997–1998 season.[4] The elimination of NBC and its hit programming as well as the more popular events in Summer Games should more clearly separate the impact of on-air promotion from these other factors.

Hypotheses

Based on the positive results reported in the Eastman, Newton, and Pack (1996) study for continuing programs promoted in sports and the relatively close distance from promotion to promoted programs in these Winter Games, these authors hypothesized that the within-Olympic promos for CBS's prime-time series would generate significant increases in ratings, though not at the same levels as with NBC's programs. At the theoretical level, the idea is that promos set up exciting (or not exciting) expectations that can transfer to the promoted programs and result in higher (or lower) viewing and thus be measured by ratings increases or decreases. Fundamental to such research are the assumptions that a hiatus—a break in the regular appearances of a series—invariably drives ratings down, and that programs new to the schedule (and thus unfamiliar to viewers) generally have very weak ratings.[5]

Based on the findings of Eastman and Newton (1998a, 1999), the impact of specific variables could be anticipated, and based on the conclusion of Eastman and Newton (1998b), the size of the impact could be estimated. Specifically, the authors hypothesized that

> H_1: Significantly more of the promos carried in the 1998 Nagano Games would have a positive impact on the ratings and shares of promoted prime-time programs than would have a negative impact.

> H_2: Promos' impact in the 1998 games on prime-time ratings would be less positive than in the 1996 games but more positive than in the 1992 games.

> H_3: At least 5% of ratings of programs promoted in the 1998 Nagano Games would be attributable to the collective salience variables.

> H_4: Programs promoted in promos with more salience—thus appearing in less cluttered pods, having single construction, having specific

---

[4]Just a year later (spring 1999), CBS was at the top of the ratings, winning many weeks in the season and eventually earning first place for the year.

[5]Classically, between two thirds and three quarters of new programs do not succeed in achieving competitive ratings or shares and get canceled in a few weeks or at the end of the season. In this study, one new show, *Four Corners*, was canceled before the 3 postweeks were completed.

design, being at closer distance, having greater frequency, and appearing in first or last position in pods — would have a collectively greater impact on ratings than programs promoted with less salient attributes.

Method

Promos were defined as on-air promotion for prime-time series carried on the CBS network (promos for upcoming Olympic events within these or future games were not included in this study). As in similar studies, promos for prime time were chosen over promos for other dayparts because prime time is the most watched portion of the broadcasting day and is the daypart for which hourly ratings are available.

Population

All 16 nights of the Nagano Games (February 7–22, 1998) were videotaped, resulting in 52 hours for analysis (13 nights at 3 hours plus 3 Sundays at 4 hours and one additional hour on the first Saturday of the Opening Ceremonies). A trained coder using pretested coding sheets scanned the 16 tapes for prime-time promos, and for each one identified, recorded the program carrying the promo and the program being promoted. Another graduate student independently recoded four randomly selected hours of the broadcast to establish the reliability of the coding. Using Holsti's (1969) basic formula $(2M/N_1 + N_2)$, intercoder reliability exceeded 99%.

Variables

As in previous research, nine facets of each promo were recorded. The (a) location of the promo within the Olympic coverage (pod or end-credit break/transition) and the (b) placement of the promo within its commercial break (first, middle, last — in other words, primacy/recency or surrounded by advertising messages) were logged because these variables have been shown to affect promotion's impact (see Eastman & Newton, 1998a, 1999). The (c) genre of the promoted program, whether the spot was (d) generic or specific, and its (e) construction, whether the promo was a single spot or multiple spot (promoting several programs), was noted. The (f) number of elements (commercials, promos, public service announcements) was recorded to measure the amount of clutter. When tabulating the number of elements to measure clutter, each promoted program (lasting 3 s or more) within a multiple spot was counted as one element. The (g) status of the promoted program as new (not yet aired), continuing (aired prior to CBS's Olympic telecast), or one-time-only (referring to movies, specials, and sporting events) was identified. The (h) frequency of promos (the number of times a program was promoted) was determined. Finally, the (i) distance between the promo and the promoted program's airdate was logged (operationalized as the next segment of the Olympics, a program or segment airing later that same night, a program airing later that same week, or the next week, or 2 weeks or more away).

For *continuing* programs, the rating and share for the program and its lead-in show in each of the 3 weeks preceding the Olympics were entered into the database along with the rating/share for that program and its lead-in for each of the 3 weeks following the Olympics. Ratings/shares data were obtained from *Broadcasting & Cable* magazine. Because two continuing programs, *Cybill* and *Dr. Quinn, Medicine Woman*, were on hiatus for the 2 months preceding the Olympics, time slot ratings were utilized in lieu of pre-games ratings for those programs, as in previous studies. Using the average of 3 weeks, rather than just 1 week, minimizes the impact of special programming, preemptions, and one-time sampling of episodes. Moreover, a change over 3 weeks is long enough to make a substantial difference in a network's overall ratings or shares for that season.

For *new* programs, following the lead of Eastman and Otteson (1994) and Billings et al. (1998), the first three ratings for programs new to the CBS lineup were compared to the ratings of the time slots in the 3 weeks prior to the Olympics. In instances where preemption and substitution occurred, ratings/shares were entered for the week immediately following the preemption.

Means of Analysis

Gains and losses in ratings (or shares) were calculated by averaging the rating for the 3 weeks prior to the Olympics and subtracting it from the average for 3 weeks after the Olympics, producing zero and plus and minus change scores. In previous studies, significant differences were defined as 2 full rating/share points, but in this study, 1 rating point was deemed meaningful because CBS's overall ratings had been substantially lower than NBC's and thus an average 1-point difference over 3 weeks could be considered important to the network. Share changes had to reach the 2-point difference plateau to be judged meaningful.

Results

CBS aired 267 promos during the Nagano Olympics, of which 17 were for future Olympic events, 34 were for one-time only events, and 216 were for new and continuing prime-time programs. Altogether, 24 different prime-time series were promoted in the 216 spots during the Nagano Games.

Findings for Changes in Audience Size

Table 7.2 lists 6 weeks of ratings/shares for each of the 24 prime-time programs and its lead-in promoted by CBS during the 16 evenings of the 1998 Olympics, organized from the most promoted to least promoted. The first column tells whether the program was new to the schedule after the Olympics (just 3 shows) or a continuing program (21 shows). The second column tells how many times the program was promoted in the prime-time portion of the Olympics (considerable additional promotion for these same programs would have occurred during the day, early evening, and late night periods). Following the week-by-week before-and-after ratings and shares, the final column shows the calculated difference scores. Parentheses in the table indicate that time slot ratings/shares were utilized for the before ratings and shares. The difference scores represent the amount of change in ratings or shares between the average for the 3 weeks prior to the Olympics for that program (or its time slot) and the average for the 3 weeks immediately following the Olympics. It is the change scores that are of primary interest here.

As Table 7.2 shows, 25% of ratings and 29% of shares went up, 2% of both ratings and shares went down, and 67% of ratings and 63% of shares stayed flat, supporting the first hypothesis. As expected, for all cases of continuing programs, the difference between the average rating of the 3 weeks before the Olympics and the 3 weeks after failed to reach the criterion of a 2-point change in ratings, the level used in previous studies. However, in the cases of eight programs (33%), there was a change of 1 full point or more. For the six continuing programs, *48 Hours* (+1.93), *60 Minutes* (+1.7), *Everybody Loves Raymond* (+1.06), *The Nanny* (+1.0), *Gregory Hines* (–1.53), and *Touched by an Angel* (-1.57), the direction was positive in four of the instances.[6] Among new programs, *Candid Camera* reached the plateau of a +2.0 change in ratings, and *The Closer* had nearly as high a positive change score (+1.83).

It is in the change scores for program shares that the more significant (for CBS) increases and decreases appear. Seven continuing programs and two new programs had share changes of 2 points or more (altogether, 38%). Of these nine, seven were positive changes, substantially aiding CBS's overall proportion of network viewing. The continuing shows were *48 Hours* (+5.7), *60 Minutes* (+3.0), *Everybody Loves Raymond* (+2.0), *The Nanny* (+2.0), and *Walker, Texas Ranger* (+2.3), and the new shows were *Candid Camera* (+4.0) and *The Closer* (+3.0). However, two continuing shows, *Touched by an Angel* and *Gregory Hines,* dropped in share points (by –2.3 and –3.67, respectively), consistent with their slide in ratings. Promo-

---

[6]*Gregory Hines* was placed on hiatus, so drawing conclusions about its short-term performance is most problematic.

TABLE 7.2

Ratings/Shares for Programs Promoted in the 1998 Olympics

	New or Continuing	No. of Promos	−3wk	−2wk	−1wk	+1wk	+2wk	+3wk	Change
Candid Camera	N	7	(6.9/12)	6.2/11	(5.9/11)	8.0/14	8.2/15	8.8/17	+2.00/+4.00
Lead-in			10.6/19	9.1/16	8.5/16	8.3/16	8.2/15	8.8/17	
48 Hours[a]	C	1	7.8/13	7.0/11	7.4/12	9.7/16	8.3/14	10.0/17	+1.93/+5.70
Lead-in			10.9/16	9.9/15	9.5/14	10.7/16	10.2/16	9.5/15	
The Closer	N	35	(7.6/11)	7.0/10	(8.1/12)	10.9/16	9.5/14	7.8/12	+1.83/+3.00
Lead-in			9.4/14	8.4/12	9.2/14	10.0/15	9.9/15	10.3/16	
60 Minutes	C	13	13.8/22	14.0/22	15.4/26	15.5/26	13.4/22	19.4/31	+1.70/+3.00
Lead-in			n.a.	n.a.	n.a.	n.a.	n.a.	n.a.	
Everybody Loves Raymond	C	27	9.4/14	8.4/12	9.2/14	10.0/15	9.9/15	10.3/16	+1.06/+2.00
Lead-in			10.0/15	8.8/13	10.0/16	9.9/15	10.3/16	9.8/15	
The Nanny	C	11	7.7/12	7.6/12	6.6/11	8.7/14	8.6/14	7.6/13	+1.00/+2.00
Lead-in			n.a.	n.a.	n.a.	n.a.	n.a.	n.a.	
Walker, Texas Ranger	C	2	8.8/15	8.1/14	9.2/17	10.2/19	9.3/17	8.8/17	+0.73/+2.30
Lead-in			6.6/11	7.6/13	6.9/12	7.1/12	7.6/14	6.5/12	
Chicago Hope	C	12	8.0/14	5.9/14	9.0/15	8.4/14	8.1/14	8.4/15	+0.67/+1.30
Lead-in			6.5/10	6.6/10	10.3/16	7.8/12	7.3/12	7.9/13	
Public Eye	C	1	7.9/12	6.5/10	6.6/10	7.8/12	7.3/12	7.9/13	+0.67/+1.70
Lead-in			7.2/11	6.7/10	5.5/8	9.6/15	9.3/15	9.5/15	
Dr. Quinn, Medicine Woman	C	8	(7.7/14)	7.7/14	(7.5/14)	8.2/15	8.1/15	8.0/15	+0.46/+1.00
Lead-in			n.a.	n.a.	n.a.	n.a.	n.a.	n.a.	
Brooklyn South	C	10	5.9/10	5.6/9	6.0/10	6.0/10	6.6/11	6.1/10	+0.40/+0.67
Lead-in			6.6/10	6.1/9	7.0/11	8.9/13	7.9/12	6.8/10	
Cosby	C	11	10.0/15	8.8/13	10.0/16	9.9/15	10.3/16	9.8/15	+0.40/+0.67
Lead-in			n.a.	n.a.	n.a.	n.a.	n.a.	n.a.	

	New or Continuing	No. of Promos	-3wk	-2wk	-1wk	+1wk	+2wk	+3wk	Change
Cybill	C	4	(7.2/11)	6.7/10	5.5/8)	6.9/11	7.4/12	6.2/10	+0.36/+1.30
Lead-in			7.7/12	7.6/12	6.6/11	8.7/14	8.6/14	7.6/13	
George & Leo	C	12	7.6/11	7.0/10	8.1/12	8.9/13	7.9/12	6.8/10	+0.30/+0.67
Lead-in			10.0/15	8.8/13	10.0/16	10.0/15	9.9/15	10.3/16	
JAG	C	4	8.5/13	5.9/9	8.8/14	9.1/14	5.3/9	9.6/15	+0.27/+0.67
Lead-in			n.a.	n.a.	n.a.	n.a.	8.2/15	n.a.	
Promised Land	C	1	8.4/13	9.4/15	8.8/13	9.1/14	9.5/15	8.5/14	+0.17/+0.67
Lead-in			n.a.	n.a.	n.a.	n.a.	n.a.	n.a.	
Diagnosis Murder	C	1	10.9/16	9.9/15	9.5/14	10.7/16	10.2/16	9.5/15	+0.03/+0.67
Lead-in			8.4/13	9.4/15	8.8/13	9.1/14	9.5/15	8.5/14	
Four Corners	N	23	(6.3/11)	6.6/11	4.9/8)	6.9/11	4.8/8	Cancel	0.00/0.00
Lead-in			7.4/11	8.5/13	8.8/14	9.1/14	7.8/12	n.a.	
Nash Bridges	C	2	8.5/15	7.1/12	7.4/14	7.2/13	7.1/13	n.a.	-0.53/-0.66
Lead-in			n.a.	n.a.	n.a.	n.a.	n.a.	n.a.,	
Magnificent Seven	C	4	7.7/14	7.7/14	7.5/14	7.1/12	7.6/14	6.5/12	-0.57/-1.30
Lead-in			n.a.	n.a.	n.a.	8.2/15	8.1/15	8.0/15	
Michael Hayes	C	11	7.4/11	7.9/13	6.9/9	6.4/10	6.6/11	7.0/11	-0.73/-0.30
Lead-in			9.5/15	n.a.	n.a.	6.9/11	7.4/12	6.2/10	
Kids Say the Darndest Things	C	10	10.6/19	9.1/16	8.5/16	8.3/16	8.2/15	8.8/17	-0.96/-1.00
Lead-in			n.a.	n.a.	n.a.	n.a.	n.a.	n.a.	
Gregory Hines	C	3	6.9/12	6.2/11	5.9/11	4.8/8	n.a.	n.a.	-1.53/-3.67
Lead-in			n.a.	n.a.	n.a.	n.a.	n.a.	n.a.	
Touched by an Angel	C	3	15.8/24	15.2/25	16.0/24	14.4/22	14.5/22	14.4/22	-1.57/-2.30
Lead-in			13.8/22	14.0/22	15.4/26	15.5/26	13.4/22	19.4/31	

Note. Parentheses around a number mean that it was a time slot rating or share because the program did not appear in that week (because it was new or preempted); n.a. (not applicable) means that the program appeared at the start of prime time and thus had varied lead-ins in the local markets. [a] Although only one promo for *48 Hours* appeared within prime time, it can be presumed that others appeared in daytime and late-night programming.

tion of two of the three new programs within the Olympics appeared to have created sampling (and the shows themselves apparently maintained that viewing), whereas promotion of older continuing shows generally held or improved their audience size in the post-Olympic weeks, clearly exceeding the level of impact predicted in Hypothesis 1.

Lead-In's Impact. In order to assess the impact of lead-in ratings/ shares on the promoted programs' ratings/shares (or those of the time slot) after the Olympics, the lead-in program's ratings and promoted program's ratings were correlated (Pearson product–moment correlations), as were the lead-in shares and program shares. The results were extremely low (r of ratings = +.07; r of shares = –.03) and not significant. Thus, lead-in was deemed to have no meaningful impact on the changes in CBS's prime-time ratings or shares.

Comparison of Three Olympics. As the upper pie chart in Fig. 7.1 shows, of the 24 programs promoted during the 1998 Olympics, six, or 25%, had significant increases in their shares of the audience, 67% stayed flat, and 8% went down. In two cases, the promoted programs did not air immediately after the Olympics, and NCAA basketball coverage caused a 2-month gap between promotion and airdates, much too long to render valid analysis in those two cases, but not affecting the overall conclusion. These findings compare with substantially more losses in 1996 and still more in 1992, shown in the mid and lower pie charts in Fig. 7.1. Thus, Hypothesis 2 was not supported because CBS did unexpectedly better in 1998 than in 1992 and even better than NBC in Atlanta in 1996.

Role of Program Familiarity. The 21 continuing programs were promoted much more often (about 3:1) than the 3 new programs during the Nagano Olympics, but nearly a third (65, or 30%) of all promos were for the new programs. This demonstrates a heavy emphasis on these three new shows. A comparison of the impact of promotion for new versus continuing programs was about equal, confirmed by a chi-square test (x^2 = 11.45, df = 1, p < .00). Although the very small pool of new programs makes this result merely suggestive, it does, however, challenge the presumption that continuing programs should benefit more from promotion than new programs.

Discussion of Change Scores. Although merely one of CBS's promoted programs gained 2 full ratings points, none lost 2 full ratings points. But it is in the area of "no change" that interest should perhaps focus. Eastman and Otteson (1994) as well as Eastman et al. (1996) argued that staying flat in ratings following a long hiatus is a positive achieve-

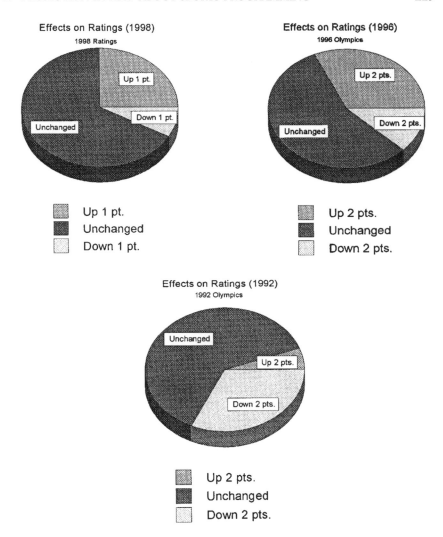

FIG. 7.1.   Proportional distribution of difference scores in 1998, 1996, and 1992.

ment. Historically, program ratings have been shown to go down after any break of 2 weeks in the regular schedule (Adams, 1988), thus supporting the claim that CBS would obtain very positive results from its promotion during the 1998 Olympics if more than half the ratings stayed flat, which was certainly the case. Altogether, 92% of its ratings either stayed flat or rose, a startling percentage. Thus, surprisingly, these findings do not wholly support Hypothesis 2, as promos in the Nagano Olympics can be evaluated as *more* effective (for CBS) than promotion in the Atlanta Olympics (for NBC), although, as predicted, Nagano's promotion was certainly far more successful than the combined results for Albertville and Barcelona in 1992.

The absence of a strong correlation between lead-in and promoted program ratings or shares is consistent with the findings in Eastman and Otteson (1994) regarding the impact of lead-in for the 1992 Olympics. Unlike in 1992, however, the ratings and shares of more than a quarter of the CBS prime-time schedule went up following the 1998 Olympics. One theoretical explanation may be the existence of a network effect, comparable to a channel effect (see Webster & Phalen, 1997). Despite persistent efforts to attract younger viewers, CBS appears to have the image in viewers' minds of being a network for older people. Its executives have long complained that their programs do not get the sampling that NBC's or ABC's do. Airing an Olympics may be a partial way out of this dilemma in that, overall, more viewers sampled and stayed with CBS's new and continuing programs following the games than had watched prior to the games. It may be that carriage of an Olympics rebranded CBS in the minds of some viewers and thus made watching its programs acceptable. Whether these audiences persisted beyond the 3 weeks that were measured is, of course, unknown, but some long-term success was apparently reflected in CBS's shift from third in overall season ratings to second in the 1997–1998 season (AP Newswire, 1998).[7]

The question is whether promotion played a key role in raising CBS's ratings or whether some other factor, for example, a schedule of more popular programs, raised the overall ratings. A comparison of the week-by-week ratings of CBS's program lineup in the 3 weeks preceding the Olympics shows three decisive facts: First, as has already been shown, only 3 programs were added to the 21 continuing programs, meaning 88% of the lineup was stable, so there was no flood of "different" shows. Second, analysis of just the 3 weeks before the Olympics shows that 16 of the 24 programs (or their slots) had downtrending or merely flat ratings and shares during the 3 weeks preceding their promotion in the Olympics. Only 8 shows trended up, and in only two of those cases was there a share change of 2 points or more. Third, 4 of the programs that were already trending up before the games received only minimal promotion in just two, three, or four spots during the games, suggesting that some other factor contributed to their positive change scores. However, of those shows trending down before promotion in the Olympics, 4 went up and 11 stayed flat in change scores. It follows that the prominence arising from

---

[7]Despite its rise to the number one ranking in the 1998–1999 season, it remained fourth among adults 18 to 49, the demographic group most wanted by advertisers (Associated Press, 1999).

being trumpeted within an Olympics operates positively but at least somewhat independently from the inherent popularity of a program.

Findings for Salience Variables

Most of the salience variables identified in previous research proved relevant to promotion in these games. About half the promos (130, or 49%) occurred within multiple spots, whereas the other half (137, or 51%) appeared as *single* spots (the *construction* variable). Contrary to conventional promotional practice, but consistent with previous Olympic promotion, a large portion of the promos were in generic form (46%) and the rest (54%) in specific form (the *design* variable).

Consistent with previous Olympic promotion, the *distance* between promos and airdates of promoted programs was quite large. The bulk (218, or 83%) were for programs airing more than 2 weeks later, whereas 25 (9%) were for shows in the next week, 17 (5%) for shows later in the same week, and 7 (4%) for shows airing the next night, resulting in 17% with a higher likelihood of impact, according to salience theory. Interestingly, it is clear that promos for prime-time shows were spread as heavily in the first week as toward the end of the Nagano Games. The average frequency of promos per program was 9.0, a high average, but the range of 1 to 35 reveals massive efforts to promote some programs and token efforts for others (at least within prime time).

Because the Olympic coverage extended beyond the prime-time hours, all promos appeared in within-program pods, and without cases of promos in transitions or end-credit pods, the variable of *location* had to be dropped from the analysis. Similarly, because merely six prime-time sporting events (all promotions for March Madness) were promoted in the sample, the variable of *genre* (operationalized as a comparison of promos for sports and other entertainment) could not be examined. Nonetheless, CBS's *placement* of the promos differed markedly from the practices of NBC in 1996 (see Billings et al., 1998). Whereas NBC balanced promos across the beginning, middle, and end of breaks, CBS relied on promoting programs at the end of breaks (76%). The remaining promos (21%) occurred in the middle of breaks, with only a small percentage (3%) aired first in breaks.

Use of Most Salient Features. Figure 7.2 shows the differences between the percentages of salience variables in 1996 and 1998. The bars represent the percentage of promos with the most salient features (first/last elements, single construction, least clutter, etc.). Interestingly, CBS utilized more salient features for three aspects of its promotion: design, fre-

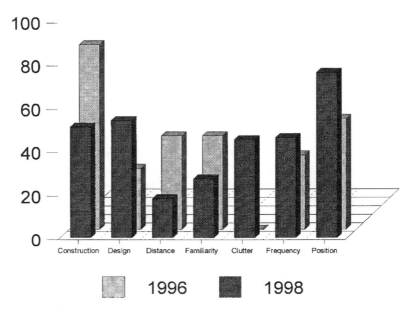

FIG. 7.2.   A comparison of salience variables impacting prime-time ratings
in 1996 and 1998.

quency, and position. These factors appear to be the three main reasons
for the success of the CBS Nagano promotional effort.

Collective Impact of Promotion.   The regression analysis in Table 7.3
shows the contribution of the salience variables in 155 promos on the ratings for the 21 promoted prime-time programs. The table reports only the
significant findings and focuses on the Adjusted R^2 value (adjusted to take
account of variable quantity and sample size). Overall, 66% of the variance was accounted for in the model, a very high percentage. Of that 66%,
56% was attributable to inheritance, a higher proportion than is typical for
prime-time programs (that hovers around 50%). What is important here is
that 10% of the variance comes from the salience variables, as shown by
subtracting the first value in the Adjusted R^2 column (.562) from the last
(.661). Thus, the contribution of promotion to the variance in ratings was
.099 (or 10%) for the programs promoted in the 1998 Nagano Olympics, a
proportion much higher than predicted in Hypothesis 3, strongly confirming the prediction.
     In addition to the well-recognized impact of the rating of the program
carrying the promotion (in this case, the nightly Olympic ratings), clutter,

TABLE 7.3
Factors Impacting Continuing Promos Carried in the 1998 Nagano
Olympics (N = 155 Promos, 21 Continuing Prime-Time Programs)

Step Variable	B	Adjusted R^2	F^*	df
Lead-in rating	.637	.562	39.95	1, 22
Clutter			14.9	1, 21
	.003	.579	3	
Position			22.2	1, 20
	.188	.600	6	
Carriage program rating			36.3	1, 19
	.490	.647	8	
Frequency of promotion			15.6	1, 18
	−.017	.651	0	

position, frequency, and distance contributed significantly to the ratings, comprising four of the six variables predicted in Hypothesis 4. In other words, less-cluttered breaks in programming (the meaning of the negative value), a first or last position within a pod, and a short distance between promo and program positively affect promoted program ratings, partially supporting the fourth prediction. Of the collective 16% contribution, most comes from the nightly rating (the carriage program rating), and the additional salience variables contributed just 2%. Thus the amount of each contribution—other than carriage program rating—appears very small, but these are statistically significant impacts and congruent with previous research findings. It must be kept in mind that an increase or decrease of 2% can shift a network to the top or the middle of the rankings. Moreover, different sizes for the contributions of the individual variables might have been found had half-hour by half-hour ratings and shares been available, rather than the published average for the Olympics in an evening.

In addition, in this study, it appears that a low frequency of promotion contributed positively. This is a puzzling finding similar to Walker's 1993 finding and contrary to industry lore. It suggests either that audiences may react negatively to repeated promotion or that some other factor (such as program familiarity) may lead to the appearance of a more positive impact for less frequent promotion. But the important point is that this analysis confirms previous research about the importance of the contribution of the salience variables, and for the first time, shows the size of the collective contribution of promotion within an Olympics.

Conclusions About Study

Overall, these findings demonstrate the relevance of two methods of assessing the impact of promotion within a lengthy event such as an Olympics. They also contribute to what is known about the impact of promotion for prime-time programs scheduled outside of prime time and within sports. More specifically, the results suggest that promoting prime-time programs may be less of a problem in a winter than a summer Olympics. Whereas Billings et al. (1998) showed that NBC had marked success promoting its new prime-time schedule in the 1996 Atlanta Olympics, CBS did relatively better in promoting continuing programming in the 1998 Nagano Games. In addition, the findings validate one thrust of NBC's decision to spend billions of dollars acquiring the rights to the Olympics long into the future: They show that an Olympics has, since the mid-1990s, become a demonstrably effective platform for advertising a prime-time schedule.

FUTURE RESEARCH IN SPORTS PROMOTION

If there is indeed a network effect, and if carrying an Olympics can change a network's image—at least with some viewers—two interesting questions to ask are whether other kinds of special programming have that effect, and if so, what kinds. There is ample evidence that a heavy schedule of major sporting events changed the image of ESPN in the mid-1980s and Fox in the late-1980s. Moreover, Fox made considerable use of its time within its NFL and other sporting events to promote its prime-time programs, and those ratings did, eventually, rise, shifting the broadcast network array from the Big Three to the Big Four in the 1990s. The role of promotion in that rise has been speculated about but not demonstrated. A comparative, descriptive study of Fox's on-air and other promotional practices over time would have value for building the historical record. Astonishingly, investigations have shown that very little remains of the decades of on-air promotion (for any kind of programs) aired in the past by the broadcast networks. Archivists tended to cut or black the promos along with the commercials when saving programs or, in a very few cases, they saved the nonprogram matter on separate tapes in isolation from the program environment. Commencing the storage of complete videotapes and analyzing what has been tried and what has succeeded or failed seems important to understanding how television markets to viewers and what the limits on viewer manipulation are.

The detailed analysis of network promotional practices conducted by Eastman and Newton (1998a) revealed ways in which the methods of promotion by the newest broadcast networks differ from those of the established networks (and from each other). Although those networks do not as yet carry any sports, once they begin to, a comparison of their promotional practices should show whether they become more like their major competitors or retain their unique practices. A comparison of the promotional practices of the cable networks carrying some sports would be revealing and aid in better formulating a model of ideal promotional strategy. Although program ratings could be obtained only with a grant, the extraordinary popularity of wrestling presents an opportunity to examine promotion within that sport (see Schlosser, 1998; Wise, 1999).

The Impact of Bias and Gender Favoritism

There are many outstanding issues related to sports promotion that remain to be investigated. Although the subject of bias toward males in sportscasts and sports coverage has received considerable critical attention, the role of slanting and favoritism in on-air and print promotion in fostering bias in upcoming sportscasters as well as audiences has not been thoroughly examined. Another topic of concern relevant to sports promotion is racial bias, because of its significance to both industry and society. If both seek fairness — for reasons of commercial value or social equity — investigating the stereotypes about race and ethnicity hidden in promotional messages becomes a crucial topic for research.

A growing body of scholarly work about televised sports examines the issues relating to gender and racial identity. In particular, the gender proportions of both the Olympic participants and the audiences have received considerable attention (see Daddario, 1998; Eastman & Billings, 1999; Jacobs, 1985; Schneider, 1998), and studies of genderized reporting in sportscasts have appeared (Eastman & Billings, 2000; Nelson, 1998, Tuggle, 1997), as well as studies of reporting by race (Eastman & Billings, in press). Because potential audiences for telecasts have many claims on their time and attention, on-air and print promotion play important roles in attracting specific groups of viewers to sporting events, but no studies have yet examined the gender appeals within on-air promotion.

Because audiences for some televised sporting events have recently acquired an increasingly large female component, the proportion of coverage devoted to women has become an increasingly sensitive issue. Whereas tennis has long had a large women's viewership, the new women's professional basketball league, the WNBA, attracts mostly women viewers, particularly young girls and teens (Brennan, 1998; Gross, 1997). The host networks for recent Olympics telecasts have recognized the increasing interest of women viewers in some sports, and both have augmented the amount of prime airtime devoted to events such as gymnastics and figure skating and boosted their promotion of those events in women-oriented promos and ads (Tuggle & Owen, 1998). For example, in their examination of NBC's coverage of women athletes in the 1996 Atlanta Olympics, Tuggle and Owen showed that women received almost as much clocktime as men. Moreover, they showed that the content of that coverage was stereotypically skewed in favor of men athletes, as also reported in an ear-

lier study of *Sports Illustrated* magazine (Kane, 1989). However, as Eastman and Billings (in press) pointed out, there has been a considerable rise
in the proportion of African American and women announcers and commentators in recent years. Scholars need to persist in looking for the effects of the changing constituents and constituencies of sportscasting. Network successes in appealing to women viewers have led to a significant
expansion of carriage of figure skating on many channels, raising the
question of how viewers are addressed in promotion for such events.

Structural and Content Effects Analyses

One area that has had very limited examination is the impact of sports
promotion outside of broadcast network television. In addition to cable
and satellite television, online sports should be a fruitful arena for research. Moreover, to date, no empirical analyses have turned the tables
and looked at sports promotion *within* network prime time—as distinct
from other promotion of other prime-time programs. The need for compatibility to maximize effectiveness may apply there as well as on weekends. Although analyses of ratings/shares changes have been conducted
for a few sports, they should be continued for a wide range of sports in addition to future Olympics. In addition, the textual content and context of
promotion has been the subject of only a few scattered comments and may
be revealing not only of marketing strategies but of embedded cultural
needs.

Although Eastman and Newton (1998a) contended that salience theory
can be used to explain promotional effectiveness or lack thereof, the specific variables that contribute to generating excitement in promotion of or
within sports or in expectations about events have not been isolated and
their impact measured. Although several salience variables have been
tested in two Olympics thus far, the heuristic value of such variables will
become even more apparent after analysis of Olympic promotion in 2000
and 2002. In addition, analysis of the change scores for ratings and shares
in subsequent Olympics should reveal longitudinal trends of interest to
the industry as well as scholars of programming.

Finally, only a very few studies to date have examined the impact of
promotion within a sport. One study focused on the promotion of the
Olympics during the Olympics in an attempt to account for the highest
rated nights of programming. Additional studies of this type, accounting
for especially high and low ratings, examining a Super Bowl evening or
televised events extending over several days, such as the World Series or
NCAA and NBA playoffs, should have value. Once such variables as team
standings, markets represented, individual records, and such were accounted for, internal (and even external) promotion might play a small

role. Similarly, researchers have taken only the briefest look at promotion within basketball and wrestling. Promotion in and about other sports should be explored on an individual and comparative basis.

Sports Beyond America

Many studies have also addressed the processes and impacts of globalization in sports marketing (see Donnelly, 1996; Sabo, Jansen, Tate, Duncan, & Leggett, 1996). Bellamy (1993), noting that the major networks have reconceptualized themselves and expanded their international presence, demonstrated the powerful role of sports in the intensification of world awareness of the major sports-providing entities. Harvey, Rail, and Thibault (1996) provided a model for studying globalization in sport in four dimensions (political, economic, cultural, and social) that permeate societies at two levels (national and global). They concluded that sport and globalization are indelibly linked, each transforming the other. The impact of the promotion of sport on television is one crucial tool in this process, and begs for studies by country and crossnationally.

Summary Remarks

In sum, whereas critical commentary on sports has been around for more than a decade, empirical research into televised sports has barely begun, and much remains to be investigated. The arena of promotion's impact on what viewers feel and tune into is merely one of a plethora of unexplored topics, but it lends itself to empirical studies because of the small (and thus convenient) size of the units, their frequency (necessary to build up sufficiently large databases for generalization), and their unique role as both miniprograms and commercial messages. Altogether, the agenda for both critical and empirical studies of sports promotion, including branding and marketing, is growing rather than diminishing. Sports promotion represents a huge financial investment on the part of sports producers and distributors, and it has subtle effects worthy of close examination.

REFERENCES

Adams, W. J. (1988). *Patterns in prime-time network television programs from 1948 to 1986: The influences of variety, churn, and content.* Unpublished doctoral dissertation, Indiana University, Bloomington.

Adams, W. J., & Eastman, S. T. (1997). Prime-time network television programming. In S. T. Eastman & D. A. Ferguson (Eds.), *Broadcast/cable programming: Strategies and practices* (5th ed., pp. 99–139). Belmont, CA: Wadsworth.

AP Newswire. (1998, April 30). The magic of Merlin helps NBC's ratings. *San Diego Union Tribune,* p. E5.

Associated Press. (1999, May 29). CBS is the season's ratings champion. *Herald Times*, p. 7.

Barnhart, A. (1998, March 7). Eat, drink, and snooze. *Kansas City Star*, p. E1.

Bellamy, R. V., Jr. (1993). Issues in the internationalization of the U.S. sports media: The emerging European marketplace. *Journal of Sport & Social Issues, 17*(3), 168–180.

Billings, A. C., & Eastman, S. T. (1998). Marketing the Olympics within the Olympics. *Ecquid Novi, 19*(2), 74–87.

Billings, A. C., Eastman, S. T., & Newton, G. D. (1998). Atlanta revisited: Prime-time promotion in the 1996 Summer Olympics. *Journal of Sport & Social Issues, 22*(1), 65–78.

Brennan, P. B. (1998, June 6–12). WNBA: The new summer games. *Washington Post*, p. 1.

Carter, B. (1996, July 29). Ratings exceed NBC's promises for the games. *New York Times*, p. D1.

Daddario, G. (1998). *Women's sport and spectacle.* Westport, CT: Greenwood.

Donnelly, P. (1996). The local and the global: Globalization in the sociology of sport. *Journal of Sport & Social Issues, 20*, 239–257.

Eastman, S. T. (1998). Programming theory under stress: The active industry and the active audience. In M. E. Roloff (Ed.), *Communication yearbook* (Vol. 21, pp. 156–178). Thousand Oaks, CA: Sage.

Eastman, S. T., & Billings, A. C. (1999). Gender parity in the Olympics: Hyping women athletes, favoring men athletes. *Journal of Sport & Social Issues, 23*(1), 140–170.

Eastman, S. T., & Billings, A. C. (2000). Sportscasting and sports reporting: The power of gender bias. *Journal of Sport & Social Issues, 24*(1), 192–212.

Eastman, S. T., & Billings, A. C. (in press). Biased voices of sports: Racial and gender stereotyping in college basketball announcing. *Journal of Sport & Social Issues, 24.*

Eastman, S. T., & Meyer, T. P. (1989). Sports programming: Scheduling, costs, and competition. In L. A. Wenner (Ed.). *Media, sports, and society* (pp. 97–119). Newbury Park, CA: Sage.

Eastman, S. T., & Newton, G. D. (1998a). The impact of structural salience within on-air promotion. *Journal of Broadcasting & Electronic Media, 42*, 50–79.

Eastman, S. T., & Newton, G. D. (1998b). Estimating the contributions of inheritance and promotion. In S. T. Eastman (Ed.), *Report on compilation valuation for distant television signals.* Copyright Board of Canada, re Retransmission 1998–2000.

Eastman, S. T., & Newton, G. D. (1999). Hitting promotion hard: A network response to channel surfing and new competition. *Journal of Applied Communication Research, 27*, 73–85.

Eastman, S. T., Newton, G. D., & Pack, L. (1996). Promoting prime-time programs in megasporting events. *Journal of Broadcasting & Electronic Media, 40*, 366–388.

Eastman, S. T., & Otteson, J. L. (1994). Promotion increases ratings, doesn't it? The impact of program promotion in the 1992 Olympics. *Journal of Broadcasting & Electronic Media, 38*, 307–322.

Farrell, T. B. (1989). Media rhetoric as social drama: The Winter Olympics of 1984. *Critical Studies in Mass Communication, 6*, 158–182.

Fortune. (1996, July 22). Fortune's Olympic fact sheet, 58–59.

Gelman, M. (1984, April 22). Fewer sponsors—But greater impact. *Advertising Age*, M6.

Goldstein, M. (1996, July 1). Analysis and commentary. *Business Week*, 33.

Gross, J. (1997, August 4). Girls gleefully claim a league of their own. *New York Times*, pp. A1, C16.

Gruneau, R. (1989). Making spectacle: A case study in television sports production. In L. A. Wenner (Ed.), *Media, sports, & society* (pp. 134–154). Newbury Park, CA: Sage.

Harvey, J., Rail, G., & Thibault, L. (1996). Globalization and sport: Sketching a theoretical model for empirical analyses. *Journal of Sport & Social Issues, 22*, 258–277.

Holsti, O. R. (1969). *Content analysis for the social sciences and humanities.* Reading, MA: Addison-Wesley.

Huff, R. (1996, December 4). Ratings: Peacock net is Thanksgiving big bird. *New York Daily News*, p. 83.

Izod, J. (1996). Television sport and the sacrificial hero. *Journal of Sport & Social Issues, 22,* 173–193.

Jacobs, V. A. (1985). *A comparative content analysis of network television coverage of the 1984 Winter Olympic Games.* Unpublished master's thesis, San Diego State University, San Diego.

Kane, M. (1989). The post-Title IX female athlete in the media: Things are changing, but how much? *Journal of Physical Education, Recreation, and Dance, 60*(1), 58–62.

Klein, R. A. (1991). Goals and concepts of promotion. In S. T. Eastman & R. A. Klein (Eds.), *Promotion and marketing for broadcasting and cable* (2nd ed., pp. 39–59). Prospect Heights, IL: Waveland Press.

Larson, J. F., & Rivenburgh, N. K. (1991). A comparative analysis of Australian, US, and British telecasts of the Seoul Olympic opening ceremony. *Journal of Broadcasting & Electronic Media, 35,* 75–94.

McAllister, M. P. (1997). Sponsorship, globalization, and the Summer Olympics. In K. T. Frith (Ed.), *Undressing the ad: Reading culture in advertising* (pp. 35–63). New York: Peter Lang.

McAllister, M. P. (1998a). College bowl sponsorship and the increased commercialization of amateur sports. *Critical Studies in Mass Communication, 15*(4), 357–381.

McAllister, M. P. (1998b, April 2). *Super Bowl advertising as commercial celebration.* Paper presented at the annual meeting of the Broadcast Education Association, Las Vegas, NV.

McCollom, R. H., & McCollom, D. F. (1980). Analysis of ABC-TV coverage of the 21st Olympiad, Montreal. *Journal of Sport & Social Issues, 4*(1), 25–33.

Moragas Spa, M., Rivenburgh, N. K., & Larson, J. F. (1995). *Television in the Olympics.* London: John Libby.

Nelson, J. (1995, August 8). NBC shells out $1.27 billion for pair of Olympics. *Herald Times,* p. B1.

Nelson, W. L. (1998). *A content analysis of the language used by NBC commentators during the 1996 Summer Olympics Games.* Unpublished master's thesis, San Diego State University, San Diego.

O'Neal, M., Finch, P., Hamilton, J., & Hammonds, K. (1987). Nothing sells like sports. *Business Week,* 48–53.

Owens, J. W., & Bryant, J. (1998, April). *The on-air promotion of college and professional football: A content analysis.* Paper presented at the annual meeting of the Broadcast Education Association, Las Vegas, NV.

Petrozzello, D. (1998, August 31). Basic cable beats broadcast networks for week. *Broadcasting & Cable,* 13.

Puijk, R. (1997). *Global spotlights on Lillehammer.* Belfordshire, England: John Libby.

Rader, B. G. (1993). *American sports: From the age of folk games to the age of televised sports* (2nd ed.). Englewood Cliffs, NJ: Prentice Hall.

Real, M. R. (1989). *Super media: A cultural studies approach.* Newbury Park, CA: Sage.

Real, M. R., & Mechikoff, R. A. (1992). Deep fan: Mythic identification, technology, and advertising in spectator sports. *Sociology of Sport Journal, 9,* 323–339.

Riggs, K. E., Eastman, S. T., & Golobic, T. S. (1993). Manufactured conflict in the 1992 Olympics: The discourse of television and politics. *Critical Studies in Mass Communication, 10,* 253–272.

Sabo, D., Jansen, S. C., Tate, D., Duncan, M. C., & Leggett, S. (1996). Televising international sport: Race, ethnicity, and nationalistic bias. *Journal of Sport & Social Issues, 20,* 7–21.

Sandomir, R. (1992, August 11). 16 days staring blearily at the TV. *New York Times,* p. B12.

Schlosser, J. (1998, August 17). Wrestling with success. *Broadcasting & Cable,* 22–27.

Schneider, S. E. (1998, April). *Is she or isn't she? Media fans address the "image problem" in women's sports.* Paper presented at the annual meeting of the Broadcast Education Association, Las Vegas, NV.

Stevenson, D. (1997). Olympic arts: Sydney 2000 and the cultural Olympiad. *International Review for the Sociology of Sport, 32*(2), 227–238.

Tuggle, C. A. (1997). Differences in television sports reporting of men's and women's athletics: ESPN *SportsCenter* and CNN *Sports Tonight*. *Journal of Broadcasting & Electronic Media, 41*, 14–24.

Tuggle, C. A., & Owen, A. (1998). *A descriptive analysis of NBC's coverage of the centennial Olympics: "The games of the woman?"* Paper presented at the annual meeting of the Broadcast Education Association, Las Vegas, NV.

Walker, J. R. (1993). Catchy, yes, but does it work? The impact of broadcast network program promotion frequency and type on program success. *Journal of Broadcasting & Electronic Media, 37*, 197–207.

Webster, J. G. (1985). Program audience duplication: A study of television inheritance effects. *Journal of Broadcasting & Electronic Media, 29*, 121–133.

Webster, J. G., & Phalen, P. F. (1997). *The mass audience: Rediscovering the dominant model.* Mahwah, NJ: Lawrence Erlbaum Associates.

Wenner, L. (1989). Media, sports, and society: The research agenda. In L. Wenner (Ed.), *Media, sports, & society* (pp. 13–48). Newbury Park, CA: Sage.

Wenner, L. A. (Ed.). (1998). *MediaSport.* New York: Routledge.

Wise, K. R. (1999, July). *Wrestling, promotion, and ratings.* Paper presented at the International Conference on Sports and Society, Northern Michigan University, Marquette, MI.

Promotion of Theatrical Movies

William J. Adams
Charles A. Lubbers
Kansas State University

Some studio executives are worried. According to Jack Valenti of the Motion Picture Association of America (MPAA), movie budgets in 1997 averaged a record $75.6 million, an increase of 21% from 1996 (Schatz, 1999). Such high costs generate worries about the very survival of some studios because a few box-office bombs can drive a marginal studio into critical financial trouble. Schatz called the current movie industry "a tale of two Hollywoods: One is enjoying the best revenues and explosive worldwide growth, while the other staggers on the verge of collapse because of runaway costs" (p. 26).

How does a studio increase the profit from a successful movie and reduce the amount of loss from a theatrical failure? Promotion. Earnest (1985) noted that "in an age of rapidly spiraling media costs, it is now the rule-of-thumb that media expenditures to launch a motion picture average two-thirds the cost of the movie" (p. 4).[1] That means a $30 million theatrical movie allots about $20 million to in- and out-of-theater marketing and promotion. For domestic movie releases, Zufryden (1996) reported that by 1995, on average, the industry was spending nearly $18 million to market a film and concluded that the cost of movie marketing had more than quadrupled in the last 15 years.

Traditionally, major studios have tried to achieve one massive hit a year (Baird, 1999). Blockbusters such as *Titanic* and *Forrest Gump* are

---

[1]According to Earnest (1985), the break-even point is 2½ times production costs, a multiple that has spiraled up in recent years.

known as "tent-pole" movies because they financially supported everything else at their studios. As in the trade book business and network prime-time television, one financial success permits a number of box-office failures. Baird (1999) reported that Kieran Breen, U.K. marketing director of PolyGram Film International, consistently hammered in the importance of marketing in the movie business today because "the budgets are so big that you can't afford to get it wrong" (p. 29).

Promotion is one of three elements in the overall marketing effort for a movie. The other two are advertising and distribution to theaters. Although advertising and distribution have been the traditional mainstays of movie marketing efforts, recent trends have seen a growth in promotion to the point where it has become as important as advertising. According to Friedman (1997), the amount spent on movie promotion by the big studios at least equals the cost of advertising, adding up to more than $4 billion annually.

This chapter focuses on the promotional aspect of marketing new movies. Because movie promotion differs in many respects from the kinds of promotion discussed in other chapters, and because so little has appeared in the scholarly literature, this chapter provides an extended discussion of promotional techniques in the movie business. Then, one specialized characteristic — the role of the critic — is examined in an original study prepared for this book. As with other chapters, this one concludes with a detailed outline of needed research in movie promotion.

MOVIE PROMOTION RESEARCH

To date, less than a dozen published studies — amid the wealth of academic writing about movies — have dealt directly with aspects of movie promotion. Table 8.1 summarizes the method and findings relevant to promotion for eight of these studies. Although four of the studies are at least 15 years old, and thus their conclusions may not be current, they provide some insight into facets of marketing and suggest varied approaches and hypotheses for subsequent studies.

Although there were some early studies with implications for movie promotion (see, e.g., Burzynski and Bayer's 1977 experiment testing the effects of prior information on subjects' appreciation for motion pictures), few scholars addressed movie marketing (or promotional materials) until the mid-1980s. In the early 1980s, Litman (1983) tested several factors that might account for variations in movie rental revenues. He found that both production costs and critical reviews (as operationalized by the usual star system) had the most impact on rental income, but that the season of release and whether the movie was an Academy Award nominee or winner

TABLE 8.1
Studies of Movie Promotion

Author(s)	Year	Method	Relevant Findings
Litman	1983	Using 125 movies from the 1970s, assessed the importance of plot type, MPAA rating, cast, production cost, type of distributor, and critical reviews to video rental revenue using regression analysis.	Found that production costs of a movie and critical reviews were both positively related to rental income, in particular for science fiction and horror movies; also found that awards and season of release were related to greater rental income.
Faber and O'Guinn	1984	Surveyed 295 students on their use of such sources of information as critical reviews, TV ads, radio ads, magazine ads, previews, friends' comments, spouses' comments, and friends'/experts' comments in relation to potential influence, frequency of use, perceived credibility, and general importance.	Found that interpersonal sources rated higher than mass media sources, but that movie previews were the most useful and important media sources; results showed that previews and all interpersonal sources were used more frequently and viewed as more credible than other sources, and that previews most influence the intention to attend a movie.
Earnest	1985	Case study of the marketing of the first *Star Wars* movie, focusing on prior and postrelease marketing research.	Explained the process of prerelease testing of movie titles, concepts, advertisements, and trailers, and how such testing built buzz and ultimately increased ticket sales; showed how postrelease research and marketing fueled multiple ticket sales to individuals and aided the rerelease of the movie 2 years later.
Eastman, Bradbury, and Nemes	1985	In-theater field experiment with 134 adult subjects using before-and-after questionnaires and manipulating the length and content of movie teasers and trailers for *Thief*.	Showed that previews do increase audience expectations compared to their absence and affect the strength of expectations but not their type on six measured dimensions.

(Continued)

TABLE 8.1
(Continued)

Author(s)	Year	Method	Relevant Findings
Wyatt and Badger	1990	Five-condition experiment testing the influence of level of information (high/low) and kind of evaluation (positive, mixed, negative) on 226 students' self-reports of interest in attending 1 of 12 movies.	Found that reviews with both high information and positive evaluation of a movie led to the most interest in attending the movie, and that reviews with high information alone raised nearly as much interest in attending the movie.
Eliashberg and Shugan	1997	Analysis of box-office revenues for 172 movies and 2,104 reviews by 181 critics to assess support for an influence model and/or a predictor model of critical impact.	Found no significant relationship between content of reviews and first 4 weeks' revenues, but found that the content of reviews modestly predicted box-office revenues. Concluded that the prediction model had merit, but not the influencer model.
Gupta and Lord	1998	Lab experiment using 274 undergraduates that tested placement of products (prominent/subtle) in *Big* and *Project X* compared to a 30-s TV spot; also compared audio, visual, or both stimuli.	Found that prominent placements elicited higher recall than advertisements, which in turn had higher recall than subtle placements; explicit mentions by voice without video reinforcement led to better recall than subtle visual placement without audio reinforcement.
Zufryden	1996	Tested a proposed three-part marketing model using tracking data collected by a market research firm for movies shown in 1993 in France.	Demonstrated the effectiveness of the model's three elements of awareness response, intention response, and ticket response for developing advertising and distribution strategies for films.

impacted rental revenues. This was one of the first studies to illuminate the roles of critics and awards.

About the same time, Faber and O'Guinn (1984) surveyed college students about the mass media and interpersonal sources of information about movies they were exposed to and the degree of influence each had on such factors as frequency of use, perceived credibility, and general importance. Not surprisingly, their results showed that interpersonal sources mattered far more than any mass media sources, but of the latter, previews ranked most influential and credible and were used the most.

Earnest (1985) undertook a case study of the marketing of the original *Star Wars* movie. Analyzing marketing research before and after the movie's release, he concluded that marketing a movie is unlike marketing toothpaste or fast food for four significant reasons. First, a movie is a luxury item. The public does not need movies to ensure its health or well-being. Second, attending a movie usually is an impulse decision. Typically, very little time passes between the decision to attend a movie and the purchase of a ticket. This lack of time means that consumers do little "research" about the product and that decisions generally are based on casually available information within a narrow window of opportunity.[2] Because movie attendance is often on impulse and also because of movies' third unique characteristic — short shelf life — they are heavily advertised in the week prior to release. Moreover, movies usually stay in wide release for only a month or two. Box-office receipts drop substantially after the first week and continue to drop in successive weeks; thus, money must be made quickly — especially on lower quality movies, as poor word of mouth might reduce ticket sales very rapidly. For releases during summertime and the winter holidays, the opportunity for sales peaks, but the competition is stiffest.[3] The fourth special characteristic of movie marketing identified by Earnest is that no brand leaders exist, unlike most consumer or industrial goods and even broadcast and cable television (see discussion of television branding by Bellamy & Traudt, chap. 5, this volume). Earnest pointed out that marketers (and buyers) of other consumer products are aware of the leading competitors, but in the movie industry,

---

[2]Robert Harper, president of worldwide marketing for 20th Century Fox, emphasized the narrow window of opportunity for movie marketing when he noted that "in movie marketing, you're starting from ground zero every week. What you're competing against is other entertainment prospects. You have to convince [the consumer] that the movie is the thing that they want to do above all of the other options that they have. You have to make it urgent and competitive" (quoted in Busch, 1999a, p. S2).

[3]The fact that movie marketing has a very short window of opportunity was echoed by Robert Levin, Sony Pictures Entertainment marketing president, who said that "it [movie marketing] all happens in a very swift period of time. You start with something no one has ever heard of, and then you have to get people to sit up and say that's something I want to see" (quoted in Busch, 1999b, p. S10).

it is difficult to gauge the competition. He concluded that effective postrelease marketing driven by market research actually helped fuel multiple ticket sales to individuals and served effectively as advance promotion for the rerelease of the movie 2 years later.

Recent changes in the industry, however, have challenged Earnest's (1985) assumptions about branding. For example, trade columnist Friedman (1999a) noted that the Imagine studio took the unusual step of promoting itself in a television advertisement. Its :60 spot aired during the 1999 Super Bowl attempted to develop a brand image for the studio as a provider of adult-oriented mainstream comedies. Given the tough competition in the movie industry, other specialty studios may try promoting their images in the media, adopting the classic techniques of branding outlined in chapter 5.

Looking also at previews, a field experiment by Eastman, Bradford, and Nemes (1985) took a very different approach to researching movie promotion by manipulating the theatrical previews for a regional movie premiere of *Thief*. The goal was to assess trailers' impact on audience expectations. Using convenience samples at a suburban first-run theater, Eastman et al. (1985) surveyed 134 incoming attendees on three successive nights about their expectations for the upcoming film. After filling out the pretest questionnaire, one audience was shown a short teaser, another a full-length trailer, and another no preview at all (functioning as a control group). After screening the movie, audience members filled out a posttest questionnaire. Although the researchers expected the longer trailer (as opposed to the teaser or no preview) to heighten audience expectations on six dimensions, to lead to reports of greater strength of expectations, and to generate greater unfulfilled expectations, they found that length was not a significant variable. However, having some kind of preview, compared to none at all, significantly affected audience expectations about suspense, suffering, violence, and romance, but not about action or adult sexual content (although all aspects appeared in the teaser and trailer). Interestingly, all subjects reported that the actual movie more than fulfilled their expectations on most dimensions. They got more action and violence, but less romance and adult sexual content, than they expected. Because audience expectations may have been influenced by such factors as the stars' previous movies as well as by the previews they saw, these results are merely suggestive. Not surprisingly, Eastman et al. (1985) concluded that the previews were not accurate indicators of the movie's content.

In 1990, Wyatt and Badger conducted an interesting experiment in which college students were given brief descriptions of 12 movies and asked to rate their level of interest in seeing each movie. After their initial evaluation, the students were given a review of one movie (included among the 12 in the pretest), and, after reading it, they were asked to rate their level of interest in attending the movie. The reviews varied in level of information (high and low) and evaluation of the movie (positive, mixed, and negative), and a control group received no reviews. Analysis of the posttest responses showed that, not surprisingly, reviews with high information and positive evaluation led to the most interest in attending the reviewed movie, but what was more startling was that higher amounts of information—regardless of evaluation—led to more interest in attending the movie. Wyatt and Badger concluded that actors' and producers' complaints about the negative impact of some critical reviews on box-office revenues were not justified by this research.

In a related study, Cooper-Martin (1992) also looked at the role of movie previews. As in Faber and O'Guinn (1984), Cooper-Martin concluded that previews have much more influence than paid advertising on the decisions of moviegoers.

In their examination of the literature, Eliashberg and Shugan (1997) found few empirical investigations into the factors affecting the box-office success of movies, especially studies accounting for the role of critics. They noted that Burzynski and Bayer (1977) concluded that critics have the greatest impact early in the life of a movie when fewest interpersonal sources of information are available. Eliashberg and Shugan proposed and tested two models: In the first model, critics are presumed to serve as opinion leaders for (influencers of) public opinion because they are regarded by many people as having expertise about movies. In the alternative model, critics can be thought of merely as leading indicators (predictors) of what the subsequent audience response to individual movies will be, and critics can be presumed to have no influence on attendance. To determine whether critics either influence or predict movie attendance, Eliashberg and Shugan collected box-office ticket data for 172 films released in 1991 and early 1992 and 2,104 reviews of the same movies published from 1990 to 1993. Their results revealed no significant relationships between reviews and early (first 4 weeks) box-office revenues, thus failing to support the influencer model, but they found some support for the predictor model. Cooper-Martin (1992) also found no significant connections between critics' reviews and the choices of moviegoers.

Because the subject had drawn considerable media attention, Gupta and Lord (1998) looked at the placement of commercial products with visible logos and company names in movies and television shows (see also Gupta & Gould, 1997). They argued that most evidence for the effectiveness of product placement has come from anecdotes to date, even though advertisers spend millions of dollars placing their wares in films and programs (see also Karrh, 1994; Vollmers & Mizerski, 1994). Gupta and Lord's laboratory experiment, using recall of a product as the dependent measure, compared various placements within a movie to the usual :30

television commercial and involved manipulating the salience of the product as well as the type of stimulus. They demonstrated the advantages of prominent over subtle product placement and the effectiveness of explicit audio mentions of a product over merely showing it on the screen without reinforcement. Television commercials were found to be less effective than prominent placement of the item but more effective than subtle placement, perhaps because they usually combine multiple reinforcements.

In another recent analysis, Zufryden (1996) examined the relationship of advertising to ticket sales for new movie releases using commercially collected tracking data from a huge sample (400 moviegoers per week) who attended any of 63 movies that played in the French theaters during the period from January to June of 1993. He analyzed the factors of awareness and intention to attend a movie using these data, in addition to information on ticket sales, number of screens, advertising expenditures, and genre classification for each film obtained from studio research departments. Zufryden showed how his three-part model involving awareness, intention, and ticket purchasing was effective for developing strategies for advertising and distribution of movies.

Collectively, such studies reveal a variety of directions for research but merely scratch the surface of what can be explored. Because readers have probably been exposed to very little research on movie marketing, the next section of the chapter provides some general background on conventional practices in the area of movie promotion.

MOVIE MARKETING

Drawing primarily on trade sources, this section looks first at the kinds of content in promotional messages, next at general techniques for promoting entertainment, and finally at techniques specific to the movie business. Altogether, this section provides a crash-course in movie promotion that is essential as background to understanding the business and conducting applied research that will be meaningful.

Promotional Content

Although the kinds of content included in advertising and promotion for a movie depend to some extent on the nature of the movie, generally, the two broad content elements that are emphasized are the production and the stars. These emphases usually apply in both domestic and international marketing.

Anything unusual or trendy about the movie or its production process makes excellent fodder for promotion. For example, press releases for movies normally include an outline of a movie's plot, but they will focus on the story's historical foundation or its connection to real happenings or current events, discuss unusual production achievements or problems, give facts about (enormous) production costs, and so on. Any information that can help create anticipation for the movie is appropriate. The movie *Waterworld* provides an example of how even bad press can help a movie. An incredible amount of media attention was devoted to the movie's schedule delays and budget overruns, but such media attention helped to spur public awareness and probably led to an increase in box-office receipts (Giobbe, 1995).

The bulk of promotional material, however, profiles or highlights the actors in a movie. Hollywood learned long ago that it can sell movies by selling their stars. Very famous stars (and some directors) have great box-office appeal, and these stars become the focus of promotional efforts. Granatstein (1998) commented on the varied ways movie stars and other celebrities are featured on magazine covers, noting that the promotion often has little or nothing to do with the star's role in a particular movie, although the movie's promoters supply the photographs and information to the magazines. Their goals may be merely to draw attention to a particular star or to manipulate the star's image with moviegoers.

Some cynics in the promotion business suspected that actor Hugh Grant's arrest for soliciting a prostitute was an orchestrated event to promote the release of his next movie, *9 Months*, and to modify his "good boy" image. Media requests to cover the film's opening soared following the incident (Michael, 1996). In another example, Paul Reubens, aka Pee-wee Herman, temporarily dropped out of public view following his 1991 arrest for exposure in an adult theater. Even though he had played some television and movie roles during the 1990s, he chose not to talk about the incident for nearly 8 years. Then, shortly before the release of *Mystery Men*, his 1999 comeback movie, Reubens spent a great deal of time discussing the 1991 incident with reporters. The resulting coverage in newspapers and magazines and on television shows was part of the promotional strategy for the movie (Peyser, 1999).

Traditional Promotional Techniques

Certain promotion techniques can be used to promote just about anything. Table 8.2 highlights the traditional techniques of entertainment promotion, many of which apply to television programs as well as theatrical movies.

As the table shows, print tactics are the foundation of the promotion field and consist of three main types. First, news releases can be used to discuss everything from celebrity marriages to drug and alcohol treatment. Second, feature stories supply details about prominent and aspiring stars or provide background on a social or political issue that is addressed

TABLE 8.2
Traditional Promotional Techniques

Print Tactics

1. News releases: "Ready-to-print" news stories written in journalistic style.
2. Feature stories: Longer stories profiling individuals or providing background information on some aspect of a movie.
   a. Bios: Brief biographies of the stars or director, usually including pictures and filmographies.
   b. Backgrounders: Printed handouts elaborating on a movie's history, relevance to a social issue, or relationship to current events.
3. Media kits: Packets of print, audio, and video materials provided to the media, often in conjunction with news conferences, movie premieres, or other media events.

Audio/Visual Tactics

1. Satellite media tours: Interviews with movie stars and directors conducted via satellite, avoiding travel by either the subjects and the interviewers, but providing access by entertainment reporters around the world.
2. Media interviews: Face-to-face or telephone interviews with media reporters to drum up interest in and awareness of a new movie.
3. Press parties and junkets: Receptions for the press in social settings that permit the reporters to interact informally with stars and have pictures taken. A junket is a more extravagant version of a press party in which reporters are transported to some other location for a special event, such as a news conference or a movie premiere.
4. Video news releases: Packages of video materials distributed via tape or satellite providing a full-motion video news story, accompanied by a number of supporting materials useful for composing stories about the movie.
5. Web pages: Portions of Internet sites that give members of the media and the public extensive promotional material about a movie, generally maintained by a studio, distributor, or group of fans. Some sites incorporate e-mail to provide the appearance of direct access to stars and producers/writers.

in an upcoming movie or that ties the movie to current events. Such promotion creates public awareness that should lead to ticket sales.

Most movie consumers are familiar with the tactics listed in the Audio/Visual section of Table 8.2. The first three consist of ways that actors and directors interact with the media. Satellite media tours, for example, offer entertainment reporters and talk-show hosts the opportunity to conduct interviews without the expense of travel to Southern California. Studios will buy satellite time and set up times for local television entertainment reporters to conduct individual video interviews with stars from a movie being promoted. The studio's expense is minimal considering that such satellite time usually results in lengthy stories about a new movie on television stations in major markets.

Stars often make the talk-show circuit as a way of promoting a movie, and such traveling appearances are written into some actors' contracts. A press party or junket reverses the process, bringing the reporters to a location to interact with a movie's cast or crew in a more-or-less social setting. Often as part of the junket, stars are made available to reporters for one-on-one interviews. The usual pattern is that individual reporters are brought into video-equipped rooms to conduct a short, carefully timed interview with one star, and each reporter is handed a tape of the interview as he or she leaves (or the tape is sent back to the reporter's station). One star can do up to 100 of these seemingly "personal" interviews in a weekend.

As noted in Table 8.2, video news releases (VNRs) are sets of promotional materials distributed via tape or satellite that offer full-video news stories featuring such aspects of production as innovations in special effects, the difficulties of filming in exotic locations, and so on. The Nielsen ratings show that television viewers who watch entertainment news programs find such stories extremely interesting, and, of course, VNRs fill airtime at no cost to the station. Although the cost of producing a VNR can be considerable for smaller organizations, the payoff for large studios wishing to promote a release can be considerable. For example, Disney hired Perri-Pharris to produce a 1988 VNR that highlighted Mickey Mouse's trip to Moscow for the purpose of announcing the release of several Disney movies in the (former) Soviet Union (Perri, 1992). Stories from this VNR appeared in hundreds of television news programs, including on CNN and *Entertainment Tonight.* Media Link, a viewership monitoring organization, estimated that the stories reached 57 million viewers in the United States and an additional 155 million viewers internationally (Perri, 1992). This information had the added bonus of being carried as news, not advertising. Thus, the stories were seen as "objective news" by television viewers, although they had negligible cost to Disney.

The fifth of the traditional audio/video techniques has now become the use of web pages. Although web pages are relatively new compared to the other traditional tactics (see Ferguson, chap. 11, this volume), the Internet has quickly become an integral part of many promotional campaigns, including the promotion of movies. Internet writer Evans (1997) reported that Warner Bros.' web site attracted as many as 30 million users, and it had the practical value of cutting promotional costs.[4] Evans noted that 60 television news broadcasts covered an online chat with actor Kevin Costner. He also pointed out that marketing directors are particularly interested in the web because its demographics resemble those of moviegoers and because the web is particularly good at reaching the college student market. Prochnow (1998) discussed several marketing applications of web pages.

---

[4]According to Evans (1997), "Less than two years after its November 1995 launch, the Warner Bros. Online site is attracting 30 million visitors a month. . . . Don Buckley, senior vice president of theatrical marketing and new media, found the site to be cost-effective in the way it has helped build interest in Kevin Costner's new film, *The Postman,* scheduled for a Christmas release. . . . The expenses were minimal, requiring only a few thousand dollars' worth of satellite time" (pp. 50–51).

They can be used as electronic fan magazines or as a single-focus site devoted to the hype of an upcoming movie; such sites usually appear about a month before the movie opens. Other movie sites, often associated with major studios, increase box-office sales by promoting online chats, much as studio web sites do for some television series (see chap. 11).

Sacharow (1997) lamented the Internet's lost potential as its own unique entertainment medium. As she put it, "Rather than using the net as a new entertainment medium, a new place to pull in eyeballs with proprietary content, the web remains, for most studios, a pure promotional vehicle for movies" (p. 31). The success of *The Blair Witch Project*, a 1999 sleeper hit, may have signaled a new direction. This offbeat mystery was reportedly shot for only $30,000, and according to Leland (1999), because it earned about $48 million in its first week, it may have been the most successful movie ever based on its production-cost-to-revenue ratio. Leland argued that the real lesson learned by Hollywood executives from *Blair Witch* was that the Internet has incredible power. In his words, "The film's web site—with its police reports and newsreel-style interviews—is no more or less the work of art than the movie itself, and it creates the illusion that everything in *Blair Witch* was real" (p. 51). Leland also reported that one studio marketing head said that ". . . this was a web site that was an entertainment experience in itself. The movie was an extension of the website, not the other way around. That's what was new" (p. 55).

Movie-Specific Techniques

Although the entertainment industry employs all the traditional promotional techniques, what makes movie promotion so interesting is the use of specialized techniques. Table 8.3 summarizes eight of the more common specialized techniques.

Premieres, Awards, Cross-Media, and Previews

Publicists use movie premieres, or opening nights, to generate media coverage about motion pictures. A premiere is an example of a pseudo-event—an event created to attract media attention. The publicist orchestrates the event to showcase the stars, hoping that the resulting publicity will help to persuade individuals to see a movie. At a premiere, stars are often led through a line of reporters to be photographed and to answer questions. Another method is to have stars field questions in the format of a news conference in hopes of increasing the number of stories about the movie. In 1995 alone, there were over 400 opening nights in Hollywood (Michael, 1996).

Award shows, such as the Academy Awards and Golden Globe Awards, attract enormous live television audiences and large amounts of media

TABLE 8.3
Specialized Movie Promotion Techniques

Movie premieres: Staged events (pseudoevents) designed to showcase the celebrities in a movie and to draw media attention to the fact that a movie has opened.

Award shows and festivals: Staged presentations of awards, usually televised, that are sponsored by film critics, trade associations, or individuals in the movie industry, and film festivals (especially juried festivals), offering the studio opportunities for creating awareness and increasing interest in a movie.

Cross-media promotion: Advertising and publicity about movies on television programs, online, and in newspapers and magazines devoted to covering entertainment.

Previews/trailers: Short clips of movies shown prior to another feature film to encourage audience interest.

Merchandising: Creating (or licensing others to create) merchandise based on a movie, ranging from coffee mugs and T-shirts to elaborate live attractions at theme parks.

Promotional tie-ins: Partnerships between movie producers and other commercial companies (or groups) designed to promote and financially benefit both organizations, most commonly between movie studios and fast-food and beverage companies.

Product placement: Using real products or services in a movie so that business names/logos are incorporated into the story line.

Critics: Reports, generally brief, about the content of new movies, usually including a ratings system (1 star, 2 stars, etc.), creating awareness about a movie and often serving as a component in the process of selecting a movie for some moviegoers. Longer reviews evaluate movies' value and place them within the context of the broad history of cinema.

---

coverage. In addition, such prestigious film festivals as Cannes and Sundance offer increased awareness of individual theatrical movies. Awards can increase audience size and thus box-office receipts. It is commonly thought that, in addition to increasing movie attendance, winning a major award predicts a movie's likelihood of winning other awards. The more awards, the greater the media buzz associated with a movie. Festivals offer the added advantage of allowing small independent companies the opportunity to attract a distributor for their films (see Schamus, 1999, for a description of how the Cannes Film Festival was the springboard for his film, *Happiness*).

It is becoming increasingly difficult to draw the boundaries between the various media. One of the most obvious examples of media melding occurs in movie coverage in newspapers, magazines, television, and web pages. These media devote a great deal of attention to entertainment, in general, and movies, in particular. Most of the efforts devoted to traditional promotional tactics — those described in Table 8.2 — are attempts to generate coverage in other media. News releases, for example, can lead to newspaper and magazine stories; a VNR can become a segment on a popular television entertainment program.

Previews, on the other hand, are within-medium promotion. In the forms of teases and trailers, they directly target moviegoers at a time when they have already expressed interest in attending at least one movie. Previews of upcoming movies appear weeks, even months, prior to the movie's release, and last merely 2 to 5 min (Eastman et al., 1985). Their purpose is to provide exciting moments from the film in an attempt to develop audience awareness and ultimately lead to attendance (Burzynski & Bayer, 1977).

Arthur Cohen, president of worldwide marketing for Paramount Pictures, explained movie promotion in terms of closure of incomplete circles (Friedman, 1999c). According to Cohen, when a circle is not completely drawn, viewers will continue to complete it, which he likened to the operation of previews. Ideally, a preview provides enough material to tease consumers, but not so much as to create undue expectations. The marketing effort for the 1998 release of *Godzilla* failed Cohen's undue test and was harshly criticized by the press for being overhyped (Busch, 1999b).

Merchandising, Tie-Ins, and Product Placements

The phenomenon of business synergy in support of profit is particularly apparent in the movie industry, as the profitability of merchandising, product tie-ins, and product placement reveals. Merchandising refers to creating or licensing others to create merchandise based on a movie. Although adult moviegoers pay little attention to this aspect of modern movie promotion, it offers large financial rewards for studios and their licensees. The king of merchandising, Disney, produced an extraordinary 186 items associated with *The Lion King*. A year after its release, the movie was turned into a Broadway show, and the *Economist* reported that the only way out of the theater was through a shop selling *Lion King* merchandise (Business, 1998). It is clear that the major media organizations have moved beyond making movies and publishing books into creating brands — such as Viacom's *Rugrats* and Time Warner's *Batman* — to exploit through movies, broadcast and cable television, publishing, theme parks, music, the Internet, and merchandising (see Bellamy & Traudt, chap. 5, this volume). Soter (1992) noted that while the movie *Batman* earned its original owner, Warner Bros., $251.1 million in its initial theatrical release, "an additional $500 million came from the sale of licensed t-shirts, coffee mugs, soundtrack albums, cereal, and other gimmicks tied into the movie" (p. 10).[5]

---

[5]Although merchandising appears to be a great asset to a studio's bottom line, the same cannot be said for all the merchandise licensees. According to Friedman (1999c), flops with toy ventures for *Godzilla* and *Babe II* drove Equity Marketing, a major toy licensee, out of show business merchandise. David Lieboweitz of Burnham Securities offered a concise reason for Equity Marketing's failures: "If you don't succeed on the silver screen, it's very hard to have merchandise jump off the shelves" (Friedman, 1999c, p. 12).

Merchandising takes other directions, too. Studios with extensive archives of old movies are now making money by offering video collections through discount stores (Scally & Heller, 1998), and theme parks and movie-based adventures are another source of income (Oliver, 1998). But the hottest new profit center is in music tied to movies. In 1998, 61 million (8.6%) of the 711 million units of music sold in the United States were soundtracks (Freeman, 1999), revealing the immense popularity of the soundtracks from such movies as *Hope Floats*, *Titanic*, and *Dr. Dolittle.*

Closely allied to merchandising is the use of promotional tie-ins, which are partnerships developed with other organizations designed to promote both of the organizations. Product tie-ins are most common between film studios and fast-food or beverage companies, and one recent success for Burger King was its tie-in with *Rugrats*. In an interview, Burger King's head of marketing said the tie-in led to significant increases in Kid's Meal sales and that "Rugrats wrist-watches are flying out of our restaurants" ("Play Food," 1999, p. 16).[6] Successes with toys for children have led fast-food chains to broaden their marketing ties with movie studios and go beyond offering movie-based premiums (Edwards, 1999). Recent industry efforts have targeted adults with tie-ins (Wood, 1996) and new technology organizations (Warner, 1998). Traditionally peaking in the summertime, for a recent year, Friedman (1997) reported that "industry estimates are that $750 million to $1.5 billion in consumer promotions will be tied-into movies between Memorial Day and Labor Day" (p. 37). Driven by intense competition, studios have lately begun expanding into tie-ins in other seasons of the year.

The third prong of the marketing fork, product placement, refers to the use of real products or services with recognizable business names/logos in an entertainment medium. In movies, real cans of Coke, boxes of Cheerios, or BMW cars can be incorporated into the story line, with payoffs for the supplier in increased brand awareness, reinforcement of existing images, and improved brand definition (Hart, 1996), while the studio benefits from free or low-cost products and the creation of realistic props and atmospheres.[7] For example, the U.S. military cannot pay cash for

---

[6]This success followed an earlier hit tie-in with *The Lion King*. "Put simply, the eight-week BK–Lion King promotion, with its integrated advertising and merchandising bells and whistles, gets scored as one of the most profitable events in BK history: total customer traffic up 19%; kids' meal unit volume up 25% and sales up 10%; and a whopping 50 million premiums blown out the doors" (Benezra, 1995, pp. 21–22).

[7]For enhancing the bottom line, product placement makes a great deal of sense. BMW vehicles and Omega watches reaped benefits from their placement in the recent James Bond movie, and Bond's use of several BMW vehicles was valued as being worth $100 million by BMW, and Omega saw a 40% increase in sales after the film was released (Stewart-Allen, 1999).

product promotion, but it can offer the military hardware necessary for movie realism (Newman, 1997). According to Stewart-Allen (1999), because movies reach a younger audience, they are a particularly effective promotional vehicle for the military. Product placement necessarily threads a fine line between advertising and entertainment.

To effectively build a brand image, scholars have concluded that a product's appearance in a film must be subtle. In his review of *Austin Powers, The Spy Who Shagged Me*, Corliss (1999) called the product placement and cross-promotion in this film anything but subtle: "Some stars might balk at product placement; Myers not only puts a Heineken joke in the film . . . but touts the beer in print ads and TV spots. There's also a plug for 'Virgin Shaglantic' " (p. 71).[8]

The growing popularity of product placement has led some movie studios to pitch packages that combine placement and tie-in promotions. Stanley (1998) noted that Warner Bros. lined up a number of partners for the 1998 release of *Lethal Weapon 4*. Most of the partnerships were ". . . pitched to brands as a placement/promotion deal, an approach that's gaining momentum in Hollywood" (p. 3). Merchandising, promotional tie-ins, and product placement are all ways for the movie studio to promote an upcoming movie and to increase the profits generated by the movie. The goal, of course, is to create a box-office hit. If the box-office performance fails to meet expectations, merchandising, tie-ins, and product placement offer revenue to offset losses. A recent investigation by Pardun and McKee (1999) showed that public relations firms are also becoming active players in the decision about whether to use product placements in various media.

Critical Evaluation

Movies, as a product for promotion, are unlike other consumer products in one special way: Neutral — or not so neutral — evaluations rarely have much influence on the public's decisions to purchase most consumer products. However, critics blanket newspapers, magazines, and television with evaluations of movies, and many viewers say critical opinion is extremely important to making their viewing choices.

---

[8]Consumer products are not the only placements in movies. For example, the international accounting firm KPMG made deals to have its name slotted into 18 movies destined for international release. KPMG paid a fee for this and also made their offices in 147 countries available as shooting locations. According to KPMG's international marketing chairman, films are so attractive as a marketing outlet because "they are seen in so many countries. Not only that, they have a seven-to-ten-year life span because they go from cinemas to video, then to cable and satellite. Finally, they get repeated on television" (Edwards, 1997, p. 14).

That some movie critics are seen as highly credible sources by many American moviegoers is unquestionable, and critic Gene Siskel's death was mourned by many television viewers and newspaper readers. Fitzgerald (1999) summarized the influence of Siskel and Ebert as follows: "Combining the depth and knowledge of their newspaper reviews with an entertainingly bickering on-air style, the taller, thinner Siskel and the shorter, portly Ebert went on to create the thumbs up/thumbs down judgments that became a 'see it/don't see it' signal for millions of moviegoers" (p. 25). Silver's 1995 review of a book written by legendary *New Yorker* movie critic Pauline Kael provides further evidence of critics' influence: "The notion of the movie critic as 'consciousness-raising' guru is indissolubly linked to the name of Pauline Kael. In her generation-long career at the *New Yorker*, Kael acquired a following second to none among literate moviegoers" (p. 57). Although most movie critics lack the prestige and authority of a Siskel or Kael, the advent of Internet movie review sites ("Screen Surfer," 1996) and the plethora of broadcast and print outlets providing movie reviews has made critical comment abundant and easily available to moviegoers. Evidence that the studios continue to believe in their power comes from the fact that, when favorable, movie promotional materials prominently feature critical reviews (Reina, 1996).

AN ASSESSMENT OF THE CRITIC'S PROMOTIONAL ROLE

Because it is widely believed in the industry that critics have some impact on how a motion picture does in the marketplace (see Litman, 1983; Faber & O'Guinn, 1984), critics are given free access to early screenings of new movies, and good reviews often lead to the overhaul of promotional campaigns or the creation of a second wave of posters and advertisements that take advantage of what the critics had to say. Critics are thought to influence the giving of motion-picture awards and to set trends in movie attendance. Inasmuch as the amounts of violence and sexual content in the American media are issues of widespread public concern, the degree of critics' influence on the choices made by millions of moviegoers is of significance to society as well as to the movie industry.

Although public access to critical opinion has also increased dramatically over the last few decades, the studies detailed earlier in this chapter revealed only modest empirical evidence supporting the assumption that critical opinion has a significant impact on movie attendance. Eliashberg and Shugan (1997) found that critics merely give advance notice of public opinion rather than influence audiences themselves; Cooper-Martin (1992) also found no significant connection between critics and the choices of moviegoers. Indeed, Cooper-Martin and Faber and O'Guinn (1984) found that movie previews were more important in influencing movie-goers' choices than critics' reviews. However, Wyatt and Badger (1990) demonstrated that reviews—even mixed and negative reviews—can increase readers' interest in seeing movies. Although Reddy, Swaminathan, and Motley (1998) found that critics do have a significant impact on the success of Broadway shows, the differences between live theater in one metropolitan area and widely released movies call into question the applicability of this research. Similarly, in addition to the passage of time, differences between video rentals and theater attendance make Litman's (1983) findings problematic when generalized to movie attendance. Nonetheless, Litman showed that the star system of ratings assigned by critics had a positive and significant impact on revenue from movies and that being either an Academy Award nominee or winner was significantly and positively related to the movie rental income. Moreover, Litman noted that each additional star in a rating increased video rentals of a movie by over $3 million. In the same vein a decade later, Sochay (1994) showed that awards, the movie's genre, MPAA ratings, and time of release were all significant predictors of box-office returns.

To date, evidence for critics' influence on audiences—either directly or via awards or revenues—has been sketchy and somewhat contradictory. Indeed, most research has been anecdotal, qualitative, or proprietary. Reliable assessment of critics' roles necessitates large samples of critical opinons, not just the commentary of a handful of superstars such as Kael or Siskel and Ebert, and requires evaluation over an extended period of time to avoid short-term effects. By far, the preponderance of academic studies of motion pictures adopts a critical or cultural perspective, examining movie content, genres, or a director's oeuvre. A few studies have focused on the financial side of national and international distribution and the economic and cultural impact of foreign imports (see Waterman, 1998/1999). Although these issues are doubtless important, critics' role in influencing American moviegoers should be examined because what they say affects tens of millions of dollars in annual expenditures by studios and producers and, presumably, patterns of movie consumption by audiences.

Using archival methods, this empirical study expands on previous research by exploring the relationship between critical comments and movies' success. Taking a two-pronged approach, it looks at critical commentary in relation to audience behavior as measured by theater attendance and at the influence of critics' predictions about motion pictures.

Research Questions

Three particular sets of questions appeared susceptible to investigation using available archival data, and their answers should provide strong foundations for subsequent empirical studies of critics' roles. First, it seemed important to ask whether positive or negative critical comment actually has affected movie ticket sales on a very large scale. This question might be answered by comparing the content of a large number of reviews with box-office revenues over an extended period of time. Second, the relative impact of different critical media could be assessed. Because newspapers may attract more eminent writers than magazines, and because television attracts more theatrical personalities — seemingly necessitating very different skills than written criticism — a second set of questions arise. Amenable to investigation are what differences a critic's medium makes in impact on movie ticket sales and how nearly critics from different media agree with each other.

Third, because critics are presumed to be experts in the field, their opinions about the quality and importance of particular motion pictures might be expected to have a high degree of accuracy. One set of their opinions that is widely reported in the print and electronic press each year are their predictions for the winners of the Oscars in the annual Academy Awards. But do critics' opinions closely correspond to the awards that are given? Because elements of intra-industry politics affect any one year's winners, this question can best be addressed by comparing critical predictions by major industry groups over many years for the most celebrated of awards, the Oscars.

R1: What is the degree and direction of correlations between ticket sales and critical reviews of major motion pictures?

R2: Are newspaper critics more or less effective than critics for magazines or on television as measured by correlations with box-office attendance?

R3: What percentage of predictions by prestigious critical associations correctly identify the annual Oscar winners?

Methods of Analysis

As operationalized in this study, critical effects on motion pictures were assessed as significant positive correlations between the critics' scores on a scale and total box-office revenues in the United States or internationally. In the second portion of the study, critical effects were assessed as the percentage of the critics' collective ability to predict who won the Oscar each year.

Assessing Revenue Impact

Data for measuring the impact of critical comment on ticket sales were taken from two trade magazines: *Premiere*, which provides a wrap-up of reviews for 100 films from 17 critics in the annual April issue, and *Variety*, which provides a breakdown of domestic and international box-office revenues for each movie. Under the system of evaluation used by *Premiere*, each critic can award 1 to 4 black stars to each film, with 4 stars being the best possible recommendation. Critics may also award 1 to 2 white stars, which mean "A Must to Avoid," in other words, the lowest possible recommendations, thus forming a 6-point scale. The critics represent such magazines as *Time* and *Newsweek*, such newspapers as the *Los Angeles Times* and *USA Today*, and such television programs as *Siskel & Ebert* and *Good Morning America*.

Altogether, evaluations of 400 movies were reported by the magazine. But because some critics reviewed only some of the movies, only a portion of the films could be used in this analysis. If one critic in a division did not review a movie, then the film was recorded as having missing data for that group. If two groups were missing data, however, the film was dropped from the study. Given the small number of critics in the sample, cutting movies with missing data was necessary because the missing data point might have powerfully affected the correlations between critical scores in each group and the two dependent measures: domestic and international box-office revenues. Because of missing data, the study analyzed 189 movies reviewed by all magazine critics, 176 movies reviewed by all newspaper critics, and 200 movies reviewed by all television critics.

Seventeen critics' scores for about 200 individual movies for the 4-year period from 1995 through 1998 (a total of 3,400 evaluations) were summed, by medium, for this study, thus providing sufficient data for tests of statistical significance. The sample of 17 critics consisted of 7 who wrote for newspapers, 6 who wrote for magazines, and 4 who reviewed for television. Each movie could thus have three scores, falling between –14 and 28 for the 7 newspaper critics, between –12 and 24 for the 6 magazine critics, and between –8 and 16 for the 4 television critics, creating a potential total of 600 composite scores.

Total domestic and international revenues generated through ticket sales for each of these pictures was taken from *Variety*'s year-end summaries. But because some movies overlapped 2 years, it was necessary in those cases to research the weekly reports and take the total box-office receipts from the last week in which the film appeared on the chart. Pearson product correlations were used to cross-compare box-office revenues, critical scores, domestic and international revenues, and the three media of magazines, newspapers, and television.

Assessing Award Predictions

Variety also provides a yearly wrap-up of Academy Award predictions made by the five major professional associations comprised of critics: the National Society of Film Critics (NSFC), the New York Film Critics Circle

(NRFCC), the National Board of Review (NBR), the Los Angeles Film Critics Association (LAFC), and the Foreign Press association (FP). For the last 26 years, just before the Oscar ceremony, *Variety* has listed the picks by the NSFC, the NRFCC, the NBR, and GG (meaning the Foreign Press) for best actor, best actress, best supporting actor, and best supporting actress.[9] Twenty years ago (in 1979), *Variety* added the predictions of the Los Angeles association (LAFC), and 10 years ago (in 1989), its editors asked these associations of critics to predict best picture and best director as well. This long record of predictions provided an opportunity to evaluate the accuracy of the critics as groups by comparing the predictions to the Oscar results over a 26-year span.

Results

To answer the three research questions, and of course provoke new questions, the archival data on ticket sales were correlated with the critics' aggregated scores, providing the results immediately below. Following that, the proportions of the Academy Awards correctly predicted by critics employed in each medium are reported.

Results of Revenue Analysis

Table 8.4 shows the correlations between critical scores given collectively by magazine critics, by newspaper critics, and by television critics with the revenues generated at the box office in the United States ("Domestic $" category) and in other countries ("International $" category). In each grouping, the first (top) number is the coefficient for the Pearson correlation between the critics' collective score and another medium (or self if a perfect 1.0) or the revenues reported for the domestic or international market. The second (middle) number is the significance level, and the third (bottom) number tells the quantity of movies evaluated by the critics who work in that medium and who were able to be included in the analysis.

As Table 8.4 shows when examining the bottom section of the table, domestic box-office revenues fail to correlate significantly with magazine critics' scores ($r = -.024$, $p = .743$), with newspaper critics' scores ($r = -.021$, $p = .787$), or with television critics' scores ($r = .057$, $p = .427$). The correlations between critical scores and box-office returns are not only not significant, they approximate zero, meaning that the analysis revealed no relationship (and

---

[9] Because the Foreign Press traditionally makes its Oscar predictions in connection with the association's own annual motion-picture awards, the Golden Globes, the industry tends to refer to these predictions as "the Golden Globes predicting the Oscars." Because of their close connection, *Variety* uses the abbreviation GG instead of FP when referring to the Foreign Press association.

TABLE 8.4
Correlations Between Critics' Scores and Movie Box-Office Revenues

	Critics' Scores			Revenues	
	Magazines	Newspapers	Television	Domestic $	International $
Critics' Scores					
Magazines	$r = 1.0$				
	$N = 189$				
Newspapers	$r = .678$	$r = 1.0$			
	$p = .000$				
	$N = 163$	$N = 167$			
Television	$r = .517$	$r = .563$	$r = 1.0$		
	$p = .000$	$p = .000$			
	$N = 187$	$N = 174$	$N = 200$		
Revenues					
Domestic $	$r = -.024$	$r = -.021$	$r = .057$	$r = 1.0$	
	$p = .743$	$p = .787$	$p = .427$		
	$N = 187$	$N = 174$	$N = 198$	$N = 200$	
International $	$r = .042$	$r = .042$	$r = .040$	$r = .841$	$r = 1.0$
	$p = .584$	$p = .592$	$p = .591$	$p = .000$	
	$N = 171$	$N = 162$	$N = 183$	$N = 184$	$N = 184$

the positive or negative valences have no meaning), providing a tentative answer to the first research question. On the other hand, domestic box office was significantly and positively correlated to international box office ($r = .841$, $p = .000$), a finding that is consistent with previous research (see Waterman, 1998/1999). It corroborates the view that films that are financially successful in the United States are likely also be successful in the rest of the world. If a movie fails here, it will also usually fail elsewhere.

Examination of the correlations between the three media of magazines, newspapers, and television provide an interesting insight. It appears that the critics were generally in agreement about the movies they evaluated. All coefficients exceed 50% ($r = .678$, $r = .517$, $r = .563$), are positive, and are statistically significant. This finding implies that magazine, newspaper, and television critics evaluate movies very similarly nowadays and that there are no outstanding differences in quality or effectiveness between them. The fact that the correlation coefficients were not related to box-office performance suggests that, in the aggregate, critics have had little to do with financial success or failure in the movie business, at least in the last 5 years.

However, financial success is only one way of measuring critical influence. It is not appropriate to conclude that the critics are unimportant to a particular film or to film promotion in general. They may have power over things other than ticket sales. For example, critical opinion is thought to influence major awards.

Results for Award Predictions

This possibility was tested using *Variety*'s annual list of critical predictions for the Oscars by the major trade associations for critics. Their collective predictions were compared to the actual Oscar winners over the 26-year period from 1972 to 1998. Table 8.5 shows the percentage of instances for which each association correctly predicted the Oscar winner in each division. A "+" in the table means that the names of two or more possible winners were regularly submitted for that award. A multiple submission was deemed *regular* when two or more names were given at least 75% of the time. In the case of the Foreign Press, two were always given for most awards.

The results reveal that, over the preceding 10 to 26 years, the top critics in the country have been able to predict Oscar winners, on average, overall, over one third of the time (39%). As Table 8.5 shows, for example, the NSFC members chose the correct winners for best picture an average of just 20% of the time, whereas they chose the correct winners for best actress over 30% of the time (30.8%). On average, overall, the NSFC was correct 25% of the time; the NYFCC was correct 31% of the time; the NBR was correct 38% of the time; the LAFC was correct 38% of the time; and the Foreign Press (GG in the table to conform to industry practice) was correct a whopping 64% of the time. The answer to the third research question thus appears to be 39%, an amount probably much smaller than most experts would estimate.

The Foreign Press (GG in the table), interestingly, shows by far the best record in all categories except best supporting actress. These results seem to corroborate the widespread assumption that the Golden Globe Awards predict the Oscars.

However, this analysis reveals some of the potential pitfalls that face researchers. Because it uses secondary data, the findings are limited by the

TABLE 8.5
Percentage of Correct Oscar Predictions by Critics

	Best Picture	Best Director	Best Actor	Best Actress	Best Supporting Actor	Best Supporting Actress
NSFC	20%	30%	23.1%	30.8%	19.2%	26.9%
NYFCC	20%	20%	46.2%	38.5%	34.6%	26.9%
NBR	50%+	30%	46.2%	34.6%	34.6%+	34.6%+
LAFC	20%	20%	60%+	35%	45%	50%+
GG	70%+	70%+	80.8%+	69.2%+	57.7%+	34.6%

Note. A "+" after a percentage means that more than one name was submitted by that association for that award.

way *Variety* chose to collect the information. In this case, the magazine did not require only one choice for each prediction. The Foreign Press usually submitted two to five names as possible winners, one of whom usually did win. Multiple submissions were also the practice for the National Board of Review and the Los Angeles Film Critics Association in some categories. The percentages in Table 8.5 that are marked with a cross (+) are the cases where more than one name or title was regularly put forth by an association, and the cases of multiple-name submission versus those with only one specific winner dramatically slant the results toward the Foreign Press. In the case of best supporting actress, for some reason, the Foreign Press traditionally submitted only one name, and as a result, its predictions were no more accurate than those of the other associations.

In sum, what the chart actually shows is that when allowed a range of possible winners, the critics can usually pick the Oscar just over half the time (58%), but, when limited to a single name, critics identify the right answer less than one third of the time (31%). That is sufficient to suggest that there may be a positive relationship between awards and critical opinion, but a much weaker one than some in the industry might expect.

Discussion of This Study

Do the results of these analyses imply that critics are largely irrelevant to motion-picture success? Possibly, but such a sweeping conclusion is hardly merited without a great deal more research. It may be that critical evaluations are compelling for some segments of the audience, such as adults with high educational levels and/or high incomes, or with moviegoers who prefer foreign films or art films. This sort of finding would be obscured by the aggregate analysis over time conducted here. Indeed, a year-by-year analysis might isolate different patterns than long-term analyses. An audience group of particular interest to the industry are those enthusiasts who see the same film many times. Critical opinion might be less important than word of mouth for such moviegoers or, on the other hand, it might be the spur to multiple theater visits for some demographic or psychographic subgroups. In conjunction with previous studies, the research presented here provides a start for investigating such questions, but it is evidence that skepticism about movie industry truisms is well warranted.

SUGGESTIONS FOR RESEARCHING
MOVIE PROMOTION

Doing research on movie promotion, as with much of media investigation, is a two-edged sword. On one side, a great deal is going on, and enormous amounts of material are available. Data regarding attendance, ratings, demographics, awards, and so on are regularly compiled and are accessible at relatively low cost in print and online. Thus, the field is wide open for research.

On the other side, very little published research is available. Perhaps even worse, to paraphrase Arnold Becker's comments about television, the promotion people actually doing the work "assume they already know everything of importance and do not want facts that might get in the way of what they already 'know' works" (Gitlin, 1983, p. 60). With hundreds of millions of dollars at stake, it appears that the industry cannot afford a bunch of academics messing around. In short, a great many assumptions persist in the business with very little to back them up. As a result, grant money is scarce, and scholars get only minimal industry encouragement when it comes to working in this field.

As little has been published in the journals, it is also hard to generate interest in the academic world. Researchers find themselves fighting the old catch-22 assumption: If the studies were really important, someone would already be doing them. This means, as far as motion-picture promotion is concerned, that nearly all studies break new ground and must be rooted in general theory about cognition and/or promotion (as discussed by Perse, chap. 2, this volume) as opposed to building narrowly on previous studies.

At the same time, a multitude of interesting questions exist. Which assumptions by the business will hold up? How does movie promotion affect different audiences? Is marketing affected by genre? Which designs work best, and how does the process of influence work?

Locating Research Materials

Researchers need to seek out sources other than journals to build reviews of pertinent literature. Fortunately, such materials exist in abundance. The biggest sources are the popular and trade presses. *Variety*, for example, provides an enormous amount of data concerning movies and marketing. On a weekly basis, it publishes information on the top 60 films in the United States and the rest of the world. It includes lists of distributors, the number of theaters showing the film, the average amount of money being made each week per screen, total box-office take, percentage changes in income from one week to the next, how long each picture has been in release, and so on. Yearly wrap-ups for the top 250 films, breakdowns by studios, direct comparisons of international and domestic box-office revenues and ticket sales, and market shares for each studio are also provided. In addition, feature articles provide a good deal of marketing information, not in terms of how well a campaign worked, but in terms of what it was suppose to achieve.

Such general interest magazines as *Premiere* provide marketing case studies, awards and nominees, examples of promotional materials, and yearly summaries of critical reviews. Video stores stock trade magazines, and movie theaters can supply examples of promotional materials aimed at the industry as well as the public. Promax and C-TAM, two industry trade associations specializing in promotion marketing, can provide a great many examples of movie trailers, press kits, and printed advertising. Other promotional items, such as the posters used to promote films to audiences, are now considered collectibles and a source of merchandising income for the industry. Although widely available, each poster will cost between $15 and $20. Lobby cards, complete press kits, and foreign posters vary in cost from $10 to $50 for new films. The price for materials related to older films usually increases substantially.

Another useful source are the fan clubs centered around individual stars. They can provide materials related to specific motion pictures (much of it accessible online), and broadcast and cable shows about the entertainment business can provide a great deal of video promotional material, usually available only in the few weeks just before the release of a movie. *Austin Powers: The Spy Who Shagged Me*, for example, dominated time on two cable networks, a number of award shows, and every major network and syndicated entertainment show in the week before it was officially released. Many movie studios now maintain official websites for most new pictures, containing press releases as well as streaming video, and accompanied by chat lines, all available for research. So, although the academic world may not as yet be of much direct help, there is no shortage of material for developing studies of movie promotion or its effects.

Research Problems

Although the wide range of available data and materials about movies and the limited amount of existing research leaves virtually any avenue open to study, particular problems need to be taken into account. For starters, because of the limited history of scholarly investigation, many terms used casually in the industry have not yet been well defined. For example, the line between promotion, advertising, and merchandising is very thin and often seems nonexistent (see Eastman, Ferguson, & Klein, 1999). Also universally accepted definitions of such terms as success are lacking, although many assumptions about how promotion works and what it does are widely believed. Researchers must provide their own working definitions based on background research before getting into such practical questions as how to improve a particular type of campaign or which movie content promotion will work best with teenagers. Doing basic research testing widely held industry beliefs has particular scholarly appeal because it ties promotion to the larger theoretical areas of cognitive, perceptual, and effects research, and may make contributions to theory with implications far beyond the field of media promotion.

Questions for Research

The research to date suggests that experimental, survey, interview, and archival approaches, among others, might be fruitful in researching the promotion of movies. For example, a study might follow up on Burzynski and Bayer's 1977 experiment testing the influence of positive and negative prior information about a movie. A word-of-mouth study might look first at the cognitive literature for clues on which to base hypotheses and could then be enlarged to test a variety of current promotional materials. Another needed follow-up should apply Zufryden's 1996 model to American audiences and those of countries other than France. It is possible, even likely, that cultural and economic differences will reveal differential effectiveness for the model. More field testing of different kinds of movie trailers using intact groups of moviegoers should examine the impact of such variables as age, level of education, and place (such as urban, suburban, small town, etc.). Surveys should delve into the use of promotional media related to movie attendance and measure self-reports of the impact of critical opinion. Interviews with retired and practicing professionals in the movie business can help to build up the historical record. In the next section, two sets of empirical studies are described in detail that could be undertaken with readily available materials.

Individual Critics and Genres.   The study previously reported in this chapter dealt with critics and movies in general, and it did not claim that critics lack influence with particular audiences defined demographically or by the genres of films they prefer. The study also did not deal with individual critics. Questions on those topics could be answered relatively easily using the same data sources used to produce the results previously reported in this chapter.

To begin, researchers would first need to categorize films, which presents the first problem, because movies, like television programs, have no universally accepted, or widely used, system for categorizing genres. Any system used would have to take into account obvious categories like Art, Action, Drama, Science Fiction, Comedy, and Romance, as well as whether the film was aimed at children, teenagers, or adults. For example, there is no reason to assume a "sophomoric" comedy like *Animal House* would behave the same as a "romantic" comedy like *Jerry Maguire* in relation to critical influence. Researchers always have to tentatively resolve the tension between having a large number of categories to describe differences and few enough categories so that large samples of each can be located.

Much popular literature also assumes critics have more influence with foreign-made films than with domestic products, so such a basic separation should be considered. MPAA film ratings should also be taken into account. Do parents consider critical reviews more important when deciding on movies for their children than for themselves? On the other hand, perhaps adults especially want a critical stamp of approval when deciding to attend a "dirty movie." The motion-picture rating code might help provide some answers in these areas.

Brief descriptions of the film essential to categorization can be found regularly in *Premiere* magazine or in *Variety*. Critical evaluations, both in depth (for researchers who may wish to analyze the content of the reviews themselves) and by rankings, are published each April in *Premiere* (as used in the study reported in this chapter) and can be found weekly in *Entertainment* magazine and *Variety,* or in any number of major newspapers. The *Premiere* magazine ranking system is very easy to use and goes back well over a decade, covering literally thousands of films.

As reported in the study in this chapter, both international and domestic box-office grosses are reported weekly in *Variety*, and are summed up yearly by that publication, but rather than use the yearly summaries, it is more useful to work backward through the weekly reports looking for the last appearance of a film on the top 100 chart (domestic and international weeks will be different). Once these data and categories are combined with the summed rankings of the critics, correlation analysis will reveal any differences related to genre. Individual critics' rankings can also be separated out to see if one is better at predicting box-office success than another. As the rankings only represent a 6-point scale, analysis of correlations is not the best way to evaluate individual critical ability. However, clustering pictures, say as 1 to 10, 10.1 to 20, 20.1 to 30, and so on, and then using simple F tests to locate significant differences between the critics' mean rankings, would be a possible method for determining individual success rates.

Although demographic data would be ideal for this type of study, the kinds of data described above are what is available. And even though a great many assumptions about "who attends the movies" can be found, very little demographic information exits. Unlike television audiences, such data are not regularly collected for filmgoers. What does exist is proprietary and is often centered around specific films.

Movie Promotion on the Web.   Researching the web should be a useful approach to evaluating theatrical movie promotion. For example, Kuchinskas (1999) argued that although promotional sites have become more and more elaborate, no one knows whether they bring people into theaters. Kuchinskas claimed that the major studios have not yet tried to measure the efficacy of their web sites. Although anecdotal evidence and statistics on the number of hits or length of visits can be collected, to date, no one has related web-site hits to ticket sales. The efficacy of movie web sites is a topic crying for hard data and is certainly amenable to scholarly investigation.

To start with, nearly all U.S.-made movies, most studios, and most medium-to-major acting talents have individual web sites. Nonetheless, little by way of descriptive data has been collected, and it should be understood from the outset that a definitive study of movie promotion on the web is impossible because the medium changes so fast that by the time the study is finished, the web will have already been transformed into something else. That means what are needed are satisfactory benchmark studies to provide a base for tracking change over time — in short, studies that supply snapshots that can be compared to future snapshots. In addition, researchers can begin the process of ascertaining what works and what doesn't when talking about promotion of movies via the web.

First of all, a basic content analysis of web sites should assess the types of information that various entities provide and develop a scale for determining the degree of standardization. Other obvious questions concern the ways in which actors, studios, and specific movie sites relate to each other: What links do they provide? How often are they updated? What happens in their chat rooms? How much does movie genre affect sites? Although such a study would be time-consuming, it would lend itself to student participation after a pilot study had developed the parameter, and a large, in-depth study should provide the benchmark against which future studies would be compared. Secondarily, it would supply the means for studying cross-media uses of the web.

Locating sites is a rather simple process, accomplished with any search engine using movie titles, names of actors and actresses, and studio names. *Premiere* prepares regular reports on upcoming movies that should be useful in tracking when, in the process of releasing films, the web site first appears, how it changes as the actual release date approaches, how long the site stays up, and how it changes based on box-office success or failure. Sites would, of course, have to be distinguished by the producer as either official studio-owned sites or those produced by fans, but tracking the number and type of links between official and fan sites would be an interesting element to include in a base study.

Content analysis should probably begin with the categories used to analyze content in other media. Several category systems have been used in previous research (see, e.g., Walker, chap. 4, this volume), although little of it has been related to promotion on the web of theatrical movies, and thus would have to be adapted based on the findings of a pilot sampling of sites. Despite requirements for breadth and depth, such a study should be limited by a time frame, such as one quarter's upcoming releases (e.g., *Premiere's* fall listing of upcoming winter movies), and then focus on tracing those films through the three stages of prerelease, release, and postrelease. Such an analysis should show how movie web sites develop, mature, and end—a convenient framework.

Another study might focus on the elements comprising successful web-site design. One archival approach might use box-office revenues from *Variety* to separate successful films from financial failures. The related web sites could then be content analyzed to see whether the two kinds reveal significant differences.

Because of the lack of foundational research in this area, the best approach might be to combine focus groups and survey methodology to assess both success in web design and the best media for movie promotion. Such an approach would involve selecting a random sample of web sites, having subjects view them, and then directing discussions about what they like and dislike. The results of the focus groups could then be used to prepare survey instruments that could be used on larger random groups of subjects. These subjects might then be exposed to different types of material and surveyed to produce questionnaire data that could be statistically analyzed to determine which elements and which media seem to be most effective (or salient, see Perse, chap. 2, this volume) when it comes to web promotion.

Participants for focus groups and survey respondents could be recruited at multiplex theaters, thus making sure they were moviegoers. Catching them after a movie would probably ensure that they had some leisure. In focus groups, respondents should be encouraged to discuss how they decide which films to attend, including the impact of trailers, posters, word of mouth, newspaper and television advertising, star appeal, media interviews, news reports, web sites, and so on. Participants could also be polled as to their web use and general knowledge of movie promotional efforts.

Such groups should provide some idea of which aspects of promotion have the most influence on the public, and this information could then be used to develop surveys of larger groups of moviegoers or some demographic group, or could be used to formulate experiments to test individual promotional techniques to see how they work, how they are affected by genre, and how to better use limited resources. Such basic research should show which techniques are overrated, outdated, or ineffective with some groups.

Although the studies described here barely scratch the surface of possible research, they can all be done with existing archival resources. They will also prepare the ground for when more complex analyses are undertaken. Another point to be considered is that such studies as those proposed here would be relatively inexpensive, sometimes a major consideration. In contrast, studies involving real theatrical posters or press kits are certainly possible but costly because of the need to purchase a large sample of materials. An additional point is that much of the work might be accomplished by students who do content analysis or structural coding for a grade. The potential for innovative work in this field is enormous, and because of the lack of competitors at present (as compared to scholars researching children or violence, e.g.), theatrical movie promotion is a field where tyro researchers can make names for themselves while providing a great deal of useful information.

REFERENCES

Baird, R. (1999, January 21). Head for the hills. *Marketing Week*, 26–29.

Benezra, K. (1995, March 20). Burger King/The Lion King. *BrandWeek*, 21–22.

Burzynski, M. H., & Bayer, D. J. (1977). The effect of positive and negative prior information on motion picture appreciation. *Journal of Social Psychology, 101*, 215–218.

Busch, A. M. (1999a, February 1). Creating a cult for "Something about Mary." *Advertising Age*, S2.

Busch, A. M. (1999b, February 1). Package-goods marketing meets retail sales push. *Advertising Age*, S10.

Business: Size does matter. (1998, May 23). *Economist, 347*, 57–59.

Cooper-Martin, E. (1992). Consumers and movies: Information sources for experiential products. In J. F. Sherry & B. Sternthal (Eds.), *Advances in consumer research* (Vol. 19, pp. 756–761). Provo, UT: Association for Consumer Research.

Corliss, R. (1999, June 21). Austin Powers: The spy who shagged me [motion picture review]. *Time*, 71.

Earnest, O. J. (1985). Star Wars: A case study of motion picture marketing. In B. A. Austin (Ed.), *Current research in film: Audiences, economics and law* (Vol. 1, pp. 1–18). Norwood, NJ: Ablex.

Eastman, S. T., Bradbury, D. E., & Nemes, R. S. (1985). Influences of previews on movie viewers' expectations. In B. A. Austin (Ed.), *Current research in film: Audiences, economics and law* (Vol. 1, pp. 51–57). Norwood, NJ: Ablex.

Eastman, S. T., Ferguson, D. A., & Klein, R. A. (Eds.). (1999). *Promotion and marketing for broadcasting and cable* (3rd ed.). Boston, MA: Focal Press.

Edwards, C. (1999, January 4). McD's broadens marketing ties with Disney. *Marketing News*, 27.

Edwards, S. (1997, June/July). Here's looking at you, KPMG. *CA Magazine*, 14–16.

Eliashberg, J., & Shugan, S. M. (1997, April). Film critics: Influencers or predictors? *Journal of Marketing, 61*, 68–78.

Evans, J. (1997, December). Entertainment on demand. *Internet World*, 50–51.

Faber, R. J., & O'Guinn, T. C. (1984). Effect of media advertising and other sources on movie selection. *Journalism Quarterly, 61*, 371–377.

Fitzgerald, M. (1999). Gene Siskel, movie critic. *Editor & Publisher, the Fourth Estate*, 25.

Freeman, L. (1999, February 1). Soundtracks send loud message to bottom line. *Advertising Age*, S12.

Friedman, W. (1999a, February 8). New movie ads build brand of Imagine studio. *Advertising Age,* 18.

Friedman, W. (1999b, February 1). Much more than an iceberg for Paramount mogul. *Advertising Age,* 56.

Friedman, W. (1999c, January 11). Saying goodbye to Hollywood. *Advertising Age,* 12.

Friedman, W. (1997, May 19). Films for all seasons. *BrandWeek, 38*(20), 37–46.

Giobbe, D. (1995, August 19). What is fair game for critics? *Editor & Publisher, the Fourth Estate,* 9–10.

Gitlin, T. (1983). *Inside prime time.* New York: Pantheon.

Granatstein, L. (1998, June 29). Celebrity Jeopardy. *Mediaweek,* 22–23.

Gupta, P. B., & Gould, S. J. (1997). Consumers' perceptions of the ethics and acceptability of product placements in movies: Product category and individual differences. *Journal of Current Issues and Research in Advertising, 19,* 37–50.

Gupta, P. B., & Lord, K. R. (1998). Product placement in movies: The effect of prominence and mode on audience recall. *Journal of Current Issues and Research in Advertising, 20,* 47–59.

Hart, P. (1996, November 18). Product placement come of age in Canada. *Marketing,* 20.

Karrh, J. A. (1994). Effects of brand placements in motion pictures. In K. W. King (Ed.), *Proceedings of the 1994 Conference of the American Academy of Advertising* (pp. 90–96). Athens, GA: American Academy of Advertising.

Kuchinskas, S. (1999, February 8). If studios build them . . . *Mediaweek,* 38–40.

Leland, J. (1999, August 16). The Blair Witch cult. *Newsweek,* 44–51.

Litman, B. R. (1983). Predicting success of theatrical movies: An empirical study. *Journal of Popular Culture, 16*(2), 159–175.

Michael, D. (1996). Hollywood magic. In *CNN Presents.* Atlanta: CNN.

Newman, R. J. (1997, September 1). A few good men with a few good scripts. *U.S. News & World Report,* 32.

Oliver, B. (1998, November 12). Road movies. *Marketing,* 37.

Pardun, C. J., & McKee, K. B. (1999). Product placements as public relations: An exploratory study of the role of the public relations firm. *Public Relations Review, 25*(4), 481–493.

Perri, T. (Producer). (1992). *Demo reel #1* [Video]. (Available from Perri-Pharris Productions, 4590 MacArthur Boulevard, Suite 620, Newport Beach, CA, 92660)

Peyser, M. (1999, August 9). Pee-wee squeaks. *Newsweek,* 72.

Play food. (1999, January 15). *Restaurants and Institutions,* 16.

Prochnow, D. (1998, July/August). Lights, cameras, action. *Link-Up,* 25.

Reddy, S. K., Swaminathan, V., & Motley, C. M. (1998, August). Exploring the determinants of Broadway show success. *Journal of Marketing Research, 35*(4), 370–383.

Reina, L. (1996, August 31). Why movie blurbs avoid newspapers. *Editor & Publisher, the Fourth Estate,* 23.

Sacharow, A. (1997, November 24). That's inter-tainment. *BrandWeek,* 31–32.

Scally, R., & Heller, L. (1998, November 9). Studios trolls archives for anniversaries. *Discount Store News, 37*(21), 42–43.

Schamus, J. (1999, April 5/12). The pursuit of *Happiness:* Making an art of marketing an explosive film. *The Nation,* 34–35.

Schatz, T. (1999, April 5/12). Show me the money: In search of hits, the industry may go broke. *The Nation,* 26–31.

Screen surfer. (1996, May 27). *People Weekly,* 63.

Silver, D. J. (1995, April). She lost it at the movies. *Commentary,* 57–59

Sochay, S. (1994). Predicting performance of motion pictures. *Journal of Media Economics, 7*(4), 1–20.

Soter, T. (1992). At the movies: Marketing lessons from tinseltown. *Management Review, 81*(11), 10–15.

Stanley, T. L. (1998, March 23). Placement/promo deals lure Lethal partners. *BrandWeek,* 3.

Stanley, T. L. (1995, January 30). Movie goes bust. . . . Promo goes boom. *BrandWeek,* 20–24.

Stewart-Allen, A. L. (1999, February 15). Product placement helps sell brand. *Marketing News,* 8.

Vollmers, S., & Mizerski, R. (1994). A review and investigation into the effectiveness of product placements in films. In K. W. King (Ed.), *Proceedings of the 1994 Conference of the American Academy of Advertising* (pp. 97–102). Athens, GA: American Academy of Advertising.

Warner, B. (1998, November 30). Who oughtta be in pictures? *BrandWeek,* 42–44.

Waterman, D. (1999). Digital television and program pricing. In D. Gerbarg (Ed.), *The economics, technology, and content of digital TV* (pp. 181–195). Boston: Kluwer. (Reprinted from *Prometheus,* 1998, *16*(2), 185–195)

Wood, N. (1996, December). Real promos for adults: Movie promotions grow up and target Hollywood's over-18 crowd. *Incentive,* 38–39.

Wyatt, R. O., & Badger, D. P. (1990). Effects of information and evaluation in film criticism. *Journalism Quarterly, 67,* 359–368.

Zufryden, F. S. (1996, July/August). Linking advertising to box office performance of new film releases: A marketing planning model. *Journal of Advertising Research, 36*(4), 29–41.

9

Television Newscast Promotion and Marketing

Joseph G. Buchman
Utah Valley State College

Perhaps no area of mass media marketing has generated more unresolved controversy than that of the promotion and marketing of broadcast news (Barnow, 1966; Spragens, 1995). Conflicts between objective journalism, or the role of the media as a "fourth estate" of government, and the marketing strategies required for audience acquisition, audience retention, and revenue maximization during news programming appeared as issues in the very earliest literature of broadcasting and journalism (Lippmann, 1922). Discussion of these issues has been addressed in foundational scholarly research (see Bogart, 1980) and has served as the basis for fictional plots for such contemporary mainstream entertainment as the movies *Network* and *Broadcast News* as well as episodes of such television programs as *The Mary Tyler Moore Show*, *WKRP in Cincinnati*, *Murphy Brown*, and *NewsRadio*.

Similarly, the line between news and marketing *within* newscasts has been controversial since the very inception of broadcasting (Small, 1970). Distinctions between news content and marketing materials in the form of both promotion and advertising have become even more blurred over time (Boorstin, 1961; Geller, 1996). Today, news promotion is commonly presented as if it were news itself, especially when promoting subsequent news-related programming. Is it news or promotion, for example, when Peter Jennings tells his audience what is coming up on *Nightline*, when Tom Brokaw spends a minute describing a new weeklong investigative series, or the local 6:00 p.m. anchor teases a new story for the 11:00 p.m. newscast?[1]

After a brief review of current U.S. industry practices related to news promotion, this chapter examines some of the recent research about television newscasting and applies its results to station and network news promotion. This section is followed by a detailed review of those few studies that deal directly with television newscast promotion. Next, the chapter reports a content analysis of local television news promotion, and it closes with questions that future research about news promotion might address.

NEWS PRACTICES AND RESEARCH

For the vast majority of television stations offering local news, the newscast itself has become the primary tool for creating the station's overall image or brand (Minnucci, 1991). This newscast-created brand serves as the benchmark for the station's overall marketing strategy. Often station newscasters are used in general station promotion as embodiments of the desired brand image of the station itself. Moreover, promotion within a newscast is likely to be perceived as more credible than promotion offered within entertainment programming. Indeed, some advertising professionals actually prefer a news environment for their commercials (Buzzard, 1990). The same effect holds true for promos, which are basically commercials for the station itself or its programs. Synergistic effects have been demonstrated between the commercial announcement and newscast program material. This effect is typically seen in heightened audience attentiveness during news-related programming and increased subsequent recall (Buchman, 1999; Warner & Buchman, 1993). Making use of a newscast environment for promotional purposes is not limited to broadcasters within the United States. A 5-year study of the *CNN World Report* found international broadcasters tended to choose stories that, in effect, marketed their nations to potential tourists and investors by presenting their nations in more favorable lights (Lee, Algan, & Flournoy, 1997).

The extraordinarily low production cost of news programming, on average one tenth the cost of a network dramatic or sitcom series, provides a

---

[1]One potent sign of the closer relationship between promotion and news can be found in the offering of sessions at professional meetings of the major news associations (Richter, 1997). For example, recent Radio-Television News Directors Association (RTNDA) and Promax conventions have offered such news promotion-oriented topics as, "News & Promotion: Creating a Winning Team," "News Promos That Make Your Audience Laugh . . . And Your Competitor's Weep," and "Three Steps to Winning the Late Night News War: From Positioning Your Late News Attributes to Maintaining All-Out Episodic/Topical Blitzes" (RTNDA, 1999; Promax, 1999). Such conference topics illustrate the industry's recognition of the importance of positioning and promoting.

powerful monetary incentive to broadcasters to tailor some news programming, or programming positioned as news, to advertiser and audience desires (Kneale, 1989). Active promotion becomes the means for
gathering the audiences for those advertisers. In recent years, stations and
networks have adopted audience-flow strategies that encourage a seamless transition from daypart to daypart, from program type to program
type, and thus from entertainment to news, and news back to entertainment (Eastman & Ferguson, 1997). One method to encourage audience
flow employed by the television networks has been to minimize the
abruptness of program transitions (Eastman, Newton, Riggs, & Neal-
Lunsford, 1997). As adapted by local stations, this strategy can be seen in
the transformation of news teasers, and, to some degree, of the newscast
itself, into a kind of program-transition-friendly infotainment (Sherman,
1995). Some stations appear to have intentionally blurred the lines of distinction between program content and promotion (McDaniel, 1997). Some
marketers have sought to take advantage of the desire for more entertaining information in newscasts by offering video news releases (VNRs) to
local stations. In practice, VNRs have become a way of, in effect, planting
public relations material within television newscasts (Vine, 1983). The
vast majority of news consumers are unaware of the sources of VNRs, and
many of them, although presented as unbiased information, are likely to
have been supplied by marketing professionals and designed to achieve
some group's specific advertising and promotional goals.

Another method for inserting marketing communications within newscasts has been the creation of pseudoevents. A *pseudoevent* is an occurrence created with explicit promotional or advertising goals; it is designed
to bias the news judgment of station gatekeepers at times convenient for
live broadcast or videotaping by network and local television news crews
(Boorstin, 1961; Peale & Harmon, 1991). In short on-air promos there is little time to separate hard news from pseudonews. Moreover, promos also
take advantage of the audience's preference for visuals, and the best visuals — wherever they come from — often dominate promotional spots.

Audience Research

Many factors are known to influence viewers' choice of a newscast. In addition to the appeal (or lack thereof) of a particular night's stories, other
nontopical news-related factors include the nature of the station-created
images of the personalities of the newscasters and reporters; the tenure of
the newscasters, reporters, and station in the market; past professional
recognition and awards earned or won by the station; issues related to
state-of-the-art technology; and the station's record of timeliness of delivery of past breaking news events. The specification of such identifiable

benefits of newscast consumption as those just detailed has been identified as essential to effective promotion (Crippens, Sutton, & Eastman, 1991; Weisberg, 1991). However, little scholarly attention has been paid to factors external to the newscast itself (Bryant & Zillmann, 1986).

The vast majority of newscast research, both within industry and scholarly venues, has focused primarily on factors within the newscast that indirectly or directly lead to audience involvement, audience size maximization, and revenue maximization. The most commonly researched internal factors include story placement, audio/video redundancy, story format, presentation style, use of graphics, story length, and viewer perceptions of the personalities of the newscasters. External-to-the–newscast variables, such as station on-air promotion activity both within and external to the newscast itself, and off-air marketing strategies, including the effects of external media campaign strategies, have to date been virtually ignored in peer-reviewed scholarly literature.

The Focus on Audience Size

Nearly 2 decades ago, Poltrack (1983) identified the temptation to focus on audience size and revenue maximization over objective reportage as being driven in part by high station monetary demands and personal managerial career stakes, two pressures that have intensified in the past 2 decades. News professionals and station managers must achieve ever more demanding ratings and revenue success to be assured of their own job security. Minnucci (1991) reported that the promotion of local newscasts has a higher priority than the promotion of any other form of programming on local television stations.

Unlike academic researchers, television news consultants and other television industry researchers have focused primarily on the relationship between newscast elements and demographic target audience size maximization. Industry research has tended to examine the effects of such characteristics as audience perceptions of newscaster and reporter personality type (or Q-ratings), station news-gathering credibility, station branding or image creation, and multidimensional perceptual mapping of one station's newscast position relative to the positions of other stations in the market. Just as the economics of program production drove local stations to affiliate with networks in the 1920s, management's demands for effective local news production and delivery have driven local stations to affiliate with news consultants. The news consultancy market in the United States is dominated by four firms: Frank N. Magid & Associates, Audience Research & Development, McHugh-Hoffman, and Broadcast Image Group (Jacobs, 1999). Most television stations offering locally produced newscasts enter into an exclusive long-term contract with one of these news research and consulting firms (Ferguson & Moses, 1999). News consultants tend to emphasize presentation over news content, resulting in common station positioning strategies across local markets (Blumenthal & Goodenough, 1991; Harmon, 1989). The impact of news consultants has been criticized for contributing to a striking cross-market similarity in the presentation and promotion of local news and other programming.

Effects and Motivational Research

Whereas industry researchers have tended to be driven by an examination of variables directly affecting the maximization of target audience size, scholarly studies have tended to focus on the more traditional dependent measures first developed by psychologists. The preponderance of academic studies examine audience effects of, and self-reported perceived motivations for, news exposure. Such studies examine viewer uses and gratifications-sought, audience activity and involvement, effects of congruent and noncongruent audio and video information, viewer affective responses, and recall of information as a result of the experimental manipulation of various experimenter-created fictitious newscast elements, audience motivations, issue conflict, and agenda-building and agenda-setting functions. Those foundational studies that have specific implications for research into news promotion have been summarized in Table 9.1.

Order Effects

An experimental study by Lang (1987) examined the relationship between the order of the presentation of information within broadcast news stories and news-consumer recall of salient information. Two news reports within an experimenter-produced newscast were manipulated into either a chronological presentation or a typical "broadcast style" (nonchronological) presentation. Dependent measures included unaided and two forms of aided recall of the topics of newscast stories and within-story facts. Results of this study indicated that chronological news story presentations dramatically increased news consumers' short-term ability to recall information from the newscast, whereas nonchronological presentation (the traditional broadcast-style newscast style) was shown to be less efficient at fostering short-term recall. Similarly, Gunter (1985a) identified narrative structure as an important variable in news-consumer recall, finding that narrative versions of news stories are remembered better than standard broadcast presentations.

Gunter (1985b) also examined serial position in relation to newscast structure and packaging. Results indicated that news consumers tended

TABLE 9.1
Research Studies About Television Newscasts

Author	Year	Data Source and Sample	Relevant Findings
Lang	1987	Two-condition experiment testing recall of stories.	Found that chronological presentation of information increases recall.
Brosius	1991	Two-condition experiment about recall of story content.	Examined talking-heads versus video-clip news presentation and found that mixed formats most enhanced recall.
Rubin and Perse	1987	30-item questionnaire answered by evening-class college students about news-viewing motives.	Demonstrated two distinct news-viewing orientations: instrumental and ritualized use of news.
Perse	1990a 1990b 1990c	Stratified samples of adults responding to self-administered scaled statements of reasons for watching local evening newscasts.	Explored both cognitive and affective reactions to newscast content and established connections between cognitive involvement and feelings of anger (utilitarian motive) and happy (diversionary) affective states during television news consumption.
Leshner, Reeves, and Nass	1998	Two-condition experiment about channel branding.	Analysis of effects of preexposure description of new channel image demonstrated positive effects on perceptions.
Newhagen	1998	Three-condition experiment about recall of news stories.	Showed that negative emotions such as anger increase recall.
Brosius, Donsbach, and Birk	1996	Four-condition experiment about recall of news stories.	Showed that congruent audio and video maximally increase recall.
Thorson and Lang	1992	Two-condition experiment about recall of news stories.	Found that videographics reduced recall for unfamiliar or complex information, but increased recall for familiar or simplistic information.
Zillmann, Gibson, Ordman, and Aust	1994	Three-condition experiment about newscast perceptions.	Demonstrated that viewer perceptions of an entire newscast were impacted by the emotional state created by the last news story and that humorous stories caused entire newscast to be perceived as less credible.
Aust and Zillmann	1996	Three-condition experiment about the perception of news problem severity.	Showed that the use of victim exemplars significantly increased perceptions of problem severity and increased perceptions of the likelihood of risk to self and sense of distress.

to remember the last stories in the newscast best, the first stories interme-diately, and the middle-of-newscast stories worst. However, consistent with Brosius (1991), emotional stories and stories with compelling video were shown to overcome the serial position effect. Clustering similar sto-ries was shown to enhance confusion, likewise supporting a mixed-for-mat presentation style.

These findings demonstrate the effectiveness of chronological or narra-tive presentation in subsequent aided and unaided viewer recall. Al-though the experimenter-manipulated newscast stories were significantly longer than a typical station promo (150 s vs. 30 s), the studies suggest that chronological presentations of on-air promotion elements will aid newscast-consumer recall of gratifications-promised within news promo-tional campaigns. In other words, the appeals in promotional copy should remain chronological ("Tonight Channel 4 brings you 'A,' then 'B,' then 'C' ") rather than typical broadcast style ("A big story tonight in sports, but first we'll give you news from Washington and the local weather forecast").

An experimental study by Brosius (1991) examined the impact of news-cast presentation style on the comprehension of television news. The two variables manipulated were talking-head versus video-clip formatted presentations, and mixed format (some talking head and some video) ver-sus same format (either all talking head or all video). Results indicated that recall was best for mixed-format newscast presentations. However, in the same-format condition, video presentation recall scores were higher than for the talking-heads condition. The implications for the design of station promotional campaigns were unclear because of the significant difference in duration between newscasts and on-air promos. It is doubt-ful that the presentation of both video clips and talking heads within a sin-gle promo can enhance recall or overall promotion effectiveness, espe-cially in promos with durations of 30 s or less. However, the results of this study, especially in relation to other commensurate research, suggest a va-riety of promotional appeals and styles, within a coordinated overall cam-paign strategy, is likely to prove more effective than a single style- or sin-gle appeal-based campaign.

Human Exemplars

Many studies have shown the apparent impact of marketing-related goals on television news content, where emphasis has been given to those stories that lent themselves to visual depictions over those that did not (Brosius, 1991; Cross, 1983; Findahl, 1981; Gunter, 1979, 1980). One com-mon form of visual imagery is found in the use of "exemplars," or human examples, over baseline statistics and other nonvisual content (Aust &

Zillmann, 1996; Zillmann, Gibson, Ordman, & Aust, 1994). These studies showed a heightened awareness of information related by or about the human exemplar over all other sources of information within television news broadcasts. A typical study might experimentally manipulate a story within a newscast related to recent damage from an earthquake. In one condition statistics relating the number of people killed, the magnitude of the quake, the dollar amount of damage, the size of the area affected, and the like would be presented. In a second condition, the story would focus on a brief interview with a victim (human exemplar) of the earthquake. Subsequent recall measures would typically show greater information retention from the story that focused on the human exemplar.

From a news promotion perspective, these studies suggest the importance of using actual viewers as human exemplars in station promotional messages. Rather than show the journalistic awards won by the station or statistics regarding the accuracy of station weather forecasts, promos that focus on viewers who benefited in some direct way from the station's newscast would probably be more effective. Promos depicting viewers who avoided a flood because of a newscast warning, showing government addressing a concern raised in a local investigative report, or showing viewers having a special vacation thanks to the station's weeklong travel feature are examples of effective use of exemplars in promotion.

Viewer Activity Level

A much-cited study by Rubin and Perse (1987; see also Perse, chap. 2, this volume) explored the nature of activity levels for television newscast consumers. Two nondiscrete news-consumption orientations emerged in the forms of instrumental and ritualized news consumption. The instrumental orientation was characterized by more active television news viewing behavior and related positively to perceived news realism, affinity, intentionality, and involvement. On the other hand, those television news consumers with a ritualized orientation tended to be motivated by habitual behavior and time-consuming or time-passing viewing patterns. Ritualized consumption was negatively related to news affinity, selectivity, and intentionality and positively related to co-viewing distractions. Ritual-oriented news consumers tended to focus on filling time regardless of newscast content. Rubin and Perse's study concluded that media uses and effects are at least in part a function of audience activity level and that the activity of news consumption relates in largely predictable ways to media use motives and attitudes. The instrumental news orientation was shown to be consistent with prior expectancy-value uses and gratifications research, such as those by Palmgreen (1984) and Palmgreen and Rayburn (1979).

In their 1987 study, Rubin and Perse also pointed out that the ritualized and instrumental orientations are not discrete classifications. Their results imply that promotional campaigns will probably be most effective when targeted to the fulfillment of the gratifications-sought by prospective news consumers along the full range of target-audience activity levels, from fully ritualized (inactive) to fully instrumental (active).

Affecting the behavior of low-involvement or low-activity consumers is a difficult goal to achieve in all forms of product and service marketing, and especially so for intangible services such as broadcasting (Hawkins, Best, & Coney, 1997). However, the behavior of those potential viewers who tend toward low-activity ritualized orientations is likely to be reinforced by marketing strategies equivalent to those used to increase product brand loyalty among low-involvement consumers. Reinforcement of well-established behavioral patterns in on-air promotional campaigns may well appeal to news consumers with a ritualized orientation. Loyalty to station newscasts among ritualized news consumers can be reinforced by marketing efforts over time. Such copy appeals as "Stay with Channel 11, we'll continue to give you everything you've come to expect" are likely to appeal to viewers with a passive news-consumption orientation.

Those newscast consumers who tend toward a more active instrumental orientation tend to be motivated primarily by the perceived realism of the newscast and appear similar to high-involvement, low-brand-loyalty product consumers. To attract news consumers with this orientation, promotional elements containing documentary or pseudodocumentary visual depictions would likely prove most effective. Perceptions of news realism will likely be enhanced by promotional campaign elements, including live remotes, interviews with victim exemplars, and opinions offered by a wide variety of political, scientific, religious, and educational authority figures or opinion leaders. Stations desiring to build brand loyalty among potential newscast consumers with an instrumental orientation will likely be best served not only by positioning their newscast as the "most real" but also by repositioning their competitors as out of touch, behind the times, or superficial. Promotional themes appealing to these viewers are likely to include such phrases as "Channel 4 gives it to you as it is, real, live, raw, unedited coverage of Anytown" or "While the others are still playing with their editing decks, we're on the air, live and unrehearsed. Get real, and get real news with Channel 4."

In a series of subsequent studies, Perse (1990a, 1990b, & 1990c) examined audience involvement as a function of both cognitive and affective dimensions. Again, two nondiscrete orientations to television news consumption emerged, labeled utilitarian and diversionary news consumption. Utilitarian news consumption was associated with higher cognitive involvement and feelings of anger during newscast exposure. Diversionary television news consumption was associated with feeling happy during newscast exposure. Just as with other well-established psychographic measures, such as Stanford Research Institute's Values and Lifestyles–VALS II, promotional campaign strategies can be developed to appeal to identifiable news-consumer targets along the full range of the diversionary to utilitarian news-gratifications-sought orientations. Promised gratification within promotional campaign elements may include appeals to concurrent and postexposure positive affective diversionary states (for example, "Watch Channel 4 and we'll bring you a touching story of love you'll never forget"), as well as appeals to cognitive gratifications ("Watch Channel 4 and impress your boss [spouse, kids, etc.] with all you've learned"). Utilitarian affective states associated with anger, such as "We'll show you something on tonight's Newscast 4 that'll really leave you steamed," can also be developed as part of the overall mix of a strategic station marketing plan targeted to each of the four main orientations of news consumers.

In a subsequent extension of this research, Perse (1990c) found that the utilitarian/instrumentally oriented viewers reported feelings of parasocial interaction (pseudofriendship) between themselves and their marketing-enhanced, self-created perceptions of the station newscasters. News-consumer affective responses of pseudofriendship with station personalities were first thought to be a function of social isolation (Horton & Wohl, 1956; Rubin, Perse, & Powell, 1985). However, later studies have indicated that parasocial interaction as expressed in a form of pseudofriendship toward television personalities is a common form of viewer affective response to prolonged television exposure (Perse & Rubin, 1989). Unlike diversionary viewers, those news consumers seeking useful information (utilitarian viewers) were linked more strongly to affective responses typified by feelings of anger. These differences in viewer affective states support the theory that preexposure viewing-gratifications-sought strongly influence television news consumers' postexposure affective states.

Promotional strategies directed at potential news consumers seeking gratification in the form of parasocial interaction could heighten the sense of pseudofriendship with copy explicating the nature of a variety of idealized parasocial relationships (for example, "With Kelsey Newscaster, you've got a true friend on Channel 4," "Isn't it good to know that you are a special part of our Newscast 4 family," or, "Together with the Newscast 4 family, we make a terrific team").

On-air promotion campaigns can be designed to reach each involvement orientation by using targeted program placement strategies. Utilitarian-oriented news consumers are likely to self-select exposure to other news and information-oriented programming where "learning-gratifications-promised" news promotion campaigns can be placed for maximum effectiveness. Likewise diversionary-oriented news consumers are likely to self-select other types of entertainment programs. Newscast promos with a "feel-good gratifications-promised" appeal are likely to prove most effective in reaching diversionary-oriented news consumers when placed within entertainment programs.

Image

An experimental study by Leshner, Reeves, and Nass (1998) investigated audience perceptions of newscasts as a function of two differentiated channel images presented to participants prior to exposure. Participants were informed that each channel was exemplary in either "specialist" or "generalist" approaches to their news coverage. Although program presentation across channels was identical, as predicted, those channels presented prior to exposure as specialist scored higher on perceptions of news attributes than channels branded prior to exposure as generalist. The authors concluded that "this pattern of results is consistent with the notion of channel as a place where television programs — and the people and action in them — exist" (p. 28).

Such research illustrates a fundamental axiom of marketing — that *perception creates the consumer's experience of reality* (Kotler, 1996). Potential news consumers who, prior to exposure, were led to perceive a given channel as specialized in certain news attributes, following exposure, rated the news elements of the specialized channel higher on a variety of measures than they rated the generalist channels. The implications for promotional strategy are apparent. Potential newscast consumers who are led prior to consumption to perceive a station's newscast as excelling in some comparative dimension, largely without regard to the actual newscast content, will act to avoid cognitive dissonance by seeking consistency between their a priori perception and postexposure evaluation of the experience. Promotional appeals can be designed to reduce the potential for cognitive dissonance by reinforcing desired news consumer pre- and postexposure perceptual consistency. Copy appeals can be designed to accentuate the gratifications-promised, as in "When you make the choice to watch Newscast 8, you know you'll experience the very best local news coverage."

In a pioneering study by Newhagen and Reeves (1992), newscast consumers were exposed to a variety of compelling negative news images within newscast stories. Dependent measures included recall for both visually and aurally presented material. Recall for visually presented information in newscasts was shown to be improved during and following compelling negative images in news stories. Recall for visual information presented before compelling negative images and memory for audio information before and during the compelling negative images were shown to be worse. Each of a series of studies by Newhagen and Reeves (1992), Lang, Newhagen, and Reeves (1996), and Newhagen (1998) that examined news-consumer recall for stories that induce negative affective states found recall highest for stories that induce a variety of negative emotional states.

In Newhagen (1998), recall following the induction of the specific affective states of anger, fear, and disgust was analyzed. Recall was found to be highest for information associated with the induction of anger, intermediate for fear, and lowest for newscast presentations inducing disgust. Remarkably, in this study the author explicitly stated one implication for station marketing campaign strategies involving the placement of promotional and commercial material. The author concluded that "the implications of the study also have bearing on news story production strategies. . . . Producers can use [images that elicit fear and anger] to first draw attention to a story, and then insert information they think viewers will want to remember right after them" (p. 274). Newhagen's study thus suggests that news-consumer recall will be highest for promotional material placed immediately after program material that elicits a news-viewer affective state of anger and that recall should also be enhanced for promotional materials placed immediately after program materials that elicit fear. Program material that elicits an affective response of disgust, however, may cause news consumers to turn away from newscasts and other announcements. Such turning away may come in the form of a cognitive or emotional disconnection from the program or manifest itself in channel-changing behavior. Newhagen concluded, "Thus a producer's intuition that information worth remembering should go after images evoking disgust may be exactly the wrong strategy" (p. 275).

Audio/Visual Congruency

In a series of studies by Brosius (1989), Drew and Grimes (1989), Graber (1990), Brosius (1993) and Crigler, Just, and Neuman (1994), stories with visual depictions were found to cause increased recall and comprehension of newscast story information. Brosius, Donsbach, and Birk (1996) compared stories where the video illustrated the audio, was mildly related to the audio, was not related to the audio, or was absent (audio only). As predicted, results demonstrated the highest recall level for the exposure condition where the audio and video were redundant. These studies suggest that station marketing and promotion campaigns should make use of graphic visual depictions with redundant audio. In essence, simplistic production values are likely to prove most effective. More discordant or complex promotion production approaches, with discrete audio and video, are less likely to generate sufficient recall to motivate program sampling.

A study by Edwardson, Kent, Engstrom, and Hofmann (1992) examined the relationship between recall of audio-presented information and video changes in television news. Their results indicated that introducing graphics into news stories decreased memory for the simultaneous audio information. However, graphics-enhanced newscast stories resulted in increased overall recall for the story, and news consumers' self-reported enjoyment and overall comprehension of the stories. Thorson and Lang (1992) examined the effects of television graphics and lecture familiarity on adult orienting responses and memory. Their study looked at memory for both the verbal and visual content of messages before, during, and after the appearance of a redundant videographic. Results indicated that when the topic of the story was unfamiliar or complex, the videographic reduced recall for information presented while the graphic was on screen. When the content was familiar or simplistic, recall ability was increased for information presented during the videographic. The results of these two independent studies suggest that the use of videographics within news promotion campaigns should be limited to those portions of the on-air promo that present the most familiar or simplistic information. The portion of the promotion campaign that requires the presentation of unfamiliar or more complex material is likely to be most effective in the absence of simultaneous presentations of videographic information.

Humor

Zillmann et al. (1994) examined the effects of ending a newscast with either an upbeat or humorous story on news-consumer perceptions of the entire newscast. In an experimental study, newscast consumers were exposed to newscasts that concluded with one of three variables: a humorous story, a human-interest story, or no additional story. Results indicated that news consumers' perceptions of the entire newscast were affected by the affective state induced by the last story. In the humorous-newscast-ending story condition, earlier newscast stories were perceived as less important or less severe than in the other two exposure conditions. Results of this study indicate that news consumers' perceptions of the entire newscast can be affected by the emotional state induced by the last story in the newscast. Use of a humorous story in the humorous-newscast-ending story condition caused earlier stories, and thus the newscast itself, to be perceived as less important. Portions of the overall promotion campaign designed to appeal to diversionary-oriented prospective news consumers may thus benefit from the use of humor within on-air station promotion, but that portion of the promotion campaign designed to target prospective newscast viewers with instrumental or utilitarian orientations is not likely to be served by a humorous approach. Furthermore, Zillmann et al.'s results suggest that humorous promos, if used at all, should be placed in programs watched primarily by diversionary-oriented viewers.

Victim Exemplification

Aust and Zillmann (1996) examined the effects of the use of victim exemplification in television news on newscast-consumer perceptions of problem severity, likelihood of local involvement, and probability of personal risk. The three exposure conditions were: newscast presentations without victim exemplification, with unemotional victim exemplification, and with emotional victim exemplification. Results indicated that the use of emotional victims increased news consumer's assessment of problem severity, perceived probability of risk to self, and sense of distress. In another experimental study by Aust and Zillmann (1996), the use of victim exemplars in television news stories was demonstrated to have a significant effect on news-consumer perceptions of the degree of importance of the issues examined in the report. Consistent with advertising research that shows the effectiveness of the use of human spokespersons over impersonal, factual presentations (see Wells, Burnett, & Moriarty, 1998), this study points to the potential effectiveness of the use of human exemplars in station promotional campaigns. The recruitment of consumer exemplars who can deliver such credible copy as "I watched Newscast 4's feature on car safety and it saved my life," or "If I hadn't been watching Newscast 8 when they flashed that tornado warning, I'd have been blown away with my house," is implied by the results of this study.

RESEARCH ON THE PROMOTION OF NEWS

Only a very few studies have looked directly at newscast promotion, and they are summarized in Table 9.2. Most of the studies focus on news teasers and bumpers, a small portion of what is usually meant by promotion.

Teasers and Bumpers

A pioneering experiment by Schleuder and White (1989) examined the effects of newscast teasers used within the network newscasts of ABC, CBS, and NBC. As shown in Table 9.2, results of this study showed that news consumers paid more attention to and had heightened recall for the verbal information presented in those newscast stories that had been promoted in teasers prior to the story presentation. Cameron, Schleuder, and Thorton (1991) significantly extended the prior study by examining the impact of news teaser placement prior to a commercial break, or pod, on viewer

TABLE 9.2
Studies of Promotion of Television Newscasts

Author	Year	Data Source and Sample	Relevant Findings
Schleuder and White	1989	Two-condition experiment manipulating network news teasers to measure attention and recall.	Found that more attention paid to and recall increased for verbal information that had also been presented in prior teasers.
Cameron, Schleuder, and Thorton	1991	Experimental manipulation of news teaser placement.	Found that news teasers in pods enhanced primacy and recency effects on viewer recall.
Schleuder, White, and Cameron	1993	Experimental manipulation of bumpers within newscasts and of before-newscast teasers.	Found priming effects for within-newscast bumpers on viewer attention and memory and that newscasts having teasers or bumpers-and-teasers (but not bumper alone) were attended to more than newscasts lacking teasers or bumpers.
Chang	1998	Four-condition experiment about the impact of the presence/absence and styles of news teasers on recall.	Found that news teasers increased recall and comprehension, but found no effects for reference or for style of teasers.
Peale and Harmon	1991	Content analysis of local newscasts focusing on nonpromotional elements.	Showed that consultants and cross-pollination effect created predictable styles of local television newscasts.

processing of the commercials. News teasers immediately prior to a pod acted in part to separate the commercial pod and the newscast into two discrete units. This strategy for news teaser placement appears to enhance primacy and recency effects on news-viewer recall. In this study, verbal recognition of the first commercial in the pod and visual recognition of the last commercial in the pod were enhanced in the split-pod condition.

In an extension to the Schleuder and White (1989) study, Schleuder, White, and Cameron (1993) examined the priming effects of within-newscast television news promotion on newscast-viewer attention and memory. Using the spreading activation model of information processing (Berkowitz & Rogers, 1986), the study examined the effects of bumpers (typically a verbal "table of contents" presented at the beginning of a newscast, sometimes with an accompanying videographic) and teasers (precommercial highlights of coming attractions). The results of this study indicated that news stories that included teasers or bumpers-plus-teasers were attended to more than news stories that had neither bumpers nor teasers. However, those stories that had been promoted by bumpers alone did not receive more attention. Memory of information that had been presented verbally in the story was better for news reports that had been promoted by bumpers, teasers, or both.

Chang (1998) examined the effects of news teasers on news-consumer processing of television news. He utilized four discrete types of news teasers along the two dimensions of program reference (presence vs. absence) and style (talking head vs. visual). Recall was measured with a factual, three-item questionnaire that was multiple-choice in format; comprehension was measured with an inferential, three-question, multiple-choice questionnaire. Consistent with expectations, the presence of a news teaser prior to the newscast enhanced news-consumer recall and comprehension as measured by the questionnaires. However, no effects were demonstrated for the interaction of program reference and style. Overall, this study serves to reinforce prior research on the causal relationship between newscast promotion exposure and news-consumer recall, attentiveness, and comprehension.

News Consultants

A content analysis of television newscasts by Peale and Harmon (1991), primarily designed to explicate nonpromotional newscast characteristics such as story length, geographic orientation, story voice, and story initiative, also controlled for other production elements that encroached on the actual newshole of a newscast, including transitions, teasers, and promotion, coded identically as "bumpers" by the researchers. The term *newshole* refers to the portion of a newscast (or newspaper) that carries the hard and soft news; the time (or space) not part of the newshole is filled with advertising, promotion, and public service announcements. Peale and Harmon concluded that, while not statistically significant in their sample, using bumpers was a fairly consistent marker of affiliation with such news consultants as Audience Research & Development and Frank N. Magid Associates, both companies that have recommended bumpers extensively. Stations using the consulting services of Primo Newservice used bumpers much less frequently, according to Peale and Harmon, whereas stations without consultants did not use a single bumper. Interestingly, the authors found few other differences among consulted and nonconsulted newscasts and concluded that the use of consultants "may be a result of what Harmon (1989) described as the 'cross-pollination effect' [that] leads to local TV newscasts of very predictable style and content" (p. 7).

A DESCRIPTIVE ANALYSIS OF LOCAL NEWS PROMOTION

As this review of the news research shows, typically, studies have examined either producer-controlled news variables within experiments or survey-based self-reports of motivational and personality influences on patterns of news consumption. Much of what needs to be known about television news promotion at the local or network levels remains to be investigated. This study begins by describing the content of news promotion on local television stations.

Research Questions

Drawing on previous findings in the research literature and suggestions in the trade literature, three research questions concerned with the quantity, appeals, and presentation of newscast promotion guided the analysis:

R1: How much of nonprogram content in and around local early-evening newscasts is promotional, and what differences exist in the quantity and placement of news promotion for affiliates of different networks?

R2: What persuasive appeals appear in local newscast promos, and which appeals dominate the time allotted to promotion?

R3: What presentational formats are utilized in local newscast promos and in what proportions?

Method

The study reported here examined the nature and content of local television news promotion within the programs leading into early-evening newscasts and then within the newscasts themselves. Altogether, the promotion by 36 network-affiliated commercial television stations in nine U.S. television markets was analyzed. The term *promos* is used to refer to preproduced on-air spots, whereas the term *promotion* encompasses live talk about upcoming news features or later programs in teases, bumpers, and promotional comments by newscasters.

Sample

A convenience sample of 10 markets was chosen based on ease of access to volunteers for simultaneous videotaping of all network-affiliated stations offering local newscasts in each market. Every station in each of the 10 markets was videotaped at approximately the same time on the same midweek weekday afternoon in early March 1999. Taping occurred for at least 2 hours prior to and then during the early-evening local newscast. However, one market had to be eliminated from the study because of the apparent loss of the tapes in transit. Another market was rerecorded on the next day (also a midweek weekday) because of technical difficulties with the original recording, and thus the final sample consisted of the stations in nine markets.[2]

In all, 36 tapes were returned containing approximately 182 hours of recorded video, and the content of approximately 6,480 min. was analyzed. In each case, tapes were cued to the beginning of the early-evening local news, and then rewound 120 min. For those tapes with program content at that point, the content analysis began. Those tapes with nonprogram (commercial or promotional) content at the –120-min. mark were rewound to the beginning of that commercial pod, and the content analysis began from there. All video prior to this point on each of the tapes was not subjected to analysis for the purpose of this study, other than to measure the total duration of the prerecorded material, as noted above.

Coding Procedures

Three types of coders were recruited and trained. The first set of coders were trained in the process of screening the tapes to identify all station promotions, to log the time of broadcast of all commercial pods (in minutes prior to the newscast) and promotional content within the pods, and to rerecord all potential promotional material onto a set of promotion-only master tapes. The second set of coders was trained to code the promos on the master tapes by persuasive appeal and presentation format. The third set of coders was trained in the analysis of promotional material within the newscast itself, recording teasers, bumpers, and promotional comments by anchors and reporters — exclusive of preproduced promos presented within the commercial pods.

Each screening coder was equipped with both a VHS playback and a VHS record deck. To maintain distinctions among stations and markets, prior to dubbing station materials, screening coders dubbed a short slate with the station's call letters and market from a prerecorded VHS set of vid-

---

[2]Markets in the database, Denver, Houston, Indianapolis, Kalamazoo, Knoxville, Louisville, Phoenix, Salt Lake City, and Seattle. Eliminated due to no data, Augusta. Stations in the database, KCNC-CBS, KCPQ-Fox, KDVR-Fox, KHOU-CBS, KING-NBC, KIRO-CBS, KMGH-ABC, KNXV-ABC, KOMO-ABC, KPHO-CBS, KPNX-NBC, KPRC-NBC, KRIV-Fox, KSAZ-Fox, KSL-NBC, KSTU-Fox, KTRK-ABC, KTVX-ABC, KUSA-NBC, KUTV-CBS, WATE-ABC, WAVE-NBC, WBIR-NBC, WDRB-Fox, WHAS-ABC, WISH-CBS, WLKY-CBS, WOOD-NBC, WRTV-ABC, WTHR-NBC, WTNZ-Fox, WVLT-CBS, WWMT-CBS, WXIN-Fox, WXMI-Fox, and WZZM-ABC.

eotaped slates. As each commercial pod was encountered, the screening coders made note of the time of the beginning and ending of the pod and then rewound the tape to dub all station promos (newscast, program, and station image) onto the promotion master tape in the record deck for later evaluation. Because of time and budget constraints, all program material was scanned by the screeners in fast-forward with the exception of program end-credits, which were viewed at normal speed because they occasionally contained audio-only, voice-over promos. All commercial pods were evaluated by the screening coders at standard speed, sometimes more than once. Over 280 minutes of commercial pod and end-credit video and audio were dubbed by the screening coders for subsequent evaluation by the content coders. Of this 280 minutes, approximately 262 minutes depicted actual station promos, the remaining 18 minutes were of station program material immediately adjacent to the commercial pods.

Analysis

To assess the quantity and types of news promotion, for each newscast, this study measured (a) the total commercial minutes (nonprogram inventory) available for newscast promotion in the 2 hours prior to the newscast and in the newscast itself; (b) the scheduling patterns and durations for newscast promos appearing prior to the newscast; (c) the scheduling patterns and durations for promotion appearing within the newscast itself, including that presented by the newscasters themselves; (d) the persuasive appeals in the copy and visuals of news promos; and (e) the audio and video techniques used in promotional messages about local newscasts.

To analyze the content of the collected promos, an initial content-coding schema based on newscast motivations noted in prior research and established promotion appeals identified in advertising literature was developed and embodied in a coding sheet with space for "other" as appropriate. Following content-coder training, a trial content analysis was conducted. Content coders evaluated 45 randomly selected station promos by type of appeal and presentation format into 20 categories. Intercoder reliability during the trial reached 96.4%.

Following minor modifications to the content-coding schema, content coders evaluated the master promotion tapes of promos for the presence or absence of 11 persuasive appeals: topical appeals (in other words, content focused on a specific news story) and generic appeals, such as pseudofriendship, ritualized/pastime, diversionary/feel happy, utilitarian/cognitive appeals, utilitarian/anger appeals, instrumental/nontopical news realism, humor, call to action, newscaster biography, and gratitude. Although these categories are not wholly exclusive, and one promo might exhibit more than one of these appeals, these 11 groupings represent the main types isolated in pretesting and derive from the previous research on news audiences. The coders also recorded which of the four presentation formats each promo used: full-screen audio and video, audio only, video only, and split screen.

Finally, the third group of coders looked for all other promotional elements present within the newscasts, timed them, and recorded their type in one of four categories: bumpers, promo videographics, audio-only voice-overs, and "pseudonews" promotions. The latter were typically delivered by anchors in such curt phrases as, "We'll check back with (reporter's name) on that story at the end of this newscast," "All this week we're covering (name of issue)," and "We'll have more tonight on (name of station's late local newscast)."

Results

The news promotion from 36 network affiliates analyzed for this study provided a plethora of descriptive information. The results provide some answers to basic structural and content questions about promotion that make a foundation for future research.

Early-Fringe Promotion

Looking first at promotion in the 2-hour period preceding local news (early fringe), Table 9.3 shows that almost *half* (48%) of all promos aired during that period were for news, and they represented a solid 10% of the stations' total commercial inventory. Stations in the sample, without regard to network affiliation or market size, devoted a remarkably consistent proportion of total on-air inventory to promotion.

As Table 9.3 shows, on average, news promotion consistently occupied about 10% of stations' total inventory and almost half the time devoted to promotion of all kinds (20% of availabilities), with the other 10% going to image and program promotion. As is usual, by far the bulk of nonprogram time was devoted to commercials (80%). On average, stations allotted 206 sec. to news promotion and 224 sec. to promotion of other program/station images during the 2 hours preceding early-evening newcasts. Interestingly, the affiliates of the four networks invested identical proportions of time to promotion irrespective of variations in the total amount of nonprogram time that could have been used. For example, on average, CBS affiliates had more inventory (2,295 sec.) in the 2 hours preceding local evening news, whereas Fox affiliates had about 4 min. less total time (just 2,050 sec.). NBC-affiliated stations, allied to the top-rated network at the time, devoted slightly more time (merely an additional 1%) to commercials and proportionately less to news promotion. Moreover, no significant differences by market were found.

TABLE 9.3
Duration of Nonprogram Time (in Seconds) and Proportion
of Time Devoted to Promotion During Early Fringe (the 2 Hours
Prior to Early-Evening Newscasts; N of Stations = 39)

| | Network Affiliation | | | | |
Prior to Newscasts	ABC	CBS	Fox	NBC	Average
Total nonprogram availabilities (in seconds)	2,155	2,295	2,050	2,125	2,156
Seconds allotted to news promotion	210	220	195	200	206
%	10%	10%	10%	9%	10%
Seconds allotted to other program promotion	240	230	215	210	224
%	11%	10%	10%	10%	10%
Seconds allotted to commercials	1,705	1,845	1,640	1,715	1,726
%	79%	80%	80%	81%	80%
Total % news promotion	10%	10%	10%	9%	10%
Total % promotion	21%	20%	20%	19%	20%

Within-Newscast Promotion

Looking now inside the newscasts, average durations in seconds of news and program promotion and commercials are reported in Table 9.4. Consistent with the early-fringe analysis, results within the newscasts show that about 9% of the newscast was devoted to news promotion (5.4% delivered by anchors and reporters and 3.3% in promos carried within commercial breaks). Typical promotional messages delivered by newscasters consisted of such phrases as "coming up after the break . . . ," "On the 10 p.m. newscast tonight . . . ," or "Thanks for watching Action News. We'll see you again tomorrow night." Other promotional material coded with this category consisted of brief video-only slides and short clips outlining upcoming stories. What is startling is how closely the total time devoted to news promotion of all kinds within the newscasts (an average of nearly 9%) matches the proportion of time alloted just to news promotion in early fringe (10%).[3] Again, no significant differences across markets or network affiliations appeared.

Some newscast elements, however, were not easily classified into discrete news or promotional presentation categories. One station offered a

[3]The tiny amount of time given to promos for entertainment programs appearing within the newscasts was lumped with commercial spot time, so no separate figure for the proportion of nonnews promos is available, but it was minuscule and certainly not approaching the 10% occurring during early fringe.

TABLE 9.4
Duration of Time (in Seconds) and Proportion of Time Devoted
to Promotion During Local Newscasts (N of Stations = 39)

Within Newscasts	Network Affiliation				
	ABC	CBS	Fox	NBC	Average
Total newscast duration (in seconds)	3,600	3,600	3,600	3,600	3,600
Newshole (in seconds)	2,030	2,068	2,130	2,125	2,085
%	56.3%	57.4%	59.2%	59.0%	58.0%
Seconds of commercials, PSAs, nonnews promos	1,295	1,215	1,130	1,170	1,202
%	35.9%	33.7%	31.4%	32.5%	33.4%
Seconds allotted to news promotion delivered by news anchors	198	188	185	200	193
%	5.5%	5.2%	5.1%	5.5%	5.4%
Seconds allotted to news promos	120	119	125	115	120
%	3.3%	3.3%	3.5%	3.2%	3.3%
Total % news promotion	8.8%	8.5%	8.6%	8.7%	8.7%

news story about its own success in a local community charity drive. Another covered one of its reporters accepting a community-service award on behalf of the station. For purposes of this analysis, these stories and other similar content were coded as soft/hard news, not promotion, although they clearly shared a promotional function.[4] Nonetheless, the overall consistency in news promotion across stations and markets may be a function of the well-established influences of news consultants, network advisories to stations, or program syndicators, which have resulted in the "cross-pollination" effect identified by Harmon (1989).[5]

Content and Persuasive Appeals

Results of the content and persuasive-appeal analysis for promos carried in early fringe are depicted in Fig. 9.1. The first striking element is that the majority of station news promotion (69%) contains topical information about imminent newscasts (add the top four percentages in Fig. 9.1). Of

---

[4]Although not directly part of this study, analysis showed that less than 60% of affiliates' early-evening newsholes actually contained news; over 40% consisted of nonprogram material.

[5]Networks provide frequent directives to their affiliated stations in the form of "suggestions" or "advice" on how to promote news and programs. Similarly, major program syndicators advise stations licensing their shows on how best to promote them.

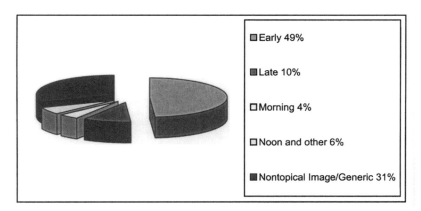

Early 49%

Late 10%

Morning 4%

Noon and other 6%

Nontopical Image/Generic 31%

FIG. 9.1.   Distribution of topical and generic promos carried in early fringe.

that total, most is for the early-evening news (49%). Not all topical promos target the next-to-be-broadcast newscast, however; a significant quantity contains vertical promotions for the late local news (10%), the next day's early morning news (4%), and in more than a handful of cases, the next day's noon newscast (6%). The remaining promos consist of generic image promotion either for the station or for its newscasts (31%).

Among generic (nontopical) news promos, the largest percentage employed a news-realism appeal (15%), as shown in Fig. 9.2. An appeal to news realism was identified by Rubin and Perse (1987) as a function of an instrumental (high activity) orientation to news consumption. Brief biographies of station newscasters (including sportscasters, weathercasters, and reporters) surfaced in approximately 6% of station promos. Utilitarian appeals combined for 9% of total promos, with slightly more than half (5%) enticing potential newscast consumers to experience some form of anger over a soon-to-be-broadcast story of injustice, and the other 4% promising a cognitive-based benefit—such as the lure of learning something of value from a given story in the newscast or from the viewing of the newscast in its entirety.

Other identified persuasive appeals included humor (4%), appeal to pseudofriendship with one or more station newscasters (3%), and a promise of "happy feelings" (Diversionary, 3%). Approximately 3% of station promos invited some form of call to action on the part of potential news consumers. Typical appeals included "You'll want to call your representative in Congress after you hear tonight's report on (subject matter)" and "A recall on a popular toy. You'll want to take yours back after you see our report tonight on (name of local newscast)." Other less common persuasive appeals included promos extolling the station's technical superiority (1%) and awards (1%). Nearly all newscasts (94.4%) ended with a

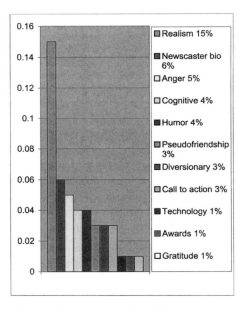

FIG. 9.2. Distribution of content appeals within generic promos carried within early fringe. Note that the categories of persuasion appeals are non-exclusive, resulting in percentages totaling more than 100 because of multiple appeals within some promos.

brief expression of appreciation such as, "Thank you for watching (name of newscast)." These appeals were coded as "gratitude" and comprised approximately 1% of all generic news promotion in early fringe. As might be expected, no appeals to "pass time" or diversionary viewing motives were noted in any topical station promos.

Presentation Strategies

Figure 9.3 illustrates the proportions of the four main presentation strategies used in promos for local news. Consistent with studies noting the importance of congruent audio and video presentation on news-viewer recall (see Brosius et al., 1996), the vast majority of station news promotions (89%) were full-screen audio and video presentations. Approximately 8% offered split screens, typically with program end-credits scrunched into a nearly unreadable glob to one side of the screen. Ironically, the split- screen presentation format risks viewer distraction because of the negative impact of noncongruent presentation, although the likely intent of such split-screen formatting is to minimize distraction and focus attention on the promotional presentation, while meeting the station's minimum commitment to program providers (to show credits or other information).

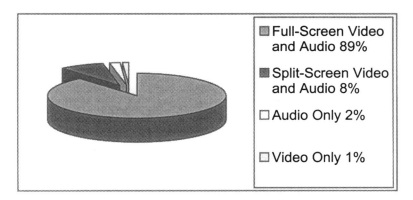

FIG. 9.3.   Proportions of presentation formats in news promos.

Although commonly used, audio-only promotions over end-credits were typically very short in length and thus comprised only about 2% of total news promotion as a percentage of total promotion duration. Video-only news promotion presentations were rarely used (1%), and coders noted in comments that at least some of the video-only presentations appeared to be the result of technical difficulties stations had had with the audio.

Discussion of This Study

As expected, this descriptive study powerfully illustrated the priority that commercial television stations give to local news promotion as part of their branding strategy. It demonstrated that news promotion occupied a substantial portion not only of overall station promotion but of the content of the newscast itself. Consistent with theories about the efficiency of a highly competitive marketplace, newscast on-air marketing strategies appeared to reflect, at least in part, predictable patterns of potential news-consumer motivations and viewing orientations (Shimp, 1997). The instrumental, utilitarian, and pseudofriendship appeals that had been distinguished in prior research were clearly present.

However, several factors limit generalization from this study. Most important is that data collection occurred late in the first quarter of the broadcast fiscal year, a time when commercial inventory pressures are likely to be at or near their lowest levels (Warner & Buchman, 1993). Stations typically respond to decreases in demand not only by lowering rate levels, but also by increasing their commitment to schedule promotion. Thus, the annual average commitment to promotion may be less than the 20% of total inventory identified in this study. Similarly, annual news promotion commitments may be less than 10% of total nonprogram time.

Time-of-day inventory pressures also affect the ability to generalize from this study, but in a positive way. Station inventory pressures are not only seasonal, but also vary significantly with daypart, with highest pressure on inventory occurring during prime time (Warner & Buchman, 1993). This sample included the early-fringe lead-in to the local early-evening newscast as well as the newscast itself. This time period should be fairly representative of the typical station's average daylong commitment to promotion scheduling, and future research may confirm the averages reported in this study.

Generalizations based on the analysis of persuasion appeals should also consider the limitations of the sample. Because of the impact of news consultants, networks, and syndicators, and the resulting cross-pollination, very careful consideration should be given to the effects of time of day on persuasive-appeal strategies. As identified earlier, local news lead-in-programming choices are strongly influenced by audience-flow considerations (Eastman et al., 1997). Persuasive strategies used within news-compatible programming can be expected to emphasize appeals to potential news consumers with information-seeking or news-based-entertainment desires and orientations. News promotional appeals in daytime or prime-time dayparts may emphasize entertainment-based persuasive-appeal strategies that are typically not scheduled in the early-evening-news-lead-in-daypart.

SUGGESTIONS FOR FUTURE RESEARCH INTO NEWS PROMOTION

Local television news promotion is a markedly undeveloped area in the literature. Subsequent studies should expand on the descriptive analysis reported in this chapter by controlling for issues of daypart, seasonality, inventory pressures, ratings, revenues, cost-per-point, and perhaps most important, station relationships with news consulting firms. Along with a firm descriptive foundation, research should investigate the effects of news promotion from the perspectives of viewer motives and activity levels and take a closer look at the content of all forms of news promotion—both on-air and external to the station or network. Comparisons of promotion by broadcast and cable networks could also be undertaken.

Viewer Orientations

Among stations with more developed marketing strategies for their newscasts, persuasive-appeal strategies in promotion are likely to be tailored to a variety of highly specific viewer orientations and motivations. These viewer orientations are likely to be evidenced in self-selection of program content. Stations that fund access to audience research are likely to utilize the results in developing targeted promotional appeals, a process that could be tracked in interviews, surveys, and case studies, as well as tested in field research. Specific research questions in this area might include whether fewer topical news promotion appeals are used during entertainment programming than in information-oriented programming, and whether there is evidence of persuasion-appeal strategies having been developed based on program type. On a slightly different front, researchers might ask about the interactions that occur between program environment and promotional strategies. In other words, which types of viewer orientations are most likely to respond to particular promotion appeals? This subject should be of especial interest to the industry if the viewer targets that generate the greatest benefit to stations can be identified.

The academic research to date identifies specific orientations of subgroups of newscast consumers characterized by a variety of parasocial-interaction-gratifications-sought. Subsequent studies could explore the effectiveness of a variety of highly targeted pseudofriendship appeals in promotion. Research issues to be examined might include the specific forms of pseudofriendship that are sought by potential news consumers and whether potential consumer subgroups seek parent–child, child–parent, child–child, or parent–parent parasocial interaction. The basic question is whether the nature of desired parasocial interaction is essentially uniform—at present an open question. Looking in a more industry-oriented direction, researchers could find out which interactions occur among parasocial promotion appeals and commercial sponsorships? Stations will want to know whether existing news viewers who are undesirable to advertisers can be persuaded to watch a competitor's newscast. On the surface, such promotional strategies appear unethical—an issue to be addressed in essays and interviews.

Although humor in television advertising has been the subject of substantial research by Sutherland and Sethu (1987) and Belch and Belch (1983), little research has yet examined the interaction of humorous approaches to the marketing of television news. Outstanding research questions include whether humorous appeals can serve effectively in marketing television news and whether some program environments for news promotion serve better for humorous appeals. More directly, scholars can address the question of whether humorous appeals can be used effectively to reposition television news competitors and test experimentally the kinds of humorous appeals that work.

Audience Activity Research

The schema of potential news consumers offered by the theories about audience activity levels suggest many opportunities for exploring significant questions using news promotion materials. Studies could be designed to examine the relationship between activity level and persuasive strategy. Is it possible, for example, to attract pastime or diversionary-oriented potential news viewers through on-air promotion campaigns without offending other viewer targets? Do stations appear to utilize on-air promotional appeals targeted to the full range of news-consumer activity levels? If so, is there an interaction between such activity-level based promotion and program formats or dayparts?

Lesher et al. (1998) demonstrated the effect of two forms of channel image (generalist and specialist) on newscast-viewer perceptions in a laboratory setting. Several opportunities for replication and extension of this research at both the network and local levels are evident. In the natural setting offered by a local television station's change in brand image (resulting from changes in call letters, network affiliation, ownership, etc.), researchers can investigate whether prior perceptions of channel images identified in the laboratory are sufficiently robust to be replicated. Can other brand image effects — such as, for example, unedited-realism or subjective-but-valuable-contextual-analysis-and-editorial brands — be duplicated in real-world settings?

Context and Content

Newhagen (1998) demonstrated the impact of television newscast depictions of stories eliciting an affective response of anger, fear, and disgust, with anger showing a positive impact on both recall and approach behavior. The results of his research at least imply the potential for ratings success in newscasts offering stories that elicit an angry response from the audience. Although reminiscent of the motion picture *Network* ("I'm mad as hell and not going to take it anymore"), and possibly a portent of things to come, several avenues of research are suggested. Research questions might include whether there is a saturation point for anger-based stories in newscasts and what levels of "angry stories" maximize viewer interest. In general, what kinds of anger-based appeals work best in on-air news promotion at the broadcast network, cable network, and local levels?

One unobtrusive experimental method for the exploration of these effects would be to expose participants to a variety of news campaigns for particular channel brand images, and then allow participants to self-select newscast exposure on an experimenter-controlled cable television system. An apparently unobserved environment can be created by telling participants they have to pass some time while waiting for a research study to begin. This experimental method is more fully explicated in Meadowcroft and Zillmann (1987).

Research in the use of victim exemplars by Aust and Zillmann (1996) suggests several avenues for research into television news promotion.

Scholars know little about the degree to which the use of a victim exemplar in television news promotion heightens news consumer's intentions to view a newscast. There are interesting theoretical as well as practical applications to learning which interactions in victim-exemplar depictions maximize the effect. For example, do interactions between co-depicted "mastering" or "sympathetic" news reporters, or between "mastering" or "co-suffering" cohort victims in multiple victim-exemplar depictions, maximize impact, and for what demographic and psychographic groups?

This set of questions just scratches the merest surface of what could be investigated about news promotion and using news promotion. For example, scholarly research has yet to touch on the effects of off-air, external-to-the-station on-air, online, and other mediated news promotion. Examinations of print, radio, outdoor, telemarketing, web-site interactions, direct mail, and telemarketing will surely find their way into the future scholarly literature of broadcast promotion. Comparisons of promotion by regional cable news channels and all-news cable networks with promotion of news by broadcasters should be another fruitful area for research. The raw data is readily available, and most kinds of analyses lend themselves to coding by undergraduate students so that very large samples can be analyzed. This is a field deserving of substantial attention and development by the academic community.

REFERENCES

Aust, C., & Zillmann, D. (1996). Effects of victim exemplification in television news on viewer perception of social issues. *Journalism Quarterly, 73*, 787–804.

Barnow, E. (1966). *A tower in Babel*. New York: Oxford University Press.

Belch, G., & Belch, M. (1983). An investigation of the effects of repetition on cognitive and affective reactions to humorous and serious television commercials. *Advances in Consumer Research, 11*, 4–10.

Berkowitz, L., & Rogers, K. (1986). A priming effect analysis of media effects. In J. Bryant & D. Zillmann (Eds.), *Perspectives on media effects*. Hillsdale, NJ: Lawrence Erlbaum Associates.

Blumenthal, H., & Goodenough, O. (1991). *This business of television*. New York: Billboard Books.

Bogart, L. (1980). Television news as entertainment. In P. H. Tannenbaum (Ed.), *The entertainment functions of television*. Hillsdale, NJ: Lawrence Erlbaum Associates.

Boorstin, D. (1961). *The image: A guide to pseudo-events in America*. New York: Atheneum.

Brosius, H. (1989). Influence of presentation features and news content on learning from television news. *Journal of Broadcasting & Electronic Media, 33*, 1–14.

Brosius, H. (1991). Format effects on comprehension of television news. *Journalism Quarterly, 68*, 396–401.

Brosius, H. (1993). The effects of emotional pictures in television news. *Communication Research, 20*, 105–124.

Brosius, H., Donsbach, W., & Birk, M. (1996). How do text-picture relations affect the informational effectiveness of television newscasts? *Journal of Broadcasting & Electronic Media, 40*, 180–195.

Bryant, J., & Zillmann, D. (Eds.). (1986). *Perspectives on media effects*. Hillsdale, NJ: Lawrence Erlbaum Associates.

Buchman, J. (1999). Radio promotion. In S. Eastman, D. Ferguson, & R. Kline (Eds.), *Promotion and marketing for broadcasting and cable*. Boston: Focal Press.

Buzzard, K. (1990). *Chains of gold: Marketing the ratings and rating the markets*. Metuchen, NJ: Scarecrow Press.

Cameron, G., Schleuder, J., & Thorton, E. (1991). The role of news teasers in processing TV news and commercials. *Communications Research, 18*, 667–684.

Chang, H. (1998). The effect of news teasers in processing TV news. *Journal of Broadcasting & Electronic Media, 42*, 327–339.

Crigler, A., Just, M., & Neuman, W. (1994). Interpreting visual versus audio messages in television news. *Journal of Communication, 44*(4), 132–149.

Crippens, D., Sutton, J., & Eastman, S. (1991). *Promotion and marketing for broadcasting and cable* (2nd ed.). Prospect Heights, IL: Waveland Press.

Cross, D. (1983). *Mediaspeak: How television makes up your mind*. New York: Coward-McCann.

Drew, D., & Grimes, T. (1989). Audio-visual redundancy and TV news recall. *Communication Research, 14*, 452–461.

Eastman, S., & Ferguson, D. (1997). *Broadcast/cable programming: Strategies and practices*. Belmont, CA: Wadsworth.

Eastman, S., Newton, G., Riggs, K., & Neal-Lunsford, N. (1997). Accelerating the flow: A transition effect in programming theory? *Journal of Broadcasting & Electronic Media, 41*, 265–283.

Edwardson, M., Kent, K., Engstrom, E., & Hofmann, R. (1992). Audio recall immediately following video change in television news. *Journal of Broadcasting & Electronic Media, 36*, 395–410.

Ferguson, D., & Moses, B. (1999). Local station television promotion. In S. Eastman, D. Ferguson, & R. Klein (Eds.), *Promotion and marketing for broadcasting and cable* (3rd ed.). Boston: Focal Press.

Findahl, O. (1981). The effect of visual illustrations upon perception and retention of news programs. *Communications, 7*, 151–167.

Geller, V. (1996). *Creating powerful radio: A communicator's handbook: News, talk, information, personality*. New York: M Street Publications.

Graber, D. (1990). Seeing is remembering: How visuals contribute to learning from television news. *Journal of Communication, 40*(3), 134–155.

Gunter, B. (1979). Recall of brief television news items: Effects of presentation mode, picture content and serial position. *Journal of Educational Television, 5*, 57–61.

Gunter, B. (1980). Remembering televised news: Effects of visual format on information gain. *Journal of Educational Television, 6*, 8–11.

Gunter, B. (1985a). Telling the story effectively. In B. Gunter (Ed.), *Poor reception: The misunderstanding and forgetting of broadcast news*. Hillsdale, NJ: Lawrence Erlbaum Associates.

Gunter, B. (1985b). Packaging the program. In B. Gunter (Ed.), *Poor reception: The misunderstanding and forgetting of broadcast news*. Hillsdale, NJ: Lawrence Erlbaum Associates.

Harmon, M. (1989). *Local television news gatekeeping*. Unpublished doctoral dissertation, Ohio University, Athens.

Hawkins, D., Best, R., & Coney, K. (1997). *Consumer behavior: Building marketing strategy*. Boston: Irwin.

Horton, D., & Wohl, R. (1956). Mass communication and para-social interaction: Observations on intimacy at a distance. *Psychiatry, 19*, 215–229.

Jacobs, T. (1999, February 8). Industry news doctors lack diversity. *Electronic Media*, 41–43.

Kneale, D. (1989). TV is going tabloid as shows seek sleaze and find profits, too titillating channels. In S. Biagi (Ed.), *Media reader: Perspectives on mass media industries, effects, and issues.* Belmont, CA: Wadsworth.

Kotler, P. (1996). *Marketing management: Analysis, planning, implementation, and control.* Englewood Cliffs, NJ: Prentice Hall.

Lang, A. (1987). Effects of chronological presentation of information on processing and memory for broadcast news. *Journal of Broadcasting & Electronic Media, 33,* 441–452.

Lang, A., Newhagen, J., & Reeves, B. (1996). Negative video as structure: Emotion, attention, capacity, and memory. *Journal of Broadcasting & Electronic Media, 40,* 460–477.

Lee, S., Algan, E., & Flournoy, D. (1997, July). *CNN world report: A five-year content analysis.* Paper presented at the annual meeting of the International Association of Mass Communications Research, Oaxaca, Mexico.

Leshner, G., Reeves, B., & Nass, C. (1998). Switching channels: The effects of television channels on the mental representations of television news. *Journal of Broadcasting & Electronic Media, 42,* 21–33.

Lippmann, W. (1922). *Public opinion.* New York: Macmillan.

McDaniel, L. (1997, May/1999, May 15). Promoting for success [46 paragraphs]. *Radio-Television News Directors Association Communicator* [Online]. Available: http://www.rtnda. org/prodev/articles/promoting.htm.

Meadowcroft, J., & Zillmann, D. (1987). Women's comedy preferences during the menstrual cycle. *Communications Research, 14,* 204–218.

Minnucci, G. (1991). Promoting the news. In S. T. Eastman & R. A. Klein (Eds.), *Promotion and marketing for broadcasting and cable* (2nd ed.). Prospect Heights, IL: Waveland Press.

Newhagen, J. (1998). TV news images that induce anger, fear, and disgust: Effects on approach-avoidance and memory. *Journal of Broadcasting & Electronic Media, 42,* 265–276.

Newhagen, J., & Reeves, B. (1992). The evening's bad news: Effects of compelling negative television news images on memory. *Journal of Communication, 42*(2), 25–42.

Palmgreen, P. (1984). Uses and gratifications: A theoretical perspective. In R. Bostrom (Ed.), *Communication yearbook* (Vol. 8). Newbury Park, CA: Sage.

Palmgreen, P., & Rayburn, J. (1979). Uses and gratifications and exposure to public television: A discrepancy approach. *Communications Research, 6,* 155–179.

Peale, B., & Harmon, M. (1991). *Television news consultants: Exploration of their effect on content.* Paper presented to the annual conference of the Association for Education in Journalism and Mass Communications, Boston, MA.

Perse, E. (1990a). Audience selectivity and involvement in the newer media environment. *Communication Research, 17,* 675–697.

Perse, E. (1990b). Involvement with local television news: Cognitive and emotional dimensions. *Human Communication Research, 16,* 556–581.

Perse, E. (1990c). Media involvement and local news effects. *Journal of Broadcasting & Electronic Media, 34,* 17–36.

Perse, E., & Rubin, R. (1989). Attribution in social and parasocial relationships. *Communication Research, 16,* 59–77.

Poltrack, D. (1983). *Television marketing.* New York: McGraw-Hill.

Promax Convention Program. (1999, August 20). [Online]. Available: http://www.promax. org/northamerica/sanfrancisco/schedule.html.

Radio and Television News Directors Association (RTNDA) Convention Programs. (1999, August 20). [Online]. Available: http://www.rtnda.org/standing%20convention/index. htm.

Richter, K. (1997, November/December/1999, 15 May). TV/radio: Bonding and branding [6 paragraphs]. *Columbia Journalism Review* [Online]. Available: http://cjr.org/year/97/ 6/rtnda.asp.

Rubin, A., & Perse, E. (1987). Audience activity and television news gratifications. *Communications Research, 14,* 58–84.

Rubin, A., Perse, E., & Powell, R. (1985). Loneliness, parasocial interaction and local television news viewing. *Human Communications Research, 12,* 155–180.

Schleuder, J., & White, A. (1989). *Priming effects of television news bumpers and teasers on attention and memory.* Paper presented at the annual conference of the International Communication Association, San Francisco, CA.

Schleuder, J., White, A., & Cameron, G. (1993). Priming effects of television news bumpers and teasers on attention and memory. *Journal of Broadcasting & Electronic Media, 37,* 437–452.

Sherman, B. (1995). *Telecommunications management: Broadcasting/cable and the new technologies* (2nd ed.). New York: McGraw-Hill.

Shimp, T. (1997). *Advertising, promotion, and supplemental aspects of integrated marketing communications.* Hinsdale, IL: Dryden.

Small, W. (1970). *To kill a messenger: Television news and the real world.* New York: Hastings.

Spragens, W. (1995). *Electronic magazines: Soft news programs on network television.* Westport, CT: Praeger.

Sutherland, J., & Sethu, S. (1987). The effect of humor on television advertising credibility and recall. In F. Feasley (Ed.), *Proceedings of the 1987 Convention of the American Academy of Advertising,* R3–R8.

Thorson, E., & Lang, A. (1992). Effects of television videographics and lecture familiarity on adult cardiac orienting responses and memory. *Communication Research, 19,* 346–369.

Vine, D. (1983). [Television news directors surveyed about video news releases]. Proprietary research. (Summary of results can be obtained by writing to DVA Research, P.O. Box 2161, Princeton, NJ 08543)

Warner, C., & Buchman, J. (1993). *Broadcast and cable selling* (2nd ed., rev.). Belmont, CA: Wadsworth.

Weisberg, R. (1991). *Promotion and marketing for broadcasting and cable* (2nd ed.). Prospect Heights, IL: Waveland Press.

Wells, W., Burnett, J., & Moriarty, S. (1998). *Advertising: Principles and practice* (4th ed.). Englewood Cliffs, NJ: Prentice Hall.

Zillmann, D., Gibson, R., Ordman, V., & Aust, C. (1994). Effects of upbeat stories in broadcast news. *Journal of Broadcasting & Electronic Media, 38,* 65–78.

Promotion of Radio

Gregory D. Newton
University of Oklahoma

Robert F. Potter
University of Alabama

There is little doubt that radio is a significant player in the media landscape and a vital ingredient in the daily media menu of most individuals. There are more than 12,500 radio stations in the United States (FCC, 1999).[1] Up to 80% of adults listen to one or more of those stations each day, compared to 73% who watch television daily (Merli, 1998), and cumulatively, radio reaches 95% of all Americans every week (Bunzel, 1999). Advertisers are expected to spend more than $16 billion on radio time in 1999 (Ditingo, 1999). In the face of such audience and revenue projections, the value of station properties continues to rise.

Given the size of the audience and the money invested in and on radio stations, there is little doubt that both the public and the business community take the medium seriously. Nonetheless, published academic research into radio — and in particular radio promotion — is sparse, to put it gently. Pease and Dennis (1995) noted that researchers have spent little effort investigating the industry or how audiences process purely auditory information. According to Williams (1998a, 1998b), academic researchers have ignored promotion's central role both historically and in current practice, despite the fact that "the modern radio station pays almost as much attention to advertising and promotion as to programming" (Alexander, 1997, p. 370). The industry itself has contributed little more to the

---

[1]Figures as of May 31, 1999, including all AM, FM, and FM educational licenses. Total does not include 3,190 licensed FM translators and boosters, or unlicensed operations.

literature. When discussing promotion, trade journals and industry convention panels tend to focus anecdotally on tricks of the trade (e.g., Borzillo, 1996a, 1996b) and on outlining the strategies that worked for an individual station or network (see McKinsey & Co., 1985).

In contrast, a recent surge of research on television promotion focuses on structural variables and the effectiveness of various promotional strategies (Billings, Eastman, & Newton, 1998; Eastman & Newton, 1998, 1999; Eastman, Newton, Riggs, & Neal-Lunsford, 1997; Walker, 1993; see Eastman & Bolls, chap. 3, this volume). However, the results of that research are not necessarily applicable to radio because of significant differences in television's and radio's approaches to both programming and promotion and the audience's uses of the respective media. Television promotion most frequently targets audiences for a specific episode of a given program. Furthermore, some television programs would be unlikely to receive promotion within certain other shows on the same station or network because they share little audience.

THE SPECIAL CASE OF RADIO

Radio's approach is different. Radio promotion emphasizes branding the station and programming throughout the day rather than focusing primarily on individual program units. Norberg (1996) described three possible purposes of radio promotion as "(1) to recycle or extend the listening of the station's audience, thus building the station's audience share; (2) to attract new listeners, thus building the station's cumulative ratings; or (3) to establish and enhance the station's image and listener expectations without a specific immediate rating goal" (p. 95). Note especially the focus on *the station* rather than a specific program, and the recognition of potential value beyond immediate ratings in the third purpose (similar to the broad focus on branding in Bellamy & Traudt, chap. 5, this volume). Indeed, Norberg later suggests that stations are best served when promotion efforts are targeted toward "enhanc[ing] the long-term listening expectations of the audience" rather than targeting short-term ratings gains. In other words, "[t]he one thing that is absolutely necessary for the successful business operation of a radio station is to establish an identity" (Warren, 1997, p. 63). In creating this identity, promotion's content aims to reflect the lifestyle and interests of the target audience (Keith, 1993) to enable the station to develop a relationship with the audience. Each element of the promotion must support the overall image of the station (Hausman, Benoit, & O'Donnell, 1996).

Radio stations have a variety of promotional vehicles available, divided between off-air and on-air. Off-air venues include print ads, outdoor advertising (billboards, transit signage, station vehicles), appearances and event sponsorships (including various "guerilla" tactics; see Buchman, 1991), direct mail, telemarketing, television advertising, and web sites. On-air promotion opportunities include spot announcements, contests and giveaways, and live remote broadcasts. Both commercial and non-commercial stations utilize combinations of these various approaches, although the execution is often quite different because of differences in the audiences for commercial and noncommercial radio, as well as the budgets and promotion goals of the station involved (see Piper-Aiken, 1997).

THE IMPORTANCE OF ON-AIR PROMOTION

Because budgetary constraints have an especially large impact on off-air promotional practices, even among large-market stations, the industry has placed increasing emphasis on creating effective on-air promotion ("Interview: Tom Owens," 1998). By conducting research on the effectiveness of on-air promotional announcements, not only can scholars investigate an area where the research results have a practical application, but also where such an application can have an immediate and substantial impact. When considering the "Four P's of Marketing"—Product, Place, Price, and Promotion (Berkowitz, Kerin, Hartley, & Rudelius, 1992)—it is primarily in the area of promotion where local radio managers have the most control. As Buchman (1991) argued, in the American radio marketplace station owners and programming consultants often dictate the station's product in terms of format and music titles played; individual listeners determine the place where radio content is consumed; and radio is free (aside from the cost of a receiver and the periodic inconvenience of ads on commercial stations or underwriting and fund drives on noncommercial stations). Creative control over the design and execution of promotional campaigns and the production of on-air promos, however, remains primarily in the hands of local program directors, promotion managers, and production directors. This is the case even at individual stations that are part of large conglomerates (Vigil, 1998).

Perhaps more important, establishing which variables can positively affect listeners' perceptions of a station, or determining how to make station identifying information more memorable, could translate into significant increases in ratings and revenue. Meeske and Maunez-Caudra (1992) pointed out the immense monetary value of call letters and positioning slogans, probably the most visible and familiar elements of a station's identity. This is largely a result of the way Arbitron (and their competitors) measures listening. Arbitron mails paper diaries covering a 1-week period to a random sample of listeners in each covered market (Webster, Phalen, & Lichty, 2000). A listener is counted if she or he reports tuning to the station for at least five continuous minutes within any quarter hour. Of course, it has been a frequent criticism of diary methodology that many respondents fill out the diaries for the entire week on the day they have to be returned, rather than hour by hour, day by day. In that case, actual listening may not be as important as the diary keeper's perception of a particular station and the ease with which the station's call letters, dial position, and/or positioning statements can be recalled. Thus, listener association with — and recall of — identifying characteristics is essential. As Buchman (1991) argued,

> [M]any promotion managers and broadcast marketing consultants believe that the positioning of a station relative to the positions occupied by its competitors is vastly more important for ratings success than actual station listening. Because they are unlikely to recall all of their listening accurately, many Arbitron diary keepers will respond in the survey by naming the station that presents the image with which they most closely identify, rather than with an accurate description of their actual listening behavior. (p. 142)

The telephone recall methodology used by AccuTrack (Strategic Media Research, 1996), which now competes with Arbitron in 70 markets, asks respondents about their radio listening over the past week in a phone interview rather than by their filling out a diary. This method places a great deal of importance on listeners' memory, up to a week later, of call letters, dial position, key programming elements, exact format, and/or slogans that clearly identify the station(s) they claim to listen to.

Regardless of the ratings service or methodology, the central point is that effective use of on-air promotion should produce better audience recall of station identifying characteristics and more positive perceptions of the station itself, which in turn should mean better ratings results.

RADIO PROMOTION STUDIES

As previously noted, relatively few published studies address issues specific to radio promotion. As Table 10.1 shows, approaches taken by authors in this area vary greatly, although there are some commonalties. All of the existing research looks at on-air promotion. It deals primarily with practices in the present radio marketplace (with the exception of Williams, 1998a). Most of the studies have relied on limited data. And finally, nearly all of the research focuses on U.S. commercial radio, with the lone exception of Piper-Aiken's study (1997) of public radio fundraising and marketing. That survey provided evidence that, frequent grousing notwithstanding, listeners understand the need for on-air fundraising and membership drives and are willing to support (or at least tolerate) those efforts. Such aggressive techniques as telemarketing, however, received strong disapproval.

TABLE 10.1

Summary of Radio Promotion Studies

Author(s)	Year	Database and Sample	Relevant Findings
Piper-Aiken	1997	Fundraising and marketing to 442 members of public radio audience for two stations.	Found a positive attitude among listeners toward direct media marketing strategies and on-air announcements employed by the two stations, but disapproval of telephone contacts.
Potter	1998	Experiment analyzing reactions to nine radio promotional spots using heart rate, skin conductance, and memory data from 62 participants.	Demonstrated that listeners automatically applied cognitive resources to process promotional messages following the onset of laser production effects and vocal echo effects; results implied that using such effects may improve memory for the promo.
Potter, Lang, and Bolls	1998	Within-subjects experiment using 12 min of radio messages and measuring heart rate, skin conductance, and memory data for 39 participants.	Found that listeners automatically applied cognitive resources to processing radio messages following announcer changes, jingle onset, production effects, and sound effects; recognition memory improved following these structural features.
Watt	1994	Mall-intercept experiment testing day-after-memory for 76 radio commercials played for 200 participants during a distractor task.	Showed that auditory structure variables that varied in dynamic complexity were significant predictors of radio spot recall, independent of content-based predictors.
Williams	1998a	Historical analysis of NBC network radio promotion using archival material for 1940–1948.	Showed that following the sale of the B network, NBC began to focus on building a network identity; on-air promotion of programs emerged as a way to build network image with listeners.
Williams	1998b	Case study of 12 radio stations in one large southern market, examining effects of cash giveaway promotions.	Confirmed that cash giveaways are an important marketing tool for some formats when promotion focus is on audience acquisition and maintenance rather than recycling; off-air portions of a campaign often varied significantly from managers' ideal for the promotion.

Chosen methods range from survey (Piper-Aiken, 1997) to case study (Williams, 1998b) to historical analysis (Williams, 1998a). If a dominant approach exists among the small group of studies in Table 10.1, it would be the experimental inquiry into the impact of various structural characteristics on audience memory and behavior (Potter, 1998; Potter, Lang, & Bolls, 1998; Watt, 1994). For example, Watt conducted an experiment in which 200 participants were recruited using a mall-intercept procedure and asked to respond to a consumer preference questionnaire while sitting in a small testing room. The questionnaire was actually a distractor task, with the experimental manipulation being a series of radio commercials played over loudspeakers in the room. After a 24-hour period, participants were contacted by telephone and asked to recall the radio commercials that had been played. Results showed that structural auditory variables were significant predictors of commercial memory regardless of content.

Potter et al. (1998) designed an experiment that used physiological indices to confirm Watt's (1994) findings. Heart rate and skin conductance measures were collected from 39 participants while they listened to 12 min. of actual broadcast radio messages. After listening, recognition memory tests were administered. Results showed that listeners automatically applied cognitive resources to processing the messages immediately following specific structural features such as sound effects. This automatic processing improved recognition memory for information that followed the structural feature.

Finally, Potter (1998) designed a study to apply these findings specifically to promotional messages. In an experiment using a within-subjects design, nine radio promos were interspersed between actual radio messages to replicate a typical listening experience. Three of the promos were produced with laser effects, three with echo vocal processing, and three were plain voice reads. Heart rate, skin conductance, and memory data were collected from 62 participants. Results show that both echo and laser effects caused listeners to automatically allocate cognitive resources to processing the promos and suggest that this may improve memory for the information contained in them. Taken altogether, these studies have produced evidence that production effects (sound effects, vocal processing), vocal effects (multiple voices), and other auditory structural features can dramatically impact a listener's ability to recognize and recall information in radio spot announcements.

A STUDY OF THE EFFECTS
OF AUDITORY COMPLEXITY

Much of this experimental work has employed a limited-capacity model of cognition. This model conceptualizes listeners as cognitive processors with a single, finite pool of cognitive resources (Lang, 2000; Lang, Geiger,

Strickwerda, & Sumner, 1993). The execution of any act of cognition, including the processing of mediated messages such as promotional spots, requires resources to be allocated from the limited pool and applied to at least three cognitive tasks: encoding, storage, and retrieval. Encoding is selecting information from the multitude of details in the environment and allowing it to pass into short-term memory. Storage is the transfer of information from short-term memory into long-term memory. Retrieval is the ability to acquire the information from long-term memory for use and further processing at a later point in time. This model can be used to predict listeners' physiological responses to, and subsequent memory for, auditory signals such as radio messages. Promos that are more likely to trigger the desired cognitive responses may more frequently lead to desired listening (and ratings report) behaviors.

Application of Theory to Radio

When using media, how well an individual encodes, stores, and retrieves information is affected by several factors. Of course, one key variable is the importance or pertinence of the message to the audience member. However, the limited-capacity model conceptualizes a mediated message as containing various structural features, several of which elicit a call for an automatic allocation of cognitive resources to encoding. For example, research on video messages has shown that viewers automatically allocate resources to message encoding in response to unrelated cuts (Lang, Bolls, Potter, & Kawahara, 1999), related cuts (Lang, Zhou, Schwartz, Bolls, & Potter, 2000), the onset of graphics (Thorson & Lang, 1992), and picture motion (Detenber, Simons, & Bennet, 1998). Radio messages can be similarly conceptualized as consisting of a number of different structural features, some of which may elicit automatic resource allocation to encoding by listeners. Specifically, sound effects, production effects, vocal processing, character voices, music onset, and announcer voice changes have been identified as structural features that lead to resource allocation in both actively involved and passive listeners (Potter, Lang, & Bolls, 1997; Potter et al., 1998). The next logical question is whether higher levels of automatic encoding result in more effective processing of messages.

Dependent Measures

Research into the effectiveness of television promos has frequently used the Nielsen rating of the promoted episode as the dependent variable. This design works well in that setting because of television's emphasis on promoting a specific episode that will air at a specific date and time. However, such a research design is less practical in the case of radio because modern radio programming less frequently delivers regularly scheduled program episodes in a manner similar to television. Instead, radio programming is based on providing a 24-hour format—a style of music, news, or information—designed to appeal to a specific demographic and psychographic audience (Keith, 1987). Most radio promos, therefore, do not direct the audience to listen at a particular day and time. Instead, as described earlier, they are designed to create a strong image of the radio station that listeners will identify with. Because of this fundamental difference in the goals of most on-air radio and television promotional campaigns, it is necessary to employ dependent variables other than ratings data when designing radio promotional experiments. Potter and Callison (2000), for example, varied the audio structural complexity of radio promos and measured changes in (a) listener attitudes toward the promos, (b) listener attitudes toward the stations that produced the promos, and (c) listener memory for the promos after varying the level of auditory complexity in the audio productions.

Hypotheses

A promo's level of auditory structural complexity can be defined as the number of resource-eliciting auditory structural features it contains. It is predicted that spots with a comparatively high number of these features will cause listeners to experience a series of calls for automatic resource allocation to encoding, whereas promos with comparatively fewer of these features will not lead to such a series of calls. As a result, it is expected that information in highly complex radio promos will be better encoded than information in simple promos. Since past research has used recognition memory as a measure of encoding effectiveness (Lang, 1995; Zechmeister & Nyberg, 1982), the following hypothesis was made:

H_1: Participants will have better recognition for information in complex promos compared to simple promos.

Media scholars have noted the important role that audience arousal plays in media processing (Christ, 1985; Perse, 1996; Singer, 1980; Zillmann, 1982). Traditionally, audience arousal has been viewed as resulting primarily from programming content. However, television viewers' self-reported arousal levels have also been shown to rise due to higher structural complexity of the message, regardless of the content (Lang, Bolls, et al., 1999). These results support the following prediction:

H_2: Complex radio promos will be more arousing than simple promos when measured by self-reported arousal levels.

When people are aroused, they automatically allocate a portion of their limited cognitive resources to storing information in long-term memory (Lang, Bradley, & Cuthbert, 1997), resulting in better free recall of information processed during periods of high arousal (Bradley, 1994). This effect has been demonstrated in both television viewers (Bolls, Potter, & Lang, 1996) and radio listeners (Bolls, Lang, Potter, & Snyder, 1999). Therefore:

H_3: Listeners will demonstrate better free-recall memory for more complex radio promos than simple promos.

Petty and Cacioppo's (1986) Elaboration Likelihood Model (ELM) of persuasion provides a theoretical basis for predictions about the effects of promotional spot auditory complexity on listener attitudes. The ELM postulates two different types of cognitive processing: central and peripheral. Central processing refers to careful cognitive deliberation on points made by a message source. Peripheral processing, on the other hand, employs simple cues in the message in order to form attitudes toward the topic. Radio promos are not the type of message that listeners are likely to become extremely involved with; rather, they are more likely to result in peripheral processing. Therefore listeners will be quite susceptible to manipulations of cues such as auditory structural features when forming attitudes about the promos and the radio stations they represent. Lutz (1985) used the ELM to develop a measure of general attitude toward the ad (A_{ad}) that has proven to be a good index of whether a person responds "in a favorable or unfavorable manner to a particular advertising stimulus during a particular exposure" (p. 46). Yoon, Bolls, and Lang (1998) have shown that television viewers have more favorable attitudes toward structurally complex ads compared to simple spots. It was predicted that radio listeners will respond in similar fashion.

H_4: Listeners will have more positive perceptions of promos produced with many auditory structural features compared to those with only a few structural features.

Television research has also shown that greater structural complexity improves viewers' attitudes toward the brand being advertised (Yoon et al., 1998). Assuming that the station in a promo is analogous to the brand in an advertisement, and that radio listeners will respond similarly to television viewers, it made sense to predict:

H_5: Listeners will think more positively about stations featured in complex promos compared to stations promoted in structurally simple spots.

Design, Subjects, Stimuli, and Pretest

An experiment was designed that varied the level of auditory structural features in radio promotional announcements and measured listeners' responses to them. The experiment employed a mixed 2 (complexity) × 5 (message) × 2 (order of presentation) factorial design. Complexity was a within-subjects, two-level (high and low) factor. Message was also a within-subjects factor, with five levels representing the five promos used in each level of complexity. Order of presentation was the only between-subjects factor and represented two systematic tape orders created for experimental presentation.

Participants were 41 undergraduates (19 females, 22 males) at a large southeastern university. They all provided informed consent and received course credit for their participation in the study. All participants were unaware of the specific purposes of the experiment, but were told the study would investigate how people process mediated messages.

Stimulus messages were chosen from cassette tapes obtained through a subscription to *Radio and Production* magazine. This monthly publication targets radio production professionals and includes discussions of the latest in audio production techniques and equipment. A regular feature of the magazine is a tape that features exemplary samples of work created and submitted by subscribers. The promos used in this study were included on cassettes mailed to subscribers between November 1997 and September 1998. Stimuli were selected from this source for two reasons. First, doing so allowed for the selection of promos from radio stations well outside the listening area where the experiment took place. Second, it can be assumed that the spots fairly represent contemporary production techniques because they were submitted by production directors and chosen for distribution as worthy examples by the editors of an industry trade magazine.

All of the promos on the cassettes were initially judged according to the extent to which they used six auditory structural features shown to cause automatic cognitive resource allocation (see Potter, 1998; Potter, Lang, & Bolls, 1997, 1998). These features were defined as voice changes (replacement of one voice by another in the audio stream), sound effects, production effects, vocal processing, character voices, and music onset. Promos containing a high number of these features were identified as structurally complex. Promos using only a few of these structural features were considered structurally simple.

Ten spots were chosen for inclusion in this experiment, 5 representative of the high-complexity level and 5 representative of the low-complexity level. Each condition contained one promo from each of the following formats: alternative rock, classic rock, top 40, oldies, and news/talk. Spot duration ranged from 30 to 75 sec. However, length was balanced across levels of the complexity factor by including one promo between 30 and 39 sec., two between 40 and 49 sec., one between 50 and 59 sec., and one longer than a minute.

Because the initial determination of auditory complexity was made subjectively, a pretest was conducted using participants ($n = 19$) similar to those who would later complete the final experiment. The pretest consisted of listening to the 10 promos and completing four semantic differential scales after hearing each. The 7-point scales were designed to assess complexity using the following semantic poles: complex/simple, extreme/mild, complicated/basic, and extravagant/plain. Pretest data were combined into a complexity index for each promo (alpha = .94). These indices were then submitted to a mixed $2 \times 5 \times 2$ MANOVA (the factors for this analysis were the same as discussed earlier). Results confirmed the classification of promotional announcements. High-complexity spots were rated significantly more complex ($M = 4.66$, $SD = .58$) than low-complexity spots ($M = 2.85$, $SD = .69$), $F(1, 17) = 130.53$, $p < .000$.

Two presentation orders were created, one beginning with a high-complexity promo, the other beginning with a low-complexity promo. Both then alternated between high- and low-complexity spots. The orders were systematically designed to prevent any two promos from being heard sequentially in both presentations. Also, to prevent possible primacy or recency effects, no promotional spot appeared exclusively in the first or last quarter of both orders.

Experimental Procedure and Scales

Two experimenters conducted the final study following the same experimental protocol. Research participants were randomly assigned to one of the two orders of presentation, and completed the experiment in groups of three to twenty. Participants were instructed they would hear 10 promotional announcements from actual radio stations and would be asked to respond to a short questionnaire following each spot.

The promos were played one at a time on a portable stereo cassette player. Between each announcement, the tape was paused while participants filled out self-report attitude measures consisting of several 7-point scales. The scales included the following:

Complexity of promo: Research participants were asked how they would evaluate the production elements used in the promotional message. The anchors of the scales were complex/simple, extreme/mild, complicated/basic, and extravagant/plain. Data obtained in this section served as a manipulation check.

Overall attitude toward the promotion: Participants were asked how they would evaluate the promotion overall. The anchors of the 7-point scales were unattractive/attractive, depressing/refreshing, unappealing/appealing, unpleasant/pleasant, dull/dynamic, and not enjoyable/enjoyable.

Overall attitude toward the station: Research participants were also asked three individual questions concerning their impressions of the radio station that produced the promo. The anchors of these scales were unprofessional/professional, dull/exciting, and a station I would NEVER listen to/a station I would ALWAYS listen to.

Finally, participants provided ratings of their emotional responses to each promo using the SAM (Self-Assessment Manikin) scale (Lang, Greenwald, Bradley, & Hamm, 1993). The SAM is a series of three 9-point pictorial scales used to evaluate self-reported emotional responses to stimuli along the dimensions of arousal, valence, and dominance (Bradley, 1994). The scale has been found to be a valid and reliable measure of emotional responses to advertising (Morris, 1995; Yoon et al., 1998; Bolls & Potter 1998) and research in cognitive psychology has shown it to be reliable and valid in responses given to purely auditory stimuli (Bradley, 1994; Verona et al., 1997).[2]

After listening to the promos and completing the questionnaires, participants were asked to review a series of four magazine advertisements and answer questions concerning their appropriateness for a college audience. This procedure was designed as a distraction task and intended to purge the participants' short-term memory for the radio spots. Following completion of the distraction task, participants were told that the researcher was interested in testing their memory for the promos. Participants were first instructed to list all the station names and promotion descriptions they could remember on a free-recall form. The single-page form consisted of 10 blank lines for station names and 10 blank lines for promotion descriptions. After participants had completed the free-recall section, they were asked to answer a series of four-option multiple-choice questions designed to test recognition memory of the information given in the promos. The multiple-choice test was comprised of 10 sheets of paper, each containing three questions about a particular promo. The questions regarding each announcement were derived from content in each third of the total duration of the spot. The recognition test packets themselves were created in three different orders of presentation to control for serial order effects in the recognition data. Participants were instructed to an-

---

[2]Although data were collected for participants' arousal, valence, and dominance responses to the promos, only the arousal data are reported here to address Hypothesis 2.

swer all 30 questions, and to guess rather than leave any of the questions unanswered.

Upon completion of the memory portions of the experiment, participants were asked to provide their telephone number and a convenient time for them to be contacted by the researchers during the next 2 to 4 days. They were then thanked for their participation and told they could leave.

During the delayed-recall phase of data collection, participants ($n = 36$) were contacted via telephone and asked to list any of the station names, call letters, and promotional spot descriptions they could remember from the promos they had heard during the experiment. Researchers recorded these responses, thanked the participants, and terminated the call.

Analyses

Mean scores were calculated for all of the scales. The pictorial SAM arousal ratings were converted into their appropriate numeric values and mean scores obtained. The data from each self-reported category were submitted to a 2 × 5 × 2 repeated measures ANOVA. No significant effects were found for order of presentation, the only between-subjects factor.

For the immediate and delayed free-recall measures each station call letter/name and promotional description recalled was scored and then categorized as either high or low complexity. The answers given to the recognition multiple-choice questions were coded as either correct or incorrect. Participants' recognition scores for each promo, therefore, ranged from 0 (no information correctly recalled) to 3 (all information correctly recalled), up to a total of 15 (five promos, 3 points possible for each). All memory data were analyzed using a 2 × 5 × 2 repeated measures ANOVA.

Results

Although pretests showed significant differences in the perceived structural complexity of the two groups of promos, a manipulation check was conducted to ensure that the experiment participants experienced the same perceptions. Using the same semantic differential scales, the participants found the high-complexity promos ($M = 5.14$, $SD = .70$) significantly more complex than the low-complexity spots ($M = 3.21$, $SD = .78$), $F(1, 39) = 313.49$, $p < .001$.

Results supported the first hypothesis, which predicted that participants would have significantly better recognition memory for information in complex promos compared to simple promos. There was a significant main effect for complexity on the recognition data, $F(1, 39) = 11.89$, $p < .001$, $\varepsilon^2 = .2140$. As depicted visually in Fig. 10.1, listeners had a higher per-

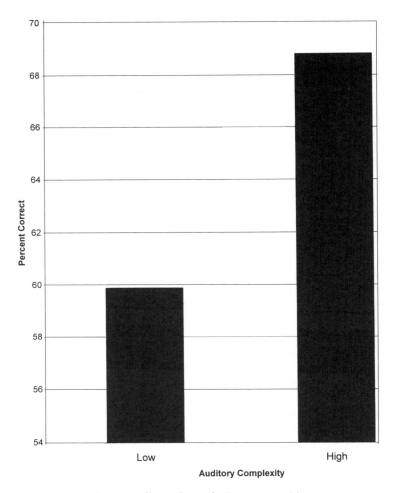

FIG. 10.1.   Effects of complexity on recognition.

centage of correct recognition responses for complex promos (*M* = 68.81, *SD* = 14.21) compared to simple ones (*M* = 59.84, *SD* = 13.94).

The second hypothesis, that listeners would report feeling more aroused by promos with a high number of structural features, was also supported (see Fig. 10.2). Complexity had a significant effect on the SAM arousal ratings, $F(1, 39) = 105.99$, $p < .001$, $\varepsilon^2 = .7158$. As predicted, participants reported higher arousal in response to the complex spots (*M* = 6.46, *SD* = 1.13) compared to the structurally simple announcements (*M* = 4.22, *SD* = .98).

Based on the limited-capacity model, hypothesis three predicted that the increased arousal in the structurally complex condition would contrib-

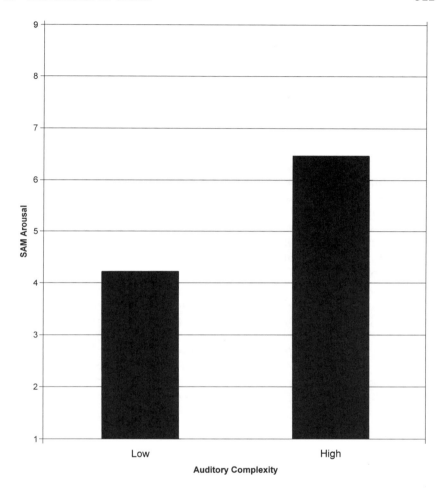

FIG. 10.2. Effects of complexity on arousal.

ute to better free-recall of the messages. There was a main effect of complexity on the ability to recall the promos, $F(1, 39) = 32.56$, $p < .001$, $\varepsilon^2 = .4200$. Listeners were able to recall a greater number of complex promos ($M = .51$, $SD = .21$) than simple spots ($M = .25$, $SD = .21$). The delayed free-recall results indicate that this effect was robust. Respondents were contacted an average of 109 hours (approximately 4.5 days) after their participation in the experiment. Even after this period of time, there was a significant main effect for complexity on the ability to recall the spots, with participants able to recall more of the complex promos ($M = .48$, $SD = .22$) than the structurally simple promos ($M = .19$, $SD = .20$), $F(1, 34) = 36.22$, $p < .001$, $\varepsilon^2 = .4923$. However, the data showed structural complexity had no effect on listeners' ability to recall the call letters or individual station names either at the time of the experiment or several days later.

Hypothesis four, that greater auditory complexity would produce more favorable attitudes toward the spot, was also supported. Because the alpha level for the attitude toward the ad scale questions was sufficiently high (.95), a mean attitude score was created for each participant. The analyses of these scores show the predicted main effect, $F(1, 39) = 14.86$, $p < .001$, $\varepsilon^2 = .2408$, with complex promos resulting in significantly more favorable attitudes ($M = 4.74$, $SD = .59$) than simple promos ($M = 4.27$, $SD = .88$).

To address the fifth hypothesis, that listeners would think more positively about stations that produced more structurally complex promos, participants were asked to respond to three semantic differential scales. Responses were analyzed separately. Listeners did not report that there was a significant difference in the level of professionalism between stations that produced simple promos compared to those that produced complex ones. As Fig. 10.3 shows, however, there was a significant effect of complexity on the perceived excitement of the stations, $F(1, 39) = 96.08$, $p < .001$, $\varepsilon^2 = .7037$, with stations that produced complex promos ($M = 5.69$, $SD = .69$) perceived as more exciting than stations represented by simple ones ($M = 4.01$, $SD = .94$).

Furthermore, participants were significantly more likely, $F(1, 39) = 42.77$, $p < .001$, $\varepsilon^2 = .5014$, to say they would always listen to the stations that produced complex promos ($M = 4.99$, $SD = .85$) rather than to stations that produced simple spots ($M = 3.90$, $SD = .89$), as shown in Fig. 10.4.

Discussion of Study

This experiment explored the predictive ability of a limited-capacity model of cognition on listeners' memory for radio promotional announcements and attitudes toward the stations that produce them. Specifically, it was predicted that increasing the auditory structural complexity of radio promotional announcements would increase listener memory and lead to more positive evaluations of the promos and the stations they represent. The results provided strong support for these predictions. Increasing the structural complexity increased listeners' ability to recall promotional messages and recognize detailed information that was presented. Furthermore, this effect was robust over time. Tested an average of more than 4 days later, participants still recalled significantly more of the complex spots.

One possible mechanism for this recall effect is variance in the participants' autonomic arousal responses to the announcements. As predicted, participants reported that complex promos made them feel more aroused

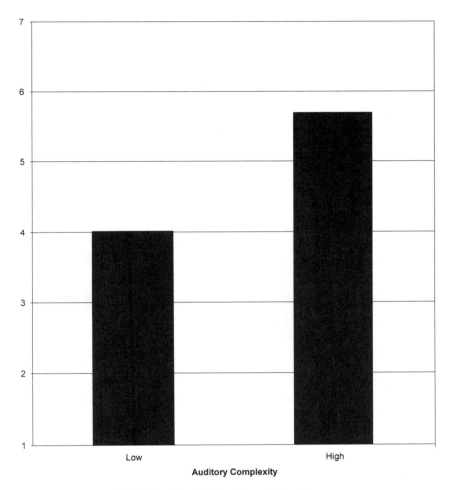

FIG. 10.3. Perceived excitement of station.

than simple spots. This is consistent with the literature on television message processing. However, the video studies have also demonstrated
physiological reactions that parallel the self-reported assessments of
arousal. Future studies may wish to employ physiological measurements
to replicate the effects of structural changes on listener arousal.

The current results also show that auditory complexity has a substantial effect on college-age listener attitudes toward the promos and the stations that they represent. Participants reported more favorable attitudes
toward the structurally complex promos. They also said that stations using complex spots were more exciting, and were more likely to be the type
of station they would listen to often.

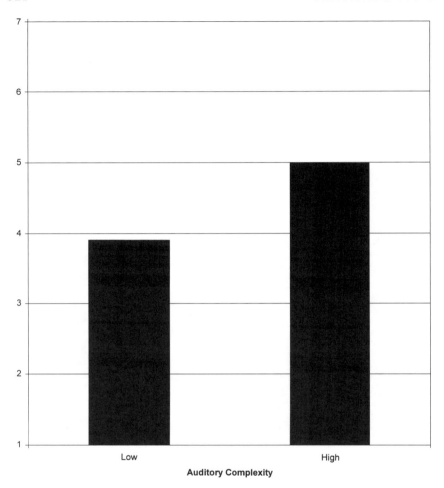

FIG. 10.4. Estimated time-spent-listening.

Unfortunately, the results showed no effect for complexity on the ability to recall the positioning statements or call letters of specific stations. In hindsight, this is not surprising because of the audience's limited exposure to the set of promos. All of the spots were taken from stations well outside the local market, so the participants only heard the call letters a few times before they were asked to recall them. As a result, free recall of call letters from both complex and simple promos was very low.

Still, the clear effects of auditory complexity on both spot recall and listener attitudes should be of utmost interest to industry professionals, considering the substantial role that memory and attitude play in the current radio ratings system. Because the design was balanced for other factors across the levels of complexity, it seems reasonable to suggest that something as simple as adding appropriate music or sound effects to an on-air promotion, or using a second announcer, will result in a better station image in the minds of listeners and better recall of the promo.

SUGGESTIONS FOR FUTURE RESEARCH

Given the relative paucity of published research in this area, much remains to be done. Four broad lines of inquiry, although by no means exhaustive, are suggested here: further experimental research in a vein similar to the study presented here, other investigations into different aspects of promo content and listener responses, marketing studies focusing on brand management in a radio context, and case studies and historical research.

Structure and Content in Radio

Although the effects just described are both interesting and potentially useful for professionals, this specific experimental design isolated the promotional spots from their normal context and involved a relatively narrow group of participants and a limited sample of radio formats. Subsequent research should try to achieve a more normal listening experience. This could involve playing the promos between music and commercials to see how surrounding programming interacts with the structure of the promos, or having the participants complete other tasks while listening. Further research should also investigate possible interactions among format appeals, audience demographics, promo content, and structural complexity (e.g., are more complex promos better suited to particular formats and audiences, whereas other audiences are best reached through less structurally complex spots?). And the critical question of the effect of promo complexity on call letter and slogan recall remains open. Given the importance of station identification in ratings methodologies, studies that further explore how (or whether) structural complexity affects recall of identifying information are needed.

Spot Content and Listener Response

The number of questions dealing with content variables and their effect on listeners is as endless as the ways to stylistically describe a spot or campaign. Nevertheless, the issues are important ones. Structurally, most stations are playing with essentially the same features. In many markets, the biggest differences between competitors' promotional efforts are likely to be in the content aspects of the campaign. However, these differences are likely to be among the most difficult questions to address methodologically because so many content variables are inherently subjective. In addition, it is difficult to separate content variables from contextual variables in order to study the effect of a particular spot or campaign. Humor, for example, is one variable that could affect promotion's impact. Gathering stimulus material is not particularly difficult—tapes of radio and TV spots, copies or tear sheets of print ads, billboard layouts, and so on, can all be had with relative ease beyond the sometimes substantial costs of time and tape. The study design itself is the real challenge. This is an area where context is likely to play an extremely crucial role. The audience perception of "humor" often may be affected by other contextual variables—the surrounding material, the listening setting, or the listener's mood and general receptiveness to humor.

Brand Marketing

Brand marketing efforts are a significant (perhaps dominant) component in the activities of contemporary radio stations, directly affecting all areas of station operation, including programming and staffing decisions (Barrett, 1999). Other industries devote significant attention to brand research (as described for television, e.g., in Bellamy & Traudt, chap. 5, this volume), yet communications scholars and marketing researchers have done little work beyond the broad prescriptions in programming and promotion texts to address branding issues in the context of radio.

Current marketing theory is dominated by the relationship metaphor, the idea that consumers form bonds with their chosen brands (Fournier, 1998). This idea has significant implications for radio promotion and programming. How do audience members bond with selected stations or formats? How tightly connected are those relationships as they develop and mature? Hiber (1998), for example, pointed to segmentation studies as the key to drawing the "emotional map" of a radio market in order to successfully connect the station brand with the audience's needs. Indeed, the symbolic meaning of goods and the role played by brands are important parts of self-identity in a postmodern consumer society—the consumption of branded products can convey information about a number of cultural categories, such as social status, age, gender, and values (Elliott & Wattanasuwan, 1998). Future research should try to explicate the relationships between various format elements and audience demographics and psychographics and test the effectiveness of different types of appeals, media mixes, and spot construction for gaining and maintaining the desired audience.

Research is also needed on the relationships within companies between the brand, management, and employees. Station consolidation in the

United States and similar pressures in other countries have created an environment where promotion directors and station creative staffs often find themselves in the position of sharing resources among co-owned and sometimes competing stations, frequently with little guidance on how to handle the situation (Reese, 1997). Meanwhile, marketing research has suggested that companies willing to construct their entire organization around a concept can boost their ability to communicate and to establish their identity (Tilley, 1999). How do stations (and groups) communicate the brand (or brands) within the company, and how do the brand characteristics impact managerial processes? Research has begun to look at the ways merging radio companies address various employee concerns (e.g., Fox, 1999), but the role of branding and promotion remain largely unexplored.

Historical and Case Approaches

Finally, other methods, such as case studies (as in Fournier, 1998; Williams, 1998b) or ethnographic research describing audiences' relationships with the media they use (as in Riggs, 1996), could provide a potential wealth of information for both practitioners and academics, but relatively few have been published to date in a radio context. Either on an individual case basis or on a broader scale, the results of that research would offer guideposts for the industry as well as additional theory-building evidence in this area. This method in particular might lend itself to studying the relationship between on-air and off-air promotion practices, and how each influences results, by capturing all of a campaign by one station or a group of stations, or studying an entire market during a set period of time. Case studies could also track a single station or group over time, exploring the development of promotion as the station responds to the results of previous campaigns and changes within the market.

As Williams (1998a) pointed out, there has been little work done exploring the historical development of radio promotion. A detailed historical record of promotion practices, from a single station to the broader industry, could provide scholars with valuable information regarding the development of both on-air and off-air promotion practices as well as offering the industry new insights into the tools available for their work. How have the changes in industry and social structures affected the development of promotion and programming, and what might those changes tell us about appropriate strategies today and next year?

Summary of Significance

The thousands of stations, millions of listeners, and billions of advertising dollars that constitute the radio marketplace in the United States suggest that radio continues to be a very important player in the evolving media environment. Competition for audience share and advertising dollars is steadily growing, both among stations within the radio industry (FCC, 1999)[3] and for radio within the broader media marketplace. It therefore remains somewhat surprising that so little research has been published on radio, and specifically in the area of promotion.

Given the importance of promotion for stations in a competitive market, understanding its processes, its role, and its effect is essential for academics as well as industry professionals. For academics, research on promotion can contribute to the development of mass communication processing theory. Moreover, it offers valuable insights into the industry that communication scholars study and describe to future professionals in the classroom, insights about how audiences react and why and how different strategies can affect station performance.

These same insights can benefit professionals as well. More than any other area of station operations, local managers can significantly affect the sound and image of their station through promotion (see Buchman, 1991; Vigil, 1998), and those efforts can directly contribute to a station's success (or failure). The results of research into the mechanisms that contribute to effective promotion can help drive more successful programming and sales. The study presented here, for example, suggests some practical rules of thumb for production directors, program directors, and promotion directors. Complex promos are good—more aurally complex spots lead to a more exciting station image in the listener's mind, for example—and the type of complexity involved in the studied spots is easy to accomplish for even relatively inexperienced producers. The winners will need every available edge, with promotion often playing the crucial role, in the ever more competitive radio marketplace.

REFERENCES

Alexander, N. (1997). Music radio programming. In S. T. Eastman & D. A. Ferguson (Eds.), *Broadcast/cable programming: Strategies and practices* (5th ed., pp. 351–376). Belmont, CA: Wadsworth.

Barrett, L. (1999, January 14). Why Emap axe fell at Kiss. *Marketing*, 9.

Berkowitz, E. N., Kerin, R. A., Hartley, S. W., & Rudelius, W. (1992). *Marketing*. Boston: Irwin.

Billings, A., Eastman, S. T., & Newton, G. D. (1998). Atlanta revisited: Prime-time promotion in the 1996 Summer Olympics. *Journal of Sport & Social Issues, 22,* 65–78.

Bolls, P. D., Lang, A., Potter, R. F., & Snyder, J. (1999). *How can I tell if you love me when I'm afraid to ask? The effects of message valence on emotional and cognitive responses to radio.* Paper presented to the Information Systems division at the annual convention of the International Communication Association, San Francisco, CA.

---

[3]FCC totals report 222 new radio stations during the 12 months preceding May 31, 1999.

Bolls, P. D., & Potter, R. F. (1998). I saw it on the radio: The effects of imagery evoking radio commercials on listeners' allocation of attention and attitude toward an ad. In D. D. Muehling (Ed.), *Proceedings of the 1998 Conference of the American Academy of Advertising* (pp. 120–130).

Bolls, P., Potter, R., & Lang, A. (1996). Television arousal and memory: The effects of production pacing and arousing content on encoding, storage and retrieval of television messages. In M. Gasser (Ed.), *Online proceedings of the 1996 Midwest Artificial Intelligence and Cognitive Science Conference* [Online]. Available: http://www.cs.indiana.edu/event/maics96/Proceedings/Bolls/bolls.html.

Borzillo, C. (1996a, May 18). Beyond hot dogs: Promotion a la Harris. *Billboard*, 95.

Borzillo, C. (1996b, August 3). Promax execs share some strategies. *Billboard*, 95.

Bradley, M. M. (1994). Emotional memory: A dimensional analysis. In S. Van Goozen, N. E. Van de Poll, & J. A. Sergeant (Eds.), *Emotions: Essays on emotion theory* (pp. 97–134). Hillsdale, NJ: Lawrence Erlbaum Associates.

Buchman, J. (1991). Commercial radio promotion. In S. T. Eastman & R. A Klein (Eds.), *Promotion and marketing for broadcasting and cable* (2nd ed., pp. 139–167). Prospect Heights, IL: Waveland Press.

Bunzel, R. (1999). Do you know who your listeners are? *Gavin* [Online]. Available: http://www.gavin.com/industry/radio/listener_profiles.shtml.

Christ, W. (1985). The construct of arousal in communication research. *Human Communication Research, 11,* 575–592.

Detenber, B. H., Simons, R. F., & Bennet, G. G. (1998). Roll 'em: The effects of picture motion on emotional responses. *Journal of Broadcasting & Electronic Media, 42,* 113–127.

Ditingo, V. M. (1999, January 4). Radio. *Broadcasting & Cable,* 39

Eastman, S. T., & Newton, G. D. (1998). The impact of structural salience within on-air promotion. *Journal of Broadcasting & Electronic Media, 42,* 50–79.

Eastman, S. T., & Newton, G. D. (1999). Hitting promotion hard: A network response to channel surfing and new competition. *Journal of Applied Communication Research, 27,* 73–85.

Eastman, S. T., Newton, G. D., Riggs, K. E., & Neal-Lunsford, J. (1997). Accelerating the flow: A transition effect in programming theory. *Journal of Broadcasting & Electronic Media, 41,* 265–283.

Elliott, R., & Wattanasuwan, K. (1998). Brands as symbolic resources for the construction of identity. *International Journal of Advertising, 17*(2), 131–144.

Federal Communications Commission. (1999). Broadcast station totals [Online]. Available: http://www.fcc.gov/mmb/asd/totals/.

Fournier, S. (1998). Consumers and their brands: Developing relationship theory in consumer research. *Journal of Consumer Research, 24,* 343–373.

Fox, K. (1999). *Should I take this job and shove it? An analysis of the effects of radio acquisitions on job satisfaction.* Paper presented to the Management & Sales division of the Broadcast Education Association, Las Vegas, NV.

Hausman, C., Benoit, P., & O'Donnell, L. B. (1996). *Modern radio production.* Belmont, CA: Wadsworth.

Hiber, J. (1998). How research can help you brand your station. *Gavin* [Online]. Available: http://www.gavin.com/industry/radio/981016/branding.shtml.

Interview: Tom Owens. (1998). *Radio and Production, 11*(3), 8–12.

Keith, M. C. (1987). *Radio programming: Consultancy and formatics.* Boston: Focal Press.

Keith, M. C. (1993). *The radio station.* Boston: Focal Press.

Lang, A. (1995). Defining audio/video redundancy from a limited capacity information processing perspective. *Communication Research, 22,* 86–115.

Lang, A. (2000). The information processing of mediated messages: A framework for communication research. *Journal of Communication, 50*(1), 46–70.

Lang, A., Bolls, P. D., Potter, R. F., & Kawahara, K. (1999). The effects of production pace and arousing content on the information processing of television messages. *Journal of Broadcasting & Electronic Media, 43*, 451–475.

Lang, A., Geiger, S., Strickwerda, M., & Sumner, J. (1993). The effects of related and unrelated cuts on viewers' memory for television: A limited capacity theory of television viewing. *Communication Research, 20*, 4–29.

Lang, A., Zhou, S., Schwartz, N., Bolls, P. D., & Potter, R. F. (2000). When an edit is an edit can an edit be too much? The effects of edits on arousal, attention, and memory for television messages. *Journal of Broadcasting & Electronic Media, 44*, 1–18.

Lang, P., Bradley, M., & Cuthbert, M. (1997). Motivated attention: Affect, activation, and action. In P. Lang, R. Simon, & M. Balaban (Eds.), *Attention and orienting: Sensory and motivational processes* (pp. 97–136). Mahwah, NJ: Lawrence Erlbaum Associates.

Lang, P. J., Greenwald, M., Bradley, M. M., & Hamm, A. O. (1993). Looking at pictures: Evaluative, facial, visceral, and behavioral responses. *Psychophysiology, 30*, 261–273.

Lutz, R. J. (1985). Affective and cognitive antecedents of attitude toward the ad: A conceptual framework. In L. F. Alwitt & A. A. Mitchell (Eds.), *Psychological processes and advertising effects: Theory, research, and applications.* Hillsdale, NJ: Lawrence Erlbaum Associates.

McKinsey & Co. (1985). *Radio in search of excellence: Lessons from America's best-run radio stations.* New York: McKinsey & Co.

Meeske, M., & Maunez-Caudra, J. (1992). Protecting radio call letters and slogans as trademarks. *Journal of Broadcasting & Electronic Media, 36*, 267–277.

Merli, J. (1998, May 4). Radio beats TV during the day: Interep usage study finds wide variety of listening patterns. *Broadcasting & Cable*, 117.

Morris, J. D. (1995, November–December). Observations: SAM: The self-assessment mankin, an efficient cross-cultural measurement of emotional response. *Journal of Advertising Research*, 63–68.

Norberg, E. G. (1996). *Radio programming: Tactics and strategy.* Boston: Focal Press.

Pease, E. C., & Dennis, E. E. (1995). *Radio — The forgotten medium.* New Brunswick, NJ: Transaction Publishers.

Perse, E. M. (1996). Sensation seeking and the use of television for arousal. *Communication Reports, 9*, 37–48.

Petty, R. E., & Cacioppo, J. T. (1986). The elaboration likelihood model of persuasion. In L. Berkowitz (Ed.), *Advances in experimental psychology* (Vol. 19). New York: Academic Press.

Piper-Aiken, K. S. (1997). Listener-member perceptions of marketing strategies employed by public radio stations. *Journal of Radio Studies, 4*, 15–19.

Potter, R. F. (1998). *The effects of voice change and production effects on attention to and memory for radio messages.* Unpublished doctoral dissertation, Indiana University, Bloomington.

Potter, R. F., & Callison, C. (2000). Sounds exciting! The effects of audio complexity on listeners' attitudes and memory for radio promotional announcements. *Journal of Radio Studies, 7*(1).

Potter, R. F., Lang, A., & Bolls, P. D. (1997). Orienting responses to structural features in media. *Psychophysiology, 34*(Suppl. 1), S72.

Potter, R. F., Lang, A., & Bolls, P. D. (1998). Orienting to structural features in auditory media messages. *Psychophysiology, 35*(Suppl. 1), S66.

Reese, D. (1997, June 21). Radio execs upbeat at Promax confab. *Billboard*, 75.

Riggs, K. E. (1996). Television use in a retirement community. *Journal of Communication, 46*(1), 144–156.

Singer, J. (1980). The power and limitations of television: A cognitive-affective analysis. In P. J. Tannenbaum (Ed.), *The entertainment functions of television.* Hillsdale, NJ: Lawrence Erlbaum Associates.

Strategic Media Research. (1996). *Methodology* [Online]. Available: http://www.rronline.com/SMRCASES/arovervi.htm.

Thorson, E., & Lang, A. (1992). Effects of television video graphics and lecture familiarity on adult cardiac orienting responses and memory. *Communication Research, 19,* 346–369.

Tilley, C. (1999, January–April). Built-in branding: How to engineer a leadership brand. *Journal of Marketing Management,* 181.

Verona, E., Curtin, J. J., Levenston, G. K., Bradley, M. M., Lang, P. J., & Patrick, C. J. (1997). Psychopathy and physiological response to emotionally evocative sounds. *Psychophysiology, 34*(S1), 92.

Vigil, J. (1998, January). Eric Chase. *Radio and Production,* 6–15.

Walker, J. (1993). Catchy, yes, but does it work? The impact of broadcast network promotion frequency and type on program success. *Journal of Broadcasting & Electronic Media, 37,* 197–207.

Warren, S. (1997). *Radio: The book.* Washington, DC: National Association of Broadcasters.

Watt, J. H. (1994). *Radio commercial sound quality and recall: Effects of form novelty and complexity* (NAB Research Report). Washington, DC: National Association of Broadcasters.

Webster, J., Phalen, P. F., & Lichty, L. (2000). *Ratings analysis: The theory and practice of audience research* (2nd ed.). Mahwah, NJ: Lawrence Erlbaum Associates.

Williams, G. C. (1998a). *Building a network image: On-air promotion and NBC radio 1940–1948.* Paper presented at the Broadcast Education Association, Las Vegas, NV.

Williams, G. C. (1998b). *Money, music, and marketing: Promoting local radio with cash.* Paper presented at the Broadcast Education Association, Las Vegas, NV.

Yoon, K., Bolls, P., & Lang, A. (1998). The effects of arousal on liking and believability of commercials. *Journal of Marketing Communications, 4,* 101–114.

Zechmeister, E. B., & Nyberg, S. E. (1982). *Human memory: An introduction to research and theory.* Monterey, CA: Brooks/Cole.

Zillmann, D. (1982). Television and arousal. In D. Pearl, L Bouthilet, & J. Lazar (Eds.), *Television and behavior: Ten years of scientific progress and implications for the eighties* (Vol. 2). Washington, DC: U.S. Department of Health and Human Services.

Online Program Promotion

Douglas A. Ferguson
College of Charleston

In July 1999, Polon wrote online: "The whole point of a web site is to increase viewer loyalty to your station and its services, thus counteracting declining numbers for network television." Using the Internet to promote to local radio and television audiences has grown as web design has developed over the last decade. Once a simple listing and a few links, the local broadcaster's online presence has evolved into a sophisticated promotional tool. Broadcast viewers can now use the Internet to find audio and video content that they missed on-air and to tie into conventional broadcast programming. The assumption broadcasters make is that those people who find satisfying material online are more likely to watch on-air in the future.

Nonetheless, few studies have looked at aspects of online promotion by broadcasters. This chapter examines the literature to date and presents an original study looking at the degree to which Internet promotion of programs is akin to traditional print and on-air promotion of shows and in what ways it is dissimilar. The chapter concludes with a discussion of issues in researching online promotion and some methodological problems for scholarly investigation into online program promotion with the goal of encouraging more disinterested academic research in this area.

USES OF ONLINE

Although the literature on the Internet is already enormous and swells daily, very little has been published—online or on paper—about media promotion via the web. The issue is important because trade reports suggest that as many as 84 million adults in the United States accessed online services in 1999, up from 66 million adults the previous year (IntelliQuest, 1999). Because of technological convergence, the web appears to be changing very rapidly. As Bucy, Lang, Potter, and Grabe (1999) report, much of the research about online sites has been conducted by commercial services and is proprietary, or it has been qualitative and anecdotal in nature. Aside from studies of such phenomena as bulletin boards and news groups (see, e.g., James, Wotring, & Forrest, 1995), most academic surveys of online media sites tend to be broad and to disregard program promotion or subsume it within analyses of much larger units dealing with a media company's entire web site. Coffey and Stipp (1997) found that computer use does not compete directly with television use, implying that online can serve as a path feeding into broadcast and cable use.

Most of the growing number of studies examine the use of the web from the audience standpoint. In particular, the availability of news content on station web sites has become one focal area (see Niekamp, 1997; Rosales & Pitts, 1997). Atkin, Jeffres, and Neuendorf (1998) studied online communication using a diffusion of innovations approach. They found that attitudinal variables were not more explanatory than demographics, but they did find the lack of use of computers online to be associated with a "local media" orientation, perhaps suggesting that many local stations may be missing their most ardent audience by not putting information online. Advertising and e-mail have also been of considerable interest (see Niekamp, 1996), but only a very few studies look at online promotion of television programs—although a great many comments about program promotion appear in chat rooms and in station feedback (see http: //www. promolounge.com).

Any analysis of online promotion must consider many design elements and features of online services. One of the most interesting to researchers, because it has important implications for communication theory, is the interactive capacity of the web that permits communication directly between consumers and businesses and consumers. When Ha and James (1998) studied 110 web sites, they found that service companies had failed to capitalize on connecting with customers where there was no transaction for goods, suggesting that media web sites are envisioned merely as showcases of company accomplishments. Yet increasing audience size— the primary function of program promotion—remains one of the powerful forces driving broadcast and cable networks to utilize the web at the present time.

Online communication has also been examined from a uses-and-gratifications perspective. Perse and Dunn (1998) studied a national random telephone sample of 1,071 people and found that computers were not one of the main channels used to fill media-related needs. Ferguson and Perse

(2000) surveyed 250 respondents and reported that one key difference between television use and online communication is that the latter is not a relaxing way to pass time. Although these studies shed some light on audience use, they do not provide information for the senders of online messages, particularly with regard to improving media promotion.

From a theoretical perspective, Bucy et al. (1999) pointed to media research connecting such messages attributes as attention, arousal, memory, and preference with attributes of content and form (see Lang, 1990; Lang, Bolls, Potter, & Kawahara, 1999; and Perse, chap. 2, and Eastman & Bolls, chap. 3, this volume). In addition, interactive capability and audio and video streaming are characteristics contributing to perceptions of ease of use and appeal of web pages. Studies that analyze the content and form of media web sites can provide guidelines for web designs that have greater value for the industry and, at the same time, lead to sites of more value to users. Research into meaningful guidelines may, ultimately, contribute to understanding the workings of cognitive processes.

RESEARCH ABOUT ONLINE PROMOTION

Previous research has identified three distinct areas of online media promotion: web pages that promote individual television programs or station lineups; web pages that promote media companies, such as NBC's or Time Warner's online sites or those of individual local television and radio stations; and web pages that promote new forms of entertainment—comparable to programs—on the web itself. This chapter concentrates on program promotion by stations via the web and includes findings about the other two topics whenever possible. Clearly, most research so far has focused on promotion by television stations, although Bucy et al. (1999) looked more broadly at popular sites of all kinds and Murphy (1998) looked at the value of radio station web sites in the sole study of that medium.

Although scholars such as Bucy et al. (1999) have asked whether the capabilities of the web are being fully exploited in media sites, the larger underlying issue about web promotion is whether the television channel model for media content is really applicable to the Internet. Broadcasters seek to buy their way into the future (via mergers, buyouts, joint-operating agreements, etc.), but it is not clear what the future is. Are thousands of web-age "channels" really comparable to the broadcast/cable model of dozens of channels? This question was posed in a cover story in *Internet World* on measuring advertising on web sites (Virzi, 1998). It follows that the attributes of web pages promoting programs may need to differ from the attributes of print and on-air promotion.

Just as Rank (1991) and other authors of advertising texts laid out the primary strategies and tactics of persuasion in advertising, in similar fashion, Eastman, Ferguson, and Klein (1999) spelled out the primary practices and strategies of promotion by broadcasters and cable operators. But whether these strategies and tactics fit the online world is an open question. In one notable case study, Wolfe (1997) recounted NBC's history of web promotion and concluded that web use has matured to the stage where web users expect sophistication in design and have little tolerance for such things as errors or delays in page updates. There is no comparable research about traditional print and on-air promotion.

Studies of Station Sites

Table 11.1 summarizes the nine research articles and papers that analyzed online promotion by television stations.[1] Five of these studies examined local television stations' use of the web, including how the viewing of programs can be promoted; three studies considered more specialized subtopics, and one ranged beyond media-only sites.

Looking at all 3,316 pages of the 1995 web sites of 61 television stations, Bates and King (1996) sought to discover how the early innovators and adopters among television stations were using the World Wide Web. They asked what content their web sites contained and were particularly interested in whether the stations saw online communication as offering promotional opportunities, such as by providing guides, information about talent and programs, and/or the opportunity to obtain information previously aired, such as transcripts of special reports or news stories. Second, they asked whether stations were taking full advantage of the features of the Internet and whether they were providing the kinds of content that users tend to find interesting, attractive, and/or useful. The answers to these questions came in the form of numerous tables that reported the values for the many variables they measured (page size, use of graphics, and use of interactive hypertext), some of which are summarized in the tables assembled later in this chapter. But the overall finding (see Table 11.1) was that chronologically early (meaning mid-1990s) web sites were unsophisticated and used only portions of the capacity of the web. Bates and King concluded that web sites were mostly used for self-promotion by the station, rather than as conduits for information.

Niekamp (1996) analyzed the 1996 web sites of 123 television stations to assess their features in relation to network affiliations and market size. He found that e-mail was the most common form of feedback and appeared commonly on news pages and most general pages, especially on sites of

---

[1]Bucy et al. (1999) included television stations but also had many nonmedia sites in their study.

TABLE 11.1
Summary of Online Promotion Studies

Author(s)	Publication Year, Data Year	Database and Sample	Selected Findings
Bates and King	1996 1995	Analysis of web sites of 61 U.S. TV stations, examining all 3,316 pages for features.	Found that early TV station web sites lacked advanced characteristics and were not sophisticated, did not make full use of Internet functionality, and were dominated by station self-promotion, as opposed to being conduits of information.
Niekamp	1996 1996	Analysis of 123 web sites for U.S. TV stations to describe features, uses, revenue sources, and roles of network affiliation and market size.	Found that e-mail feedback is prevalent for news and general pages for most sites and text versions of news stories were the most common content with links to station's local news operations; showed that Big Three affiliates had the strongest web presence, but little support by advertisers.
Bates et al.	1997 1996	Investigated 416 TV stations with web sites and coded up to two levels, including main (home) page for features used by stations.	Located improvements in the use of the web and inclusion of web features compared to 1 year before, but noted that audio and video features were largely unused and that sites lacked nonpromotional content; found more graphic and visual elements in sites.
Rosales and Pitts	1997 1996	Analyzed 47 TV station web sites to look for e-mail, clips, pictures, links, graphics, news, station promotion, and programming information.	Reported the percentages of sites with particular features and concluded that all stations used their sites to promote the station itself; found that 81% offered programming information, but did not distinguish program promotion from station promotion; concluded that stations' intent was to target users who might be potential audiences for on-air, using contests, merchandising, and info about station personnel and mission.
Niekamp	1997 1997	E-mail survey of 108 responding stations (34%) asking about their features, interactivity, quantity of e-mail in relation	Found that hot links in news stories significantly predicted the number of page reads per day, whereas the presence of audio and video clips, interactive features, length of time

(Continued)

TABLE 11.1
(*Continued*)

Author(s)	Publication Year, Data Year	Database and Sample	Selected Findings
		to market size, audio and video in news content, and frequency of redesign, using multiple regression analysis of usage.	online, frequent redesign, and small and midmarket size did not predict use of pages (although large market stations were more heavily used, as well as stations with more hot links); concluded that users might be "news junkies."
McClung	1997 1996 & 1997	Conducted a secondary analysis of Bates and King's and Bates et al.'s data in order to assess the efficiency of sites.	Revealed that TV web sites became increasingly efficient in presenting information to end users by adhering to more precise document representation, with the outcome of making information retrieval easier for users; concluded that the trend was toward user efficiency.
Kiernan and Levy	1999 1997	Surveyed commercial TV stations about the features of web sites and degree of competition in local markets.	Found that the content of web sites varied widely in the kinds of news and other content offered and in the types of interactive features supplied; calculated web competition as content diversity (a breadth measure) and site diversity (a measure of formats utilized in sites), but found no significant relationship between diversity and station characteristics such as market size, financial resources, or network affiliation.
Bucy et al.	1999 1997	Analyzed home pages of 496 sites drawn from top-100 most-used sites to find out if web capabilities were exploited; compared commerical and noncommercial sites and the relationship between traffic and site complexity.	Described a large set of site features in detail and by kind of source (commercial or not); included nonmedia sites, so results go beyond TV stations; found significant relationships between the amount of site traffic and home-page structure for both commercial and noncommercial sites; concluded that site packaging will become increasingly important to gaining users' attention.
Atkin et al.	1998 1998	Conducted a regional telephone survey of 377 randomly selected adults about the role of the Internet in their media choices.	Found that Internet access did not figure significantly in most consumers' orientation toward the local media; the rank of TV web sites was far less prominent than that of more traditional media.

stations affiliated with ABC, CBS, or NBC. However, Niekamp (1996) found far less advertising content than anticipated, and he did not analyze the promotion of programs.

A subsequent study of the 1996 web sites of 416 television stations by Bates et al. (1997) provided an opportunity for comparisons over time with the findings in Bates and King (1996). The results showed a general improvement in the station web sites, especially with regard to graphic and visual elements, and a higher level of use of sites for station promotion, although the employment of audio and video features remained very low.

Rosales and Pitts (1997) located 47 television stations with web sites in 1996 out of 360 randomly selected stations, concluding that only a small percentage (13%) of stations were actually making use of the web as of May 1996. Their study focused on whether existing sites had such features as audio and video clips, pictures, graphics, and links, and they reported that virtually all the sampled stations lacked audio and video clips but had graphics and links. Only one third or so carried pictures and had links to networks, but few linked to sister stations. However, Rosales and Pitts found the links distracting and confusing for users. They concluded that most stations used sites for promotion but concentrated on such station self-promotional information as mission/vision statements and lists of personnel and such activities as contests and giveaways. Although they located a sizable proportion of sites with programming information, their study did not distinguish station from program promotion.

In a second study conducted in 1997, Niekamp (1997) attempted to predict site traffic (the "pages read" by consumers) using features of television web sites, and he found that hot links were the primary significant predictor. Other characteristics, such as the presence or absence of audio or video clips or e-mail, length of time that the station had had a web site, frequency of redesign of the site, did not predict site traffic. Not surprisingly, he did find that large market stations were more heavily used than the sites of small or midsized market stations. Niekamp (1997) concluded that web users probably tended to be "news junkies."

Reanalyzing the data previously collected by Bates and King (1996) and Bates et al. (1997), McClung (1997) focused on features related to ease of use—which he defined as efficiency for the user. He found that stations had become more efficient by standardizing their pages, but concluded that stations' self-representation was both inadequate and misleading.

Looking in another direction, in a study of the 1997 web sites of 62 U.S. television stations, Kiernan and Levy (1999) focused on the characteristics of sites in relation to the amount of local competition, in the assumption that high competition would result in more elaborated web sites, an assumption ultimately refuted by their analysis. When they evaluated journalistic competition among web sites, they found no relationship between site characteristics and numbers or kinds of competitors. Assessing such attributes as whether the site carried local news, network news, weather reports, sports information, program scripts, archives, and audio and video clips, Kiernan and Levy found no relationship between their measures of diversity and such station characteristics. They also found that the content of web sites was not related to station financial resources, market rank, or network affiliation. They concluded that stations may not be competing journalistically, at least in ways that are reflected in web sites.

One of the most sophisticated studies of site attributes to date comes from Bucy et al. (1999), and it is particularly useful because it spells out in detail many of the formal features related to the promotional characteristics of web sites. Bucy et al. coded the home pages of 496 randomly selected high-volume web sites in 1997, encompassing some media sites but stretching beyond to include educational and other commercial sites. Bucy et al. concluded that web-page designers have failed to make much use of the interactive and audio/video capabilities of the medium, but that more complex web sites seem to foster increased web traffic. They also concluded that web pages tended to conform to accepted design rules largely by default because most were so technologically simple. This study provides a model for future research of entire web sites or more selective pages of media and nonmedia sites.

Atkin et al. (1998) undertook a random telephone survey of 377 television stations to understand the ways that the 1998 media sites of local stations fit into the public's communication orientation and how they ranked as sources of current information. They found that media web sites played only a very small role in the minds of most consumers at the time the survey was conducted.

The gaps in the kinds of data collected in these studies and their apparently contradictory findings, as well as the rapid changes in computer technology and increased consumer adoption of faster equipment, suggested that it was time for another study of the design features of web sites. The study reported in this chapter was limited to television station sites in order to focus on program promotion, a critical aspect of web communication overlooked in several previous studies.

A STUDY OF ONLINE STATION PROMOTION

The broadcasting industry has taken a keen interest in what stations are doing online, particularly with regard to program promotion, and the weekly trade journal *Broadcasting & Cable* has begun devoting a section to the "Site of the Week" (Tedesco, 1998). Because stations devote so many of their human and dollar resources to the improvement of their web sites, continuous measurement of sites helps practitioners track the latest developments and scholars estimate their impact on society and the media industry. The study reported in this chapter analyzes features of current program promotion in the online medium with the goal of adding to the developing database about web-site characteristics. It also lays a foundation for further research in areas heretofore unexplored by providing a 1999 snapshot of how television stations are adapting multimedia to an old-fashioned one-to-many model of media communication, at least in terms of marketing and promotion.

Research Questions

Taken together, the available trade press and scholarly reports suggest that station web sites should have become more sophisticated by 1999 because of the industry footrace to outdo the competition by offering advanced online features. Rather than focus on hypotheses, however, this study explored the ways in which television stations were using online web sites in 1999 to promote their programs. Five research questions guided the research:

R1: What stylistic elements characterize television station web sites and what do they contribute to online promotion of programs?

R2: In what ways have web features and online promotional practices of television stations varied over time?

R3: How do the features and promotional aspects of station web sites vary in relation to network affiliation?

R4: What sources of promotion (local, syndicated, network) do affiliates draw on?

R5: What proportion of stations conduct contesting and merchandising online?

These questions were tackled by collecting data as closely matched as possible to that in previous studies as well as collecting new facets of sites that relate to the ways popular television programs carried by local stations are promoted online.

Method

This study used both quantitative and qualitative content analysis to assess television stations' use of the web to promote their programs. The content of a sample of 290 television station sites, including their use of links to the seven broadcast networks of ABC, CBS, NBC, Fox, UPN, WB, and PBS.[2]

Sample

In February of 1999, a systematic random sample was drawn from the sampling frame of all U.S. television stations, including translator frequencies, appearing on the FCC web site (www.fcc.org). The list appeared as a binary file formatted as an Excel spreadsheet of station frequency assignments for digital television (HDTV). For this study, every fifth listing was marked from a random starting point, and a sample of 291 stations was generated, of which 179 had web sites (62%). Because the original FCC database listed only the channel number and the city of license, individual station's call letters were located using http://www.ultimatetv. com. Another site (http://www.tvfind.com) provided the call letters in combination with the network affiliations of stations without web sites.[3]

Variables, Coders, and Analysis

Unlike many previous studies that designated the home page as the unit of analysis, this study followed the example of Rosales and Pitts (1997) and used the entire web site for each station. However, the study's focus was on the pages in each website that promoted specific television programs, not on the pages that provided generic lineup information or background material on the station's history or management, talent, or technology.

The methodology and features of web sites examined in this study drew on studies by Bucy et al. (1999), Bates and King (1996), Niekamp (1996), and Bates et al. (1997). The variables studied included the same six variables collected in previous research: number of pages and percentage using frames for each web site, the number of photographs, text and graphic links, full-motion video, and merchandising pages. Seven additional variables were measured in order to focus on program-page design attributes: the use of background colors, the warmth or coolness of colors, animation, sources of text content, and degree of scrolling (also called blinking), as well as interactive features such as feedback and e-mail directly related to the programmer. Some variables used in previous studies (e.g., advertising and news content) were not collected, in order to focus on program promotion. Two other variables, such as the selling of mer-

---

[2]Pax TV was not included, as its programming largely consists of off-network reruns at this time.

[3]In July 1999, the most comprehensive site was located at http://www.metronet.com/~chipk/usatv.

chandise (used only by Rosales & Pitts, 1997) and conducting contests, were added to better understand the kinds of promotional activities that have become popular since the earlier studies were conducted.

Coders were recruited from a class of senior-level students familiar with broadcasting research, with each of 33 students examining the web sites of 10 stations or fewer. After coding, intercoder reliability was measured using a double-coded subsample of 30 sites. The average reliability across all items coded was .82, an acceptable level for exploratory research.

Quantitative data were collected for each station web site and entered first into a spreadsheet, along with short qualitative descriptions of each site. The final step was the collapse of quantitative information from raw counts into categories for statistical analysis. Qualitative information was examined separately, and focused on general comments about each web site made by the coders.

Results

The sample of 179 station sites provided a wealth of data for analysis. The section below compares the findings in this study (called "Ferguson" in the tables) to the findings in previous studies, before introducing the new material.

Comparative Station Site Attributes

Although the original studies are far richer in detail than outlined in Tables 11.2 and 11.4, the summarized information permits comparisons of congruent findings in the current study (labeled "Ferguson 1999" in the tables) with the studies by Bates and King (1996), Niekamp (1996), Bates et al. (1997), Rosales and Pitts (1997), McClung (1997), Kiernan and Levy (1999), and Bucy et al. (1999). The studies are listed in the order of oldest to most recent data in order to illustrate changes over time.

Tables 11.2 and 11.3 identify studies by the year that the data were collected rather than publication date, because change happens so swiftly in the computer business that a delay in publication might confuse the time order of online developments.

Table 11.2 shows the percentage of the web sites studied by the various researchers in relation to the network affiliation of the stations,[4] also including the data from the current study. The data show that in 1995, ABC, CBS, and, perhaps surprisingly, PBS stations accounted for a substantial

---

[4]As previously mentioned, Bucy et al. (1999) assessed sites as either commercial or noncommercial but included more than just television stations, thus no data is reported for that study in Table 11.2.

TABLE 11.2
Comparative Percentage of Network Affiliations
for Television Web Sites

Study/Year of Data Collection	Affiliated Network									
	ABC	CBS	NBC	Fox	WB	UPN	Pax	PBS	Indie	Other
Bates/1995	26.7	22.9	16.4	4.9		1.6		21.3		6.2
Bates/1996	15.5	16.7	20.7	10.6	2.1	4.5		11.8	4.0	14.1
Niekamp/1996	23.5	28.4	25.2	14.6	2.4	4.1		none	1.6	0.2
Rosales/1996	21.3	14.9	23.4	6.4	4.3	4.3		none	2.1	23.3
Rosales/1997[a]	17.8	20.5	21.2	9.0	2.6	3.8		none	7.5	17.6
Kiernan/1997	31.0	24.0	26.0	13.0	5.0	2.0		none		
Ferguson/1999	18.2	13.1	17.2	10.3	3.1	2.4	1.7	15.5	8.9	9.6

[a]Addendum to 1996 study.

number of web sites, but most studies reveal the early dominance of NBC stations and the later strengthening of CBS's and ABC's sites.[5] Some of the differences in proportions in this table can be explained by sampling methods, but the general trend is that the web-site shares approximate the commercial networks' audience shares. The public network, however, tends to be better represented online than its average audience share might suggest, perhaps because its upscale audience contains more web users. Use of the web is likely to increase substantially in the future as stations perceive sites as less peripheral to the promotional effort and more central to the distribution of their content. Conceived as a pie chart, Fig. 11.1 distinguishes the current study to illustrate the distribution of the affiliations of the web sites that were examined.

Table 11.3 displays the number of stations analyzed, the average length of the pages, and the proportion of pages using the device called frames. (*Frames* are sections of the screen that may encircle the center of the screen, but more probably occupy the side or bottom or top in a band that alters independently of the main part of the screen. Such devices increase the information-carrying capacity of the screen and make it a better tool for promotion.) As the table shows, there are large gaps in data collection and widely differing methodologies among these studies, although they are the most closely related available. The number of pages (or screen length) was not commonly measured because it varies so widely depending on the receiver's technology; even with the same equipment, the user's browser settings affect the number of screens displayed on a site with vertical-scrolling content. Congruent with trade reports, most authors have

---

[5]Bates and King's (1996) first small sample did not reveal the shift in network dominance because the total depended on number of pages per site (and one ABC station had 600 pages).

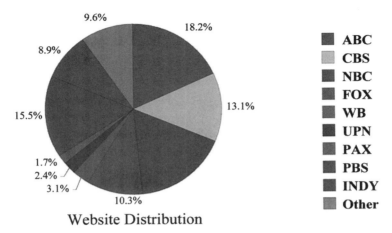

Website Distribution

FIG. 11.1. Proportions of stations affiliated with networks.

concluded that web sites are growing only slightly in sheer size. Bates and King (1996) found an average of 54 pages per site (calculated later by McClung, 1997) and Bucy et al. (1999) reported that the average home page consumed three or fewer screens (86%). At the same time, the two studies that collected data on the use of multiple frames suggest that it may be declining. If so, simplification of web sites is addressing the needs of the user by increasing the speed at which pages appear and mini-malizing the need for advanced software and hardware.

In addition, Table 11.3 provides stronger data on the number of photo-graphs on the pages examined, and reveals that the quantity appears to be greatly increasing, although the appropriateness of photographs naturally varies according to the kind of content examined. One would expect few photos on home pages, for example, but many on program promotion pages. In addition, both studies by Bates and others use subcategories (e.g., small photo, medium photo, large photo) that defy direct compari-sons, but the trend appears to be toward more photographs. This coin-cides with industry recommendations for effective promotional practice; display advertisements with photographs attract more attention (see East-man et al., 1999).

Table 11.3 also reports the average percentage of web sites examined with links to other sites. The results show an increase over time, peaking at 80% or 90%, but with the expected variation with the kind of page ex-amined. Clearly, most home pages will have links, whereas pages pro-moting programs or other information will have fewer links. Rosales and Pitts (1997) made particular note of the distraction and confusion arising from having frequent highlighted links inside paragraphs. They refer to the practice as cumbersome and confusing for users. Studies that go be-

TABLE 11.3
Number of Pages per Web Sites, and Percentage
With Frames, Photographs, Links, Blinking Technology,
Animation, and Streaming Video Clips

Study	Data Year	No. of Stations	Average No. of Pages/Screens	% With Frames	% With Photos	% With Links	% With Blinking	% With Animation	% With Video
Bates and King	1995	61	54[a]	NA	13.8%	46.7%	NA	NA	0.2%
Niekamp	1996	123	NA	NA	7.3%	62.6%	NA	NA	0.8%
Bates et al.	1996	416	?	NA	5.8%	67.7%	NA	20.5%	6.9%
Rosales and Pitts	1996	47	NA	NA	36.2%	98.0%	NA	NA	36.2%
Kiernan and Levy	1997	62	NA	NA	40.7%	81.3%	NA	NA	18.9%
Bucy et al.	1997	496	3 or less, 86%[b]	79.4%	31.9%	97.8%	9.7%	11.9%	NA
Ferguson	1999	177	NA	23.4%	86.0%	80.4%	29.4%	55.9%	36.9%

[a]Average total number of pages per site. [b]Average percentage of sites having the home page completed in three screens or fewer.

yond the counting of links into particular types in relation to particular content are clearly needed.

Table 11.3 includes the percentages of sites with blinking capability, animation, and video streaming, insofar as these researchers reported them. The simple device of blinking text appears to be an effective technique for attracting attention, so it was counted separately. The present study gave wide latitude to coders to define blinking and animation, but limited the category of video to real-time streaming in this study (generally, it was called either archived material or real-time in previous studies). Surprisingly, over one third of station sites in the current study took advantage of browser features such as RealVideo that permit streaming video. Seven types of streaming-video content were identified: audio feeds, skycam views, news stories, local radar screens, sports, program promos, and movie reviews.

In sum, this portion of the findings demonstrates a marked increase in the use of all three advanced technologies over the mid-1990s. Because faster servers and computer connections will speed up the reception of photographs, animation, and other complex elements, they will facilitate greater use of such elements in future web promotion.

Sources of Promotional Content and Interactions

Table 11.4 looks at the sources of promotional content and the interactive features found in the various studies. It illustrates the relative paucity of data on the use of local, syndicated, and national content. Some previous studies did collect information on the use of program schedules and station logos, but none of the earlier studies counted the instances of local program promotion. The meaning of the leap from 7% to 57.3% in syndicated content is not clear, nor are the variations in levels of network content, though it can be expected to be increasing. Ferguson found that rate of network pages went up among affiliates of the Big Four networks to 74.6% of the content. Bates and King (1996) did report, however, that 37.7% of the pages they investigated were promotional.

Table 11.4 also reports the percentages (or stations) that use interactive communication with the audience. The two studies by Bates and others (1996; 1997) use each page as the unit of analysis, so direct comparisons to other research are invalid. Even so, the table shows dramatic increases in the availability of e-mail and other kinds of interactions on station web sites. Bucy et al. (1999) found an average of 27.1 asynchronous elements per home page, including text links (98%), picture links (66.1%), e-mail links (49.4%), phone numbers (14.5%), addresses (8.5%), and survey forms (4.2%). It has always been clear that getting feedback of some kind from the viewers and listeners is crucial to a successful promotional effort—

TABLE 11.4
Percentage of Pages With Promotion From Local,
Syndicated, or Network Sources, and With E-Mail
Feedback, and Other Means of Interaction

	Source of Promotion			Interactive Features	
Study	% Local	% Syndicated	% Network	E-Mail	Other Interaction
Bates and King	NA	NA	NA	12.3%	0.1%
Niekamp	NA	NA	NA	82.1%	NA
Bates et al.	NA	7.0%	46.2%	39.4%	1.5%
Rosales and Pitts	NA	NA	78.7%	NA	NA
Kiernan and Levy	NA	NA	NA	27.4%	NA
Bucy et al.	NA	NA	NA	49.4%	9.7%
Ferguson	98.3%	57.3%	69.1%	92.1%	19.8%

whether that feedback came in the form of handwritten letters, telephone calls, or ratings. Online sites appear to be changing the way broadcasters conceive their programming service to audiences because with interactivity stations can tailor their messages, including those that promote programs. As shown in Table 11.4, e-mail remains the most simple form of two-way communication, but newer forms of real-time interactivity (e.g., chat rooms) were becoming more popular by the end of the decade.

Program Promotion Online

In the data collected for this chapter, 166 individual local, syndicated, and network programs were promoted online. Of those, most of the promotion, by far, was for local shows. As in previous research, three common threads of local shows were commonly touted: local news (e.g., News 10, WB20 News), area team sports, and weather. The promotion of an occasional local talk show or public affairs program was the exception. The next table of findings reports the kind of promotion carried online (in other words, whether the content was for local programs such as early-evening and late newscasts, syndicated reruns, or first-run network programs). The findings spell out the proportion of each of the three kinds of programs that television stations with different affiliations chose to promote on their web sites. The goal was to see if web promotion was unusually selective by type of program and whether the pattern of affiliates of some networks differed markedly from their competitors's patterns. No comparable data was reported for earlier studies.

Table 11.5 demonstrates that nearly all affiliates focus on local programming in their web sites. Only in the case of the WB (83.3%), whose affiliates are often the fifth or sixth stations in the market, is the affiliates' commitment less than total to promoting local programs. (In this table, the lower

TABLE 11.5
Cross-Tabulation of Aired Promos by
Network Affiliation and Promo Source

1999 Data	n	% Local	% Syndication	% Network
ABC	36	100.0	58.3	61.1
CBS	30	96.7	67.7	74.2
NBC	44	100.0	52.3	81.8
Fox	15	100.0	80.0	86.7
UPN	3	100.0	100.0	66.7
WB	6	83.3	66.7	100.0
PBS	32	96.9	36.4	48.5

percentages mean that affiliates of that network promoted fewer of their programs of that kind online, irrespective of what they did in print and on the air.)

Syndicated programming provides another story entirely. The four most commonly cited syndicated shows were *Home Improvement, Oprah, Ricki Lake*, and *Jerry Springer*. Only UPN affiliates promoted all their syndicated programs (100%). Fox affiliates, traditionally the oldest of the once-independent stations in each market, were more likely to promote local programs (local = 100%, syndicated = 80%, network = 86.7%), which is rather surprising because many Fox affiliates lack much by way of local programs. NBC affiliates, often the earliest in their respective markets to have a strong web presence, were very unlikely to promote their syndicated shows (52.3%). With regard to promotion of network shows, the six commercial stations in the 1999 sample showed strong commitment to promoting most network shows, although public stations apparently felt no such obligation. The four network shows that were most commonly cited were *ABC World News Tonight, Late Night With Conan O'Brien, The Tonight Show With Jay Leno*, and *JAG*.

Because merchandising and contesting are other aspects of promotion, tracking their use is an important aspect of understanding how web sites are used to promote programming, but the sole study before this current one to report such data was Rosales and Pitts (1997). They reported that all the stations they sampled used their sites for station promotion, and noted that 47% used web sites for marketing such products or services as station souvenir items and social activities.

Merchandising and Contesting

In the current study, the researcher found that about one fourth of stations (24.3%) were pushing the envelope of standard banner-and-listing program promotion by merchandising their stations using commercial tie-ins to product sales. Merchandise offers ranged from program-related items (T-shirts, ball caps, souvenirs, videos) to flowers, magazines, and advertising coupons. More unusual offerings—defying classification—were free slide shows, virtual station tours, free live psychic readings, tax assistance, instant polls, job boards, recipes, games, and kids' clubs. In some instances, the stations stepped out of the realm of broadcast content entirely in order to take full advantage of a different type of medium. For example, advertising banners and product tie-ins were pitched to local merchants as business opportunities on stations' web sites, showing that they targeted more than the usual audience with online content.

Although contesting, in the form of giveaways and sweepstakes, has been used on-air and in print media for decades by promotion managers, 27% of the web sites in this analysis also contained contest information. Stations that ran online contests used the same sort of trivia question or sweepstakes approach used on-air, with the usual prizes ranging from trips (e.g., to Las Vegas) to concert and sporting event tickets. More interesting was the fact that two stations exploited the graphic/textual nature of web pages to offer crossword-type puzzles. The findings about merchandising and contesting suggest that traditional promotional practices are beginning to move to a new venue.

Discussion of This Study

In addition to some general features tracked in most studies of web sites, this study assessed the sophistication of the parts of station web sites devoted to programs—which may be the part that draws most users (see Ferguson, 1999) and thus which should have the most promotional value for stations. The first research question asked about the stylistic elements characterizing online promotion at the present time and the second research question asked about changes in features over time. The results showed that stylistic elements have been measured in such different ways that comparison becomes problematic, but the general trend seems to be that sites have become more visual (with photographs, streaming video) and more interactive (more e-mail, more features), while at the same time becoming less cluttered and probably promoting program (and stations) more effectively.

Nowadays, stations that are more effective at promotion strive to simplify the promotional message instead of trying to do too much (see Eastman's 1999 guidelines in which "less is more"), and this message seems to have moved to the online world. It may be that limiting the length of scrolling pages and cutting back on text are effective ways for stations to create an uncluttered web site, at least as suggested by the recent industry practices tracked here.

Comparisons of online and on-air practices can illuminate the special characteristics of web sites and the promotion they carry. One of the main dissimilarities (and a clear benefit) between web-based promotion and conventional on-air promotion, for example, is the ready availability of free space online. Web sites can go on and on with little additional cost, whereas on-air promotion has a time-scarcity value, and spots are frequently bumped to make room for paid commercial messages, with the uncommon exception of fixed-position promotion (see Ferguson & Moses, 1999). Moreover, display space in newspapers, on outdoor billboards, and on the radio is also not free. On-air and print promos conserve scarce resources by grouping program promos into multiple spots, a seldom-used practice on the web, where space is always plentiful and promotion is usually fixed position.

One problem, however, is that the chronologies of program schedules are not reinforced by the use of stand-alone promotional messages on web sites. Another drawback is that proper rotation of promotional messages is not maintained at present on web sites, often because updating online material has not been a high priority (not, at least, in comparison to stations' emphasis on keeping on-air promos current). Until the number of people who are regularly exposed to web promotion approaches parity with on-air and print promotion, attention to online promos is not likely to become a high priority.

Another dissimilarity is the widespread use of generic promotion online as compared to the use of specific promos on-air. One of Eastman's (1999) design guidelines reads, "Use specifics more often than generics for programs" (p. 53). Clearly, web promotion should use more specific promotion of programs, but it is unlikely to do so until stations see the need to have better rotation of messages. It may be that the greatest similarity between contemporary online promotion and conventional offline promotion is in the way that online message layout resembles outdoor advertising. Billboards along busy roads need to grab audience attention quickly and without much detail. Many online promos are designed like billboards; even web advertising markets itself as a "billboard" service because of the strong similarities to outdoor advertising. Thus, the web promotional strategy of many stations is to create or reinforce awareness through a simple listing of program titles, rather than persuading through a unique selling proposition, a far more effective approach.

Another way to identify the similarities and dissimilarities is to examine the promotional activities that local television stations do "off-web." For example, the amount of local news promotion online is probably very similar to offline promotion. Ferguson and Moses (1999) identify local news promotion as key to the local effort, and not surprisingly, this study found local news promotion quite prominent on a very large number of local sites.

The third research question asked about the role of network affiliation, and the findings for 1999 suggested that the quantity of web sites, if not quality, seemed to track station's Nielsen ratings, in that large market stations and top-rated stations were more likely to have web sites and to have developed program promotion on them. As network web sites become more sophisticated, stations are more likely to link to (or even be subsumed by) the national effort. Until 1998, ABC affiliates in particular had no network-originated umbrella service like NBC.com. NBC was an early adopter of web sites and continues a high level of sophistication. CBS and Fox have been quick to follow, and the WB site has strongly challenged the big networks while easily outperforming the UPN and Pax pages. All of the Big Three networks (ABC, CBS, NBC) were busy in the late-1990s acquiring Internet services and becoming web portals (e.g., ABC's go.com and NBC's snap.com), suggesting that the networks will only become more active in promotion online.

The fourth research question addressed the sources of promotion, and they were shown to be poorly indicated in previous studies, only sketchily revealed in this study, and a fruitful area for future research. The last research question asked about the prevalence of online contesting, and results showed that just over a quarter of television stations in 1999 attempted it, but this approach to promotion can be expected to grow because it can make innovative use of the unique features of online in new types of games and contests.

DIRECTIONS FOR FUTURE RESEARCH

Ferguson, Eastman, and Klein (1999) identify three basic strategies for promotional messages: acquisitive, competitive, and retentive. In other words, stations seek to acquire more audience, take away their competitors' audiences, and retain their loyal audience. The relative importance given by stations to these goals differs according to the medium. For example, commercial television is much more tilted to acquisitive strategies than are commercial radio stations, which focus more on retentive strategies (Ferguson, Eastman, & Klein, 1999). This present examination of 1999 promotional practices online suggests that building loyalty (retentive strategy) may be most important as web usage proliferates, further indicating that online promotion has a closer similarity to the radio model than to the television model. Certainly, the use of competitive strategies has not reached its potential (Kiernan & Levy, 1999).

Cross-Media Promotional Analyses

Researchers should undertake to compare web promotion with nonweb promotion for particular media. One way to assess the importance of the web as a promotional tool for the electronic media is to survey the people directly involved with on-air and on-web promotion and ask them about their strategies, as opposed to inferring station goals from the promotional messages and practices, the approach that most studies cited in this chapter have taken. In any case, the identity that a web visitor can associate with a specific station site is more important than the image the station projects. Constantly reinventing the web interface and tinkering with the page appearance may actually work against a strong web identity. Promotion managers need to know the reasons why broadcast audiences initially visit station web sites, a subject accessible using such conventional research methods as focus groups and surveys.

Furthermore, stations need to give the web visitors good reasons to make repeat visits, and unlike with conventional promotional practices (such as on-air promos, display advertising, billboards), the intended audience must seek out the information. This fact may constitute the most important dissimilarity between web-based promotion and all the rest, and again, evidence might best be gathered directly from the promotion staff for the various electronic media, and compared to reports of users of two paired kinds: those who stay long and short lengths of time with a station's pages and those who repeatedly visit a site or visit just one time.

Finally, web promotion and nonweb promotion are similar in their attention to the use of logos, wordmarks, identifiers, and slogans. The main associated dissimilarity lies in the unity of purpose, or lack thereof. A web page often tries to do everything at one time, rather than accomplish one thing at a time and let the user choose a direction. In this sense, the web site is more like a yellow pages advertisement in that both pack as much information together as possible because it may be a while before the messages are revised.

Improving Methodologies and Reporting

Although quantitative content analysis reduces data to comparable counts and categories, it is usually ineffective for getting a complete descriptive picture of complexities. For example, the finding that nearly all stations promote local programs does not speak to the range of activity. In the analysis conducted for this chapter, the kinds of promotion ran the gamut from a great deal to very little, but all were coded nominally (as "yes"), when interval-level data (or qualitative reports) might have been more useful.

Table 11.6 summarizes various statistics about the features of the 179 web sites analyzed for this chapter in the hopes that future studies will also report more details. Reporting means, standard deviations, and ranges provides insights not available in simple proportions of presence and absence. For example, the use of photographs averaged 25.3 per station site studied, but the skewed distribution put the median at only 12

TABLE 11.6
Statistical Summary of Stylistic Elements Related to Web Sites

	Mean	Mode	Median	SD	Minimum	Maximum	n
Screen count	56.4	1	36	62.8	1	350	173
Frames	31.3	0	3	58.8	0	298	175
Photos	25.3	0	12	36.5	0	234	178
Paragraphs	113.3	0	50	155.6	0	975	175
Bullet points (links)	65.4	0	16	125.4	0	883	179
Streaming video	5.9	0	0	17.6	0	130	179

pictures because of outliers having hundreds of photographs, indicating the range of variation is enormous. Moreover, more sites by far utilize graphics in preference to real photographs, although indexes that combine elements to create estimates of complexity or sophistication may weigh the absence of photographs negatively. Also, the average number of streaming videos (5.9) per site in this study should not be confused with the percentage of stations with streaming video reported in Table 11.3. What the table shows is very little use of streaming video, although all experts predict the technology will rapidly become more common.

Future research must contend with the selection of meaningful data. Some studies, including this one, chose things to count merely because they could be easily counted. In investigating promotion, for example, it would seem advisable to move away from the focus on home pages to look at whole sites, and to move away from the page as the unit of analysis and more toward the station's total effort in all media. It may be that expenditure in one area — such as online — actually results in a reduction in another area such as print or display promotion. Although the number of channels (and web sites) are likely to remain relatively slow growing when compared to the number of web pages and links, investigating all the pages will result in larger, more complete databases and force researchers to develop a nomenclature for the different kinds of promotion happening online. Then, tightly focused studies looking at a single set of variables can be conducted, if it is clear what the set comprises and excludes. Besides, keeping track of fewer variables than in "site description studies" is more parsimonious and likely to be associated with more theoretically based research. Qualitative data can be collected alongside the numerical data and associated with categorical findings if necessary to provide a context or interpretation.

Sampling, however, remains an issue in most kinds of content analysis, and the study of web sites is no different. Unfortunately, no perfect sampling frames for web sites are possible because of all the shared promotion on sister (translator) stations and statewide public television networks.

Should two identical web sites for two different FCC-licensed stations be counted twice (as was done a few times in this study)?

Enough exploratory research has been done to start testing some assumptions about web pages. For example, what goals are being realized (or not) by stations on their web pages? Researchers need to confirm the role of market size in relation to assumptions about end user technology and the resulting utilization of advanced features in sites. Looking in another direction, how do online techniques used in promotional messages trigger such cognitive processes as memory, arousal, and recognition? In laboratory experiments, online promotion could more readily be manipulated in realistic and undetectable ways than print or videotape, thus lending itself to investigations into cognitive processing.

With regard to the use of web sites by networks and production companies, there is a stunning lack of published research. The topic of branding has received much industry attention in the 1990s, and trade magazines have devoted considerable attention to the ways such well-known companies as NBC and Disney associate their names with new products and services, especially online, but Bellamy and Traudt, (chap. 5, this volume) report the first scholarly look at the branding phenomenon in media. As over-the-air broadcasting fades as the dominant means of distribution of television and radio, brand-name entertainment industries will need to increase and enhance their online presence. On the economic front, big media companies will need to expand into ownership of as many channels of online distribution as possible, just as mergers and buyouts have consolidated the broadcast and cable fields. Future research should address this likely direction by collecting baseline data before big changes become evident, and the developments in online promotion are relevant aspects.

Significance of the Research Ahead

The results of a half-decade of research seem to demonstrate that the Internet will become central rather than peripheral to stations' promotional efforts. Although the station promotion director may have been content to think of the Internet as a medium that was a supplement to on-air and print in 1995, by the turn of the century its importance is clearer. In the near future, web pages will soon become of equal (or greater) importance than more traditional venues for station promotion, especially for attracting the young viewer so desired by advertisers (and thus stations). The key element is interactivity. The Internet permits the broadcast audience to "pull" information about a station, rather than follow the old "push" model. The ease with which stations can poll the audience can also help in schedule planning and decisions about promotional approaches. As the quotation at the start of this chapter suggests, the

Internet makes the old network-affiliate model less relevant and the model of a locally oriented station more important.

To move to this point of a more local orientation, stations must commit more resources to web sites (Polon, 1999). Station engineers must provide better servers, and promotion staffs must find better ways of presenting and updating information. As the usability of site content improves, the possibilities inherent in advertising and merchandising suggest the means for funding a deeper commitment to an online presence. Above all, reasons must be found for web users to visit the station's web site on a regular basis, and cross-promotion between on-air and on-web messages, following the models of *ABC World News Tonight* and the Public Broadcasting Service, both of which have given cross-promotion a high priority on the air. Research about what kinds of cross-promotion is being undertaken is needed, as well as studies looking at its impact on viewing and web usage. Researchers should assess the implications of current trends in online promotion from the perspectives of media companies and from the perspectives of the end users.

REFERENCES

Atkin, D. J., Jeffres, L. W., & Neuendorf, K. A. (1998). Understanding Internet adoption behavior as telecommunications behavior. *Journal of Broadcasting & Electronic Media, 42,* 475–490.

Bates, B. J., Chambers, L. T., Embery, M., Jones, M., McClung, S., & Park, J. (1997, August). *Television on the web, 1996: Local television stations' use of the World Wide Web.* Paper presented to the Association for Education in Journalism and Mass Communication, Chicago, IL.

Bates, B. J., & King, R. E. (1996, April). *Television and the web: How local television broadcasters are using the World Wide Web.* Paper presented to the Broadcast Education Association, Las Vegas, NV.

Bucy, E. P., Lang, A., Potter, R. F., & Grabe, M. E. (1999). Formal features of cyberspace: Relationships between web page complexity and site traffic. *Journal of the American Society for Information Science, 50*(13), 1246–1256.

Coffey, S., & Stipp, H. (1997, March/April). The interactions between computer and television usage. *Journal of Advertising Research, 37*(2), 61–67.

Eastman, S. T. (1999). Designing on-air, print and on-line promotion. In S. T. Eastman, D. A. Ferguson, & R. A. Klein (Eds.), *Promotion and marketing for broadcasting and cable* (3rd ed., pp. 29–53). Boston: Focal Press.

Eastman, S. T., Ferguson, D. A., & Klein, R. A. (1999). *Promotion and marketing for broadcasting and cable* (3rd ed.). Boston: Focal Press.

Ferguson, D. A. (1999). Network television promotion. In S. T. Eastman, D. A. Ferguson, & R. A. Klein (Eds.), *Promotion and marketing for broadcasting and cable* (3rd ed., pp. 89–96). Boston: Focal Press.

Ferguson, D. A., Eastman, S. T., & Klein, R. A. (1999). Marketing the media: Scope and goals. In S. T. Eastman, D. A. Ferguson, & R. A. Klein (Eds.), *Promotion and marketing for broadcasting and cable* (3rd ed., pp. 1–28). Boston: Focal Press.

Ferguson, D. A., & Moses, B. A. (1999). Local station television promotion. In S. T. Eastman, D. A. Ferguson, & R. A. Klein (Eds.), *Promotion and marketing for broadcasting and cable* (3rd ed., pp. 97–126). Boston: Focal Press.

Ferguson, D. A., & Perse, E. M. (2000). The World Wide Web as a functional alternative to television. *Journal of Broadcasting & Electronic Media, 44*(2), 155–174.

Ha, L., & James, E. L. (1998). Interactivity reexamined: A baseline analysis of early business web sites. *Journal of Broadcasting & Electronic Media, 42*, 457–474.

IntelliQuest. (1999, April 19). *IntelliQuest study shows 83 million U.S. internet users and 56 million online shoppers* [Online press release]. Available: http://www.intelliquest.com/press/release78.asp.

James, M. L., Wotring, C. E., & Forrest, E. J. (1995). Exploratory study of the perceived benefits of electronic bulletin board use and their impact on other communication activities. *Journal of Broadcasting & Electronic Media, 39*, 30–50.

Kiernan, V., & Levy, M. (1999). Competition among broadcast-related web sites. *Journal of Broadcasting & Electronic Media, 43*, 271–279.

Lang, A. (1990). Involuntary attention and physiological arousal evoked by structural features and emotional content in TV commercials. *Communication Research, 17*(3), 275–299.

Lang, A., Bolls, P. D., Potter, R. F., & Kawahara, K. (1999). The effects of production pace and arousing content on the information processing of television messages. *Journal of Broadcasting & Electronic Media, 45*, 451–475.

McClung, S. R. (1997, October). *Information representation and local TV stations on the web: Building a better web site.* Paper presented to the Ohio University Communications Research Conference, Athens.

Murphy, R. (1998, April). *The value of radio station web sites.* Paper presented to the Broadcast Education Association, Las Vegas, NV.

Niekamp, R. (1996, August). *Television station sites on the World Wide Web.* Paper presented to the Association for Education in Journalism and Mass Communication, Chicago, IL.

Niekamp, R. (1997, August). *Television station web sites: Interactivity in news stories.* Paper presented to the Association for Education in Journalism and Mass Communication, Baltimore, MD.

Perse, E. M., & Dunn, D. G. (1998). The utility of home computers and media use: Implications of multimedia and connectivity. *Journal of Broadcasting & Electronic Media, 42*, 435–456.

Polon, M. (1999, July 19). You are what your website says you are. *TV Broadcast* [Online]. Available: http://www.TVBroadcast.com/99.7.16.7.htm.

Rank, H. (1991). *The pitch: A simple way to understand the basic pattern of persuasion in advertising.* Park Forest, IL: Counter-Propaganda Press.

Rosales, R. G., & Pitts, G. (1997). *A content analysis of U.S. television stations' web sites.* Paper presented to the Broadcast Education Association, Las Vegas, NV.

Tedesco, R. (1998, July 27). Site of the week: www.kron.com. *Broadcasting & Cable, 128*, 46.

Virzi, A. M. (1998, March 9). Webcasts not ready for prime time yet. *Internet World*, 1.

Wolfe, S. (1997, September 29). NBC and the net: The honeymoon's over. *Media Central Digest* [Online]. Available: http://www.enliven.com.

Author Index

Subject Index

359